D1608135

BEST PRACTICES SERIES

Network Design

Design

Principles and Applications

THE AUERBACH
BEST PRACTICES SERIES

Broadband Networking, James Trulove, Editor,
ISBN: 0-8493-9821-5

Electronic Messaging, Nancy Cox, Editor,
ISBN: 0-8493-9825-8

Financial Services Information Systems, Jessica Keyes, Editor,
ISBN: 0-8493-9834-7

Healthcare Information Systems, Phillip L. Davidson, Editor,
ISBN: 0-8493-9963-7

Internet Management, Jessica Keyes, Editor,
ISBN: 0-8493-9987-4

Multi-Operating System Networking: Living with UNIX, NetWare, and NT, Raj Rajagopal, Editor,
ISBN: 0-8493-9831-2

Network Manager's Handbook, John Lusa, Editor,
ISBN: 0-8493-9841-X

Project Management, Paul C. Tinnirello, Editor,
ISBN: 0-8493-9998-X

Server Management, Gilbert Held, Editor,
ISBN: 0-8493-9823-1

Enterprise Systems Integration, John Wyzalek, Editor,
ISBN: 0-8493-9837-1

Web-to-Host Connectivity, Lisa Lindgren and
Anura Guruge, Editors
ISBN: 0-8493-0835-6

Network Design, Gilbert Held, Editor,
ISBN: 0-8493-0859-3

AUERBACH PUBLICATIONS

www.auerbach-publications.com
TO ORDER: Call: 1-800-272-7737 • Fax: 1-800-374-3401
E-mail: orders@crcpress.com

Network Design

Principles and Applications

Editor

GILBERT HELD

AUERBACH

Boca Raton   London   New York   Washington, D.C.

Library of Congress Cataloging-in-Publication Data

Network design : principles and application / editor, Gilbert Held.
    p. cm. -- (Best practices series)
    Includes bibliographical references.
    ISBN 0-8493-0859-3
      1. Computer networks. I. Held, Gilbert, 1943- II. Best practices series (Boca Raton,
Fla.)

    TK5105.5. N4654 2000
    004.6--dc21

00-023724

© 2000 by CRC Press LLC
Auerbach is an imprint of CRC Press LLC

No claim to original U.S. Government works
International Standard Book Number 0-8493-0859-3
Library of Congress Card Number 00-023724
Printed in the United States of America   2 3 4 5 6 7 8 9 0
Printed on acid-free paper

Contributors

AL BERG, *Director, Strategic Technologies, NETLAN Inc., New York, New York*

HOWARD C. BERKOWITZ, *Principal Consulting Engineer, Corporation for Open Systems (COS), McLean, Virginia*

EILEEN BIRGE, *Research Director, The Concours Group, Houston, Texas*

ELLEN BONSALL, *Marketing Director, U.S. Operations, ActivCard, Inc., San Francisco, California*

FRANK J. BOURNE, *Senior Applications Engineer, StrataCom, Atlanta, Georgia*

RANDALL CAMPBELL, *Product Line Manager, Token Ring Switching, Cisco Systems, Inc., Research Triangle Park, North Carolina*

TIM CLARK, *Vice President, Sales, Tavve Software Company, Durham, North Carolina*

DOUGLAS G. CONORICH, *Internet Security Analyst, Internet Emergency Response Service, IBM Corporation, Clearfield, Utah*

ANDREW CSINGER, *Founder, Xcert Software Inc., Vancouver, British Columbia, Canada*

DAVID CURLEY, *Vice President, Worldwide Marketing, Mitel Corporation, Kanata, Ontario, Canada*

G. THOMAS DES JARDINS, *Senior Software Engineer, Inbound Technology Group, FORE Systems, Inc., Warrendale, Pennsylvania*

NICHOLAS ECONOMIDES, *Professor, Stern School of Business, New York University, New York, New York*

MATTHEW FELDMAN, *Chief Technology Officer, Intellect Visual Communications, New York, New York*

JOHN FISKE, *Independent Writer, Prides Crossing, Pennsylvania*

MICHEL GILBERT, *Senior Member, Technical Staff, Hill Associates Inc., Colchester, Vermont*

KEVIN M. GROOM, *Senior Technical Associate, AT&T, Cincinnati, Ohio*

FRANK M. GROOM, *Professor, Center for Information and Communication Sciences, Ball State University, Muncie, Indiana*

ANURA GURUGÉ, *Independent Technical Consultant, Meredith, New Hampshire*

ROOHOLLAH HAJBANDEH, *Manager of Business Development, American Communications Consultants, Inc., Madison, Wisconsin*

GILBERT HELD, *Director, 4-Degree Consulting, Macon, Georgia*

Contributors

JIM HEWITT, *Principal Consultant, Brainstorm Technology, Cambridge, Massachusetts*

SVEN JAMES, *President, CompuSven, Inc., Naples, Florida*

DOUG KAYE, *Director of Marketing, Magellan Networks, Northern Telecom, Richardson, Texas*

TIM KELLY, *Vice President, Cygnus Communications, Battleground, Washington*

MICHAEL KENNEDY, *Enterprise Vendor and Service Provider, Strategic Networks, Sunnyvale, California*

GARY C. KESSLER, *Director, Information Technology, Hill Associates Inc., Colchester, Vermont*

WILLIAM R. KOSS, *Consultant, Sonoma Systems, Marlboro, Massachusetts*

LISA M. LINDGREN, *Independent Consultant, Meredith, New Hampshire*

ANDRES LLANA, JR., *Telecommunications Consultant, Vermont Studies Group, Inc., King of Prussia, Pennsylvania*

PHILLIP Q. MAIER, *Program Manager, Secure Network Initiative, Lockheed Martin, Sunnyvale, California*

MICHAEL MCCLURE, *Vice President, Marketing, Marketwave Corporation, Seattle, Washington*

COLIN MICK, *Consultant, Palo Alto, California*

NATHAN MULLER, *Independent Consultant, Huntsville, Alabama*

THOMAS OSHA, *Director, Corporate Communications, Cincinnati Bell, Cincinnati, Ohio*

CHRISTINE PEREY, *Independent Consultant, PEREY Communications & Consulting, Placerville, California*

BRYAN PICKETT, *Vice President, Enterprise Networks, Training and Documentation, Nortel, Richardson, Texas*

JOY PINSKY, *Vice President of Marketing, FreeGate Corporation, Sunnyvale, California*

RICHARD RAUSCHER, *Senior Systems/Network Analyst, H. Lee Moffitt Cancer Center and Research Institute, University of South Florida, Tampa, Florida*

LARRY SCHESSEL, *Cisco Systems, Research Triangle Park, North Carolina*

DAVE SCHNEIDER, *Chief Technology Officer, Internet Dynamics, Inc., Westlake Village, California*

ROSHAN L. SHARMA, *Principal, Telecom Network Science, Dallas, Texas*

DUANE E. SHARP, *President, SharpTech Associates, Mississauga, Ontario, Canada*

SCOTT T. SMITH, *Senior Partner, CSC Consulting, Waltham, Massachusetts*

PETER SOUTHWICK, *SMTS, Hill Associates Inc., Colchester, Vermont*

MARTIN TAYLOR, *Vice President of Technology Strategy, Madge Networks, San Jose, California*

DICK THUNEN, *Marketing Representative, Sync Research, Inc., Irvine, California*

JAMES S. TILLER, *CISSP, Network Security Consultant, Lucent Technologies, Tampa, Florida*

GOPALA KRISHNA TUMULURI, *Software Test Engineer, FORE Systems, Pittsburgh, Pennsylvania*
JOHN R. VACCA, *Information Technology Consultant, Pomeroy, Ohio*
TRENTON WATERHOUSE, *Marketing Manager, LAN Switching Systems, Cabletron Systems, Rochester, New York*
COLIN WYND, *Account Manager, H–P OpenView, Hewlett–Packard, Mountain View, California*

Table of Contents

Introduction

NETWORK DESIGN IS A COMPLEX PROCESS, requiring knowledge of several disciplines to include engineering, financial analysis, and computer science. Although the network design process was never simple, advances in technology and the introduction of new networking communications facilities and products resulted in a difficult endeavor becoming more difficult. Today the network manager and LAN administrator face many difficult decisions when designing a network. Unlike many occupations where knowledge in one area is sufficient to perform a job, network managers and LAN administrators must be knowledgeable concerning multiple disciplines. For example, it is difficult to interconnect geographically separated LANs without knowledge of how WANs operate and the transmission facilities that can be used to facilitate the interconnection of local area networks.

Recognizing the fact that the search for reference material in itself can be a time consuming project, this handbook was created as a reference to network design principles and applications. As you will note from the contents, this handbook is subdivided into an introduction followed by eight distinct network design related sections. Within each network design related section are a series of section topic related chapters selected to provide you with a firm foundation concerning an important aspect of modern network design.

In Section I we begin our coverage of network design by obtaining a firm foundation of the role of LANs to include how they operate, when to consider the migration of one type of LAN to another, and LAN-to-mainframe connectivity options. Once we obtain an appreciation for the role of LANs and their technical and operational characteristics, we will turn our attention to WANs.

In Section II we will examine the wide area network. This examination commences with a review of the voice network and continues by focusing upon such WAN-related topics as routing protocols, remote access, and the convergence of IP, ATM, and SONET/SDH at the backbone.

Once we have a firm foundation concerning the operation and utilization of LANs and WANs, we turn our attention to a troika of networking methods used to interconnect LANs. In Section III we focus our attention on the role of Virtual Private Networks (VPNs), and intranets and extranets, with a series of chapters that enlightens us concerning each networking method.

In Section IV we will become acquainted with one of the bedrocks of network design, traffic analysis and performance. In this section a collection of chapters are presented that provides detailed information concerning performance monitoring and traffic analysis for both LANs and WANs. While it is not possible to monitor a network to be constructed, many times the monitoring of a similar or equivalent existing network can alert us to the fact that we may need to alter or modify our design. In addition, traffic analysis and performance monitoring provides invaluable information concerning the operational status of an existing network and whether that network should be modified.

Unlike an Egyptian pyramid that was constructed for the eternal rest of a noble, networks can rapidly become obsolete. Recognizing this fact, it is important to consider how and when to migrate from one type of network to another. In Section V we turn our attention to this timely topic, examining the transition of SNA to IP and frame relay as well as methods to implement a successful cutover.

Because it is important to be knowledgeable concerning the use of different networking tools and techniques, Section VI is focused on this topic. In Section VI we will turn our attention to simulation as well as methods to determine bridge and router delays and how to use baselining as a planning tool.

No book on network design would be complete without a discussion of security. Thus, Section VII is focused upon this topic, providing us with a series of chapters covering highly relevant information that must be considered to correctly design a secure network. In this section we will examine both authentication and encryption as well as methods required to secure different types of networking devices.

In concluding this handbook we will turn our attention to the rapidly emerging future of communications. In Section VIII we will consider evolving technologies, since knowledge of the future is instrumental for creating a network design that is flexible enough to support emerging technologies.

As a professional author I highly value reader feedback. Please feel free to send your comments concerning the chapter selection process, topics covered, or suggestions for new topics or sections either to the publisher or directly to this author whose email address is gil_held@yahoo.com.

Section I
Understanding LANs

LOCAL AREA NETWORKS (LANs) can be considered to represent the building blocks upon which modern networks are created. Because readers are commonly employees of organizations with different networking requirements, a number of LANs were developed over the past two decades to satisfy diverse networking requirements. This section focuses attention on obtaining a degree of familiarity with different types of LANs and their roles in satisfying different networking requirements.

In Chapter 1, author Nathan Muller begins the exploration of LANs with his chapter titled **LAN Connectivity Options for the Small Business**. In this chapter, Muller acquaints us with cabling, the use of media converters and network adapters, how hubs provide the building blocks of LAN connectivity, and the use of different types of network operating systems. With a foundation concerning the interrelated components of a LAN, Chapter 2 introduces the manner by which voice and LAN networks are merging. In the chapter titled **Integrating Voice and LAN Infrastructures and Applications**, author David Curley first acquaints us with the rationale for running voice traffic over a LAN. Once this is accomplished, Curley discusses the different technologies that can be used, examining RSVP, ATM, and other protocols, as well as discussing migration issues that need to be considered.

Chapter 3 commences with an examination of specific LAN technologies, turning attention to **High-Speed Token Ring**. In Chapter 3, author Martin Taylor examines the need for high-speed Token Ring networks, describes the technology, and introduces the quality-of-service capability (QoS) provided by Token Ring through its frame format, which includes eight levels of priority. Because some readers with existing Token Ring networks may elect to consider their replacement with Ethernet, the next chapter is focused on this timely topic. In Chapter 4, **Should You Migrate Your Token Ring Network to Ethernet?**, author Randall Campbell first examines the two networking technologies. Once this is accomplished, Campbell examines the use of Ethernet to operate Token Ring applications and migration issues one needs to consider. By providing information on long-term and short-term advantages in converting Token Ring to Ethernet as well as the features and functions users need to consider, this chapter provides the foundation for readers to make applicable decisions based on their current and future networking requirements.

The next two chapters in this section provide detailed information concerning two important versions of Ethernet. In Chapter 5, author Colin Mick, in his chapter titled **Introduction to 100BASE-T: Fast (and Faster) Ethernet**, provides detailed information concerning the different types of Fast Ethernet and their use in different networking environments. Continuing the tour of modern versions of Ethernet, Mick's chapter, **Gigabit Ethernet** (Chapter 6), first provides a technical overview of this latest version of Ethernet. Once this is accomplished, Mick acquaints us with cabling and topology rules that are essential knowledge for constructing Gigabit Ethernet networks.

Although ATM at one time was considered to represent a universal LAN-to-WAN technology, from a practical standpoint, low-cost Ethernet captured the LAN market. However, ATM's switch-based infrastructure enables it to be effectively used to interconnect LANs as well as provide a quality-of-service backbone networking environment. Chapter 7 focuses attention on a scheme required to allow LANs that use one type of addressing to be routed through an ATM backbone that employs a different type of addressing. This scheme is **ATM LAN Emulation**, which is the title of Chapter 7 and is co-authored by G. Thomas des Jardins and Gopala Krishna Tumuluri. In Chapter 8, author Doug Kaye provides additional information about ATM in his chapter entitled **InterLAN Switching**. In this chapter, Kaye examines the role of ATM in local networks and describes methods to transport IP and other protocols over an ATM infrastructure.

The two chapters that conclude this section provide insight into timely topics many LAN operators must consider. In Chapter 9, author Lisa Lindgren's chapter, **LAN-to-Mainframe Connectivity Choices,** introduces methods that facilitate the connection of distributed LANs to centralized mainframes. Because reliability is a topic few can afford to ignore, this section concludes with author Richard Rauscher's chapter, **Building Highly Reliable Computer Networks**. In this chapter, Rauscher provides a series of techniques and networking strategies to consider that can be a blessing when the unexpected occurs.

Chapter 1
LAN Connectivity Options for the Small Business

Nathan J. Muller

SMALL BUSINESSES OF 2 TO 100 USERS are part of the fastest-growing segments of the networking market. According to various industry estimates, there were about one million networked companies with 100 or fewer employees in 1996 and 300,000 more in 1997. The number of such companies has grown to more than two million during the year 2000. The major networking vendors and many second-tier vendors are targeting this market with product lines that feature entry-level hubs, switches, printer servers, integrated services digital network (ISDN) routers, and other networking products that offer ease of use, clearly written and illustrated documentation, and technical support specifically aimed at novices.

The most popular network topology among small businesses is Ethernet because it is relatively inexpensive, easy to set up and use, and very fast. There are currently three categories of Ethernet. Standard Ethernet operates at 10M bps, which is quick enough for most networking tasks. Fast Ethernet moves data 10 times faster at 100M bps, making it ideal for desktop video, multimedia, and other bandwidth-hungry applications. The latest category of Ethernet is Gigabit Ethernet, which moves data 100 times faster than standard Ethernet, making it suited for uplinks among high-capacity hubs or switches as well as links among high-capacity servers.

Although there are other types of LANs available, (e.g., token ring, fiber distributed data interface, and asynchronous transfer mode, this chapter focuses on Ethernet because it is the network of choice among small businesses and will continue to be well into the future. As in any type of network, several elements merit consideration when building an Ethernet network, including cabling, media converters, network adapters, hubs, network operating systems, and routers for LAN-to-LAN communication over the wide area network (WAN).

CABLING

For standard 10Base-T Ethernet, the most popular type of network cabling is Category 5 unshielded twisted-pair (UTP) cable. This type of cable looks like the coaxial cabling that is often used to connect a VCR to a TV set and usually has eight wires. It can be used at a maximum distance of 328 feet. A modular plug at each end (RJ45) of the cable makes interconnecting the various network devices as simple as plugging them in. Fiber-optic cabling (also known as 10Base-FL) can be used as well at a maximum distance of about 607 feet.

Fast Ethernet, or 100Base-T, is the standard that is most compatible with 10Base-T. It uses the same contention-based media access control method — carrier sense multiple access with collision detection (CSMA/CD) — that is at the heart of 10Base-T Ethernet. This level of compatibility means that no protocol conversions need to be done to move data between the two types of networks.

There are several media standards for implementing 100Base-T. They can be summarized as follows:

- 100Base-TX: a two-pair system for data grade (Category 5) UTP and STP (shielded twisted-pair) cabling
- 100Base-T4: a four-pair system for both voice and data grade (Category 3, 4, or 5) UTP cabling
- 100Base-FX: a two-strand multimode fiber system

All these cabling systems can be interconnected through a hub, which helps organizations retain their existing cabling infrastructure while migrating to Fast Ethernet.

Companies with small networks usually standardize on Category 5 cabling because it is inexpensive, flexible, and adequate for short distances. It also allows companies to easily migrate to higher-speed networks without having to rewire the building. For networks that span multiple offices or floors — or must traverse noisy environments such as manufacturing facilities — fiber-optic cabling is the best choice because it offers immunity to electromagnetic interference, provides virtually error-free transmission, and is more secure than copper-based media. The maximum length for a 100Base-FX segment is about 1,300 feet.

Gigabit Ethernet, also called 1000Base-T, is limited to 328 feet per segment using Category 5 cabling. Media extensions to the Gigabit Ethernet standard use multimode fiber at up to 1,500 feet (1000Base-SX) and single-mode fiber at distances up to 9,000 feet (1000Base-LX). Optical fiber is mostly used as an uplink between stackable Ethernet hubs, but it can also be used for interconnecting servers. Gigabit Ethernet will not see widespread use among most small businesses unless they are engaged in specialized work such as computer-aided design/computer-aided manufacturing or three-dimensional modeling.

MEDIA CONVERTERS

All three types of media — twisted pair, thin coax, and optical fiber — can be used exclusively or together, depending on the type of network. There are even media converters available that allow segments using different media to be linked together. For example, some media converters link 10Base-T to 10Base-2 and 10Base-T to 10Base-FL (single or multimode). There are also media converters that link 100Base-T to 100Base-FX (single or multimode). Because media conversion is a physical layer process, it does not introduce significant delays on the network.

NETWORK ADAPTERS

A computer — whether configured as a client or server — is connected to the network with an adapter called a network interface card (NIC), which comes in internal and external versions. Typically, the NIC is installed inside the computer: It plugs directly into one of the computer's internal expansion slots. Most older computers have 16-bit Industry Standard Architecture slots, so a 16-bit NIC is needed. Faster computers, such as Pentium-based machines, come standardly equipped with several 32-bit PCI slots. These PCs require 32-bit NICs to achieve the fastest networking speeds.

If a computer is going to be used with a Fast Ethernet network, it needs a network adapter that specifically supports 100M bps as well. Some NICs offer an "autosensing" capability, enabling them to determine the speed of the network and whether to run at 10M or 100M bps in half-duplex or full-duplex mode. In half-duplex mode, the computer can alternately send and receive. In full-duplex mode, the computer can send and receive at the same time, effectively doubling its throughput on a dedicated segment.

Some NICs support multiple types of media connectors. In addition to RJ45, they might also include a connector for the older British Naval Connector (BNC) interface. If a PC lacks vacant expansion slots, an external network adapter may be used, which plugs in to the computer's printer port. The adapter usually has LED indicators for such things as polarity, signal quality, link integrity, and power.

Portable computers can connect to the office LAN via a PC Card network adapter. This credit-card-size adapter communicates with the portable computer using special software drivers called socket and card services. Another set of drivers, called network drivers, enable the PC Card to communicate with the network at large. Some client operating systems, such as Microsoft Corp.'s Windows 95, provide these sets of drivers, which enables

Plug-and-Play operation; otherwise they must be installed by the user from the vendor's installation disk. Some PC Card adapters include an integral 56K bps modem that can be used for remote dial-up connection to the office LAN.

HUBS

Although it is possible to network PCs together in serial fashion using NICs with BNC T-connectors and terminators, most Ethernet networks installed today use a hub, which centralizes the cable connections from computers and other networked devices.

A hub is basically a box with a row of jacks into which the cables from the NIC-equipped computers are plugged. Most small office hubs have 4 to 16 jacks, but some may have more. Most hubs also have a dedicated uplink port, which allows the hub to be connected to other hubs as a means of accommodating growth.

Like network adapter cards, hubs are available in both standard Ethernet and Fast Ethernet versions. However, more than two hubs cannot be linked together without using some kind of switch or repeater to boost the interim signal. If three, four, or more standard hubs are uplinked together without regard for signal strength, data becomes corrupted and applications fail.

But this situation applies only to standard hubs joined together through RJ45 ports, where each hub is seen by the network as a separate entity. Stackable hubs, on the other hand, are designed to appear as a single hub to the network — regardless of how many are connected together. The linkages are implemented with one or more stacking cables that actually join the backplanes of each hub through a dedicated high-speed port. Because information does not pass through the hub's regular RJ45 ports, it is not slowed down by error correction and filtering. The result is a minimal slowdown when data moves from one hub to another.

Some switching hubs allow both 10M and 100M bps networking hardware to be used on the same network. An autosensing feature associated with each port determines the speed of the NIC at the other end of the cable and transparently bridges the two speeds together.

A small business that wants to network only a few computers together will be able to get by with a hub, some network adapters, and 10Base-T cables. If the organization anticipates significant growth in the future, a stackable 10/100 Ethernet hub is the better choice. It provides tighter integration and maximum throughput and the means to scale up to a few hundred nodes if necessary without the need for external repeaters or switches.

Hubs also come in managed and unmanaged versions. Hubs that are not manageable are easy to set up and maintain. They offer LED indicators that show the presence of send-and-receive traffic on each port, collisions, and hub utilization and power status. However, unmanaged hubs do not offer the configuration options and administrative features of managed hubs.

A management system offers ways to configure individual ports. For example, address filtering can be applied to ports to limit access to certain network resources. A management system can also provide performance information about each port to aid troubleshooting and fault isolation. Most hubs of this type support the Simple Network Management Protocol (SNMP) and the associated Remote Monitoring (RMON) standard, which makes possible more advanced network monitoring and analysis. In supporting SNMP, the hub can also be controlled and managed through a major management platform such as IBM's NetView, Hewlett-Packard Co.'s OpenView, and Sun Microsystems, Inc.'s Solstice SunNet Manager.

A small business with less than 25 PCs can get by without a managed network for a limited time. But when the number of PCs increases, it becomes more economical over the long term to have a management system in place that can facilitate daily administration and provide information for troubleshooting purposes. Although this might require a dedicated administrator with technical expertise, the expense of this additional employee is more than offset by improvements in productivity made possible by high-network availability and reliability. An alternative would be to subscribe to the remote monitoring services of a vendor or carrier, in which case an SNMP-based hub management system would still be required.

NETWORK OPERATING SYSTEM

Every computer that is attached to a network must be equipped with a network operating system (NOS) to monitor and control the flow of information between users. NOSs are of two types: peer-to-peer or client/server. Examples of peer-to-peer NOSs that are commonly used by small businesses are Windows 95, Artisoft LANtastic, and Novell Inc.'s NetWare Lite. These NOSs are useful for sharing applications, data, printers, and other resources across PCs that are interconnected by a hub. Examples of client server NOSs are Windows NT and NetWare, which are used by large organizations whose users require fast network access to a variety of business applications.

PEER-TO-PEER

A simple peer-to-peer network can be built inexpensively with thin coax cabling and a 10/100 Ethernet switching hub. After the networking hardware has been installed, a peer-to-peer network software package must be installed in all the PCs. If the PCs come with Windows 95, the basic proto-cols for peer-to-peer networking are probably already installed in each sys-tem and it is a matter of configuring them through the operating system's control panel. If a different NOS is preferred, a separate package, such as Artisoft LANtastic or NetWare Lite, can be installed separately.

Most NOSs allow each peer-to-peer user to determine which resources will be available to other users. Specific hard and floppy disk drives, direc-tories or files, printers, and other resources can be attached or detached from the network via software. Access to each resource can be controlled in a variety of ways. For example, when configuring Windows 95 for peer-to-peer networking, a password can be applied to each shared resource. Alternatively, specific users and groups can be granted access to each shared resource.

When one user's disk has been configured so that it is "sharable," it appears as a new drive to the other users. Because drives can be easily shared between peer-to-peer PCs, applications need to be installed only on one computer instead of all computers. If the company relies on a spread-sheet application, for example, it can be installed on one user's computer and be accessible to other computers whenever it is not in use. If the spreadsheet program is not used continuously by all potential users, it makes more sense to share one copy rather than buy one for each machine. Of course, sharing applications over a peer-to-peer (or client/server) net-work might require a network license from the vendor, or the company risks a penalty for copyright infringement.

Peer-to-peer networks have several advantages over client/server. They are easy and inexpensive to set up and maintain, and there is no require-ment for a dedicated network administrator. Many vendors offer documen-tation that is geared for the novice, and they offer telephone support when the occasional problem is encountered.

CLIENT/SERVER

In a client/server environment such as Windows NT or NetWare, files are stored on a centralized, high-speed file server PC that is made available to client PCs. Network access speeds are usually faster than those found on peer-to-peer networks. Virtually all network services such as printing and electronic mail are routed through the file server, which allows networking tasks to be tracked. Inefficient network segments can be reworked to make them faster, and users' activities can be closely monitored. Public data and applications are stored on the file server, where they are run from client PCs' locations, which makes upgrading software a simple task — network administrators can simply upgrade the applications stored on the file server rather than having to physically upgrade each client PC.

In the client/server network, the client PCs are subordinate to the file server. The clients' primary applications and files are stored in a common location. File servers are often set up so that each user on the network has access to his "own" directory, along with a range of "public" directories where applications are stored. If two clients want to communicate with each other, they must go through the file server to do it. A message from one client to another is first sent to the file server, where it is then routed to its destination. A small business with 100 or more client PCs might find that a server-centric network is the best way to meet the needs of all users.

Take a simple task such as printing, for example. Instead of equipping each desktop or workgroup with its own printer, it would be more economical for many users to share a few high-speed printers. In client/server networks, network printing is usually handled by a print server, a small box with at least two connectors: one for a printer and another that attaches directly to the network cabling. Some print servers have more than two ports — they may, for example, support two, three, or four printers simultaneously. When a user sends a print job, it travels over the network cabling to the file server where it is stored. When the print server senses that the job is waiting, it moves it from the file server to its attached printer. When the job is finished, the print server returns a result message to the file server, indicating that the process is complete.

Another simple task that can be more economically handled by a server-centric network is the provision of gateway access to the outside world. This involves a remote-node server, which provides remote access and modem sharing. Most remote-node servers attach directly to the network cabling. They provide a bridge between the network, a modem, and an ordinary telephone line.

Remote access allows users to dial in to their home networks from anywhere in the world. Once a connection has been established over ordinary phone lines by modem, users can access any programs or data on the network as if they were locally attached to the LAN. Some remote access servers provide only access to a file server's disk drives. Others can provide access to both the file server and direct access to any PC's hard disk on the network, which saves time because it allows a remote user to communicate directly with any network user without having to go through the file server.

To prevent unauthorized access to the corporate network, the remote access server can be configured to implement appropriate security features. Password protection is the most common security feature, but hackers using automated tools can easily discover passwords. The remote access server's modems might be able to offer better protection by supporting a dial-back capability. Incoming calls are prompted for a password, and the modem calls back the originating modem using the associated number stored in its security table.

More advanced security systems are available, such as the Remote Authentication Dial-In User Service (RADIUS), which is considered one of the most effective security protocols for dial-in access. RADIUS provides a client/server architecture that supplies authentication, authorization, and session accounting for users of remote access networks, including the Internet and corporate intranets. The remote access server acts like a client to the RADIUS server.

An administrator creates user profiles, which are stored at the RADIUS server. These profiles determine the authorizations that are given to remote dial-up users. A challenge/response protocol is used during user log-on to avoid sending passwords in plain text over the communication line. When a user dials in to the network, the RADIUS server responds with a challenge. The remote client uses the challenge to perform a cryptographic operation, the result of which is sent back to the RADIUS server. At the server, a similar operation is performed, and if the result matches the client's result, the user's identity is verified. If not, access is denied.

Developed by Livingston Enterprises, RADIUS has achieved status as the worldwide *de facto* standard and is the Internet Engineering Task Force's proposed standard for dial-in access security (RFC 2138).

Modem sharing lets local network users dial out from their individual network computers to access the Internet, bulletin boards, and other services. After launching their favorite communications software, local users establish a link with the remote-node server over the network, which opens up an outgoing telephone line. Users' individual PCs do not need modems. Because only a few modems and phone lines are required to support a small company, this method of remote access can provide significant cost savings on equipment and lines. In the case of peer-to-peer networks, by contrast, every PC requires its own modem for access to the outside world.

ROUTERS

For LAN-to-LAN communication between remote sites, a router is needed. A router can be a stand-alone device or it can come in the form of a module that plugs in to a managed hub. Routers operate at layer 3 of the OSI reference model (the network layer). Basically, they convert LAN protocols into wide-area packet network protocols such as Transmission Control Protocol/Internet Protocol (TCP/IP), and perform the process in reverse at the remote location.

ISDN-based routers provide high-quality dial-up connections to a local Internet service provider (ISP) so that LAN traffic can be carried economically between far-flung locations over the public TCP/IP-based Internet. Some products come with scripts that detect the specific type of ISDN connection the company has before setting up the TCP/IP information on the network (70 types of ISDN circuit configurations are available, each with its own order code). Some routers even offer firewall software to protect the corporate network from intruders who might attempt to enter through the Internet.

A stand-alone ISDN access router comes with an Ethernet port for connection to the hub. It also has an ISDN port for connection to the company's network termination point at which the carrier has connected a digital line for ISDN service. Some ISDN routers also have "plain old telephone service" ports, which also allow the unit to be used for faxing. In some cases, two phone lines capable of supporting 56K bps modems can be aggregated to achieve bandwidths close to ISDN's 128.8K bps. This type of router typically costs around $500.

Some stand-alone routers offer a high degree of configuration flexibility. Depending on the software package ordered with the unit, the device's WAN port can be configured for use over leased lines, ISDN, frame relay, switched 56K service, switched multimegabit data services and X.25. This type of router typically costs around $1,000.

GETTING STARTED

One of the easiest ways for a small business to set up a LAN is to buy a starter kit. Some vendors offer starter kits for both 10Base-T and 100Base-T networks. This is a convenient, affordable solution that comes complete with the necessary hardware and cabling needed to create a two-node network.

The typical kit includes a four- or five-port stackable hub, two autosensing Ethernet 10/100 NICs, and two thin coax cables. A 10Base-T starter kit typically sells for less than $100, whereas a 100Base-T starter kit costs less than $200. Additional NICs can cost between $25 and $60. An autosensing 10/100 PC Card for portable computers costs less than $100. Starter kits for switched Ethernet are also available for under $250. A two-port switch offers two autosensing 10/100Base-T ports, two NICs and cables. The starter kits are ready to run with all major network operating systems.

To make LAN-to-LAN communication easier for small businesses, some vendors have bundled equipment together into a basic network package for secure Internet access. A package from Cisco Systems, Inc., for example, consists of a firewall, a hub, and a router for approximately $2,000. A similarly provisioned package from 3Com Corp., specifically designed for nontechnical users, features a World Wide Web browser interface that can step the user through all configuration and addressing tasks.

Another way for a small business to get started with a LAN is to buy products from a local value-added reseller (VAR), which will install and configure the network to meet specific business needs. Usually, the VAR specializes in providing products from a single vendor and its authorized partners, so the offerings are tightly integrated and have a record of proven performance. A key advantage to dealing with VARs is that they also offer technical support. And if a company cannot afford the upfront cost of installing a LAN, the VAR can usually arrange an equipment lease.

CONCLUSION

Just a few years ago, building a corporate network was a daunting task undertaken only by seasoned professionals. Small businesses that could not afford to spend lavishly on technical assistance either had to struggle along without a network or try to put the pieces together themselves, often on a trial-and-error basis, until they got it right. Recognizing the growing importance of this market, many interconnect vendors have started to design products that are easy for ordinary people to install and use. In some cases, the equipment is ready to use out of the box or is self-configuring after installation. In the few instances in which manual procedures are still necessary to get the equipment configured properly, a graphical interface steps the user through the process.

Although this chapter has focused on the LAN connectivity options for small businesses, the same connectivity options are available for the home, where it is increasingly common for several desktop computers to reside. In addition to computers for one or more students, there might be one for a telecommuter, along with a docking station for a mobile professional's laptop computer. All these computers can be networked together to save money on printers and other resources, as well as the cost of Internet access.

Chapter 2
Integrating Voice and LAN Infrastructures and Applications
David Curley

INTEGRATION OF VOICE AND LAN NETWORKS will be an essential IT strategy for many businesses in the next three to five years. Consolidating the long-separate voice and data networks has implications not only for the network infrastructure, but also for the PC, the telephone set, the PBX, and the IT organization itself. This chapter is a road map to guide organizations in making the right voiceLAN-related investment decisions.

PROBLEMS ADDRESSED

VoiceLAN is the transmission of voice traffic over a LAN infrastructure. VoiceLAN enables server-based telephony architecture for voice switches, terminals/phone sets, and applications.

Today, voice traffic is transmitted across a separate circuit-switched infrastructure with a PBX or key system (for smaller offices) serving as a centralized switch. Under a voiceLAN scheme, both data and voice traffic are interleaved and switched as frames or cells over the same data network.

Organizations should consider running their voice traffic over the LAN infrastructure for several reasons:

- **Single infrastructure.** VoiceLAN eliminates the need for a cabling plant dedicated to voice only. Converged voice/data traffic running over a single wire reduces the upfront cost of equipment procurement (e.g., cable, patch panels, racks, installation), cable plant management (i.e., dealing with moves, adds, and changes), and maintenance.

0-8493-0859-3/00/$0.00+$.50

- **Single organization.** VoiceLAN allows enterprises to consolidate and streamline separate support organizations for data and voice networks. This convergence produces a more efficient, less costly management structure that spends less time "coordinating" and more time delivering network services and applications to users.
- **Breaking PBX lock-in.** For the most part, PBXs are proprietary, single-vendor systems, which usually means they are inflexible and expensive to maintain. VoiceLAN deployment paves the way for an open client/server model to be applied to telephony, creating a less rigid vendor-client relationship.
- **New level of CTI.** Current CTI systems allow data and voice application environments to "talk" to each other by means of computer-to-PBX links. CTI is included implicitly in the voiceLAN model. VoiceLAN also distinguishes itself from CTI because data and voice applications actually share the same set of standards and software interfaces. Thus voiceLAN leverages both media far beyond what is possible under present CTI systems, and has the potential to give organizations a distinct competitive advantage in the marketplace.

MIGRATING THE LAN INFRASTRUCTURE

Migration to voiceLAN is likely to encompass a number of smaller elements or activities. Migration cannot happen overnight, but is an evolutionary process that includes beneficial steps along the way. Over time, organizations can focus on improving elements of their network infrastructure, their desktop workstations, and their organizations in addition to their telephone systems.

A first step in deploying voiceLAN is to upgrade the present LAN infrastructure to support the demands of voice traffic without affecting the flow of existing data traffic. Infrastructure refers to the cabling plant and the local networking equipment used to carry traffic from end station to end station (i.e., hub, bridge, router, switches, and network adapters). The PBX is not considered part of the infrastructure in a voiceLAN environment; rather, the PBX will evolve into a call server that can be considered another type of end station on the LAN.

Solutions for Delay-Sensitive Applications

Voice bandwidth is not usually of much concern when using LANs for transmission. An uncompressed high-quality voice conversation needs only 64 Kbps, and compression or packetization reduces bandwidth requirements further. This represents only a small fraction of a dedicated 10 Mbps Ethernet LAN segment.

More important, voice is a delay-sensitive application that demands minimal latency (or minimal variations in latency, otherwise known as "jitter") in communications. The vast majority of LANs today are based on shared-bandwidth media. With Ethernet LANs, all users contend for bandwidth on a first-come, first-served basis. Token ring LANs are somewhat more deterministic since each end station transmits only when that end station holds the token, which passes from end station to end station at more or less regular time intervals. However, under both of these shared-bandwidth schemes, significant transmission delays, as well as variations in transmission delay, occur — severely disrupting a real-time voice conversation between end stations.

Desktop Switching

Part of the solution to this problem is to provide dedicated bandwidth to each user end station through desktop LAN switching. In a fully switched network, end stations do not contend (as in Ethernet) or wait (as in token ring) for bandwidth with other users; instead, each user workstation gets its own dedicated LAN segment for connectivity into the network. Migrating to a fully switched network (i.e., a single workstation or server per dedicated switch port) entails replacing existing shared-media LAN hubs with LAN switches.

Dedicated LAN switching has become affordable. Commodity Ethernet switches currently sell for less than $200 per port ($US), and ATM25 switches can be obtained for less than $400 per port ($US).

Minimize Routing

LAN switching only addresses bandwidth contention to the desktop. Links between desktop switches, or from desktop switches to building/campus switches, must also provide predictable, minimal delays for voice communications.

In most enterprise networks, routers are used to calculate paths and forward packets between LAN segments at Layer 3 of the OSI model. These routing algorithms introduce significant delay and usually add noticeable latency to voice communications. By contrast, switching involves a much simpler and faster process. Segmenting the network at OSI Layer 2 through switching, rather than at Layer 3 through routing, increases the capacity of the network to support delay-sensitive applications such as voice.

Although routing will continue to be necessary, especially in larger enterprise environments, implementation of voiceLAN requires minimizing routing in favor of switching. If deployed properly, switching removes the delay-inducing routing process from the path of most network traffic.

In many cases, this migration step entails replacing a collapsed backbone router with a backbone switch. The routing function can either be centralized through a one-armed router (or route server model) or distributed in switches providing desktop or departmental connectivity. In either case, traffic is typically switched through the network and only passes through a routing function when absolutely necessary.

Controlling LAN Backbone Traffic

Migrating the network from shared-access LANs and routing to switching is a prerequisite to voiceLAN implementation. However, a major challenge remains in ensuring that voice can be properly supported on the backbone links (e.g., trunk) between LAN switches.

Supporting both data and voice over a common backbone LAN infrastructure is essentially a bandwidth-contention issue — determining how to make sure that delay-sensitive voice traffic is not preempted by other data traffic traversing the same links. Various techniques for prioritizing different traffic, reserving bandwidth, or guaranteeing network-delay characteristics may be applied. Two solutions to this problem are roughly categorized as the frame-switching/IP and ATM-centric approaches.

Frame Switching/IP-based Solution. Because of the rapid decline in price of Ethernet switches and the large installed base of Ethernet adapters, switched Ethernet has become the most popular solution for organizations deploying desktop switching. It is only natural for many organizations to consider Ethernet (especially Fast Ethernet) trunks for interconnecting desktop switches to each other or to LAN backbone segment switches.

However, as Ethernet frames are switched across the network, delay problems may still occur for voice. Ethernet frames are variable in length, and Ethernet has no mechanism for prioritizing one frame over another. Therefore, as network traffic increases, small frames carrying a voice payload may often have to wait in switch buffer queues behind large frames carrying data. Because voice has a delay tolerance of only 75 milliseconds, the lack of prioritization across a switched Ethernet network may degrade the quality of voice communications. Furthermore, this fundamental problem will not disappear with expanded bandwidth under Fast (or Gigabit) Ethernet.

RSVP. Among the most promising solutions to Ethernet's lack of prioritization or guaranteed latency is to handle the problem at Layer 3 via the RSVP. RSVP, which was developed by the IETF and leading network product vendors, operates by reserving bandwidth and router/switch buffer space for certain high-priority IP packets such as those carrying voice traffic.

In effect, RSVP enables a packet switching network to mimic certain characteristics of a circuit-switching multiplexer network. However, RSVP is still only able to set up paths for high-priority traffic on a "best effort" basis; thus it cannot guarantee the delay characteristics of the network. Furthermore, as an OSI level 3 protocol, RSVP support requires that routing functionality be added to switches.

RSVP's best-effort capability is sufficient for several delay-sensitive applications, such as non-realtime streaming video or audio. However, it is questionable whether RSVP can support real-time voice communications over the LAN to a level of quality and reliability that is acceptable in a business environment.

ATM-Based Backbone Solutions. An alternative solution for delivering voiceLAN over a common data infrastructure is ATM. ATM was designed specifically to support both voice and data traffic over a common infrastructure and provides multiple QoS levels.

ATM's CBR service guarantees a virtual circuit of fixed bandwidth for high-priority traffic such as voice. In addition, ATM uses a relatively small, fixed-length cell (53 bytes) rather than a variable-length frame to transport traffic, thereby limiting the maximum time any one cell must wait in a switch buffer queue. The use of ATM links/trunks between LAN switches neatly solves the problem of supporting both voice and data traffic for that portion of the network.

ATM to the desktop is more problematic, however. The most common standard for ATM LANs operates at 155 Mbps over Category 5 UTC cable or optical fiber. However, deploying 155 Mbps ATM to every desktop is currently too expensive for the vast majority of organizations (although it is beginning to be deployed as a LAN backbone technology).

In order to deploy a reliable voiceLAN solution cost-effectively using ATM, a lower-cost access technology must be deployed to the desktop. However, this access technology must also be able to extend the benefits of ATM's QoS from the ATM backbone all the way to the desktop.

An organization can choose from among several potential access solutions, including ATM25, Ethernet using IP/RSVP, or Ethernet/CIF.

ATM25 Access. ATM25, as its name implies, is a 25 Mbps version of ATM designed specifically for desktop connectivity to a 155 Mbps ATM backbone. ATM25 provides all of the QoS benefits of higher-speed ATM and can be used to build end-to-end ATM networks. ATM25 can also operate over Category 3 UTC cable, whereas 155 Mbps ATM and Fast Ethernet require organizations to upgrade their UTP cabling to Category 5 UTP cable.

The downside of ATM25 is that it requires replacing all legacy network adapters where voiceLAN will be deployed. In addition, ATM25 adapters and switches are still considerably more expensive than 10Base-T Ethernet adapters and switches.

Yet, if deploying voiceLAN is a top priority for your company, installing a network featuring 155 Mbps ATM in the backbone and ATM25 to the desktop may be the most reliable and logical solution. Although ATM25 is a more expensive option than switched 10 Mbps Ethernet, the cost of an ATM25 connection (including adapter and switch port cost) fell substantially in 1996 to an average street price of $400 to $450 ($US).

Ethernet RSVP/IP Access. The most popular desktop connectivity option for data networking continues to be Ethernet, and the addition of desktop switching and Fast Ethernet technology only continues this trend. The challenge is combining IP over Ethernet network access links with ATM in the backbone in such a way that voiceLAN performance requirements can be satisfied.

One solution requires Ethernet-to-ATM desktop switches to include routing and RSVP support. The desktop end station sends voice in IP packets (further encapsulated inside Ethernet frames) to the switch, using RSVP to request bandwidth to be reserved for the voice conversation. The desktop switch then terminates the IP connection and converts the voice payload to ATM cells for transmission across the backbone (or the desktop switch may forward these IP datagrams across the ATM backbone without terminating the IP connection). The desktop switch is also responsible for mapping the RSVP bandwidth reservation request (at the IP level of the architecture) to an appropriate ATM QoS for the ATM connection.

Although this approach appears to provide the best of both worlds by combining an ATM backbone with the popularity of switched Ethernet to the desktop, it has not been demonstrated to be capable of guaranteeing the necessary quality of service needed for voice communications.

Ethernet CIF Access. CIF allows a desktop application to place voice traffic in ATM cells that are subsequently inserted into Ethernet frames by the network adapter driver for transport over the link from the adapter to switch. At the Ethernet switch, cells are extracted from the frames and sent across the ATM backbone.

CIF's primary advantage is that high-priority traffic, such as voice, can be given the necessary QoS from the desktop across the ATM network without having to actually install ATM end-to-end in the network. Furthermore, because voice does not utilize IP, the desktop Ethernet switch can be simpler and need not include more expensive and computer-intensive routing functionality. In this way, CIF may be a potential alternative to RSVP/IP for organizations migrating to switched Ethernet to the desktop but also interested in deploying voiceLAN.

CIF's ability to guarantee quality of service comes at a price. CIF requires installation of special software or NIC drivers in workstations to accomplish the framing of ATM cells. In addition, transporting traffic inside of ATM cells, which are in turn encapsulated by frames, entails significant overhead, reducing the usable bandwidth on an Ethernet segment to 6 Mbps to 7 Mbps.

CONSOLIDATION OF THE CABLING PLANT

A consolidated cabling plant that supports both voice and data is one of the primary benefits of implementing voiceLAN. With voiceLAN, the cabling plant supporting voice communications (e.g., cabling runs, patch panels, cross-connects) becomes a redundant, backup infrastructure that can be removed when the voiceLAN network stabilizes.

No matter what technology is used for voice transport (i.e., ATM or IP), voiceLAN deployment requires optical fiber in the risers of buildings for backbone connectivity. Most large organizations have already installed fiber for their LAN backbone and therefore no upgrade to the cabling plant is necessary. Exhibits 2-1 and 2-2 depict a consolidation of cabling plants through voiceLAN technology for a typical organization.

MIGRATING THE DESKTOP

The deployment of voiceLAN also entails a migration of the desktop PC to become telephony-enabled. Exhibit 2-3 illustrates the voiceLAN-enabled desktop environment. This migration has two components: hardware and software.

Hardware Upgrades

In a pure voiceLAN architecture, all voice calls are received via a PC and its LAN adapter card rather than via a desktop telephone wired to a PBX or voice switch. There are two alternative human interfaces for people to interact with the PC to receive voice communications: the PC itself and the traditional desktop telephone.

By using the PC as the interface, voice traffic is processed by a PC sound card and the user employs a PC-attached microphone and headset. This solution is appropriate for users who are already using a microphone and headset to keep their hands free for typing (e.g., telemarketers, travel agents, help desk operators). Disadvantages of this setup include the fact that voice packets are processed by the PC's CPU, potentially hampering performance of other applications that might be running simultaneously. In addition, if the PC locks up, the user's conversation may be interrupted.

For most users the desktop telephone is still appropriate as their voice communications interface. However, in a voiceLAN solution, this phone set must be able to connect directly to the PC so that voice traffic can be received directly from the network adapter card without having to pass

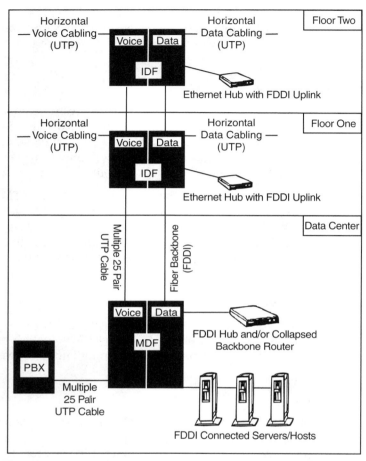

Key:
FDDI   fiber distributed data interface
IDF   intermediate distribution frame
MDF   main distribution frame
PBX   private branch exchange
UTP   unshielded twisted pair

Exhibit 2-1. Legacy voice and data cabling infrastructures.

through the CPU. Today this can be accomplished through a third-party plug-in card.

Universal Serial Bus. A more elegant solution for accomplishing a direct connection is the USB interface, originally developed by Intel. The motherboards of most new PCs included USB interfaces as standard features.

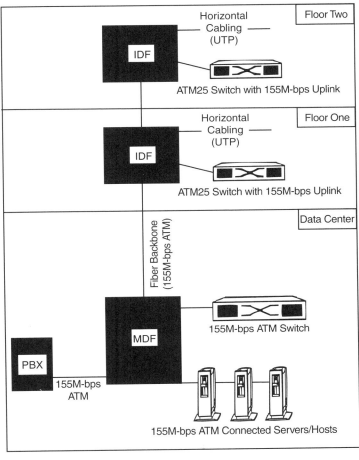

Key:
FDDI   fiber distributed data interface
IDF   intermediate distribution frame
MDF   main distribution frame
PBX   private branch exchange
UTP   unshielded twisted pair

Exhibit 2-2. Consolidated cabling infrastructure.

The USB supports 12 Mbps of throughput and allows USB-compatible telephone sets to connect directly to the PC without the need for an additional plug-in card. This alternative greatly reduces the cost of deploying voiceLAN. Several vendors have released or will soon release telephones conforming to the USB standard.

Firewire Bus. An alternative standard called Firewire — originally developed by Apple Corp., but currently being promoted by Sony and other consumer electronics companies — is also being introduced in new products.

21

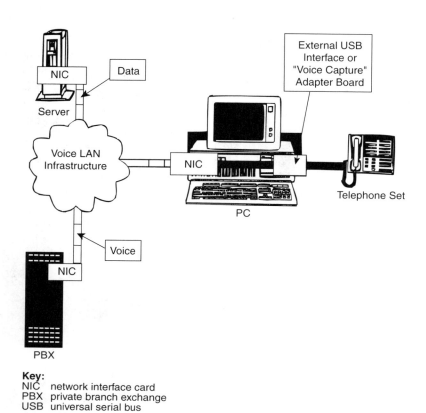

Exhibit 2-3. The VoiceLAN-enabled desktop.

The Firewire bus runs at speeds of up to 400 Mbps, which makes it appropriate for video traffic as well as voice. This high level of performance also may make Firewire too expensive for ubiquitous deployment, particularly if voiceLAN, not video, is the driving application. PC vendors may also be slower to develop Firewire-compatible telephones because of the Macintosh's declining share of the business market. Therefore, deploying USB-compatible phones is currently the most prudent choice for voiceLAN migration at the desktop.

Software Upgrades

To take maximum advantage of voiceLAN technology, PC-resident applications need to communicate with the PBX and PC-attached desktop phone sets. For this, a standardized software interface is required.

Most PBXs today support several such software APIs, though many of these interfaces provide translation of commands between the PBX and mainframe hosts for use in CTI applications such as call center applications. For Windows applications, most PBXs support Microsoft's TAPI. TAPI is available for Windows 95.

Microsoft Corp. has introduced a newer API, combining its Windows data transmission API (Winsock) with its voice communications API (TAPI). This consolidated API, known as Winsock 2, makes it even easier for developers to write integrated voice and data communications applications.

Clearly, the migration to a voiceLAN architecture is made much easier for organizations planning a substantial (Wintel) PC procurement in the next six months. These PCs are considered "voiceLAN ready" because they include both USB motherboards and systems software supporting TAPI/Winsock 2 APIs. Legacy PCs would need to have TAPI/Winsock 2 software and a third-party adapter board (for handset connectivity) installed.

MIGRATING THE PBX

Legacy Telephony

Today's PBX and telephony systems are analogous to the host and dumb terminal model of the mainframe era. PBXs are relatively inflexible, proprietary, and expensive to maintain and upgrade in the same way mainframes are. Phone sets are still the most ubiquitous desktop instrument for telephony communications, but the PC offers the most intuitive interface to advanced features. Moving from the traditional PBX model to a server-based telephony model represents the final stage in the migration to a fully integrated voice and data network.

Linking Distributed PBX Components

For organizations with large campus environments, an intermediate step between the legacy PBX and server-based telephony may be an architecture featuring multiple PBX components distributed throughout the campus.

This type of architecture has traditionally required a dedicated fiber backbone to connect multiple units. Under a voiceLAN solution, these units, outfitted with network adapter cards, can be connected over a LAN backbone infrastructure. This infrastructure is already in place in most larger campus network environments. In this case, the horizontal connection between the PBXs and the telephone sets at the desktop can continue to use the traditional voice network infrastructure.

There are two advantages to this architecture:

1. Distributed PBXs scale more cost-effectively than a single, large PBX.
2. The necessity for installing and maintaining dual backbones, one for voice and one for data, is eliminated.

Because this architecture does not implement voiceLAN to the desktop, it represents only a partial step toward a server-based telephony architecture. However, it also does not necessitate replacing old PCs with new ones outfitted with USB interfaces.

Server-Based Telephony

A server-based telephony architecture allows for the traditional functions of the PBX to be broken down into its components and distributed on the voiceLAN network. The switching function of the PBX can be handled by the frame or cell switches of the data network, whereas the call control function can be moved to a server. Specific telephony applications can also be moved to distributed application servers and integrated with other networked data applications.

Initial Implementation Tips. Implementing the ultimate voiceLAN architecture (depicted in Exhibit 2-4) cannot be accomplished through a wholesale changeover, except perhaps when an organization moves to a new building. Rather, this new architecture is typically deployed alongside the legacy PBX/dedicated voice network in the same way that organizations have deployed distributed servers running alongside centralized mainframes.

Server-based telephony should be implemented initially in specific workgroup environments. The best candidates are those workgroups that can best leverage server-based telephony applications that are available today.

Where a voiceLAN model is implemented, the user's port on the legacy PBX should be left unchanged until the voiceLAN deployment has stabilized and has been thoroughly tested. This is recommended because it provides, during the migration, redundancy and a backup system that can deliver phone service to the user.

The first phase of server-based telephony applications installed at the desktop is relatively basic. This configuration is similar to desktop PCs running terminal (i.e., phone handset) emulation and communicating with a LAN-attached mainframe (i.e., the PBX). While the integration with networked data applications is limited compared to a full-scale, server-based telephony architecture, it does give users an intuitive GUI interface for voice communications and allows the users a certain level of integration with their desktop applications.

Desktop Telephony Applications. Following are some examples of desktop telephony applications that should be considered for implementation in this initial phase. In these examples, the applications are enhanced by voiceLAN in that they are melded with real-time voice communications:

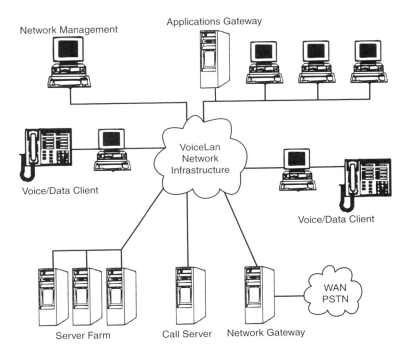

Key:
PSTN   public switched telephone network
WAN   wide area network

Exhibit 2-4. VoiceLAN architecture.

- **GUI phone.** At its basic level, this application running on the desktop provides a phone handset interface on the PC. The GUI phone prompts users to take more advantage of advanced call features that they are reluctant to utilize today simply because of the nonintuitive interface of existing phone handsets.
- **Integration with PIM software.** Integrating the GUI phone with PIM software provides a seamless link between the user's PIM application (e.g., an advanced electronic Rolodex) and the user's actual communications interface (e.g., the GUI phone). This application offers functionality similar to call center applications to general users right at their desktops.
- **GUI voice mail.** Voice mail can easily benefit from a graphic representation. At the click of a mouse, users scroll through a list of voice mail messages — saving, deleting, or forwarding messages. With this type of application, voice messages are treated as objects that can be manipulated in the same way data files are. For users, this method is potentially far more user-friendly and time-efficient than using the keypad of a phone handset.

25

- **Integrated messaging.** When voice mail is decoupled from the PBX architecture, full integration with other types of messaging applications (i.e., e-mail) can more easily take place. VoiceLAN simplifies the process of combining message media and potentially reduces the cost of integrated messaging.

MIGRATING USERS

As the voiceLAN network is tested for its reliability as a dedicated voice network, the organization can begin to migrate the general population of users. Individual users or entire workgroups can be moved on a line-by-line basis by installing a USB PC and USB handset at the desktop, eventually eliminating the legacy phone set connected via the dedicated voice network. The order in which users/workgroups are moved depends on each user/workgroup's ability and willingness to take advantage of integrated voice/data applications.

While the general population of users is being migrated, the organization should also begin to deploy more advanced applications in the original testbed workgroups. These applications can be tightly integrated with networked data applications (as opposed to desktop applications). The client/server applications that can be deployed in this final stage include:

- **Collaborative applications.** A server-based telephony architecture facilitates the integration of voice communications to collaborative software that allows multiple people to work on the same document while communicating.
- **Voice/database applications.** At present, computer telephony integration permits a certain level of integration between PBXs and databases; however, deploying such applications is expensive and generally reserved for telemarketing or customer service applications. A server-based telephony architecture allows high-end CTI functionality to be deployed on a much wider scale and to be made accessible to the general user population.

CONSOLIDATING THE VOICE AND DATA ORGANIZATIONS

One of the biggest advantages of deploying voiceLAN is the integration of voice and data network support teams and the eventual reduction in support costs. Many organizations have already begun consolidating their support organizations for voice and data without deployment of a voiceLAN architecture. Migrating to voiceLAN and to a server-based telephony architecture forces organizational consolidation among personnel from the voice and data environments.

Infrastructure Maintenance and Support Staff

The first operational element that needs to be integrated is the maintenance and support of the network infrastructure. In many organizations, these teams function separately. Initially, the voice team continues to maintain the legacy voice infrastructure, but that task should gradually disappear as users/workgroups move to the voiceLAN infrastructure.

The lighter burden for infrastructural maintenance allows personnel previously dedicated to supporting voice systems to be placed into applications development teams with members from both the data and voice environments. This blending of organizations mitigates some of the potential conflicts between groups of people from the voice and data environments. The consolidation of staff from the voice and data environments is also necessary to develop applications that tightly integrate voice and data. Furthermore, it may also reduce worries about job security on the part of voice-only staff, who may fear they have become expendable. Above all, a consolidated organization that supports all forms of network communications in the enterprise is better able to deliver increasingly sophisticated network services and applications to users.

RECOMMENDED COURSE OF ACTION

Achieving the end goal of voiceLAN implementation requires a series of logical steps. Individual organizations may start the migration at different points depending on their installed base of equipment, economic issues, or other decisions made to meet customer service demands and strategic business goals. The course of implementation may take three to five years. During that time, many technology hurdles will be overcome with standards development. Other issues, such as bandwidth congestion and the need for cost-efficiencies, are causing organizations to take a close look at convergent technologies that can solve problems today.

Various compelling events may precipitate these voiceLAN migration steps. Examples of such events, often designed to simplify management, satisfy growth, or save money, may include:

- Maintenance contract renewal
- Growth of new locations or branch offices
- Voice or data system upgrades
- Hiring of new personnel with new skills
- Reorganization (e.g., downsizing or substantial moves and changes)
- New bandwidth requirements (backbone and often selected user work groups)
- Optimizing wide-area access
- Delivery of training (i.e., video) to the desktop
- Improvements in communications via voice-annotated text or other media

Exhibit 2-5 summarizes, in table format, the key decision points in the migration to a voiceLAN network. The table is a broad road map for organizations that wish to begin factoring voiceLAN into their network architecture planning today. Decisions about information technology or services investments and their implications, are grouped in four areas — IT strategy, enterprise requirements, workgroup requirements, and desktop applications.

VoiceLAN in the backbone is the first logical step that can be implemented now to satisfy immediate business goals — notably, cost-efficiency and network management — and lay the framework for a converged network in the future. Implementing voiceLAN in the workgroup and at the desktop are steps that will be taken in the medium- to longer-term.

When selecting a vendor to work with as a business partner in the development of a voiceLAN implementation, corporate network managers should evaluate the vendors':

- published plans for voiceLAN implementation
- actual delivery of products included in these plans
- inclusion of voice as an integral component of an overall strategy rather than as a future possibility
- commitment to emerging voice-enabling standards

Voice system vendors — or those vendors providing the call servers, telephony sets, and voice software components — must meet additional criteria, including:

- migration to open, standards-based products
- track record in investment potential
- demonstrated experience in CTI
- partnerships with IT leaders for "best in class" solutions
- defined migration path to ATM (e.g., describing which telephony products can be leveraged and used in the new infrastructure and which products are no longer needed)

Exhibit 2-5. Decision points/recommendations for VoiceLAN migration.

Decision Points / Migration Steps	Typical Situation	Recommendation	Impact
Strategy	• Voice not a part of IT strategy • Separate budgets • Separate planning • Separate organizations	• Ensure voice and voiceLAN are embedded in IT strategy • Voice must be considered integral component of overall plan	• As compelling events occur and decisions are made, organization continually moves closer to voiceLAN goal
Enterprise	• More bandwidth required for workgroup or user applications • Corporate pressure to reduce costs and provide productivity improvements • Cost savings or simplicity (elimination of duplicate infrastructures) sought	• Evaluate opportunity to converge voice/data on single backbone • Upgrade or replace existing backbone LAN • Converge voice/data functional organizations	• Bandwidth issue resolved • Simplified infrastructure • Organization positioned for voiceLAN
Workgroup	• Application-specific bandwidth requirements • Productivity improvements and competitive advantage sought • Remote offices demanding "head-office" type functionality and access	• Voice-enable applications • Evaluate server-based telephony solutions • Exploit opportunity to trial voiceLAN technology on workgroup basis • Extend voiceLan-capable technology to workgroup via ATM or switched Ethernet access network	• Maximize productivity • Move another step closer to voiceLAN • Force a break from traditional voice model
Desktop	• Disparate voice and computing instruments and applications • Dual wiring infrastructure • Lost productivity	• Ensure strategy supports evolution to single wiring to the desktop • Opportunity to evaluate computer-attached telephones • Roll out in logical manner (starting with R&D organization, then general business groups, finally call centers)	• Final leg of voiceLAN convergence to the desktop • Achieve simplicity, cost savings through streamlined moves/changes • New applications deployment and enhanced productivity

29

Chapter 3
High-Speed Token Ring

Martin Taylor

ALTHOUGH THE POPULATION OF 20 MILLION DESKTOPS connected today by Token Ring may be dwarfed by the number of Ethernet connections that are out there, current users of Token Ring remain very loyal to the technology. The reasons are not hard to find — Token Ring's fault tolerance, manageability, performance, and efficient use of bandwidth get the job done. In large LAN installations where network availability is critical, one can depend on Token Ring to deliver.

The technology of Token Ring has been around for over 15 years, and it is a testament to the robustness of the original design concept that many large networks today continue to make use of essentially the same network components that powered those first, early installations. But that is not to say that Token Ring technology has stood still. The demand for increasing network bandwidth drove the introduction in 1989 of 16M bps Token Ring to quadruple the speed of the original 4M bps offering. More recently, the development of Token Ring switching increased backbone capacity to hundreds of megabits per second and added the possibility of dedicated, full duplex links carrying Token Ring traffic at 16M bps in both directions at once.

By and large, this evolution of Token Ring technology has kept ahead of the growing demand for bandwidth in most LAN installations, but the anticipation of continued growth of traffic in the future has naturally made some large Token Ring users nervous. The availability of solutions based on ATM (Asynchronous Transfer Mode) that can switch Token Ring traffic at speeds of 155M bps and beyond have provided some comfort; but to date, Token Ring users have not enjoyed a choice of high-speed solutions — unlike Ethernet, where Fast Ethernet, and more recently Gigabit Ethernet, offer a simpler and lower-cost alternative to ATM.

High-speed Token Ring (HSTR) addresses this imbalance. Supporting 100M bps and 1G bps Token Ring connections for interswitch links and for switch-to-server connections, HSTR provides the first simple and

0-8493-0859-3/00/$0.00+$.50
© 2000 by CRC Press LLC

cost-effective alternative to ATM for dealing with capacity issues in Token Ring backbones.

THE EMERGING NEED FOR HIGH-SPEED TOKEN RING

Continual growth in traffic loads is a seemingly inescapable fact of local area networks. PCs get faster and deal in more complex and information-rich data objects; intranet Web servers unlock corporate information resources for access by much wider communities of users; departmental server systems are displaced by corporate superservers. These and other trends contribute to a rising tide of data traffic that seems to devour all the bandwidth that can be thrown at it.

In Token Ring networks, switching is now the primary technology for tackling this growth in demand for LAN capacity. Shared 16M bps back-bone rings that link multiple workgroup rings with corporate mainframe and server resources can now be replaced with switching systems that handle hundreds of megabits per second of Token Ring traffic. The effect on network performance can be dramatic because user access to central resources — which was once throttled through overloaded 16M bps back-bone rings — now takes place at full wire speed through the fast backplane of a switch.

The 16M bps limitation of Token Ring does, however, limit the scalability of switched Token Ring networks. Connections between switches and con-nections from switches to servers represent traffic concentration points where 16M bps looks increasingly inadequate.

Some relief from overloaded interswitch connections can be obtained by taking advantage of the load-sharing capabilities that are inherent in Token Ring's source routing. Switches can be connected together with mul-tiple parallel dedicated 16M bps Token Ring links, and the properties of source routing will ensure that network traffic is shared approximately equally among the multiple links.

But load sharing across multiple links provides only temporary relief from network overloads as traffic continues to grow. Each additional link adds only another 16M bps of capacity and occupies another port on the switches at each end of the link. Furthermore, the use of multiple links does not provide a satisfactory solution to the problem of server access bottlenecks.

TODAY'S HIGH-SPEED OPTIONS FOR TOKEN RING USERS

To solve the problem of overloaded interswitch links and switch-to-server connections, a higher speed networking technology is needed. Up until now, Token Ring users have effectively had a choice between FDDI (Fiber Distributed Data Interface) and ATM (Asynchronous Transfer Mode).

Fast Ethernet has not, so far, provided a satisfactory high-speed backbone solution for Token Ring users. Differences in frame format, address bit ordering, and maximum frame size make it very difficult to carry out a direct translation between Token Ring and Fast Ethernet without introducing unacceptable compromises. It is possible to use routers to connect the Token Ring environment to a Fast Ethernet backbone, but the software processing overhead of routers, and the necessity to carry out packet fragmentation to deal with differences in maximum frame size, result in severe performance limitations. This is also a costly solution.

FDDI offers a fault-tolerant, shared 100M bps medium and meets many of the backbone connectivity needs of Token Ring users. Its token-passing access mechanism, which is based on that of Token Ring, enables its full bandwidth potential to be realized, and its dual reconfiguring ring topology provides very effective protection against cable or transmission link faults.

However, FDDI suffers two disadvantages that are responsible for its fall from favor among Token Ring users over the last few years. First, the FDDI frame format is different from that of Token Ring, and Token Ring switches that support FDDI links must perform a number of complex packet translation functions to support connectivity. This makes FDDI a relatively expensive solution. Second, FDDI offers no scalability options beyond the existing 100M bps standard. Other technologies such as ATM and Fast Ethernet have next-generation standards that scale into the gigabit range, and FDDI appears far less future proof by comparison.

ATM looks like a much more promising candidate for Token Ring backbone and server connections. With its ability to scale to 2.4G bps and beyond, its inherent fault tolerance, and its support for native Token Ring frame formats (in LAN Emulation mode), ATM meets all of the key needs of large Token Ring backbone installations.

But ATM is not ideal for all situations. It is a far more complex technology than Token Ring; and although it can be relatively easy to install and configure, there is too much new information for network technicians to learn if they are to be able to troubleshoot ATM networks successfully. ATM may also be regarded by some as an overkill solution for many Token Ring needs in terms of both its raw power and its sophisticated features for bandwidth reservation and quality of service support.

DEFINING THE REQUIREMENTS FOR HIGH-SPEED TOKEN RING

The requirements for a High-Speed Token Ring solution have been the subject of discussion and agreement among members of the High-Speed Token Ring Alliance, a consortium of Token Ring equipment vendors that was formed in August 1997. The objective of the Alliance is to define a simple, cost-effective, and scalable solution for switched Token Ring networks that preserves as much of the existing investment in Token Ring as possible while providing a forward evolution path for Token Ring networks that meet all foreseeable applications needs.

In particular, the Alliance agreed to the following set of needs:

- support for standard Token Ring frame formats
- speeds of 100M bps and beyond
- support for UTP, STP, and fiber cabling
- support for existing maximum packet sizes as defined in the 802.5 Token Ring standard
- support for all Token Ring bridging modes, including source routing, transparent, and SRT
- compatibility with the 802.1Q standards effort for Virtual LAN tagging

The Alliance also agreed that the most urgent needs for High-Speed Token Ring were for interswitch and switch-to-server connections. Therefore, the focus of HSTR development would be on dedicated point-to-point full duplex links rather than shared media operation. This would reduce the time taken to arrive at a new standard and make it easier for vendors to bring products to market relatively quickly.

THE TECHNOLOGY AND TIMESCALES OF HIGH-SPEED TOKEN RING

The process of developing a new LAN standard can take years, but the need for HSTR is already here and demand has grown rapidly. For this reason, the HSTR Alliance has cooperated very closely with the IEEE 802.5 committee on a "fast-track" resolution of technical issues to arrive at a completed standard.

Basing the standard as closely as possible on existing technologies is seen as the best way to get rapid agreement on the technical specification. The basis for HSTR is the existing 802.5r standard, which specifies full duplex, point-to-point, dedicated Token Ring operation at 4 and 16M bps. This will be adapted to operate first at 100M bps and then later at 1G bps.

The 100M bps speed was chosen in order to leverage the existing transmission technology on which Fast Ethernet is based. By making use of encoding schemes and transmission waveform specifications that have already been proven over both twisted pair and fiber optic cabling, the HSTR Alliance will minimize the amount of new technical thinking that needs to be done to arrive at a standard.

The first priority of the Alliance was to develop a specification for 100M bps HSTR over copper cabling, including both Category 5 UTP and IBM Type 1 STP. A specification for 100M bps HSTR over fiber cabling will follow soon after, based on the 802.5j Token Ring fiber standard adapted to run over the 100-Base-FX specification for Fast Ethernet on fiber.

Subsequent work focused on Gigabit HSTR. As might be expected, this will leverage the transmission technologies that are being developed to support Gigabit Ethernet over both copper and fiber cabling.

THE DEPLOYMENT OF HIGH-SPEED TOKEN RING

The first products supporting the new HSTR standards are likely to include 100M bps HSTR line cards for Token Ring switches, and 100M bps HSTR Network Interface Cards (NICs) for servers.

For most Token Ring users, the first application of HSTR will be for upgrading interswitch links. By installing HSTR line cards in existing Token Ring switches, interswitch links that are currently running at 16M bps can be very quickly upgraded to 100M bps.

HSTR provides full support for source routing, so backbone interswitch connections in fault tolerant networks with parallel load-sharing paths can be upgraded to 100M bps without compromising fault tolerance in any way. The HSTR connections between switches will behave in exactly the same way as existing 16M bps connections, except that they have more than six times the traffic capacity.

Some existing switched Token Ring networks make use of FDDI for inter-switch connections. Because HSTR will offer both lower cost and better performance for interswitch connections, it may be desirable to use HSTR for future upgrades to these networks and freeze any further investment in FDDI. Some Token Ring switches will support both FDDI and HSTR line cards, and this makes it relatively easy to carry out a phased migration to HSTR in the backbone while preserving current investment in FDDI.

After upgrading interswitch links, the next area that may need attention is the connection to enterprise servers. If servers are already connected directly to Token Ring switches by full duplex 16M bps links, and these links are becoming overloaded, then the server connections may be upgraded by installing a 100M bps HSTR adapter card and connecting directly to a port on a 100M bps HSTR line card in a Token Ring switch.

Some vendors are likely to introduce server NIC products that support 4, 16, and 100M bps on the same card. This provides excellent investment protection, because the server may be connected initially to a 16M bps switch port, and then moved later to a 100M bps switch port if greater throughput is needed.

HSTR is not initially targeted at desktop connections, but there is nothing to prevent it from being deployed at the desktop if needed. HSTR will be supported over both Category 5 UTP and IBM Type 1 STP cabling, and 100M bps HSTR NIC cards could be installed directly in desktop systems for connection to 100M bps HSTR switch ports. However, it is likely that adding 100M bps HSTR to the desktop would only be justifiable for exceptionally demanding applications such as very high-resolution imaging.

HIGH-SPEED TOKEN RING AND VIRTUAL LANS

In some situations, it may be useful to divide the Token Ring LAN into a number of separate broadcast domains or "Virtual LANs" that are defined logically rather than physically, and to use routers to move traffic from one VLAN to another. Typically, VLANs are defined by assigning each switch port to a particular VLAN identity. Traffic arriving at that port from end stations is deemed to belong to the VLAN associated with that port.

If making use of VLANs, then in general it is useful to be able to define VLANs that span multiple switches. The key property of a VLAN is that a broadcast or multicast packet originating within a given VLAN must only be delivered to switch ports that belong to the same VLAN. When using High-Speed Token Ring connections between switches, it becomes necessary to mark each packet with its VLAN affiliation so that one knows which switch ports this packet may be delivered to.

Where source routing is used, the originating ring number in the source routing information field of each packet is sufficient to identify the packet's VLAN affiliation, and one does not need to do anything new or special. But packets that are being transparently switched do not contain any information from which VLAN information can be deduced. To solve this problem (for both Ethernet and Token Ring networks), the IEEE 802.1Q working group is defining a packet-tagging scheme that enables VLAN information to be associated with each packet.

The emerging 802.1Q standard is fully compatible with High-Speed Token Ring, and will enable VLAN-tagged packets to be carried between Token Ring switches. The 802.1Q specification is also expected to define a standard method for identifying Ethernet packets that are being carried over Token Ring links. The implication of this is that HSTR could provide a backbone solution that integrates Token Ring and Ethernet traffic across a common high-speed infrastructure.

HIGH-SPEED TOKEN RING AND QUALITY- OF- SERVICE

Until High-Speed Token Ring arrived on the scene, ATM was the first choice of Token Ring users looking for major upgrades to backbone switching capacity. This is because ATM can provide a high-capacity, scalable, fault-tolerant backbone that handles native Token Ring frame formats and source routing.

One additional capability of ATM has also been a factor in its adoption for Token Ring backbones: quality-of-service. ATM networks can provide not only "best effort" delivery of packet data like Ethernet and Token Ring LANs, but it can also deliver time-sensitive traffic streams like voice and video with a guaranteed upper limit on end-to-end delay.

This capability of ATM is being exploited today in a minority of ATM installations to provide backbone integration of voice or video trunks across campus LANs. However, quality-of-service cannot easily be exploited for packet-based LAN traffic because it requires much more sophisticated edge switches linking Ethernet and Token Ring to ATM than are currently available. This has not been an issue so far because there are few, if any, desktop applications in use today that can exploit Quality-of- Service.

However, there is growing interest in the deployment of desktop video-conferencing and voice telephony over the LAN, and network planners making backbone evolution decisions need to take into account the possible requirements of the enterprise looking several years forward. ATM has been seen as a safe choice for the large-scale LAN backbone because it is expected to have no problem accommodating future requirements for voice and video in the LAN.

So, how does HSTR stack up against ATM for handling integrated packet-based voice and video in the LAN? The answer is that although HSTR cannot provide the same level of guaranteed service for real-time traffic streams as ATM, it is likely to be good enough for most practical needs.

PRIORITY ACCESS FOR VOICE AND VIDEO TRAFFIC

The original designers of Token Ring had the foresight to build into the standard a feature that was intended to enable support for real-time traffic in the LAN. This capability, which allows prioritization of time-sensitive data packets, has been built into every Token Ring product since 1985 that complies with the 802.5 standard, but has remained effectively dormant for lack of applications that can exploit it.

The token-passing access mechanism of Token Ring is a deterministic protocol that guarantees a station will be able to access the medium to send a packet within some fixed time limit, depending on the number of stations on the ring and the speed of the ring. Under normal operation, when there are a number of stations on the ring waiting to send a packet, the token is passed from one station to the next around the ring, granting the right to transmit a packet. The priority mechanism allows a station that is waiting to send a higher priority packet to preempt all the other stations and grab the token next. If one thinks of all the stations waiting to transmit packets on the ring as being in an orderly queue to access the medium, then a station wanting to send a higher priority packet effectively jumps the queue and can start transmitting as soon as the packet currently being transmitted by another station has finished.

The Token Ring priority mechanism supports eight levels of priority, 0–7. The code of practice adopted by the industry assigns normal data packets to Priority 0, and ring management packets to Priority 7. Packets being transmitted by a bridge port or switch port should be sent with Priority 4. This is a recognition of the fact that when a ring is connected to a Token Ring switch, a high proportion of the traffic carried on the ring will come from the switch port. So, using a higher priority for transmissions from the switch port provides users with better overall performance.

Token priority levels 5 and 6 are intended for time-sensitive applications such as voice and video. Tests carried out on Token Ring networks with various populations of users connected to a ring have shown that the use of Priority 5 or 6 for voice and video packets can guarantee access to the medium within a few milliseconds, provided that the overall bandwidth consumed by voice or video packets is kept within a reasonable proportion of the total bandwidth on the ring.

So, the token priority mechanism provides a means to support real-time traffic in the context of a single ring. But what happens when the network consists of many rings interconnected by switches? Can the switches preserve the priority of voice and video packets end to end across the network? And can they also expedite the delivery of voice and video packets over normal data packets? The answers depend on how the switches have been designed.

PACKET PRIORITY AND TOKEN RING SWITCHES

When a switch receives a packet to be forwarded to another ring, it can establish what priority the packet was transmitted with by looking in the Logical Link Control (LLC) header that is part of the packet. It is therefore possible for the switch to preserve this priority across the switch fabric and ensure that the same priority level is used to transmit the packet onto the destination ring. This ability to preserve packet priority across the switch fabric, and to transmit the packet onto the ring at the output port of the switch with the appropriate priority level, is the first prerequisite of a Token Ring switch for handling voice and video traffic.

But just preserving packet priority across the switch fabric is not enough. Token Ring switches have internal queuing mechanisms that buffer packets being sent to a particular output port when that port is congested. If there is only a single queue for an output port, then it is possible for a high-priority packet to be trapped in a queue within the switch behind several lower priority packets. The result is likely to be that voice and video packets suffer unacceptable delay variations across the network at times of heavy traffic loading.

The solution to this is to implement multiple queues within the switch fabric so that high-priority packets are sent to a different output queue than lower-priority packets. The switch must give precedence to the higher priority queues when selecting which packet to send next on a congested switch output port. This way, voice and video packets have their own queues and do not get trapped behind data packets. Provided that the total bandwidth of voice and video packets being sent to a particular switch output port is limited to a reasonable fraction of the speed of that port, there will not be a buildup of voice or video packets in the high-priority queues, so end-to-end transmission delays will be kept within acceptable limits.

This, then, is the second prerequisite of a Token Ring switch for handling voice and video traffic: the switch must implement multiple queues to enable higher priority voice and video packets to be expedited over normal priority data packets at congested switch ports.

PACKET PRIORITY AND HIGH-SPEED TOKEN RING

As explained, the priority mechanisms embodied in Token Ring work in two distinct ways. First, high-priority packets enjoy privileged access to the shared medium when there are multiple stations connected to the ring. And second, an appropriately designed Token Ring switch can make use of the priority indication within the Token Ring packet to expedite delivery of high-priority packets over those with lower priority when switch ports become congested.

High-Speed Token Ring will not, initially, provide a shared media mode of operation and, therefore, the priority mechanism that provides privileged access to shared rings does not apply to HSTR.

However, priority information embedded in Token Ring packets is preserved across HSTR links, and Token Ring switches can be designed that support multiple queues on outgoing HSTR ports. Therefore, HSTR links for interswitch or switch-to-server connections can form part of an end-to-end transmission path that supports packet prioritization and expedited delivery of high-priority packets.

MEETING THE NEEDS OF VOICE AND VIDEO IN THE LAN

Real-time interactive voice and video in the LAN requires both adequate bandwidth for the delivery of constant streams of packets containing voice and video information, and consistent low transmission delay end-to-end across the network.

ATM provides the most sophisticated solution for the delivery of voice and video in the LAN. An application can request that bandwidth be reserved for a voice or video stream, and place an upper limit on transmission delay. The ATM switches that make up the network assess whether there are sufficient resources to meet the request from the application and either accept or refuse the request. Once a bandwidth reservation request has been accepted by the ATM network, resources are set aside on each link of the end-to-end transmission path to ensure that the voice or video stream is delivered within the requested delay bounds.

All this sophistication, of course, comes at a price. ATM is a substantially more complex and more costly technology than Token Ring. Because of this, ATM has made little impact at the desktop. And the popularity of ATM in the LAN backbone is based on other attributes of ATM besides Quality of Service: capacity, scalability, and fault tolerance.

Using end-to-end packet prioritization and expedited delivery of priority packets in the LAN is a much less sophisticated solution for voice and video than ATM can offer. However, it is also much simpler, and it leverages capabilities that are already built into the Token Ring network. The only circumstances under which it will not work so well are when bandwidth is very constrained and when voice and video traffic occupies a high proportion of the available bandwidth. But bandwidth in the LAN is relatively inexpensive, and it is generally cheaper and easier to over-provision capacity in the LAN to enable good voice and video performance with packet prioritization than it is to introduce a new and different technology for this purpose.

CONCLUSION

High-Speed Token Ring offers existing Token Ring users a simple incremental upgrade path for switched Token Ring backbones. Carrying native Token Ring frame formats with support for all Token Ring bridging schemes including source routing, HSTR is a logical extension of the Token Ring environment to 100M bps and 1G bps transmission speeds.

Both HSTR and ATM can meet all the practical backbone needs of large Token Ring installations in terms of capacity, scalability, and fault tolerance. HSTR will generally cost less than ATM for equivalent network capacity and involves less new knowledge to install and manage. ATM, on the other hand, can provide guaranteed quality of service, can be seamlessly extended over public and private WAN environments, and provides for a more peaceful coexistence with Ethernet in mixed-technology installations.

Token Ring users planning backbone upgrades now have the luxury of a choice. With HSTR and ATM to choose from, network planners are more likely to find a backbone solution that precisely fits their own particular needs.

Chapter 4
Should You Migrate Your Token Ring Network to Ethernet?

Randall Campbell

TOKEN RING NETWORK MANAGERS ARE FACED WITH THE DIFFICULT DECISION of staying with Token Ring or migrating to Ethernet. Making matters worse is that analysts, consultants, and vendors do not always agree on the answer. Some recommend abandonment of Token Ring as soon as possible and a move to Ethernet. Others suggest that Token Ring is strategic and one should stay with it forever. Ultimately, one has to decide what to do. This article examines the technical and business factors that will help determine the future direction of the network.

First of all, take a look at a few of the more obvious facts about the local area networking market. Regardless of how it is measured, the Ethernet market is much larger than the Token Ring market. This has resulted in increasing choices, decreasing prices, and rapid advancement of technology for the Ethernet user. Unfortunately, Token Ring technology has not advanced as quickly and prices remain much higher. Also, fewer vendors are offering Token Ring solutions, as many view this to be a declining market.

Recently there has been much press about new high-speed alternatives for Token Ring. Some argue that Token Ring customers have not needed higher speeds until recently, therefore these new technologies are arriving just in time. This is extolled as a revival of the Token Ring market and a reason for customers to stay with Token Ring. Others, however, say that this is too little and too late to stem the tide of customers migrating to Ethernet.

There is a business to run and one needs to make the best choice possible for the company, both in the short term and for the long term. Thus, one can examine the technical and business issues that should be considered. At the end, a checklist will be provided that will help weigh those factors that are most important in making this decision.

0-8493-0859-3/00/$0.00+$.50
© 2000 by CRC Press LLC

UNDERSTANDING LANs

First, let's examine the technical issues. What are the differences between Token Ring and Ethernet? Will an Ethernet network support all applications?

DIFFERENCES BETWEEN TOKEN RING AND ETHERNET

With the current state of LAN switching technology, many of the important differences between Ethernet and Token Ring have disappeared. Both Token Ring and Ethernet can provide a full duplex, dedicated link to the desktop from a LAN switch. This gives each user his own LAN segment with dedicated 10/100 or 4/16Mbps of bandwidth. There are no collisions and no one with whom to share a token. In fact, for full duplex Token Ring there is no token and no ring. In this environment the only important differences are the speed, maximum frame size, source routing support, and IP multicast support.

Speed

The speed issue has recently become a topic of debate with the efforts of Token Ring vendors to establish a standard for 100Mbps and 1Gbps Token Ring. 10Mbps and 10/100Mbps Ethernet NICs, hubs, and switches are widely available today. Gigabit Ethernet is standardized and becoming widely available. Token Ring is widely available in 4 and 16Mbps versions.

The proposed High Speed Token Ring (HSTR) standards provide for 4/16/100Mbps Token Ring and 1Gbps in the future. There are no 100Mbps hubs planned for Token Ring because the proposed HSTR standards do not support shared media. At the time of this writing, 100Mbps HSTR NICs are just emerging and are priced at three to five times more than 10/100Mbps Ethernet NICs. Although there are stated goals to support both Token Ring and Ethernet over HSTR, initial offerings are Token Ring only. So, the only real difference in speed is 4/16Mbps vs. 10Mbps for client NICs. Server and backbone speeds for both Token Ring and Ethernet are the same.

Some vendors are providing support for Token Ring over Fast and Gigabit Ethernet links. This has the advantage of providing Token Ring frame support at or close to the price points of Ethernet. An important capability of these solutions is the ability to support both Token Ring and Ethernet over the same link at the same time. This makes migration easier by allowing installation of a single high-speed backbone for Token Ring and Ethernet clients and servers.

Maximum Frame Size

The other performance-related difference is the maximum frame size. All speeds of Ethernet are limited to 1500 bytes as the maximum frame size. The maximum frame size for Token Ring can be set as low as 516 bytes and as high as 17,749 bytes. The typical value is 4399 bytes. On the surface this appears to be a good thing. After all, the more data one can send per frame, the better the throughput, right?

As usual, things are not that simple. The benefit of large frames is most apparent on the server. Conventional wisdom states that the CPU in a server has to process each frame transmitted or received. The more bytes there are in each frame, the fewer frames are needed to send the same amount of data. This results in lower CPU utilization. This would be true if all NICs were created equal. CPU utilization depends a great deal on how efficiently data transfers occur across the bus. The NIC hardware, drivers, and operating system can impact performance and CPU utilization more significantly than frame size.

Well, if NICs are efficient, are large frames better? There is another trade-off that needs to be considered. This has to do with the number of store-and-forward hops between the clients and servers. A store-and-forward hop can be a router, bridge, or switch in either the LAN or over the wide area network (WAN). Each store-and-forward hop must completely receive the frame before it forwards it on the next hop in the path. The larger the frame, the longer it takes to receive it, and the longer it takes to transmit it. This can result in increased end-to-end latency that can negatively impact performance.

Without going into great detail about queuing theory and flow control, the net result is that larger frames work best over short, fast paths. Smaller frames work best over longer, slower paths. Typically, the network is a mix of short and long paths. For example, the LAN has short, fast paths and the WAN has longer, slower paths. Based on the author's experience, a maximum frame size of around 2000 bytes provides good performance for both the LAN and WAN. By the way, cut-through switching (in which the bridge or switch forwards the frame on the output link as it is being received on the input link) can help, but cut-through only occurs if the input and output link are running at the same speed. If they are different speeds, even a cut-through switch will use store-and-forward.

Source Routing

Source routing is a technique for bridging LANs that is not available on Ethernet. Ethernet only supports transparent bridging. There are three advantages of source routing over transparent bridging: multiple parallel paths, duplicate MAC addresses, and network management.

Source routing allows traffic to be distributed over parallel bridge paths through the network. With Ethernet, parallel paths are allowed, but all traffic will take the same path. The other paths will be inactive until the active path fails. When the active path fails, the spanning tree protocol will automatically activate another path. There is an advantage to this approach. When a source routing path fails, the end systems have to rediscover a path. This may result in the failure of sessions (for example, SNA sessions). In Ethernet, a path change is transparent to the end system (this is why it is called transparent bridging). Therefore, sessions typically do not fail when the path changes in Ethernet. Pure transparent bridging can be used on Token Ring; however, this is not typical. Some networks use Source Route Transparent (SRT) bridging where some traffic will be bridged via source routing and other traffic, such as IPX, will be bridged using transparent bridging.

Duplicate MAC address support is a technique that was developed to get around a shortcoming of SNA. SNA did not implement an address resolution protocol on the LAN. As a result, SNA users had to configure the MAC address of their SNA gateway in their client. If the gateway failed, they would have to reconfigure a backup gateway or wait for the gateway to be repaired. Since source routing bridges or switches only look at the source routing information to determine the path, it is possible to put the same MAC address on two different ring numbers. This allowed the network manager to configure two identical SNA gateways with the same MAC address on two different Token Rings (with different ring numbers). Now, the SNA gateway would connect to the first gateway that responded to the client explorer frame (this is pretty much a random choice). If that gateway failed, the session would fail, but the client could immediately reconnect to the other gateway. This technique has been widely used in SNA to provide backup and load distribution between gateways.

Ethernet does not support source routing. All forwarding decisions in bridges and switches are made by looking only at the destination MAC address. As a result, a MAC address can only appear on a single Ethernet segment. Duplicate MAC addresses are simply not supported. One way to provide SNA gateway backup on Ethernet is to use a protocol in the gateway to activate a backup with the same MAC address if the primary fails, or a protocol in the client to reconfigure it to a different gateway. One can also use a single source route/translational (SR/TLB) bridge between the Ethernet network and the Token Ring attached SNA gateways as shown in Exhibit 4-1. Another alternative is to change from pure SNA clients to the tn3270 or tn5250 protocol. Tn3270/5250 runs over TCP/IP and uses TCP/IP for alternate path support.

Source routing is helpful for network management in that each frame contains the bridging path from source to destination. This is useful when looking at traces since one can tell on which ring number a frame originated and where it is headed. On Ethernet, one must keep up with where MAC addresses are located. This can also be automated via a variety of tools and can include Layer 3 addresses such as IP, IPX, or NetBIOS.

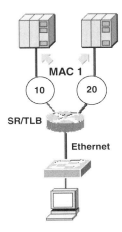

Exhibit 4-1. SNA gateway backup using SR/TLB.

Source routing has its share of headaches as well. Because the procedures for discovering a source route were never well standardized, there are a variety of problems that occur with different implementation of protocol drivers and protocol stacks. Recently there was a situation where the client was configured to use source routing and the server was not using source routing. With this configuration, the server should not send or respond to source-routed frames. However, when the client and server are on the same ring, the server would actually respond to a source route frame from the client. When the client and server were on different rings it no longer worked. There are other cases where clients will send excessive explorers and flood the network when connections are lost to their servers. Ethernet is much simpler because it only supports transparent bridging. This is why some network managers have moved to transparent bridging on their Token Ring networks.

IP Multicast

IP multicast is increasingly being used for distribution of live or scheduled multimedia information over the network. A server can send a single multicast packet of voice, video, or data to the network that multiple clients can receive. The network will duplicate this multicast packet as needed to get a copy to each client registered to receive it. This technique greatly reduces the load on the server and the amount of traffic sent through the network.

Unfortunately, IP multicast is very difficult to do effectively on Token Ring networks. The reason has to do with the way different multicast

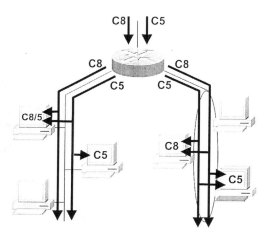

Exhibit 4-2. Token ring IP multicast using functional address.

streams are identified at the MAC layer. Think of a multicast stream as a TV channel. On Ethernet, each channel uses a different MAC group address as the destination address of the frame. Ethernet NICs can support multiple group addresses at the same time. Therefore, an Ethernet NIC can tune in to Channels 8 and 5 and ignore all other channels. It does this by only copying frames destined to the MAC group address for Channels 8 and 5.

Unfortunately, most Token Ring NICs support only a single group address. Equally unfortunate is that most of them do not support the universally administered group addresses used by IP multicast. Therefore, on Token Ring, all IP multicast data is typically sent to the broadcast MAC address or a functional address. If the functional address is being used, a Token Ring NIC will either receive all of the channels or none of them, as illustrated in Exhibit 4-2. If the broadcast MAC address is being used, all Token Ring NICs on the LAN will receive all of the channels if any one is tuned in to a single channel. These received multicast frames are sent to the CPU in the client or server regardless of whether there is any application running to process them. This can result in significant unnecessary use of the CPU.

WILL AN ETHERNET NETWORK SUPPORT ALL OF MY APPLICATIONS?

The short answer is yes. The author cannot think of any applications that only run over Token Ring. For years SNA only ran over Token Ring, but SNA over Ethernet abounds today. One might have devices that only support Token Ring interfaces, such as 3174 control units. Source route translational bridging can be used to connect these Token Ring devices to an Ethernet network.

The only function Ethernet cannot provide is duplicate MAC address support. If one relies on this feature of source routing on Token Ring, it will be necessary to either migrate the SNA to TN3270/5250 or automate the gateway backup via other means. The other main difference between Token Ring and Ethernet is the maximum frame size. This may provide some performance advantage for Token Ring over Ethernet, but with the increasing performance of clients and servers these differences will be less noticeable.

If one has decided Ethernet can support the applications, what are the migration issues that need to be considered?

Migration Issues

The first migration issue is cabling. If one already has unshielded twisted pair (UTP) cabling for the Token Ring network, one is in good shape. For Category 5 UTP cable, one can run both 10Mbps and 100Mbps Ethernet; for Category 3 cable one can run 10Mbps Ethernet. What if one is currently using the IBM cabling system with Type 1 or 2 cable? This is a shielded twisted pair (STP) cable with 150-ohm impedance instead of the 100-ohm impedance for UTP. One cannot directly connect an Ethernet NIC or port to the IBM Type 1 or 2 STP cable.

There are a few choices in this situation. For IBM Type 2 cable, one can use the UTP Category 3 telephone pairs for Ethernet. It will be necessary to wire these cables to an RJ45 jack in the office. For IBM Type 1 cable and no UTP cable, one can either rewire the building (no fun) or use baluns to convert the impedance from 150 ohms to 100-ohm. These baluns have an RJ45 female connector and an IBM cabling system connector. One will need one of these baluns at each end of the cable.

The second migration issue is interoperability during the migration. The length of the migration will determine how best to provide this. There are two basic approaches. One is to migrate as quickly as possible by replacing the current Token Ring NICs and installing an Ethernet switched network. The other is to move to Ethernet as devices are replaced; when a new PC comes in the door it is installed on the Ethernet network. The existing PCs remain on the Token Ring network until they are replaced.

To migrate quickly, simply leave the current Token Ring backbone in place and install the new Ethernet backbone. Typically, one would use existing routers to interconnect the Token Ring and Ethernet backbones. As clients and servers are upgraded with new NICs, they are connected to the Ethernet backbone. This will likely require changing the client's or server's network address, which can be done automatically with DHCP for TCP/IP. For IPX, the clients will automatically find their nearest server, but servers will have to be reconfigured manually.

To migrate gradually, a single high-speed backbone that can support both the Token Ring and Ethernet users is desirable. The choices for a high-speed backbone are ATM, Fast/Gigabit Ethernet, or HSTR at some point in the future. When using ATM as a backbone, it is easy to support both Token Ring and Ethernet. If Fast/Gigabit Ethernet is used for the Ethernet network, then look for a vendor that can support full Token Ring capability over this backbone. It will be a nonstandard implementation, but it can provide an easy way to migrate to Ethernet without building separate Ethernet and Token Ring backbones. HSTR may be an option in the future, but at the time of this writing it only supports Token Ring frames at 100Mbps. Even if it does support Ethernet frames and 1Gbps in the future, it will likely be much more expensive than a Fast/Gigabit Ethernet solution.

Next, one needs a way to interconnect the Token Ring and Ethernet network. The best solution is to use routing, either in a router or in a switch. Protocols that are routable such as IP and IPX should be routed, with the Ethernet and Token Ring networks configured as different subnets or networks. Nonroutable protocols such as SNA and NetBIOS can be translationally (SR/TLB) bridged. Typically, routers will support both routing and SR/TLB bridging between Token Ring and Ethernet. Routing will block broadcast and explorer traffic between the LANs and thereby reduce the impact of any broadcast storms.

Many customers are eliminating nonroutable protocols. NetBIOS can be run over TCP/IP very effectively and provides superior scaling to the native version. SNA traffic can be converted to tn3270/5250 and therefore also run over TCP/IP. This eliminates the need to have SNA session routing in the network. Even Novell is migrating Netware to run over TCP/IP. Migration to TCP/IP as the only networking Layer 3 protocol is a good goal to set because it eliminates the complexity of managing multiple Layer 3 protocols and allows the use of high-speed, Layer 3 switching technologies that tend to be IP only.

For the routable protocols, parallel routers can be used between subnets and networks. The routing protocols will provide for automatic path selection and backup. For any nonroutable protocols, parallel paths can only be used if there is the capability to run spanning tree end-to-end across both the Ethernet and Token Ring network. This can be a tricky function to implement, so it is usually best to provide a single path for bridging between the Token Ring and Ethernet network. Network management can be used to activate backup paths in the event of a failure.

One of the issues sometimes mentioned by Token Ring vendors about mixing Token Ring and Ethernet is the maximum frame size differences. Some will claim that this can cause a severe problem with either dropped frames or degraded performance. It is true that there could be some problems in this area; however, there are effective ways to handle this issue.

For TCP/IP, there are two mechanisms available to solve mismatches in frame sizes. Modern TCP protocol implementations will negotiate the frame size down to the smallest supported on either end of the connection. If a Token Ring user is connecting to a server on Ethernet, the maximum frame size will be set to 1500 bytes and all will be fine. If TCP is not being used and the Token Ring user sends a frame larger than 1500 bytes, the router can perform IP fragmentation and convert the large frame into multiple frames that are no larger than 1500 bytes.

For nonroutable protocols, the SR/TLB function can use the routing information field (RIF), which is part of source routing, to bring the frame size down to 1500 bytes. This will result in the Token Ring client only sending 1500 byte frames to an Ethernet server while still being able to send larger frames to a Token Ring server. In most cases, these mechanisms will effectively resolve frame size differences.

To summarize, the main issues for migration are to choose a backbone technology that can support both Token Ring and Ethernet and the use of routing and translational bridging to support interoperability between the LANs. One should always be aware of possible issues with the different frame sizes, but in most cases this will happen automatically. If the application does not automatically adjust, one will need to configure the maximum frame size for the application on Token Ring to 1500 bytes.

BUSINESS ISSUES

Thus far, the technical differences between Token Ring and Ethernet and the issues involved in migration have been discussed. Understanding these issues will help in dealing with the business issues that usually revolve around satisfying a wide variety of demands from users and corporate management. How many times has one heard the following?

- The network is too slow, we are losing productivity.
- The network is critical; we lose lots of money every minute the network is down.
- We have a new application that we are rolling out. Can the network handle it?
- We keep getting a lot of dropouts when we play audio and video streams over the network.
- My new PC came with an Ethernet interface; why can't I use it?
- The CFO says we are spending too much on the network, so he has cut our budget.

It always seems that everyone wants the network manager to do more with less, but the network manager has problems to deal with as well. It will be necessary to manage the network, define and deliver service levels, train employees so that they are effective in dealing with problems, and make the most cost-effective use of the budget available. When faced with all of these requirements and pressures, the typical reaction is to try to tweak the current network architecture to meet the needs with the least amount of change.

There is no doubt that simply upgrading the existing Token Ring network will provide the least amount of change. Migration to a new technology is difficult, time consuming, and will likely result in some problems during the migration. The most conservative approach is simply to enhance the existing Token Ring network.

On the other hand, the network manager may not be able to meet all of the requirements placed on him by simply upgrading the Token Ring network. For example, if there are definite needs for Ethernet connectivity, heavy requirements for IP multicast, or requirements for high-speed backbones and Layer 3 switching today, one will at least need to provide an integrated Token Ring and Ethernet network. Most of the short-term requirements can likely be met by upgrading the Token Ring network or providing the integration of some Ethernet technology.

The real issue is the long-term viability of Token Ring. It is doubtful that Token Ring will ever increase in popularity or catch up with Ethernet in terms of technology or price. HSTR is unfortunately too late to attract the interest of many vendors other than traditional Token Ring NIC vendors. Since the number of Token Ring vendors is not likely to grow significantly, Token Ring customers will always have fewer choices than Ethernet customers. Over the long term, an Ethernet network clearly provides more choices, both in terms of vendors and technologies.

If one cannot, or does not want to migrate to Ethernet, then the best choice is to build the switched network so that one can easily support both Token Ring and Ethernet users. The short-term solution may be to only support Token Ring users. If one builds an infrastructure that can support both, one can add Ethernet users in the future if the requirements change. Therefore, choose vendors that can provide a single backbone for both Token Ring and Ethernet, whether it be ATM, Fast/Gigabit Ethernet, or even HSTR. Ideally, you should not have to pay more for a backbone infrastructure that can support both Ethernet and Token Ring than you would pay for one that only supports Ethernet.

SUMMARY

It is possible to migrate to Ethernet from Token Ring, and there are short-term and long-term advantages in doing so. One can build higher capacity LANs at lower cost with Ethernet than with Token Ring. There are a few features and functions that one has to work around (e.g., duplicate MAC address support), but one gains better support for IP multicast. So, should one migrate?

Exhibit 4-3. Determining factors for your network..

Rank	Criteria	Advantage
____	New equipment cost must be kept as low as possible	Ethernet
____	CPU utilization must be kept as low as possible	Token Ring
____	Non-ATM, high-speed backbone and server connections are desired	Ethernet
____	Duplicate MAC address support is needed	Token Ring
____	IP multicast applications required	Ethernet
____	Active parallel switching path is needed	Token Ring
____	Layer 3 switching required	Ethernet
____	Minimize change to the network	Token Ring
____	Need to exploit latest technology for business advantage	Ethernet
____	Must use IBM type 1 or 2 cable	Token Ring

This is a decision that only the network manager can make. If one needs to keep up with the latest networking capabilities and new applications, migration to Ethernet is a wise choice. If one has limited resources and no major needs to change, enhancing the existing Token Ring network may be best. If one chooses to stay with Token Ring in the short-term, make sure that the backbone solution can support Ethernet users in the future. This will minimize headaches if one decides to migrate to Ethernet in the future.

Exhibit 4-3 summarizes a series of factors that can be used to determine which issues are the most important in your network. After ranking the items, sort them from high to low and see which technology best satisfies the most important items. Enter an importance factor for each item (1 is low; 5 is medium; 10 is high).

Chapter 5
Introduction to 100Base-T: Fast (and Faster) Ethernet
Colin Mick

FAST ETHERNET (100BASE-T), an extension to the IEEE 802.3 Ethernet standard to support service at 100M bps, is virtually identical to 10Base-T, in that it uses the same media access control (MAC) layer, frame format, and carrier sense multiple access with collision detection (CSMA/CD) protocol. Network managers can use 100Base-T to improve bandwidth and still maximize investments in equipment, management tools, applications, and network support personnel.

INTRODUCTION

Fast Ethernet (100Base-T) is an extension to the IEEE 802.3 Ethernet standard to support service at 100M bps. It is virtually identical to 10Base-T in that it uses the same media access control layer, frame format, and carrier sense multiple access with collision detection (CSMA/CD) protocol. This means that network managers can use 100Base-T to improve bandwidth and still make maximum use of investments in equipment, management tools, applications, and network support personnel.

100Base-T is designed to work transparently with 10Base-T systems. Switches (high-speed, multiport bridges) are used to connect existing 10Base-T networks to 100Base-T technology. By building networks with 100Base-T and 10Base-T linked with switches and repeating hubs, network designers can build networks that provide four levels of service:

1. Shared 10M-bps service
2. Dedicated (switched) 10M-bps service
3. Shared 100M-bps service
4. Dedicated 100M-bps service

Operating at higher speeds with the same frame size and the CSMA/CD protocol requires that 100Base-T collision domain diameters be smaller — typically about 200 meters. In 100Base-T, larger networks are built by combining collision domains by way of switches. Fiber (100Base-FX) links are used to support long (i.e., 412 meters in half duplex, 2 kilometers in full duplex) cable runs. Within a single collision domain, port density is increased by using modular or stacking hubs.

The 100Base-T standard (IEEE 802.3u, 1995) currently defines four physical layer signaling systems:

1. 100Base-TX supports operation over two pairs of Category 5 unshielded twisted pair (UTP) or shielded twisted pair (STP) cables
2. 100Base-T4 supports operation over four pairs of Category 3, Category 4, or Category 5 UTP or STP cables
3. 100Base-T2 supports operation over two pairs of Category 3, Category 4, or Category 5 UTP or STP cables
4. 100Base-FX supports operation over two 62.5-micron multimode fibers

Products for 100Base-TX and 100Base-FX are available from a wide range of manufacturers. Products for 100Base-T4 are supported by a smaller group of manufacturers, and no products have yet been offered for 100Base-T2.

In addition, the Fast Ethernet standard has recently added support for full-duplex operation and flow control. Full-duplex operation is broadly available in current 10Base-T and 100Base-T products.

HOW IT WORKS: AN ISO VIEW

Exhibit 5-1 depicts an ISO seven-layer diagram comparing 10Base-T and 100Base-T. Both 10Base-T and 100Base-T defined operations at the lower half of the data link layer (known as the Media Access or MAC layer) and the physical layer. Extension of the Ethernet standard to 100M-bps operation required one small change to the MAC layer operation specified in the IEEE802.3 standard. Originally, timing was defined in absolute terms (i.e., an external reference clock). As a result, timing specifications were defined in milliseconds, nanoseconds, and picoseconds. To support 100M-bps operation, timing was respecified relative to the internal clock of the MAC. This meant that specifications were defined in bit times.

Several changes were made at the physical layer. In 10Base-T, coding (i.e., conversion of data bits to symbols) is done in the PLS layer, directly below the MAC. A mechanical interface called the attachment unit interface (AUI) is situated directly below the PLS. Below the AUI is the PMA layer, which converts the digital symbols into analog symbols that can be

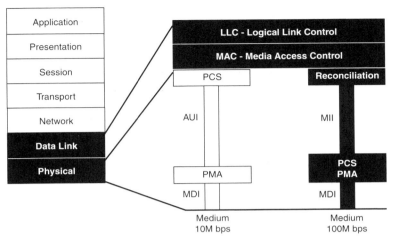

Key:
AUI   Attachment unit interface
MDI   Media dependent interface
MII   Media independent interface
PCS   Physical coding sublayer
PMA   Physical medium attachment sublayer

Exhibit 5-1. 100M bps standards model.

sent across the wire, and a media-dependent interface (MDI) — a socket for connecting the cable.

100Base-T puts the coding, called the physical coding sublayer (PCS), below the mechanical interface. This is done to make it possible to offer a variety of coding systems that can be packaged in a transceiver along with the analog/digital circuitry for connection via the mechanical interface. The mechanical interface used for 100Base-T is called the Media Independent Interface (MII). It is similar to the AUI, but offers a larger data path and the ability to move management information between the PHY and the MAC. A simple mapping function, called the Reconciliation Sublayer, handles linking the MII to the MAC. As noted previously, 100Base-T currently supports four signaling systems (see Exhibit 5-2): 100Base-TX, 100Base-T4, 100Base-T2, and 100Base-FX.

Two 100Base-T signaling systems — 100Base-TX and 100Base-FX — are based on the transport protocol/physical medium dependent (TP/PMD) specification developed by the ANSI X3T12 committee to support sending fiber distributed data interface (FDDI) signals over copper wire (see Exhibit 5-3). TP/PMD uses continuous signaling, unlike the discrete signaling used with 10Base-T. In 10Base-T, when a station is finished sending a

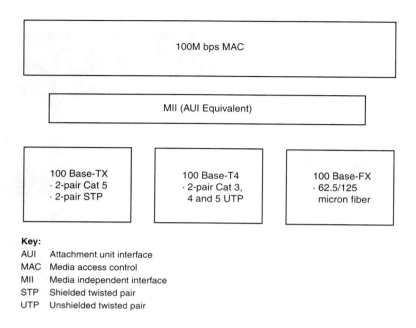

Exhibit 5-2. 100Base-T physical layers.

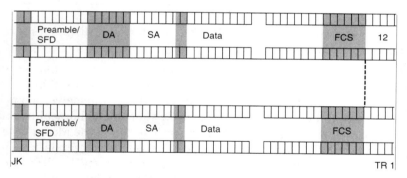

Exhibit 5-3. 100Base-T (TX and FX) frames.

frame, it sends a few idle signals and then goes quiet except for a link pulse which is sent every 16 ms to indicate that the link is still good.

In TP/PMD, a continuous stream of idle symbols is sent when data is not being transmitted. To ease the transition between data and idle signals, a JK symbol sequence is added to the front of a data frame and a TR symbol sequence is added to the end of the frame before transmission of idle symbols begins. The JK, TR, and idle transmission patterns must be added to Ethernet frames when they are transmitted via the TP/PMD specification.

Exhibit 5-4. 100Base-T-FX.

• Uses 2-strand, 62.5/125 micron fiber
• Connector: MIC, ST, SC (converters available)
• Uses FDDI TP/PMD specification
— Continuous signaling scheme
— 4B5B coding scheme
• Transmits over 1-fiber and receives over 1-fiber
• 100M bps data rate
• Full- and half-duplex
• Detects and signals far end faults

Both 100Base-TX and 100Base-FX use 4B5B coding. This means it takes 5 baud (signal transitions on the wire) to transmit 4 bits of information. This is vastly more efficient than the Manchester coding used for 10Base-T, which requires 2 baud to send each bit across the wire.

Exhibit 5-4 summarizes the attributes of 100Base-FX. It uses two strands of 63.5-micron fiber. All standard connectors are listed in the specification — different manufacturers support different types of connectors. 100Base-FX uses the FDDI TP/PMD specification with continuous signaling and 4B5B coding. The data clock runs at 125 MHz, providing a signaling rate of 100M bps with the 80 percent efficiency of 4B5B coding. One fiber is used for transmitting data, the other for receiving data. It can support both half-duplex and full-duplex operation and has automatic link detection.

100Base-TX

Exhibit 5-5 summarizes the attributes of 100Base-TX. It operates over two pairs of Category 5 UTP or STP, and uses Category 5 certified RJ-45 connectors. It uses the 125-MHz data clock, continuous signaling, and 4B5B coding of 100Base-FX, but adds signal scrambling and MLT-3 conditioning to deal with noise problems associated with sending high-frequency signals over copper. 100Base-TX uses exactly the same connector pinouts as 10Base-T. It transmits over one pair and receives over the other. It supports half-duplex and full-duplex operation.

100Base-T4

100Base-T4 (see Exhibit 5-6) is a more complex signaling system because it must support a 100M-bps data rate over cable certified for operation at 16 MHz. This is accomplished by increasing the number of cable pairs used for data transmission and using a more sophisticated coding system. 100Base-T4 starts with the two pairs used for 10Base-T — one for transmit and one for receive — and adds two additional pairs that are used

- Uses 2-pair Category 5 twisted pair cable
- Connector: Category 5 certified RJ-45 (IEC 603-7), or DB-9
- Uses FDDI TP/PMD specification
  - Continuous signaling scheme
  - 4B5B coding scheme
  - Scrambled symbols
  - MLT-3

- Transmits over 1-pair and receives over 1-pair
- 100M bps data rate
- Full and half duplex modes
- Identical connector pin-out

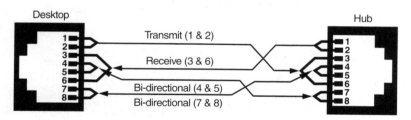

Desktop

Transmit (1 & 2)

Receive (3 & 6)

Hub

Exhibit 5-5. 100Base-TX.

- Uses 4-pair Cat 3, 4, or 5 cable
- Transmits over 3-pair
- Connector: Standard RJ-45 (IEC 603-7)
- Uses an 8B6T coding scheme
- Signaling: 100M bps = 3-pair x 25 Mhz x (133% for 8B6T encoding)
- Half Duplex

Desktop

Transmit (1 & 2)

Receive (3 & 6)

Bi-directional (4 & 5)

Bi-directional (7 & 8)

Hub

Exhibit 5-6. 100Base-T4.

bidirectionally. This means that when transmitting, 100Base-T4 always transmits over three pairs (one dedicated and two bidirectional) while listening for collisions on the remaining pair. It uses a much more sophisticated coding system called 8B6T.

Unlike other coding systems that use binary (0, 1) codes, 100Base-T4 uses ternary (+1, 0, –1) codes which enable it to pack 8 bits of data into 6 ternary symbols. By using 8B6T coding and three wire pairs for transmission, 100Base-T4 provides a 100M-bps data transmission rate with a clock speed of only 25 MHz (8 bits transmitted as 6 ternary symbols over three

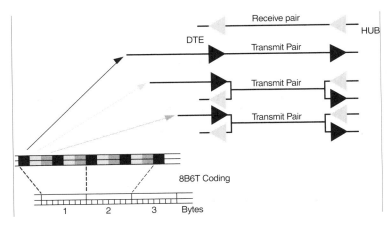

Exhibit 5-7. 100Base-T4 signaling.

wire pairs at 25 MHz). This process is diagrammed in Exhibit 5-7: 1 byte (8 bits) of data is encoded into 6 ternary symbols, which are transmitted sequentially across three wire pairs. Unlike 100Base-TX and 100Base-FX, 100Base-T4 does not support full-duplex operation.

100Base-T2

100Base-T2 provides a more robust and noise-resistant signaling system capable of operating over two pairs of Category 3, Category 4, or Category 5 UTP, or over STP links and supporting both half-duplex and full duplex operation. It uses an extremely sophisticated coding system called PAM5X5 which employs quinary (five-level — +2, +1, 0, –1, –2) signaling. In addition, it uses hybrid circuitry to enable simultaneous bidirectional transmission of 50M-bps data streams over each of the two wire pairs (see Exhibit 5-8).

Because of its robust encoding, 100Base-T2 emits less noise during use and is less susceptible to noise from external sources. When used with four-pair Category 5 cable bundles, it can coexist with other signaling systems. A single four-pair bundle can carry two 100Base-T2 links, one 100Base-T2 link, and one 10Base-T link, or one 100Base-T link and one voice (telephone) link.

Media-Independent Interface (MII)

The Media-Independent Interface is a mechanical interface to the Ethernet MAC, similar to the AUI, which is used to connect transceivers (see Exhibit 5-9). The MII supports a nibble-wide data path, a station management interface, and command and status registers. It uses a 40-pin connector,

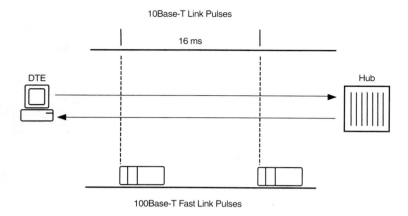

Exhibit 5-8. Media-independent interface (MII).

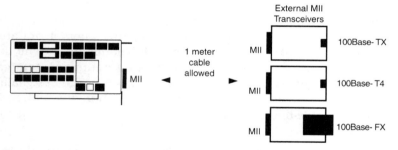

Exhibit 5-9. 100Base-T auto negotiation (2).

similar in appearance to mini-small computer systems interface (mini-SCSI) connectors.

Auto-Negotiation

Auto-negotiation provides automatic link testing and configuration for UTP signaling systems. All 100Base-T systems using UTP or STP go through Auto-Negotiation prior to establishing a link. During this start-up process, 100Base-T systems on each side of a link:

- Check the link.
- Exchange coded information defining the abilities of each link partner (e.g., 10Base-T half duplex operation, 10Base-T full-duplex operation, 100Base-TX half-duplex operation, 100Base-TX full-duplex operation, 100Base-T2 half-duplex operation, 1000Base-T2 full-duplex operation, or 100Base-T4 operation).
- Go to an internal lookup table to determine the highest common operation mode.
- Configure themselves as per the table.
- Turn off Auto-negotiation.
- Open the link.

If one end of the link is a 10Base-T system that does not support Auto-negotiation, the partner is automatically configured for 10Base-T half-duplex operation (default mode). When confronted with another networking technology that uses the RJ-45 connector (e.g., Token Ring), Auto-negotiation will automatically fail the link.

Auto-negotiation is based on the link pulse used in 10Base-T. For Auto-negotiation, the link pulse is divided into 33 fast link pulses that are used to carry pages of coded information between link partners.

Full Duplex Operation

Full-duplex operation supports simultaneous signaling in both directions over dedicated links by turning off the CSMA/CD collision detection circuitry. It provides some increase in bandwidth over links that have a high proportion of bidirectional traffic, such as switch-switch and switch-server links. In addition, full-duplex operation increases the maximum length of fiber links. Whereas a half-duplex link is limited to 412 meters by the need to detect collisions, full-duplex operation supports links of up to 2 kilometers because no collision detection is required. This increased link length is only useful for fiber links, signal attenuation limits, and copper link length to 100 meters for both half- and full-duplex operation.

Flow Control

Flow control provides a method for controlling traffic flows between intermediate devices (primarily switches and routers), and between intermediate devices and servers to avoid dropping packets. Currently, two-speed (10/100 or 100/1000) operation requires large buffers to reduce the probability of dropping packets when a continuous stream of packets is sent from a high-speed to a low-speed device (e.g., 100M bps to 10M bps, or 1000M bps to 100M bps). In such a scenario, when the buffers fill, the intermediate device drops the unbuffered packets.

Flow control provides a management alternative to having large buffers. When a buffer approaches full, the receiving device can send a flow control

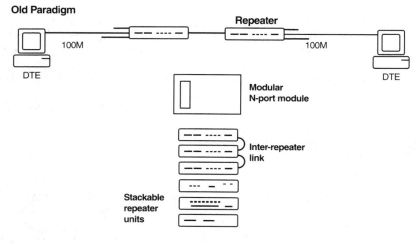

Exhibit 5-10. Repeater connection styles.

packet back to the sending device to stop the incoming packet stream. When the buffers of the receiving device empty, packet transmission starts again. This eliminates dropped packets and allows manufacturers to build switches with smaller buffers, which reduces costs.

Repeaters and Repeater Connections

Repeaters provide for shared media operation in 10Base-T and 100Base-T via the CSMA/CD protocol. 10Base-T networks have a collision domain diameter of 1000 meters. This permits building large, single-collision domain networks using hierarchical, cascaded repeating hubs to increase port density. 100Base-T does not permit hierarchical cascading of hubs because the maximum collision domain for UTP is slightly more than 200 meters (see Exhibit 5-10).

Two techniques can be used to build large, single-collision domain networks (i.e., increase port density). One technique is to use modular hubs where ports can be added by inserting additional multiport cards into the hub chassis. A second is to use stackable hubs — standalone repeaters that can be connected via high-bandwidth stacking ports that do not impact the collision domain.

Topology Rules

Topology rules for half-duplex 100Base-T networks are shown in Exhibit 5-11. Copper links are limited to 100 meters by the U.S. cabling standard EIA/TIA-568-A. A collision domain containing two copper links can

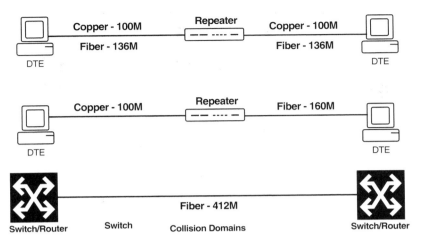

Exhibit 5-11. 100Base-T topologies.

contain one Class I repeater and two 100-meter copper links; or two Class II repeaters, two 100-meter copper links, and a 5-meter copper inter-repeater link. A collision domain containing a Class I repeater with two fiber links can support two fiber links of 136 meters, for a collision domain diameter of 272 meters. A collision domain containing a Class I repeater can also support one copper link of 100 meters and a single fiber link of 160 meters.

A fiber DTE-DTE half-duplex collision domain (e.g., switch-to-switch or switch-to-server) can support a 412-meter fiber link. Links of up to 2 kilometers can be supported over fiber by operating in full-duplex mode, which turns off the CSMA/CD portion of the protocol and requires a dedicated link (see Exhibit 5-12).

Gigabit Ethernet

Work to extend the Ethernet family to 1000M-bps (gigabit) operation is well underway. The first products using the new technology were demonstrated at Networld + Interop Las Vegas in May 1997, and the first products started shipping during the summer of 1997. Initial products support operation over 62.5-micron multimode fiber (1000Base-SX), 50-micron single-mode fiber (1000Base-LX), or short lengths (to 25 meters) of coaxial cable (1000Base-CX). The operation of these products is being defined in a supplement to the IEEE 802.3 standard entitled 802.3z

It was scheduled for completion in 1998. A second supplement, entitled 802.3ab, will define gigabit Ethernet over 100-meter, four-pair Category 5 copper links (1000Base-T). It was scheduled for completion in late 1998.

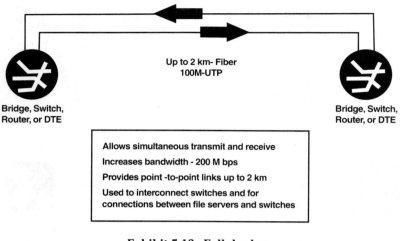

Up to 2 km- Fiber
100M-UTP

Bridge, Switch,
Router, or DTE

Bridge, Switch,
Router, or DTE

Allows simultaneous transmit and receive

Increases bandwidth - 200 M bps

Provides point -to-point links up to 2 km

Used to interconnect switches and for
connections between file servers and switches

Exhibit 5-12. Full duplex.

IMPACTS ON NETWORK DESIGN

Fast Ethernet is a family of 100M-bps signaling systems for use with the standard Ethernet MAC layer. The family consists of four signaling systems (100Base-TX, 100Base-T4, 100Base-T2, and 100Base-FX) and technologies that support automatic startup (Auto-negotiation), shared media operation (Repeaters), full-duplex operation, and flow control to manage traffic flow.

Fast Ethernet devices work seamlessly with legacy Ethernet systems: they have the same MAC layer, the same frame format, and the same CSMA/CD protocol for shared media operation. Auto-negotiation ensures that all 100Base-T devices operating over copper links automatically config- ure themselves to operate with link partners. This makes 100Base-T a very economical technology for adding high-bandwidth links to legacy systems.

Higher-speed operation reduces the diameter of 100Base-T shared media collision domains to approximately 200 meters for copper. Collision domains can be extended through the use of fiber and connected via switches to build large, complex networks. Full-duplex operation improves bandwidth for bidirectional links and increases the maximum length of fiber links to kilometers. Port density within a single collision domain is expanded through the use of modular and stackable hubs.

100M bps is not the endpoint for Ethernet. 1000M-bps (gigabit) devices were demonstrated in the spring of 1997 and began shipping in the summer of 1997. Targets for Gigabit Ethernet operation are 700 meters for full- duplex single mode fiber links, 25 meters for short-haul copper coax links, and 100 meters for Category 5 copper links.

Chapter 6
Gigabit Ethernet
Colin Mick

ALTHOUGH MOST ORGANIZATIONS ARE JUST BEGINNING TO ADOPT FAST ETHERNET, a newer, faster Ethernet technology is already entering the marketplace and some users are already preparing to use it. Gigabit Ethernet may seem overkill to those who are still running with shared or switched 10M-bps networks, but more than 100 network component and systems vendors are betting that there is already a market for an Ethernet technology that offers a full two orders of magnitude improvement in data rate.

The initial market for Gigabit Ethernet will be primarily to upgrade network infrastructures by providing high bandwidth links for backbones and server connections. A second market consists of vertical markets with specialized applications that require high bandwidth to the end user station.

Gigabit Ethernet is a logical backbone technology to connect existing networks built with both Fast Ethernet and 10Base-T. Modern network design practices, with their need for anywhere-to-anywhere connectivity, require high-bandwidth backbone support to ensure that users can reach servers anywhere in the organization. Today most networks use 100M-bps backbones based on asynchronous transfer mode (ATM), Fast Ethernet, or fiber distributed data interface (FDDI) technology. As requirements for bandwidth to end users increase, backbone capacity must be scaled up. Compared with other options, Gigabit Ethernet offers the simplest backbone upgrade for Ethernet-based networks; there is no translation, no fragmentation, and no frame encapsulation. New standards under development will augment Gigabit Ethernet backbones with Class of Service (COS) support.

Centralization of servers into server farms and the provision of anywhere-to-anywhere service both increase the demands on server performance. Gigabit Ethernet offers a simple upgrade to improve server performance. New Peripheral Component Interconnect (PCI) bus servers are capable of delivering data bursts at more that 1G bps and continuous data well in excess of 100M bps. Today, most servers and server farms are connected to the network via Fast Ethernet links. Gigabit Ethernet offers a low-

0-8493-0859-3/00/$0.00+$.50
© 2000 by CRC Press LLC

Exhibit 6-1. Application bandwidth table.

Object	Bandwidth/Size	Compression ratio	Required Bandwidth
ISOCHRONOUS STREAM			
Full Motion Video (HDTV)	150M bps	50:1 (MPEG)	3M bps
Full Motion Video (NTSC)	45M bps	50:1 (MPEG)	1M bos
Voice	64K bps	8:1 (voice)	8K bps
DATA			
X-ray image	120Mbits	2:1	60M bits
24 bit computer image	800M bits	100:1 (JEPG)	8M bits
20-page document with graphics	40M bits	$:1	10M bits
1 page letter	5K bits	4:1	1.3K bits
1 page scanned FAX image	1M bits	14:1	75K bits

cost upgrade that can potentially double the throughput of each server; all this takes at the server end is installation of a Gigabit Ethernet network interface card (NIC) and driver. (You also will have to add a Gigabit Ethernet repeater or switch to connect your servers to your existing network.)

Graphics, image, multimedia, and video-based applications offer a ready market for Gigabit Ethernet now. Exhibit 6-1 shows the bandwidth requirements of a variety of applications.

TECHNICAL OVERVIEW

Gigabit Ethernet extends the ISO/IEC 8802-3 Ethernet family of networking technologies beyond 100M bps to 1000M bps. The bit rate is faster and bit times are proportionately shorter, reflecting the 10× bit rate increase. In full-duplex operation, packet transmission time has been decreased by a factor of 10; in half-duplex operation the improvement is smaller because of changes made to ensure operation over a reasonable collision domain diameter. Cable delay budgets are similar to those seen in 100Base-T. Base and the achievable topologies for half-duplex operation are similar to those available for half-duplex 100Base-T.

HOW IT WORKS

Gigabit Ethernet combines the tested and true Ethernet Media Access Control (MAC) and two different physical layer signaling technologies: 1000Base-X and 1000Base-T (see Exhibit 6-2). It also takes advantage of full-duplex operation and flow control, new capabilities added to the Ethernet MAC by the 802.3x Media Access Control sublayer, partitioning, and relationship to the ISO Open Systems Interconnection (OSI) reference model.

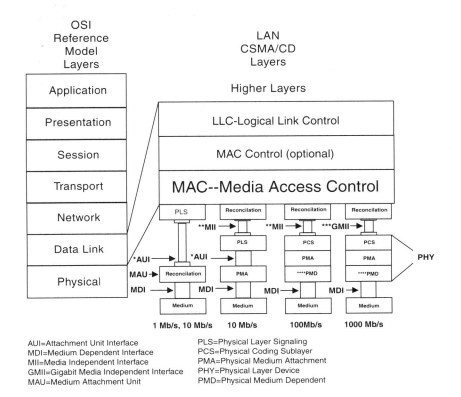

AUI=Attachment Unit Interface
MDI=Medium Dependent Interface
MII=Media Independent Interface
GMII=Gigabit Media Independent Interface
MAU=Medium Attachment Unit

PLS=Physical Layer Signaling
PCS=Physical Coding Sublayer
PMA=Physical Medium Attachment
PHY=Physical Layer Device
PMD=Physical Medium Dependent

NOTE: The four types of layers below the MAC sublayer are mutually independent.
*AUI is optional for 10Mb/s systems and is not specified for 1 Mb/s, 100 Mb/s or 1000 Mb/s systems.
**MII is optional for 10 Mb/s DTEs and for 100 Mb/s systems and is not specified for 1 Mb/s or 1000 Mb/s systems.
***GMII is optional for 1000, 100 or 10 Mb/s DTEs and is not specified for 1 Mb/s systems.
****PMD is specified for 1-BASE-X and 1000Base-X; 100Base-T4 does not use this layer.

Exhibit 6-2. Media access control sublayer partitioning and relationship to the ISO open systems interconnection (OSI) reference model.

1000Base-X Signaling Systems

The 1000Base-X family couples the Ethernet MAC with hardware originally developed for Fibre Channel (ANSI X3.230). This approach follows the one used for developing 100Base-X, where the Ethernet MAC was coupled with ANSI X3T12, encoding physical medium dependent specifications designed to carry FDDI over copper and fiber links.

Adoption of the Fibre Channel

The physical layer required modification of the interface to the Ethernet MAC, the use of 8B10B coding, and a 17 percent increase (from 1.0625M baud to 1.25M baud) in the speed of PHY operation to accommodate the 1000M bps data rate.

The MAC interface change was accomplished by adding a Gigabit Media Independent Interface (GMII) between the MAC and PHY layers. Similar in operation to the Media Independent Interface (MII) found in 100Base-T, the GMII is capable of supporting operation at 10M bps, 100M bps, and 1000M bps through transmit and receive paths up to 8 bits wide. A reconciliation sublayer maps signals between the MAC and the GMII.

The 1000Base-X family consists of three physical layer signaling systems: short wavelength (1000Base-SX) fiber, long wavelength (1000Base-LX) fiber, and a short-haul copper system using twinaxial cable (1000Base-CX). The signaling systems incorporate the Physical Coding Sublayer (PCS) and Physical Medium Attachment (PMA) sublayer.

1000Base-SX specifies operation over a pair of optical fibers using short-wavelength (770-860 nm) transmission and either 62.5 micron or 50 micron multimode fiber. 1000Base-LX specifies operation over a pair of optical fibers using long-wavelength (1270-1355 nm) transmission and either 62.5 micron or 50 micron multimode fiber or 10 micron single-mode fiber.

1000Base-CX specifies operation over two pairs of 150-ohm shielded, balanced tw-style cabling. This system would typically be used for jumper cables to connect devices in an equipment rack or machine room. Cables use either shielded DB-9 subminiature connectors as specified by IEC 807-3 or the 8-pin shielded ANSI Fibre Channel connector (HSSDC) with the mechanical mating interface defined by IEC 61076-103.

1000Base-T uses a DSP-based signaling system that supports operation over 100 m of 4-pair Category 5 UTP cabling as specified in EIA/TIA 568-A and ISO/IEC 11801 — the same Category 5 links used for 100Base-TX operation. This portion of the standard was developed by a separate Task Force (802.3ab).

Auto-negotiation

All Gigabit Ethernet signaling systems use some form of Auto-negotiation to configure both ends of the link for proper operation at start-up. 1000Base-T uses the same Auto-negotiation technology pioneered by Fast Ethernet. This technology, described in clause 28 of IEEE 802.3u, supports operation over copper links with RJ45 connectors. It ensures that stations at both ends of the link are compatible and, if so, configures them for optimal operation.

In addition to ensuring proper connection and operation and start-up, 1000Base-T Auto-negotiation can support multi-speed (100/1000M bps) capable devices, much like the 10/100 devices available for Fast Ethernet.

1000Base-X uses a different form of Auto-negotiation, developed by the 802.3z task force, to support full-duplex continuous signaling using 8B10B coding over 1.25-GHz links. As with the copper link version of Auto-negotiation, it provides a means for stations at two ends of a link to exchange information describing their abilities and to then use this information to configure themselves so they can operate with one another in an optimal configuration. The auto-negotiation information is exchanged via special frames as part of the start-up process.

Once Auto-negotiation is complete, the link is opened for communication. The basic information exchanged as part of the 1000Base-X Auto-negotiation process is contained in a "base page" and includes support of full-duplex operation, support of half-duplex information, support of asymmetric and symmetric PAUSE control (needed for flow control), provision of remote fault codes to report Auto-negotiation problems, acknowledgment that the base page has been received, and notification of additional or next pages to be sent.

The next pages are used to exchange optional or vendor-specific information as part of the Auto-negotiation process.

Half-Duplex/Full-Duplex

Gigabit Ethernet supports two modes of operation: the traditional half-duplex mode which uses carrier sense multiple access with collision detect (CSMA/CD), and a full-duplex mode similar to that provided by Fast Ethernet. The two modes operate and behave quite differently.

Half-duplex operation requires modifications to the MAC layer which change the treatment of small packets and can limit performance. At operating speeds above 100M bps, the MAC appends a sequence of carrier extension bits to short frames to ensure that the length of each frame event equals or exceeds the slot time. This means that the minimum frame size for half-duplex operation at 1000M bps is 4096 bit times or 512 bytes. A minimum frame size of 512 bytes ensures half-duplex operation with a collision domain of 200 — the same as that provided by 100Base-T. (Failure to extend the frames would limit the collision domain to approximately 20 meters.) Extension bits are not data and are automatically stripped from frames at receipt.

A second change to the MAC enables sending a burst of frames. When operating in half-duplex mode at speeds greater than 100M bps, the CSMA/CD MAC may optionally transmit additional frames (up to a total of 65,536 bits) without relinquishing control of the transmission medium. This improves the throughput during half-duplex operation — assuming there are multiple packets in a queue waiting to be sent and that upper layer protocols permit packet bursting.

Exhibit 6-3. Gigabit Ethernet link distances.

PHY	IEC 807-3 TW-style copper cable	EIA/TIA-568-A Category 5 copper cabling	62.5 micron multi-mode fiber	50 micron multi-mode fiber	10 micron single mode fiber
1000 Base-SX	na	na	260 meters	500 meters	na
1000 Base-LX	na	na	440 meters	500 meters	3,000 meters
1000 Base-CX	25 meters	na	na	na	na
1000 Base-T	na	100 meters	na	na	na

Full-duplex operation provides for simultaneous data flow in both directions by turning off CSMA/CD as per clause 31 of IEEE 802.3. Turning off CSMA/CD allows the links to operate at full bandwidth, maximizing performance. In 10Base-T and 100Base-T, full-duplex operation is possible only on dedicated or switched links, but 1000Base-T also supports shared media full-duplex operation via Full Duplex repeaters, which are described later in this chapter.

CABLING AND TOPOLOGY RULES

Gigabit Ethernet signaling systems are designed to work with a variety of fiber and copper links.

Fiber links are dependent on the interaction between the optics and the fiber; the distances shown in Exhibit 6-3 are minimum distances. The TW-style copper users should be aware that the electrical requirements for 1000Base-CX support are more stringent than the IEC-807-3 specifications.

Gigabit Ethernet link distances assume ISO/IEC 11801 compliant fiber. Distances will vary depending on the modal bandwidth of the installed fiber. Additional details on the impact of modal bandwidth on fiber link distances are provided in clause 38 of the standard.

Supporting 1000M-bps operation over Category 5 links raises concerns about both return loss and crosstalk, performance areas that have previously been unspecified in the U.S. EIA/TIA-568-A cabling standard. A new addendum to that standard specifies how to measure return loss and crosstalk for both component and field testing. By the time 1000Base-T products reach the market, commercial cable testing devices should be capable of evaluating these cable characteristics. Cabling experts have indicated that cabling plants that are compliant with the current version of

Exhibit 6-4. Maximum collision domain diameters for half-duplex operation.

Model	TW-style cable	EIA/TIA-568-A Category 5 copper	Fiber	TW-style and fiber (CX & SX?LX	Cat 5 fiber (T&& SX/LX)
DTE-DTE	25	100	320	na	na
One repeater	50	200	220	210 [b]	220 [c]

Notes:
[a] In meters, no marin
[b] Assume 25 meter of TW-style cable and fiber link of 195 meters.
[c] Assume 100 meters of CAT-5 and one fiber link of 10 meters.

EIA/TIA-568-A should have no problem meeting appropriate return loss and crosstalk performance levels.

Exhibit 6-4 provides collision domain diameter information for 1000Mbps half-duplex operation. Maximum collision domain diameters for half-duplex operation assume 25 m of TW-style cable and one fiber link of 195 m.

BUILDING NETWORKS WITH GIGABIT ETHERNET

Gigabit DTEs can be connected via a direct link, via CSMA/CD repeaters for shared media solutions, via full-duplex repeaters for shared media solutions, and with switches for dedicated bandwidth solutions.

Half-duplex repeaters are the traditional means for providing shared bandwidth to Ethernet users. The standard defines operation of a half-duplex CSMA/CD repeater, which supports collision domains of up to 200 m in diameter. Only one repeater can be contained within a single collision domain. Half-duplex repeaters offer an extremely low-cost method for sharing access to 1000M bps service, but they also offer reduced performance, compared with full-duplex repeaters (FDR) and switches.

FDRs, also called buffered distributors, offer the traditional low-cost shared media operation of repeaters, but with support for full-duplex operation. They utilize the full-duplex flow control mechanism to arbitrate access instead of Ethernet's traditional CSMA/CD. On-board buffers store incoming packets until they can be repeated to other ports. Asymmetric flow control is used to temporarily halt the flow of incoming packets when the input buffers fill. When the buffers empty, the halted transmitting units are allowed to resume transmission. The combination of full-duplex operation, input buffers, and flow control means that FDRs can support effected shared media operation at close to 1000M bps, providing much higher throughput than traditional half-duplex repeaters.

Switches provide dedicated bandwidth connections and a means for connecting networks with different bandwidths. Each link in a collision domain represents a separate collision domain, and since there are no collisions, links can operate at either half-duplex or full-duplex.

Gigabit Ethernet switches fall into two categories: aggregating and backbone. Aggregating switches are used to connect one or two gigabit links to a number of 100M-bps ports. Flow control is used to keep the gigabit links from overwhelming the switch buffers when a gigabit flow is directed to one or two 100M-bps ports. Backbone switches provide multiple gigabit ports and have multi-gigabit backplanes to provide wire-speed connectivity between ports. They typically have larger buffers than aggregating switches and may offer advanced features such as Layer 3 switching and virtual LANs.

MANAGEMENT OF GIGABIT ETHERNET

As with 100Base-T, Gigabit Ethernet makes use of the current 802.3 Ethernet management suite as defined in clause 30 of 802.3u. The basic Ethernet frame format, CSMA/CD operation, and both the RMON and Simple Network Management Protocol MIBs remain virtually unchanged (although some minor changes were made.) This means most management tools should continue to work seamlessly with Gigabit Ethernet products.

SUPPORTING ORGANIZATIONS

Two multi-company organizations are significant contributors to Gigabit Ethernet technology: the Gigabit Ethernet Alliance and the Gigabit Ethernet Consortium. The Gigabit Ethernet Alliance is an organization composed of more than 120 companies to facilitate the development of the standard and provide technology marketing support. Headquartered in Silicon Valley, the GEA has supported technology development by providing mechanisms to facilitate progress on the standard between formal IEEE-sponsored meetings and to develop test suites to ensure product conformance and interoperability. The technology marketing arm of the GEA has focused on promoting Gigabit Ethernet technology through press releases, a World Wide Web site, technology demonstrations, and seminars. Since the major goal of the GEA is to support the development of the Gigabit Ethernet standard, it has a limited lifespan and may disband.

Until it disbands, the GEA will maintain a Web site (*www.gigabit-ethernet.org*), which provides information about the technology, standards status reports, and links to GEA member company sites.

In the summer of 1997, a GEA team working with staff members of the University of New Hampshire Interoperability Laboratory established the Gigabit Ethernet Consortium. Founded July 7, 1997, with 15 member companies, the GEC provides an independent forum for testing Gigabit Ethernet products for conformance and interoperability. This program will provide vendors with critical development information and provide users with the confidence that first-generation products will have a high degree of interoperability. Unlike the GEA, the Gigabit Ethernet Consortium is intended for long-term operation.

ENABLING TECHNOLOGIES

The diffusion of Gigabit Ethernet into the marketplace will be done in parallel with several enabling/facilitating technologies, much as Fast Ethernet diffused in parallel with switching. Some of these enabling technologies — full-duplex operation, flow control, and full duplex repeaters — have already been discussed, as they operate via Ethernet standards. Other enabling technologies emerging from other standards groups include Layer 3 switching, classes of service, support for time-sensitive applications, and virtual LANs.

Layer 3 switching extends the speed and power of switching technology to Layer 3 routing and is a natural outgrowth of the switching technology that appeared in the early 1990s. Until recently, most switches have operated at ISO Layer 2 — making decisions based on MAC addresses. Layer 3 switches extend the speed of switching technology to Layer 3 addresses (usually based on Internet Protocol (IP)), allowing better network management and segregation of network traffic while eliminating the bottleneck of long router processing latency.

Class of service technology provides the ability to assign priorities to messages to assure the delivery of time-sensitive information. Although priorities and time-sensitive delivery have been available with other networking solutions, such as Token Ring, FDDI, and ATM, Ethernet has traditionally remained a single priority system. Work by the IEEE 802.1 High Layer Working Group (project 802.1p) and in 802.3 (proposed project 802.3ac) have provided a standards-based approach to attach priorities to Ethernet frames.

Transmission of voice, video, and multimedia content over networks brings its own set of problems. Solutions to these problems are coming from the Internet Engineering Task Force (IETF) via technologies such as IP Multicasting, RSVP, and RTSP. IP Multicasting is an extension to the standard IP network level protocol (RFC 1112) to facilitate the one-to-many delivery of time-sensitive information to a group of users by broadcasting datagrams to a host group identified by a single IP destination address. RSVP, the Reservation Protocol, provides a way of creating multi-hop connections across routers with a specified quality of service level to support specific data streams or traffic flows. RTSP, the Real Time Streaming Protocol, is an application-layer protocol for controlling the on-demand delivery of time-sensitive data such as audio and video. These protocols require intermediate device (router, switch) support.

VLANs are a management tool for organizing users into logical groups rather than physical ones. Since the organization is logical, individual users can be swiftly transferred from one VLAN to another via management tools. Many manufacturers already offer proprietary VLAN implementations for switches.

SUMMARY

Gigabit Ethernet is an extension of the IEEE 802.3 Ethernet family of local area networking technologies. It was designed to integrate smoothly with legacy Ethernet systems, just like 100Base-T. Gigabit Ethernet offers an easy-to-use, scalable technology to expand and update legacy Ethernet Networks. Gigabit Ethernet uses the traditional Ethernet format and size and supports half-duplex (CSMA/CD) and full-duplex operation.

Gigabit Ethernet management uses the same management definition and MIBs, which means that most management tools should be able to work with Gigabit Ethernet products. Gigabit Ethernet supports operation over most LAN links including 50 and 62.5 micron multimode fiber, 10 micron, single-mode fiber, short runs of and standard EIA/TIA-568-A Category 5 copper links. This means it will work with most existing fiber and copper installations.

Gigabit Ethernet is supported by a large number of vendors. Conformance and interoperability test mechanisms for Gigabit Ethernet are already in place and tests are being developed in parallel with the standards process.

The Ethernet family of local area networking standards is developed under the IEEE 802.3 working group. The standard consists of a base volume and supplements. Fast Ethernet is currently described in a 1995 supplement containing Clauses 21-30. An additional supplement was published in late 1997 containing Clause 31 (Full Duplex and Flow Control and Clause 32 — 1000Base-T2) and a supplement covering Gigabit Ethernet (with the exception of 1000Base-T) was published in late 1998 (see Exhibit 6-5).

Exhibit 6-5. Ethernet standards status and coverage as of Summer 1997.

Clause	Publication	Covers	Contents
1	ISO/IEC 8802-3 (1996)	General	Introduction
2	ISO/IEC 8802-3 (1996)	General	Media Access Control (MAC) service specification
3	ISO/IEC 8802-3 (1996)	General	MAC frame structure
4	ISO/IEC 8802-3 (1996)	General	Media Access Control
5	ISO/IEC 8802-3 (1996)	General	Layer Management
6	ISO/IEC 8802-3 (1996)	General	Physical Signaling (PLS) service specification
7	ISO/IEC 8802-3 (1996)	1/10M bps	Physical Signaling (PLS) and Attachment Unit Interface (AUI) specifications
8	ISO/IEC 8802-3 (1996)	10M bps coax	Medium Attachment Unit and basebaud medium specifications, Type 10 BASE5
9	ISO/IEC 8802-3 (1996)	10M bps	Repeater unit for 10M bps base band network
10	ISO/IEC 8802-3 (1996)	10M bps coax	Medium attachment unit and baseband medium specifications, Type 10BASE2
11	ISO/IEC 8802-3 (1996)	10M bps broadband	Broadband medium attachment unit and broadband medium specifications, Type 10BROAD36
12	ISO/IEC 8802-3 (1996)	1M bps coax	Physical signaling, medium attachment and baseband medium specifications, Type 1BASE5
13	ISO/IEC 8802-3 (1996)	10M bps topology	System consideration for multi-segment 10M bps baseband networks
14	ISO/IEC 8802-3 (1996)	10M bps CAT 3, 4, 5	Twisted medium attachment unit (MAU) and baseband medium, Type 10BASE-T
15	ISO/IEC 8802-3 (1996)	10M bps fiber	Fiber optic medium and common elements of medium attachment unit and star, Type 10BASE-F
16	ISO/IEC 8802-3 (1996)	10M bps fiber	Fiber optic passive star and medium attachment unit, Type 10BASE-FP
17	ISO/IEC 8802-3 (1996)	10M bps fiber	Fiber optic medium attachment unit, Type 10BASE-FB
18	ISO/IEC 8802-3 (1996)	10M bps fiber	Fiber optic medium attachment unit, Type 10BASE-FL
19	ISO/IEC 8802-3 (1996)	Management	Layer Management for 10M bps baseband repeaters
20	ISO/IEC 8802-3 (1996)	Management	Layer Management for 10M bps baseband medium attachment units
21	IEEE 802.3u (1996)	100M bps	Introduction to 100M bps baseband networks, Type 100BASE-T
22	IEEE 802.3u (1996)	100M bps	Reconciliation Sublayer (RS), and Media Independent interface (MII)
23	IEEE 802.3u (1996)	100M bps CAT 3, 4 , 5	Physical Coding Sublayer (PCS), Physical Medium Attachment (PMA) sublayer and baseband medium Types 100BASE-T4
24	IEEE 802.3u (1996)	100M bps CAT 5, fiber	Physical Coding Sublayer (PCS), Physical Medium Attachment (PMA) sublayer, Type 100BASE-X
25	IEEE 802.3u (1996)	100M bps CAT 5	Physical Medium Dependent (PDM) sublayer and baseband medium, Type 100BASE-TX
26	IEEE 802.3u (1996)	100M bps fiber	Physical Medium Dependent (PDM) sublayer and baseband medium, Type 100BASE-FX
27	IEEE 802.3u (1996)	100M bps	Repeater for 100M bps baseband networks

Exhibit 6-5. *(Continued)*

28	IEEE 802.3u (1996)	100M bps 100M bps CAT 3, 4, 5	Physical Layer link signaling for 10M bps and 100M bps Auto-Negotiation on twisted pair
29	IEEE 802.3u (1996)	100M bps topology	System considerations for multi-segment 100BASE-T networks
30	IEEE 802.3u (1996)	Management (all of Ethernet	Layer Management for 10M bps and 100M bps
31	IEEE 802.3x (in prep)	10/100/1000M bps	Full Duplex and Flow Control
32	IEEE 802.3y (in prep)	100M bps Cat 3, 4, 5	100BASE-T2
33	IEEE 802.3ac (in dev.)	VLAN tagging	New clause to be added to support VLAN tagging
34	IEEE 802.3z (in dev.)	1000M bps	Introduction to 1000M bps baseband networks
35	IEEE 802.3z (in dev.)	1000M bps	Reconciliation Sublayer (RS) and Gigabit Media independent Interface (GMII)
36	IEEE 802.3z (in dev.)	1000M bps fiber & short-haul copper	Physical Coding Sublayer (PCS) and Physical Medium Attachment (PMA) sublayer, type 1000BASE-X
37	IEEE 802.3z (in dev.)	1000M bps	Auto-Negotiation for 1000BASE-X
38	IEEE 802.3z (in dev.)	1000M bps fiber	Physical Medium Dependent (PDM) sublayer and baseband medium, type 1000BASE-LX (Long Wavelength Laser) and type 1000BASE-SX (Short Wavelength Laser)
39	IEEE 802.3z (in dev.)	1000M bps Short-haul copper	Physical Medium Dependent (PDM) sublayer and baseband medium, type 1000BASE-CX
40	IEEE 802.3z (in dev.)	1000M bps CAT 5	1000BASE-T
41	IEEE 802.3z (in dev.)	1000M bps	Repeater for 100M bps baseband networks
42	IEEE 802.3z (in dev.)	1000M bps topology	System considerations for multi-segment 1000M bps baseband networks

Chapter 7
ATM LAN Emulation
G. Thomas des Jardins
Gopala Krishna Tumuluri

THIS CHAPTER DESCRIBES ONE SERVICE USED TO PROVIDE INTERWORKING between asynchronous transfer mode (ATM) networks and the installed base of 802.3 (Ethernet) and 802.5 (Token Ring) network equipment — LAN emulation, or LANE.

LAN emulation allows users of an ATM network to run any higher-layer protocol in its existing state without requiring any changes. LANE is a method of performing basic bridging functionality between a host on an ATM-attached bridge and an ATM-attached host, or between two ATM-attached hosts. Because LANE masks much of the complexity from users while allowing them to benefit from ATM, it has become the standard of choice for transporting data traffic across heterogeneous networks.

TRANSPARENT AND SEAMLESS BRIDGING AND OTHER GOALS OF LANE

The overarching goal for LANE is to provide seamless and transparent bridging between an arbitrary number of hosts, where the hosts may be ATM native or connected to the ATM cloud via an interworking device. Therefore, many of the features of the emulated technology are specifically replicated, as are some of the design constraints posed by bridging.

To support the goal of transparent operation, the connection-oriented nature of ATM is concealed. To allow seamless operation, features found in the shared-medium domain such as broadcast are emulated.

Ease of use is addressed at the outset by designing in support for services, including automatic configuration and address registration, that allow true plug-and-play operation. A secondary goal is simplicity of design.

DESIGN

Packets on 802.3 or 802.5 networks typically can be grouped into two broad categories — unicast and multicast.

0-8493-0859-3/00/$0.00+$.50
© 2000 by CRC Press LLC

Unicast and Multicast. A unicast packet has a single intended destination and frequently is only one of several packets for that destination. By contrast, a multicast or broadcast packet has multiple destinations and is typically intended for the whole broadcast domain.

Once established, a virtual circuit between two end points, the source and the destination, would enable them to have point-to-point bidirectional communication, thereby emulating the 802 network for unicast packets. What is more difficult to imagine is how multicast might be replicated in a point-to-point connection-oriented technology such as ATM.

For that matter, the mechanisms of actually creating even a single point-to-point connection might give the reader pause. In fact, much of the complexity of LANE resides in simply preparing to exchange unicast and multicast data; the actual transfers themselves are relatively straightforward and not much different from any bridging technology.

Connections

ATM networks are connection-oriented by design. This design has the desired benefit of allowing ATM hardware to rapidly perform forwarding based on routing decisions determined when the call was set up. Because this function is not processor-intensive as routers are, very high throughput rates can be easily achieved.

Broadcast

The types of network technologies meant to be supplanted or augmented by ATM networks run LANE-provided connectionless service as a by-product of their design. ATM does not offer a similar feature, although there are ways it could be implemented. LANE specifies a simple and straightforward method for providing a broadcast facility using multicast support.

Emulated LANs

An emulated LAN is a group of ATM-attached stations that are logically grouped. This logical group is equivalent to a LAN segment on a traditional shared-media network.

This group of ATM stations belongs to the same broadcast domain. Of course, this broadcast domain is completely logical and does not have anything to do with the physical hardware connections. Later in this chapter we will discuss how to implement multiple emulated LANs on a single physical ATM network and also how a single ATM station can be part of multiple emulated LANs.

MAC Driver

LAN emulation is intended to provide an interface to the network-layer protocols that is identical to the one provided by traditional IEEE 802

LANs. The higher-layer protocols must function as though they are running on a traditional network. This virtual interface must be provided by the LANE implementation.

Interworking with Existing LANs

As mentioned previously, LAN emulation can be used to achieve interworking between devices attached to ATM networks and devices on traditional networks. Interworking devices (typically called *ATM access bridges*) must be used that can understand both the ATM and IEEE 802 networks. These devices implement the bridging functionality on the IEEE 802 interfaces, as is done in traditional networks.

On the ATM interface, however, they make use of LANE to implement bridging. (How such devices transparently bridge 802 stations and ATM stations by acting as proxies is discussed in more detail later in this chapter.)

Protocol Layering

In an IEEE 802 network there is the physical layer, media access control (MAC) layer, and the logical link control (LLC) layer. In an ATM network there is a physical layer, ATM layer, and the ATM adaptation layer (AAL). Any application needs to be implemented on top of the AAL layer. LAN emulation is just another application as far as the ATM network is concerned, thus it is implemented over the AAL layer. In particular, LAN emulation makes use of the AAL 5 layer.

LAN emulation also makes use of the signaling mechanism provided by the underlying ATM network to establish the switched virtual circuit (SVC) connections. LAN emulation in turn provides the functionality of the MAC layer and the logical link layer to the network layer.

Exhibit 7-1 illustrates how LAN emulation, ATM layers, and signaling all work in comparison with the Open Systems Interconnection (OSI) protocol stack.

COMPONENTS OF LANE

Now let's turn our attention to the implementation of the LAN emulation protocol. First, we describe the components that constitute an emulated LAN, then we explain how these components fit together and how the entire LAN emulation works.

LANE has the following components:

- LAN emulation client (LEC)
- LAN emulation server (LES)
- Broadcast and unknown server (BUS)
- LAN emulation configuration server (LECS)

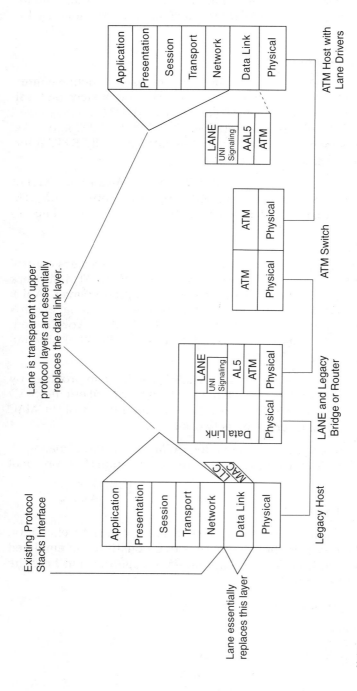

Exhibit 7-1. Open system interconnection (OSI) and LANE protocol stacks.

Notes:
Routing occurs at the network layer; is protocol independent, and is complex to administer. Some protocols, like SNA, are not routable.
Bridging occurs at the data link layer, is independent of protocols, and is simple to administer.
Hubs and routers operate at the physical layer.

The last three components — the LES, LEGS, and BUS — are often thought of as the LE services, because together they support the client's data exchange.

There are three steps to the process of exchanging data: LANE registration, address resolution, and data exchange. This process is explained further in a later section of this chapter titled "LAN Emulation in Action."

For now, however, a complete examination of the components, beginning with the client, is called for.

LAN Emulation Client (LEC)

- An LEC is the interface between the ATM world and the legacy world.

For any meaningful network communication to take place, there must be nodes that need to communicate. These nodes must be willing to participate in an emulated LAN that is a single broadcast domain. These entities are called LAN emulation clients, or simply LE clients.

Because an emulated LAN has meaning only in an ATM environment, the LE clients must be ATM-attached hosts or proxies for hosts that are sending data across an ATM network. These nodes can be host workstations or other interworking devices, such as bridges or routers with ATM interfaces that are acting as proxies for the MAC addresses in the non-ATM environment.

Data transfer takes place between two clients participating in an emulated LAN. Before exchanging data, the clients make use of the address resolution mechanism and the underlying signaling mechanism (discussed in greater detail in the section "LAN Emulation in Action").

Each LE client has a registered MAC address it represents. This address is an IEEE 802 network address that the LAN is emulating. For example, for emulated Ethernet LANs, this address would be a 6-byte hardware MAC address.

Each client is also equipped with an ATM address for it to be able to communicate with other clients that are ATM stations. Proxy clients, such as routers and bridges, extend this concept somewhat and will be addressed later.

LAN Emulation Server (LES)

- The LES tracks emulated LAN membership.
- The LES provides address resolution.
- The LES supplies the LEC with the address of the BUS.

In traditional networks, membership in a LAN is directly tied to a physical network topology. Membership is achieved by connecting the nodes using some sort of physical medium, which repeats signals throughout the medium, forming a broadcast domain.

In an ATM network, however, membership in a LAN has an explicitly defined relationship. Complexity arises because an emulated LAN is not a group of physically connected machines but a mesh of virtual circuits. An emulated LAN is completely virtual.

Network topology and emulated LAN membership are disjointed. This concept may be confusing at first; what is important to remember is that ATM networks define data paths using a concept of a virtual circuit and allocate resources according to defined policies of quality of service.

In this virtual environment, it becomes necessary for some entity to keep track of the membership of LE clients in an emulated LAN. This entity is called the LAN emulation server (LES), or the LE server.

This server is responsible for registering LE clients that would like to be part of a single emulated LAN. However, the LES has additional responsibilities to fulfill apart from maintaining the membership in an emulated LAN.

In an emulated LAN environment, for two LE clients to communicate with each other they need to establish an ATM virtual circuit, which requires the clients to know their ATM addresses. However, LAN emulation clients use IEEE 802 MAC addresses in the data frames they send to each other. So it becomes necessary that a client resolve a MAC address to an ATM address before any data transfer can take place.

This ATM address is then used to establish the necessary virtual circuit over which the IEEE 802 frames with source and destination MAC addresses can be sent. The LES provides a mechanism for the clients to resolve the MAC addresses to ATM addresses using the LAN emulation address resolution protocol (LEARP).

The LES also provides the LE clients with the ATM address of the broadcast and unknown server, which is the second-most important entity in an emulated LAN.

Broadcast and Unknown Server (BUS)

- BUS is used for unknown unicast traffic.
- BUS provides broadcast or multicast.
- BUS can be a bottleneck.

In traditional shared-media networks such as Ethernet, no "connections" exist. Rather, broadcast is achieved by all stations on the network listening to all traffic.

ATM networks, however, are point-to-point or connection-oriented networks that require an explicitly defined connection for traffic through a network, as well as a defined quality of service that this virtual connection should receive.

To emulate a traditional connectionless shared-media LAN on an ATM network, we need to define how the ATM layer will emulate a broadcast mechanism. This is extremely important because most of the network-layer protocols used today rely heavily on broadcasts. For example, IP uses the address resolution protocol (ARP) to resolve IP addresses to MAC address, and ARP uses broadcasts. In addition, bridges and other interworking devices use the same broadcast mechanism to send unknown unicast frames for which the address-to-port mappings are not resolved.

The entity that provides this mechanism is called a broadcast and unknown server (BUS). This entity makes use of the point-to-multipoint virtual connections provided by ATM networks to provide the broadcast mechanism to all LAN emulation clients.

A point-to-multipoint VC is a VC that replicates the traffic on one incoming VC to many outgoing VCs. This capability is standard in most ATM switch equipment. The clients send all the broadcast or unknown unicast frames to the BUS, which in turn sends the frame to all the clients over the point-to-multipoint VC.

LE Configuration Server (LECS)

- The LECS maps emulated LAN names to LES addresses.
- The LECS provides information about how an emulated LAN is configured.
- The LECS is reached via a well-known default address.

In an ATM network, every single entity needs to have its own ATM address for it to be uniquely identified. Therefore the LE clients, the LES, and the BUS all have their own unique ATM addresses that are obtained during the configuration phase when a client joins the emulated LAN.

The LE clients need to know the ATM addresses of the LES and the BUS. As discussed previously, the LES provides the clients with the ATM address information of the BUS. However, the clients need to be initially configured with the LES address if they are to successfully take part in an emulated LAN.

It would be difficult to configure each client with the 20-byte ATM address of the LES for each emulated LAN the client wishes to join. Therefore, LAN emulation specifies a service that provides a mapping of emulated LAN names to the LES ATM addresses. This entity is called the LAN emulation configuration server, or the LECS.

The LECS can respond at either a specified ATM address for security reasons (in which case all the clients need to be configured with this information), or the LECS can be configured to respond at a well-known

ATM address, allowing all the clients to use this globally known LECS ATM address for simple plug-and-play operation.

LAN emulation provides both mechanisms for clients to communicate with the LECS. The LECS maintains a data base that has a name of the emulated LAN and the ATM address of the LES that is serving that emulated LAN, and responds to client queries by providing this information.

LAN emulation also provides flexibility because it directly configures the LE clients with the ATM addresses of the LES. The function of the LECS is similar to an IP network's name server. It is easier to address something by name rather than a number.

The LECS can also be optionally used to provide additional information about the characteristics of a particular emulated LAN. For example, one can query the LECS to find out what type of IEEE 802 LAN is being emulated by a particular LES.

ATM ADDRESSES

Each of the LAN emulation components — the LE clients, LE server, BUS, and LEGS — needs a unique ATM address. This section explains how these addresses are partly obtained and partly formed.

In the 20-byte ATM address, the last byte is called the *selector byte* and is reserved for use by different entities implemented on the same network interface. This selector byte can be given a different value, which gives users the choice of having 255 unique ATM addresses on the same physical interface.

By using a different selector byte, all of the LAN emulation components can be present on the same physical interface and yet have unique ATM addresses. In fact, multiple instances of the same LANE component can be implemented on the same physical interface.

VIRTUAL CONNECTIONS

Virtual connections form the basic component in LAN emulation and in any ATM implementation. Without VCs, no communication is possible. Exhibit 7-2 shows LANE components and their virtual connections.

LANE communication occurs between the LE clients and one of the other entities (possibly another LE client). Collectively the LECS/LES/BUS can be considered the LAN emulation services because their sole purpose is to serve the LE clients in one form or the other.

Connection 1: The Configuration Direct VC

The LE clients initially communicate with the LECS to retrieve the address of the LES of an emulated LAN that the client wishes to join. This

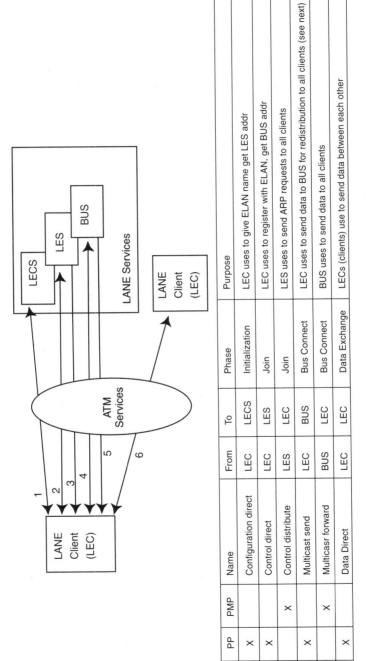

#	PP	PMP	Name	From	To	Phase	Purpose
1	X		Configuration direct	LEC	LECS	Initialization	LEC uses to give ELAN name get LES addr
2	X		Control direct	LEC	LES	Join	LEC uses to register with ELAN, get BUS addr
3		X	Control distribute	LES	LEC	Join	LES uses to send ARP requests to all clients
4	X		Multicast send	LEC	BUS	Bus Connect	LEC uses to send data to BUS for redistribution to all clients (see next)
5		X	Multicasr forward	BUS	LEC	Bus Connect	BUS uses to send data to all clients
6	X		Data Direct	LEC	LEC	Data Exchange	LECs (clients) use to send data between each other

Exhibit 7-2. LANE components and their virtual connections.

emulated LAN name can be null in case the client wishes to join any emulated LAN. This communication with the LECS is a point-to-point communication between one client and the LECS and takes place on a virtual connection called the configuration direct VC.

Once the client retrieves the required information and the necessary characteristics of a particular emulated LAN, it does not need to communicate with the LECS further until there is a change in configuration.

Connection 2: The Control Direct VC

The LE client then needs to become a member of an emulated LAN by registering with the LES. This registration and other one-to-one communications between the LE client and the LES takes place over another VG called the control direct VG.

The name of this virtual connection derives from the fact that all of this communication involves purely control messages and not any useful data transfer. In addition, this VC is a direct point-to-point VC between the LES and the LEC and is therefore called a control direct VC.

Connection 3: The Control Distribute VC

The LES uses a point-to-multipoint VC to communicate with all the clients in an emulated LAN. This virtual connection is called the control distribute VC. (The use of this VC is described in more detail later.)

Connection 4: The Multicast Forward VC

LE clients that wish to send broadcast frames to all the clients in the emulated LAN need to first forward them to the BUS. To do this, the clients use a point-to-point VC to the BUS called the multicast send VC. The BUS then uses a point-to-multipoint VC called the multicast forward VC to forward these frames to all the clients. All the clients would be part of this multicast VC.

Connection 5: The Data Direct VC

So far we have only talked about how control frames and broadcast frames make it through the ATM network. The ultimate use of the emulated LAN is for two clients to exchange data directly between them. This exchange is carried over another virtual connection called the data direct VC, which is established once the MAC addresses are resolved to ATM addresses.

LAN EMULATION IN ACTION

Now that we have some understanding of the reasons for using LAN emulation and what components are required to implement LAN emulation, let's turn our attention to how all this works together and finally to how two

ATM stations transfer data between them as if they are attached to an IEEE 802 LAN. Exhibit 7-2 also shows how LANE components and their virtual connections fit in the phases of data exchange.

Phase 1: LANE Registration

Step 1: Initialization. The LE clients are the final beneficiaries of LAN emulation, and they need to pass through several phases before they can actually communicate with each other.

First comes the initialization phase, during which the LEC establishes a configuration direct VC to the LECS and obtains the ATM address of the LES. If the LES address is manually provided to the LEC, then this initialization phase will be null and will not be executed. At the end of the initialization phase the LEC is supposed to know the ATM address of the LES to which it needs to connect and join the emulated LAN.

Step 2: Joining Emulated LANs. The second phase is the join phase. In this phase the LEC connects to the LES and expresses its interest in being part of the LAN being emulated by this LES.

Upon connecting to the LES, the LEC registers two addresses. One is the 6-byte MAC address that LEC represents in the emulated LAN; the second is the client ATM address at which the servers and other clients can connect in order to send data frames to the given MAC address.

The LES completes the join phase by saving this information in its data base and establishing a point-to-multipoint VC (i.e., the control distribute VC) to the client. If any of the connections fail or if the address registration does not take place correctly, the join phase is aborted and restarted.

Step 3: Connecting to the BUS. Once the LE client joins the emulated LAN successfully, it needs to connect to the BUS in order to be able to send or receive broadcast multicast and unknown unicast frames.

This phase is called the BUS connect phase. During this phase the LE client queries the LES for the BUS address using the LAN emulation ARP protocol (described later). The LES responds to the LE clients with the ATM address of the BUS, which it knows right from configuration time.

LE clients, after obtaining the BUS ATM address, establish a point-to-point VC (i.e., the multicast send VC) to the BUS. The BUS then establishes a point-to-multipoint VC (i.e., multicast forward VC).

Once all these connections are successfully established the emulated LAN is declared to be operational according to the LE clients. When any of these control connections to the LES or the BUS get dropped, the join phase is restarted. Until a successful join occurs, no communication can take place between any pair of clients.

Phase 2: Address Resolution

In any network, address resolution is the key for successful communication. This address resolution is required because of different types of addresses used by different protocol layers. MAC layers use MAC addresses, network layers use network-layer address (e.g., IP), and transport layers use ports. No matter what layer it is, each layer has its own addressing mechanism to distinguish itself from its peer.

In LAN emulation, there are two layers between the network layer and the physical layer. One is the MAC layer that is being emulated; the other is the LAN emulation layer, which is actually on top of an ATM network.

Since the MAC layer addressing and ATM network addressing are different, two levels of address resolution are needed. One is a network-layer-to-MAC-address resolution, which is done in a manner identical to the traditional networks by the network layer. The other is the MAC-address-to-ATM-address resolution, which is done by the LAN emulation layer. This second form of address resolution is called the LAN emulation address resolution protocol (LEARP).

This level of address resolution is completely transparent to the network layers. The network layers only see the MAC layer being emulated and therefore only see the traditional ARP.

How Two Levels of Address Resolution Work Together

Suppose one host is running some network protocol and wants to communicate with its peer. This host will first resolve the network address to MAC address just as if it were running on a traditional IEEE 802 network. Then the network layer uses the virtual MAC interface provided by LANE (which is identical to the traditional MAC interface) to send the data in the form of a MAC frame. This MAC frame is received by the LEC (running LANE).

Now the LEC needs to transmit this frame to its peer LEC, for which it needs to establish a connection. Establishing this connection requires an ATM address.

The transmitting client uses the services provided by the LES to resolve the MAC address to a unique ATM address. Once this resolution is done in a completely transparent way, the client establishes a virtual connection and delivers the original MAC frame intact to the other end as if nothing happened in the middle.

Thus, each MAC address must be resolved into a unique ATM address. This ATM address must be the address of the client that represents the MAC address.

It is possible and perfectly legal for many MAC addresses to map to a single ATM address, but not vice versa. Interworking devices may act, however, as proxy LE clients and represent more MAC addresses per each ATM address.

LEARP Requests and Responses

We described the reason and mechanism for using LEARP — or LAN emulation address resolution protocol — in the previous section. Now let's explain exactly how it works.

Each LEC that wants to resolve a MAC address to an ATM address sends out a LEARP request to the LES. This request contains the following information:

- MAC address the requesting client represents
- ATM address the requesting client represents
- MAC address the client is trying to resolve

The LE client uses the control direct virtual connection to send the LEARP requests. The LES, after getting the LEARP request, looks it up in the database.

If the MAC address is registered and there is an ATM address associated with it, the LES responds to the LE client with positive information. If the LES fails to find the requested information in its database, then it forwards the LEARP request to all the clients in the emulated LAN (using the control distribute VC).

If all clients are supposed to register the MAC address they represent with the LES, then how is it possible for the LES to fail in its search? That question will be answered in the section on "Proxy LE Clients." Some LE client would respond to the LES for the LEARP request that was flooded to all the clients. The LES now uses that information to respond to the original client that requested the information.

Phase 3: Data Exchange

LANE Data Frames. Each client sends IEEE 802 frames to the other client. These IEEE 802 frames need to be encapsulated in what is called a LANE data frame.

The LANE data frame has a 2-byte header with one field in it; the rest is the MAC frame. This 2-byte field is called the LEC-ID, which is a unique number assigned by the LES when the LE client registers in the emulated LAN.

In traditional networks, physical ports give a unique identity; however, in a virtual environment like LANE, there needs to be a way to identify and differentiate between LE clients. This LEC-ID is useful for the clients in recognizing the frames sent by them in case the response comes back to them through the BUS.

Data Transfer. There are three kinds of data frames that could be transmitted in the IEEE 802 LAN.

One is the unicast frame that a station wants to send directly to another station after the address resolution is done. The second is the unknown unicast frames that are destined for a particular client and are still awaiting address resolution. The third type is the broadcast and multicast frames; these are destined to all or a group of stations in the LAN. (Remember, we are not discussing address resolution at the network layer. We are only concerned with the LE address resolution, which involves resolving the MAC addresses to ATM addresses.)

Broadcast Frames. The broadcast frames received by the virtual MAC driver are encapsulated in LANE frames and are sent to the BUS for broadcast to all the clients in the emulated LAN. This is the most simple form of transferring the frames. If all the frames could be sent in this way, life would be simple, but at the same time it would be very inefficient.

Unknown Unicast Frames. These are the frames for which there is no ATM address that has been resolved for the destination MAC address in the MAC frame. For these frames the LE clients send a LEARP request to the LES and forward the frame to the BUS to be broadcast to all the clients.

To keep the performance of the BUS from degrading there is a limit imposed on the LEARP requests and the number of unknown unicast frames that can be forwarded to the BUS for broadcast. This limit is typically one frame per second for each unresolved destination MAC address.

Directed Unicast Frames. All the unknown frames would become directed unicast frames once the LE client gets a response to its LEARP request. At this point the MAC address is resolved and direct communication between the clients can start. Also at this point the transmitting client establishes a data direct virtual connection to the destination client and the unicast frames are sent over it.

LEARP Cache and Virtual Connection Cache. By now we know that LE clients resolve MAC addresses to ATM addresses using the services of the LES and then establish a virtual connection to the peer clients to transfer the actual data. It would be too inefficient for the LE clients to do LEARP requests and VC establishment for each unicast frame they get from the virtual MAC driver.

To be more efficient, the LE clients cache the LEARP entries and also the VCs associated with each MAC address. These cache entries are subject to aging based on a time-out period, which is a configurable parameter. The sizes of the caches can vary, depending on the implementation.

Flush Message Protocol. The unknown unicasts are forwarded to the BUS at a very slow rate until the LE address resolution completes. Once this LEARP is completed, the rest of the frames go through a direct virtual connection between the LE clients.

Because the BUS is a different entity running elsewhere in the ATM network, it is quite possible that the unknown unicast frames sent to the BUS would reach the destination client more slowly, and in some cases after the unicast frames sent on the direct VC reach it. If this happens then the frame ordering is not maintained; this situation could lead to unnecessary retransmissions.

To avoid this potential problem, each LE client implements a flush message protocol. After resolving an address and before transmitting data on the direct VC, each LE client sends a flush request to the BUS. The BUS, upon getting this request, transmits any frames pending for this client on the multicast send VC and sends a flush response to the client. The LE client, upon receiving this response, starts transmitting the unicast frames on the direct VC.

COMMON QUESTIONS ABOUT LAN EMULATION

How Many Emulated LANs?

Not only is it possible for multiple clients to be part of a single emulated LAN, but it is also possible for a single client to be part of multiple emulated LANs. Imagine an end station with two IEEE 802 network interface cards connected to two disjointed LAN segments. This station can in fact belong to multiple networks. However, in traditional networks the end station would require two physical interfaces and should be part of two physically disjointed LAN segments.

In LAN emulation, however, because the network is a virtual one and is purely a mesh of VCs over a physical ATM network, it is not difficult to imagine two or more virtual emulated networks. In this case the mesh of VCs needs to be disjointed and not the physical ATM network.

How Many Clients per Emulated LAN?

How many LE clients can be part of a single emulated LAN? As mentioned earlier, the LE frames have a 2-byte header that carries the unique LEC-ID in it. This limits the number of clients per emulated LAN to 216-1.

How Many MAC Addresses per Client?

Proxy LE Clients. The single most important goal of LAN emulation is to have seamless and transparent interoperability between legacy networks and ATM networks. We know that LAN emulation can be used to emulate an IEEE 802 LAN on top of a connection-oriented point-to-point ATM network.

How can this emulated LAN operate seamlessly with a legacy network? This is a tricky question because legacy networks do not understand LAN emulation.

A proxy LEC can solve this problem. A proxy LEC is a LAN emulation client that represents all the MAC addresses on the legacy network and does the bridging conversion from legacy network to LANE network. The proxy LEC incorporates some intelligence to do this.

There are few differences in the way proxy LE clients operate in comparison with their non-proxy counterparts. During the LE join phase, each LE client registers a MAC address it represents and the ATM address that other clients can connect at. If a proxy LEC has to register the MAC addresses it represents, then the database of the LES can be huge (depending on the number of such clients and the number of addresses they represent).

There is another problem with registering all the addresses with the LES. Imagine transparent bridges that would like to act as proxy LECs. These bridges learn the MAC addresses on different ports slowly, as they see frames from different sources. When these proxy clients want to join the emulated LAN at the beginning, they do not know all the MAC addresses they would like to represent.

LAN emulation provides for all these problems. Any proxy LEC is only allowed to register one MAC address during the join phase just as any other LE client. However, the proxy LEC should register itself as a proxy with the LES. The proxy LEC should never register any more MAC addresses at any time. The LES forwards unresolvable LEARP requests to all the proxy LE clients and the proxy clients respond to these requests dynamically, as and when needed. Other than these differences, all the other functions and operations are the same.

How Can LE Clients Participate in Multiple Emulated LANs?

The LE clients need to obtain as many unique ATM addresses and MAC addresses as the number of emulated LANs they would like to be part of. Remember, an LEC can only represent one MAC address, and each MAC address should map to a unique ATM address.

The magic of LAN emulation lies in the fact that neither the ATM address nor the MAC address needs to have physical relevance. This makes the life of an LE client simple. It can use the selector byte in the ATM address to form more unique ATM addresses and generate multiple unique MAC addresses from their hardware address by following a deterministic algorithm.

Once these addresses are formed or generated, the LE client needs to locate a LES/BUS pair for each emulated LAN it would like to be part of and establish the necessary connections. Then the client needs to maintain the list of VCs and addresses associated with each emulated LAN and should make sure complete isolation of all traffic among emulated LANs is maintained.

What is the limit on the number of emulated LANs that a single client can be part of? The theoretical limit is 255, since the selector byte can be used to generate 255 unique ATM addresses.

However, a more practical limit would depend on the realistic number of network interfaces an end station or an interworking device would like to have. In most current implementations this limit is 16.

SUMMARY

LAN emulation, like most protocol implementations, is standards-based. Standards ensure proper interoperability between the implementations by different vendors. Just as the IEEE standardizes most of the IEEE 802 networks and their implementation, the ATM Forum has standardized the implementation of LAN emulation.

The ATM Forum has released a document that contains every single detail on how LAN emulation must be implemented. This document is called the "LAN Emulation over ATM, version 1.0." This specification can be ordered directly from the ATM Forum (phone: [415] 578-6860; e-mail:info@ atmforum.com).

The ATM Forum LANE specification provides a mechanism to emulate only IEEE 802.3 (Ethernet) and IEEE 802.5 (Token Ring) networks. There is no specification yet to emulate fiber distributed data interface (FDDI) networks on top of ATM, though this does not preclude vendors from having proprietary implementations.

Chapter 8
InterLAN Switching
Doug Kaye

A REVOLUTION IS IN PROGRESS that is dramatically changing the way information networks are designed. Although shared-media LANs have been widely deployed, these are increasingly being upgraded to switched, dedicated LANs to maximize application performance and to reduce complexity in the local environment. In the wide area, virtual-circuit switching is exploding in popularity in the form of frame relay.

Asynchronous transfer mode (ATM) is a new form of switching being introduced in both local and wide area environments that will revolutionize the way switching networks of the future operate. ATM switching will extend LAN application performance across the wide area, making network capacity more scalable, simplifying network management, and improving bandwidth price performance (through the consolidation of other traffic including voice and video).

The personal computer revolution that has taken place offers some insight into how this might happen. Desktop computers have come a long way in a little more than a decade. The same technology (very large scale integrated circuits) that supported the PC revolution is behind the ATM switching revolution. By reducing the size and the cost of switching circuits and integrating them on computer chips, switched networks will provide the high performance connectivity for desktop workstations and enable the distribution of client/server applications.

Network operators are faced with many complicated issues in the area of interLAN switching. This chapter discusses the growing complexity of interLAN connectivity and highlights the emergence of switching and the role of ATM in local area networks. The convergence of routing and ATM switching are also demonstrated.

COMPLEXITY OF LAN INTERCONNECTIVITY

In all networks, complexity tends to grow exponentially as the number of interconnections rises. The multiplication of interconnections and switches rapidly reaches a very high level of complexity. Many enterprise networks are rapidly approaching this limit, driven by the explosion of

0-8493-0859-3/00/$0.00+$.50
© 2000 by CRC Press LLC

interconnected LANs. If handled improperly, this complexity can result in increased costs, as well as degradations in performance, scalability, and management.

Performance

Complex networks, if not managed properly, can result in long latency times, frequent congestion conditions, and bottlenecks that affect user response times, application effectiveness, and the ability to utilize computing assets to their fullest potential.

Cost

The operational implications of these complex networks are that they can be expensive to maintain, and often demand the time and attention of more experienced — higher-salaried — members of the IS team. In addition, there is limited or no accountability for bandwidth used inefficiently on a per-application basis.

Scalability

Complete product replacement may be required to accommodate higher-speed connections (e.g., adding T3 or ATM ports).

Management

Network design, inventory tracking, support, and maintenance are all negatively influenced by the complexity of the overall network.

THE SWITCHING SOLUTION

Switching has emerged as the technology of choice to alleviate cost, scalability, and management problems, among others.

Emergence of Switched LANs and the Role of ATM in Local Networks

ATM is a high-speed multimedia networking technology that is being embraced by both local and wide area networking communities. This is demonstrated by the large number of products and services being announced and rolled out, and by the unprecedented participation of over 600 companies in the ATM Forum.

The values being sought from ATM are:

- performance for a broad range of applications
- scalability from multimegabits to multigigabits and from the workgroup to the wide area
- simplification through multimedia networking consolidation and through simplified management inherent in connection-oriented environments

The rollover of PCS toward higher-performance desktop platforms and more bandwidth-intensive multimedia applications is driving the need for higher capacity to the desktop. This is being accomplished primarily by the movement beyond shared-media LANs to switched Ethernet and Token Ring solutions. Ethernet and Token Ring switches based on ATM (including ATM LAN emulation) are becoming the technologies of choice. They provide a high degree of scalability in speed, reach, and application support. LAN switching helps to eliminate complexity by enhancing application performance and traffic scalability while decreasing the administrative complexity of shared-media LANs and router configurations.

In cases where 16M bps is insufficient, there are numerous desktop technologies available, such as multiple versions of 100M-bps Fast Ethernet, 100VG-AnyLAN, fiber distributed data interface (FDDI), and ATM.

Key ATM Attributes for InterLAN Connectivity

ATM offers high performance by providing:

- low-latency, low-overhead, switched virtual circuit connectivity
- end-to-end signaling
- rate-based flow control based on emerging available bit rate (ABR) standards
- simultaneous support for different applications via ATM classes of service on a per-connection basis
- scalable capacity and management simplification via connection-oriented operation

LAN Emulation

ATM LAN emulation (LANE) is used to make the ATM network appear to be a collection of virtual Ethernet and Token Ring LANs. The replication of most of the characteristics of existing LANs means that LANE enables the LAN applications to run over ATM transparently. LANE is independent of particular LAN protocols, so that other protocols can use ATM-emulated LANs.

ATM LANE advantages include:

- An Ethernet or Token Ring network interface card (NIC) can be replaced by an ATM NIC with no impact on the network applications in use in the workstation.
- Most unicast LAN traffic moves directly between clients over direct ATM virtual circuits (VCs), while multicast traffic is handled via a server.
- Bridges are used to interconnect real LANs and emulated LANs running on ATM.
- Source routing bridges can interconnect a real Token Ring LAN and an emulated Token Ring LAN.

- Routers can interconnect ATM emulated LANs and other wide-area or LAN media for purposes of routing scalability, protocol spoofing, or security firewalls.

The ATM Forum LANE implementation agreement discusses client devices and end systems connected to an ATM network, including:

- computers with ATM interfaces that operate as file servers
- end-user workstations or personal computers
- Ethernet or Token Ring switches that support ATM networking
- routers and bridges with membership in an emulated ATM LAN server supporting ATM LANE service

To the extent that desktop ATM penetrates the market, four existing or emerging protocol stack/application standards are relevant:

1. LAN emulation client
2. Native ATM
3. ATM adaptation of voice/data/video pipes
4. Classic IP and multiprotocol over ATM (MPOA) clients

These application environments can coexist in any given workstation by using different ATM virtual circuits supporting the appropriate class of service.

Routing Requirements

Routing is required to support communication with the installed base of shared-media LAN bridge/router networks and to manage broadcasts and unknown address flooding over the wide area. Applications using ATM LAN emulation require multiprotocol routing to support connectivity between emulated LANs, while classic IP requires multiprotocol routing, at least in the context of address resolution. In contrast, ATM switching provides high-speed connectivity for classic IP, MPOA, and ATM LAN emulation and for emerging native ATM applications. It will provide circuits for the network consolidation of voice, data, and video.

The introduction of Ethernet or Token Ring switches into wiring closets will maximize application performance in the local area, and be an important next step in the process of reducing administrative complexity in the local environment. An important enterprise networking issue is how ATM switching will extend application performance across the wide area. The objective is to make network capacity more scalable, simplify the network management, and improve bandwidth price performance (through consolidation of other traffic including voice and video), while allowing routing to co-exist and evolve to leverage the inherent advantages of switching.

Classic IP and MPOA

RFC 1483 defines an encapsulation technique for carrying IP traffic over ATM VCs, which is used in three types of environments:

1. For ATM PVCs between routers.
2. To carry LAN traffic transparently between bridges.
3. For individual workstations to use ATM to carry IP traffic in IP virtual LANs. This is an important ATM application because these users need the larger capacity provided by ATM.

RFC 1577 describes how to construct a logical IP subnet (LIS) so that high-performance workstations and supercomputers can use ATM as a virtual LAN. In this process:

- A protocol supporting automatic address resolution of IP addresses is defined.
- Each LIS supports a single ATM ARP server.
- Each LIS client is configured with the unique address of the ATM ARP server.
- A subset of the IP protocol suite is supported.

The MPOA subcommittee of the ATM Forum is defining standards to provide RFC 1577 capabilities in a protocol-independent manner and to address the routing issues associated with minimizing multiple router hops in ATM networks.

THE EMERGENCE OF CELL-BASED ROUTING AND SWITCHING

The next section discusses the various ways ATM and routing can evolve outside of the wiring closet for campus and wide area connectivity and the emergence of a new class of functionality.

An important objective is to build networks that maximize application performance and enhance service predictability through the support of various classes of service, for managing delay and throughput variations. Most Ethernet switches boast latencies in the 10 to 100 microsecond range, with pure ATM switches at the low end of this range. With ATM switching exhibiting latencies at least a hundred times better than routers, it seems obvious that latency can be minimized by integrating router functionality into switching.

A number of approaches can be used to combine routing and switching in the wide area. Routers can be interconnected over an ATM network, but this does not eliminate the latency introduced by routers. This approach does not fully exploit the attributes of switching (i.e., ATM serves as a pipe), because there is only a loose coupling between routing and the management of ATM connections.

A second approach has been proposed by a number of vendors and it relies on routing to link switched networks. In this case, routing functionality is distributed between centralized route servers and workgroup level packet forwarders. Many VCs travel across the single high-speed interface to the route server, which establishes connections among virtual and emulated LANs and also takes care of conventional tasks like firewalls and segmentation. This approach establishes a single point of failure and a potential bottleneck in the route server and could have a negative impact on network latency by introducing extra hops. Backbone traffic will increase because interdepartmental traffic needs to travel down to the router and back up.

A third approach calls for a single device that integrates conventional routing and ATM switching. This device is sometimes called a cell-based or ATM router, or an ATM enterprise network switch (ENS) because adaptation and switching of non-LAN traffic is also incorporated. An ATM ENS offers low application delay by choosing optimal switched paths and eliminating multiple networking devices between end systems. It integrates routing, address resolution, packet forwarding, and ATM connection, traffic, and quality of service management. Furthermore, it can consolidate the full range of wide area connectivity needs including voice and video.

The remainder of this chapter discusses the interLAN switching capabilities of enterprise network switches in a number of key application environments. The key values of interLAN switching are:

- multiple application-based qualities of service
- high-performance cell-based routing and switching
- scalable networking
- network simplification

ENTERPRISE NETWORK SWITCHING

An effective enterprise network switching tool supports interLAN switching and ATM adaptation and switching on a single, high-speed platform. InterLAN switching is an implementation of cell-based routing and switching in an ATM enterprise network switch. InterLAN switching is integrated with its capability of consolidating voice, data, video, and ATM on a single platform.

Multiple Application-based Classes of Service

An ENS supports multiple application-based qualities of service to provide more predictable application performance and to optimize the use of network resources. The full suite of ATM classes of service should be supported by an ENS, including constant bit rate (CBR), variable bit rate (both real-time and non-real-time VBR), unspecified bit rate (UBR) and available bit rate (ABR, initially using end-to-end signaling and forward-congestion signaling). Classes of service are based on a queuing structure that supports three hardware emission priorities and four discard priorities. In addition to these mechanisms, a logical network topology can be configured that rides on top of the physical wide area network topology. A multicast facility is also provided to broadcast packets to all members of a logical network.

This logical network capability provides the following benefits:

- bandwidth effectiveness, because trunk bandwidth can be pre-allocated to certain applications to provide guaranteed minimum performance, while taking full advantage of statistical sharing for peak loads
- mapping of different classes of service to different logical networks
- automatic reconfiguration without affecting users because the physical structure of the WAN is decoupled from the logical structure
- provision of statistics for the bill back of end users and applications

High-Performance Cell-based Routing and Switching

An appropriately configured cell-based routing and switching platform can deliver high-performance operation at the switch and network levels. In addition to the standard LAN and interLAN services, such a network optionally provides a distributed switching and routing system that supports the low-latency transmission of interLAN switched packets across a network. An internal address structure is used to support very high-speed, low-latency forwarding at transit nodes. A particular network protocol only has to be supported at the edge of the network.

Scalable Networking

Cell-based routing and switching offers scalable networking, providing an integrated solution from the campus to potentially very large global networks operating over narrowband to broadband facilities. Cell-based routing and switching platform vendor offerings are available in five and 16-slot versions to economically serve different site sizes. In addition, interfaces operating at speeds from 56K bps to 155M bps can be provisioned on either the user interface or network sides on a plug and play basis. At speeds up to T3, such a network supports frame and frame/cell trunking, which dramatically reduces the overheads associated with ATM adaptation.

InterLAN switching can offer switch capacity, simplified internal addressing, OSPF-based routing, and hierarchical network support, which are all enablers for building very large networks. It can also provide an evolution path to ATM by supporting a separation between routing and high-speed packet forwarding functionality. Routing is the process of finding paths through a network made up of interconnected nodes and links, and forwarding is the process of physically passing user data through a network node based on the topology information gathered by the routing protocol.

Network Simplification

InterLAN switching provides simplification through multimedia network consolidation based on:

- resource sharing across multiple networks
- dynamic bandwidth management across multiple applications
- integrated network management on open platforms
- accommodation of new traffic patterns without the necessity of major network reconfigurations, though there may be an opportunity for some reoptimization
- introduction of new applications without the necessity of a new networking infrastructure, though greater bandwidth may be required as these applications grow

In addition, interLAN switching provides:

- simplified network configuration due to autodiscovery of nodes
- fewer routing boxes to manage
- progressive integration of bridges and routers onto a high-speed ATM platform

Open Architecture

InterLAN switching is open and consistent with LAN internetworking and emerging ATM LAN standards. Multivendor interoperability over LAN interfaces is well established, this being the preferred method used to connect to the existing router base. Multiprotocol encapsulation over PPP, frame relay, and SMDS for remote access have been defined and are supported. Frame relay to ATM service interworking will allow frame relay-attached branch routers to connect to an interLAN network over a single high-speed ATM interface to the public network.

INTERLAN SWITCHING APPLICATIONS

The general deployment strategy for a switched interLAN is to achieve the immediate benefits of interLAN switching in a manner that provides minimal disruption to the embedded LAN/router network, and then to add ATM wide-area and local interfaces on a plug-and-play basis as the need arises. The manner in which such a network delivers the values associated with interLAN switching is best illustrated by examining a number of application scenarios.

In the first application, interLAN switching is integral to an enterprise network consolidation role. The second application focuses on campus networking and could be stand-alone or integrated with the first. The third application discusses evolution to ATM of integrated campus, metropolitan area, and wide area networks.

High-Performance InterLAN Connectivity via an Enterprise Network Consolidation Vehicle

While router networks have been deployed widely in enterprise environments, there are two quite different environments in which router functional integration into an interLAN may be desirable. Some users have very large router networks. Although a necessary and well used technology, the increasing complexity of router networks, especially in large, distributed environments can significantly affect performance, manageability and network scalability. Multiple hop requirements, increased latency in routers, and congestion due to router table updates can have serious impacts on the performance of the network.

Other users have multiple interconnected router networks that they may be in the process of reengineering because their bridged networks are reaching their operational limits.

In both cases, the installed base of routers may be reaching a capacity limit necessitating an outright replacement. Enterprise users who have deployed a switched-interLAN or are interested in the network consolidation of their voice, video, SNA, and inter-router traffic via an ATM ENS, need to also address their requirements for high-performance interLAN connectivity. InterLAN switching provides two methods for consolidating interLAN traffic across the wide area, and provides the benefits inherent in ATM (improved performance, simplified network design, management, administration, and scalability).

In the first approach, interLAN switching interfaces to the installed base of routers via a native LAN (Ethernet, Token Ring, FDDI, and, ultimately, ATM running LAN emulation) interfaces and makes a non-broadcast, multi-access network look like a wide-area emulated LAN. Native LAN interfaces to routers provide the best price and performance, the highest application throughput, and lowest latency, and keep the router configuration simple, easing operational complexity. InterLAN switching provides any-to-any connectivity among LAN-attached routers located at the edge of the network. This application makes routers connected to the network appear to be one hop away from each other. A multicast facility is used to broadcast packets among the routers and a spanning tree is maintained to ensure that packets are not replicated unnecessarily. This application operates independently of network layer protocols. For example, the routers can use a proprietary routing protocol such as IGRP, or a standard such as RIP or OSPF.

In the second approach, the network provides connectivity to multiple network layer protocols while hiding the details from these protocols. The network layer protocols view the network as a single hop topology with traffic being transparently switched through the interLAN network.

In addition to the overall benefits of network consolidation, interLAN switching provides the following benefits:

- high capacity cell-based routing
- high-performance (high throughput and low latency) application networking
- simplified network design and improved network scalability
- effective operations, management, and administration via network management

InterLAN Switching and Virtual LANs

A virtual LAN (VLAN) is a logical LAN segment that spans end-station connections attached to different physical LAN segments. Virtual LANs:

- decrease the costs of moves and changes
- enhance performance by eliminating unnecessary broadcasts
- increase manageability through placement of mission-critical servers at centralized locations

The concept of extending VLANs over the wide area is just emerging in the industry, using vendor-specific implementations. Passport will support wide area VLANs once these standards are defined.

The VLAN concept has also been defined for the ATM environment. In this case, the extension of emulated LANs across the wide area can be accomplished via ATM virtual circuits, providing high-speed, low-latency connectivity. ATM LAN emulation standards define mechanisms to allow a single VLAN to be made up of ATM and Ethernet or Token Ring workstations.

In both cases, routing between VLANs can be provided by interLAN switching, providing firewalls and media conversion.

Campus Networking via InterLAN Switching

Another application area is campus networking, which is presented here as a stand-alone application, but can be integrated with wide area network consolidation.

Campus networks are generally characterized by:

- a layered architecture built on a structured wiring scheme
- stackable or chassis LAN hubs in the wiring closet
- intermediate concentrators such as multiport bridges (optional)

- LAN backbones based on Token Ring, FDDI, or ATM
- some level of redundancy (not shown) at various levels of the architecture in larger sites

This campus environment creates management and control complexity for the network operations staff, particularly because a high degree of redundancy is not economically practical in many cases. More significantly, the ever-increasing application and traffic demands cause risks and difficulties in the expansion of the campus backbone. High-performance switching architectures provide an alternative to meeting the problems associated with highly complex campus networks. A high-performance ATM switching platform combined with cell-based routing and high fanout can support up to 10 ATM OC-3c interfaces, 14 FDDI, 56 Token Ring LANs, or 84 Ethernet LANs as a nonblocking 1.6G-bps campus switch.

The operational cost, space, and power requirements are reduced by consolidating multiple multiport bridges and routers onto a single platform. Downtime for software and hardware upgrades can be eliminated because of inherent robustness. For end users, the results are improved application throughput, lower latency, and higher network availability. Further operational benefits can be achieved by integrating the campus, MAN, and WAN environments.

Evolution to ATM Networking

As public network ATM services become available with competitive price and performance, public network ATM interfaces can be provided on a switched interLAN wherever required. These will support network-to-network communications for all classes of service supported, as well as connectivity to routers and muxes that support standard ATM adaptations (AAL1 for circuit emulation, AAL5 for data).

SUMMARY

The major challenges associated with LAN networking are performance, scalability, management, and cost. In the local environment, users are rapidly moving to switched LAN architectures and ATM.

In response to user requirements for LAN interconnectivity across the campus or over an international wide area network, interLAN switching has been developed. An effective ATM enterprise network switch delivers the benefits of switching architectures across the wide area, making network capacity more scalable and simplifying network management. Cell-based routing and switching is the next wave making possible the benefits of ATM-to-LAN interconnection.

Chapter 9
LAN-to-Mainframe Connectivity Choices

Lisa M. Lindgren

THE MAINFRAME HAS BEEN THE JEWEL IN THE CROWN OF THE ENTERPRISE NETWORK since its introduction in the 1960s. It is the repository for 70 percent of the mission-critical data and applications of enterprises. In the late 1980s and early 1990s, most industry visionaries predicted the demise of the mainframe. In its place, enterprises would adopt client/server architecture, implemented with low-cost servers based on industry standard technology like UNIX and Intel processors. In fact, one major industry publication actually ran a contest for readers to estimate the date on which the last mainframe would be unplugged.

It is now known, of course, that those visionaries were overly optimistic about client/server technologies. They seriously underestimated the costs and problems of downsizing mainframe applications to open system platforms. And they grossly overestimated the technical capabilities and scalability of client/server solutions. Finally, the visionaries overlooked one possibility in formulating their conclusions — that the mainframe would become dramatically less expensive and offer support for open technologies like UNIX and TCP/IP. Today's mainframe offers a lower cost, smaller footprint, and support for even greater redundancy and fault tolerance than the mainframe of the past. Better yet, the mainframe leverages the vast investment already made in the processes for the comprehensive backup and disaster recovery capabilities that have, as yet, eluded the client/server environment.

So, rather than selling their mainframes off for scrap metal, enterprises around the world have made the investment in retooling the mainframe-based applications for Y2K. As the IBM rising stock price will attest, enterprises have continued to invest in new mainframe processors. Many large enterprises have installed TCP/IP on the mainframe to support new applications, the transfer of data to and from other servers, and host access by TCP/IP-based clients. Enterprises have deployed multiple mainframes and tied them together with parallel sysplex to support complete redundancy and fault tolerance.

In short, the mainframe is not dead. It is not even sick. It will continue to play a vital and viable role in large enterprises for many years to come. But it is playing a different role than it did in the early days. Rather than serving as the master of the enterprise IT infrastructure, it now participates on more equal terms with other servers. In addition to serving in its traditional role as an interactive transaction processor, the mainframe is now also sending and receiving large amounts of data via file transfers and participating in client/server and object-oriented applications. Because of this changing role, there are new types of devices that provide connectivity between the mainframe and the enterprise network. The traditional channel-attached devices do a fine job of handling traditional traffic flows and volumes, but new types of devices are required to meet the new demands for high-volume data transfers and for new software capabilities.

TRADITIONAL IBM (AND COMPATIBLE) DEVICES

IBM Systems Network Architecture (SNA) is the predominant network architecture implemented in enterprises with IBM (and compatible) mainframes and midrange systems. IBM introduced SNA in 1974, and it gained widespread deployment through the late 1980s and early 1990s. SNA is a hierarchical architecture. ACF/VTAM, the SNA software that runs on the mainframe, is the master of the SNA network, "owning" all devices and serving as the primary end of all sessions. Traditional IBM devices that connect to the mainframe channel and communicate with ACF/VTAM are the cluster controller (e.g., 3174) and the communication controller, also referred to as a front-end processor (e.g., 3745).

Since the late 1980s, many enterprises have begun to integrate TCP/IP into the enterprise network, including in many cases the installation of a TCP/IP stack and applications on the mainframe. IBM introduced the 3172 Interconnect Controller in 1990 to provide LAN-to-mainframe interconnection, initially only for TCP/IP traffic.

With the addition of the 3172, IBM had three different platforms that would provide connection from the network to the mainframe. The 3174 provided channel connection for a small workgroup of terminal devices or PCs emulating terminals. The front-end processor formed the backbone of the SNA network and provided mainframe access to the majority of devices in the enterprise. The 3172 provided access to mainframe-based TCP/IP applications for TCP/IP-based workgroups. Exhibit 9-1 depicts a typical data center environment of the early 1990s.

Over time, however, each of the platforms evolved to the extent that the lines between the platforms have blurred. In fact, IBM spent a lot of time

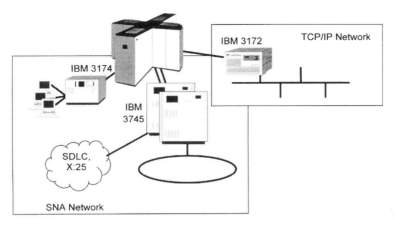

Exhibit 9-1. Typical mainframe data center, circa early 1990s.

and effort in the 1990s trying to position the three platforms at user group meetings and in individual customer presentations. Although IBM is no longer actively marketing these traditional connectivity devices for new installations, it is still relevant to discuss their positioning, strengths, and weaknesses. There is a massive installed base of each device type, and organizations evaluating LAN-to-mainframe options often need to decide whether to upgrade, maintain, or replace these devices.

3174 ESTABLISHMENT CONTROLLER

The early cluster controller provided I/O, session, and presentation services to a limited number of coaxial-attached "dumb" terminals. The upstream connection was either a communication line (e.g., SDLC) or a channel connection. Since the early days of SNA, the controller (now called the 3174 Establishment Controller by IBM) has evolved to support LANs, PC clients, Advanced Peer-to-Peer Networking (APPN, SNA successor), TCP/IP, Frame Relay, and other advanced features.

Despite the introduction of advanced features, both remote and channel-attached controllers have been and are being replaced by other equipment, primarily gateways and routers. This is due primarily to the diminishing installed base of traditional terminal devices and split-stack emulators that require a controller to complete the session with the mainframe. Many organizations find that upgrading an existing controller to support new LAN clients and new gateway functions is more expensive than implementing more modern solutions. The goal of enterprises should be to stabilize the controller installed base, keeping them only where they are required to support legacy devices or specific features. Over time, as the end systems are upgraded, the controller should be phased out.

3745 Communication Controller (and Related Products)

Prior to the proliferation of multi-protocol, bridge/router-based backbones, the 3745 Communication Controller (and its predecessors) formed the backbone of the majority of large enterprise SNA networks. The 3745 runs ACF/NCP software, which is responsible for routing SNA traffic and managing the communication lines in the backbone network, among other tasks. These devices were deployed in the data center, channel-attached to mainframes, and in remote locations. The remote 3745s have largely been replaced by bridges, routers, gateways, and Frame Relay Access Devices (FRADs), but most large enterprises still have channel-attached 3745s, referred to as FEPs.

The FEP is an excellent platform for consolidating a large number of serial lines and for handling terminal-oriented sessions and traffic. It also supports unique features for interconnection of two SNA networks (i.e., SNI), support for X.25 networks (i.e., NPSI), support for ASCII devices (i.e., NTO), and support for bisynchronous (BSC) devices and hosts.

However, as LANs and multi-protocol environments grew, IBM tried to adapt the FEP to the new environments with patchy success. Initially, IBM offered a Token Ring interface on the 3745. This has been quite successful, since most IBM-oriented data centers utilized Token Ring technology. The Token Ring interface on the FEP (called the TIC) was the dominant LAN-to-mainframe path for SNA traffic until the recent success of channel-attached routers.

IBM offered Token Ring support, and later Ethernet, directly on the 3745 frame itself. However, as the need for LAN support grew and the requirement for higher-speed channels (i.e., ESCON) and lines increased, the capacity of the 3745 could not really keep up with the demands. The 3746 Model 900 Expansion Unit (3746-900) was introduced to meet these demands. The 3746-900 is connected to the 3745 and provides support for additional X.25 and SDLC lines in addition to ESCON channels, Token Ring, Ethernet, ISDN Primary Rate Interface, and ATM networks. Originally, the 3746-900 relied on the ACF/NCP code in the 3745 for all software functionality, but it has recently been updated to support autonomous APPN and IP routing. The 3746-900 frame has sold very well, in large extent due to the ESCON channel and enhanced LAN and line support.

The ultimate end goal in the IBM FEP strategy was to migrate customers from ACF/NCP-based 3745 FEPs to a stand-alone APPN and IP router. The 3746 Model 950 (3746-950) was this targeted platform. The 3746-950 is, quite simply, a 3746-900 that no longer has a connection to the ACF/NCP on the 3745 and that supports native APPN and TCP/IP routing. The migration story for large enterprises from the 3745 to the 3746-950 was outstanding; but the implementation was terrible and, consequently, the 3746-950 has had very limited success. In essence, the platform was too late, too slow, and does not support leading-edge interfaces and software functionality. While IBM still sells the product, it has turned its attention and marketing focus on its own channel-attached router, the 2216.

So where does that leave enterprises with an installed base of 3745 and 3746 devices? The goal should be to minimize the ongoing investment in them. The hardware maintenance fees on these devices can be quite high, and the ACF/NCP software on the 3745 incurs a monthly software fee that can be as high as $2000 per CPU, depending on the number of connections. Newer platforms (e.g., channel-attached routers) can accommodate most of the SNA and TCP/IP traffic and all of the connection types (plus more!) supported by the 3745/3746. However, certain functions can only be provided by a 3745 (e.g., SNI, NPSI, NTO). Organizations should plan to move the majority of SNA and IP traffic to newer channel-attached platforms and keep the 3745/3746 devices for these special-purpose functions until the need for them no longer exists. It should be noted that the used market for 3745 and 3746 devices still exists (but values are rapidly falling), so organizations can sometimes partially fund new channel equipment through the sale of the used 3745 and 3746 devices.

3172 Interconnect Controller

IBM positions the 3172 Interconnect Controller as a LAN/WAN-to-mainframe gateway for TCP/IP and SNA devices. The 3172 is essentially a PC server, based on the MicroChannel Architecture (MCA) bus, that has been packaged for the rigors of the data center. The model 3, which is the only remaining model of the product available to the market, was introduced in 1992. It offers a base 25-MHz 80486 processor but offers a 90-MHz Pentium processor option. This device is, for the most part, a straight passthrough device for TCP/IP and SNA traffic, performing little in the way of protocol processing. The exception to this is its TCP/IP Offload feature, which offloads some cycles from the mainframe for TCP/IP traffic. The device supports parallel and ESCON channels; Token Ring, Ethernet, FDDI, and ATM LANs; and SDLC and Frame Relay WAN links. Its five slots can accommodate up to two mainframe channel connections and up to four LAN or WAN connections.

As is obvious from the product specification, the 3172 has not kept up with PC server technology. Its 90-MHz Pentium is grossly under-powered by today's standards. The MCA bus is anachronistic in today's PCI/Compact PCI world. The device cannot provide the raw power and throughput required for file transfers, given the increasing size and number of file transfer operations to and from the mainframe. Organizations with relatively new mainframes, an up-to-date LAN switching architecture in the data center, and high throughput requirements should consider replacing existing 3172 devices with channel-attached routers (which emulate the 3172 but offer much higher throughput). On the other hand, organizations with older and smaller mainframes and light throughput requirements should hold onto existing 3172s until they become a performance bottleneck or until the end of their useful life.

CHANNEL-ATTACHED GATEWAYS

As traditional fixed-function SNA terminal devices were replaced with PCs at end users' desktops, a new host connectivity market was formed — the emulation software market. Initially, the PC was outfitted with a coaxial card and emulation software, then attached directly to the cluster controller via coaxial cable. The software was fairly limited and only mimicked a traditional terminal device. Over time, the emulators became much more feature-rich, incorporating:

- APIs to allow the creation of new PC programs to access mainframe data
- user customization capabilities like keyboard and color remapping
- automation features like scripting and record/playback
- support for multiple hosts in a single package
- support for various host connectivity choices and protocols

As departmental LAN servers (e.g., Novell's NetWare) proliferated, vendors began to offer new LAN-to-mainframe gateway software. This software is installed on a LAN server, and LAN-based PCs running emulators utilize the gateway to access the host rather than a traditional cluster controller. Novell's NetWare for SAA is a very successful example of this server-based gateway software. It is estimated that Novell alone had an installed base of more than 75,000 gateway servers in the early 1990s.

Several vendors in the early 1990s began to offer PC servers that were packaged in the factory with gateway software and mainframe channel cards. These channel-attached gateways appealed to organizations with a lot of departmental and remote gateways because they offered better cost-per-user figures, more complete manageability, a turnkey and pre-tested platform, and often redundancy features. The channel-attached gateways often offer greater scalability, supporting more sessions than remote servers do because they are built using high-end components. There are a number of different solutions available on the market today, most supporting either Novell NetWare for SAA (with is now marketed by IBM), IBM Communications Server for NT, or Microsoft SNA Server. Some vendors (e.g., Bus-Tech) offer a choice of gateway software.

These new channel-attached gateways, then, are a very good option for organizations that have a large number of remote gateways. Organizations can consolidate on fewer, high-end gateways that are more manageable.

These gateways do not, however, serve competently as a general-purpose LAN-to-mainframe connectivity device. They do not offer the same config-uration flexibility, routing capabilities, networking protocol support, and high performance offered by channel-attached routers and switches. Another area of caution is scalability. While some gateway vendors claim to support tens of thousands of concurrent sessions on a single PC server, real-life experience suggests that these claims are boastful at best. Organi-zations planning to deploy new channel-attached gateways should care-fully test the platforms with a traffic profile that closely mimics that orga-nization's production environment in order to estimate equipment requirements.

A final, niche set of channel-attached gateways must be mentioned for completeness. Early on in the emulation market, some vendors focused on providing PC-to-mainframe access over a TCP/IP network. The IETF stan-dard for this type of emulation is called TN3270 (or now, TN3270E). Some vendors opted to offer TN3270 client software (the PC emulator software) and a channel-attached TN3270 server (the gateway) in lieu of the full-func-tion SNA clients and gateways. In the United States, OpenConnect Systems, Apertus, and CNT were the dominant TN3270 vendors. These products offer a rich set of features but are being surpassed in price/performance and connectivity options by IBM and Cisco channel-attached routers. In other instances, organizations are also choosing to forego external TN3270 gateways in favor of running that function on the mainframe itself. Organi-zations should maintain these products while they remain viable, but look to new platforms or the mainframe-based option for expansion of TN3270 services to new TCP/IP-based users.

CHANNEL-ATTACHED ROUTERS AND SWITCHES

The multi-protocol router became the dominant backbone-networking device by the early 1990s. Initially, routers were deployed to bridge and route TCP/IP and other LAN protocols. By the early 1990s and led by Cisco Systems, routers had advanced to support traditional SNA and other legacy protocols in a variety of different ways. As those integration technologies matured and became accepted in the enterprise, a wide variety of devices (remote controllers, gateways, and even 3745 Communication Controllers) were de-installed in favor of routers. Small, inexpensive routers were deployed in branch and remote locations. Medium-capacity routers were deployed as distribution points in regional locations. High-end routers with lots of slots and very fast buses were deployed in central locations like data centers.

Once the high-end routers were located in data centers and supported SNA and TCP/IP traffic, it was a natural extension to attach those routers to the mainframe channel. Cisco Systems led the way, announcing the Channel Interface Processor (CIP) for the Cisco 7000 router series in 1993. The CIP initially emulated the IBM 3172 Interconnect Controller, supporting TCP/IP traffic (with some optional mainframe offload for IP) and SNA. Later, a TN3270 server (i.e., gateway) function and additional mainframe offload were added. Cisco has extended the product line with the Channel Port Adapter (CPA) for the 7500 series. IBM was late to the channel-attached router game but now offers channel attachment for its 2216 router. The 2216 offers support for SNA, TCP/IP, and TN3270 traffic.

The channel-attached router has become the conceptual replacement for front-end processors. Like FEPs, these routers provide attachment to multiple mainframes and routing of traffic between multiple mainframes, mainframe partitions, and data centers. Like FEPs, routers support advanced software features and complex networking capabilities. Like FEPs, they are becoming the *de facto* standard solution for mainframe channel attachment.

However, there are instances in which the advanced software features of routers are not required for mainframe-bound data. For example, a TCP/IP-based file transfer from a UNIX system in the data center to a single mainframe requires simple connectivity over a high-speed LAN and no protocol processing. In these cases, network-based switches or integrated mainframe adapters are good solutions for channel attachment.

CHANNEL-ATTACHED SWITCHES

Bay Networks announced the industry's first channel attachment for a switch with its 5745 Enterprise Switching Module (ESM) for the 5000 Switching Hub. Although the first to market, this product has had very limited success due to Bay's slipping enterprise router market share and technical problems with the product. IBM, on the other hand, has released channel attachment for its capable 8265 ATM switch.

Because switches operate at a lower layer in the protocol stack than routers, these platforms cannot provide the protocol routing, encapsulation, and other software features that routers can and do provide. Therefore, organizations should look at channel-attached switches as possible solutions when simple and direct connectivity to the mainframe from the high-speed LAN and WAN switching environment is required.

INTEGRATED MAINFRAME ADAPTERS

All of the solutions discussed thus far (even the traditional IBM devices) are external boxes that bring the network to the mainframe. IBM offers an integrated device that ships with all new G4 and G5 mainframes called the Open Systems Adapter. Conceptually, this device is a 3172 that is "under the covers," inside the mainframe. However, IBM has enhanced the OSA beyond its original 3172-like capabilities. The OSA supports Token Ring and Ethernet (including full-duplex for switched environments), FDDI, and ATM (155 Mbps) for SNA and TCP/IP traffic.

The OSA is and will continue to be successful; it is a "no-brainer" for organizations buying new mainframes to utilize this integrated networking technology. As a "free" component for new mainframes, it offers immediate LAN-to-mainframe attachment and a direct pipe into the mainframe. Organizations should embrace the OSA, particularly in environments where simple and direct connectivity to the mainframe is desired. They should look to channel-attached routers, on the other hand, when offload of IP protocols from the mainframe is important and when external routing of traffic is required.

MAKING YOUR SELECTION

Enterprise organizations now have a number of different choices when they are trying to integrate the modern high-speed LAN environment with the mainframe. They can continue to maintain traditional IBM (and compatible) connectivity devices where necessary. Or, they can augment or replace those systems with a new generation of platforms that offer higher throughput and advanced hardware and software capabilities. Exhibit 9-2 summarizes the strengths and weaknesses of the seven different types of platforms discussed in this article and provides a recommendation on where or when to maintain or deploy each of the types.

Exhibit 9-2. Seven different types of platforms.

Platform	Strengths	Weaknesses	Recommendation
3174 Establishment Controller	Terminal device and split-stack emulator connectivity	Price/performance; lack of many internetworking features found on gateways and routers	Limited to traditional legacy device connectivity; attach "downstream" of router to gain advanced routing and encapsulation
3745 Communication Controller, 3746-900, 3746-950	Serial SNA line concentration; traditional SNA routing (PU_T4); unique functionality (SNI, NTO, NPSI)	Price/performance; support for modern LAN interfaces and complete TCP/IP function; low throughput	Isolate in data center to perform only those functions not performed by other platforms (e.g., SNI); move standard traffic to more cost-effective platform; minimize ongoing fees and expenses
3172 Interconnect Controller	Inexpensive platform offering basic LAN-to-mainframe connectivity	Low throughput compared to newer platforms; lack newest LAN/WAN connections; lack newer software features	Maintain until performance needs exceed throughput capabilities; look to newer platforms for advanced features
Channel-attached gateways	Less costly than multiple remote gateways; rich set of gateway features and protocol options	Not suitable as a generalized LAN-to-mainframe connectivity device; scalability can be an issue	Install to eliminate multiple remote gateways, especially when traditional gateway software features required; if only TN3270 needed, consider using TN3270 in mainframe or channel-attached router
Channel-attached routers	Rich and up-to-date LAN/WAN connectivity choices; rich routing and security software features; cost-effective; high-performance	May have more functionality than required in certain instances	Look to as the conceptual replacement for FEPs; implement when routing between multiple mainframes/partitions and main-frame offload required

Exhibit 9-2. *(Continued)*

Platform	Strengths	Weaknesses	Recommendation
Channel-attached switches	Simple connectivity from very high-speed, switched LANs and WANs	Unproven in market; lack of protocol offload features; lack of routing	Implement for specific needs (e.g., 155 Mbps ATM direct to mainframe)
Open system adapter (OSA)	Bundled with new mainframes; integrated within mainframe; simple connectivity	Lack of protocol offload features; lack of routing	Implement where simple, direct mainframe connectivity is required

Chapter 10

Building Highly Reliable Computer Networks

Richard Rauscher

HIGHLY RELIABLE COMPUTER NETWORKS are becoming increasingly essential in industries in which real-time transactions occur. The healthcare industry depends on information systems not only for business operations but also for critical care: Patient monitoring systems now rely on computer networks for communications. What would happen if the nurses' station didn't get a message indicating that a patient was in cardiac arrest? Law enforcement and emergency services are using information systems for every part of their function: A working computer at the dispatchers' office can be the difference between a police officer knowing if the car he just pulled over was simply committing a speeding violation or contains a wanted murderer. In these and many other instances, the computer network can be the difference between life and death.

Vendors sell products based on performance. Engineers often buy products based on performance. With the speed of common local area networks (LAN) increasing tenfold every few years, "more power" should be the slogan for the network architect of the 1990s. Does all this increased bandwidth *really* translate to any tangible benefit? That depends on network utilization and applications. Maintaining good utilization statistics helps the network engineer make this decision. These statistics may also indicate that there is no current requirement for more bandwidth. Budget money would be better spent elsewhere. It may be time to concentrate on making the computer network more reliable rather than faster.

If the network architect is building a network on which others' lives will depend, she must ask herself if she would let her life depend on this network. If the answer is "no," she needs to make immediate changes: either to the network infrastructure or to her choice of careers.

0-8493-0859-3/00/$0.00+$.50
© 2000 by CRC Press LLC

The reader may already be an expert in finding network *performance* bottlenecks. This chapter helps the reader to identify *reliability* bottlenecks. The chapter focuses strictly on network infrastructure components and only briefly mentions server and client issues. It discusses the following issues: device reliability, environmental issues, physical layer issues, link layer issues, network layer issues, and network management. The reader should have a good understanding of the functions of the Open Systems Interconnection (OSI) stack before perusing this chapter. Purchasing reliable equipment and installing redundant equipment will help the network architect build a highly reliable network.

DEVICE RELIABILITY METRICS AND RATINGS

A computer network is simply a collection of cables and electronic devices connected in a particular way to facilitate communications between two or more computers. Examining each of the components in a computer network helps readers analyze the risk (probability) of network failure.

An important but often overlooked and understudied device specification, the *mean time between failures (MTBF)*, can be used by network planners to maximize the reliability of their design. The MTBF is the only metric supplied by the manufacturer that can be used to evaluate the expected reliability of a product. In most cases, the vendor is self-reporting this information. But even assuming that the vendor is honestly disclosing its MTBF numbers, what does this number mean? Let us first examine the ways in which vendors compute their MTBF number and then use these numbers to calculate our own MTBF odds based on the network model below.

1. To get a product to market quickly (which is necessary in the competitive marketplace), the vendor is likely to take a large number of devices and run them continuously for some predetermined period. The MTBF is calculated by taking the total, cumulative running time of each device and dividing it by the number of failures. For example, if a vendor ran 10 devices for 1,000 hours each and 2 failed during that time, the total number of hours is 10,000/2 = 5,000 MTBF.
2. Vendors often do not consider an initial "burn-in" period (the initial period that a device is powered and running).
3. Vendors may or may not consider real-world effects, such as applying and removing power on a regular basis, handling during shipping, handling during installation, and so on.
4. Vendors may or may not be computing the MTBF as a function of the combined MTBF of all the devices' components, plus some operational probability of failure.
5. Vendors expect the unit to degrade below the stated MTBF after the period stated as its usable life has elapsed.

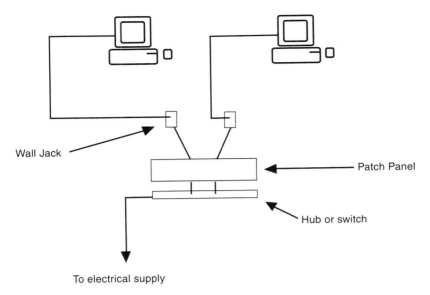

Exhibit 10-1. A simple network diagram.

The responsible network engineer will ask vendors how they compute their MTBF ratings. The engineer should not be surprised if the salesperson needs to call headquarters to obtain this information. A few rules of thumb should apply:

1. Do not trust the vendor's self-reported MTBF exclusively; read trade magazine articles about that vendor.
2. Allow a burn-in period for every device placed on the network; to effectively "burn-in" a new device, no activity is required — the device just needs to be turned on.

Analysis of a Simple Network

It would be helpful to examine the simple network model in Exhibit 10-1.

Exhibit 10-1 represents a simplified LAN model in which two computers are communicating via a hub. For simplicity, assume that this network is based on Ethernet. What can go wrong with this network? Ignoring the computers, the component parts of this network are the following:

1. both cables from computer to wall
2. both cables from wall, through wall, to back of patch panel
3. both cables from patch panel to hub

4. the hub's internal electronics
5. the hub's power supply
6. the power feeding the hub's power supply

Six of the nine components of this network are cables. Without any MTBF data on the rate of failing cables, common sense is necessary. Three assumptions are necessary: (1) cables that move are more likely to break than cables that do not; (2) cables that do not move and will not break; and (3) before a cable is put into production, it is tested. Given these assumptions, cables that are subject to human interaction are more likely to move; therefore, cables that are subject to human interaction are more likely to break. Therefore, the cables that connect the back-of-the-wall jack to the back-of-the-patch panel are the least likely points of failure. If we can further assume that one of these computers is a server and one is a client and that the server is seldom subject to human interaction, we can also deduce that the cable from the server to the wall jack carries a reduced probability of failure.

Given the lack of supporting data, assume that the hub has a significantly higher probability for failure than any cable in the network. This may be because the hub is an active, electromechanical device. The hub is considered mechanical because it contains (usually) an electrical fan. That fan may have been constantly accumulating dust since the day it was turned on. That dust will clog the low-power motor. Over time, that motor may slow down or shut down completely. When the fan stops, the unit operates outside its design specifications and it probably stops running. In real networks, there may be tens or hundreds of interdependent network devices at various levels of the OSI stack.

REDUNDANCY

Often the outage of a single component, device, or link in the network can cause a larger outage. Therefore, it is useful to have a second item in place to provide service in the event that the primary item fails. This use of more than one item to perform the same task is called redundancy. Although it is true that a network functions without redundancy, a redundant network, which decreases the probability of failure, is more reliable. If redundancy is properly implemented, it can protect the network from debilitating device or link failures. The following sections of this chapter discuss how to have redundancy at a variety of levels. These levels loosely correspond to the three lower layers of the OSI stack. The lower three layers are physical, link, and network.

PHYSICAL LAYER ISSUES (OSI LAYER ONE)
Environment

Network architects occasionally have the ability to plan the construction of a new building. This can be very satisfying if done correctly. However, more often than not the network architect must construct a network in a preexisting structure. Most of these structures, particularly older buildings, did not consider data communications during the design. Thus, communications closets may be in electrical closets, broom closets, or even ceilings and floors. The network architect must consider the total environment when analyzing the space in which the computer equipment will live. Are there any water pipes? The risks associated with water pipes are somewhat obvious. If one of them springs a leak, the organization does not want the network to go down the drain. Also, although less obvious, plumbers may occasionally need to access these pipes. In general, it is a good idea to stay away from areas in which other building infrastructure is concentrated, for it is in these areas that the most work will be done.

(As an aside, network architects should consider all building infrastructure maintenance people armed and dangerous. During the days of thick coaxial cable, this author had several run-ins with the heating and air-conditioning duct workers. At a thin coaxial cable installation, a team of painters seemed to thrive on unplugging Ethernet loopback connectors. Whether it is envy or a malicious plot to ruin the architect's good name, these people are out to destroy the network. Architects be warned.)

Power

In general, the network architect should have some basic understanding of how the power systems in the facility work. The equipment for which he is responsible must be powered. This section explores some of the power issues:

1. Is there an uninterruptible power supply (UPS)? A UPS is a mechanism that typically sits between the network devices and the facility's power supply (wall current). The UPS passes power through special circuitry that detects failures in the electrical supply and switches (within 1/60 of second) to its on-board battery. Unless the power systems have centralized redundancy, a UPS is a must. It not only keeps the network devices functioning in the event of an outage, but it can also condition the electrical current going into the network devices so to not cause unnecessary wear and tear on the device's power supply.

2. How many power supplies does the network devices have? Most modern network devices have an optional redundant power supply. If the facility has opted for the redundant power supply, the network architect should be sure that the power that feeds it is not the same power that supplies the other power supply. For example, if a communications closet has several devices, each with a redundant power supply, a reasonable UPS scheme would be to plug the primary power supply of each device in to one UPS and the second power supplies of the other devices in to another UPS.

3. Do multiple, independent power systems feed the communications closet (e.g., power systems that come off of multiple circuit breakers)? If so, network architects should take advantage of this by partitioning the power strategy across the two separate supplies.

Exhibits 10-2 through 10-5 illustrate the various tiers of power supply redundancy. Exhibit 10-2 shows a typical, nonredundant configuration. Exhibit 10-3 shows the next most expensive step, the installation of a

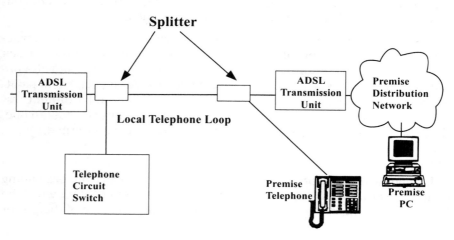

Exhibit 10-2. No redundant power.

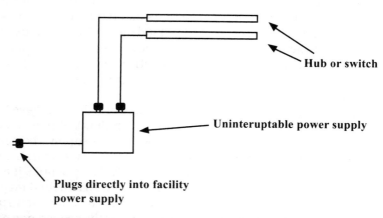

Exhibit 10-3. UPS for temporary redundancy for main power supply.

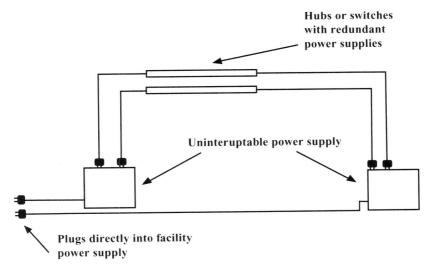

Exhibit 10-4. Hubs with redundant power supplies and UPSs.

UPS. Exhibit 10-4 shows the installation of redundant power supplies into the hubs. Exhibit 10-5 shows the addition of a redundant power conduit system.

After addressing power redundancy, the next logical layer in the network stack is the physical layer. The physical medium over which bits travel (typically twisted pair or multi- or single-mode fiber optics) does not usually wear out. The breaking of a physical connection is usually caused by human activity. Construction or changes being made to other parts of the building's infrastructure (i.e., heating/air conditioning, plumbing, and electricity) can cause accidents in which the network's physical links are cut. In extreme circumstances, interference from electrical and magnetic sources can interfere with copper-based transmission media. Severe moisture can adversely affect some types of fiber-optic media.

Like power systems, various levels of redundancy can be achieved to avoid problems with physical lines being cut. Exhibit 10-6 illustrates a simple star network.

Each physical connection (represented by a line) is a possible point of failure for one or more clients. In this picture, there are two servers, one central switch and two closets from which clients are connected. The physical connections that can affect users here are the connections from server to switch, the connections from the primary switch to the closet switch, and the connections from the closet switches to the clients. Adding additional

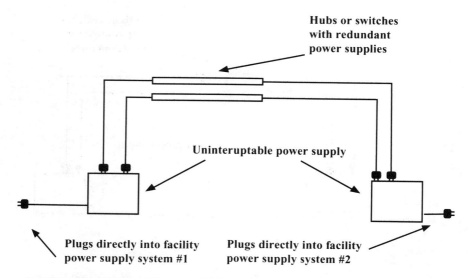

Exhibit 10-5. Hubs with redundant power supplies, UPSs, and power feeder systems.

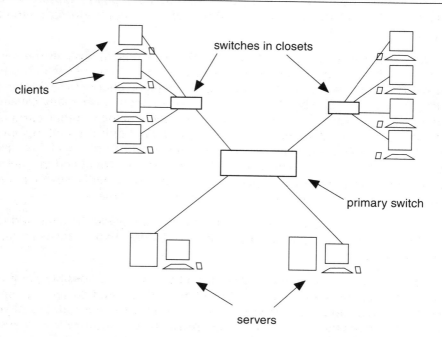

Exhibit 10-6. Typical collapsed star topology.

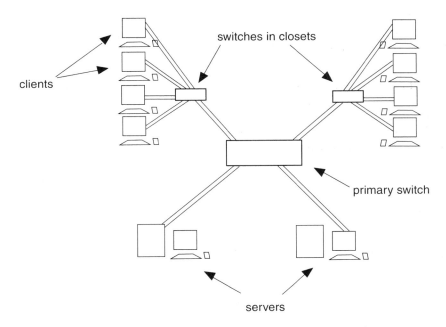

Exhibit 10-7. Addition of redundant physical connections.

cables from the servers to the primary switch and from the primary switch to the closet switches reduces the probability of a failure that would affect more than one network node. It should be noted that these additional, redundant connections should follow a different physical route through the building from point A to point B. This is called route redundancy. Because cables usually fail as a result of some sort of local physical interference, there is a significant chance that the same interference would affect the redundant cable if it were to follow the identical route. The network can be made further redundant by adding additional links from the computers to the closet switches (see Exhibit 10-7).

These redundant physical paths must have software support. That support is discussed in the section on Layer 2 and 3, which follows.

LINK LAYER ISSUES (OSI LAYER TWO)

The Wide Area Networks

For wide area networks (WAN), the network engineer must usually secure connectivity from point A to point B via some service provider. In the world of deregulation, this service provider may be a telephone company, a power company, a cable company, or anyone willing to sell networking infrastructure. Because this is usually the telephone company, telephone company terminology is used here.

It is important for network architects to have some understanding of how their equipment is interacting with that of the local telephone company. Telephone companies coordinate all of their local connectivity for a geographical area from a central office (CO). Network architects must understand how their telephone company's COs are organized. The better they understand how the telephone company's network is configured, the more intelligently they will be able to request route redundancy through their network. Request that redundant WAN connections be routed through different COs. The section on Layer 3 provides more information about the use of redundant leased-lines

The Local Area Networks. Layer 2 (the link layer) is defined primarily by LAN definitions. These are standardized by the IEEE committee 802 and by ANSI. The IEEE 802.3 subcommittee has defined a set of standards known commercially as Ethernet. Because Ethernet is the most prevalent LAN topology type, it is used here as the primary example.

Shared Ethernet. Several vendors offer facilities for redundancy in shared Ethernet environments. These facilities vary among vendors and are not typically interoperable. Because all shared Ethernet redundancy solutions are vendor-dependent, they will not be discussed here.

Switched Ethernet. One of the more influential developments in LAN technology has been the overwhelming shift from shared media technologies to switched media technologies. An Ethernet switch is nothing more than a bridge with many ports. These ports may connect to other switches or hubs or directly to end devices. For the purposes of this chapter, the widespread use of switches has introduced a powerful tool for redundancy: the Spanning Tree Protocol.

Spanning Tree Protocol. The Spanning Tree Protocol (STP) was originally developed by IEEE subcommittee 802.1d to overcome the inability to have redundant bridges. Because Ethernet switches are simply multiport bridges, the STP can be used to facilitate the construction of highly link-redundant networks. To construct a redundant network that uses STP as a "safety net," it may be useful for readers to understand how the STP works.

Exhibit 10-8 provides a network diagram. It is a simple example in which three switches are connected via a link to one another. There is a cycle in this network. The cycle must be eliminated for the Ethernet network to function correctly. The STP algorithm works as follows:

1. Through the use of Ethernet multicast packets (called bridge protocol data unit, or BPDU), a "root" switch node is elected; this election is based on the switch with the lowest "bridge ID." The bridge ID is usually based on the media access control address of the switch.

2. For each segment that is common to more than one switch, a decision is made about which switch will forward packets to the root node. This decision is based on the switch that is closest (based on the number of hops) to the root node. The redundant links are put in "standby" mode.

3. Switches exchange BPDU packets that contain data indicating the number of hops to the root node.

4. As each switch receives BPDU packets, it evaluates the packet and compares the information to its stored perception of the network. If the new information leads to a shorter path to the root node, a new root port is identified and the old one will be shut down.

5. If a switch detects a change in the configuration of the network, a new root node may be elected (if necessary) and the calculation starts again.

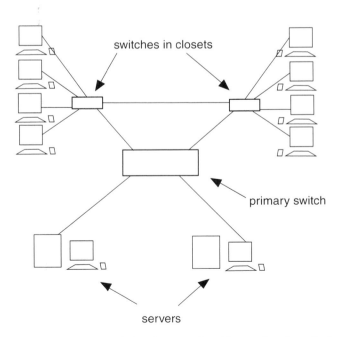

Exhibit 10-8. The switched network with a redundant link.

Assume that the primary switch is elected to be the root node. The link that interconnects to the two closest switches would be furthest from the root node and therefore be turned off on both switches.

Recovery times when using the STP vary depending on the number of nodes in the tree, the speed of connectivity to those nodes, and various tunable parameters associated with the STP. A typical network takes more than 30 seconds to recover from a root-port outage. Many users perceive this 30-sec. delay as unacceptably long. To increase the attractiveness of Ethernet, various vendors have implemented proprietary methods to obtain a much smaller convergence time. Some vendors have claimed to reduce convergence times for large networks to less than five seconds.

STP is no longer limited only to Ethernet switches. Vendors have begun making network interface cards (NIC) that also recognize redundant connections. Using this technology, we can extend the use of redundancy to the leaf nodes of the network as in Exhibit 10-7. The obvious problem with Exhibit 10-7 is that the failure of any one switch would affect many computers. Exhibit 10-9 adds the redundant link between the closet switches and an additional primary switch. The failure of the primary switch, a single-server-to-switch link, or any one switch-to-switch link, does not result in downtime.

LAYER THREE: THE NETWORK LAYER

In this section, readers examine Layer 3 methods for redundancy to build highly reliable networks. The Internet Protocol (IP) is the subject examined. Although only IP examples are cited, many of the same or identical concepts can be seen in Internet Packet Exchange (IPX) and Xerox Network Services (XNS) networks.

The basis of achieving IP redundancy is in learning new routes to old destinations. Exhibit 10-10 shows a corporate WAN with three sites. Site A is the primary facility and sites B and C are secondary facilities. All three sites are connected via T1 lines. For redundancy, add a third link connecting facilities B and C. Now the failure of any one link will not result in the isolation of any node. But how does IP handle this? The answer depends on the routing protocol. The simplest way to configure routing is to statically identify routes. There is one pro and several cons to static routes. The pro is that it is extremely simple and difficult to make a mistake. The con is that it is impossible to learn new routes when the primary route fails.

There are three popular routing algorithms for small to medium-size networks (<500 subnets): RIP (routing information protocol), RIP2 (an

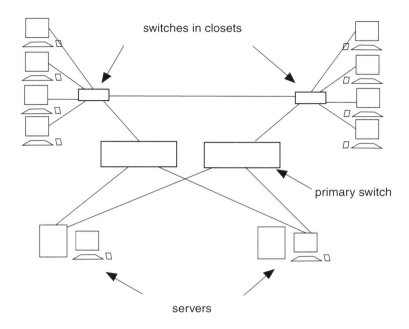

switches in closets

primary switch

servers

Exhibit 10-9. Redundant primary switches and server connections.

---

improved version of RIP), and OSPF (open shortest path first). RIP sends periodic updates; OSPF updates its neighbors when something changes. Thus, if a node or link becomes inactive, OSPF will propagate that fact more quickly. For this and other reasons, OSPF will converge to a complete layer three network much faster than RIP.

NETWORK MANAGEMENT AND TESTING

The wonderful thing about automated, redundant fault-tolerant systems is that entire devices and power supplies, for example, can fail and no one will notice. Of course, at least one person needs to notice: the network manager. To build a completely fault-tolerant system would be a fool's errand if there were no network management system to inform someone that a fault had occurred. Once a fault occurs, the system is on its backup systems and just one fault away from being nonfunctional.

After a supposedly reliable network has been configured and installed, one should always test the points of failure for which one planned

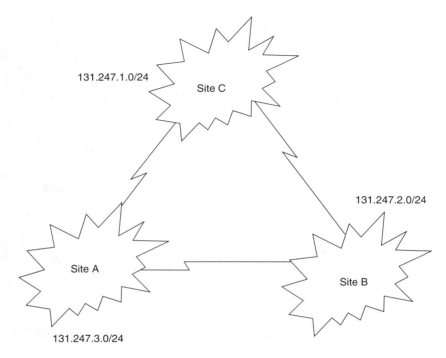

131.247.1.0/24

Site C

131.247.2.0/24

Site A

Site B

131.247.3.0/24

Exhibit 10-10. IP networks with a redundant path.

redundancy. This test can be as simple as disconnecting a plug. If all goes well, the redundant systems should engage and the network management system will be notified.

BUSINESS JUSTIFICATION

Network redundancy is not inexpensive. The need for redundancy must be weighed against the cost of downtime to the organization. Redundancy can, in extreme cases, double the cost of networking. When calculating the cost of downtime, take into account not just the lost salaries of idle employees but also the indirect costs such as the public relations expenses of not being able to service customers.

THE ULTIMATELY RELIABLE NETWORK

The ideal is a LAN that will not go down under any noncataclysmic conditions (see Exhibit 10-11). To keep the complexity of the drawing minimal, the exhibit describes only a single client. There are two servers. Also assume that those servers are OS-level redundant for each other. In other words, one server can be down and some software mechanism will cause

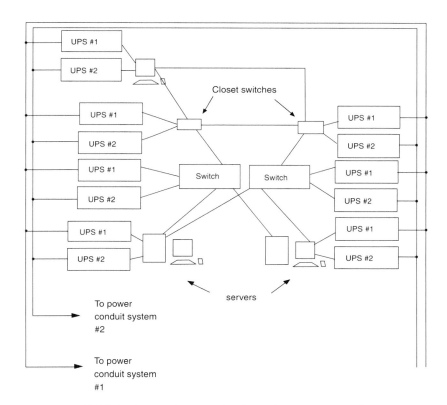

Exhibit 10-11. The completely redundant network.

the client to look to the other server for resources. Every device on the network has two UPSs that connect to it. Every device has a redundant power supply, and two UPSs and is powered from two independent power systems. The client computer is the only single point of failure. Assuming that is a spare client computer, and that any user could do the job equally well from the second computer, there should be no significant work loss in the event that the client computer failed.

Section II
Understanding WANs

THE SECOND PILLAR OF NETWORK TECHNOLOGY IS THE WIDE AREA NETWORK (WAN) used to interconnect geographically separated locations. The use of WANs has considerably evolved over the past two decades. Originally, the lack of competition in the long-distance transmission market limited the ability of organizations to consider the use of different transmission facilities due to a lack of offerings. With the divestiture of AT&T and its operating companies during the 1980s, competition for long-distance transmission accelerated, resulting in the expedient development and implementation of new technologies as one communications carrier attempted to gain an advantage over another carrier. Due to the number of networking facilities available for WANs, it is important to understand the use of different networking facilities, which is the focus of this section.

Because wide area networking is based on many factors to include federal, state, and local regulations, this section begins with a chapter that covers conditions in the U.S. telecommunications sector. In Chapter 11, **U.S. Telecommunications Today,** author Nicholas Economides discusses the impact of technological and regulatory change on market structure and business strategy. In this chapter, Economides points out the major driving forces in U.S. telecommunications, reviews the Telecommunications Act of 1996 and its impact on the industry and consumers, and discusses local services and the entry of Regional Bell Operating Companies (RBOCs) into the long-distance market. This chapter concludes with an overview of the Telecommunications Act of 1996 and its impact on wireless communications and cable technology.

With an appreciation for the state of the U.S. telecommunications industry, one can turn attention to the bedrock of the industry — the voice network. In Chapter 12, **The Voice Network: Communications with Sky's-the-Limit Versatility,** author Bryan Pickett provides detailed information concerning the public switched telephone network (PSTN). In this chapter, Pickett describes in detail the features and functions associated with the voice network to include the role of PBX, messaging, wireless service, and Centrex service. Continuing the examination of WAN facilities, author Roohollah Hajbandeh's chapter, titled **T1, T3, and SONET Networks,** introduces high-speed wide area networking in Chapter 13. In this chapter, Hajbandeh first introduces T1 functional elements to include the role of channel service units, channel banks, repeaters, and digital access, and cross-connect systems. Once this is accomplished, attention is focused on different versions of pulse code modulation (PCM), T1 framing and the multiplexing of voice and data onto T1 and T3 networks, and the use of optical transmission to obtain relatively high data transmission rates with relatively low error rates.

After obtaining a solid overview of WAN facilities in prior chapters in this section, the next two chapters introduce different network access techniques. In Chapter 14, **Remote Access Concepts and Techniques,** author Peter Southwick introduces the use of the public switched telephone network to remotely access LANs. In this chapter, Southwick examines several networking scenarios as well as describes the use of different protocols to obtain a remote access capability to include security-related protocols and devices. The second access-related chapter in this section is authored by William R. Koss. In Chapter 15, titled **ATM Access: The Genesis of a New Network,** Koss first provides an overview of key ATM features, followed by discussion and description of ATM access devices that end users can consider to obtain access to an ATM backbone infrastructure being deployed by most communications carriers.

In Chapter 16, author Tim Kelly introduces the use of Frame Relay. In the chapter **Transport over Frame Relay: Issues and Considerations,** Kelly first reviews the rationale for Frame Relay and examines the transport issues as they relate to the quality of the underlying service. This chapter is followed by the chapter titled **Emerging High-Bandwidth Networks** (Chapter 17). In this chapter, authors Kevin M. Groom and Frank M. Groom, Ph.D., focus attention on several high-speed networking technologies to include ATM, frame relay, and the transmission of frame relay over an ATM backbone.

Because one of the newer areas of interest of network managers and LAN administrators is the convergence of voice and data, the next two chapters in this section focus on this topic. In Chapter 18, Larry Schessel's **Voice and Data Network Integration** introduces voice over IP technology as well as gives several examples that illustrate the benefits of the technology. Chapter 19, **ATM Circuit Emulation Services,** authored by G. Thomas des Jardins, provides information concerning the use of ATM to emulate voice-transporting circuits. This information provides the ability to better understand how one can use ATM to transport both voice and data on a common infrastructure.

Concluding our introduction to wide area networking are two chapters — one covering routing while the second covers the convergence of different WAN technologies. In Chapter 20, Michael Gilbert's chapter, **Routing and Routing Protocols,** introduces the method by which routers can automatically determine alternate routes between networks in the event one or more path connections should become inoperative. In Chapter 21, entitled **Convergence of IP, ATM, and SONET/SDM at the Backbone,** John R. Vacca covers the rationale for the use of each communications technology. This chapter also illustrates how their use is converging for providing different methods to access a backbone infrastructure that provides the capability to interconnect geographically separated locations.

Chapter 11

U.S. Telecommunications Today*

Nicholas Economides

THIS CHAPTER EXAMINES THE CURRENT CONDITIONS in the U.S. telecommunications sector (April 1999). It discusses the impact of technological and regulatory change on market structure and business strategy. The chapter touches on, among other issues, the impact on pricing of digitization and the emergence of Internet telephony. It also takes a brief look at the impact of the 1996 Telecommunications Act on market structure and strategy in conjunction with the history of regulation and antitrust intervention in the telecommunications sector. The author expresses concern about the derailment of the implementation of the 1996 Act by the aggressive legal tactics of the entrenched monopolists (the local exchange carriers), and he points to the danger that the intent of Congress in passing the 1996 Act to promote competition in telecommunications will not be realized. After discussing the impact of wireless technologies, the chapter comments on the wave of mergers in the industry and ventures into some short-term predictions.

INTRODUCTION

The U.S. Telecommunications sector is going through a revolutionary change. There are three reasons for this. The first reason is the rapid technological change in key inputs of telecommunications services and in complementary goods, which have reduced dramatically the costs of traditional services and have made many new services available at reasonable prices. Cost reductions have made feasible the World Wide Web (WWW) and the various multimedia applications that "live" on it.

The second reason for the revolutionary change has been the sweeping digitization of the telecommunications and the related sectors. The underlying telecommunications technology has become digital. Moreover, the consumer and business telecommunications interfaces have become more versatile and closer to multifunction computers than to traditional telephones. Digitization and integration of telecommunications services with computers create significant business opportunities and impose significant pressure on traditional pricing structures, especially in voice telephony.

The third reason for the current upheaval in the telecommunications sector is the passage of a major new law to govern telecommunications in the United States, the Telecommunications Act of 1996 (1996 Act). Telecommunications traditionally has been subject to a complicated federal and state regulatory structure. The 1996 Act attempted to adapt the regulatory structure to technological reality, but various legal challenges by the incumbents have so far delayed, if not nullified, its impact.

Before going into a detailed analysis, it is important to point out the major driving forces in U.S. telecommunications today.

- dramatic reductions in the costs of transmission and switching
- digitization
- restructuring of the regulatory environment through the implementation of the 1996 Telecommunications Act coming 12 years after the breakup of AT&T
- move of value from underlying services (such as transmission and switching) to the interface and content
- move toward multifunction programmable devices with programmable interfaces, such as computers, and away from single-function, nonprogrammable consumer devices, such as traditional telephone appliances
- reallocation of electromagnetic spectrum, allowing for new types of wireless competition
- interconnection and interoperability of interconnected networks; standardization of communications protocols
- network externalities and critical mass

These forces have a number of consequences:

- increasing pressure for cost-based pricing of telecommunications services
- price arbitrage between services of the same time immediacy requirement
- increasing competition in long-distance services
- the possibility of competition in local services
- The emergence of Internet telephony as a major new telecommunications technology

TECHNOLOGICAL CHANGE

The last two decades have witnessed (1) dramatic reductions in costs of transmission through the use of technology, (2) reductions in costs of switching and information processing because of big reductions of costs of integrated circuits and computers, and (3) significant improvements in software interfaces. Cost reductions and better interfaces have made feasible many data- and transmission-intensive services. These include many applications on the WWW, which were dreamed of many years ago but only now have become economically feasible.

The general trend in cost reductions has allowed for entry of more competitors in many components of the telecommunications network and an intensification of competition. Mandatory interconnection of public telecommunications networks and the use of common standards for interconnection and interoperability created a "network of networks" (i.e., a web of interconnected networks). The open architecture of the network of networks allowed for entry of new competitors in markets for particular components, as well as in markets for integrated end-to-end services. Competition intensified in many, but not all, markets.

Digital Convergence and "Bit Arbitrage"

Entry and competition were particularly helped by (1) the open architecture of the network and (2) its increasing digitization. Currently, all voice messages are digitized close to their origination and are carried in digital form over most of the network. Thus, the data and voice networks are one, with voice treated as data with specific time requirements. This has important implications on pricing and market structure.

Digital bits (zeros or ones) traveling on the information highway can be parts of voice, still pictures, video, or a database or other computer application, and they appear identical — "a bit is a bit is a bit." However, because some demands are for real-time services while others are not, the saying that "a bit is a bit is a bit" is only correct among services that have the same index of time *immediacy*. Digitization implies arbitrage on the price of bit transmission among services that have the same time immediacy requirements.

For example, voice telephony and video conferencing require real-time transmission and interaction. Digitization implies that the cost of transmission of voice is hundreds of times smaller than the cost of transmitting video of the same duration. This implies that if regulatorily imposed price discrimination is eliminated, arbitrage on the price of bits will occur, leading to extremely low prices for services, such as voice, that use relatively very few bits. Even if price discrimination remains imposed by regulation, arbitrage in the cost and pricing of bits will lead to pressures for a de facto elimination of discrimination. This creates significant profit opportunities for the firms that are able to identify the arbitrage opportunities and exploit them.

Internet Telephony

The elimination of price discrimination between voice and data services can lead to dramatic reductions in the price of voice calls, precipitating significant changes in market structure. These changes were first evident in the emergence of the Internet, a ubiquitous network of applications based on the TCP/IP. Started as a text-based network for scientific communication, the Internet grew dramatically in the late 1980s and 1990s, once not-text-only applications became available.[1] The Internet now reaches about half a billion computers, most of which are connected to it through the telephone network. Internet-based telecommunications are based on packet switching. There are two modes of operation: (1) a time-delay mode in which there is a guarantee that the system will do whatever it can to deliver all packets and (2) a real-time mode, in which packets can, in fact, be lost without possibility of recovery.

Most telecommunications services do not have a real-time requirement, so applications that "live" on the Internet can easily accommodate them. For example, a number of companies currently provide facsimile services of the Internet where all or part of the transport of the fax takes place over the Internet. Although the Internet was not intended to be used in real-time telecommunications, despite the loss of packets, telecommunications companies presently use the Internet to complete ordinary voice telephone calls. Voice telecommunications service started on the Internet as a computer-to-computer call. As long as Internet telephony was confined to calls from a PC to a PC, it failed to take advantage of the huge network externalities of the public switched telephone network (PSTN), and was just a hobby.

About four years ago, Internet telecommunications companies started offering termination of calls on the PSTN, thus taking advantage of the immense externalities of reaching anyone on the PSTN. In 1996, firms started offering Internet calling that originated and terminated on the PSTN (i.e., from and to the regular customers' phone appliances). The last two transitions became possible with the introduction of PSTN-Internet interfaces and switches by Lucent and others. In 1998, Qwest and others started using IP switching to carry telephone calls from and to the PSTN using their own network for long-distance transport as an Intranet.

Internet calls are packet-based. Because they utilize the real-time mode of the Internet, there is no guarantee that all the packets of a voice transmission will arrive at the destination. Internet telephony providers use sophisticated voice-sampling methods to decompose and reconstitute voice so that packet losses do not make a significant audible difference. Because such methods are by their nature imperfect, the quality and fidelity of an Internet call crucially depend on the percentage of packets that are lost in transmission and transport. This, in turn, depends, among other factors on (1) the allocation of Internet bandwidth (pipeline) to the phone call and (2) the number of times the message is transmitted.[2] Because of these considerations, one expects that two types of Internet telephony will survive: (1) the low-end quality, carried over the Internet, with packets lost and low fidelity, and (2) a service of comparable quality with traditional long distance, carried on a company's intranet on the long-distance part.

Internet-based telecommunications services pose a serious threat to traditional national and international long-distance service providers. In the traditional US regulatory structure, a call originating from a computer to an Internet service provider (ISP) (or terminating from an ISP to a computer) is not charged an "access charges" by the local exchange carrier. This can lead to substantial savings.

The Federal Communications Commission (FCC), in its decision of February 25, 1999, muddies the waters by finding that "Internet traffic is intrinsically mixed and appears to be largely interstate in nature" on the one hand; while, on the other hand, it validates the reciprocal compensation of ISPs which were made under the assumption that customer calls to ISPs are treated as local calls. If Internet calls are classified as interstate (i.e., as long-distance data calls), the price that most consumers will have to pay to reach the Internet would become a significant per minute change and it is likely that the Internet will stop its fast growth. In fact, one of the key reasons for Europe's lag in Internet adoption is the fact that in most countries, unlike in the United States, consumers are charged per minute for local calls.

In response to the Internet telephony threat, in January 1998 AT&T announced that it would offer a new long-distance service carried over the Internet and AT&T's intranet. AT&T's service, offered at 7.5 to 9 cents per minute, will originate and terminate on the PSTN and therefore will appear to customers like a regular call; no computer will be required. Several months earlier, Deutsche Telecom (DT) introduced Internet long-distance service within Germany. To compensate for the lower quality of voice transmission, DT offered internet long-distance service at one-fifth of its regular long-distance rates. Internet telephony remains the most important challenge to the telecommunications sector.

THE TELECOMMUNICATIONS ACT OF 1996 AND ITS IMPACT

Goals of the Act

The Telecommunications Act of 1996 attempts a major restructuring of the U.S. telecommunications sector. The 1996 Act will be judged favorably to the extent that it allows and facilitates the acquisition by consumers of the benefits of technological advances. Such a function requires the promotion of competition in all markets. This does not mean immediate and complete deregulation. Consumers must be protected from monopolistic abuses in some markets as long as such abuses are feasible under the current market structure. Moreover, the regulatory framework must safeguard against firms exporting their monopoly power in other markets.

In passing the Telecommunications Act of 1996, Congress took radical steps to restructure U.S. telecommunications markets. These steps may result in significant benefits to consumers of telecommunications services, telecommunications carriers, and telecommunications equipment manufacturers. But the degree of success of the 1996 Act depends crucially on its implementation through decisions of the FCC and state public utility commissions and the outcome of the various court challenges that these decisions face.

The 1996 Act envisions a network of interconnected networks that are composed of complementary components and generally provide both competing and complementary services. The 1996 Act uses both *structural* and *behavioral* instruments to accomplish its goals. The 1996 Act attempts to reduce regulatory barriers to entry and competition. It outlaws artificial barriers to entry in local exchange markets in its attempt to accomplish the maximum possible competition. Moreover, it mandates interconnection of telecommunications networks, unbundling, nondiscrimination, and cost-based pricing of leased parts of the network, so that competitors can enter easily and compete component by component and service by service.

The 1996 Act imposes conditions to ensure that de facto monopoly power is not exported to vertically related markets. Thus, the 1996 Act *requires* that competition be established in local markets *before* the incumbent local exchange carriers are allowed in long distance.

The 1996 Act preserves subsidized local service to achieve "universal service" but imposes the requirement that subsidization is transparent and that subsidies are raised in a competitively neutral manner. Thus, the act leads the way to the elimination of subsidization of universal service through the traditional method of high access charges.

The 1996 Act crystallized changes that had become necessary because of technological progress. Rapid technological change has always been the original cause of regulatory change. The radical transformation of the regulatory environment and market conditions that is presently taking place as a result of the 1996 Act is no exception.

History

Telecommunications has traditionally been a regulated sector of the U.S. economy. Regulation was imposed in the early part of this century and remains until today in various parts of the sector.[3] The main idea behind regulation was that it was necessary because the market for telecommunications services was a natural monopoly, and therefore a second competitor would not survive.

As early as 1900, it was clear that all telecommunications markets were *not* natural monopolies, as evidenced by the existence of more than one competing firm in many regional markets, prior to the absorption of most of them in the Bell System. Over time, it became clear that some markets that may have been natural monopolies in the past are *not* natural monopolies any more, and that it is better to allow competition in those markets while keeping the rest regulated.

The market for telecommunication services and for telecommunications equipment went through various stages of competitiveness after the invention of the telephone by Alexander Graham Bell. After a period of expansion and consolidation, by the 1920s, AT&T had an overwhelming majority of telephony exchanges and submitted to state regulation. Federal regulation was instituted by the 1934 Telecommunication Act, which established the FCC.

Regulation of the U.S. telecommunications market was marked by two important antitrust lawsuits that the U.S. Department of Justice brought against AT&T. In the first one, *United States* v. *Western Electric*, filed in 1949, the U.S. Department of Justice (DOJ) claimed that the Bell Operating Companies practiced illegal exclusion by buying only from Western Electric, a part of the Bell System. The government sought a divestiture of Western Electric, but the case was settled in 1956 with AT&T agreeing not to enter the computer market but retaining ownership of Western Electric.

The second major antitrust suit, *United States* v. *AT&T,* was started in 1974. The government alleged that (1) AT&T's relationship with Western Electric was illegal, and (2) that AT&T monopolized the long-distance market. The DOJ sought divestiture of both manufacturing and long distance from local service. The case was settled by the modified final judgment (MFJ). This decree broke away from AT&T seven regional Bell operating companies (RBOCs). Each RBOC consisted of a collection of local telephone companies that were part of the original AT&T. RBOCs remained regulated monopolies, each with an exclusive franchise in its region.

Microwave transmission was a major breakthrough in long-distance transmission that created the possibility of competition in long distance. Microwave transmission was followed by technological breakthroughs in transmission through satellite and through fiberoptic wire.

The breakup of AT&T crystallized the recognition that competition was possible in long distance, while the local market remained a natural monopoly. The biggest benefits to consumers during the last 15 years have come from the long-distance market, which, during this period was transformed from a monopoly to an effectively competitive market. However, often consumers do not reap the full benefits of cost reductions and competition because of an antiquated regulatory framework that, ironically, was supposed to protect consumers from monopolistic abuses and instead protects the monopolistic market structure.

Competition in long distance has been a great success. The market share (in minutes of use) of AT&T fell from almost 100 percent to 53 percent at the end of 1996. Since the MFJ, the number of competitors in the long-distance market has increased dramatically. There are four large facilities-based competitors: AT&T, MCI–WorldCom, Sprint, and Frontier.[4] There are also a large number of "resellers" that buy wholesale service from the facilities-based long-distance carriers and sell to consumers. For example, currently, about 500 resellers compete in the California interexchange market, providing strong evidence for the ease of entry into this market. At least 20 new firms entered the California market in each year since 1984. At present, there are at least five "out of region" RBOCs providing service in California through affiliates. In California, the typical consumer can choose from at least 150 long-distance companies.

Prices of long-distance phone calls have decreased dramatically. The average revenue per minute of AT&T's switched services has been reduced by 62 percent between 1984 and 1996. AT&T was declared "nondominant" in the long-distance market by the FCC in 1995.[5] Most economists agree that presently the long-distance market is *effectively competitive.*

Local telephone companies that came out of the Bell system (RBOCs) actively petitioned the U.S. Congress to be allowed to enter the long-distance market, from which they were excluded by the MFJ. The MFJ prevented RBOCs from participation in long distance because of the anticompetitive consequences that this would have for competition in long distance. The anticompetitive effects would arise because of the control by RBOCs of essential "bottleneck" inputs for long-distance services, such as orginating access of phone calls to customers who live in the local companies' service areas to long-distance companies. Hence, RBOCs monopoly franchises.

A long-distance phone call is carried by the local telephone companies of the place it where originates and the place it terminates, and only in its long-distance part by a long-distance company. Thus, "originating access" and "terminating access" are provided by local exchange carriers to long-distance companies and are essential bottleneck inputs for long-distance service. Origination and termination of calls are extremely lucrative services.[6] Terminating access has an average cost (in most locations) of $0.002 per minute. Its regulated prices vary. A typical price is $0.032 per minute, charged by NY Telephone. Such pricing implies a profit rate of 1,500 percent.[7] Access charges reform is one of the key demands of the pro-competitive forces in the current deregulation process.

The great success of competition in long distance allowed the U.S. Congress to appear "balanced" in the 1996 Act by establishing competition in local telephony while allowing RBOCs into long distance after they meet certain conditions. However, the transition of local markets to effective competition will not be as easy or as quick as in the long-distance markets. This is because of the nature of the product and the associated economics.

Many telecommunications companies are presently trying to be in as many markets as possible so they can bundle the various products. Companies believe that consumers are willing to pay more for bundled services for which the consumer receives a single bill. Bundling also discourages consumers from migrating to competitors, which may not offer the complete collection of services, so consumer "churn" is expected to be reduced.

Entry in Local Services as Envisioned by the Act

At the time this chapter was written, the "last mile" of the telecommunications network that is closest to the consumer (the "local loop") still remains a bottleneck controlled by a local exchange carrier (LEC). The 1996 Act boldly attempts to introduce competition in this last bottleneck, and, before competition takes hold, the 1996 Act attempts to imitate competition in the local exchange.

To facilitate entry in the local exchange, the 1996 Act introduces two novel ways of entry other than through the installation of owned facilities. The first way allows entry in the retailing part of the telecommunications business by requiring incumbent local exchange carriers (ILECs) to sell to entrants at wholesale prices any retail service that they offer. Such entry is essentially limited to the retailing part of the market.

The second and most significant novel way of entry introduced by the 1996 Act is through leasing of unbundled network elements from incumbents. In particular, the 1996 Act requires that ILECs (1) unbundle their networks and (2) offer for lease to entrants network components (unbundled network elements, or UNEs) "at cost plus reasonable profit."[8] Thus, the 1996 Act envisions the telecommunications network as a decentralized network of interconnected networks.

Many firms, including the large interexchange carriers AT&T and MCI–WorldCom, attempted to enter the market through "arbitration" agreements with ILECs under the supervision of state regulatory commissions, according to the procedure outlined by the 1996 Act. The arbitration process proved to be extremely long and difficult, with continuous legal obstacles and appeals raised by the ILECs. By the time of this writing, just over three years after the signing of the 1996 Act by President Clinton, arbitrations have been concluded in only a few states, and entry in the local exchange has been minimal.

Entry of RBOCs in Long-Distance Service

RBOCs (Ameritech, Bell Atlantic, BellSouth, SBC, and US West) have 89 percent of telephone access lines nationwide. Most of the remainder belongs to GTE and independent franchise holders. Competitive access providers (who did not hold a franchise monopoly) have less than one percent of residential access lines nationwide. Besides providing access to long-distance companies, LECs also provide lucrative *custom local exchange services*, such as call waiting, conference calling, and automatic number identification. Basic local service provided by LECs is considered not to be particularly profitable.

The 1996 Act allows for entry of RBOCs in long distance once a list of requirements has been met and the petitioner has proved that its proposal is in the public interest. These requirements can be met only when the market for local telecommunications services becomes sufficiently competitive. If the local market is not competitive when an incumbent LEC monopolist enters into long distance, the LEC can leverage its monopoly power to disadvantage its long-distance rivals by increasing their costs in various ways and by discriminating against them in its pricing. If the local market is not competitive when an incumbent LEC monopolist enters into long distance, an ILEC would control the price of a required input (switched access) to long-distance service while it would also compete for customers in long distance. Under these circumstances, an ILEC can implement a *vertical price squeeze* on its long-distance competitors whereby the price to cost ratio of long-distance competitors is squeezed so that they are driven out of business.[9]

In allowing entry of local exchange carriers into the long-distance market, the 1996 Act tries not to endanger competition that has developed in long distance by premature entry of RBOCs in the long distance market. However, on this issue, the 1996 Act's provisions guarding *against premature entry* may be insufficient. Hence, to guard against anticompetitive consequences of premature entry of RBOCs in long distance there is a need of a deeper analysis of the consequences of such entry on competition and on consumers' and social welfare.

THE IMPACT OF WIRELESS (CELLULAR, SATELLITE, AND PCS) AND OF CABLE TELEVISION

During the last 15 years there has been a tremendous (and generally unanticipated) expansion of the mobile phone market. This significant growth has been limited by relatively high prices resulting from (1) the prevention of entry of more than two competitors in each metropolitan area and (2) the standard billing arrangement that imposes a fee on the cellular customer for *receiving* (as well as initiating) calls.

However, during the last three years, the FCC has auctioned parts of the electromagnetic spectrum that will enable the transmission of personal communication services (PCS) signals.[10] The auctioned spectrum will be able to support up to five additional carriers in the major metropolitan markets.[11] Although the PCS spectrum band is different than the traditional cellular bands, PCS is predicted to be a low-cost, high-quality, mobile alternative to traditional phone service. Other wireless services may chip away at the ILECs markets, especially in high-capacity access services.[12] The increase in the number of competitors has already created significant decreases in prices of mobile phone services.

By its nature, PCS is positioned between fixed local service and traditional wireless (cellular) service. Presently there is a significant price difference between the two services. Priced between the two, PCS will first draw consumers from cellular in large cities and later on will be a serious threat to fixed local service. AT&T has recently announced that it will use some of the spectrum that it acquired in the PCS auctions to implement a fixed wireless service ("telepoint"), a close (and maybe superior) substitute to fixed wire service.[13]

Industry analysts have been predicting the impending entry of cable television in telephony for many years. Despite numerous trials, such entry in traditional telecommunications services has not materialized. There are a number of reasons for this. First, to provide telephone service, cable television providers needed to upgrade their networks from analog to digital. Second, they need to add switching. Third, most of the cable industry has taken a high debt load and is unable to make the required investments in the short run.

If and when it is able to provide switching, cable television will have a significant advantage over regular telephone lines. Cable TV lines that reach the home have a significantly higher bandwidth capacity than do regular twisted pair lines. This is not important for regular voice telephony, but it is crucially important for applications on the World Wide Web that require high bandwidth capacity. Companies such as @home and WebTV are utilizing this capacity to provide bundles of Internet and traditional TV services. Often these services do not allow for two-way communication but rather rely on a telephone line for transmissions from the home to the ISP which are expected to require only low bandwidth. The merged AT&T–TCI plans to provide telephony, broadband video, and Internet services over the cable line to the home.

THE CURRENT WAVE OF MERGERS

The various legal challenges have derailed the implementation process of the 1996 Act and have increased the uncertainty in the telecommunications sector. Because the arbitration process that started in April 1996 has resulted in final prices in only a handful of states, long-distance companies have been unable to enter the local exchange markets by leasing UNEs. As of this writing, no state has completed the implementation of the Telecommunications Act of 1996, and only 15 of the 50 states have adopted permanent prices for unbundled network elements.[14]

In the absence of final prices, given the uncertainty of the various legal proceedings, and without final resolution on the issues of nonrecurring costs and the electronic interface for switching local service customers across carriers, entry in the local exchange through leasing of UNEs has been minimal. Moreover, entry in the retailing part of the business through total service resale has also been minimal, because the wholesale discounts have been small.

In the absence of entry in the local exchange market as envisioned by the 1996 Act, the major long-distance companies are therefore buying companies that give them some access to the local market. For example, MCI has merged with WorldCom, which had just merged with Brooks Fiber and MFS, which in turn also own some infrastructure in local exchange markets. MCI–WorldCom is focusing on the Internet and the business long-distance market.[15]

AT&T has acquired TCG, which owns the local exchange infrastructure that reaches business customers. AT&T has also recently unveiled an ambitious strategy of reaching consumers' homes by using cable TV wires for the "last mile." With this purpose in mind, AT&T bought TCI with the intent of converting the TCI cable access to an interactive broadband, voice, and data telephone link to residences. AT&T has also entered in an agreement with Time Warner to use its cable connection in a way similar to TCI's, and in April, 1999, AT&T announced its bid for MediaOne, the cable spin-off of US West, which had earlier announced its merger with Comcast.

TCI cable presently reaches 35 percent of U.S. households. Together with Time Warner and MediaOne, AT&T would be able to reach a bit more than 50 percent of U.S. households. Without access to UNEs, to reach all residential customers, AT&T would have to find another way to reach the remaining U.S. households. Further cable conversion is one strategy that can accomplish this. AT&T has also announced, but not yet implemented, a wireless telepoint technology, similar to cellular mobile technology, but only suitable to immobile or slow-moving receivers.

The provision of telephony, Internet access, broadband, data, and two-way video services exclusively over cable lines in the "last mile" requires significant technical advances, significant conversion of the present cable networks, and an investment of at least $5 billion (and some say $30 billion) just for the conversion of the cable network to two-way, switched services.

Moreover, there is some inherent uncertainty in such a conversion, which has not been successful in the past. Thus, it is an expensive and uncertain proposition for AT&T, but, at the same time, it is one of the few remaining options of entry in the local exchange.

Early attempts of the RBOCs to maximize their foothold, looking forward to the time when they would be allowed to provide long-distance service, include SBC's acquisition of Pacific Bell and Bell Atlantic's merger with NYNEX, despite antitrust objections. SBC also bought Southern New England Telephone (SNET), one of the few companies that, as an independent (not part of AT&T at divestiture), was not bound by MFJ restrictions and had already entered into long distance.

Two additional significant mergers that were announced in 1998 are still being reviewed by antitrust and regulatory authorities at this time. Bell Atlantic announced its intention to merge with GTE, and SBC has announced its intention to buy Ameritech. At the present, the DOJ has conditionally approved the SBC–Ameritech merger, and the FCC has announced its own requirements to approve the merger. However, the GTE–Bell Atlantic merger may be much harder to approve as this merger may allow the combined entity to bypass existing rules. GTE is already providing long-distance service because it was not part of AT&T and is not bound by the MFJ restrictions. On the other hand, the Telecommunications Act of 1996, amending the MFJ, prohibits Bell Atlantic from offering long-distance service until a number of conditions are met and Bell Atlantic shows that its entry into long distance is in the public interest. One option is for GTE to spin off its long-distance voice and data assets. If the Bell Atlantic–GTE merger is approved without such a condition, the combined entity can engage in a vertical price squeeze, cross subsidization and raising rivals costs — all the reasons that led to the prohibitions of the MFJ and the 1996 Act.

If all the LEC mergers pass antitrust and regulatory scrutiny, the eight large local exchange carriers of 1984 (seven RBOCs and GTE) would be reduced to only four: Bell Atlantic, Bell South, SBC, and US West. The smaller ones, Bell South and US West, already feel the pressure, and have been widely reported to be in merger/acquisition talks with a number of parties. For example, BellSouth has announced a pact with Qwest to sell Qwest's long-distance service once BellSouth is allowed to sell long-distance service.

THE COMING WORLD

The intent of the 1996 Act was to promote competition and the public interest. It will be a significant failure of the U.S. political, legal, and regulatory systems if the interests of entrenched monopolists rather than the public interest as expressed by the U.S. Congress dictate the future of the

U.S. telecommunications sector. The market structure in the telecommunications sector two years ahead will depend crucially on the resolution of the LECs' legal challenges to the 1996 Act and its final implementation.[16] Already, we have seen significant vertical integration into the cable industry, as AT&T found it extremely difficult to enter the local exchange market.

Whatever the outcomes of the legal battles, the existence of arbitrage and the intensification of competition necessitate cost-based pricing and will create tremendous pressure on traditional regulated prices that are not cost based. Prices that are not based on cost will prove unsustainable. This includes access changes that LECs charge to IXCs, which have to become cost based if the vision of a competitive network of interconnected networks is to be realized.

Computers are likely to play a bigger role as telephone appliances and in running intermediate size networks that will compete with LECs and intensify the arbitrage among IXCs. Computer-based telephone interfaces will become the norm. Firms that have significant market share in computer interfaces, such as Microsoft, may play a significant role in telephony.[17] Hardware manufacturers, especially firms such as Cisco, Intel, and 3Com, that make switches and local networks will play a much more central role in telephony. Internet telephony (voice, data, and broadband) is expected to grow fast.

Finally, I expect that, slowly but steadily, telecommunications will drift away from the technical standards of signaling system seven (SS7) established by AT&T before its breakup. As different methods of transmission and switching take a foothold, and as new interfaces become available, wars over technical standards are very likely.[18] Such wars will further transform telecommunications from the traditional quiet landscape of regulated utilities to the mad-dash world of software and computer manufacturing. This change will create significant business opportunities for entrants and impose significant challenges on traditional telecommunications carriers.

Notes

* For this chapter, "today" is April 1999. Portions of this article are based on "US Telecommunications Today," *Business Economics*, April 1998.

1. Critical points in this development were the emergence of GOPHER in the late 1980s and MOSAIC by 1990.
2. A large enough bandwidth increases the probability that fewer packets will be lost. And, if each packet is sent a number of times, it is much more likely that each packet will arrive at the destination at least once, and the quality of the phone call will not deteriorate. Thus, the provider can adjust the quality level of an Internet call by guaranteeing a lot of bandwidth for the transmission and by sending the packets more than once. This implies that the quality of an Internet call is *variable* and can be adjusted upward using the variables mentioned. Thus, high-quality voice telephony is immediately feasible in intranets

because intranets can guarantee a sustained large-enough bandwidth. There is no impediment to the quality level of a phone call which is picked from the PSTN at the local switch,
carried over long distance on leased lines, and redelivered to the PSTN at the destination
local switch, using the recently introduced Lucent switches. For Internet calls that originate or terminate in computers, the method of resending packets can be used on the Internet to increase the quality of the phone call, as long as there is sufficient bandwidth
between the computer and the local telephone company switch. The fidelity of calls can
also be enhanced by manipulation of the sound frequencies. This can be done, for example, through the *elemedia* series of products by Lucent.

3. The telecommunications sector is regulated both by the federal government through the
FCC and by all states, typically through a public utilities commission (PUC) or public service commission. Usually a PUC also regulates electricity companies.
4. Frontier is a new name for Rochester Telephone.
5. *See* Federal Communications Commission (1995).
6. These fees are the single largest cost item in the ledgers of AT&T.
7. Termination pricing varies. Pacific Bell, under pressure from the California Public Utilities
Commission, recently had an access charge of $0.016 per minute, giving it a profit rate of
700 percent.
8. The FCC and state regulatory commissions have interpreted these words to mean total element long-run incremental cost (TELRIC) which is the forward-looking, long-run, (minimized) economic cost of an unbundled element and includes the competitive return on
capital.
9. Avoiding a vertical price squeeze of long-distance competitors, such as MCI, was a key rationale for the 1981 breakup of AT&T in the long-distance division that kept the AT&T
name and the seven RBOCs that remained local monopolists in local service. *See* Economides (1998, 1999).
10. Despite this and other auctions of spectrum, the FCC does not have a coherent policy of
efficient allocation of electromagnetic spectrum. For example, recently, the FCC gave for
free huge chunks of electromagnetic spectrum to existing TV stations so that they may
provide high-definition television (HDTV). Some of the recipients have publicly stated
that they intend to use the spectrum to broadcast regular TV channels and information
services, rather than HDTV.
11. We do not expect to see five entrants in all markets because laxity in the financial requirements of bidders resulted in default of some of the high bidders in the PCS, prompting a
significant dispute regarding their financial and other obligations.
12. The so-called wireless loop proposes to bypass the ILECs' cabling with much less outlay
for equipment. Trials are under way to test certain portions of the radio spectrum that
were originally set aside for other applications: MMDS for wireless cable and LMDS as cellular television.
13. The second impediment to wider use of mobile phones seems also likely to disappear. In
January 1998, AT&T announced that it will offer mobile service with billing of incoming
calls to the originator of the call.
14. These were Colorado, Delaware, Florida, Georgia, Kentucky, Louisiana, Missouri, Montana, New Jersey, New Hampshire, New York, Oregon, Pennsylvania, Texas, and Wisconsin. Of the states that have adopted permanent prices for UNEs, five are in the Bell
Atlantic/ NYNEX territory (Delaware, New Hampshire, New Jersey, New York, Pennsylvania). Also note that only four states have adopted permanent rates in arbitrations of entrants with GTE (Florida, Montana, Oregon, and Texas). For more details, see Hubbard and
Lehr (1998).
15. The MCI-WorldCom merger was challenged by the European Union Competition Committee, the DOJ and GTE on the grounds that the merged company would have a large market
share of the Internet backbone and could sequentially target, degrade interconnection,
and kill its backbone rivals. Despite (1) a lack of an economically meaningful definition of
the Internet backbone, the fact that (2) MCI was unlikely to have such an incentive because any degradation would also hurt its customers, and (3) it seemed unlikely that such
degradation was feasible, the Competition Commission of the European Union ordered
MCI to divest of *all* its Internet business, including its retail business, when it was never
alleged that the merging companies had any monopoly power. MCI's Internet business
was sold to Cable and Wireless, the MCI-WorldCom merger was finalized, and MCI-World-
Com is using its UUNET subsidiary to spearhead its way in the Internet.

16. In one of the major challenges, GTE and a number of RBOCs appealed (among others) the FCC (1996) rules on pricing guidelines to the Eighth Circuit. The plaintiffs won the appeal; the FCC appealed to the Supreme Court, which ruled on January 25, 1999. The plaintiffs claimed (among other things) that (1) the FCC's rules on the definition of UNEs were flawed, (2) the FCC default prices for leasing of UNEs were so low that they amounted to confiscation of ILEC property, and (3) that FCC's "pick and choose" rule allowing a carrier to demand access to any individual interconnection, service, or network element arrangement on the same terms and conditions the LEC has given anyone else in an approved local competition entry agreement without having to accept the agreement's other provisions would deter the "voluntarily negotiated agreements." The Supreme Court ruled for the FCC in all these points, thereby eliminating a major challenge to the implementation of the Act.
17. Microsoft owns a share of WebTV and has made an investment in Qwest.
18. A significant failure of the FCC has been its absence in defining technical standards and promoting compatibility. Even when the FCC had a unique opportunity to define such standards in PCS telephony (because it could define the terms while it auctioned Spectrum), it allowed a number of incompatible standards to coexist for PCS. This led directly to a weakening of competition and higher prices wireless PCS consumers have to buy a new appliance to migrate across providers.

Recommended Reading

Crandall, R. W. 1991. *After the breakup: U.S. telecommunications in a more competitive era.* Washington, DC: Brookings Institution.

Economides, N. 1996. The economics of networks. *International Journal of Industrial Organization* 14(2):675–699.

Economides, N. 1998. The incentive for non-price discrimination by an input monopolist. *International Journal of Industrial Organization* 16(March 1998):271–284.

Economides, N. 1999. The Telecommunications Act of 1996 and its impact. *Japan and the world economy* 11(September) forthcoming.

Economides, N., Lopomo, G., and Woroch, G. 1996. Regulatory Pricing policies to neutralize network dominance. *Industrial and Corporate Change* 5(4):1013–1028.

Federal Communications Commission. 1995. In the matter of motion of AT&T Corp. to be reclassified as a non-dominant carrier. CC Docket No. 95-427, order, adopted October 12, 1995.

Federal Communications Commission. 1996. First report and order. CC Docket No. 96-98, CC Docket No. 95-185, adopted August 8, 1996.

Hubbard, R. G., and Lehr, W. H. 1998. Improving local exchange competition: Regulatory crossroads, mimeo, February.

Mitchell, B., and Vogelsang, I. 1991. *Telecommunications pricing: Theory and practice.* Cambridge: Cambridge University Press.

Noll, R. G., and Owen, B. 1989. The anti-competitive uses of regulation: *United States v. AT&T.* In *The antitrust revolution*, edited by J. E. Kwoka and L. J. White. New York: Harper Collins, 290–337.

Chapter 12
The Voice Network: Still the Bedrock of the Wide Area Network

Bryan Pickett

FOR DECADES, THE VOICE NETWORK HAS BEEN THE BEDROCK OF ENTERPRISE COMMUNICATIONS, determining much of the efficiency with which co-workers communicate with one another as well as the first impression received by outside callers.

The voice network is still the bedrock, but it is demonstrating a lot of exciting new abilities that boost productivity, make companies appear more receptive to callers, simplify employees' lives, and make the whole company more effective. These new features rest on the following:

- The digital technology that has taken over the private branch exchanges (PBXs) and key systems that provide telephone service within enterprises. Digital technology, built into voice switching and access fabrics, gives them the same kind of "sky's-the-limit" versatility that it gives to data networks.
- The capability of enabling existing voice systems to support Internet Protocol-based traffic. Most PBX vendors have made available or have at least announced upcoming availability of line and trunk cards that provide access to IP networks or external IP gateways. This interim capability is a precursor to converged systems that will have platforms based on open standards and will support voice and data over a single IP network.

The two networks, voice and data, are increasingly cooperating in various tasks, further boosting the organizations' effectiveness and the level of customer service they deliver.

0-8493-0859-3/00/$0.00+$.50
© 2000 by CRC Press LLC

Much of the bridging is done over a computer telephony integration (CTI) interface, which is frequently used to integrate data operations with voice applications. Examples include a call center operation that retrieves customer files and presents them to customer service agents along with incoming calls, a voice mail system that transfers recorded messages into data storage and then retrieves them for presentation in the voice format. Other CTI examples include a messaging system that combines presentation and retrieval of voice, fax, and e-mail messages, a desktop program on the PC that allows workers to make and receive telephone calls via keyboard or mouse commands, and voice-response units that collect customer commands entered on keypad, then pass that string of commands, such as account number, to a call center agent.

THE VOICE NETWORK

A voice network serving an enterprise and owned by it can be thought of as similar in structure to a data network that consists of five basic elements:

- **Servers**: One or more switches — PBXs or key systems — and perhaps adjunct applications software or processors that handle specific tasks such as messaging, automatic call distribution (ACD), and interactive voice response.
- **Clients**: Telephone sets or terminals, which may vary widely in their features and capabilities. Although the switch serving them is probably digital, the telephones may be digital or analog; that is, they may accept voice signals from the switch in either digital or analog form. Newer terminals might be PCs with telephone cards and software that provides a graphical user interface, fully software-based, or may communicate through an IP-based LAN connection.
- **Local network fabric**: The means of transmitting calls within the enterprise. This fabric may include copper, fiber, or radio links operating at rates from 56 Kpbs up to TI (1.5 Mpbs) or even higher. In addition, the fabric may incorporate various network architectures (both voice and data may travel over the same links), various network protocols such as integrated services digital network (ISDN), and CTI.
- **Wide-area network fabric**: The means of transmitting calls outside of the enterprise or from one campus or location to another (often shared with data transmission). It may include the public-switched network and actual and also virtual private networks (VPNs), operating at rates from 56 Kbps up to gigabit-per-second synchronous optical network (SONET) rates.
- **Network management**: Network administration and maintenance, including provisioning of lines, troubleshooting, routine diagnostics, security, fraud detection, and traffic and performance monitoring.

An enterprise also may obtain voice services similar to those provided by such a private network from the local telephone service provider. This type of service, called Centrex, is provided by full-scale switches and facilities that are owned by the local exchange company (LEC) and are part of the public switched telephone network (PSTN). Centrex service emulates the features available from a private network. With this type of service, only the clients reside on customer premises. The servers, local and wide-area access, and network management are the responsibility of the LEC, perhaps working with an interexchange carrier (IXC).

SERVERS

The heart of an enterprise private voice network is the switching system. This is normally a key system for smaller organizations or a PBX for larger ones.

Key systems typically serve between just a few employees, beginning with two or three incoming lines, to several hundred employees with over a hundred incoming lines. Key systems and PBXs share lines among extensions rather than providing an incoming line to each extension. Sharing is possible because not all employees will use their phones simultaneously. However, the number of lines should be carefully engineered to the number of users. Systems must be designed and sized to prevent incoming and outgoing calls from being blocked for lack of capacity, taking into account such parameters and events as maximum call length, busy day and busy hour, and disposition of call trafficking (intra-office, interoffice, and incoming and outgoing call traffic.)

PBXs typically overlap with the upper range of key systems. They may handle only a few dozen incoming lines and fewer than 50 users at the low end; at the high end they may serve up to 100,000 users with several thousand incoming lines.

Smaller PBXs or key systems may be networked together or to a large central PBX to provide voice service among different buildings on a campus. This enables a very large organization such as a manufacturing or office compound, a university or hospital complex to have a single inbound number and presents a uniform interface to outside callers. The outlying buildings may be miles apart or spread around a city.

PBXs and key systems provide significant benefits in addition to a single inbound enterprisewide phone number. They enable employees to use a uniform dialing plan and dial each other within the enterprise with just four or five digits as well as share trunks for both local and long-distance services. They also provide uniform software-based calling features such as call forwarding, conference calling, caller line identification, and voice messaging, as well as uniform access to these features.

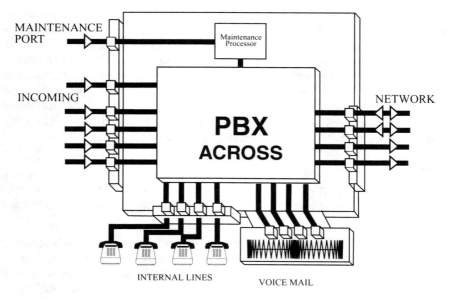

MAINTENANCE
PORT

INCOMING

NETWORK

INTERNAL LINES

VOICE MAIL

Exhibit 12-1. PBX traffic.

How PBX traffic is handled is shown in Exhibit 12-1.

BASIC SYSTEM COMPONENTS

PBXs and key systems contain three major elements:

1. **The terminal interface** comprises the line cards that terminate lines to individual extensions, trunk cards that terminate incoming PSTN or private trunks, and miscellaneous service cards such as tone generator cards that generate dial tone, rings, and busy signals; and special announcement cards that play recorded announcements when activated by a call.
2. **Switching fabric** is the hardware and software that switches conversations between various terminal interfaces within the enterprise or between individual extensions and the trunks. Digital PBXs use the same technology as central office switches, called TDM-time-division multiplexing for converting analog voice signals into digital signals for transmission either to the central office switch or to another location. (The standard voice channel in public and private networks in North America is 64 Kbps).
3. **Control complex** is the central processor and memory, and includes the software, which controls the operation of the switch. This control complex may include adjunct software packages that perform various applications.

The switch may be linked to other switches in the enterprise network or to the PSTN by T1 or T3 lines, asynchronous transfer mode (ATM) transmission or IP-based networks, most commonly at 155 Mbps.

FITTING THE SYSTEM TO THE ENTERPRISE

PBXs and key systems should be carefully sized to fit the enterprise and provide room for growth. They should also offer features that match the needs of the specific enterprise. The five chief factors that affect the fit are as follows:

1. **Configuration** — The particular types of software loaded into the system, including operating software, feature packages, and other software specific to a given brand, model, and software release. The configuration may include software for particular applications. Enterprise customers should make certain that their PBX or key system vendor has or is moving toward the capability to support traffic over IP networks. An IP trunk on a PBX, for example, helps protect the significant investments that organizations have made in existing equipment while providing increased capability.
2. **System capacity** — The number of calls likely to be made and the ability of the system to handle all calls even at peak hours. Systems do not usually have one line per extension, to save on expense, but should be designed for virtual nonblocking — in nearly all circumstances, no caller in or outbound should ever get a busy signal.
3. **Processor speed and capacity** — The processor speed controls how quickly the PBX or key system can process requests for service, such as call connection, feature activation and advanced applications such as ACD, messaging services, and network call routing.
4. **Memory** — Should be adequate to serve operations requirements, system features, and individual features such as individual speed calling lists and personal directories.
5. **Hardware** — The physical size of the system must be adequate to handle all the line cards, memory, and processing needed for the enterprise.

Each factor should be examined to ensure that a key system or PBX will successfully serve the enterprise. Together, they comprise the features and applications that can be provided or supported by the switch.

FEATURES AND APPLICATIONS

The primary tasks of the PBX or key system are as follows:

- **Route** incoming calls to the desired extension — or increasingly to the desired party anywhere on premises or off.
- **Convey** calls made by employees either within the system or out onto the enterprise's private network or the PSTN.

- **Provide** features that enable employees to handle calls effectively and efficiently.

Digital PBXs and digital key systems typically offer hundreds of features that help companies and employees handle calls at the desktop, starting with basics such as call hold, call transfer, call forwarding, conference calling, speed dialing, and last number redial. (See the section below on clients.) Some features may be represented by dedicated buttons on the telephone set; others can be accessed through programmable buttons or special codes interpreted by the PBX or key system. In addition, PBXs and key systems typically give each extension dual line appearances. Although an extension is in use, the switch can route a second call to it, the new call appearing as a call waiting indicator on the telephone set. The user can put the first call on hold and answer the second.

PBXs and key systems can usually work with Caller ID to present the caller's number and often name on the telephone's display screen. This enables the user to manage calls even more effectively.

Other call management features available on PBXs and key systems offer capabilities such as setting up call hunt groups. (If one member of a group or department is on the phone, an incoming call will automatically be routed to a *predefined answering location*.)

Employees are usually given access to personal directories, which may be based in their own desk telephones, programmed in the switch's memory, or — with CTI — on their PCs.

Some PBXs and key systems work with display phones to guide users through telephone features. Research shows that this visual aid significantly increases use of call-management features, and, thus, employee efficiency.

Today's PBXs and key systems go far beyond personal call management from the desk. They also can provide applications such as interactive voice response, automated call distribution, and messaging services that enable organizations to manage calls more efficiently on an enterprisewide basis. Some of these applications may be provided by applications modules or processors, perhaps servers or PCs, linked to the PBX, or may be integrated software modules that are part of the PBX.

Automatic Call Distribution

Automatic call distribution (ACD) distributes calls evenly among a group of employees set up to interact with incoming callers for a specific purpose. Examples include catalog sales, taking reservations or orders, or answering queries. Perhaps the most well-known applications are large telemarketing operations, or call centers, or help desks.

The applications of ACD are increasing. Companies are using ACD to handle tasks such as making appointments, responding to account or help desk queries, and managing inventory — any business function that receives a significant number of incoming calls with a specific purpose can benefit from ACD capabilities.

ACD systems may support anywhere from just a few agents to more than 1000 agents. The agents may be located in different buildings or geographical locations, served by the same PBX or by geographically dispersed PBXs networked together. The ACD applications usually work with Caller ID, so customer records or simply names and phone numbers can be automatically presented to the answering agent. Agents can even work at home using a telephone set that is linked back into the central call center.

ACD systems can offer many features that keep incoming callers satisfied and that prevent call abandonment. For example, the system can play announcements while callers are on hold, informing them about specials or the estimated time they can expect to wait. The systems can also act as automated attendants, allowing callers to choose to remain on hold or go to an interactive voice-response system, a specific extension, or a voice mail system. With sophisticated CTI connections, the customer is identified using his phone number, and as he is on hold, he can be treated to specialized messages or menu choices suited to his "customer profile." In more recent systems, advanced skills-based routing capability has become an important capability. With this, the system can route a call to the agent most appropriately skilled to handle that particular call. This means the customer gets quicker, more-efficient service, and there is much less chance of the customer being transferred multiple times before finding an agent properly skilled to deal effectively with his or her call.

Callers typically respond well to having a choice about how their individual calls are handled, and, of course, an associated interactive voice-response system may well serve for many routine queries well. In addition, with the advent of Web-based call centers, customers surfing companies' Web sites can click on "call-me" buttons to connect directly to a call center. Thresholds can be built in to the system to minimize delays while on hold or divert calls to alternate queues, ensuring that no one waits too long. Alternatively, some companies may want to allow customers to leave a message instead of holding for long periods as a way to improve customer service and decrease 800-line charges. This increases customer satisfaction. ACD systems may also capture calling numbers for later callback if callers do hang up.

These systems can generate a variety of real-time and comprehensive historical reports that assist in call and call center management. For example, they can typically document busy hours and numbers of calls as well as calls answered, average time in queue, number of calls handled by individual agents, duration of time spent on each call, and the number of abandoned calls. Such reports help managers to ensure that the right numbers of agents are available to handle calls. Managers can even reconfigure the call center in real time by linking in selected additional agents from other departments or locations to handle a sudden influx of calls. They can also correlate data, such as time spent on calls and sales generated, that may help supervisors measure effectiveness.

Customer-Defined Routing

Basic ACD systems manage calls like a queue at a bank — they allocate calls, in the order of arrival, to the next available agent or answering device. As mentioned earlier, more advanced systems offer a variety of customer controlled routing (CCR) features skill sets that work with an ACD system and Caller ID or dialed number identification system (DNIS) to allow specific routing instructions to control the destination of individual calls, while still pooling ACD resources to ensure the most efficient use of all resources.

For example, the ACD system can give priority to long-distance calls, emergency calls, or calls to certain extensions numbers, which is useful if, for example, preferred customers are given a specific number to dial. Calls to certain extensions numbers (DNIS), calls from certain areas, or calls those associated with certain specific customer numbers can be sent to certain targeted agents, allowing selection of destination by variables such as skill level sets of the agent or fluency in a foreign language. Specific classes of callers, such as wholesalers and retail customers, can be routed to specific agents so callers do not wait in the same queue.

One typical application is routing by a credit card company of calls from its regular, gold, or platinum card holders to different groups of agents, or a utility company might give priority during a power outage to calls from certain customers organizations, such as hospitals, defined as needing uninterrupted service. Calls from the outage area might be routed to an announcement giving specifics of service restoration that could give an expected wait time. This empowers the customers to hold or call back, increasing their satisfaction and decreasing 800-number costs.

Time of day and day of week can also be factored into routing instructions. Weekend calls might be routed to the one help desk designated to take them or routed to receive a recorded announcement.

Agents need not even be on the premises. Those in remote locations can become integral parts of the same call center through seamless reporting, call routing, and management structures.

Links to the call center can be extended from the PBX or central office via integrated service digital network (ISDN) lines, which combine two voice channels and one data channel on an ordinary twisted copper wire pair. This type of wiring serves most residences, most small businesses, and most desktops within an enterprise. The ISDN line permits the simultaneous use of the remote agent's telephone and PC. This solution is especially appropriate for telecommuters and satellite offices.

Interactive Voice Response

Interactive voice response (IVR) systems are another important way to handle incoming calls within a call center or separate from it. An IVR system may also be offered as an adjunct to the PBX or key system or as an associated server. These systems can handle many types of calls that do not require human intervention, for example, queries about account balances, order status, prices, and product specifications. Because such calls can consume a significant portion of the service representatives' time, the IVR system can boost an enterprise's effectiveness and stimulate the best use of its resources.

In addition, an IVR system can increase customer satisfaction because callers can use it to complete transactions, rather than leaving a voice-mail message that requires a follow-up call. Well-designed IVR systems can also be used for more complex transactions such as fund transfers and the taking or confirmation of orders.

IVR systems can also offer such capabilities as automated speech recognition. Callers can simply speak their requests. In addition, IVR systems can provide features such as multilingual capabilities and links to a fax service to provide a written information or confirmation of the transaction to the caller.

Increasingly, the IVR system is being used as the gateway into the call center. All callers are questioned by IVR and attend to routine business before opting to speak with an agent. IVR applications can even be used to interface to Web servers, so a bill pay program created on IVR can be used by the Web server to reduce development time and costs.

Voice Mail

Voice mail capabilities can also extend the flexibility of the voice network. Voice mail can enable inbound callers to accomplish their business more easily and enable callers within the enterprise to work together more effectively.

Voice mail systems now go far beyond simply recording messages for later playback. They also have the ability to act as an auto attendant, provide custom call routing, and offer additional messaging features such as priority notification and capture of calling numbers. If the caller tags a message as priority, for example, the PBX or key system may put it at the head of a queue of waiting messages and play it back first.

The system can also direct the recipient's telephone to indicate the presence of an urgent message. If the recipient is away from the office, he or she can direct that all messages with "urgent" tags be forwarded to another extension, an off-premises phone number, or a pager. Messages can also be forwarded after being heard to one or multiple extensions. Users can also direct the PBX or key system to send messages to several different numbers after them. Systems will try up to five different telephone numbers in sequence or automatically activate a pager.

To personalize handling of incoming calls, some voice mail systems allow users to set up guest mailboxes for specific customers or clients; the users can personalize messages for specific clients. These mailboxes are linked to incoming numbers delivered by Caller ID.

Key systems also provide automated attendant service through the voice mail system, during or outside of business hours. Callers can be routed to their choice of extensions or individuals or to an operator. Outside of business hours, the system can continue to answer the phone and play announcements. Some systems can also reroute calls according to a programmed sequence if the dialed extension is busy or route incoming calls to specific extensions according to instructions defined for certain exchanges or incoming numbers.

Unified Messaging

PBXs and key systems may also help users manage voice, fax, and e-mail messages. Adjunct systems can enable users to handle voice as well as e-mail messages and faxes on their PCs, select both oral and written messages to be heard now or saved for later, direct selected voice messages to a phone, view entire fax or e-mail messages or just their headers on their PCs or just their beginnings, and manage messages in other ways. Users may send faxes from the PC to one or to many recipients and leave information in mailboxes to be faxed in response to customer inquiries.

Faxes and e-mail messages may be stored separately from voice mail to prevent voice mailboxes from being filled with written material. Unified messaging systems can also integrate voice calls with dialing via PC-based directories.

Adjunct servers may also support data services — even multimedia conferencing — that travel over an Intranet or other high-speed data networks to be delivered by the PBX to the user's desktop PC. Applications using CTI features may be developed using Microsoft's Windows Telephony Application Programming Interface (TAPI) or Novell's Telephony Server Applications Programming Interface (TSAPI).

Personal Directories

Some systems also allow users to create personal directories that are stored in the system memory or in an associated PC accessed through a CTI interface. Such directories can contain names, phone numbers, and addresses of important contacts or customers as well as information that people want at their fingertips, such as parts numbers or prices. Typically, the user pushes a button on the phone to bring the directory up to the display and then scrolls down to find an entry or, alternatively, keys in the first few letters of the name desired. Setting up directories can be made easier with the use of templates that are provided by some systems.

Wireless Service

PBXs and key systems also can support in-building or campuswide wireless systems that allow employees to move around the building and still make and receive phone calls. The wireless system may be integrated with the PBX or key system so that calls to the user's regular desk phone extension are either routed to the wireless phone simultaneously or forwarded if the desk phone is not answered. Users can employ features such as call forwarding, conference calling, voice mail, call transfer and others. These wireless systems can work with Caller ID, so users can identify who is calling. They may also use a CTI link to access customer records, which appear on an associated PC or server, or to access a corporate directory so that they have telephone numbers at their fingertips while they roam.

The adjunct wireless system usually employs radio base stations throughout the premises, even including outdoor areas, such as a sales yard or walkways between buildings on a campus. Some systems cooperate with the public wireless carrier's network, so the same phone can be used by employees within the building and outside as they are traveling.

Centrex Service

Some companies choose not to operate their own switches, but obtain PBX-like features from their local telephone service provider. Such service is called Centrex, and it is delivered from the service provider's central office (CO) switch, part of the PSTN. Desktop call management features are to a great extent comparable to those available from a PBX or key system. For example, users can forward and transfer calls, set up a conference call, and see multiple line appearances. The central office switch may not, however, offer all features available in a PBX or key system.

Nonetheless, there are advantages to Centrex service. The enterprise need not get into the business of running a phone system, bear the capital costs of purchasing its own PBX or key system and lines and trucks, or dedicate space to the system. The LEC may be able to extend additional capacity when needed more easily than the enterprise can upgrade its private switch.

However, PBXs and key systems tend to have more features and capabilities, such as unified messaging, in-building wireless service, and extensive ACD and CCR options. Moreover, they tend to move more quickly with the times and technological developments than central office switches, so they offer more state-of-the-art features.

CLIENTS

Access devices (clients) for key and PBX systems range from simple units with one incoming line to complex sets that support thousands of lines, while also serving receptionists and call center agents. Sets may offer just basic capabilities or hundreds of features. Many now have screens and liquid crystal displays. In addition, telephone sets based on PC software applications or IP are now becoming available.

General Purpose Telephone Sets

General purpose sets range from the very basic to sets that have a broad variety of features. The most basic, suitable perhaps for lobbies, cafeterias, warehouses and other locations where people do not require many call management features, may have only one incoming line, a few features such as conference, transfer, and call forward, and a few programmable buttons that can be set to dial extensions — for example, security or front desk — automatically.

Stepping up from this basic level, sets may have more programmable buttons, speakerphone, call timer, liquid crystal display, well over 100 call-management features, personal directories, and additional call appearances. These more feature-rich phones may maintain a roster of the last incoming and outgoing calls, especially if the set works with Caller ID to capture names and numbers of external callers. Names and extensions of internal callers are routinely displayed. With some phones, to return a call, the user just scrolls through the list of incoming calls and pushes a button.

Displays can range from a one-line alphanumeric screen that delivers simple messages such as "message waiting" or the number of the caller to a multiline display capable of delivering instructions on how to use various call-management features or presenting directory or call roster listings.

Telephone sets are also available for a wide variety of special purposes, such as call centers, operator or attendant consoles, and positions where a particularly smart phone is desired. ISDN hookups and links to PCs can also be incorporated into phone sets.

Call Center Sets

Sets designed for call centers may have displays that present a caller's name and other identifying information, allowing a personal greeting; jacks that accommodate the user's choice of headsets; dual headset jacks so supervisors can coach attendants; language options so information is available in the attendant's own language; and adapters that link the set to a PC or other server so customer files can be associated with calls.

Attendant Consoles

The attendant console should help the attendant guide calls through the organization efficiently. Sets designed for this position typically feature high-volume call handling, a large directory, message center capabilities or links, and perhaps dial-by-name capabilities. These sets usually show line appearances for many or even all phones in a department or enterprise and indicate whether each is busy or not.

ISDN Telephones

An ISDN set typically allows the user to link the phone to a desktop PC and make use of the two ISDN B-channels and perhaps the D-channel as well. The phone–PC link allows the user to carry on voice and data calls simultaneously, perhaps sharing data with a colleague, customer, or supplier while discussing the file.

Intelligent Telephones

Performance-oriented phones may help boost the productivity of busy managers and executives. These phones may offer aids to efficiency such as context-sensitive feature appearances — instructions or features appear only at the time they may be needed. For example, the option of transferring or forwarding a call only appears on a screen when the user is answering or on a call. An intelligent phone may also provide prompts and icons that guide the user through voice-mail options.

Wireless Telephones

Wireless sets served by a PBX or key system through an adjunct wireless system can offer a wide range of call management features as well as data adapters and LCD displays.

PCs and Workstations

Desktop PCs and workstations can be served through the PBX with the addition of a communications adapter that links the computer to a telephone or the PBX via built-in RS232, or V.35, Universal Serial Bus (USB) or IP interfaces interfaces. These adapters can eliminate the need for dedicated data facilities because data can be carried to the desk over standard telephone wiring. Adapters are also available that work with ISDN protocols. PC screen phones enable the use of PC speakers and microphones to simulate telephones.

LOCAL-AREA ACCESS

The access fabric is considered to include both media for transporting signals and protocols for encoding them.

Media in a voice network may include both copper and fiber cabling as well as microwave and radio links. Wiring to the desk in the voice network is traditionally copper twisted pair. This is still a viable option, even, if broadband applications are delivered by the PBX to the desk. Twisted pair can carry hundreds of megabits per second of bandwidth. Fiber installed to the desk or floor may also carry voice along with data traffic. Microwave links are typically used in large private networks that traverse considerable distances and carry both voice and data traffic.

Radio links usually support digital wireless communications. They may operate according to various protocols, including code-division multiple access (CDMA), time-division multiple access (TDMA), or wavelength-division multiple access (WDMA). Some systems interwork with public digital wireless networks, which typically use either CDMA or TDMA.

Wiring architectures usually include the star design sometimes found in data networks. There are usually direct runs from the main distributing frame collocated with the PBX or key system or from intermediate distribution frames located in equipment closets on each floor or in other areas throughout the premises. The intermediate distribution frames are connected to the main frame by backbone risers.

Increasingly, voice networks may share facilities with data networks, and increasingly those networks include fiber capable of carrying very high transmission rates. It is not uncommon for very large enterprises to handle voice traffic over LAN backbones operating at SONET rates of hundreds of megabits per second or even gigabits per second (Gbps).

As transmission media are changing, so are transmission formats. Historically, PBXs and key systems have used the circuit-switched time-division (TDM) multiplexing format employed in the PSTN, formatting signals into 64 Kbps bit streams. These 64 Kbps streams were usually multiplexed into a 24-channel 1.5 Mbps signal, so that voice calls could be fed directly into that network. Now, however, as public networks are incorporating different types of transmission rates and protocols, some PBXs and even key systems are being equipped to interwork with systems and networks operating with those rates and protocols. Rather than just a single-purpose access fabric dedicated to the TDM format, these systems may have fabrics capable of handling signals in a variety of formats.

Some protocols and transmission rates finding a place in the enterprise voice network are ATM which is cell-switched and usually operates at 155 Mbps; circuit-switched SONET rates into the gigabits per second; ISDN and Internet protocols. These operate from 128 Kbps up to 1.5 Mbps; and even traditional data formats and speeds such as 16 Mpbs token ring, 10 Mbps Ethernet, and TCP/IP.

ISDN can provide great versatility, and it already uses the standard TDM 64 Kbps increments. The basic service, called basic rate interface (BRI), provides two 64 Kbps channels that may be used for voice and data, perhaps linking a telephone and PC. An additional low-capacity data channel, called the D-channel, may sometimes be used for control and signaling or even data transfers. PBXs and key systems may be able to supply ISDN bandwidth in 64 Kbps increments up to the Primary Rate Interface (PRI) limit of 11.5 Mbps, a full DS1 signal. This is enough capacity to accommodate many wideband applications such as multimedia, high-speed file transfer or video conferencing.

PBXs may also provide interfaces or busses to LANs operating under standard protocols such as Ethernet (10 or 100 Mbps), Token Ring (16 Mbps), and perhaps even Fiber Distributed Data Interface (FDDI, 100 Mbps). These interfaces work with a CTI interface (see below) to link data files and transactions to voice calls.

Perhaps the most important trend is the changeover that is beginning from circuit-switched to IP-based transmission or packet-switched transmission. Many enterprises are building packet-switched IP ATM networks to handle all traffic, including voice, data, and video. Voice-over-ATM is one possible direction of the future for the public network, stimulated in part by the trend to ATM for private enterprise networks and ATM switches are being marketed for central offices. To be compatible with both public ATM networks as well as internal ones, some PBXs are already equipped to interface with ATM switches, or frame-relay switches, and IP-based networks. Getting consistent toll-quality voice-over-IP networks is still a problem, but most observers predict that this problem will gradually dissipate as technological advances continue. Converged IP-based networks offer the potential for toll-cost savings, savings both in network equipment and because of simplified network management, and more powerful applications.

ATM switches are usually employed as edge switches, sitting at the edge of a local enterprise network and interfacing with either a public network or with dedicated or virtual private circuits to an enterprise's other locations. ATM is becoming justifiably popular because of its tremendous capacity and because it can handle all kinds of traffic in any combination — voice, ISDN, video, fax, and all data formats. It gives the network manager the greatest flexibility.

Adjuncts to PBXs can consolidate all types of traffic and convert them to the cell-switched ATM format, or frame relay format, or IP-based traffic (re: both external and integrated IP gateways).

Computer Telephony Integration Interface

A key part of a PBX or key system's access fabric is likely to be a CTI interface, which links the phone to a PC, workstation, or server. This link is useful in a wide range of applications such as call centers, desktop video-conferencing, messaging, and wireless systems.

CTI interfaces may automatically identify a caller's telephone number, using Caller ID or automatic number identification, and retrieve pertinent files from the PC or server. In call centers, they can work with ACD systems to bring up files while calls are being routed to call center representatives, enabling them to access a caller's account history, greet the caller by name, and transact necessary business immediately.

Having a customer's file available also enables businesses to deliver very personalized service; for example, a hotel or restaurant can offer to provide the same type of room or table the customer had on a previous visit, or a medical office can present a receptionist or nurse with a patient's file so the individual can immediately schedule an appointment or verify test results.

The CTI interface is also involved in linking messaging systems with a PBX, helping the system to bring faxes, e-mail, and voice mail together into one unified presentation. It is also an integral part of desktop videoconferencing, again linking the PC to the PBX, which handles the voice call. In addition, this interface may be used in wireless systems, allowing users to call in to their home base to retrieve faxes or direct them to a nearby fax machine for printout. The USB interface can also be useful.

WIDE-AREA ACCESS

Wide-area access links one location to another within a corporate private network, or it links the location or private network to a public, local or long-distance network. It is similar to local-area access, using the same formats and media.

Companies may establish dedicated private networks or VPNs that use public facilities. Economics may favor one or the other, depending on the amount of traffic between any two given sites. Typically, a public carrier will operate a "cloud" or backbone network, on which it sells a certain level of capacity as a VPN, perhaps with occasional higher levels permitted when demand soars (think of the first day of sales to popular concerts).

Either type of network may make use of switched facilities operating at rates from DS1 up to SONET gigabit levels. Voice signals may also travel over cell-switched ATM or frame relay facilities. WANs my also transmit voice via data protocols such as Transmission Control Protocol (TCP) IP, for example, in the nascent trend to voice over the Internet. Using this technology, voice may also begin to be sent over corporate intranets.

NETWORK MANAGEMENT

Tools are available for many PBXs and key systems that give network managers a wide range of capabilities. Specific tools are available from various third-party vendors, or a comprehensive group may be available from the switch vendor. A comprehensive package from the vendor may make the management job simpler by working from the same database as the switch and giving a unified picture of operations. Tools may employ an intuitive GUI or commands based on strings of alphanumeric characters.

Management tools may handle tasks, including station management, call accounting, traffic and performance management, alarm management, call tracking, and maintenance. There is a trend now toward evolving network management systems to the point that a single management system can manage voice and data networks.

Station Management

Station management includes configuration of phone sets, programming them with features, assigning directory numbers or terminal numbers for single or multiline sets, and adds, moves and changes. Station management tools may offer shortcuts, such templates that can be established for configuring phones with features needed by specific groups of employees or job categories such as receptionist or salesperson. Then, the manager simply calls up the template to provision a given phone — much easier than keying in commands to provision each feature on each phone. The tools may also offer options such as a menu of all available numbers or automatic assignment of numbers. With some tools, station changes can be programmed offline and then executed instantly, reducing down time for users.

Call Accounting

Call accounting includes call detail recording, generation of call accounting reports, and toll fraud management. A call accounting package may record call details such as call duration, ring time, call frequency, and total use of phone by extension. It may also manage notification of certain alarms, perhaps even going down a list of phone numbers, including voice, fax, pager, and modem, to reach a system administrator. Alarms may be set to indicate when conditions are reached that may indicate security has been breached and fraud is present — for example, an unusual number of calls to a certain geographical area or from a given extension or department. Any such alarm maybe continuously presented on a graphical interface.

Call detail recording can help telecommunications departments bill back phone charges to individual departments or help the company contain costs by generating complete reports that track phone usage, especially for long-distance calls. Call accounting programs can create and graph customized reports that include or exclude information such as date and time of call, cost, authorization code, and other criteria as desired.

Traffic and Performance Analysis

These tools report on usage of network resources such as trunks and network loops. Their analyses help the network manager monitor operations and detect problems before they affect service. Some tools also allow the manager to play out various scenarios for adding capacity or reconfiguring the network and simulate their effects.

Alarm Management

These tools manage and report alarms, perhaps in graphical format. They may prioritize and sort alarms and set alarm thresholds. They can also create a log of all system events, summarize major, minor, and critical alarms, indicate when a problem is being worked on, and filter alarms so only those needing action are brought to the attention of management personnel. Many PBXs now offer an SNMP connection to the data network, which allows a company to use one unified network management system to monitor all voice and data nodes in their network.

Call Tracking

Call tracking tools monitor calling patterns, in part to detect fraud. They can deliver a wealth of information about how the voice network is being used to help forecast future needs and ensure that the current network is being used as efficiently as possible. For example, they can track the number and duration of calls to specific areas or countries, indicating when dedicated trunks might be an economy measure. And they can identify unusual calling patterns that might indicate toll fraud — unauthorized usage of a company's transmission facilities.

Maintenance

Maintenance tools provide information on the status or hardware and perform diagnostic tests. These tools may enable network personnel to identify individual hardware units such as line cards or trunks that cause problems, run diagnostic tests, and enable and disable these devices.

The management tools may reside on a PC or workstation with a GUI, and link to the PBX and other network elements via TCP/IP–Ethernet links or other protocols.

SUMMARY

The direction of voice networks in the future is already clear from the trends cited. Perhaps the most monumental is the ongoing shift toward the Internet and IP-based networks. In addition, the incredible versatility enabled by CTI interfaces the extension of high-end features into even relatively small key systems, and the increasing involvement of the PBX or key system in a broad variety of operations, particularly those involving data.

Chapter 13
T1, T3, and SONET Networks

Roohollah Hajbandeh

BROADBAND NETWORKS ARE CONFIGURED through the use of several types of digital communications links. The most common of these, which have been in use by communications carriers for approximately 20 years and available to users for approximately a decade, are T1 and T3 links. These will be superseded eventually by the synchronous optical network (SONET), a set of standards for broadband networks that operate over fiber-optic links and that will provide more versatile bandwidth to both carriers and users.

T1 NETWORKS

T1 is a digital communications system for simultaneously transmitting 24 voice, data, and video signals over the same circuit. The original users of T1 were telephone companies and government agencies. Because each T1 is equivalent to 24 voicegrade circuits, the telephone companies' savings from using T1 were substantial. At first the cost of T1 to end users was prohibitive; since T1 services were tariffed during the 1980s, however, competition among major carriers has brought the prices down significantly. In addition, at first the need for higher bandwidth and additional services and capabilities increased the demand for T1 circuits such that the waiting time for installation was several months.

Advantages of T1

Each T1 is equivalent to 24 separate circuits between two sites, an advantage for T1 because multiple lines and multiple-site networks are expensive and hard to manage. The end-user equipment at each site can be PBXs, videoconferencing systems, imaging systems, or host computers. T1s connecting two PBXs are called tie trunks. For some old PBXs that cannot directly receive a T1 signal, a T1 line must first be terminated at a channel bank.

Analog lines are subject to noise and signal deterioration, and equipment that is used for reconstructing the analog signal cannot make them suitable for data transmission, because analog lines amplify both original signal and noise. T1 circuits are more immune to noise and distortion than multiple lines. T1 signals can also be corrupted, but because they are digital, processing will regenerate the original signal without amplifying the noise.

User-to-Network Access

Because T1s are dedicated point-to-point circuits, each customer pays a fixed rate for that service. The T1 charges depend on the distance between the two locations and each location's distance to the carrier's closest point of presence or local central office. However, the closest connection may not be the least expensive one. Recently, interexchange carriers have started offering switched T1 services. With switched T1, customers pay for the portion of bandwidth they use. In either case, the connection between the customer's site and the closest central office is a dedicated circuit and has a fixed cost. U.S. telephone serving areas are divided into about 200 local access and transport areas (LATAs). A LATA can include part or all of one state. The transmission between LATAs is done by long-distance or interexchange carriers even if both LATAs are part of the same local exchange carrier's serving area, so a T1 circuit may involve more than the local exchange carrier.

T1 Functional Elements

Channel Service Unit. The channel service unit is the first interface between the user and the network and the last regeneration point for the incoming signal before it is delivered to customer premises equipment. (In the past, channel service units were part of the network, but now they also are considered as customer premises equipment.) The channel service unit is responsible for general line monitoring functions, discussed later in this chapter. If a T1 multiplexer or piece of customer premises equipment fails, the channel service unit sends streams of 1s to the network to keep the connection alive until the customer premises equipment recovers. Some T1 multiplexers and PBXs have built-in channel service units.

Current intelligent channel service units provide, by supporting the extended superframe format, sophisticated line monitoring and diagnostic capabilities. Basic channel service units have limited diagnostic and monitoring capabilities. If the long-distance carrier provides T1 service in the extended superframe format, the channel service unit should also support it. FCC Part 68 local tariffs require that each T1 be terminated on a channel service unit. Channel service units are also responsible for:

- protecting the network from the surge of a long stream of 0s
- signal monitoring
- interfacing with remote network testing equipment

- the loop back to the network, which is also used for testing and monitoring

Digital Service Unit. Digital service units are for digital circuits what modems are for analog circuits. The analog line transmission rate is limited to 19.2K bps, but digital service units can accept a full T1 rate (i.e., 1.544M bps). Channel service units and digital service units functions may be combined into a single unit or both can be built into terminal equipment. The physical interface between carrier and user equipment is through an RJ-48C or a DB-15 connector.

Channel Banks. Channel banks are a special kind of T1 multiplexer. The main function of channel banks is to convert analog voice signals into digital signals and combine the digital signals from 24 channels into a single channel. A basic channel bank multiplexes voice and data, but it is not software driven, and to reconfigure it the unit must be physically rewired. An intelligent channel bank is software driven and can be reconfigured through a local or remote terminal. Not all channel banks are compatible with all long-distance carriers, nor are all PBXs compatible with the T1 services of all carriers. Some channel banks can interface only with standard services and not with such advanced services as MEGACOM and MEGACOM 800.

Digital Access and Cross Connect System. The digital access and cross connect system (DACS) is used for multiplexing and routing T1s at the central office switch. The routing is done at both full T1 and individual circuit levels. Newer DACS route services such as MEGACOM, MEGACOM 800, Accunet, ISDN H channels, fractional T1, and T1. The more advanced DACSs are software driven and can be accessed and controlled by customers. Usually, they are designed to accommodate at least 64 incoming and 64 outgoing T1s.

Regenerators/Repeaters. Voice traffic signals are converted into 0- and 1-bit streams and are formatted in a specific order. During transmission the original data mixes with line noise (which depends on wire material and environmental factors such as temperature and electromagnetic fields), but because the noise signal does not follow any particular format it is distinguishable from the original data. Regenerators/repeaters retrieve data and discard the noise. Usually, one regenerator/repeater is required for every 6,000 feet of cable.

T1 Integration of Voice and Data

The main advantage of T1 is that voice and data can be simultaneously transmitted over the same line. This is done by digitizing the voice signals using a digitizing process called pulse code modulation (PCM) (see

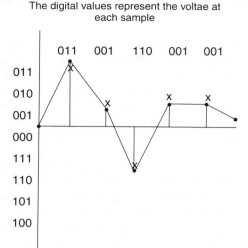

Exhibit 13-1. Analog-to-digital conversion.

Exhibit 13-1). For a human speaking voice to be audible, the upper frequency is about 3,500 Hz. To maintain the integrity of an analog signal after digitizing it must be scanned at at least twice its upper frequency. Therefore, a voice signal is scanned 8,000 times per second. Each scanned segment is called a pulse.

Based on the amplitude or the height of each pulse, it is assigned an equivalent 8-bit binary value. In the absence of a signal, a value of 0 is assigned. The total rate of each channel on a T1 link is derived by multiplying samples per second by the number of bits in each sample (i.e., 8,000 samples × 8 bits per sample = 64,000 bps).

Voice frequencies that are substantially above 3,500 Hz are filtered out; otherwise, they create noise on the line. Filtering adversely affects the adjacent frequencies. As a result the effective frequencies scanned are between 300 and 3,300 Hz.

Variations of PCM

Vector Quantizing Code. Vector quantizing code reduces the bandwidth required for a voice channel from 64K bps to 16K bps. Voice transmission quality is lowered but is acceptable in some applications. After the voice signal is scanned, 0s and 1s are grouped together and form strings, or vectors. A vector is compared with a set of vectors stored in the system's lookup table. When the closest match to its bit pattern is found, a shorter code signifying that vector is transmitted. At the receiving side, the shorter code is replaced with the string of 0s and 1s it represents.

Differential Pulse Code Modulation. Differential pulse code modulation (DPCM) uses 4 bits per sample, instead of 8. This technique requires less bandwidth for transmitting voice signals. DPCM is suitable when there is not much variation in volume from one sample to another. Otherwise, it cannot accurately reproduce the original voice signal.

Adaptive Differential Pulse Code Modulation. Several proprietary adaptive differential pulse code modulation (ADPCM) techniques and the standard CCITT G.721 version are in use. ADPCM's scanning rate is 8,000 times per second, but there are 4 bits per sample. By assigning a different significance to each of the 4 bits, ADPCM can produce as true a representation of voice signals as PCM does.

Continuously Variable Slope Delta Modulation. Continuously variable slope delta modulation (CVSD) uses a 1-bit word per sample. A 1 bit indicates the presence of a signal but gives no indication of the signal's strength. The sample represents the slope or variation in slope of the curve. (The slope is the rate of change in height divided by the rate of change in run.) Before transmission, slopes are compared with the reference values in a lookup table. If the slope is greater than the reference value, a 1 is transmitted. If the slope is less than the reference value, a 0 is transmitted. A rising curve is presented by a series of 1s. The receiver functions in reverse and reconstructs an approximation of the original curve. CVSD reduces the bandwidth required for a voice channel to 32K bps.

The availability of several PCM techniques has created many incompatibility problems, and the T1 equipment using the ADPCM technique cannot be directly connected to a central office that only uses PCM.

AMI and Bipolar with 8-Zero Substitution. In a binary format, a 1 value (i.e., a pulse) is represented by a square wave and a 0 value (i.e., the absence of a pulse) by a straight line (see Exhibit 13-2). To change from +1 to –1 the wave must take the value of zero first. In a proper T1 signal, the value of two consecutive pulses alternate between positive and negative, a scheme known as alternate mark inversion (AMI) (see Exhibit 13-2). Two or more consecutive pulses of the same polarity (known as a bipolar violation) is an indication that the incoming data is corrupted or that there is noise on the line. The timing for scanning the voice signal is derived from pulses received by the end user equipment. A long stream of 0s causes the scanning process to lose its synchronization. Different applications have different tolerances for violations of the 1s density rule. Generally, if the number of consecutive 0s exceeds seven, the timekeeping and operation

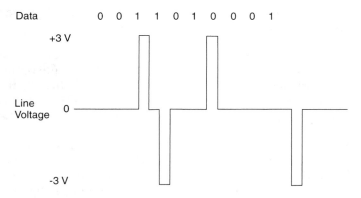

Exhibit 13-2. Alternate mark inversion and bipolar signal format on a T1 line.

---

of regenerators/repeaters is disrupted. To allow a legitimate long stream of 0 bits (i.e., a stream that represents valid data), the bipolar eight-zero substitution (B8ZS) technique is used. B8ZS inserts additional 1s into the data stream at the eighth bit and bipolar variation indicators. At the receiving end the additional 1s are discarded and the original data is regenerated.

Time Division Multiplexing

PCM is for voice traffic only. To transmit over a single T1 link, the combined bit streams generated from PCM and other sources of data are multiplexed (i.e., combined). Multiplexing is done by sequentially accepting data from each of the 24 time slots on the T1 link, allowing the transmission of 8 bits of data onto each time slot. If a channel is idle and has no data to transmit, the time slot will be wasted. By definition, one frame of data consists of 24 8-bit words, or 192 bits. At the end of every 192 bits, a 1 bit is inserted to separate one frame from the other.

The T1 bandwidth works out as follows:

(24×8) information bits per frame + 1 framing bit = 193 bits per frame.
193 bits per frame $\times$ 8000 samples per second = 1,544,000 bps.

Because of variations in scanning rate, the 1,544,000 bps rate varies by ±50 bps.

D4 Framing

Each of the 24 T1 channels is assigned an 8-bit time slot, and the channels are numbered in the same sequence that their data appears on the bit stream. To separate one frame from the next, one bit (called the F bit) is inserted at the end of each frame. The values given to the F bits for the first 12 frames are 100011011100, and the same sequence is repeated for the next 12 frames. Separation of frames with the 193rd bit is called frame level synchronization, or D4 framing. To identify the start of each T1 frame, the receiver postulates the beginning of a frame to be at point X. If after 192 bits another framing bit is found and the above sequence is repeated, the receiver knows that point X is the beginning of the frame. If not, the system tries $X + 1$ as the beginning of the frame. This process is repeated until the beginning of the frame is located. This method, which is the simplest form of T1 service, uses 8,000 bps of the available bandwidth and has limited monitoring and network management capabilities. To test or monitor a T1 with D4 framing, the network should be temporarily taken out of service.

To use some of the overhead bits for network management capabilities, 12 individual frames can share the same signaling information bit. For 12 frames to share the same signaling bit, D4 framing uses a process called robbed bit signaling, and the summation of 12 frames is also called superframe. In a superframe, the sequence 10001 1 01 1 100 is repeated in the first 12 frames. The overhead bits freed by this process can be used for test and monitoring, allowing out-of-band signaling and monitoring of a T1 circuit without bringing the circuit down. To allow more network management capabilities, extended superframe is created. With extended superframe only every fourth frame (frame 4, 8, ..., 24) carries the synchronization bit and the 001011 sequence is used. This reduces the overhead from 8,000 bps to 2,000 bps. Of the remaining 6,000 bps, 2,000 bps is used for error checking and 4,000 bps for monitoring the line condition. The channel used for monitoring and testing is called the facility data link. The facility data link also provides the following information:

- *Errored seconds.* The number of seconds that contain one error.
- *Bursty seconds.* The number of seconds that contain 2 to 319 errors.
- *Severely errored seconds.* The number of seconds that contain 320 or more errors. That is equivalent to 96 percent of frames having at least one error.
- *Failed seconds.* The number of seconds in which the error rate was so high that the link had to be taken down.

Compatibility Issues

For a T1 circuit to be compatible with a public network, its bit stream must have the following characteristics:

- If the channel service unit and central office use different PCM techniques, a conversion must be made between them.
- A framing bit is inserted after every 192 bits. If the public network uses the extended superframe format, the customer premises equipment (i.e., the channel service unit, channel bank) should also support it.

UNDERSTANDING WANs

- The 24 channels are numbered sequentially, 1 to 24.
- B8ZS and alternate mark inversion techniques are used.

Means of Transmission

Transmission of T1 signals can be by copper wire, microwave, satellite, or fiber-optic networks. Because transmission is handled by the telephone companies, users might not have a choice, but they should be aware that each medium has its advantages and limitations. Terrestrial networks have shorter delays than satellite channels, but they are subject to service interruption. Generally, for distances longer than 500 miles, satellite rates are lower than other alternatives, but each round trip introduces an additional 0.5-second delay. If the transmitting and receiving devices are not configured to accommodate the delay, data transmission is disrupted. Terrestrial wiring can be twisted-pair or coaxial cable. Over copper wire, repeaters/regenerators are placed at each mile interval. Error rates on fiber networks are much lower, and transmission of data over distances to 25 miles without repeaters is possible. Microwave networks are more immune to noise and do not have cable breaks (e.g., by backhoes) and do not need as many repeaters as terrestrial cables, but they are less secure.

Fractional T1

When the cost of a full T1 circuit is not justified, customers can subscribe to fractional T1 or to as many DS-0 channels as they need. Once a fractional T1 is terminated on customer premises it can be broken down into smaller subrates. But there is a limit on how the bandwidth can be subdivided. If the rates required are 9.6K, 4.8K, 2.4K, and 1.2K bps, the DS-0 is divided into multiples of the highest rate, 9.6K bps in this case; the bandwidth assigned to lower rate devices is not fully used. Generally, if customers need more than five or six DS-0s between two points, it is more cost effective to subscribe to a full T1. Usually, the DS-0s of a fractional T1 circuit are channelized and not contiguous. For example, by subscribing to two DS-0 channels, customers have access to two separate channels of 64K bps each and not a single 128K-bps channel. To bundle a number of DS-0s together, a customer has to subscribe to the ISDN primary rate interface (PRI) and have an ISDN-compatible device on the customer premises. Fractional T1 is available with 56K and 64K-bps channels. Some carriers charge extra for providing clear 64K-bps channels.

Cost-Justifying a T1 Circuit

The following factors should be considered in justifying a dedicated T1 link versus switched access:

- the bandwidth required during peak hours
- the use of bandwidth during each day

- the cost of dedicated circuits including the connection to the local central office at both ends
- the cost of customer premises equipment for terminating the T1
- Tthe cost and availability of other services such as ISDN PRI and switched T1

T3 NETWORKS

The next level above T1 in the digital service hierarchy is T3. Each T3 link is the equivalent of 28 T1s. The multiplexing of T1s to form a T3 signal is done in two steps.

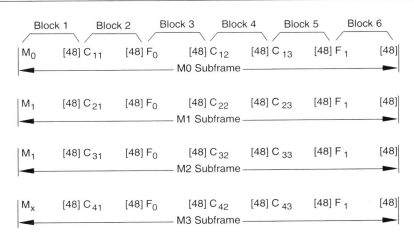

Notes:
$M_0 M_1 M_1 M_x$ is the multiframe aligment signal. $M_0 = 0$, $M_1 = 1$ and M_x may be a 0 or a1.
$C_{11} C_{12} C_{13}$ = stuffing indicators for DS-1 input 1.
$C_{21} C_{22} C_{23}$ = stuffing indicators for DS-1 input 2.
$C_{31} C_{32} C_{33}$ = stuffing indicators for DS-1 input 3.
$C_{41} C_{42} C_{43}$ = stuffing indicators for DS-1 input 4.
$F_0 F_1$ is the frame alignment signal. $F_0 = 0$ and $F_1 = 1$.
[48] represents 48 information bits from each DS-1.

Exhibit 13-3. DS-2 frame format.

Step 1. Four DS-1s are multiplexed to form a DS-2 signal (see Exhibit 13-3). Each DS-2 consists of four subframes (also called M frames), numbered M1 through M4. The four M frames do not represent each DS-1 on a one-to-one basis. This is just a way of interleaving the bit streams from four DS-1s into a single bit stream. The DS-2 frame format is as follows:

- Each M frame contains 6 blocks.
- Each block has 48 bits of data.

- Each block contains 12 information bits from each four T1s.
- After every block of data there is one bit of overhead.
- Each M frame consists of 294 bits.
- Each DS-2 frame contains $4 \times 294 = 1{,}176$ bits, including 24 bits of overhead.

DS-2 service to each DS-1 is synchronous. That means equal time slots are assigned to each DS-1 regardless of their data rates. Because the four DS-1s do not generate the same data rate, to adjust for different data rates the bit stuffing or pulse stuffing technique is used. The bits used for this function are called C bits. Each DS-2 subframe contains three C bits. If all three C bits in a subframe are zero, no stuffing is done and the zeros in those positions are part of the DS-1 data. When stuffing has occurred all three C bits in a subframe are set to 1.

The normal output rate for each DS-1 is 1.544M bps, and four DS-1s amount to 6.176M bps. The output rate selected for a DS-2 is 6.312M bps. Because there are 1,176 bits per frame, the number of frames per second is:

6.312M bps ÷ 1,176 bits per frame = 5,367.35 frames per second
5,367.35 frames per second × 24 overhead bits per frame
   = 128,816 bits of overhead

The available space for stuffing is:

Total DS-2 bandwidth	6,312,000 bps	
Overhead bits	−128,816 bps	
Four DS-1s (4 × 1,544,000	−6,176,000 bps	
Stuffing Bits	7,184 bps	(1,796 bits per DS-1)

If no stuffing has occurred, the maximum available rate is:

$6{,}312{,}000 - 128{,}816 = 6{,}183{,}184$ bps per DS-2 or 1,545,796 bps per DS-1.

Step 2. Seven DS-2s are multiplexed to form one DS-3 signal (Exhibit 13-4). To form a DS-3 from seven DS-2s two standards are available: the M13 format (Exhibit 13-5) and C-bit parity format (Exhibit 13-6). M13 is similar to D4 framing for T1 and has limited monitoring and error correction capabilities. It uses all 21 C bits for bit-stuffing. Each DS-3 frame using M13 standards is structured as follows:

- Each DS-3 frame contains seven subframes.
- Each subframe consists of eight blocks.
- Each block consists of 84 bits of data (12 from each 7 DS-2s).
- After every 84 bits of information, there is 1 bit of overhead.
- Each DS-3 frame consists of $8 \times 85 \times 7 = 4{,}760$ bits.

The seven subframes do not represent the seven DS-2s on a one-to-one basis. Because each DS-3 consists of seven DS-2s, its transmission rate

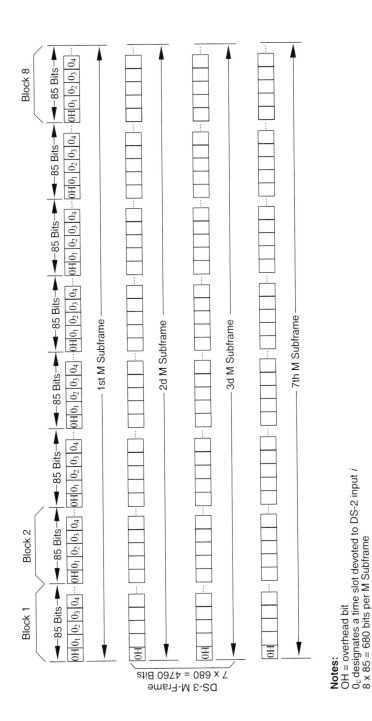

Exhibit 13-4. DS-3 framing format.

Notes:
OH = overhead bit
0_c designates a time slot devoted to DS-2 input i
8 × 85 = 680 bits per M Subframe

185

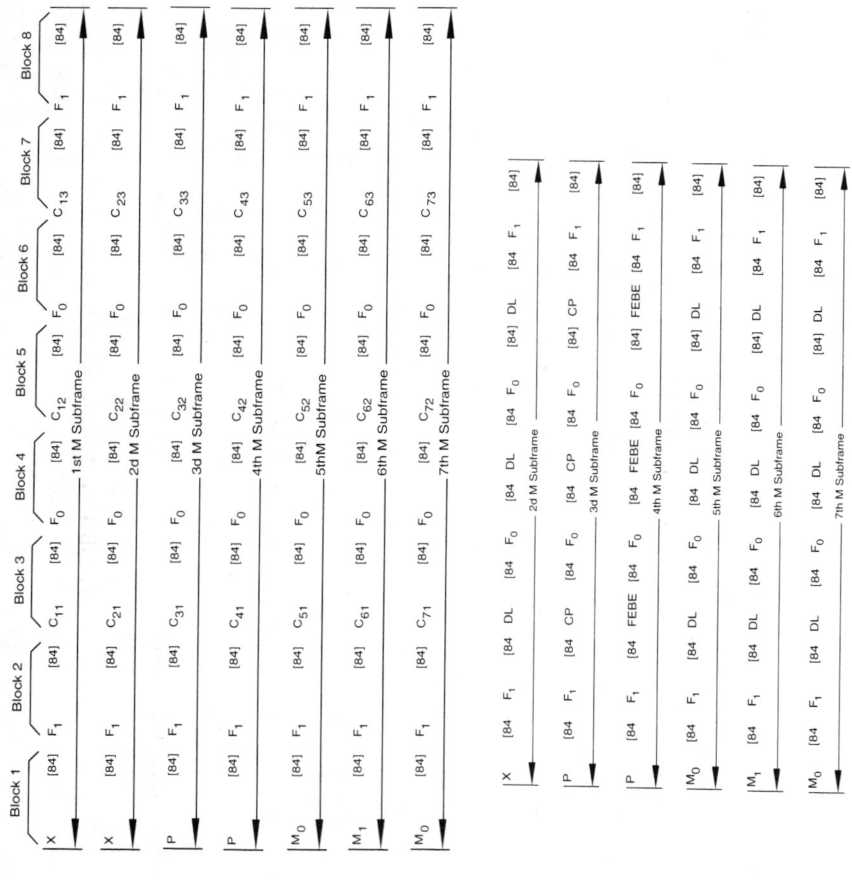

Exhibit 13-5. M13 signaling format.

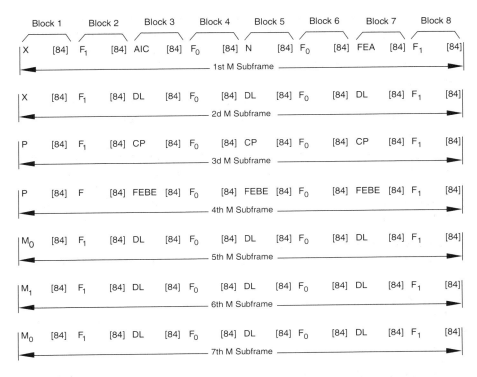

Notes:
The X bits transmit a "degraded second" indicator from thr far end to the near end.
$M_0 M_1 M_1$ is the multiframe aligment signal. M_0 = 0, M_1 = 1.
$F_1 F_0 F_0 F_1$ is the frame alignment signal. F_0 = 0 and F_1 =1.
C-bit definitions:

      AIC   = Application identification channel =1.
      NA   = Reserved network application bit.
      FEA   = Far-end alarm channel.
      DL   = Data link.
      CP   = C-bit parity.
      FEBE = Far-end block error
P is the parity information bit.
[48] represents 48 information bits from each DS-1.

Exhibit 13-6. DS-3 signal using C-Bit parity format.

should be: 6.312M bps per DS-2 × 7 DS-2s = 44.182M bps. But the assigned rate is 44.736M bps. The additional capacity is used for bit-stuffing and overhead. Each DS-2 in a DS-3 is treated synchronously. That means equal time slots are assigned to each DS-2 whether it has data to transmit or not. Since not all DS-2s have the same bit rates, to adjust for varied transmission rates among DS-2s the bit-stuffing technique is used. The three C bits in a subframe are used as bit-stuffing indicators. For example, if all C bits in the fourth subframe are 0, no stuffing is done for the fourth DS-2. But if all

C-bits in the fourth subframe are 1, bit stuffing is performed in the fourth DS-2. By using three C bits as bit-stuffing indicators, the possibility of mis-identifying the DS-2s that are bit-stuffed will be significantly reduced. The amount of bandwidth used for this function is 526,306 bps, as shown by the following calculation:

44,736,000 bps ÷ 4,760 bits per frame = 9,398.32 frames per second
56 overhead bits per frame × 9,398 frames per second
= 526,306 bits of overhead per second

The C-bit parity format redefines the C bits and X bits (the message bits) to be used for additional monitoring capabilities. The C-bit parity format is for DS-3 what extended superframe is for T1. M bits are located at the first position of subframes 5 (value = 0), 6 (value = 1), and 7 (value = 0). Signaling in a C-bit parity format is described in the following sections.

Message Bits (X Bits). The X bits are at the beginning of subframes 1 and 2. They both have the same value (either 1 or 0) and their function is to carry in-band messages.

Parity Bits (P Bits). P bits are located at the first positions of subframe 2 and 4. Their function is to provide an in-band parity check for the data. If the data in the DS-3 contains an odd number of bits, P is set to 0; otherwise, P is set to 1. All P bits have identical functions.

Framing Bits (F Bits). Each DS-3 frame contains 28 F bits, 4 per subframe. The sequence of their respective value is 1001. F bits are also used by the receiving equipment to locate the boundary of a DS-3 frame.

The C bits and X bits can also be defined to perform the following functions.

Application Identification Channel. This field is used for identifying the framing standard that is used. For the M1 3 standard, the application iden-tification channel is set to 0, and for the C-bit parity format it is set to 1.

X Bit. The value of this bit is usually 1. If the receiving device detects any signal degradation for longer than one second, it sets the X bits to 0 and sends them back to the transmitter.

Far-End Alarm Control Bits. These bits are used for loopbacks and test-ing. If an alarm condition is detected at the receiving device, these bits are used to send a status signal to the transmitting device.

T3 Users

DS-3 circuits have been less than successful as a commercial communi-cations service. Primary users have been a few major corporations. The reasons are the high cost and lack of a commonly accepted standard among manufacturers of equipment, network providers, and other broadband networks. Other broadband technologies will eventually take the place of T3 service.

SYNCHRONOUS OPTICAL NETWORK

Although the principle of using light waves for communications is an old one, the use of fiber optics for transmitting communications signals became technically acceptable and economically feasible only after the development of laser technology. An optical fiber is a fine wirelike structure made of a glass or plastic dielectric. It consists of the core, which reflects the light waves; the cladding, which protects the core; and the primary and secondary coatings, for more strength and protection.

Fibers used in communications are of two kinds: single mode and multimode. Single-mode fiber is used in public networks, and the multimode fibers are used in private networks and LANs. These two types of networks are based on two different standards and use different transmission rates. The fiber distributed data interface (FDDI), which uses multimode fiber, is the basis for private backbone networks and is limited to 100M bps and a maximum diameter of 60 miles. The SONET uses single-mode technology; its transmission rate can be as high as 13G bps, and its maximum network size is almost unlimited.

Fiber-optic-based networks have the following advantages:

- Fiber-optic signals are immune to and do not cause electrical and environmental interference.
- Fiber-optic communications are secure because an attempt to tap the signal causes the error rate to climb and can be easily detected.
- Fiber-optic bandwidth is wide, starting at 51.84M bps and climbing to 13G bps. The first phase of SONET will provide 2.488G bps, the equivalent of 32,000 telephone circuits.
- Optical cables do not corrode and are strong; optical fiber has the same tensile strength as steel wire of the same gauge. Cables are reinforced with protective shields to withstand severe conditions.
- The error rate of fiber-optics is less than IO-1', approximately 100 times lower than that of a typical copper wire. Such a low error rate reduces the number of retransmissions and transmission overhead, and simplifies error checking.
- Optical signals can travel 25 to 54 miles without needing to be regenerated or repeated. T1 signals transmitted on copper wire should be regenerated after every mile.
- Optical fiber becomes increasingly cost effective with the development of new technologies. As the demand for higher bandwidth

increases, there will be no technical or economical alternatives to optical fiber.

- Fiber-optic interfaces are being standardized. Because there is no standard DS-3 interface, connections to other broadband networks are made over proprietary interfaces. This limits equipment choice. In addition, DS-3 networks do not provide enough bandwidth for network management.

SONET is a North American standard. Its first phase is specified in American National Standards Institute (ANSI) documents T1.105 and T1.106. SONET circuits are software defined and can be assigned and provisioned quickly and without the need for physical rewiring. Only SONET can accommodate future high-bandwidth services (e.g., high-definition TV, broadband ISDN, and interactive videoconferencing).

SONET Applications

SONET is a transmission medium with many applications. Local exchange carriers use SONET for connecting their central offices, interexchange carriers use it for their trunks, and private corporations use SONET for connecting high-speed workstations.

SONET Transmission Rates

SONET is designed to multiplex T1, T3, and higher rates. Lower rates can also be transmitted, but they should be multiplexed to higher rates before being connected to SONET. The SONET optical carrier (OC) line rates defined so far are:

- OC-1: 51.840 M bps (equivalent to 810 DS-0s)
- OC-3: 155.520M bps
- OC-9: 466.560M bps
- OC-12: 622.080M bps
- OC-18: 933.120M bps
- OC-24: 1.244G bps
- OC-36: 1.866G bps
- OC-48: 2.488G bps

Provisions are being made for the transmission rate to reach 13G bps in the future.

SONET Definitions

SONET is a transport system that can be compared to a system for moving physical objects. It breaks the load into smaller pieces, palletizes, labels, transmits, unloads, and reassembles the shipment at its destination. The following sections define some SONET characteristics.

OC. This is the applicable SONET data rate.

Synchronous Transport System (STS). This is the frame structure. STS has 51.84M-bps (STS-1) and 155.520M-bps (STS-3) formats, or it can achieve higher capacity by interleaving several STS-1s. Each STS-1 frame consists of 90 rows and 9 columns of data with 8 bits in each cell. Each frame is repeated 8,000 times per second. The data rate for STS-1 is derived as follows:

90 rows × 9 columns × 8 bits per cell × 8,000 frames per second
= 51.84M bps

Synchronous Payload Envelope (SPE). This is an area within the STS frame. STS consists of two parts: the payload, or capacity, part and the overhead part. Three columns or 27 bytes of each STS are set aside for transport overhead and one column or 9 bytes for path overhead. The remaining 86 columns by 9 rows or 774 bytes are the payload part of the STS frame. SPE is the payload part of the STS, so the useful data rate is derived as follows:

86 columns × 9 rows × 8 bits per cell × 8,000 frames per second
= 49.536M bps

Virtual Tributary (VT). An area within the SPE that is allocated based on the data rate or services assigned. The standard transmission rates for VT are as follows:

- VT-1.5: 1.728M bps
- VT-2: 2.304M bps
- VT-3: 3.456M bps
- VT-6: 6.912M bps
- VT6-N: $N \times 6.912$M bps
- Asynch DS-3: 44.736M bps

Building Blocks of SONETs

The major functional components of a SONET, as defined by Bellcore or ANSI standards, are:

- digital loop carrier
- terminal multiplexer
- regenerator
- digital cross connect system
- add/drop multiplexer

The references to published standards for these components are given in Exhibit 13-7.

Exhibit 13-7. Bellcore SONET specifications.

SONET digital loop carrier	Bellcore TR-TSY-000303
Add/drop multiplexers	Bellcore TR-TSY-000496
Regenerators, terminal multiplexers	Bellcore TA-TSY-000917 and TR-TSY-000253
Digital cross connect system	Bellcore TR-TSY-000499

Digital Loop Carrier System. The digital loop carrier concentrates low-speed traffic before it enters the SONET or a central office switch. This technique is also called optical remote switching. If the remote users are connected to the central office without their data streams being concentrated, the capacity of the central office would be limited by its total number of ports. For the interface between digital loop carrier and end users, from 1 to 2,016 DS-0s are used, while the interface between the digital loop carrier and the central office is at OC-3 (155M bps), equivalent to 2,430 DS-0s. The main application of the digital loop carrier is for telephone companies to connect remote switches to their host switches. This capability allows customers at remote sites to be served as effectively as customers on the main switches. The digital loop carrier reduces cabling costs substantially, increases service choices, makes more bandwidth available, and increases switch capacities.

Terminal Multiplexer. The terminal multiplexer is for multiplexing T1, E1, T3, broadband ISDN, and their subrates onto a SONET channel. The transmission rate for a terminal multiplexer is usually OC-12 (622M bps) and higher. As the terminal multiplexer performs both the multiplexing and switching functions, it accepts a wide range of bandwidth and can assign alternative routes to each incoming channel. Because of its high capacity, it is considered part of the network.

Add/Drop Multiplexer. The add/drop multiplexer is capable of adding and dropping DS-1, DS-3, and OC-n signals onto other OC-n circuits. An add/drop multiplexer is a combination of terminal multiplexer and digital cross connect system. Multiplexing of interfaces at DS-0 rates is not part of the current add/drop multiplexer requirements.

Regenerators. After conversion and multiplexing, a signal can travel 25 to 54 miles without being degraded. Beyond those distances, regenerators are used. They convert the incoming optical signal to an electrical signal. They also measure amplitude, shape, density of zeros and ones, and timing. Distorted signals are corrected, then converted from electrical to optical, and retransmitted onto the SONET. The distance signals travel before they need regeneration depends on the wavelength and the kind of fiber being used. It is expected that as new materials and amplifiers come into use the distance between repeaters will substantially increase. Repeaters also have network management, monitoring, and alarm capabilities.

Digital Cross-Connects. The digital cross-connect system is part of the carriers' networks and is the first point of deployment of SONET. It operates at the OC-12 level (622M bps), and its function is to separate voice, data, switched, and nonswitched signals. The multiplexing and demultiplexing schemes are not the same as for combining T1s to T2s and then to T3s and do not consume as much overhead.

SONET Customer Premises Equipment. Essential to deployment of SONET is an intelligent T1 multiplexer that can interface the customer's DS-0, fractional T1, T1, ISDN PRI, and subrate equipment with OC-1 or higher channels on the public network side of the interface. The equipment connected to this multiplexer can be PBXs, LAN bridges, or similar facilities.

SONET Switch. The SONET switch is the last element in the hierarchy of the SONET network. Its function is to multiplex rates from DS-0 to OC-48. These functions are performed in the digital interface unit, which is an adjunct processor to the switch. The use of the digital interface unit eliminates the need for M13 multiplexers and their associated space and wiring.

SUMMARY

Currently, there are few devices that can consume all the bandwidth SONET can provide. Until such devices become available, demand for T1 service and T1 multiplexers will rise. As carriers install more fiber and create more transmission capacity, T1 prices are bound to fall, which leads to more demand. In addition, for many applications T1 is quite sufficient. Availability of ISDN will not diminish the demand for T1, fractional T1, and their related equipment. As carriers continue to offer ISDN H channels (which are 6, 12, and 23 contiguous B channels), the use of T1 will be stimulated.

Chapter 14
Remote Access Concepts and Techniques
Peter Southwick

ONE OF THE FASTEST GROWING SEGMENTS OF THE ENTERPRISE NETWORK is the area of remote access. Whether it is to access the Internet for fun and games or the corporate intranet for mission-critical information, the concerns and possible solutions are the same. In this chapter remote access is presented from three separate views. The first is a presentation of remote access scenarios and the concerns and solutions present in those scenarios. Each reader will recognize his own problems from those presented. The second view is an analysis of the platforms that are available today to solve those problems. The final view is of the options possible for the implementation of the solutions.

TYPICAL REMOTE ACCESS SCENARIOS

Considering the broad range of meanings that can be associated with "remote access," it is best to narrow the scope of what remote access means in this chapter. Remote access is a means by which a remote user (someone who is physically removed from direct connection to the corporate network) gains connectivity to the resources of a network. A further definition of remote access, for the principal focus of this chapter, is that the users utilize dial-up facilities for access.

Two distinct types of remote access are being used today. The first is when a user creates a dial connection to a device directly connected to the desired network. This type, which we will call direct-dial access, has been the cornerstone of remote access systems for the last decade. The second access type is when a user dials in to an intermediate service provider and is connected to the destination network via the Internet or some private network. This scenario, which we are calling indirect access, is becoming more common, especially where long distances are concerned.

Remote access is being used for a wide variety of applications today. School-age children are dialing into schools to pick up homework assignments and perform research. College students are attending online classes, performing collaborative research and doing administrative tasks. In the corporate sector, remote access supports telecommuting, hoteling, remote (branch) offices, and Small Office/Home Office (SOHO) installations. It is said that the key to a successful telecommuting environment is access to the same resources in a similar manner as those personnel located at the corporate locations. Remote access is the key to this success. The same is true for all the applications using remote access. For the purpose of this chapter, our focus application is remote access to a corporate network. Remote access in scholastic applications have the same concerns and architecture as those described here.

In order to further define the architecture and protocols found in remote access situations, three distinct remote access scenarios must be explored. The first of these is the scenario in which the remote user has a local area network (LAN) and remotely connects this LAN to the corporate network. The second scenario is when a user has a PC in a fixed location (at their home or remote office) and via an attached communicating device (a.k.a. modem) connects to the corporate network. The final scenario is when an intermediate network provider carries the traffic between the remote access user and the corporate LAN.

LAN-TO-LAN DIRECT-DIAL SCENARIOS

In the case of the branch office, or SOHO, the typical implementation is that the office contains a LAN providing connectivity between the devices in the office (refer to the upper portion of Exhibit 14-1). The goal of the remote access is to connect the devices on this LAN to those at the corporate (main) location. At the remote location, the interconnection device of choice is the remote access router. This device is programmed to recognize a request for service for the main location and create a connection for the duration of the request. Once the request has been satisfied, the connection is terminated. At the corporate location, a similar device accepts the incoming request for service and provides connectivity to the resources of the corporate LAN. This type of remote access scenario is called dial-on-demand routing and provides an economical alternative to full period connectivity options. LAN-to-LAN scenarios have the benefit of having dedicated devices assigned to the task of providing connectivity. The remote access chore is transparent to the end users and their computers. A further benefit is that LANs are typically geographically fixed, allowing better security measures.

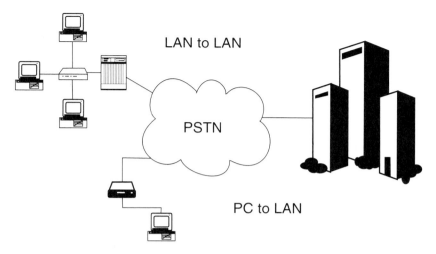

Exhibit 14-1. Remote access scenarios.

Fixed User-to-LAN Direct Dial Scenarios

The second scenario is that of the SOHO user who does not have a LAN (refer to the lower portion of Exhibit 14-1). The user's computer doubles as a remote access device and a computing system. When the user wishes to access information or an application on the corporate LAN, the PC creates a connection to a server on the corporate LAN and a connectivity is achieved. If the operating system and the applications are savvy enough, the remote connectivity is transparent to the human user. If not, the user must establish the connection prior to the request. Two types of remote access sessions are possible in this scenario. The first is termed remote control. In a remote control session, the remote computer is acting as a remote terminal attached to the "server" or host computer attached to the corporate network. Once attached, the user has the full capabilities of the computer attached to the LAN. A possible scenario would be that you install a modem on your computer attached to the corporate LAN, leave it running, and go home. From home you dial into this computer and run specialized, but available, software that allows you to control that computer. As one might surmise, remote control poses a great security risk. Could anyone else control this computer? For this reason, remote control has fallen out of favor for most corporations.[2] The second type of PC-to-LAN connection is called remote node. In this scenario, a remote computer is connected to a network access server or a communications server. Once verified, the user has full access to the resources of the corporate network. The remote node scenario allows the users access in a controlled fashion.

197

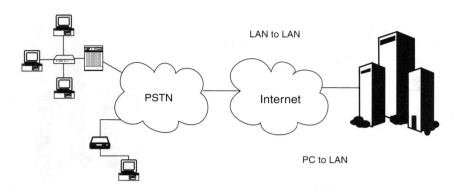

Exhibit 14-2. Indirect dial remote access.

A benefit of the remote node access is that the same computer can be used directly attached to the corporate LAN and remotely attached. Another benefit is that the network access server of the communication server has controlled pieces of equipment that can be secured from unauthorized access.

Indirect-Dial scenarios

This scenario, as depicted in Exhibit 14-2, could be employed in either a LAN-to-LAN environment or a PC-to-LAN setting. In either case, the requesting device is not directly attached to the corporate LAN. Instead, the remote device connects to a network access server supplied by an Internet service provider (ISP) or an interconnect service provider. The remote access traffic is tunneled through this intermediate network (the Internet as shown in Exhibit 14-2) and delivered to the destination network. This scenario allows an assortment of equipment complements (routers or PC) to access the corporate network in a common fashion. It also allows the use of local ISPs for international remote users. In most cases, higher speed connections can be made to a local ISP than over an international direct-dialed call. Security is achieved through the use of tunneling protocols which can provide encryption and possibly compression for the remote access traffic.

CONCERNS AND SOLUTIONS

In all remote access scenarios regardless of the application, security is the number one concern. Security is followed closely by response time (speed) and, finally, a concern that has recently been giving network managers headaches, Addressing. In the following paragraphs, these concerns are discussed, along with an assortment of solutions.

Security

Exhibit 14-3. Security issues.

Security Threat	Network Solution
Hacking	Authentication, call back, caller ID
Spoofing	Digital signatures, digital certificates
Interception	Encryption, tunneling

Today entire volumes are being written about security on corporate networks. Other chapters in this volume provide the details of firewalls and other security-related topics. For the purposes of remote access, two areas of security are discussed. These topics are presented in relationship to the threats found in remote access systems. The first threat is the uninvited user. If a modem is attached to a corporate network, it will be found by a curious user and it will be hacked. To counter this threat, authentication protocols and software can be installed. The second threat is the interception of valuable information by an eavesdropper. To counter this threat, encryption protocols are available. Exhibit 14-3 provides a summary of the security threats and their solutions.

Authentication systems today are available in two forms. The first and most common is the software-based authentication systems. The second, and more exotic, is hardware-based systems.

The software-based systems use an authentication protocol at link establishment to verify the user's identity and a digital signature associated with the information is used to verify that the information has not been tampered with. These protocols can be combined with caller identification and call-back options to create a very secure access environment. Once a user is connected and authorized, a threat still exists that someone could intercept information exchanged and insert unwanted data. To assure that what is sent is received, digital signatures are employed. The international standard for digital certificates is X.509. This system is more robust than password-based schemes.

Hardware authentication systems are based on the concept of the smart card. Each time a remote user dials in to the corporate LAN, the smart card is queried for an identifier/password. This code must match the code generated by the corporate mate to the smart card. This system, although costly, provides a very high degree of security.

Encryption is the second issue associated with securing the information requested or generated by the remote access user. Like authentication systems, encryption systems can be hardware-based or software-based.

Encryption can be performed at the link level (encrypt everything going between the remote location and the corporate location) or at the data level (encrypt only the message, leaving the headers clear). The encryption key length is a critical element in the security of your information. The longer the key length, the better the security: A key of 128 bits is considered unbreakable, whereas a key of 24 bits can be broken in a matter of minutes by a determined party.

Speed

If network managers are concerned principally with security, remote access users are concerned about access speeds. A corporate user is connected to his resources by a multimegabit-per-second LAN; the typical remote user must deal with multiple kilobits per second access speeds. Recently, technologies have been introduced that are increasing the speeds possible for remote access users. Plain Old Telephone Service (POTS) modems have increased in speed and decreased in cost to the point where a 33K bps modem is the standard and 56K bps modems are readily available. The 56K bps modems offer an asymmetrical access, 56K bps in the downstream direction and 33K bps in the upstream direction.

An alternative to POTS is an Integrated Services Digital Network (ISDN) Basic Rate Interface access line. This technology offers speeds up to 144K bps and a combination of packet- (up to 16K bps) and circuit-switched (2 x 64K bps) access options. A new application of ISDN access is called Always-On/Dynamic-ISDN (AO/DI). In an AO/DI scenario the packet access is continuously connected to the corporate network; low-speed applications (i.e., e-mail and text-based browsing) use this access. When higher-speed access is required, the circuit-switched channels are activated, first one, then the other. When the requirements for the bandwidth are no longer needed, the circuit-switch channels are released and the packet-switched access is again used.[3]

The newest technologies for remote access are the Digital Subscriber Line (DSL) technologies. This family of access technologies is delivered to remote users on existing twisted pair (the same as POTS and ISDN). But due to specialized signaling techniques, they offer speeds that are predicted to hit 10M bps in the network-to-user direction. The common designator for the DSL technologies is xDSL, where x can be one of many letters. A (asymmetrical) DSL — one pair up to 8M bps to the user and up to 1.5M bps to the network; H (high bit rate) DSL — two pair 1.5M bps bidirectional; S (single line) DSL — one pair 786K bps bidirectional; RA (rate adaptive) DSL — one pair up to 12M bps to the user. The list is being updated and added to daily.

High speeds can also be achieved by the aggregation of multiple lower-speed circuits. This technique is generically called inverse multiplexing and can be performed in hardware as well as software. The most common hardware approach is defined by a protocol created by the Bandwidth On Demand Interoperability Working Group (BONDING). BONDING was designed around digital access technologies (i.e., ISDN) and provides the capability of aggregating multiple channels into a single high-speed access link. Software-based inverse multiplexers are based on an aggregation scheme called multilink point-to-point protocol (MP). This standard allows aggregation of channels of any type at any speed. MP can be implemented by most remote access devices, and it is by far the more common inverse multiplexing approach for remote access users.

Other options for remote access are appearing constantly; cable modems, wireless packet networks, and satellite-based networks are all possible today.

Addressing

Addressing has become a constant nag for network managers. Remote users must have a proper address, unique and with the correct network identifier in order to access the resources of the corporate network. If the network is based on the Transmission Control Protocol/Internet Protocol (TCP/IP) protocol suite, then other elements are also needed with the address, including the address mask, the address of the router, and the address of the name server. All of these addresses must be entered into the remote user's computer. If a LAN-to-LAN remote access scenario is being used, the task is lessened. But if the PC-to-LAN scenario is in use, and the PC is mobile or accessing the corporate network via the Internet, the problems increase. For the PC to LAN scenario, the problems associated with IP addresses can be resolved with the use of the Dynamic Host Configuration Protocol (DHCP). This protocol allows a remote access PC to access an address server, receive the required addresses, then access the network as a directly connected user. DHCP has an added benefit in that it allows the reuse of IP addresses (sometimes IP addresses are in short supply) between remote users. A small pool of addresses can be shared by a larger group of remote users. Another solution to the addressing problem is the use of address translation devices. With this system, the user maintains a single address and each time the user is connected to the network, the user's address is translated to a valid network address.

CHANNEL PROTOCOLS

The key to the success of the LAN has been the simplicity of the channel protocols found on the LAN. The MAC protocols provide all the services needed for access and control. In the remote access environment, no single protocol is available. Presented here are six classifications of protocols commonly found in the remote access environment. The first two classifications are used for basic transport on a single (simple protocol) channel or multiple (inverse multiplexing) channels. The third and forth classifications are security-based protocols providing authentication and encryption services to the remote access user. The final two classifications, tunneling and compression, provide value-added capabilities to a remote access environment.

1. Simple Protocols

The Serial Line Internet Protocol (SLIP) and the Point-to-Point Protocol (PPP) provide basic datalink protocol support for remote access users. SLIP is the minimalist's approach to a protocol. The user's information is framed with two known flag patterns, one at the beginning and another at the end. Whatever the user inserts between these two flags is transported across the access link. In certain situations, SLIP is the perfect solution for remote access. In opposition to SLIP, PPP has a suite of data link functions. PPP is based on a High-level Data Link Control frame format. As such it has bit error detection capabilities, protocol identification capabilities, and follows a strict data link initialization procedure. PPP has an additional capability of initializing network layer sessions as well. Multiple network layer protocols can be simultaneously supported on a single PPP data link. PPP has become the default and de facto standard for remote access users.

2. Inverse Multiplexing Protocols

When the bandwidth on a single channel is insufficient, two options exist: buy a bigger channel or add more channels. Due to economics, the second solution is often the only feasible one. If a second channel is added between the remote location and the host location, some mechanism must be employed to associate the information found on these two channels. This mechanism is called an inverse multiplexing protocol. The principal inverse multiplexing protocol is the MP. This is a frame-based inverse multiplexing protocol used in conjunction with PPP. In an MP scenario, the two ends of the connection (PC and network access server) agree on the number of channels being used and the characteristics of the channels. Once this handshake is performed, the devices statistically multiplex information over all the active channels. Modifications to MP can be found in the MP+ protocol described in RFC 1934 and in the ITU-T standard for inverse multiplexing H.323. One limitation of the MP protocol is the lack of a dynamic bandwidth allocation scheme that can add or subtract channels on an as-needed basis. To resolve this limitation, the Bandwidth Allocations Control Protocol and the Bandwidth Allocation Protocol were developed. These two protocols allow the negotiation of additional channels on the fly between a remote access device and a network access server.

3. Authentication and Integrity Protocols

To solve the problems associated with verifying the user's identity and the integrity of the information sent from a valid user, authentication protocols are employed. During PPP or MP session establishment, two adjunct protocols are employed to verify the identity of the users. These protocols, the Password Authentication Protocol (PAP) and the Challenge Handshake Authorization Protocol (CHAP) are used to pass user identities and passwords between remote access devices. When combined with caller identification and or a call-back scheme (the remote user dials in to the network access server, and the server releases the call and places a call back to the user) PAP and CHAP provide a very secure authorization mechanism.

An additional problem exists in that an authorized user gains access only to have his information intercepted, appended to, and resent, the appendage being some sort of a tool for later exploitation. To prevent this type of intrusion, an upper layer integrity protocol is employed. Integrity protocols are commonly called digital signatures in the sense that they seal a packet of information. Digital signatures typically employ some form of a hash algorithm that appends a binary value to the sent information that is generated by the content of the information. At the receiver, this value is verified, and if correct, the information is tamper-free. Some digital signature standards are the Secure Hash Algorithm (SHA-1) Message Digest 2 through 5 (MD2.. MD5) and the Distributed Authentication Security Service.[4]

4. Encryption Protocols

The principal use of remote access is for corporate network access. Often, mission-critical information is being passed between the remote locations and the corporate locations. To prevent this information from being stolen, encryption protocols are employed. Two types of encryption can be employed in a remote access scenario. The first is the use of a link level encryption device. This type of device is engaged once the remote access call is answered and encrypts all data sent between the devices. Link level encryption devices are typically hardware-based and expensive to use and deploy. The second type of encryption is an upper layer encryption protocol. This software is engaged once the remote access link is established and encrypts only the information being transmitted. Framing information is passed in the clear. These systems are the more common. Examples of upper layer encryption standards are Data Encryption Standard, Pretty Good Privacy, and Secure IP (IPsec). One final issue with encryption standards is that the U.S. federal government considers them to be national secrets and allows only the export of certain protocols. For international remote access users, this means that restrictions must be adhered to. In recognition of this restriction, most encryption protocols

---

are available in export and U.S.-only versions, the difference being the length of the encryption keys.

5. Tunneling Protocols

When an Internet-based remote access scenario is used, the best security mechanism is the use of a tunneling protocol. The concept is simple: encapsulate your data in the normal full stack of corporate protocols, encrypt it, then reencapsulate this entity in a tunneling protocol that resides in a transport layer protocol that is routed as data through the Internet. With so many layers of protocol, who can find your data? Tunneling protocols are classified as Layer 2 or Layer 3 tunneling protocols. In a Layer two protocol, the user's information to include the Layer 2 frame (i.e. PPP) is tunneled through the Internet. In Layer 3 tunneling, only the network layer is passed between devices. Layer 2 protocols are based on the RFC-1701 description called the Generic Routing Encapsulation (GRE). GRE defines the basics of tunneling information through the Internet. Implementations of the concept defined in the GRE specification are Microsoft Corp.'s point-to-point tunnelling protocol (PPTP) and Cisco System Inc.'s L2F. These two protocols have been combined into the L2TP standard, which is currently a draft RFC. Layer 3 tunneling protocols are newer and less stable than the Layer 2 protocols. An example is IPsec, which defines a mechanism for tunneling IP traffic over the Internet.

6. Compression Protocols

The final classification of protocols found in the remote access environment are the compression protocols. Compression provides an increase in throughput without an increase of bandwidth. Compression standards take one of two forms, the first being the file compression standards (i.e., PKZIP from PKWare, Inc.). These standards squeeze a file prior to transmission. At the destination, the file is expanded prior to use. The second type of compression system is a real-time compression. Data to be transported is compresses prior to encapsulation. At the receiver, the expansion takes place when the data is received, not when it is used. Examples of this real-time compression are Stac, Inc.'s LZS compression and Microsoft's compression tunneling protocol. Both of these are proprietary in nature. A standards-based real-time compression scheme is proposed for the IPsec standard.

SECURITY AND AUTHENTICATION DEVICES

One of the most varied segments of the remote access technology market is the security segment. The technology currently spans between simple password and biometrics information (voice, finger print, face recognition). In the following paragraphs we will explore three key elements of

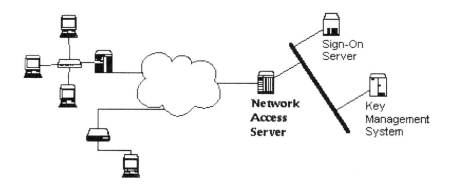

Exhibit 14-4. Security devices.

this segment. These elements are graphically depicted in Exhibit 14-4. The first is the network access server, which is the first line of defense in any security system. The second is the authentication server. These devices allow or deny users based on stored information. Finally, key management systems allow secure transfer of information over the remote access links.

1. Network Access Server

Network access server is a generic term used to define a group of components that bridges the gap between remote access users and the corporate network. Components of a network access server might perform: routing, encryption, tunneling, filtering (firewall), and also authorization. What a network access server definitively does is respond to a remote access request for services, verifies the identity of the user, and connects that user to the corporate network. It can also be the light at the end of the tunnel. In a remote access system using the Internet, the network access server terminates the tunneling protocol and passes the original protocol to the corporate LAN.

2. Single Sign-On (SSO) Standards

A remote access system needs a standards-based remote authorization database that matches client information (i.e., user ID, password, and calling line identification) to the accessed system (corporate network). An SSO is used as opposed to a local authentication system. Two standards are supported today, the Remote Authentication Dial-In User Service (RADIUS) and the Terminal Access Control Access Control System (TACACS). Both are widely supported and feature-rich.

3. Key Management Systems

If encryption is required in the remote access system, then a key management mechanism is required. Key management systems are tasked with automatically keeping encryption keys updated, eliminating the need to manually update the security keys at each location of a remote access system. The key distribution is performed by the central and remote nodes establishing a secure, authenticated session and updating the key information. Examples of key management protocols are

- Internet Security Association and Key Management Protocol (ISAKMP)/Oakley — NSA — the IETF standard for key management
- Diffie–Hellman — an encryption and key management mechanism
- Simple Key Management for Internet Protocol (SKIP) — Sun Microsystem, Inc.'s entry into key management
- A digital certificate system that includes a key management system

WHAT DO I HAVE TO DO TO GET STARTED?

A network manager tasked with setting up a remote access system actually has two options. The first option is to outsource the remote access system. Multiple companies are willing to provide the technical expertise to set up and install these systems. The second option, as always, is that the network manager can set up the system on his own. As the size, the number of simultaneous access scenarios, and the geographic reach of the system increase, the outsourcing option becomes more attractive. If the Internet is used as the remote access vehicle, again, outsourcing becomes an attractive option.

Outsourcing

One of the factors that goes into the selection of outsourcing is the geographic scope of the network. Outsourcing companies are typically regional, national, or international in scope. Because the competition is more severe in the smaller markets, a better deal could be made by staying with a regional or national provider. Identifying local outsource companies requires a small amount of sleuthing. Telephone companies, ISPs, retailer, and consultants all might have leads to a reputable regional company. At the national level, three established names are ANS, PSINet, and UUNet Technologies. At the international level, IBM's Global Network, AT&T Corp.'s WorldNet, and MCI Communication Corp.'s Concert are all possibilities. When negotiating the outsourcing deal, be sure to do the following:

- Specify what level of security is required for your system. This is a key factor in determining the remote access scenario that is correct for your installation.

- Specify the speeds required for the remote access personnel. Test various options to determine an optimum level. Because the bandwidth bottlenecks are not always the access system, a 1M bps access speed might not provide any faster throughput than a 128K bps access line.
- Determine how many simultaneous users are required at any one time. Savings can be achieved by reducing the number of access lines, but this increases the chances of a user receiving a busy tone. Exact numbers (number of access lines and blocking probability) can be found by performing a traffic engineering study.
- Determine the functions and features provided by the outsourcing company vs. what is a customer's (your) responsibility. An example is that if an Internet tunneling system is used, the customer typically provides the authorization hardware and software.
- Determine whether the equipment to be used for the remote access system will be dedicated to your company or shared with others. Shared equipment has a lower upgrade cost than dedicated equipment. Also determine the growth costs of the system.

Do it Yourself

If the setup of the remote access system is within your capabilities, then the preceding questions must be answered, and the answers will determine the type of software, hardware, and security to be used at the remote and central locations. As a memory aid, remember the "PASS" to remote access:

- Protocols — choose a Data Link and Network layer protocol.
- Access Lines — select one or more types and an appropriate number.
- Scenario — which is being used, LAN to LAN or PC to LAN?
- Security — determine the type and amount of authorization, integrity, or encryption that are required.

SUMMARY

This chapter has presented a number of critical issues surrounding a fast growing segment of the enterprise network, remote access. The concerns associated with remote access were presented along with a number of possible solutions. The goal of all remote access users is unlimited speed and ironclad security. Hopefully we have started you on a path to meet these goals.

Notes

1. Full period connectivity options include leased line circuits, frame relay, or other packet/cell access circuits.
2. In a leading high-tech company, anyone found installing a modem and remote control software on their corporate PC is dismissed.

3. Additional information on AO/DI can be found at the North American ISDN User Forum's (NIUF) Web site.
4. Further information about digital signature standards can be found in Cohen, F. B., *Protection and Security on the Information Superhighway*, John Wiley & Sons, New York, 1995.

Bibliography

Cohen, F. B., *Protection and Security on the Information Superhighway*, John Wiley & Sons, New York, 1995.

Kessler, G. and Southwick, P., *ISDN*, McGraw-Hill, New York, 1998

Cisco Systems, Inc., Router Products Configuration Guide, Cisco Systems, San Jose, CA.

References and URLs

IPSec RFC 1825, RFC 1826, RFC 1827 — http://www.faqs.org/rfcs/

Key Management — HTTP://WEB.MIT.EDU/NETWORK/ISAKMP

PPTP (Point-to-Point Tunneling Protocol) — http://microsoft.com/windows95/info/pptp4w95.htm

ANS — http://www.ans.com

PSINet (Sprint Corp.) — http://www/si/com

UUNet Technologies — http://www.us.uu.net

Internet Secure Association Key Management Protocol, Oakley was added by ARPA's Hilarie Orman, http://hegel.ittc.ukans.edu/topics/internet/index.html

Chapter 15
ATM Access: The Genesis of a New Network
William R. Koss

INTRODUCTION

DATA COMMUNICATIONS HAS COME A LONG WAY IN THE PAST SIX YEARS. In 1992, many users deploying wide area networks (WANs) still thought in terms of 56K frame relay and fractional T1 speeds as state of the art. Some six years later, the World Wide Web (WWW) has driven most of us to deploy V.90 standard modems in the home or explore the possibilities of cable modems, ISDN, and xDSL technologies. In the enterprise network, network backbones are now primarily cell-based backbones. Long gone are shared backbones such as token ring, Ethernet, and collapsed router backbones. FDDI is still around, but nobody is getting excited about DAS and SAS. The network core within the enterprise and within the service provider (LEC, CLEC, IAP, ISP, IXC, and CIXC) networks is using a cell-based technology called ATM (asynchronous transfer mode).

One may have heard of ATM — it was all the rage in 1994. Everyone went through a few years of ATM Year One, Year Two, Year Three, and then the marketing hype finally fizzled out. In its place came tag switching, voice over IP, IP over SONET, xDSL, and terabit routers. All this occurred while the service providers were deploying ATM within their network cores and most enterprise IT managers were completing the deployment of ATM backbones to service the growing demand for bandwidth and network performance. The purpose of this article is to explore the emergence of ATM into the wide area network and the outline the challenges and techniques that will used to deliver increased bandwidth for voice, data, and video services.

ATM TODAY: THE NETWORK CORE

For discussion purposes, existing ATM networks can be divided into two primary categories: (1) carrier class networks maintained by service providers, and (2) enterprise networks maintained by corporations and organizations and primarily intended for private use. To understand the deployment of ATM into the WAN, one can start by examining how ATM is deployed within each of the defined categories.

Not too long ago many people referred to the phone companies as the Telco or carrier markets. Today, this is an injustice. Such a large number of companies exist that offer some type of network access that the market they are part of is now refered to as service providers. Within the service provider market, many types of companies and market verticals can be defined. This article concentrates on the following acronyms that define the major vertical elements of the service provider market:

- **LEC:** Local exchange carrier that provides local access to telecommunication services; formally defined as regional Bell operating companies (RBOCs).
- **CLEC:** Competitive local exchange carrier. Companies that provide local access to telecommunication services. Most CLECs have emerged in past few years to compete for local telephone service against LECs.
- **IAP:** Internet access provider. Companies that provide wholesale Internet backbone transport and access. Examples are UUNET, ANS, SAVVIS, and Concentric.
- **ISP:** Internet service provider. Companies that provide local Internet access and Internet-based services.
- **IXC:** Interchange carrier. Companies that provide inter-LATA services between LATAs within an interstate or intrastate basis. AT&T, MCI Worldcomm, and Sprint are the primary IXCs within the United States.
- **CIXC:** For lack of a better term, competitive interchange carrier. This vertical represents companies that are developing inter-LATA services based on their own developing network infrastructure. The prominent players are Level3, Qwest, and IXC Communications.

Each service provider has developed a different type of network to meet its business and customer requirements. For discussion purposes, some generalities that encompass many of the service provider networks can be defined.

By the end of 1998, most service providers within the United States had deployed ATM within their networks. Those that have are typically well-established companies or aggressive young companies with a business strategy that depends on leveraging the technical advantages of ATM to compete for customers. For the purposes of this article, international service providers or small market players that have yet to establish themselves are not discussed here. The reason for this is that each international market is different, and the smaller market players have yet to develop enough mass to affect the market dynamics.

The existing IXCs and LECs are confronted with a series of challenges that can best described as legacy challenges. Most IXCs and LECs have created several networks to deliver customer services. They have networks for voice services, packet-based IP, frame relay, local access, and ATM. The emerging CLECs and CIXCs have bypassed legacy technologies and deployed ATM as their transport technology. The competitive nature of the service provider market requires that service providers be able to address the following challenges:

- provide the client an end-to-end network solution
- provide application services such as Internet access, global intranets, Web-based co-location, Web-based transaction and application support, and data warehousing
- unify their networks and provide a single managed service
- reduce duplicated costs and overall operational costs
- deliver integrated voice, data, and video services to the client
- provide unified billing and service-level agreements (SLAs) that guarantee quality of service

The IXCs and LECs that are the incumbent service providers are challenged to (1) reduce cost, (2) improve performance, (3) unify services, and (4) deliver higher quality services. Their plan is to achieve these objectives by leveraging the strengths of technologies such as ATM. The reason ATM is important is that it currently exists within many of the service provider core networks and ATM has several important elements that are driving ATM deployment, including:

- It solves the TDM problem; existing networks based on time-division multiplexing cannot support future network growth.
- It provides support for all services; ATM supports three primary services that service providers are concerned with: voice, data, and video.
- It exists and is proven; ATM is already deployed in the network core. It is proven, understood, and technical resources have been trained to support the technology.
- It reduces deployment and operational costs; ATM access equipment is less expensive and less complicated. The long-term support and operational costs of ATM networks is projected to provide significant long-term savings.

As the IXCs and LECs view ATM as the unifying network technology that is able to provide a solution from the carrier core to customer premises, the CLECs and CIXCs view ATM as the network infrastructure of choice. Nearly all CLECs and CIXCs have developed extensive network infrastructures that built upon ATM. ATM provides the universal network foundation to support all services and provide scalable bandwidth. As much as the IXCs and LECs view ATM as the future, CLECs and CIXCs view ATM as the technology that enables them to compete without the encumbrance of legacy networks.

Within the enterprise market, ATM has been widely deployed as the universal backbone of the network. Some users have invested in desktop ATM solutions, but many users have built successful network backbones using ATM solutions that encompass Ethernet or token ring switching as the final connection to the desktop. Most enterprise ATM backbones are deployed within buildings and campus networks. Using a switched cell network architecture, ATM backbones running at speeds of OC3 are capable of supporting an immense amount of traffic and adequately dealing with the challenge of performance-intensive applications. Similar to the service provider market, several important elements are driving the deployment of ATM into the WAN within the enterprise market:

1. It solves the performance problem. ATM delivers the bandwidth demanded by customers in scalable increments and meters from the customer premise to the network core.
2. It provides support for all services. ATM provides the foundation for voice, data, and video support within a defined standard.
3. It exists and is proven. ATM is already deployed in the network core. It is proven, understood, and technical resources have been trained to support the technology

ATM TOMORROW: THE ATM WAN

The deployment of ATM into the WAN has been a slow process. At present, the majority of ATM WAN installations have been for DS1 speeds. Several reasons can be attributed the slow deployment of ATM technology:

- ATM has primarily been used as a backbone technology for high-speed network trunks
- emergence of possible alternative technologies such as "Everything over IP SONET"
- service providers have been slow to develop infrastructure to support ATM-based services
- continued strong demand of frame relay-based services
- market readiness and demand has been lacking as many enterprise users complete network deployments based on core technologies such as IP, 100BT, and gigabit Ethernet and frame relay
- Y2K readiness and WWW integration have consumed IT resources, inhibiting planned network upgrades

Despite these challenges, 1998 was an important milestone in the ATM WAN market. Major service providers began announcing the availability of high-speed ATM services. Sprint announced its ATM intentions in June 1998, and UUNET announced its intention to deliver high-speed ATM-based services in 1999. To understand why ATM will grow in the WAN, one must first define the business challenges that will compel both the enterprise users and service providers to deploy ATM in the WAN.

Enterprise Network Performance

This is an important concern for enterprise IT managers. Applications are driving the expansion of networks and the need to deliver high-speed services to an increasing number of users. Enterprise managers are continually faced with the challenge of supporting an increased number of applications that require an increased amount of network resources. Collaborative group documents, business presentations, and reports are routinely sent via e-mail or the Internet as the work environment becomes increasingly mobile. The demand for increased access to information at the desktop has created a demand for better network performance. Applications that have been driven out from the network core to the remote offices require more bandwidth for better performance. The ATM core of the enterprise network is and will be pushed out to the edges of the network.

Service Provider Network Performance

Service providers are challenged with the need to deliver more services other than bandwidth and network access. They are challenged to provide services such as data warehousing, data archiving, co-location of Web services, business-class Internet access (>T1), corporate intranets or VPN services, and workgroup services. To satisfy the demands of their clients, the service providers are challenged to move ATM for their network core to the customer premise. Even today, several service providers have tariffed their ATM services at the same rate that they provide frame relay service.

Quality of Service

An important technical feature of ATM is that it provides multiple levels of quality of service, and it has internal provision to address the needs of flow control and dynamic bandwidth allocation. Clients are demanding a guaranteed level of service for network dollar, and ATM enables the service provider a mechanism to provide service-level agreements (SLAs). The classic example is of two customers, one who has contracted for 6Mbps service and one who has contracted for 10Mbps service. The flow control capabilities of ATM allow the service providers to guarantee the expected level of service for each customer, although the customers may be sharing the same network link. Clients receive a different billing rate for their service, and the service provider can maximize their network bandwidth.

Inclusion, Unification, and Expansion

The conversion of the network core to ATM within the enterprise and service provider networks provides a strong impetus to expand these networks to include other users or networks. Unifying and standardizing network technology are methods of reducing cost and improving reliability and serviceability. In order to simplify the network, ATM will move from the network core to the edge of the network.

Scalability

ATM is dynamically scalable and it provides metered bandwidth that conforms to the infrastructure of networks maintained by service providers as well as enterprise users. ATM enables the service providers to deliver bandwidth that meets the demands of users. Other competing technologies such as xDSL require bandwidth services that are asymmetrical to the network. Users will demand bandwidth in increments of 1.5Mbps, 3Mbps, 6Mbps, 12Mbps, DS3, OC-3c, and OC12.

Integrated Services

ATM provides the only standardized method for unifying network services under a single network medium. ATM supports both data and voice, as well as video services. The unification of voice, data, and video is an important long-term objective for both enterprise users and service provides. Enterprise users long for the day when they can contract for one service and one bill that includes voice, data, and video services. By deploying ATM to the customer premise, service providers can begin to unify network functions and deliver the long-sought-after "single pipe" that provides all functions.

Outsourcing Services

ATM enables service providers to deliver high-speed, transparent LAN services (TLS). TLS services provide a simple means of providing LAN-to-LAN extension without the need to deploy a complex solution. This enables service providers to provide "outsourcing" services to clients seeking to bundle network WAN services to achieve an overall lower operational network cost.

When examining how ATM will be deployed in the future in the enterprise market, one is primarily concerned with the WAN. Although the rapid emergence of switched technologies such as 100BT Ethernet and gigabit Ethernet at low cost points successfully stunted the deployment of ATM to the desktop — ATM found a home in the network core — it was in the core of the network that ATM provided the speeds necessary to reduce network congestion. It is only now that the extensive investments made in ATM backbone technology can be leveraged to deliver "in-demand" services across the network topology. Exhibit 15-1 illustrates the deployment of ATM access services within the enterprise market.

From the service provider perspective, the ATM network of tomorrow involves migration of the ATM network from the core of the network to the customer premises. By expanding the ATM as the network transport, service providers are presented with a viable strategy to modernize the components of their networks that generate profits — but at a considerable cost. The large incumbent interchange carriers such as Sprint, Williams, MCI Worldcomm and AT&T have multiple networks under management. These networks include frame relay, voice, IP, and ATM. Expanding ATM throughout their networks allows the incumbents to (1) reduce costs, (2) deliver high-speed services, (3) unify networks, and (4) provide new CPE-based services.

Without exception, the new CLECs and CIXCs have built new networks almost entirely based on ATM as the core transport. Each of these new companies has seized on ATM as their preferred transport technology. Thus, none of these companies is encumbered with legacy networks such as frame relay or circuit-switched technologies. In short, when one thinks about ATM access, one is thinking about a CPE device that is designed to be an access mechanism that transports CPE services into the ATM network for delivery across the service provider network. Exhibit 15-2 illustrates ATM access into the ATM service provider backbone network from two customer sites.

KEY TECHNOLOGIES FOR THE ATM WAN

The ATM WAN of tomorrow will be a combination of "core" ATM technologies and "transition" technologies required for supporting legacy networks. When examining the deployment strategy of ATM access equipment within the ATM WAN of tomorrow, one does so from two perspectives. The first perspective is the user or CPE side and the second perspective is the network or service provider side. Using the CPE/service provider model, one can begin to define the "system" required for ATM access. On the service provider side, ATM services will be delivered at various speeds using a variety of interfaces. Typically, ATM access devices will support the following on the service provider side:

- DS1/E1 interface
- DS3/E3 interface
- OC-3c interface
- inverse muxing over ATM (IMA) interface
- add drop mux and add drop bypass

The service provider side of ATM access devices are simple compared to the variety of services that must be supported on the CPE side. The CPE

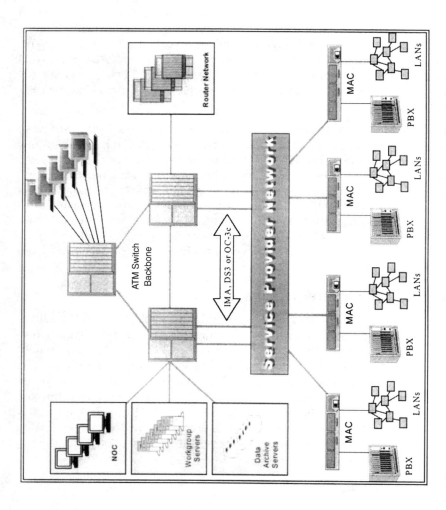

Exhibit 15-1. ATM deployment in enterprise networks.

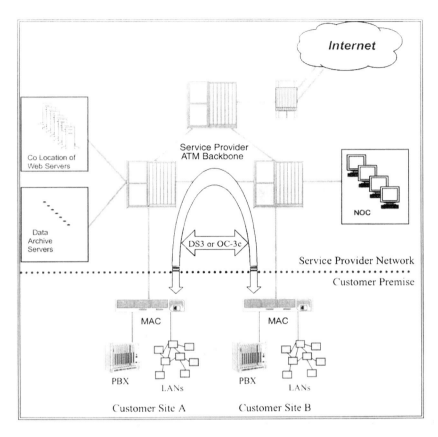

Exhibit 15-2. ATM access from customer site to service provider.

side of ATM access devices must achieve two objectives: they must support the services that customers will use going forward, and they must also support a variety of legacy network technologies and services that clients have deployed over the years. It must be remembered that a motivating component of ATM is the ability to provide a consolidation of technologies and services. The following outlines the primary CPE side requirements:

- LAN interface: 10/100 Ethernet, 4/16 Token Ring, and FDDI
- IP routing support: static routing and default gateway forwarding support
- Transparent LAN service support: bridging
- LAN client support: LAN client provides support for SVCs and bandwidth management and interoperability in enterprise networks with native ATM devices

Combining the service provider and CPE side features, one creates what can be called an integrated access device (IAD) or multi-service access concentrator (MAC). The objective of this device is to provide user-to-network connectivity. It is not a router and it is not a switch — it is an access device. In simple terms, it can be considered a fast segmentation and reassembly (SARing) engine that transports voice and data into an ATM stream. The primary objective of MACs will be to balance their cost and simplicity in order to leverage the benefits of ATM. Unified services or "single-pipe" strategy is a driving force behind the deployment of ATM; but if the devices used to provide ATM access are expensive or complicated, the compelling reasons to deploy ATM are diminished. Enterprise IT managers and service providers have a common objective that ATM and MACs must achieve — long-term operational cost reduction.

As enterprise networks and service providers begin the migration out from the network core, support for legacy technologies will be important in-demand features. Not only will the IXCs have legacy networks, but many enterprise users will have a mix of legacy technologies as well. The objective will be to provide an orderly transition to ATM, starting with the locations with critical needs. In order to achieve this process, MACs will need to provide support for legacy services such as frame relay. An essential element of this requirement will be for MACs to support Frame Relay connections from routers and FRADs, as well as FRF 5 and FRF 8 for support of Frame-to-ATM and Frame-to-ATM-to-Frame services.

As much as MACs must be data orientated to support the variety of services typically found at the remote site location, they must also be able to support a variety of voice services. A primary benefit of ATM is the integration of voice and data on a single pipe. The benefits of the technology are greatly reduced if all one can get is a faster pipe and still require a different connection for voice services. Thus, MACs need to possess strong voice services. These services include:

- circuit emulation services: structured and unstructured transmission of DS1/E1 streams for support of digital PBX interconnect
- FXO/FXS POTs: support for analog PBXs as well as dial tone, PLAR, and ring generator
- voice and silence suppression and compression
- AAL2 voice services that support dynamic bandwidth allocation through SVCs

As well as supporting a variety of services, MACs must also support a variety of network management services. MACs will be deployed by both enterprise users and service provider users. Thus, it is important for MACs to support features that enable each to manage and support the devices. The primary objective is for MACs to be "lights-out" devices that are installed, configured, and forgotten. Unfortunately, network devices rarely live up to such lofty goals and at times will be in need of management services. In this case, it will important for MACs to support a variety of "punch list" network management features. These features include:

- Web-based management
- Telnet
- SNMP
- support for popular network management platforms with MIB extensions
- CRAFT interface
- out-of-band management via modem

An important tactical capability in the deployment of MACs will be support for inverse muxing over ATM (IMA). IMA leverages two market conditions for the service provider and enterprise client. At present, many service providers are forced to deploy full DS3 circuits for clients that desire to scale above the T1 range. Unfortunately, many clients do not require a full DS3. In other cases, clients are demanding >T1 service in areas where DS3 is not readily available. The solution to this challenge can be found in IMA. IMA allows T1 lines to be bonded together to deliver access services that are >T1, but less than DS3. This elegant strategy provides a gradual scale in services and cost as network demands warrant. Exhibit 15-3 illustrates the deployment of IMA services.

ATM WAN: SHOULD YOU START NOW?

Why ATM will be important in the WAN is known; now one needs to ensure that one will be prepared to undertake the transition. From a preparation perspective, the following questions provide a starting point to determine whether or not one should initiate programs to begin transitioning the WAN transport to ATM-based services.

- Do you have remote locations that require improved performance or locations in your network that would benefit by extending your ATM backbone to include their location?
- Are you looking to reduce long-term costs and unify voice and data services?
- Do you have E-commerce, or Web-based applications that require dedicated Internet access above T1 speeds?
- Can you benefit from leveraging the infrastructure of service providers to provide data warehousing, co-location of Web servers, and high-speed intranet services?
- Do you have major application initiatives underway that will increase the demands for network bandwidth throughout your network over the next 12 to 24 months?
- Are you looking to contract for guaranteed network bandwidth for some or all of your network locations?

- Is network performance a mission-critical requirement for your business? Do you have or will you have mission-critical applications that are dependent on network performance?
- Are you interested in positioning your network infrastructure to support video-based applications such as conferencing and training?
- Are long-term cost reduction, network simplification, and performance long-term objectives for your IS organization?

CONCLUSION

The genesis of the new network has begun. The start has been slow — but the conclusion is inevitable. ATM is and will be deployed as the transport of choice for wide area networking. Service providers of all types are deploying ATM for solid business reasons. ATM provides key advantages not found in other WAN technologies: namely, quality of service, unification of services (voice, data, video), and superior scalability.

Enterprise networks are being deployed with public or private ATM backbones. This will be extended to remote offices and locations, where ATM access solutions will be deployed for the following reasons:

- **Cost/performance balance:** increase network performance in a manner that allows for scalable migration of services based on a cost/need ratio.
- **Simplified billing and service level agreements:** lower service cost, simplified billing statements, and guaranteed service that enable the enterprise users to purchase only what they require.
- **Leverage investments in public and private backbones:** effective use of ATM core infrastructures that are already deployed will lead to improved services and lower, long-term costs.
- **Reduce acquisition and operational costs:** deploy less-expensive technological solutions that provide long-term, low cost, "lights out" operational costs.

ATM is the only technology that is standards based and can be used to deliver multi-service networking throughout the wide area network. In addition, ATM is the only technology that can be used by enterprise users and service providers to reduce their equipment acquisition costs and ongoing operational costs over the long term.

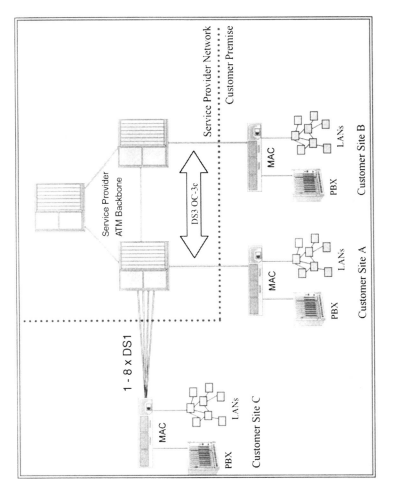

Exhibit 15-3. Deployment of inverse multiplexing over ATM (IMA) services.

Chapter 16
Transport over Frame Relay: Issues and Considerations
Tim Kelly

THE USERS OF NETWORK SERVICES (e.g., frame relay) are concerned with the end-to-end integrity of data transfer. Ensuring this integrity is the function of the transport layer. This chapter examines transport issues as they relate to the quality of the underlying service.

WHAT IS FRAME RELAY?

Frame relay and X.25 are connection-oriented services (as opposed to the Internet Protocol [IP], which is a connectionless service). Frame relay is a development of integrated services digital network (ISDN), prompted by the need to handle the standard 2 *n* by 75-bps data rates over a 64K-bps standard digital telephone channel. The general problem goes by the name of rate adaption. Several adaption schemes have been standardized. International Telegraph and Telephone Consultative Committee (CCITT) standards V.110 and X.31 are examples, but these are unwieldy schemes and require special hardware and software in the terminal or terminal adapter. Another idea was to use the ISDN D channel, which already has a link layer protocol (link access procedure D [LAP-D]) that is built into any ISDN terminal. The D channel is used for call setup of the 64K-bps B channels and for access to the packet switching function (X.25) on the basic rate interface. By modifying the LAP-D frame format slightly, a switched virtual circuit service and permanent virtual circuit service could be provided. Switched virtual service is possible because signaling packets that are sent over the D channel to set up the B channel can be used to define another type of connection (i.e., frame relay).

The idea is to take the basic LAP-D link layer frame and replace the 13-bit service access point identifier and terminal end point identifier with a value that provides the same function as the logical channel address in the

0-8493-0859-3/00/$0.00+$.50
© 2000 by CRC Press LLC

X.25 world. A 10-bit field, called the data link connection identifier (DLCI), is used. With this approach, packet switching functions no longer need to unpack the link layer frame to find the network layer address. They can route (relay) the link layer frame directly based on the DLCI. The relationship of the DLCI to the source and destination address is established when the connection is established. In ISDN, a signaling packet that contains the end point addresses is sent to the network to set up the virtual circuit connection. Currently, only permanent virtual circuit service is available over frame relay offerings, and therefore the association between end points is set up as subscription time.

The interest in frame relay stems from the frame relay switch being able to relay the frame in as little as 4 milliseconds. This is much shorter than the 30 to 100 milliseconds required by a typical X.25 packet switch. For transfer of a large file, reduced network latency is not very important, but for a transaction-oriented application (typical of local area network [LAN] applications), reducing network latency contributes directly to reduced network response time.

THE OSI REFERENCE MODEL

To set the stage for this discussion of transport issues, a review of the open systems interconnection (OSI) model is in order. Only the lower four layers are considered, because they are application independent and as a whole provide the reliable transportation mechanism generally required by applications.

The physical layer is responsible for bit transmission and, if needed, synchronization. The link layer is responsible for a series of functions that includes basic character phasing, sequencing, and acknowledgment. The list, in order of ascending value, might be as follows: character synchronization, block framing, error detection, device addressing, block sequencing, block acknowledgment, and automatic retransmission (in the case of errors or out-of-sequence conditions).

How many of these link layer functions are used depends on the application. X.25 employs all these functions to provide reliable link layer transmission between users and the network and between switching nodes within the network. The data or contents of the link layer frame are fully protected from errors during transport on the telephone lines interconnecting these network nodes.

On LANS, the link layer contains a new sublayer, called the media access control (MAC), that performs frame synchronization and error detection. This MAC layer is unique to each type of LAN (i.e., token passing bus, token passing ring, contention bus). Frame relay is a link layer function. All that is needed to connect a LAN to a frame relay service is a bridge that functions at the MAC layer.

The network layer is responsible for routing and switching. To do routing or switching, an address plan is needed that is consistent (and unique) across the network. Each addressable node has a network level address. This address is quite separate from the link layer address. The link layer address is analogous to a street address; two houses in different towns could have the same street address (e.g., 540 W. Main). Because more than one individual may be living at each address, a network layer address, which is the address of the individual, is also needed. The structure of these addresses, how they are known to the routing nodes in the network, and how they are updated when people move are topics that are beyond the scope of this chapter.

CONNECTIONLESS AND CONNECTION-ORIENTED SERVICES

There are two basic types of network layer services: connection oriented and connectionless. A connection-oriented network (e.g., the dial-up telephone network) provides the users of the network layer service with a dedicated electrical connection that is set up when the called party acknowledges the call. Data sent across the network is acknowledged by the receiving party and the connection is terminated with a call termination sequence. Both X.25 and frame relay are connection-oriented network services.

A connectionless network (such as that provided by the IP) works like the mail. A letter (i.e., data) is sent, but the sender does not receive acknowledgment of its arrival.

The transport layer is responsible for the end-to-end delivery of information. It uses the network layer for a delivery mechanism that spans the network just as the network layer uses the link layer to get the data across each link and the link layer uses the physical layer to accomplish bit transmission. Like the network layer services, those of the transport layer may be connection oriented or connectionless. If the layers associated with the user (the session, presentation, and application layers will be considered here as an undivided user layer) are involved in supporting a transaction-oriented application such as credit authorization, a failure in the underlying layers (including transport) is not critical because the user can always reenter the request. For this application, a connectionless transport layer is sufficient.

For users desiring high-integrity data transfer, a connection-oriented transport layer is needed so that delivery assurance can be provided to the user layers. The obvious question is where this connection-oriented service should be offered. The candidates are the link, network, and transport layers, either all or one. The X.25 community believes that the network layer should be responsible for the connection. The Transmission Control Protocol (TCP) and IP community believe it should be accomplished at the transport layer. The goal of this chapter is not to take sides but to point out the implications of implementations at the transport layer, given that the services provided by the underlying layer are reliable.

Perspective can be gained on the variety of opinions on this matter by looking at the OSI transport layer protocols. There are five of them, from TP0 to TP4. TP4 is a full-function, connection-oriented protocol.

THE NATURE OF TRAFFIC

All traffic through the network is bursty, meaning technically that it follows a Poisson distribution. The only apparently nonbursty traffic is that which, for lack of bandwidth, takes a long time to send. For example, a large file transfer sent over the wide area network (WAN) that takes several hours at 9,600 bps is not, for the sake of this discussion, bursty. The only reason data is sent this way is that bandwidth costs are so high that it is cost effective to send the traffic for several hours rather than pay for the cost of a high-bandwidth circuit. Another kind of nonstochastic traffic is encrypted military communications. The underlying information is in fact bursty, but the system also sends constant nonsense data to mask the transfer of actual information.

The argument can be made that video communications are continuous. This is true for current implementations because the receiving devices have no substantial storage capacity. Frame information is repeated because the receiver cannot store and display the nonchanging information. In terms of the actual information content, the signal is stochastic. Here, information is defined as changes to the signal. A constant, nonchanging signal, as far as the need for bandwidth goes, contains no information. A test pattern transmitted from a television transmitter contains all the information in the first frame transmitted; the subsequent frames contain no new information.

The point being made here is that the lack of new information means that the user at the receiving station, if the initial test pattern can be stored, needs zero bandwidth after the initial burst. Therefore, the information content of broadcast television is indeed bursty. Videoconferencing systems make use of this fact; they transmit only the changes from the previous frame. Because the information content is bursty (stochastic), the information can be sent effectively over a bandwidth-on-demand system such as frame relay.

Voice traffic at first appears to require continuous bandwidth, but if examined over short enough periods, speech is bursty; approximately 40 percent of the time when we are speaking, no sounds are being made. This fact is made use of in low bit-rate voice technology.

226

Dedicated bandwidth is available in fixed increments and there is a cost associated with each increment. This cost per increment is typically non-linear. The major cost is the initial cost of procuring the right of way and route construction; the incremental cost of additional fiber waveguides is small. Once the facility exists, its real cost is therefore its initial installation cost plus continuing maintenance cost.

The fact that bandwidth in this sense is fixed and that the traffic is bursty poses the classic problem of providing sufficient bandwidth for the burst peaks while maintaining efficiency. After all is said and done, there is no satisfactory solution to this problem. Traffic can be queued and sent later to distribute peak traffic over time. This improves efficiency (efficiency is measured as bandwidth used divided by bandwidth available). The parties waiting for their turn on the network may, however, be unhappy. An alternative is to build more bandwidth, but this will be partly (i.e., inefficiently) used most of the time.

Frame relay offers the possibility of effective solutions to the problems of bursty traffic, not in the technology per se but in its ability to differentiate between types of traffic. The goal is to identify small chunks of the types of data to be transmitted, then assign them priorities based on their need for timely delivery. They can then be interleaved on the same transmission facility. For example, voice and video data could be given transmission priority over transaction data or file transfer data. This, in effect, provides a leveling of demand on the facility. In the limit, of course, the file transfer takes longer and the response time for the transaction is extended, but these inconveniences may be acceptable if the greater overall efficiency yields lower costs.

In practice, it may turn out that this solution to peak traffic demands is ineffective. Traffic is, on the whole, stochastic, and bandwidth cost is still fixed. If users expect to receive or providers expect to offer bandwidth on demand, they will require bandwidth capacity sufficient to accommodate peak rush hour traffic. From a carrier's point of view, there may be some benefits. To the extent that the traffic's peaks for the entire range of traffic to be handled are distributed more or less evenly throughout the day, bandwidth on demand allows the carrier to more efficiently use this bandwidth throughout the day. The carrier can only add bandwidth in fixed increments (e.g., DS-0, DS-1, or DS-3), but the carrier has (theoretically at least) the ability to add bandwidth to the frame relay switches during anticipated traffic peaks and at other times to allocate that bandwidth to other kinds of traffic. Unfortunately, the demand for practically all types of traffic in the network peaks at around 10:00 a.m. and 2:00 p.m.; in the middle of the night, there is little traffic of any kind. The carriers can level demand to some extent by lowering the cost of frame relay service during off-peak times, as is done with switched telephone rates.

TRANSPORT ISSUES

Although frame relay has the potential for providing faster, more efficient delivery across the network, it presents some interesting problems to the user in its lack of flow control and congestion management. X.25 networks offer error-free, sequenced, acknowledged, connection-oriented service. Frame relay leaves the implementation of such functions to the user, but eliminates considerable overhead. Frame relay is a connectionless service, but users can implement connection-oriented services at higher layers. Frame relay is well suited to TCP/IP users, who desire maximum speed and minimum service from the underlying layers.

Nearly tenfold increases in frame routing speed are claimed for frame relay switches in comparison with conventional X.25 packet switches. These comparisons may be suspect, unless it is certain that the tests were conducted on the same hardware platform, that the code was optimized for that platform, and that other, similar adjustments were made. Also, comparing new frame relay hardware with a five-year-old X.25 packet switch is an invidious comparison.

For users not concerned that the network supply all the functions of X.25, frame relay offers the ideal link layer transportation mechanism. The only service provided is unacknowledged rapid routing with error detection. The frame itself makes provision for the frame relay switch to route it through the permanent virtual circuit and contains a cyclic redundancy check to detect errors. Thus, at least the frames received are known to be without detected error even if no mechanism is implemented (at the link layer) to request retransmission. This leaves the complete responsibility for flow control and congestion management to the upper layers. In keeping with this philosophy, the network layer is also a minimum service entity. Thus, the responsibility for all error handling falls to the transport layer.

SEQUENCE NUMBERING

Both high-level data link control (HDLC) and X.25 provide sequence numbering capability; frame relay and the IP do not. Therefore, over a frame relay network, if the user layer requires sequencing services, it is up to the transport layer to provide them. In this general case, the transport layer may make no assumptions about the underlying layers, or it must make the worst-case assumptions (i.e., segments will not be delivered in order, segments may become lost, and segments may be delayed). Because most frame relay connections are permanent virtual circuits and possess short delays, the extended sequence numbering capability of, for example, TCP is not needed.

ACKNOWLEDGMENTS

The X.25 protocols provide acknowledgments at the link layer, on a link-by-link basis, and at the network layer. Because no such acknowledgments are provided by frame relay, this task, for the same reasons given for sequencing, must be handled by the transport layer. The acknowledgment number field is the same size as the sequence number field. This allows the receiver to provide the next expected segment number. The next expected segment number is the inclusive acknowledgment for all previously received segments.

FLOW CONTROL

Flow control in an X.25 network is provided on a link-by-link basis and across the network by the network layer. Here again, the underlying layers of a frame relay implementation provide no flow control. Flow control is performed at the transport layer, using a credit window mechanism. The receiver sends a credit to the transmitter for the maximum number of segments it is willing to accept. The transmitter may send until it has exhausted the credit. This value must be chosen with great care because the underlying network may store (i.e., delay) many segments. The receiver cannot offer the transmitter too much credit because it must be prepared to receive all of the segments outstanding in the network should they be delivered all at once; it must offer enough credit so that the transmitter does not frequently exhaust its credit and have to stop and wait for more (which reduces efficiency). This is not a severe problem on an end-to-end frame relay network because the network delays are quite small. On the other hand, if the frame relay connection is one component of a greater network (i.e., the frame relay is a subnetwork concatenated with several other subnetworks), the credit value must be carefully considered. The transport layer's responsibility is end to end and transcends any underlying services.

ERROR RECOVERY

Any underlying network or subnetwork will on occasion make an unrecoverable error such that a frame or packet is lost. For this reason, transport must provide some sequencing capability. Errors manifest themselves to transport as missing segments, because an error detected by the cyclic redundancy check (CRC) at the link layer will simply cause the link layer to not deliver that frame. This is true of frame relay and HDLC, but it happens much less often with a full HDLC implementation because the link layer can request retransmission of the missing frame. This feature slows the delivery at the link layer (on an error-prone link); this additional overhead is deemed unnecessary on modern links, which are based on digital transmission technology and therefore are less error prone.

If the digital links never made errors, there would be no need for error checking or the ability to automatically retransmit frames in which errors are detected. In an HDLC frame, removing both the control field (assuming the address field is still needed) and the CRC saves three octets of overhead per frame. The reality is that errors do occur, and so the CRC is needed. Thus, the sole savings is one octet per frame. An error-free link would also not require the use of retransmission software. But errors do occur and retransmission is required, and this task ultimately falls to the transport layer, which must have these capabilities anyway.

CONGESTION MANAGEMENT

Congestion management is the heart of the transport problem. As previously discussed, all connectionless services tend to suffer from congestion, because traffic is bursty and bandwidth is fixed. To the extent that the bandwidth exceeds use, congestion is not a problem, but efficiency suffers. Networks must balance the cost of bandwidth against use; in other words, they must trade off efficiency against lower response time.

There are three possible ways to address this problem. For want of better names they could be called the smart link, the smart network, and the smart transport approaches.

The smart link approach implements flow control only at the link layer. This is acceptable for small networks. It works, for example, for a node receiving, over a single input link, traffic destined for multiple outbound links. If one of the output links is congested, the node exercises flow control on the inbound link to keep from being overrun by data it cannot deliver. The unwanted side effect is to cut off the traffic to all the outbound links.

In X.25 networks, the flow control at both link and network layers effectively provides congestion management. Should a node or link suffer from congestion, flow control can be used on that link or on some or all of the virtual circuits passing through that node to minimize congestion. Of course, response time across the network for that logical channel suffers accordingly. Other logical channels passing through that node, however, continue to operate. This is the smart network approach to congestion management.

In connectionless networks, congestion is typically handled at the network layer by discarding packets. This is acceptable because transport protocols used with unreliable connectionless networks do not have high expectations of the network layer and are capable of retransmitting these missing packets. Unfortunately, this exacerbates the congestion problem. (The IP now has a mechanism for sending a source quench packet to the source when a node is overrun by packets.) It is by no means assured that the IP will be used over a frame relay network, where the same condition exists. Work is being done to address this issue. Some of the issues and potential solutions are discussed here. The actual solution, at least in the short term, will depend on the exigencies of the network design.

With the smart transport approach, the transport layer is informed of the congestion status of the underlying network sublayers. This is comparable to noticing that United Parcel Service (UPS) acknowledgments (i.e., network layer packets) that normally flow between offices in New York and Los Angeles are not returning in the expected one day. If the UPS van is stuck in traffic on the New York end or the Los Angeles end, that is comparable to link layer congestion. If the air traffic control system is delaying flights, or if one or more of the UPS package-handling depots is overflowing with packages, that is comparable to network layer congestion. If the assumption is made that packages (i.e., packets) are lost and copies are resent, this congests the network further. One dilemma is the length of time it is appropriate to wait for acknowledgments to arrive. In a stable network with relatively uniform traffic flow, this is not a problem. But network traffic is bursty and the network is subject to sudden overloads (in the UPS example, this might be the Christmas rush). One approach (used in TCP) is to monitor the response time and store the average. But sudden increases in network delay can cause retransmissions and delays. The goal of the transport layer is to balance response time (minimum delay across the network) with maximum efficiency (high throughput).

There are two ways the transport layer can achieve these goals. One is to calculate and monitor the existing round trip propagation delay. The trick is to avoid making the system too sensitive. The retransmission timer should not respond for congestion of short duration but should be sensitive enough to identify the real network propagation delay if a serious case of congestion does occur. By implementing a congestion control scheme (e.g., Karn's algorithm), transport can dynamically adapt to changes in delay on the underlying network.

The other approach is for the underlying (i.e., the frame relay) network to supply enough buffers to temporarily store the large volume of packets. This approach works as long as the network can determine what the peak traffic is going to be and provide enough buffers. In addition, users must be willing to tolerate the attendant transit delay caused by buffering the traffic while waiting for bandwidth to become available. With buffering, frames (or packets) are not discarded during congestion, but the transit delay of the subnet varies with the load. If the transport has not properly implemented Karn's algorithm or a similar mechanism, inefficiencies are introduced as the transport layer responds to these sudden increases (and decreases) in subnet delay.

SUMMARY

Although frame relay provides low delay and efficient bandwidth on demand, bandwidth still is available only in fixed sized increments.

Because traffic is bursty, network users need to plan strategies for those temporary peak traffic conditions when the traffic exceeds the bandwidth.

There are four ways to handle the problem:

1. *Provide more bandwidth than needed so that traffic requiring network access never exceeds the bandwidth allocated.* This is the approach being taken with current frame relay offerings through the committed information rate.
2. *Limit the traffic.* This is implemented in the transport layer by having it show restraint. Restraint implies that the transport mechanism, as previously discussed, can detect congestion by sensing temporary increases in subnetwork delay. Because the transport layer has no control over subnetwork delay, it has to choose responses that will not inadvertently add to congestion.
3. *Temporarily store traffic overload in buffers.* This must be implemented in the underlying frame relay or other subnetwork.
4. *Implement flow control either at the frame relay or the network layers.* It could be argued that this problem of congestion should be handled at the lowest layer of the architecture possible (i.e., at the frame relay layer) and not at the transport layer, which is two layers removed from the problem. To this end, the frame relay standard has defined two bits for congestion management. These are called the forward explicit congestion notification and backward explicit congestion notification bits. Exactly what course of action the frame relay switches should take in response to these bits is still the subject of discussion.

Buffering data within the subnetwork runs counter to the philosophy of a low-delay fast transportation mechanism. Implementation of flow control is not just a subnetwork problem but affects the whole frame relay layer. The use of the congestion notification bits ripples back through all of the attached frame relay networks to the customer's attachment point. This implies the need for much coordination (i.e., standards activity) to provide easily interconnected frame relay services and equipment. Rather than go through the protracted process of establishing a standard, the more likely scenario is that vendors will simply let users apply the functions of the transport layer to the problem. Therefore, whatever transport layer protocol is used over frame relay (e.g., TCP or OSI TP4), it must be capable of implementing the adaptive behavior described above. Because transport layer functions are several layers removed from the problem, it is hard to make delicate adjustments. On the other hand, as long as frame relay provides the fast, low-delay delivery mechanism, it is quite usable by any robust transport layer application.

232

Chapter 17
Emerging High-Bandwidth Networks

Kevin M. Groom
Frank M. Groom

INTRODUCTION

CORPORATE USERS ARE INCREASINGLY DEMANDING FASTER TRANSPORT SPEED. This is driven by the type of media being employed and shared among workers, such as documents, images, and training material. This material is being augmented by e-mail communication and increasingly by desktop videoconferencing. Further, the access to traditional transaction data applications on servers and requests and responses from client/server applications continue to be a primary driver for network connectivity.

As personal computers (PCs) and workstations come equipped with fast Peripheral Component Interconnect (PCI) buses that can deliver data to networks at 100M bps and greater speeds; have powerful Pentium II, Power PC, or Alpha central processing units (CPUs); and have 6- to 11-Gb hard drives, the user is demanding faster transport to feed these powerful data engines. Moreover, the distribution of large data and application servers is now augmented by groupware servers such as Lotus Notes storing documents and data and World Wide Web servers storing Hypertext Markup Language (HTML) marked-up pages for access with browsers.

To transport information among increasingly diverse and distributed processors, sharply greater bandwidth is required. As the trend for workers to spend many of their hours working from home or on the road continues, fast home access to corporate information is becoming an equal partner in the high-bandwidth business environment.

Asymmetrical digital subscriber line (ADSL) high bandwidth to the home worker has emerged from trials by the Regional Bell Operating Companies

(RBOCs) and was being offered in a gradual roll-out in the 1998 to 2000 time period. ADSL is the newest and most promising high-bandwidth connection technology for access from the home. Asynchronous transfer mode (ATM) of 100M bps and Gigabit Ethernet are the emerging network technologies in the office. Frame relay is the fastest growing wide area connection technology, and the beginnings of a demand for ATM is emerging. Both frame relay and ATM are the prime interexchange carrier services offered to bridge city, state, and the national locations. Finally, world high-bandwidth connection services are emerging as corporations attempt to meld their national networks into a blend of high-bandwidth connectivity provided by such consortiums as AT&T's World Partners Frame Relay Consortium, which partner to deliver integrated world frame relay service.

HIGH-BANDWIDTH LOCAL ACCESS FOR THE HOME

Telephone, cable, and satellite companies have concentrated significant attention on basic residential connectivity. Initially, home entertainment was the application that was expected to drive customer demand for higher speed connectivity. However, with the emergence of vast interest and usage of the Internet, industry sights have turned to Internet access, work-at-home situations, and remote access to standard business Ethernet, Internet Protocol (IP), or ATM local area networks (LANs).

The general classification for the telephone company's product direction is termed digital subscriber line (DSL) service. DSL service has a basic intent of delivering higher bandwidth transport over the in-place twisted pair telephone loop plant that extends to each residence, while placing a modem on each end of the loop, one at the subscriber's location, and one at telephone central office switch center. The local loop tends to have between 20 and 33 bridge taps along the line. About 20 percent of installed lines have loading coils as well.

This gives problems to other services, such as Integrated Services Digital Network (ISDN), and limits the number of telephone lines that are ISDN equitable. DSL services — due to their more modern modulation techniques, digital signal processors, and isolation of the voice traffic to the low end of the frequency spectrum — are impervious to the bridge and load coil situation, thus allowing direct usage of a large percentage of the currently existing twisted pair local loop wire. It is estimated that 85 percent of U.S. households could be connected through DSL service with no modification of the wire pair with an equivalent 30 to 50 percentof such wire being ISDN capable. Among the array of DSL services that have been defined, telephone companies have targeted ADSL and high bit-rate digital subscriber line (HDSL) services as having the most customer demand potential.

Exhibit 17-1. Digital subscriber user service array.

Type	Data Rate	Mode	Use
Modem	28.8, 34.6, 56.4K bps	Duplex	Minimum remove
DSL	160K bps	Duplex	ISDN
ADSL	1.5–9M bps	Simple down	Internet
16–640K bps	Duplex up	Work home	
HDSL	768K bps	Duplex down	Symmetric
768K bps	Duplex up	Computer use	
SDSL	384K bps Up/D	Duplex	Minimum data
VDSL	13–52M bps	Duplex down	Heavy data processing
1.5–2.3M bps	Duplex up		

XDSL Speeds and Services

The complete array of DSL services and the traditional modem service are presented in Exhibit 17-1. These are ADSL, HDSL, very high bit-rate digital subscriber line (VDSL), and symmetric digital subscriber line (SDSL) service.

The ADSL forum has defined a standard model to be followed by telephone companies and equipment suppliers to construct an ADSL connection and to offer ADSL services. The loop plant twisted pair wire is expected to remain unchanged. Distances beyond 3.5 mi from a central office will be connected by means of a T1 line that will span the longer distance to arrive within a reasonable distance to a residence community. ADSL places a splitter at both ends of the local loop line as well as an ADSL transmission unit (ATU-C at the central office and ATU-R at the residence).

The purpose of the modems is to modulate higher speed data and video on the line. The splitter allows the plain old telephone service (POTS) telephone conversation to be modulated separately on the line after the data and video and to be isolated from these transmissions. At the central office, the telephone conversation is split off from the higher speed data and video and sent directly to a line module of the central office switch, such as a traditional analog transmission. These ATU modems and the splitters are portrayed in Exhibit 17-2.

The modems on each end modulate the traffic into very high speed (above 138 kHz to 1.1 GHz), medium speed (from 30 to 138 kHz) with the overlap accommodated by echo cancellation. The POTS telephone connection sits as it always has at the bottom frequency between 0 and 4 kHz. A guard band of 24 kHz separates the voice traffic from the higher speed frequencies.

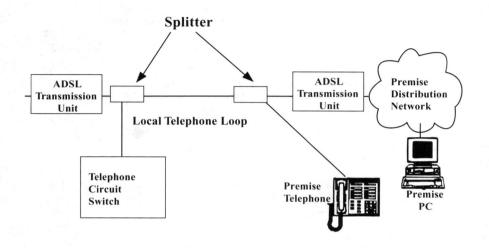

Exhibit 17-2. The standard reference model for ADSL service.

ADSL is an asymmetrical connection service. The downstream traffic is designed to be significantly faster than the upstream traffic. The service is intended for an audience with asymmetrical needs. Video-on-demand service has a limited and relatively slow request traffic, followed by massive and continuous downstream flow of a video movie. Internet traffic has been observed to follow the same pattern, with a browser-based seek request for information, followed by a sizable series of text, image, video, and sound clip information flowing downstream. ADSL can have this asymmetrical connection set up in a range from 1.5M bps downstream coupled with 64K bps upstream from the residence, to 6.1M bps downstream and 640K bps upstream.

There are four basic transmission modes for ADSL service:

1. Packet mode is essentially Transmission Control Protocol (TCP)/IP over a home Ethernet, which requires an Ethernet card in each home or remote office PC and twisted pair wire to connect to the ADSL home modem. This mode is ideal for home access to the Internet and for connection to a corporate network.
2. Cell-based ATM employs an ATM card in each home or remote office PC and is suited for remote office connection to a corporate ATM network by means of a telephone company ATM network. This connection is desirable for multimedia, videoconferencing, or home or office delivery of real-time training material.

3. Bit synchronization mode will be employed for streamed video to the home such as with video-on-demand service.
4. POTS mode is reserved for voice telephone traffic.

EMERGING OFFICE AND BUILDING CONNECTIVITY

Corporations are requiring increased bandwidth to connect to servers in the worker's building or across the campus, as well as to the distant location of other workers in the corporation. Simultaneously, they have an investment in older PCs, Ethernets and hubs, and software such as Novell, Inc.'s NetWare. To modernize their investments and satisfy a diverse set of needs, they need to accommodate both the current network technology and the emerging high-bandwidth technology.

Current Office Connectivity and Building Backbones

Most corporations have already interconnected workgroups of users on a particular floor of an office building through an intelligent hub. Up to 100 or 120 users can be connected to a hub by means of category three or five twisted pair wire over distances of no more than 100 m (330 ft). These users can then be bridged to other hubs on the same or other floors. Such interconnected office workers can share common laser printers, e-mail, file servers, and applications through their shared and commonly managed LAN hub.

To minimize the investment in intelligent hubs (which cost between $10,000 and $20,000, depending on their configuration) and to extend the user's connection beyond 100-m distance limitation, cheaper "dumb" or distributed hubs supporting up to 20 PCs can be placed close to workers for their subgroup interconnection. The distributed hubs can then be linked to a more distant floor hub by means of coaxial cable or fiber. The stacking of these simple hubs and connecting them to a central switching hub for the floor is portrayed in Exhibit 17-3.

These traditional building connections are now under pressure from a number of advanced applications. In particular, the use of multimedia and desktop videoconferencing is driving bandwidth demands to the desktop for special-case users. However, the big impetus for desktop bandwidth is the movement from personal desktop computing toward network and workgroup computing. Much of desktop usage involves sending and receiving transactions over the local network to office, building, campus, and national and international servers. To meet this demand, simple office Ethernets have been upgraded first to switched 10M-bps Ethernet, which has minimum contention, and then to 100M-bps switched Ethernet. As companies rapidly move to switched Ethernet and Token Ring LANs to reduce Ethernet collisions and the latency both experience and many move to 100M-bps Fast Ethernet on the floor, there is a general movement toward replacing the more expensive and complicated router-based fiber distributed data

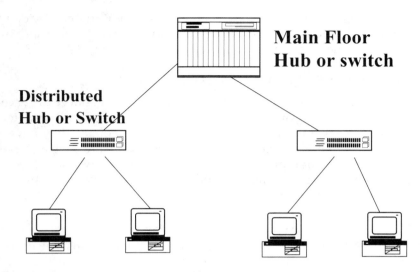

Main Floor Hub or switch

Distributed Hub or Switch

Exhibit 17-3. The distributed simple hubs connected by a smart switching hub.

interface (FDDI) backbones with a single 100M-bps Fast Ethernet switch and placing a Fast Ethernet exit card in each floor hub or switch.

ATM DESKTOP CONNECTIVITY

ATM to the desktop is driven by the requirement for a variety of media to be delivered over the same connection to the desktop applications and disk storage. Exhibit 17-4 presents the range of information sizes and speeds required for the variety of multimedia that might be delivered. Sound and motion video pose the additional requirement that they must have rapid, yet unvarying delivery speed with no lags or variation. In many cases, this mixed set of media types must be delivered simultaneously in an intermixed stream over a common connection and used as a unit by the destination device.

Exhibit 17-4. Varying bandwidth requirements for media types.

Media Type	Bandwidth (bps)
Entertainment video–real-time play	3,000,000
Videoconference	128–356,000
Image visualization–real-time	50–80,000
Engineering image	90,000
Voice	64,000
Sound	176,000–700,000
Stereo	1,400,000
Fax	64,000

Further, many of the individual media types require compression algorithms unique to the individual media type to be performed at the source and destination sites to squeeze the volume of information into any reasonable delivery protocol.

Only ATM provides the bandwidth reservation with guaranteed quality of service and a fast enough transfer rate to deliver these varying types of media to the desktop in a satisfactory fashion. In contrast, fast Ethernet provides high-speed and high-quality data transmission but cannot guarantee the delivery rate for individual media types. Many believe that a moderately loaded (less than 50 percent of capacity) 100M-bps Ethernet can carry multimedia to the desktop over the last 100 m if ATM is used for the wider backbone network.

ATM BUILDING BACKBONE NETWORKS

Unless ATM is provided all the way to ATM-equipped desktop PCs, ATM backbone networks provide only high bandwidth without the quality of service features, classes of service, and bandwidth guarantees for which ATM was created. As a backbone network, ATM competes with the newer 100M-bps and 1G-bps Ethernet and the older FDDI protocols purely on speed, simplicity of the protocol, and cost.

The simplicity and cost factors are the strength of Fast Ethernet. FDDI strength is in its embedded base and proven capability, while multimedia such as picture, video, desktop videoconferencing, and group document delivery are the features requiring ATM. If multimedia is employed locally and wide area ATM connection is provided by an interchange carrier to other distant ATM networked sites, building connectivity is moving to Fast Ethernet. ATM becomes the vehicle for interconnecting the buildings of a campus.

Where ATM is employed as building or campus backbone interconnecting 10M- or 100-bps Ethernet floor LANs, ATM acts as a bridging service and requires the employment of three LAN emulation servers, including the LAN emulation server itself, the LAN emulation configuration server, and a broadcast unknown server.

FDDI Backbone Network

The standard for campus backbone networks has been an FDDI network constructed with routers interconnected by dual fiber rings. The hubs that interconnect workgroups and workers on a given floor are connected to the FDDI by fiber links that span the greater distance from the floor to a central FDDI router. Either a passive fiber card or a full FDDI card can be placed in the hub to gain access to the backbone.

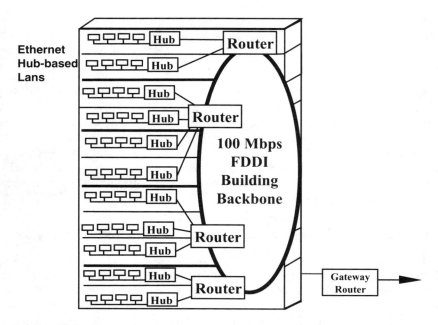

Exhibit 17-5. Connecting hubs to a router-based FDDI building backbone.

If the passive card is used, connection to the ring is at 10 or 16M bps. If the full FDDI card is placed in the hub, the connection speed from the hub to the ring router is at 100M bps. An FDDI ring is created by placing two FDDI cards (in some cases, a single four-port card can be employed) in a set of routers. These routers are then interconnected by a set of dual fiber cable to form a building or campus ring. A third FDDI card or passive fiber card is placed in the router to link back to the LAN hub. Such an FDDI backbone connection is portrayed in Exhibit 17-5, with hubs serving as the office access to the backbone ring.

HIGH-BANDWIDTH CAMPUS BACKBONE NETWORKS

Looking more closely at a campus situation, we can see quite clearly how the placement of a limited set of switches can be more cost-effective than employing router-based, shared-bandwidth, FDDI backbones. The complete FDDI campus backbone is then constructed by placing a router with two FDDI cards in the first floor of each building and stringing dual sets of multimode fiber around the campus, from building to building connected to a router in each building. One of the routers on the ring can serve as a gateway router to off-campus networks and to the Internet. Otherwise, a server is connected to the ring to perform the gateway function.

Fast Ethernet Backbone Networks

To access an FDDI ring from a hub we either need to encapsulate our LAN-addressed packet inside an FDDI-addressed packet, termed "tunneling" the LAN packet, or we need to translate Ethernet to FDDI and then back to Ethernet on the other end of the ring. This complexity, delay, and cost in such translation has led to the creation of a faster version of the standard LAN protocol, Ethernet.

Although only Pentium-class computers (or PowerPC computers) workstations can make use of 100M-bps Fast Ethernet, it is quickly finding a home as a fast backbone network connecting 10M-bps Ethernet switches. Ethernet at 100M bps can serve as fast transport between switching hubs or Ethernet switches or it can serve as a complete building backbone.

Further, Fast Ethernet can serve as fast campus backbone network interconnecting Fast Ethernet building backbones. Fast Ethernet can replace FDDI as both a building and a campus backbone, offers the same transport speed of 100M bps in a nonshared fashion, and maintains the same protocol and addressing throughout the complete campus network. The simplicity of this design as well as its low cost is quickly persuading companies to convert to this structure as an extension of what they already have installed (Exhibit 17-6).

In early release, prior to the 1998 standard specifications from the Gigabit Ethernet Alliance, a number of vendors have offered Gigabit Ethernet switches for campus and large building backbone networks. These switches employ a hybrid protocol with Layer 2 media access control (MAC) remaining traditional Ethernet, while Layer 1 is the fiber channel protocol using either multimode or single mode fiber. Gigabit Ethernet is designed to interconnect 100M-bps Fast Ethernet switches and thus will be a strong competitor to existing FDDI and the emerging ATM backbone networks.

ATM Backbones

ATM switches can be used to create a backbone network that cross-connects the hubs that interconnect the floor traffic. These ATM switches can be used to construct a building backbone network or extended to create a campuswide backbone network, much as can be constructed with FDDI and Fast Ethernet.

ATM in the Building

When an ATM switch is used to cross-connect floor hubs, an ATM access module must be placed in each hub, and a set of LAN emulation servers must be connected to the backbone ATM switches. Traditional Ethernet or Token Ring LAN packets are then segmented into ATM cells by the access modules. The access module then requests an address translation from the

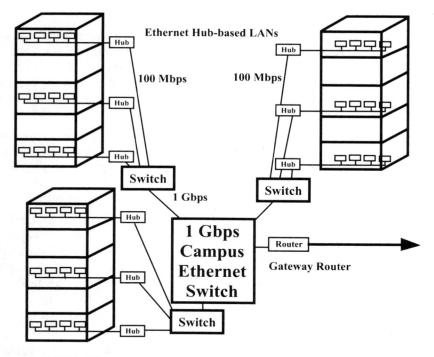

Exhibit 17-6. 1G-bps interbuilding campus backbone network.

ATM LAN emulation servers in the backbone and then readdresses the cells with ATM addresses to traverse the ATM network to the destination Ethernet segment. The reverse of this process is then performed by the ATM access module in the receiving hub. These ATM access modules, commonly called Proxy LAN emulation clients (LECs), act as bridging devices to bridge the traffic flowing from an Ethernet network to an ATM network, and bridging back again on the egress side.

ATM Campus Backbone

When the complete campus requires very high bandwidth to interconnect the buildings (155M or 622M bps) and multimedia traffic is being transported, a set of ATM switches can be placed at the heart of the campus with media, application, and file servers centrally attached to the backbone switches. These servers attract much of the traffic over the network and thus require very high entry speed between the servers and the network. LAN emulation servers are usually moved out from the building backbone to the campus ATM backbones when most of the traffic flows across campus generally supporting up to 1000 users (Exhibit 17-7).

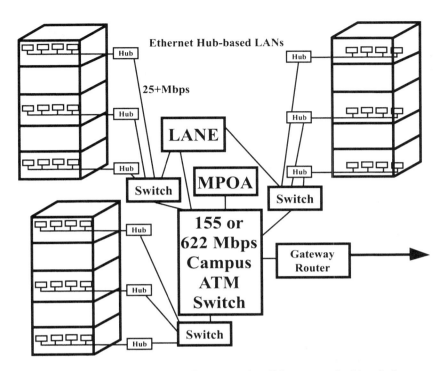

Exhibit 17-7. An ATM switch connecting Ethernet switching hubs.

Where larger communities are served, multiple separate LAN emulation servers can be created, specialized to a particular set of buildings. High-performance workgroups are separated from the regular LAN connections in the buildings and interconnected with their own workgroup ATM switch, which is then directly attached either to the campus or to a building ATM backbone network.

AVAILABLE WIDE AREA NETWORK CHOICES

Traditionally, access from the campus to wide area networking has been performed by employing a gateway router that can bridge local and wide area networks (WANs), perform required packet reformatting, and address translations and interpretations. T1 bridged routers, frame relay, and ATM networks are the current prime choices for providing high bandwidth across a wide area.

The conventional WAN is router-based, providing TCP/IP connectivity. The network is constructed as a set of autonomous networks that are interconnected by border routers. Such a network is accessed by a gateway router from individual buildings or campuses.

The individual routers that make up a TCP/IP WAN have traditionally been connected by full or fractionalized private T1 lines that have been leased from the telephone companies. Each router link requires such a connection and frequently a mesh of such lines connects all the routers. Usually the routers are located at the sending building locations, with the T1 links spanning the distance between the individual routers, providing an asynchronous bridging function.

Interconnecting many gateway routers to form an IP mesh network becomes very expensive as the distance grows. Each connection is composed of the two links on both ends to the public cross-connect network and the multiplexed usage of the public backbone over the distance to be traversed. More frequently, these building gateway routers connect only to a single central site for an application server, e-mail store-and-forward, Web sites, and a corporate file server. In this case, the private lines between the routers can be eliminated, since most traffic goes to one central site. When occasionally traffic must go end site to end site, the central router can route the traffic back over the connecting destination end site to the central router.

This network architecture, although it eliminates the interrouter connecting private lines, still creates a number of problems. First, there are a large number of links required from the distant locations to the central site. These links are very costly, each incurring many thousands of dollars per month based on the distance covered, the speed of the link, and the number of carrier companies employed in the interlinking. The farther the distance, the larger the cost. Because these separate links are not combined into a network service, these connections are difficult to manage.

A frame relay network should provide significant savings over an equivalent private line network. By employing a frame relay network to connect many locations to a central site, 20 percent savings should be achievable compared to a standard private line design regardless of the comparable speed used. This is regardless of whether we compare a 64K-bps private line to frame relay 64K-bps service or a 1.5M-bps private line vs. 1.5M-bps frame relay service.

Furthermore, for the many-to-many requirement, a still larger savings should be achievable approaching a 30 percent reduction. Frame relay service still requires the customer to lease at full price a short, private line access link to the location of the edge relay switch of the vendor. However, significant savings should be achievable over the long-haul distance with frame relay service. This results from the opportunity to statistically share the facilities and from dramatically reducing the number of individual, long-distance, end-to-end, private line links required to connect each end customer site to all the others in a many-to-many connection.

On the other hand, benefits from network management services can be achieved if the frame relay service is provided by one carrier and only short private lines connect users at each end point. Top quality network management can be achieved, since the network and its facilities are all under one carrier's control.

Using Public Frame Relay Networking to Bridge Locations

Frame relay addresses the problems raised by a national connection. Frame relay service does this by substituting a national, high-speed, public, packet-switched, shared network for the many individual private lines that would normally need to be established. Although private line links must be established from each location to the closest entry point of the national frame relay network, these links are decidedly shorter and thus much less expensive. A short T1 link to a connection may be $500 for a full 1.5M bps down to $200/month for a 32- to 64K-bps subchannel of a private line. A T1 private line from New York to Seattle, on the other hand, would cost thousands of dollars a month, mostly from the distance charges.

Charges for frame relay have been dropping. Since the public frame relay network is a shared-use network, the pricing is reduced. Ideally, frame relay is intended to be an on-demand, pay-as-you-use network with dramatically reduced price compared with building your own private network with long and leased T1 private lines. Ideally, the public frame relay network would be the equivalent of a dial-up high-speed packet network. This is considered to be a switched virtual circuit (SVC) network in terms. Such a presubscribed and pay-as-you-use public data network would require the carrier provider, on receiving a call setup message from your router, to dynamically pick each sequential link in the path of the end-to-end frame relay network that you would utilize.

Further, the carrier would need to dynamically update the route selection table in each node in the frame relay network that you temporarily use to create a virtual path for your transmission. This is projected to reduce a user's national network connectivity cost by up to 70 percent over a national, dedicated, private line network. Unfortunately, this dynamic update of switch tables is not yet a reality. What is offered is the ability to contract for a stated period of time a "temporarily permanent virtual path" or a permanent virtual circuit (PVC) in terms.

On placing an order with the carrier and leasing a line to the carrier's point of presence (POP) closest to each of your sites a company can have a 24-hr/day, 30 days/month, shared piece of a public high-speed network. This permanently shared piece of the network costs about 80 percent of what a private line network would cost. In fact, the distance portion of the private line facility is a shared portion of the carrier's digital cross-connect

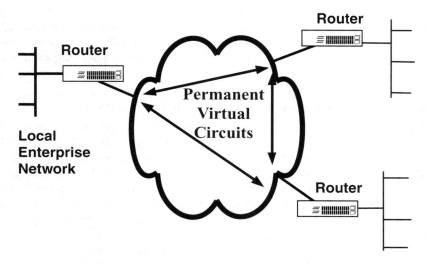

Exhibit 17-8. Frame relay network composed of permanent virtual circuits.

network anyway, with your portion being prereserved as a PVC. Exhibit 17-8 represents a frame relay network established as a set of PVCs.

To establish a "permanent circuit" between sites 1, 2, and 3, one of two modes of operation would be employed. In the standard approach, the customer would subscribe with the carrier for PVCs from site 1 to site 2, from site 1 to site 3, and from site 2 to site 3. The carrier would then provide the customer a set of frame relay addresses to place in the customer's router. This router will then translate the IP addresses to frame relay addresses and place these new addresses in each packet prior to sending them to the frame relay network to be forwarded to a specific site.

These temporary addresses are called data link control identifiers (DLCIs). Each port can specify up to 1024 DLCIs — in other words, up to 1024 PVCs per port. Fortunately, frame relay is a fully duplexed, bidirectional network requiring only one setup to establish both directions of the communication (differing from its big brother network, ATM, which requires a separate call setup for each direction of the communication path). However, like ATM, frame relay employs a different DLCI address at each end of the link (and unseen by the subscriber, a whole string of sequential DLCIs for each link along the way to the destination final leg link). To send a packet from site 1 to site 2, the customer's router must place DLCI 100 in every packet.

Customer participation in frame relay addressing has been considered enough of a hurdle that many carriers offer the preferred option of the carrier creating the frame relay addresses for the customer using the carrier's within-network router and database to perform the translation from IP to DLCI addresses. Under this option, the customer submits IP packets with IP addresses from the customer's router to the carrier's router (which is on the edge of the frame relay network). The carrier's router will then perform the address translation on both ends of the frame relay network, with the customer sending and receiving standard IP packets with which they have years of experience. As far as the customer perceives, with this approach frame relay is merely an extension of the local IP networks.

Interfacing Frame Relay with Other Networks

Since frame relay is a carrier-provided network service, existing protocols (such as the widely popular IP protocol, the IBM Systems Network Architecture [SNA], the Telco ISDN), and even voice can be carried over it with a significant reduction in cost and the added advantage of having a carrier-managed wide area linkage.

Frame Relay and ATM Interworking

The ATM and frame relay forums have approved two methods by which these two networks can be interconnected. Under network interworking, devices on the frame relay network must be knowledgeable about the ATM network and capable of performing the frame relay to ATM mapping. This includes the mapping for the frame relay service-specific convergence sublayer (FR-SSCS) functions of the ATM, AAL-5 adaptation layer at the upper portion of the ATM Layer 2 protocol. In another frame relay/ATM interworking method, the service interworking method, devices on both the ATM and frame relay networks are not required to know anything about the other network protocol.

To customer premise equipment (CPE) on a frame relay network, the entire network appears as frame relay. The same is true of CPE on the ATM network. To accomplish this protocol isolation, an FR/ATM interworking function (IWF) has been defined and performed by a device sitting as a bridge between the two networks. The IWF node must translate frame relay DLCI addresses to ATM virtual path indicators (VPIs) and virtual channel indicators (VCIs). Current public wide area frame relay and ATM offerings are provided only by setting up PVCs. In the future, it is anticipated that both frame relay and ATM networking will also be offered as "on-demand, pay-as-you-use" SVC services. Both call-setup messaging and dynamic route allocation must then be handled by the IWF interface unit for both sides of the connection.

This will be a sizable task. Exhibit 17-9 depicts frame relay connecting local networks to a wide area ATM network through a standard IWF node.

247

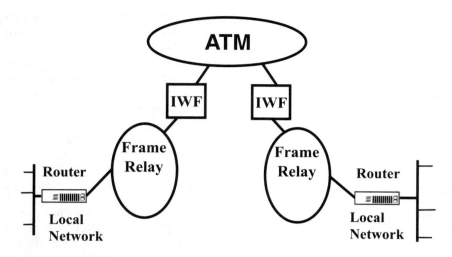

Exhibit 17-9. Frame relay connecing local networks to ATM through IWF.

This IWF node, usually a router with frame relay and ATM access cards, and the IWF address conversion and packet segmentation software.

In the early stages of ATM and frame relay interworking, most prefer to think of ATM as a low-level physical connection technology employed by frame relay service. In fact, much of public frame relay has been implemented by the RBOCs and the interexchange carriers (IE) with ATM as the actual transporting vehicle. The customer buys frame relay service, but that service is provided with an ATM backbone. Ultimately, frame relay and ATM will be considered as two services, each with its own special audience and employing IWF interconnection points as the translation and interconnection nodes between the two network protocols.

Frame relay service was designed as a data-only networking scheme due to the bursty nature of data, which in the past was incompatible with the continuous flow required for voice traffic. Now many companies are beginning to recognize the savings they could gain by employing their frame relay network to carry voice traffic along with their data traffic. Voice savings of 25 to 30 percent have been incurred by connecting a company's PBX to a common multimedia access switch that is shared with the company's data traffic.

The approach taken is to first convert the analog voice to digital form using sampling and pulse code modulation resulting in 8-b words at a 64-bps transfer rate. This digital representation is then compressed to remove pauses and hesitation (Bell estimates the average pause time per call at 2.5 s). This compressed, digitally represented voice set of bytes is then placed into packets (about 4000 bytes per packet), addressed to the appropriate destination, and sent forward on a 64K-bps link to the frame relay network. At the receiving end it is desirable to set up large buffers so the message can be reassembled with all the pauses and hesitations as they originally occurred. Generally, frame relay does not provide the same quality of voice as the public circuit switched telephone network, but for many businesses, the cost savings and management capability of voice over frame relay will override the modest quality degradation.

ATM NETWORKS: PUBLIC CARRIERS AS VIRTUAL CIRCUIT PROVIDERS

Where a company has achieved the speed and quality of service (QoS) control of transmission locally and wishes to connect dispersed locations and still maintain ATM speed and the QoS features, a public carrier's ATM networking service can be contracted to provide continuous ATM service that can be used in creating an end-to-end wide area ATM connection. Moreover, the complete range of ATM speeds from 51M to 622M bps can be publicly contracted for this wide area ATM connection. However, only the establishment of a permanent connection (PVC service) is currently publicly provided by most public carriers, although AT&T has announced a SVC ATM service.

With carrier-provided wide area PVC ATM service, businesses use the carrier as if it were providing a private line connection between their sites. They preestablish a 155M-bps PVC from one location to the other. The two end-point ATM switches treat the public connection as if it where a private line between the locations. Although they locally, dynamically create SVC connections, when they bridge sites using the public ATM network, they do not attempt to dynamically set up a circuit over the public network. What they do is only route the traffic to an available, preestablished PVC as if they were switching to a line connecting the sites.

The switches on each end dynamically establish their connection and disconnection locally, but the public connection is always available for use as a link between the local ATM switch port much like a permanently leased line. Either a single IXC (such as AT&T) or an RBOC telephone company (such as Ameritech) can provide the wide area ATM PVC connecting service.

PUBLIC CARRIERS PROVIDE JOINT ATM NETWORK

An RBOC can provide a local ATM PVC connection. However, when a company needs to cross the country, one has some choice in the connection. One can establish the PVC service either with an IXC — such as AT&T, Sprint, or MCI — or with a mixture of an IEC and two RBOCs. A major problem may occur when a business wishes to employ a mixture of carriers to create an end-to-end ATM network. The two local carriers need to create links to the national IXC, and the three companies need to set up a set of end-to-end PVCs that create a link across the multiple carriers to the destination.

This is a difficult circuit to set up initially, and it is virtually impossible to manage as a unit today due to the reluctance of the carriers to allow management across their boundaries.

EMERGING GLOBAL OPTIONS

Partnering is the strategy employed by the carriers to create global high-bandwidth connection, such as the planned AT&T and British Telecom (BT) agreement.

Sprint, France Telecom, and Deutsche Telekom have established Globe I as their joint world communication vehicle. Beyond using the carrier consortia, organizations — such as Sandia Laboratories in Arizona — are using 155M-bps ATM satellite links to interconnect their site to a number of national supercomputer research centers such as that at the University of Illinois, and to laboratories such as Lawrence Livermore in California. Sandia establishes two one-way links (one in each direction) and can interconnect locations without the problems of establishing long fiber connections to a land-based ATM network. Motorola has announced its own satellite network for providing global 56K-bps to 155M-bps data connection to and from any location on the globe.

SUMMARY

Users continue to seek faster networks for metropolitan, national, and international connection. As users, equipped with high-performance computers seek to transport more information and multimedia over faster local networks, the push for high-speed corporate networks increases. This has led toward Fast Ethernet and ATM for the local interconnection.

Moreover, the national and global distribution of corporations and a requirement to communicate with suppliers and customers, as well as distant corporate employees at a speed equivalent to local connection, are driving the deployment of fiber-based connection locally, nationally, and globally and the employment of ATM and soon 1-Gbps Ethernet protocols. As more complicated applications with distributed databases and Web server-based information are added to corporate networks, the endless cycle requiring more speed to more locations will continue.

Chapter 18
Voice and Data Network Integration

Larry Schessel

VOICE OVER INTERNET PROTOCOL (VOIP) is the enabling technology for this service integration. In short, 64Kbps voice is converted into data packets and transferred over the data backbone. The savings of voice and data over a single corporate network can be considerable and the technology exists. But where does a company begin? This article reviews the enabling technologies and presents a viable private network evolution strategy that takes advantage of current technologies and standards. Savings are realized almost immediately.

VOICE AND DATA NETWORKS

Companies with private voice networks own one or more private branch exchanges (PBXs) to deliver the service. A PBX is the switching element that link two users together in a voice connection. PBXs can be broken done into the following basic functional components:

- Wiring: PBXs require dedicated wiring to each telephone in the company. This allows employees to call other employees connected to the PBX. To gain access to the public service telephone network (PSTN), PBXs require outside lines purchased from the local public telephone company.
- Hardware: PBX hardware includes line cards terminating the local wiring, a switch network that makes the connection between two telephones, and servers for PBX software.
- Software: PBX software controls the call setup and features such as call forwarding, call transfer, and call hold; software also provides operation and maintenance support as well as per-call statistics.

Companies with multiple locations require dedicated PBXs at each site and public leased lines connecting the multiple PBXs into a single logical network.

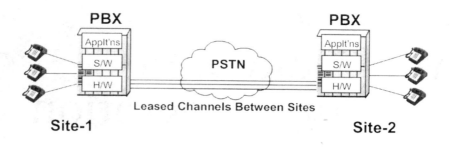

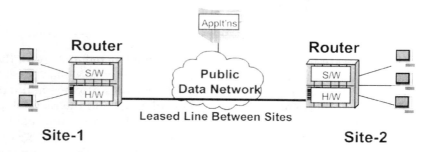

Exhibit 18-1. Comparison between private voice and data networks.

Private data networks are delivered using equipment known as routers and hubs. Similar to voice networks, data networks also require dedicated wiring between the different network elements and to each desktop. PCs, servers, printers, and scanners are some of the data devices that can be connected to the network to deliver specific services. Once networked, these devices communicate with each other, passing information in the form of data packets. Exhibit 18-1 compares the voice and data network topologies.

VOICE OVER INTERNET PROTOCOL

When a user picks up and dials the telephone, the PBX provides dial tone, collects digits, and routes the call based on entered digits. In routing the call, the PBX sets up a dedicated connection between the two users. As the users speak into their phones, the PBX converts the analog voice into digital signals and sends the digitized voice across the connection at a rate of 64Kbps. The PBX converts the analog signal to digital format by sampling the analog voice every 125 microseconds and converting the voice sample to an 8-bit digital representation. Digitized voice is converted back to an analog signal at the terminating end of the connection.

IP data networks, on the other hand, handle device communication by packaging information into logical envelopes known as packets, addressing

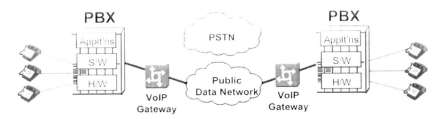

Step-1 Introduce VoIP Gateways for Inter-PBX Links

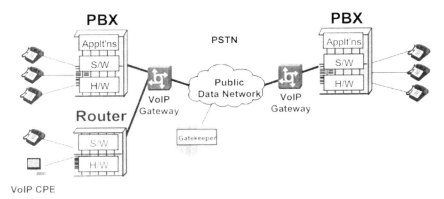

Step-2 Introduce VoIP Gatekeeper and CPE

Exhibit 18-1. *(Continued)*

the packets with destination information, and routing the packets through the network. Each network node looks at the addressing information and passes the packet onto the next network node until the packet arrives at its final destination. This routing method is connectionless because there is no dedicated connection between origination and termination as there is with a voice connection. A side benefit of connectionless communication is the fact that bandwidth is only required when there is information to send.

VoIP merges voice and data technologies into one ubiquitous voice service. Analog voice signals are sampled and digitized the same as the steps performed by the voice network. However, rather than send the 64Kbps digitized signals over dedicated voice channels, the digitized voice is packetized and sent over the IP data network. Furthermore, bandwidth efficiencies can be realized if the voice signal is compressed prior to packetization. Voice compression can lower bandwidth demands as low as 4Kbps while maintaining near toll-quality voice. This means that a single 64Kbps channel that normally carries a single voice conversation in the voice network can carry up to 16 voice conversations in the data network.

To support call control, the International Telecommunication Union (ITU-T) has standardized the H.323 protocol. H.323 describes terminals, equipment, and services for multimedia communication over a local area network (LAN), voice being just one service supported. Other recommendations within the H.323-Series include H.225 packet and synchronization, H.245 control, H.261 and H.263 video codecs, G.711, G.722, G.728, G.729, and G.723 audio codecs, and the T.120-series of multimedia communications protocols. Taken as a whole, these recommendations provide the standards to which many backbone, access, and customer premise equipment vendors are developing VoIP components and guaranteeing interoperability. Cisco, for example, has integrated H.323 protocols and voice capabilities into each of their newest routers. Microsoft and Intel also have H.323-compatible products for voice and data communications. The next section provides an overview of product categories.

VoIP PRODUCTS

H.323 VoIP products can be broken out into the following general product categories that loosely map to network layers:

- **Customer premise equipment (CPE):** Originally, H.323 CPE was mostly developed for multimedia communication. Products such as Microsoft Netmeeting, Intel Proshare®, and PictureTel LiveLAN™ were marketed for their desktop video and data sharing capabilities. More recently, however, CPE products have been developed that are more focused on IP-voice communication. The Selsius Ethernet phone, for example, resembles a standard phone but connects to an Ethernet port rather than a PBX port. Symbol Technologies has developed a wireless H.323 telephone that also connects directly into an Ethernet port.
- **Network infrastructure:** Network equipment includes standard routers, hubs, and switches. Voice, however, is very susceptible to network delays and packet loss. Router features such as random early drop/detect, weighed fair queuing, reservation protocol (RSVP), IP precedence, compressed real-time protocol, and multi-class multi-link PPP have been developed to address these issues and are prescribed in a converged network. Asynchronous transfer mode (ATM) network equipment also supports quality of service parameters and enables the administrator to set up dedicated private virtual connections (PVCs) between sites.
- **Servers:** A major VoIP benefit is the fact that it builds on the Internet model where there is a clear separation between network infrastructure and network applications. While network infrastructure provides

the packet transport, servers support the applications. The H.323 gatekeeper server, for example, supports call control functions; an accounting, authorization, and administration (AAA) server provides billing and accounting; and network management typically requires a simple network management protocol (SNMP) server.

- **Gateways:** It will still be a long time before one sees the data network handling all voice communication. As an interim step, gateways will be necessary to link the new IP-based voice services with existing public and private voice networks. Gateways also provide a good evolutionary step for companies to selectively choose how and where they will apply VoIP for low risk and high returns.

VOICE AND DATA NETWORK INTEGRATION

So, the technology, standards, and products exist to migrate voice onto the corporate data network. But where does a company begin in order to minimize network risk and optimize savings? There are two major areas for network cost savings in a voice network: PBX private service (single location and multi-location) and public service (local and long distance). There is also another category representing value-added services that are enabled due to the voice, data, and video integration. These value-added services offer potential for companies to reengineer existing services such as automatic call distribution (ACD) services and build new services such as click-to-dial, where an Internet user can access a company's operator through the Web.

The following sections discuss each category in further detail. Included is a proposed network integration plan as well as future value-added services to consider when building the next-generation converged communication network. Refer to Exhibit 18-2 for a summary of the proposed private voice network evolution.

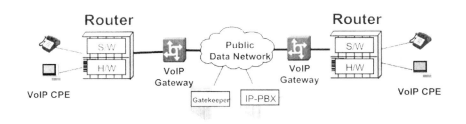

Step-3 Replace PBX with IP-PBX

Exhibit 18-2. Stepwise private voice network evolution.

Private Voice Service

Purchasing a PBX is a big decision for a company. For one thing, it is expensive; and once purchased, the company is locked into the specific PBX vendor for hardware/software upgrades and maintenance. Companies are also limited to the call control features supported by the PBX so that little differentiation is possible between themselves and their competition.

In an IP world, networks are built in layers. Companies first choose the underlying infrastructure, for example, routers, switches, or ATM equipment. Then, companies choose the application protocol; IP for VoIP. Finally, they decide the specific services, servers, and CPE that they wish to run over the network. Taken as a whole, the decision is just as important as the PBX decision. But taken separately, each decision is much lower in cost and risk; new technologies can be introduced with little or no impact to other network layers.

VoIP assumes that there is already a data infrastructure supporting IP services; IP data infrastructure is a mature market with many third- and fourth-generation products. VoIP, however, is in its infancy. The most mature of the products are VoIP gateways providing interworking between the voice and data networks. Gateways terminate voice interfaces from a PBX or public voice switch and convert the signaling and voice to IP protocol. Gateways then send the information across the IP network to either another gateway or a VoIP CPE.

Gateway-to-gateway communication is a good first step for a company introducing VoIP capabilities. Back-to-back gateways provide an alternative to dedicated inter-PBX trunks, typically leased lines — which are very expensive if purchased from a public carrier. Instead, gateway-to-gateway service allows the network administrator to redirect leased-line inter-PBX traffic over the internal corporate IP network. Gateway costs can be recovered in months, depending on the number of locations and distance.

Gateway-to-gateway communication can also be used to link a remote office to the corporate office PBX. The remote office would appear as one or more extensions off the corporate office PBX, and traffic to and from the remote office would be routed through the PBX. Cisco, for example, has integrated VoIP capabilities into both its small remote office routers as well as larger corporate office routers to support such an application.

Introducing H.323 CPE to the network is a good second step in the corporate network VoIP evolution. This enables IP users to originate and terminate calls directly from their PC, Ethernet phone, or wireless IP-phone. IP devices add a level of network complexity due to the potentially large number of users, security issues, and varying IP device types. The H.323 gatekeeper provides the needed user authorization and routing capabilities. Many vendors have introduced gatekeepers, both integrated into the router and contained on separate servers. Both solutions offer viable alternatives.

With the combination of gateway, gatekeeper, and IP device, companies can begin to introduce business solutions to work at home and CTI applications. Basically, the IP device can be logged into the corporate data network at the same time as calls are originated and terminated from the device. Help Desk operators working from home, for example, would require only a single link into the corporate data network to answer customer questions and access corporate information.

The third major step in evolving the private voice network is fully replacing the PBX with a next-generation IP-PBX. As discussed earlier, PBXs rely on wiring to the desktop and provide hardware and software for call control, accounting, etc. In a VoIP network, Ethernet wiring provides the desktop wiring, the data backbone provides the transport, and servers provide the PBX call control features. The wiring and data backbone exist, while companies such as Selsius and NBX are introducing the server and CPE components. It will not be long before IP-PBX features match and surpass capabilities of current PBXs and the IP-PBX becomes a viable alternative.

Value-Added Services

One area where IP-PBX features will surpass PBX capabilities will be value-added services. These are services that take advantage of voice, data, and video integration as well as IP network and device capabilities to delivery services not possible on a PBX. Some of these services offer significant cost savings, while others offer revenue-generating opportunities. Following are several value-added service examples to consider when implementing a VoIP network. Note that many other services are possible by adding new servers to the network similar to adding new Web sites to an IP network.

- **Unified messaging.** Most corporate managers receive voicemail, e-mail, and faxes on a daily basis. While timely information is one of the keys to a successful business, it is also difficult to manage the information, especially when it arrives in different forms and locations. Unified messaging consolidates the different information into a single mailbox accessible from a telephone, Web site, or pager. The unified messaging server supports media conversion so that e-mails can be read to phone users, faxes can be redirected to local fax machines, and voicemail can be converted to audio files and played back on a computer. Future enhancements may include videomail and interactive content.
- **IP call center/click-to-dial.** The number of Internet users and the amount of Internet commerce are growing faster than most estimates. Intel, for example, just announced that it is generating over $1 billion in revenue per month directly from the Internet. Cisco also generates

over 50 percent of its revenue from direct Internet sales. VoIP offers further opportunity to reach customers through the Internet by enabling direct and immediate interactions with customer service representatives. The click-to-dial application enables users to click a Web site button to automatically set up a VoIP call between user and operator. IP call centers extend the model so that the call completes between IP user and IP attendant, thereby lowering 800 service costs.

- **Active directory services.** There is much electronic information within a corporation and contained on public servers. Active directories enable users to interact with the directory, potentially clicking an employee name and connecting to the user through the Internet. This service integrates the data server with VoIP capabilities and strengthens the argument for integrated voice and data services.
- **Virtual second line.** Eventually, VoIP devices will be in widespread use within the corporation and residence. Much of their success will depend on how they are addressed. Dialing an IP address to reach these devices is cumbersome and doomed to failure because it changes the way people are accustomed to making a call. The possibility exists, however, to address the IP device with a standard telephone number. This strategy merges seamlessly with today's telephones and cellular phones and provides a good evolutionary path to the next-generation communication network.
- **Follow-me/find-me.** Once the IP device has an assigned telephone number, many standard telephone features can be carried over from the PSTN. Call forwarding, call transfer, and three-way calling are examples. Follow-me service allows users to predefine a search list of telephone numbers at which they may be contacted (e.g., work number, home number, and cellular number). When an incoming call arrives, the service rings each number on the list and, once located, transfers the incoming call to one's current location. It is an intuitive step to add the IP device telephone number to the list and direct incoming calls to the IP device when active.
- **Desktop video conferencing.** VoIP specifically refers to handling voice service over the IP network. The benefits of VoIP, however, extend beyond voice. If the devices at either end of a VoIP connection support voice, video, and data, then the underlying signaling will set up a multimedia connection. No user interface change is required; the user still dials a standard telephone number. For example, a company that builds an internal VoIP network can take advantage of full multimedia communication between employees. Gateways can provide the interoperability with older telephone devices and links to the public voice network. Not only are costs reduced because voice services are moved onto the private data network, but internal services are enhanced with video and data as well.

Public Voice Services

Public voice carriers have also recognized the potential cost savings and new revenue from VoIP solutions. Most carriers have ongoing trials to better define market segments and decide where best to apply internal resources. With the convergence of voice, data, and video, additional carriers are entering the foray. Internet service providers (ISPs), competitive local exchange carriers (CLECs), inter-LATA exchange carriers (IXCs), and cable companies have all begun investing in VoIP solutions. Some are looking to enhance existing services, while others are looking to compete with incumbent carriers.

This is all very good news to companies looking for competitive public service rates because increased competition is expected to drive down local and long-distance service rates. Already, VoIP-based companies such as ITXC have begun to offer cut-rate international and long-distance calling card services.

It is also good news for companies evolving their networks to VoIP solutions. In the short term, they can be assured that vendor priority is kept on standards and interoperability. Longer term, as carriers begin offering VoIP public services, company voice traffic can seamlessly transfer from private to public networks without the need for gateways, moving end-to-end via VoIP.

CONCLUSION

The communication paradigm is on the verge of change, signaling a new generation of lower-cost voice, video, and data services. Companies have the opportunity to take advantage of this paradigm shift in a low-risk and cost-effective manner. VoIP is the enabling technology to begin integrating voice, video, and data services onto a single data backbone network. VoIP to PSTN gateways are a good first step to begin the convergence because they are established products with many competitors. Gatekeepers and IP CPE are close behind, with the potential to introduce new value-added services. Finally, there is the opportunity to rebuild the infrastructure with IP-PBXs and public VoIP offerings. This enables ubiquitous voice, video, and data services over a data backbone and offers services one can only begin to imagine.

Chapter 19
ATM Circuit Emulation Services

G. Thomas des Jardins

ASYNCHRONOUS TRANSFER MODE, OR ATM, is a term in which the word asynchronous literally means "not synchronous," or "not having the same period between occurrences." In contrast, traditional POTS (plain old telephone service) circuits are designed with the assumption that they will always be used with a reference timing source and are therefore synchronous.

In order to adapt the existing equipment base of circuit-oriented equipment to ATM, it is desirable to define some method for carrying the data normally encoded by a circuit over an ATM virtual circuit. The ATM Forum has written an interoperability specification to address emulating circuits using ATM virtual circuit (VC) technology.

This document, the "Circuit Emulation Service Interoperability Specification" (CES-IS), specifies two types of constant bit rate (CBR) service:

1. Structured DS1/E1 N*64 (Fractional S1/E1) service
2. Unstructured DS1/E1 (1.544M bps/2.048M bps) service

Both services are geared toward solving different types of problems.

STRUCTURED VERSUS UNSTRUCTURED, IN BRIEF

Structured service is designed to use an ATM network to provide low-rate voice traffic at many different points and is an "edge of the cloud"-oriented technology. Unstructured service is oriented toward the interior of the network cloud and allows the user to relay traffic straight through the network, but only between two points. This circuit emulation service is distinct from using circuits to carry ATM data, which is specified by other documents. Exhibit 19-1 compares structured versus unstructured service.

The next sections describe in more detail the circuit emulation services offered, how they are implemented, and how they are used. For purposes of illustrating their implementation and use, let's assume that a company

0-8493-0859-3/00/$0.00+$.50
© 2000 by CRC Press LLC

Exhibit 19-1. Structured versus unstructured circuit emulation service.

Feature	Structured	Unstructured
Bandwidth used	Uses bandwidth in cost-effective N*64 increments	Full DS1/E1 link rate
Timing	Supplied by network	Supplied by equipment
Facility data link	Terminates	Passes through
Configuration	Somewhat complex	Simple
Framing	ESF,SF	Useful for nonstandard types of framing since it does not require framing (see note)

Note: Although framing is not required in unstructured service, an optional feature allows for performance monitoring when the unstructured service uses superframe (SF), extended superframe (ESF), or G.107 framing; however when this feature is offered, it must be designed such that it can be disabled if desired.

desires to connect circuits across an ATM cloud. These may be either DS1 or E1. Therefore let's begin with a review of the characteristics of these circuits.

DISTINGUISHING CHARACTERISTICS OF CIRCUITS

Circuits are discussed in the context of three basic characteristics: how much, when, and what. More specifically:

1. "How much" refers to bandwidth, or how much of the circuit is actually in use.
2. "When" refers to timing. A signal is used to maintain clocking so that the bits are decoded correctly.
3. "What" refers to a framing scheme used to decode the bits, and for determining what all the bits are for. In addition, signaling information can be transmitted as well.

How Much Bandwidth. Constant bit rate circuits consist of some amount of bandwidth, which is usually either broken into 64K-bps blocks or utilized in its entirety. With regard to the two different types of circuit emulation service — structured and unstructured — a primary difference is whether the user is transmitting the circuits with "visibility" — that is, knowing how much of the circuit is in use (structured) — or as an opaque data stream (unstructured).

Briefly, a comparison of bandwidth ranges for structured versus unstructured service is as follows:

Service	El Bandwidth Range	DS1 Bandwidth Range
Structured	N = 1 to 24 × 64K bps	N = 1 to 31 × 64K bps
Unstructured	1.544	2.048

262

Timing. A timing source traceable to a primary reference source (PRS) must be supplied to the CBR circuit in order to keep it synchronized with the public network.

In the case of structured service, there are several means by which this timing source may be supplied. Structured timing options include:

- ATM link-derived timing (the ATM link must in turn receive its timing from a PRS-traceable source).
- An externally supplied source.
- A single clock source. For an entirely private network it may be possible to synchronize the entire network to a single clock source that is not PRS-traceable. Since there would be no interface to the public network, no timing slips would occur between the public and private networks.

Framing. Information used to align blocks of data, or frames, is also recovered from or imposed on the circuit. The framing specified in the CES-IS is the extended superframe (ESF) format. Two forms of signaling are supported: in-band using channel-associated signaling, and out-of-band, using basic service.

CIRCUIT EMULATION SPECIFICATIONS

In addition to the ATM Forum "Circuit Emulation Service Interoperability Specification" (CES-IS), circuit emulation is specified by the following documents:

- I-363, which specifies the various ATM adaptation layers (AALs).
- Request for Comment (RFC) 1573 "Evolution of the Interfaces Group of MIB-II."
- RFC 1406 "Definitions of Managed Objects for DS1 and E1 Interfaces."

There are many other standards and interoperability specifications as well. However, this chapter elucidates the operations of devices and services specified by the CES-IS.

Circuit Services: Theory and Description

With ATM, which is "not synchronous," rate adaptation is free. Circuits assume a reference timing source and are therefore synchronous. To adapt circuit-oriented equipment to ATM, a method is needed for carrying the data normally encoded by a circuit over an ATM virtual circuit.

Structured circuit services have extensive visibility into the data being carried across the network and can carry lesser amounts. Unstructured circuit service is provided with limited visibility into the data being carried, and only the full rate of the emulated technology can be transported.

Structured DS1/E1 service is a transparent implementation useful for fractional circuits and backhauls, where knowledge of the layout of the data is important. It is, however, more complex; by allowing portions of a circuit to be mapped to different VCs, "fractions" of bandwidth can be assigned to different locations or equipment.

Unstructured DS1/E1 service is an opaque implementation. No knowledge of the structure of the data being transmitted is presumed. This has the advantage of being simple, but it requires a whole circuit to be mapped to a single VC.

Structured DS1/E1 N*64 Service Description. The bandwidth is divided into N*64 portions and emulates a Fractional DS1 or E1 circuit. The service multiplexes N time slots, where each slot uses 64K bps. For DS1 (1.544M bps), $1 <= N <= 24$, and for E1 (2.048M bps) $1 <= N <= 31$.

The order is not required to be the same at both ends. Multiple fractional circuits can use the same CBR I/F and would receive separate VCs and might go to separate destinations.

Framing describes how data and signaling bits are packed. For DS1 equipment, extended superframe (ESF) is required to be supported and SF is optional. For E1, G.704 is required to be supported. Structured data transfer mode (SDT) is required to be used.

Structured AAL1 Requirements. Structured service may perform partial cell fill to reduce payload assembly delay. It must perform controlled frame slips. In the case of extended starvation (approximately 2.5 seconds, plus or minus .5 second), it must trigger trunk conditioning (i.e., a "red" alarm). It must provide common timing to the CBR side. This could be derived from an ATM-side primary reference source, an external source, other DS1/E1 circuits, or an internal nonstratum 1 oscillator.

DS1/E1 Unstructured Service Description. Unstructured circuit emulation service emulates a complete DS1 or E1 circuit. It is opaque as far as data is concerned. It has a 1:1 VC-to-circuit mapping. It can optionally decode framing for SF, ESF, or G.704 framing standards (thereby permitting better maintenance). It uses unstructured data transfer (UDT) and has well-defined timing requirements. It requires full cell fill.

Unstructured AAL1 Requirements. Unstructured service must provide appropriate timing traceable to PRS to the CBR side, and this timing has specific jitter and wander requirements. Because of the requirements for recovering timing, some schemes that derive timing from information contained within the cells may place derived requirements upon the cell delay variation of the connection used to connect the line.

For DS1/ESF, it is a requirement that the device terminate bit-oriented messages for yellow alarms and loopback. In general the device should work with facility data link by passing on performance report messages each second with cyclical redundancy checks and framing errors.

Configuration and Operation

Management of circuit emulation service (CES) interworking devices, and the services provided by them, is divided into two categories:

1. Management of the ATM link
2. Management of the circuit side of the link

Essentially, a single task is accomplished: communicating how CBR data is mapped on and off a VC.

Management

Management of CES devices is performed through the use of the CES management information base (MIB) to define the VC to fractional mapping (according to the ATM Forum's CES-IS, as well as RFC 1442 "Structure of Management Information for SNMPv2" and RFC 1406 "Definitions of Managed Objects for DS1 and E1 Interfaces").

CES ATM Requirements

The first requirement is that sufficient bandwidth be provided for the connection. This is indicated by setting the peak cell rate (PCR) for the connection appropriately; also cell delay variation (CDV) must account for F4/F5 OAM cells, though these are limited to 1 percent of line rate. The ATM virtual circuit payload type and cell loss priority should be 0, and the connection type must be a CBR. The VC can convey timing from a primary reference source to the CES interworking facility.

Playout Buffer and Cell Fill. If there is underflow — that is, not enough bits to fill a frame before it must be transmitted, the playout buffer has been starved. If there is overflow — that is, too many bits — the playout buffer has been consumed.

Playout latency refers to the average amount of time that the playout buffer contributes to the latency. Cell fill means that cells are not required to be completely used. Partially filled cells may be transmitted more quickly, thereby lowering latency but wasting bandwidth. Both sides must agree on how full a cell should be.

Role of CDV and PCR. When designing a box to emit cells at a given rate, an algorithm called a scheduler is constructed to control the cell emission. This algorithm, which is frequently implemented as a custom integrated circuit, must consider the possible rates that may be scheduled in various combinations and must emit cells to meet each connection's rate.

Some combinations of rates do not allow precise scheduling; for instance, two rates of 1/2 and 1/3 (of link rate) will conflict. Thus the scheduler must attempt to ensure that the average service a connection receives meets the constraints of the connection — the average rate, usually described as a peak cell rate (PCR), and the cell delay variation (CDV).

The amount of variance from the ideal position of a cell is known as CDV, which is defined as the difference between the cell's reference arrival time and the actual arrival time. Each device along a path contributes a certain amount of CDV to the connection, which is accumulated and added to the total CDV of the connection from end to end.

Essentially, all devices contribute a nonzero amount of CDV to a connection. The amount of variance that can be tolerated by a given connection is dependent on several factors, ranging from the amount of buffering built into the equipment to the nature of the traffic being transported.

Cell Delay Variation Tolerance. The maximum amount of CDV a device contributes is not defined by a specification. In fact, the ATM Forum CES-IS specifically states that the "CDV tolerance [CDVT] is considered a network option and is currently not subject to standardization." However, Bellcore documents have proposed an accumulated CDV level of 750 μs for a whole connection.

The maximum CDVT that can be tolerated, however, depends on two factors:

1. How much memory the device has to buffer cells while waiting to assemble a complete frame
2. The temporal value of the data to be lost when a cell arrives at a different cell slot from the desired one

If a connection is established with a certain CDVT, the connection is expressing to the network the bounds on the delay that can be tolerated by either of these two constraining factors.

Thus, when the network sets up the switched virtual circuit (SVC) or permanent virtual circuit (PVC), the path that the connection will be routed through will consider the CDV accumulated along that path and refuse to set up a connection that does not meet the required accumulate CDV (e.g., CDV < = CDVT).

Example: Adding Up CDVs. To fully define a CBR VC's traffic contract, the peak cell rate and the cell delay variation tolerance need to be specified. For example, suppose each device adds 10 μs CDV to the CDV on the connection (ATM Forum UNI version 3.1, page 322). If there are five devices in the path of the connection, the total CDV is 125 µs. Thus, if the contract specifies 150 as the CDVT, the connection would be permitted to be established.

Using FORE Systems' equipment, the CDVT defaults to 1,000 µs, and therefore the contract would indeed pass the traffic of the cell path 300. If the CDVT is set to 250 (the stated design parameter of the cell path 300) or even to 180 (the observed value), the traffic passes without cell loss. Just to prove that the switch would police correctly, if the CDVT is set to 50 you would observe the concomitant loss of cells.

The CDVs are simply added for the purposes of this example. Because the CDV describes the displacement of the cell from the ideal position in absolute terms, there is a nonzero chance that the first switch might delay, while the next switch might actually send a cell early. Thus the two CDVs might cancel each other out. Although this possibility exists, it would be poor engineering practice to count on this occurring, and therefore the CDVs are conservatively added up.

Tip for Customers. CDV is a part of any ATM network. When a company is requesting service, the service provider will want to know the maximum, allowable cell delay variation tolerance.

Cell delay variation is applicable to any connection with a PCR or SCR, such as a variable bit rate (VBR) or CBR connection, and is a parameter the customer will need to configure when setting up the PVC or SVC.

In the reassembly function, a buffer is used in which the stream is stored before it is transmitted. The buffer must be large enough to accommodate expected CDV and small enough so that excessive delays are not occurring in the circuit. The value is the maximum cell interarrival jitter that the reassembly process will tolerate without producing errors on the CBR interface.

Chapter 20
Routing and Routing Protocols
Michel Gilbert

IN THE LANGUAGE OF THE OPEN SYSTEM INTERCONNECTION (OSI) REFERENCE MODEL, a router is a network layer device responsible for routing traffic between subnetworks that make up a data internetwork. At its heart, a router is essentially a packet switch.

This definition relies upon a number of terms that merit exploration. The term "packet" refers to the transmission unit (known as a Protocol Data Unit) that moves from the network layer software in one system, across a network, to the network layer software in another system. A packet contains, among other things, the address of the source end station and the address of the destination end station. It is on this destination address that the router bases its decisions. End stations are the devices that generate or receive the vast majority of the packets moving through the network. They are, in essence, the reason why the network exists in the first place!

The terms subnetwork and internetwork are also not all that precisely used in the industry. For the purposes of this discussion, a subnetwork is defined as a collection of network resources that can be reached without needing to go through a router. If a message has to pass through a router to go from one end station to another, those two end stations are on differing subnetworks. And an internetwork is defined as a collection of two or more subnetworks connected using routers. This relationship is depicted in Exhibit 20-1.

In this context, the role of the router is straightforward: it receives packets transmitted by end stations (and possibly other routers) and routes them through the internetwork to the appropriate subnetwork. Once the packet has reached a router attached to the destination subnetwork, this router delivers it to the intended end station. Routers can also perform more advanced functions if the network layer protocol supports those functions. Some of these include the ability to fragment packets if necessary, or to

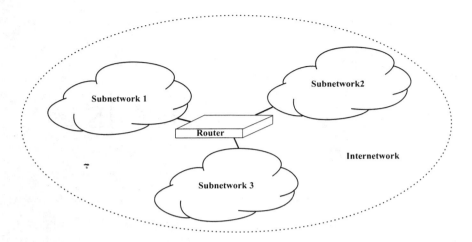

Exhibit 20-1. Routers, subnetworks, and internetworks.

---

notify transmitting end stations when packets are being discarded. Routers also provide some congestion control capabilities, although the vast majority of routers handle congestion by the simple expedient of dropping packets. Routers can also be fairly sophisticated packet filters, providing the network with a certain level of security.

Routing is sometimes confused with bridging. The distinction between the two lies in the Layer at which they operate. Routing is a network layer function. Routers operate on packets and make routing decisions based on the network layer address. Bridging is a data link layer function. Bridges operate on frames and make filtering and forwarding decisions based (directly or indirectly) on the media access control address.

It is important to note that the frame is the mechanism used to get a transmission from one end station to another within the same subnetwork. Packets ride within frames and are the transmission unit used to get a message from one end station to another anywhere in the internetwork. If the two end stations are in the same subnetwork, the packet will be placed in a frame by the transmitter and sent across the subnetwork to the intended recipient, possibly crossing one or more bridges. If the end stations are not in the same subnetwork, the packet will ride in one frame from the transmitter to a router, which will make a routing decision and forward the packet across the next subnetwork in a new frame.

Within a subnetwork, bridging software has to build tables and keep track of potentially all of the devices within the subnetwork. And those tables do not usually contain entries for any end station in a different subnetwork.

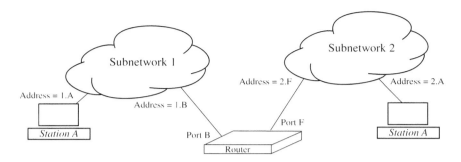

Exhibit 20-2. Routers, subnetworks, and addressing.

Routers, on the other hand, build tables that list all of the subnetworks and how to reach them.

ROUTING IN THE NETWORK LAYER

The network layer protocol in an internetwork is responsible for end-to-end routing of packets. There are many network layer protocols in the industry, but they all share some common characteristics. All of them define a packet structure and an address format. All of them specify the types of service the network can provide, which may include such things as packet fragmentation, connectionless or connection-oriented service, and packet prioritization.

Key to the operation of the network layer protocol is the network layer address. The network layer address is hierarchically structured, with at least two basic segments defined. The first of these identifies a subnetwork, and the other identifies a particular end station within that subnetwork. Some network layer protocols define additional address fields, but these two fields are always present.

Each router or end station interface is assigned a network layer address that must be unique throughout the internetwork, much like each phone in the world must have a globally unique number so the telephone network can route the call. All of the devices that connect to the same subnetwork must agree on what the local subnetwork number is, as depicted in Exhibit 20-2. This global numbering strategy is the cement that binds the internetwork together, and makes it possible for routers to route packets.

A hierarchical address structure is only one of the things most modern network layer protocols have in common. The vast majority of these protocols also provide only a connectionless service and implement datagram-based networks. A connectionless service is one in which the upper

Exhibit 20-3. Common network layer protocols.

Network layer protocol	Address length	Address fields	Additional capabilities	Used in
Internet Protocol (IP)	4 octets (32 bits)	NETID (var.), Hostid (var.)	Fragmentation, nondelivery notification, subnetting	Internet, most network environments
Internetwork packet exchange (IPX) protocol	12 octets (96 bits)	Network (4), node (6), socket (2)	Automatic client addressing	NetWare
Datagram delivery protocol (DDP)	4 octets (32 bits)	Network (2), node (1), socket (1)	Automatic client addressing	AppleTalk
VINES internet protocol (VIP)	6 octets (48 bits)	Network (4), subnetwork (2)	Fragmentation, nondelivery notification, automatic addressing	VINES

layer protocol or application has no way to request an end-to-end relationship or "connection" with another end station. All it can do is provide the data to be sent and the address to which it is to be delivered. If there is any acknowledgment, flow control, or sequencing of messages to be done, the upper layer protocol or application will have to do it.

A datagram-based network is one in which the routers are unable to establish end-to-end circuits on which to carry traffic. Every packet received by a router is routed independently of the ones that precede and follow it. That makes it difficult to provide any guaranteed quality of service or capacity because the routers cannot predict where the next packet will come from, when it will arrive, and where it will be destined. If a network supports end-to-end circuits, the routers would at least know that packets will arrive on an established circuit, and expected loads could be defined at the time the circuit is established.

Exhibit 20-3 summarizes four of the major network layer protocols in use today, and their primary characteristics. All four of these define connectionless services and implement datagram-based internetworks.

IP has one of the most complex addressing structures, largely due to its role in the Internet. The boundary between the IP subnetwork number (called the NETID) and the end station number (called the HOSTID) is not fixed. It varies depending on the class of the address and the value of the subnet mask being used. IP defines five address classes, three of which are for deploying subnetworks. These are summarized in Exhibit 20-4.

One of the more difficult concepts in IP networks is the subnet mask. Logically, the purpose of the subnet mask is to take a particular NETID and

Exhibit 20-4. IP address classes.

Address class	Value of first octet	Length of NETID/use	Number of NETID	Number of HOSTID
Class A	1–126	1 octect	126	16,777,214
Class B	128–191	2 octets	16,382	65,534
Class C	192–223	3 octets	12,097,150	254
Class D	224–239	Multicast	N/A	N/A
Class E	240–255	Reserved	N/A	N/A

divide it into smaller subnetworks connected by routers. For example the Class B address 128.13.0.0 could be divided into 256 smaller networks designated as 128.13.1.0, 128.12.2.0, 128.13.3.0 (and so forth) using the 255.255.255.0 mask. This is known as subnetting. Conversely, the mask can be used by routers to summarize routes. For example, all of the Class C networks from 199.12.0.0 to 199.12.255.0 could be advertised as 199.12.0.0 using the 255.255.0.0 mask. This is called supernetting, or Classless Interdomain Routing (CIDR).

IP addresses are typically manually assigned to all devices. There are exceptions, however. Most notably, the Dynamic Host Configuration Protocol (DHCP) permits a DHCP server to dynamically "lease" addresses to end stations as they come online. IP can perform packet fragmentation if necessary. A fragmented packet stays fragmented until it reaches the destination end station, where it is reassembled.

The Internetwork Packet Exchange (IPX) address has three portions. The first two portions identify the subnetwork (called the network) and end station (called the node). The third portion is called the socket and identifies a particular protocol, application, or upper layer process in the end station. IPX has a unique approach to address assignment. The local subnetwork identifier (called a network number) is assigned at the local routers. IPX clients learn this number by querying the routers, and then adopt their own media access control address as their end station identifier (called a node number). This means IPX client addressing is automatic; only servers and routers need to be programmed.

Like IPX, Datagram Delivery Protocol (DDP) has a three-part address, the subnetwork portion (called the network number) is assigned to local routers, and the end-station portion (called the node number) is dynamically assigned. What differs is the assignment mechanism. A DDP end station searches for an end station number that is not in use by any other local end station and adopts it.

VINES Internet Protocol (VIP) is more like IP, with a simple two-part address. However, VIP does not support the concept of subnet masking. And VIP addressing is 100 percent automated. The local subnetwork number is provided by the Virtual Networking System (VINES) server, which has the address encoded on a hardware key required to enable the server software. The VINES client requests an end station number from the local server, which provides a function similar to that of DHCP in an IP internetwork.

Like IP, VIP packets can also be fragmented if necessary. However, VIP depends on an associated protocol called the Fragmentation Protocol to do the deed. Fragmented packets are reassembled by the next router in the path before being routed onwards.

It is important to note that routing, as a network layer function, is performed by any device that implements a network layer. This includes both end stations and routers. While it may seem odd to think of an end station performing a routing function, the routing process actually begins with the device that generates the packet. This device must determine if the destination end station lies within the local subnetwork or on a different subnetwork. Destinations that lie within the local subnetwork can be reached directly via the underlying network technology. This is known as direct routing or delivery. To reach destinations that lie on a different subnetwork requires the services of a router. The end station must be able to identify a local router that can provide the service and forward the packet to that device, a process known as indirect routing.

Routers also perform direct and indirect routing, but typically this action is performed on packets generated by end stations. The router examines the destination address within a packet it has received and performs direct routing if the destination is on a local subnetwork. If the destination is not on a local subnetwork, the router performs an indirect routing operation and passes the packet on to another router.

For either a router or end station to perform direct routing, it must have a mechanism for mapping the Network Layer address of the destination end station to the corresponding address in the underlying network (e.g., the Ethernet address or the Frame Relay DLCI). IP, DDP, and VIP depend on associated protocols to build and maintain local tables that provide this mapping. Because IPX uses the value of the media access control address as part of the network layer address, it has no need for such a table. Once this mapping has been accomplished, the network layer packet is encapsulated in a frame that includes the mapped destination address and transmitted to the destination device.

To perform indirect routing, a device must have a mechanism for mapping the destination subnetwork to the network layer address of a local router that can forward the packet to that subnetwork. This mapping is typically achieved in one of three ways. First, the device can send a request to the local routers asking them to identify themselves if they are capable

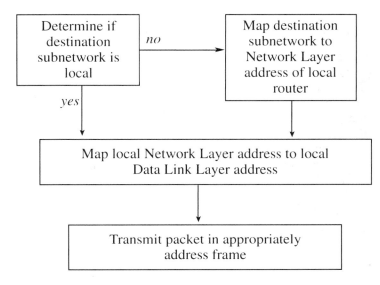

Exhibit 20-5. The routing process.

of routing a packet to the destination subnetwork. Second, a device can be programmed with a "default router" to which it will forward packets it does not otherwise know how to route. Third, the device can have a mechanism for building a table that contains the required mappings. End stations typically employ some form of the first two strategies. For example, IP end stations are commonly configured to know a default router (called a default gateway in the IP community). Routers typically employ the second and/or third approach. Of course, once the Network Layer address of a local router is known, the packet can be directly routed to it by mapping that address to the corresponding local network address. This entire process is represented graphically in Exhibit 20-5.

The routing table is the key to the routing process, especially in routers. It contains the mappings that associate destination subnetworks with the address of a local router that can forward packets to, or toward, that network. The routing table lists the next hop only and typically indicates a total cost to reach that subnetwork. Cost is a reflection of the quality of the route. In general, a smaller cost means a better route. The specific meaning of the number differs from environment to environment.

The routing table contains various types of entries, which can be classified in two ways: how the entry was placed in the table, and the scope of the routing information. Entries in a routing table can be made statically or dynamically. Static routes are manually configured, and dynamic routes are automatically entered by some process in the router or end station. Static routes cannot be overwritten by a dynamically learned route.

Routing table entries can also differ in their precision. Host-specific routes are routes to a specific end station and are fairly rare. Subnet-specific routes are routes to a specific subnetwork and are the most common. Route summaries aggregate a set of subnetworks into a single entry. The default route is an "all others go here" route. In general, a router will select the "best" or "most specific" route it finds in its routing table. If there is a host-specific route for a particular end station, that is the best match. If the best match is the default route, this is the one that will be used. If there is no match at all, the router declares a routing error and discards the packet.

ROUTING PROTOCOLS

Routing protocols are responsible for providing the dynamic entries in a routing table. It is the routing protocol that monitors the network and alters the routing table when network changes occur. There are many routing protocols in the industry, and most network layer protocols have at least two associated routing protocols that can be used to build its routing tables. These protocols can be assessed in multiple ways.

The first assessment point is bandwidth. To build meaningful routing tables, the routers must exchange information. This act consumes bandwidth that would otherwise be used by end stations. The more bandwidth consumed by the routing protocol, the less is available to the end stations to do work.

The second assessment point is the metric the router optimizes to select routes. To select between several possible routes, a router needs a way to compare their quality. Some routers use simple hop count (i.e., the number of links or routers along the path to the destination). Others use metrics such as delay, bandwidth, or packet loss. Some protocols can even use a combination of several metrics. Delay is commonly accepted as one of the better metrics a router can use.

A third assessment point is the time the routing tables take to converge. There is always a finite period of time between the moment a network changes and the moment when the routing protocol has correctly altered the routing tables. This is a critical issue. From the moment the internetwork changes until the moment all of the routing tables are correct, packets may be misrouted along old and possibly invalid routes.

Finally, routing protocols require memory space and processing power within the router. Although today's low-cost memory and high-powered processors have made this a less critical issue, there are still some environments in which these requirements should be considered, including server-based and low-end routers.

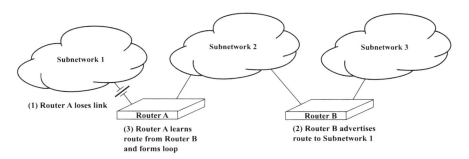

Exhibit 20-6. The counting to infinity loop.

The vast majority of modern routing protocols are classified as "distributed," meaning that the process of calculating routing tables is performed by all of the routers in the internetwork. Centralized routing protocols, in which a single system makes all of the routing decisions and downloads routing tables to the routers, have only recently begun to appear in parts of the Internet and in some asynchronous transfer mode (ATM) environments. Distributed routing protocols fall into two broad classes: distance vector (DV) and link state (LS).

DV routing protocols, also called vector distance protocols or Bellman–Ford protocols, have three important characteristics. First, the routing updates they produce contain a list of destination/costs pairs. Second, those routing updates are sent neighboring devices (i.e., devices with which they share a common subnetwork). Finally, route calculation is itself distributed, with each system performing part of the calculation. In effect, these protocols extract a list of the destinations they have learned and the cost to reach them from the local routing tables and pass that information to their neighbors. The neighbors accept this calculated cost information as correct, add to the reported costs the cost of the link between themselves and the neighbor, and compare those values to the ones already in the routing table. If any of the information is better than what currently occupies the routing table, the routing table is updated.

In early implementations, DV protocols were shown to have a propensity for forging routing loops. The "counting to infinity" problem is one such loop that neighboring systems were prone to forming under specific conditions, as depicted in Exhibit 20-6. In this diagram, Router A has a route to Subnetwork 1 and Router B uses Router A to reach this subnetwork. If Router A loses the route and Router B advertises that fact before Router A can advertise the loss, Router A will accept Router B as a new route to Subnetwork 1, forming a loop. Any packet destined for Subnetwork 1 and arriving at one of these routers will ping-pong between them until the loop resolves.

To avoid this problem, most DV routing protocols implement "split horizons." Split horizons is a rule that prevents a router from advertising routes in the direction from which they were learned (i.e., downstream). It is essentially a "don't preach to the choir" philosophy. A split horizon with poisoned reverse is a version that permits advertisement of these routes, but sets the cost to "infinity" to prevent other routers from learning.

Most existing DV routing protocols transmit complete updates at regular intervals. Restricting updates to this interval can seriously impact network convergence time if something changes or fails. To improve convergence, routers are required to send updates immediately if they change any part of their routing table. This is called a "triggered" or "event-driven" update. Unfortunately, if the table update was the result of a network problem that caused a particular route to fail or become less optimal, it is possible for a router that has not yet received information about the change to reintroduce the old route into the network. To prevent this from occurring, routers are typically required to place any route that has failed into a "hold down" state. During the hold-down interval, typically three times the normal update interval, the router will refuse to accept any further updates on that route. The result is that first news (good or bad) about changes in a route travels quickly. If the news is bad news, however, the subsequent good news (i.e., a new route) is learned much more slowly.

DV routing protocols tend to be fairly simple to implement and design for, and they demand very little in terms of memory and processing power. Unfortunately, most of them are also prone to long convergence intervals and can consume significant amounts of bandwidth as the network grows large.

LS routing protocols also have three distinct characteristics. First, the routing updates contain link characteristic and status information. Second, routing updates sent by one router can potentially be seen by all routers in the internetwork, through a process similar to flooding. Finally, complete route calculation is performed by each router running the protocol.

At the heart of the LS routing protocol is the LS database. The routing updates generated and flooded by each router are stored by all routers in a local database. This database contains sufficient information to graph the network, calculate the shortest paths, and build a routing table based on those calculations. The role of the database is critical. A significant portion of any LS protocol is devoted to ensuring that the databases at all routers are synchronized. New routers entering the network have mechanisms for requesting a copy of the database from a local router, and existing routers have mechanisms for periodically verifying their database against that of another local router. Database synchronization is performed between neighboring routers that have formed a logical relationship called an adjacency.

Clearly, the size and complexity of the network can significantly impact the size of the database and the complexity of the route calculation. And even though LS updates are relatively small and only sent when changes occur, flooding can still be demanding in terms of network bandwidth. To deal with these scalability issues, LS protocols adopt mechanisms for limiting the flood of information.

First, only select routers are permitted to pass a flooded update into the network, and these routers are required to check the update against their local database before flooding, to avoid resending updates that have already been seen. Finally, networks running a LS routing protocol can be organized into areas, and many LS updates are only flooded within their assigned area. To provide routing information across area boundaries, specific routers are designated to summarize intra-area routes to other connected areas.

LS routing protocols tend to converge fairly quickly. If correctly configured, they tend to be more bandwidth-friendly than DV routing protocols and are significantly less prone to creating routing loops than DV routing protocols. However, LS routing protocols are also significantly more complex to design for and configure than DV routing protocols, and they can consume significantly more processing power and memory.

All of the classifications and characteristics of routing protocols discussed thus far apply to pretty much any routing protocol. However, there is another way of classifying routing protocols that is specific to the Internet. The Internet is essentially an internetwork of internetworks. Each internetwork is locally administered and is generally referred to as an Autonomous System (AS). On the Internet, a routing protocol that operates completely within an AS is called an Interior Gateway Protocol (IGP). However, the Internet also needs to pass routing information between these AS to bind them into a whole. Routing protocols operating between AS are called Exterior Gateway Protocols (EGP).

SURVEY OF MAJOR ROUTING PROTOCOLS

Exhibit 20-7 summarizes the key attributes of the major DV routing protocols used in the industry today. As Exhibit 20-7 indicates, the IP version of the Routing Information Protocol (RIP) optimizes hop count and generates updates every 30 seconds. Because of the problems that surface as RIP scales, this routing protocol limits the maximum length of a learned route to 15 hops. In RIP-speak, 16 means "you can't get there from here." RIP is considered an IGP and is typically used within small AS. Because RIP does not include subnet mask information in the routing updates, it can be used only in networks that either are not subnetted or have been subnetted using the same mask for all subnets. RIP cannot be used to support Variable Length Subnet Masking (VLSM) or CIDR.

Exhibit 20-7. Summary of DV routing protocols.

Routing protocol	Used to route	Metric(s)	Update interval	Documented by:
Routing Information Protocol (RIP)	Internet Protocol (IP)	Hop count	30 s	RFC 1058
RIP Version 2 (RIP-II)	IP	Hop count	30 s	RFC 1388
Routing Information Protocol	Internetwork Packet Exchange (IPX) protocol	Delay, hop count	60 s	Novell/Xerox
Interior Gateway Routing Protocol (IGRP)	IP	Delay, bandwidth (reliability, load)	90 s	Cisco
Enhanced IGRP (EIGRP)	IP, IPX, DDP	Delay, bandwidth (reliability, load)	Event driven	Cisco
Routing Table Maintenance Protocol (RTMP)	Datagram delivery protocol (DDP)	Hop count	10 s	Apple Computer
Routing Table Protocol (RTP)	VINES Internet Protocol (VIP)	VINES Internet Protocol (VIP)	90 s	Banyan
Border Gateway Protocol Version 4 (BGP4)	IP	IP	Event driven	RFC 1771 (and others

RIP Version II (RIP-II) was introduced in 1993 and has garnered little support in the industry. The major enhancements it brings to RIP are the inclusion of the subnet mask in the routing update, an authentication mechanism for routing updates, and information to support integration with EGP. Like its predecessor, RIP-II is considered an IGP.

The Novell, Inc. NetWare (or IPX) version of RIP is much like the IP version. The three notable exceptions are the update interval, the inclusion of delay as a metric, and the fact that it builds routing tables for IPX instead of IP.

Cisco Systems, Inc. has two routing protocols of its own. The Interior Gateway Routing Protocol (IGRP) builds IP routing tables, has an update interval of 90 seconds, and can learn multiple lowest-cost routes to a particular destination and balance the load across them. More significantly, IGRP optimizes a composite metric that defaults to include the total path delay weighted by the bandwidth of the narrowest link along the route. Link delay and bandwidth are statically configured at each interface on each router. The composite metric can also factor in load and reliability, but these metrics are not typically included. Like RIP, IGRP is considered an IGP and does not include the subnet mask in its updates.

Cisco's Enhanced IGRP (EIGRP) adds four new features to IGRP. First, it can build routing tables for the DDP and IPX, as well as IP. Second, it uses only event-driven updates, eliminating all periodic updates. Third, IP updates include the subnet mask, which makes EIGRP suitable for VLSM and CIDR environments. Finally, EIGRP implements the Diffused Update Algorithm, a simple, but elegant strategy for virtually eliminating the formation of routing loops in the internetwork.

The Routing Table Maintenance Protocol (RTMP) in Apple Computer, Inc.'s AppleTalk has a reputation for being one of the chattiest routing protocols in the industry, with routing updates generated every 10 seconds. It can be used only to build DDP routing tables for an AppleTalk internetwork. In most other respects, it is very similar to the IP version of RIP.

Banyan Systems, Inc.'s VINES implements a proprietary protocol suite that uses the VIP at the Network Layer. The Routing Table Protocol (RTP) is the most commonly encountered routing protocol in these networks. RTP optimizes delay and generates updates every 90 seconds. In recent years, Banyan has introduced Sequenced RTP, a version of RTP that eliminates periodic updates, thereby reducing bandwidth consumption.

The only EGP reviewed in this survey is the Border Gateway Protocol Version 4 (BGP4). This IP routing protocol is essentially the glue that binds the Internet backbone together. Although essentially a DV routing protocol, BGP4 adds a few new twists. First, to BGP4, a neighbor is any other BGP4 system that it can directly reach in another AS, or any other BGP4 router it is programmed to recognize in the local AS. BGP4 routers do not have to share a subnetwork to be considered neighbors. The BGP4 metric is actually a collection of attributes that describe the characteristics of a route. Also, BGP4 supports policy-based routing. That is to say, BGP4 routers can be programmed to accept or reject routes and to transmit or not transmit routing information, based on defined policies.

Exhibit 20-8 summarizes the key attributes of the major LS routing protocols in use today. LS routing protocols originated in the Advanced Research Projects Agency Network (ARPANET), and it is no surprise that the most commonly cited and used LS routing protocol appears in the context of TCP/IP. Open Shortest Path First (OSPF) is considered an IGP and is used in larger AS to build routing tables for IP routers. OSPF features strong support for building routing areas within an AS, and strong support for integration with other routing protocols as well as IP multicast. OSPF optimizes a metric that is described as "dimensionless." Each OSPF interface is assigned a cost, the meaning of which is at the discretion of the network administrator. If every interface is assigned a cost of one (1), OSPF will

Exhibit 20-8. Summary of LS routing protocols.

Routing protocol	Used to route	Metric(s)	Documented by:
Open Shortest Path First (OSPF)	IP	Dimensionless	RFC 2178
Intermediate System to Intermediate System	IP, CLNS	Dimensionless	ISO DP 10589 and RFC 1142
NetWare Link Services Protocol (NLSP)	IPX	Dimensionless	Novell

essentially optimize hop count. If each interface is assigned a cost proportionate to the delay experienced on that interface, then OSPF optimizes delay. OSPF Version 2, the current version of the standard, was updated in RFC 2178 in July 1997.

Intermediate System to Intermediate System (IS-IS) originated as an ISO protocol for the Connectionless Network Service (CLNS). It has been adopted by the Internet community and is used by some Internet service providers within their backbone network. It is relatively uncommon to find IS-IS in a corporate network. Like OSPF, the IS-IS metric is dimensionless and the protocol provides strong support for area-based routing.

The performance problems historically experienced over wide area network links in NetWare internetworks was one of the primary motivating factors for Novell's development of the NetWare Link Services Protocol (NLSP), which is largely based on IS-IS. In addition to building IPX routing tables, NLSP also builds NetWare's service tables, a function normally performed by the Service Advertising Protocol (SAP). Although IPX routers running NLSP retain the ability to respond to directed RIP and SAP queries, they no longer produce the bandwidth-intensive periodic updates. Recently, Novell has backed off of its emphasis on NLSP and has started to encourage the migration of NetWare environments towards the use of IP in place of IPX.

CONVENTIONAL ROUTER IMPLEMENTATIONS

A router is essentially a computer system equipped with multiple interfaces and software to perform the routing function. Within this definition, there are several platforms that can be classified as routers. The term "software router" typically refers to the use of a generic computer to provide routing. This most often occurs within the context of a server. In fact, the Windows NT Server, NetWare, and VINES servers all have an integrated routing capability, making it possible to build internetworks without the need to purchase additional routing equipment. Using those platforms to route traffic should be done with care, however. Every CPU cycle and kilobyte of memory consumed by the routing process is not available for servicing users. Software routers are typically best used in small internetworks, in branch office environments, or on the periphery of a larger internetwork.

Dedicated routers are those that come with a fixed number and type of ports. Those systems tend to have a relatively low port density, and are primarily used in smaller networks. They are also common in branch office or departmental contexts.

Modular routers implement their ports as I/O cards that can be selected to match the needs of the environment. These systems usually have a higher base sticker price than dedicated routers and tend to have higher port densities and support higher port speeds. They are commonly used in internetwork backbones.

Many modular hubs now have routing capabilities. Initially, this required the purchase of a specialized routing card that had to be inserted in the hub. Many modern hubs, however, have migrated this function to the backplane of the hub or integrated it into multiport modules.

Finally, the industry is seeing the rapid emergence of Layer 3 switches, which are essentially high-speed routers. These come in two flavors. A wire-speed router implements an internal switching fabric. Most of these systems have application-specific integrated circuits (ASIC) on each interface and distribute the routing process to these ASICs. The CPU in these systems is typically responsible for calculating routing tables and distributing them to the ASICs. They are called wire-speed routers because the latencies through the router are extremely small. Some of these platforms can route millions of packets per second.

Hybrid Layer 3/Layer 2 switches combine a Layer 2 switch with a Layer 3 router. Routing decisions are made by the Layer 3 function, as would be expected. But if a long-term flow of packets is detected, or if the end stations have the ability to request it, the router can establish a Data Link Layer connection for that flow of traffic and bypass the packet-by-packet routing decision. These systems are most commonly associated with ATM networks.

CONCLUSION

The purpose of this chapter has been to provide IT personnel with the background information they need to make informed decisions about routing options. To that end, this chapter has provided a consistent language for discussing internetworking, described the general model for routing implemented in modern networks, surveyed the major network layer protocols and routing protocols, and described the major types of routing platforms and the contexts in which they are most commonly used.

Chapter 21
Convergence of IP, ATM, and SONET/SDH at the Backbone

John R. Vacca

IF YOU LISTEN TO TELECOMMUNICATIONS ENTERPRISES, you might think that convergence of IP, ATM, and Synchronous Optical Network/Synchronous Digital Hierarchy (SONET/SDH) at the backbone is as easy as a game of connect the dots. Sketch out lines to the right end points and presto! — you have a digital data network that seamlessly integrates text, voice, and video traffic. The dream of convergence is alluring, but reality ruins everything. Any-to-any digital networking is complex because it must accommodate a host of legacy and leading-edge technologies. Once you interconnect protocols and network layers (no easy feat) you have to make end-user applications ready for a single, global network. And what thorny technical problem would be complete without an Internet element? Will the Net be the golden cornucopia for any-to-any networking? Or will it collapse under the weight of its own success, as cynical experts have suggested? To understand the technological challenges of establishing any-to-any digital networks, we must look at these hurdles one by one.

Traditional technologies are also part of the convergence of the IP, ATM, and SONET/SDH puzzle. So, you have to factor in networking standbys like X.25, T1, Systems Network Architecture (SNA), and dial-up networks over private telephone lines.

For instance, it is generally a combination of practicality and market forces that are driving this change in philosophy regarding the convergence of IP, SONET/SDH and ATM at the backbone. At one time, voice, data, and video services were often carried on separate networks — frequently by different enterprises. Then things began to change, particularly in the United States. First, voice enterprises like the Regional Bell Operating Companies (RBOCs) — who were big fans of SONET/SDH networking — decided to get in the data and video delivery business. They also wanted to do so using their existing SONET/SDH-based networks. Meanwhile, other kinds of enterprises who were looking to expand their offerings, both in terms of service variety and geographical coverage, realized that in many cases it was better to use existing networks, most of which were SONET/SDH based, than build brand new ones. So, it became advantageous to find some way of converging SONET/SDH, IP, and ATM. SONET/SDH has proven amazingly flexible in terms of the payloads it can carry. ATM payloads are just one example — SONET/SDH is also proving capable of carrying IP payloads. In fact, the battle to watch won't be SONET/SDH versus ATM, it will be ATM versus IP.

The best example right now of SONET/SDH, ATM, and IP working as well as converging together is Sprint, which installed Cisco Gigabit Switch Routers to boost the efficiency of its fiber-based Internet transport network. GTE Internetworking also uses Cisco routers in a similar fashion. Cisco explains this approach, which it calls *Packet over SONET/SDH*. While Cisco is making the most noise in this area, you can be sure its competitors aren't far behind. IP over SONET/SDH makes a lot of sense for existing carriers who want to add Internet provision to their service portfolio. These carriers should represent a healthy market for IP over SONET/SDH routers. However, it will be interesting to see how carriers, such as level 3 communications, approach the design of their IP-centric networks. Will they opt for SONET/SDH or will they try some other tack?

Another example is how Microsoft has converged SONET/SDH, ATM, and IP technologies in a new way. Yes, you would expect Bill Gates would do nothing in a small way, and Microsoft's enterprise network in Redmond, Washington, does nothing to change this perception. The enterprise is touting the network as *the largest enterprise ATM network in the world, possibly riding over the largest private SONET/SDH backbone in the world.* These days, few enterprises other than Microsoft would need the capacity afforded by Optical Carrier level 3 (OC-3) with 155 Mb/s and Optical Carrier level 12 (OC-12) with 622 Mb/s rings in their enterprise network. However, bandwidth demands are increasing all the time, and while Microsoft is undoubtedly a trailblazer in SONET/SDH-based ATM enterprise networks, I would not be surprised if other enterprises followed a similar trail in the future.

Now, let's take a look at other SONET/SDH, IP, and ATM convergence technologies and strategies.

PACKET OVER SONET/SDH

The Telecommunications Act of 1996 aimed to eliminate the artificial distinction between inter-local access, transport area (LATA), and intra-LATA business by opening the long-distance and local markets to competition. This deregulation of the industry creates regional competition. As a result, incumbent local exchange carriers (ILECs) need to provide differentiated services to maintain and expand their existing customer base. ILECs will also need to penetrate the markets in which their customers conduct most of their business. In this newly formed competitive environment, the ability to increase revenue and earnings will determine who will survive. As a result, LECs will no longer be just local.

Yet, with the local calling market estimated at $200 billion, stakes are high and competition is fierce in the ILEC's home market. According to the consulting firm, Deloitte & Touche, 47 percent of enterprise customers are ready to walk away from their existing ILEC to such new service providers as competitive local exchange carriers (CLECs), competitive access providers (CAPs), out-of-region LECs, and cable-TV carriers. The ILECs stand to lose as much as $20 billion in annual revenue from this customer defection. Meanwhile, CLECs are aggressively expanding to bid for this market. They now have more than two million lines in service and an annualized run rate of $2 billion in local revenues.

At the same time that the local and regional market becomes more crowded, enterprise customers have begun to ask for differentiated treatment for their mission-critical services. Throwing bandwidth at this problem is no longer an economical or viable choice in today's competitive market. Thus, just as service providers are going through revolutionary changes, their networks and the nature of their services are going through an evolutionary phase as well. Service providers who play an aggressive role in this evolution and who are early adapters of new convergence technologies and services can survive this tide of change. An example is the swing toward networks based on the Internet protocol (IP), and the emergence of a convergence technology that makes the construction of such networks efficient and economical.

IP-Centric Networks

The demand for bandwidth is skyrocketing in data-service networks. With this demand comes the need for efficient bandwidth utilization, higher performance, and simplicity. As the rate of data provision begins to exceed that of the traditional voice services, the current time-division multiplexing (TDM) infrastructure becomes increasingly inefficient. The edge of the network belongs to Ethernet, requiring that networks of the future be designed for this protocol. Also in today's networks, transmission control protocol/World Wide Web traffic constitutes 86 percent of all backbone traffic.

According to The Yankee Group, Boston, the telecommunications market will grow from $206 billion in annual revenue to $371 billion by the year 2001, with data services accounting for the lion's share of this increase. As the time line is expanded, the growth in data services by 2006 will be 34 times that of voice services. This increase has already been seen in the construction of data infrastructure, which is outpacing that of voice 4 to 1.

In this context, the explosion of Internet traffic has changed the network traffic landscape. Traffic types are changing from text and e-mail to images and video. These changes affect the characteristics of the packets traversing the Internet backbone. The average packet size increased to 390 and 440 bytes in 1999 alone. In addition, the average session duration is only 14 seconds long. These factors point to exhaustive signaling connections that can overburden a connection-oriented network.

The traditional telephone enterprise network structure is also being shaken by increasing interest in voice-over-IP (VOIP) technology. Enterprise customers spend millions of dollars on international voice and fax traffic. The advent of VOIP means that these customers can spend a fraction of today's cost for voice and fax services. Internet telephony will compete effectively against the circuit-switched infrastructure, forcing the incumbent service providers to partner or build up their IP-based infrastructure before the new service providers carve away at the main source of their income. As VOIP technology evolves and the number of Web users grows to 270 million by the year 2001, more enterprises will opt to put their long-distance transactions on IP-based networks rather than on existing circuit-based ones.

These trends have brought about the birth of a new paradigm: IP transport networks. The IP transport infrastructure is an IP-based, full-service network that takes advantage of IP Layer 3 quality of service and such inherent IP characteristics as scalability, simplicity, and multicasting. Today's fast-growing service providers are investing billions of dollars to build global long-distance and local infrastructure services via an IP-based fiber network.

Most of these networks are built from an IP transport vision with a focus on coexisting with the carrier's SONET/SDH and SDH infrastructures. SONET/SDH and SDH technology is the technology of choice worldwide for providing high-capacity pipes. SONET/SDH networks provide high resiliency and availability in the face of network failures and transport valued synchronization bits that can be easily tapped into for maintaining a synchronous data network. Today's data network can build on these features and take it a few steps further by adding better use of wide area network bandwidth, support for differentiated services through Layer 3 Quality of Service (QoS), and high-performance multicasting features.

Packet Over SONET/SDH Fuels The IP Transport Infrastructure

Packet-over-SONET/SDH technology can relieve today's network from the stress of growth while paving the way for additional service features in the future. Packet-over-SONET/SDH is the serial transmission of data over SONET/SDH frames through the use of point-to-point protocol (PPP). This data mapping is done in accordance with RFC 1619, PPP over SONET/SDH,

RFC 1662, PPP in high-level data-link control-like framing, and OC-3/Synchronous Transport Module level 1(STM-1) with 155 Mbps, OC-12/stm-4 (622 Mbps), and OC-48/STM-16 (2.5-Gbit/sec) rates.

The format of IP packets in the SONET/SDH synchronous payload envelope is simple. One byte is dedicated to the packet flag at the beginning of the string and four bytes are dedicated to the PPP header (one address byte, one control byte and two protocol bytes). The IP packets are serially placed in the SONET/SDH frame, and a cyclic redundancy check is added at the end.

Clearly, the routers that form an IP transport infrastructure that can coexist with the SONET/SDH infrastructure must access various overhead bytes in the section, line, and path SONET/SDH overhead. Again, most data platforms must be able to access these bytes in order to provide a cohesive network to the service providers. Today's competitive market leaves no room for wasting precious resources. Deployment of packet-over-SONET/SDH technology will provide up to 99 percent efficient wide area network bandwidth utilization in the network.

Depending on the packet size, the ATM cell tax can create major deficiencies in bandwidth usage in the network. The cell tax could range from 15 to 51 percent of the payload. This becomes even more critical on long fiber runs, such as cross-country or transoceanic links. At OC-3 rates, the effective data bandwidth for packet over SONET/SDH is 149.76 Mbps versus that of ATM, which is 128.36 Mbps. Small packets grind hard on an ATM network.

Next, let us look at how an enterprise like Microsoft chooses SONET/SDH for their enterprise network.

CHOOSING SONET/SDH FOR AN ENTERPRISE NETWORK

When you are Microsoft, you need an engine as powerful as any telecommunications carrier to power your enterprise network. The foundation of Microsoft Corp.'s upgraded Puget Sound ring network in Redmond is a powerful SONET/SDH backbone built with 4-fiber bidirectional line-switched rings (BLSRs).

In an effort to consolidate technologies, improve scalability, and keep up with bandwidth demands, Microsoft removed its centralized Fiber Distributed Data Interface (FDDI) network and created a system that it considers the largest corporate ATM network in the world, possibly riding over the largest private SONET/SDH backbone in the world.

Before the upgrade to an ATM backbone in 1997, the Microsoft campus contained SONET/SDH equipment mostly geared toward digital signal level 3 (DS-3) with 44.736 Mbps and DS-1 (1.544 Mbps) rates. The transport backbone now contains 10 nodes of Alcatel Single Mode (SM) SONET/SDH multiplexers in a BLSR configuration. It also uses an Alcatel 1631 SX Wideband SONET/SDH Digital Cross Connect and an Alcatel 1633 SX Release 10 Broadband Digital Cross Connect.

The Legacy Network

During the five years before the upgrade, Microsoft used a centralized FDDI network consisting of 3,000 servers and 34 FDDI rings connecting 40,000 PCs and 54 buildings on the Puget Sound campus. Microsoft used Fujitsu's Fujitsu Lightwave Multiplexer (FLM) system in a unidirectional path-switched ring architecture. Digital Equipment Corp.'s Gigaswitch connected the FDDI rings for corporate data.

US West, Denver, Colorado, installed the Alcatel cross-connects in the network more than four years ago and also maintains service for the network. Before being used in conjunction with the rings in today's network, the crossconnects handled call center and voice center traffic.

Although the legacy network would be considered state-of-the-art on many campus networks, Microsoft began evaluating capacity limitations due to the architecture. Microsoft had separate voice, video, and data networks. They were converging toward the common infrastructure that supports improvements and efficiencies in the labor it takes to manage that work. This allowed Microsoft to be "out with the old, in with the new" and eliminate technologies that are no longer appropriate for them.

Change Reasoning

Much of Microsoft's product development work takes place on and around the Puget Sound campus where employees were finding that the network was slowing them down. The amount of data traveling on the network has increased over the past six years as the enterprise has grown.

The enterprise also found that its network was not scalable. A network capable of handling multimedia and multicast technologies was needed. The enterprise chose a 4-fiber BLSR approach because it has double the capacity of a 2-fiber BLSR and more bandwidth availability. In addition, only one protection switch mode is available with a 2-fiber BLSR — the ring switch. If all of the working traffic is on the protect ring, the entire ring is used up. The 4-fiber BLSR has the same protect mode as well as a protect mode called "span-switching."

Because that span switch lets you use your protect-bandwidth more efficiently, you get much better availability by using a 4-fiber BLSR. In the Microsoft case, they needed both the capacity and the availability, which drove them to the 4-fiber BLSR approach. The 4-fiber bidirectional ring is the most robust of all the ring architectures, both from ability to survive multiple failures as well as having high capacity. Those two reasons are why Microsoft chose that platform to continue the SONET/SDH architecture. Moving from DS-1 to DS-3 over to OC-3 [155 Mbps] and OC-12 [622 Mbps] rates suggested a higher-capacity ring. In fact, if OC-192 [10-Gbit/sec] technology were mature enough, Microsoft would have gone straight to that. But it was not available in ring format at the time Microsoft was doing its evaluation.

Network Upgrading

One option Microsoft originally looked at was a dark-fiber mesh network tying together ATM switches. At the time, Alcatel had just introduced its 4-fiber, bidirectional ring. Microsoft was aware of the Alcatel products because they had already deployed Alcatel digital cross-connect systems (DCSs) within the Microsoft network. They worked with Alcatel on how best to incorporate its 4-fiber bidirectional technology into the network design and come up with a three-ring configuration. One ring has four nodes, and two rings have three nodes each. The three independent rings were installed and interlocked via Alcatel's cross-connects and carry much of Microsoft's backbone ATM traffic throughout the campus.

Had Microsoft connected the rings using DS-3 or DS-1 lines, it would have been difficult for the enterprise to set up a high-capacity data network. But OC-12 at 622 Mbps gives some really large pipes that they can use to run ATM, data traffic, and the various types of local area networks that they have set up on their campus.

Lower-speed traffic rates such as DS-1 for private branch exchanges will drop to the 1631 cross-connects. Dropping an OC-12 out of the Fujitsu OC-48 nodes into the Alcatel cross-connects creates a mid-span meet. The traditional grooming and filling function that those crossconnections perform, as well as the service restoration capabilities of the digital crossconnect, is why they are there.

Cisco's Catalyst 5000 switches and its 7500 routers are at the edge of the network. The routers provide redundancy and increase port capacity, and the switches supply 10/100 Mbps Ethernet to Microsoft desktops. The Cisco routers and switches will work with ATM switches from FORE Systems in the ATM backbone.

The combination of ATM switching and SONET/SDH transport addresses scalability, manageability and reliability in the quantities that Microsoft's development enterprise requires. Essentially, Microsoft is acting as a carrier to their own development group.

Multiple runs of 144-strand singlemode fiber stretch within the Microsoft campus right-of-way. Meanwhile, 2- to 3-km runs of multimode fiber appear in lower quantities, such as 24 fiber-pairs. Microsoft feels that when they go above OC-3 rates they will be using singlemode exclusively, except for very short runs. Between racks, Microsoft can do multimode at 622 Mbps, but they have got runs of multimode that were basically distance-limited based on the FDDI specs.

Installers worked nights and weekends to accomplish the 72-building upgrade goal of five buildings per week and 11 to 21 each month. The schedule was intended to minimize the impact on product development and release schedules. Most of the buildings are on the Puget Sound campus, with approximately one-third off-site. Connecting off-site buildings with the main campus is one of the reasons Microsoft went with SONET/SDH technology.

Now, let us look at more SONET/SDH technology. Next, the major issues are covered that relate to understanding and designing a clocking system for SONET/SDH equipment.

SONET/SDH EQUIPMENT CLOCKING

The popularity of SONET/SDH technology is growing rapidly as more products demand the high bandwidth, connectivity, and scalability that SONET/SDH offers. This enabling technology is necessary in many cases for products to reach *next-generation* performance levels. SONET/SDH is thus not only well-established within the traditional telecommunications industry, but equipment vendors outside this community are now (or soon will be) offering SONET/SDH interfaces on their products.

SONET/SDH equipment requires precise clocking to function properly and to be compliant with SONET/SDH standards. However, clocking is an area that is often misunderstood, even by people specifying and deploying SONET/SDH equipment.

Synchronization Needs

SONET/SDH networks were originally designed to transport voice traffic in an efficiently scalable way. The legacy time-division multiplex (TDM) hierarchy, consisting of digital signals DS-0, DS-1, DS-3, and so on, incurs an increasing loss of efficiency as the hierarchy rate increases. This is because the TDM system is asynchronous and thus requires additional overhead each time one multiplexes up to a higher rate in the hierarchy. This occurs in order to rate match each lower-rate asynchronous source into the new higher rate.

SONET/SDH overcomes this scalability limitation by using a synchronous hierarchy, resulting in an overhead percentage that does not vary as the rate increases. Each time one multiplexes to a higher rate, the lower-rate signals are synchronously byte interleaved to produce the higher rate. Since the lower-rate signals are synchronous to one another, no additional overhead is needed (with stuffing bytes and associated signaling) to support rate matching.

SONET/SDH has a built-in overhead of 5.5 percent, which can decrease slightly in the special case where one transports concatenated payloads (such as with an OC-3c payload rate of 149.76 Mbps versus an OC-3 payload rate of 148.61 Mbps). The initial mapping of a payload into the SONET/SDH synchronous payload envelope can result in additional losses. For instance, a frame of a DS-3 (44.736 Mbps) is usually mapped into a full SONET/SDH 52 Mbps Synchronous Transport Signal 1 (STS-1) — the fundamental SONET/SDH rate and format — frame, yielding an effective loss to overhead of 14.8 percent. But when this STS-1 carrying a DS-3 is multiplexed to higher rates (for instance, to an STS-192 (corresponding to OC-192) at 10 Gbits/sec) no further losses to overhead occur.

SONET/SDH standards emanate from two different enterprises: the American National Standards Institute (ANSI) and Bell Communications Research (Bellcore). In general, the Bellcore requirements are derived from the ANSI standards. Clocking requirements are distributed throughout numerous standards. However, the key requirements common to all systems are contained within a manageable subset that includes:

- *ANSI T1-101:* Synchronization Interface Standard.
- *Bellcore GR-253-core:* Synchronous Optical Network (SONET/SDH) Transport Systems: Common Generic Criteria.
- *Bellcore GR-378-core:* Generic Requirements for Timing Signal Generators.
- *Bellcore GR-436-core:* Digital Network Synchronization Plan.
- *Bellcore GR-499-core:* Transport Systems Generic Requirements (TSGR): Common Requirements.
- *Bellcore GR-1244-core:* Clocks for the Synchronized Network: Common Generic Criteria.

Other clocking standards usually pertain to specific equipment types. So, you must search for those standards when dealing with a specific equipment type.

Stratum Level Division

Network clocks are divided into stratum levels based on their accuracy, stability, and other parameters according to Bellcore GR-1244-core. Stratum levels are expressed as a number, sometimes along with a letter. The better the clock, the lower the stratum level. The primary references used in the network meet the Stratum 1 requirements. As a clock is distributed across a network and among equipment, impairments are introduced that reduce the stability and result in the clock being classified at a higher stratum level. SONET/SDH equipment must either be synchronized with a Stratum 3 or better clock or, if the equipment is not a digital cross-connect, clocked from an oscillator with a minimum accuracy of ±20 parts per million.

Network Timing Architecture For SONET/SDH

The SONET/SDH network in the United States is timed from a limited number of Stratum 1 primary reference sources (PRSs) distributed across the country, forming timing domains. Historically, synchronization was distributed as an analog 2.048-MHz signal. With the advent of the digital network, this distribution occurred via DS-1 (1.544 Mbps) signals passed from the PRSs to network elements (NEs), which then distributed timing to other NEs in a hierarchical fashion. This architecture is evolving so that the SONET/SDH network will distribute the network timing instead of using the TDM network. In the new architecture, one point of the SONET/SDH network within a timing domain will be synchronized with the PRS. The SONET/SDH network will then distribute timing to other nodes of the SONET/SDH network and other non-SONET/SDH NEs from DS-1s timed from the SONET/SDH network.

The hierarchy allows a small number of expensive, high-accuracy clocks to be used to time an expansive network, providing reference to lower-accuracy clocks, which then provide reference to yet lower-accuracy clocks. An advantage of this system is that a detected failure of a clock high in the hierarchy will cause the clocks it feeds to enter holdover mode. This will still maintain a clock for that level and lower levels that is more accurate than the free-running clock of the level just below the failure.

Sources Of Equipment Timing

There are five different ways that SONET/SDH equipment can be timed. A subset of these is applicable in a given application:

1. External timing
2. Line timing
3. Loop timing
4. Through timing
5. Free running

External Timing. Building integrated timing supply (BITS) is the name given to the single master clock within a telephone enterprise central office. The BITS clock is derived from a timing reference that feeds the central office, typically a DS-1. Due to jitter introduced by SONET/SDH network pointer adjustments, DS-1s carried on SONET/SDH cannot be used for network synchronization distribution because they fail to meet ANSI T1.101 synchronization interface specifications. When SONET/SDH is used to distribute a timing reference, timing is derived from the SONET/SDH line rate, not from within the payload. As distributed within an office, the BITS clock can assume one of two formats: a composite clock (CC) signal or a DS-1.

The CC conveys both bit and byte synchronization (64 and 8 kHz, respectively) used in DS-0 (64-kbit/sec) signals all on a single waveform. The CC signal consists of a 64-kHz, 5/8 duty cycle, return-to-zero, bipolar signal with a bipolar violation every eighth bit. Data is clocked out on the leading edge (departure from 0V) of this signal and sampled on the trailing edge (return to 0V).

DS-1 signals used for bits typically consist of a framed "all-ones" sequence, with a bipolar return-to-zero line format, and can be either in the super-frame or extended-super-frame format. In either case, the bits clock is multiplied up using a phase-locked loop (PLL) to produce the bit- and byte-rate frequencies for SONET/SDH transmission.

Line Timing. The line timing method is used, for instance, with an add/drop multiplexer. This kind of NE has a bidirectional SONET/SDH interface on both sides. Timing is extracted from one incoming side and used as a reference for both outgoing sides.

Loop Timing. The loop timing method is a special case of line timing and is applicable to line terminating equipment. Here the NE has only one bidirectional connection to the SONET/SDH network. The transmit timing is derived from recovered receive timing.

Through Timing. The through timing mode is mostly used for regenerators. Timing recovered from the incoming signal in one direction is used to clock the transmitted signal continuing in the same direction. The same holds for the opposite direction.

Free Running. If an oscillator that is not referenced back to a network timing source is used, both the oscillator and the mode are referred to as free running. Therefore, of the various ways that SONET/SDH NEs can be synchronized, the preferred order for clock selection is as follows: bits (external timing), received timing (loop, line, or through), and local timing (free running).

Switching The Clock. If multiple clock sources, such as external timing, loop timing, and an internal free-running clock, are available to an NE, then a mechanism must be implemented to select the appropriate synchronization source. The selection can be statically provisioned or can be under hardware or software control, based on the real-time health of the various clock sources.

One must be conscious of preventing timing loops in a network (such as when NE #1 uses NE #2 as its timing reference, but NE #2 is already using NE #1 for its reference). This can be an issue if an NE can switch between external and line timing, such as upon an external reference failure. This is not a problem with network terminating equipment, since downstream equipment within the network would not look to the terminating equipment for a reference. Thus, terminating equipment can be designed to switch between external and line-timing sources. Switching can be either revertive or non-revertive. Revertive switching implies that there is a preferred clock source, and that, if it has failed (whereupon one switches away from it) and then recovers, one should switch back to the preferred source. With nonrevertive switching, once you switch to a new clock source, you stay with that source until it fails, even if the clock you switched away from recovers. Non-revertive switching is recommended by Bellcore in most circumstances.

SONET/SDH implements a messaging protocol, via synchronization status messages, to identify to the receiving NE the stratum level traceability of the clock that was used to create a given SONET/SDH signal. With this information, an NE can select the best synchronization reference from a set of available references. This can aid in automatic reconfiguration of line-timed rings and in troubleshooting synchronization problems.

Finally, let us look at how to integrate SONET/SDH and Ethernet-based service.

SONET/SDH AND ETHERNET-BASED SERVICE PROVISION INTEGRATION

Many competitive access providers and competitive local exchange carriers provide enterprise services over SONET/SDH-based fiber-optic rings. The use of SONET/SDH rings gives them significant advantages over the predominately copper-based access networks of their incumbent competitors. To date, these competitive carriers have grown by using their rings to provide high-quality, low-cost solutions for voice. However, according to industry experts, 60 percent of all backbone network traffic will be Internet-based by year-end 2001, making this one of the highest growth opportunities for competitive access providers and competitive local exchange carriers.

Supporting this growth presents voice-oriented carriers with significant challenges. These carriers are required either to implement entirely separate local area network (LAN) and voice/data fiber access networks, which increases fiber requirements and network deployment cost, or to provision Ethernet services over their SONET/SDH access networks.

In order to provide Internet connectivity over traditional SONET/SDH access networks, carriers typically employ external devices, such as bridges, Ethernet switches, or routers to support LAN-based traffic. While this approach allows carriers to deliver LAN services, it is not cost-effective in terms of capital cost and complexity at the network access point. Using two entirely separate technologies for the delivery of voice and Internet services means that carriers have to face the problems associated with multiple management systems and the different provisioning methods for SONET/SDH ring and LAN access equipment.

In addition, typical LAN access solutions are focused around "in-band" simple network management protocol-based management rather than on the "out-of-band" Open Systems Interconnection-based management architectures found in SONET/SDH-based access equipment. Finally, the skills necessary to provide field engineering support of SONET/SDH T1/T3 equipment are very different from those required to support router-based solutions. The result is that many competitive carriers are forced to run two separate support enterprises — one to support voice delivery and the other to support Internet access.

The alternative for competitive carriers is the integrated SONET/SDH broadband access multiplexer with an Ethernet mapper card, allowing carriers the ability to provide direct LAN connectivity integrated inside their enterprise service-delivery vehicle. This enables carriers to provision 10- and 100 Mbps Ethernet connections from customer locations to their Internet backbone, using techniques and management tools that are identical to those used for voice circuits. This also gives them a single platform for the delivery of enterprise services, which meets the requirements for network reliability that enterprise customers demand.

Integrated Ethernet mapper cards provide carriers with an ideal vehicle to transport 10- and 100-Mbps Ethernet services over a SONET/SDH access network by integrating the Ethernet line interface directly into the SONET/SDH add/drop multiplexer located within the customer premises and the carrier's central offices (COs). It connects to intelligent LAN equipment (customer-supplied bridges, routers, and firewalls, for example) rather than directly to customer LAN networks. It provides "native-mode" LAN connections between two Ethernet LANs via a SONET/SDH network. Thus, it is an ideal solution for both high-bandwidth Internet service delivery and for transparent LAN service (TLS) delivery over the same platform and on the same fiber routes as conventional T1 and T3 voice and data service delivery.

The Benefits

One of the key benefits of the integrated broadband access multiplexer is a reduction in the cost and complexity of the equipment needed to deliver services at the customer premises. Because SONET/SDH-based Ethernet mapping uses the SONET/SDH multiplexing hierarchy, it can be directly integrated into CO digital cross-connect-based architectures. This allows LAN traffic to be separated from voice traffic at the CO, with voice traffic routed to local switching and interexchange carrier access portions of the network, and Internet traffic to be connected directly to the Internet service provider CO routing platform. In this way one of the primary benefits of SONET/SDH-based networks is realized — the combination of multiple services with a minimum of multiplexing stages, which leads to carrier service cost reduction.

CONCLUSION AND SUMMARY

Networks must have longevity and scalability with an initial low cost of ownership. A successful network must also use bandwidth efficiently. To achieve these goals, we must design networks based on the type of traffic they can carry and choose between a connection-oriented and a connectionless network early in the design process. Choices will depend on the applications running on the network. If an IP-based network is selected because the true nature of the infrastructure is data-centric, then ample buffering must be seeded in the network to deal with the round-trip delays and packet bursts.

Packet-over-SONET/SDH technology implemented with new gigabit switch routers can meet these requirements. Consideration of IP over SONET/SDH when a enterprise model is IP-centric is essential. Packet-over-SONET/SDH leverages existing SONET/SDH technology and delivers simple and efficient bandwidth use, Layer 3 QoS, and scalability. It can synchronize off existing SONET/SDH rings and support the required bytes in the SONET/SDH overhead for reliable, cohesive integration.

For those seeking a proven, tested, and immediately available solution, there are two choices: an FDDI switch or an Asynchronous Transfer Mode (ATM) backbone. An FDDI switch is a device that provides fast switching or bridging among its many FDDI ports. While the use of an FDDI switch will increase overall network capacity, it limits the network's collapsed backbone to a single location, as the network remains operating at 100 Mbps with no option to move to a higher-speed backbone.

Using an ATM super-backbone with devices that connect each FDDI segment to ATM provides a better solution. This is because it switches between the many FDDI segment rings (similar to the way the FDDI switch does) but it also adds the ability to further expand the network and increase the backbone speed to 622 Mbps and even to the gigabit-per-second range.

In conclusion, the use of integrated broadband access multiplexers enables carriers to deploy high-bandwidth Internet services as easily and reliably as the voice services on which they have built their revenue. At the same time, these multiplexers minimize the impact of integrating enterprise-focused access platforms into their networks.

ADDRESSES OF COMPANIES

1. Sprint Corporation, 2330 Shawnee Mission Parkway, Westwood, KS 66205, 1999.
2. Cisco Systems, Inc., All Rights Reserved, 170 West Tasman Drive, San Jose, CA 95134-1706, 1999.

3. GTE Internetworking, BBN Technologies, 1300 North 17th Street, Arlington, VA 22209, 1999.
4. Level 3 Communications, Inc., 3555 Famam Street, Omaha, NE 68131, 1999.
5. Deloitte & Touche, 555 12th Street, N.W., Suite 500, Washington, DC 20004-1207, 1999.
6. Compagnie Financière Alcatel, Paris, France, 1999.
7. Fujitsu Network Communications, Inc., 2801 Telecom Parkway, Richardson, TX 75082, 1999.
8. Compaq Computer Corporation, 20555 SH 249, Houston, TX 77070-2698, 1999.
9. FORE Systems, Inc., 1000 FORE Dr., Warrendale, PA 15086-7502, 1999.
10. American National Standards Institute, 11 West 42nd Street, New York, NY 10036, 1999.
11. Bell Communications Research (Bellcore), 445 South St., Morristown, NJ 07960, 1999.

Section III
VPNs, Intranets, and Extranets

WITH A FIRM UNDERSTANDING FOR THE TECHNICAL CHARACTERISTICS, operation, and utilization of LANs and WANs, one is ready to consider a series of methods that provide modern-day internetworking capability. Those methods involve the connection of geographically separated networks via a public network, referred to as virtual private networking (VPNs), applying the TCP/IP protocol suite to a private network, referred to as an intranet, and providing a mechanism for users on a public or private network in one business environment to connect to an intranet operated by another business, a technology referred to as an extranet.

The first four chapters in this section focus on various aspects of virtual private networks. In Chapter 22, **Virtual Networking Management and Planning,** author Trenton Waterhouse first provides an overview of virtual networking and then examines the role of switching in VPNs and VPN creation and management issues associated with such switching. This chapter is followed by the chapter titled **Putting VPNs to Work for Small Businesses and Offices.** In Chapter 23, co-authors Joy Pinsky and Michael Kennedy introduce the manner by which VPNs can be used in a variety of business applications, ranging from closed user groups formed with partners, customers, and suppliers, to Internet-based customer interaction. In concluding this chapter, the authors review three main issues required for obtaining reliable transport across a network and the role of authentication, authorization, accounting, and encryption.

Continuing our investigation into virtual private networking, Chapter 24 focuses on virtual private networking occurring via the Internet. In the chapter titled **Virtual Private Networks: Secure Remote Access over the Internet,** author John R. Vacca focuses attention on the use of the Point-to-Point Tunneling Protocol (PPTP), Layer 2 Forwarding (L2F), the Layer 2 Tunneling Protocol (L2TP), and the Internet Protocol Security (IPSec) layer 3 protocol. Included in this timely chapter is an overview of the manner by which Microsoft Corporation worked together with UUnet Technologies to implement a VPN that supports all Microsoft mobile employees.

The fourth VPN-related chapter included in this section is authored by James S. Tiller. Chapter 25, entitled **IPSec VPNs,** examines interoperability and scalability issues associated with secure VPNs, extranet access considerations, internal network protection methods, and the future of IPSec VPNs.

Concluding this section are two chapters focused on intranets and extranets. In Chapter 26, titled **Integrating Data Centers with Intranets,** author Anura Gurugé provides readers with a detailed view of the manner by which 3270 applications can be converted to HTML as well as the use of applets for performing IBM 3270 and 5350 emulation. This chapter also reviews the pros and cons associated with a 3270-to-HTML solution and applet-based emulations, making us aware of the advantages and disadvantages associated with those methods to facilitate knowledge in this area. In concluding this section, author Phillip Q. Maier's chapter, **Implementing and Supporting Extranets** (Chapter 27), first provides a detailed examination of the use of extranets along with several examples of extranet architectures. This is followed by the use of application gateway firewalls and other security measures that can be used to ensure that data integrity does not become an issue when extranets are used to interconnect communications between different organizations that require the ability to communicate.

Chapter 22
Virtual Networking Management and Planning

Trenton Waterhouse

FROM THE USER'S PERSPECTIVE, A VIRTUAL NETWORK IS A DATA COMMUNICATIONS SYSTEM that provides access control and network configuration changes using software control. It functions like a traditional network but is built using switches.

The switched virtual network offers all the performance of the bridge with the value of the router. The constraints of physical networking are removed by the logical intelligence that structures and enforces policies of operation to ensure stability and security. Regardless of access technology or geographic location, any-to-any communications is the goal.

The switch could be considered a third-generation internetworking device. First-generation devices, or bridges, offered a high degree of performance throughput but relatively little value, because the bridge's limited decision intelligence resulted in broadcast storms that produced network instability. Routers, the second generation of internetworking devices, increased network reliability and offered great value with firewalling capabilities, but the trade-off was in performance. When routers are used in combination with each other, bandwidth suffers, which is detrimental for delay-sensitive applications such as multimedia.

THE BUSINESS CASE FOR VIRTUAL NETWORKING

Both the business manager and the technical manager should find interest in this new virtual networking scheme. The business manager is usually interested in cost-of-ownership issues. Numerous studies from organizations such as the Gartner Group and Forrester Research have found that only 20 percent of networking costs are associated with capital equipment acquisition. The other 80 percent of annual budgets are dedicated to items such as

303

wide area networking charges, personnel, training, maintenance and vendor support, as well as the traditional equipment moves, adds, and changes.

It is important for IS managers to remember that capital expenditure happens in year one, even though the equipment may be operating for another four years. Wide area network (WAN) charges can account for up to 40 percent of an organization's networking budget. For every dollar that the technical staff spends on new equipment, another four dollars is spent on the operation of that equipment. Therefore, focus should be on the cost-of-ownership issues, not necessarily the cost of the network devices.

Network Reliability

Business managers are also looking for increased reliability as the network plays a major role in the core operations of the organization. Networks have become a business tool to gain competitive advantage — they are mission critical and, much like a utility, must provide a highly reliable and available means of communications. Every office today includes an electrical outlet, a phone jack, and a network connection. Electrical and phone service are generally regarded as stable utilities that can be relied on daily. Networks, however, do not always provide comparable levels of service.

Network Accountability

Managers also can benefit from the increased accountability that virtual networks are able to offer. Organizational networking budgets can range from hundreds of thousands of dollars to hundreds of millions per year. Accounting for the use of the network that consumes those funds is a critical issue. There is no better example than WAN access charges. Remote site connectivity can consume a great deal of the budget, and the questions of who, what, when, and where with regard to network use are impossible to determine. Most users consider the network to be free, and the tools to manage and account for its use are increasingly a requirement, not an option.

THE TECHNOLOGY CASE FOR VIRTUAL NETWORKING

The IS manager's needs for higher capacity, greater performance, and increased efficiency can be met through the deployment of switched virtual networks. Each user is offered dedicated bandwidth to the desktop with uplinks of increasing bandwidth to servers or other enterprise networks. Rather than contending for bandwidth in shared access environments, all users are provided with their own private link. This degree of privacy allows for increased security because data are sent only to intended recipients, rather than seen by all.

The most attractive feature to the technical manager, however, may be the benefits gained through increased ease of operation and administration of virtual networks. A long-standing objective has been to deliver network services to users without continually having to reconfigure the devices that make up that network. Furthermore, many of the costs associated with moves, adds, and changes of users can be alleviated as the constraints of physical networking are removed. Regardless of user location, they can remain part of the same virtual network. Through the use of graphical tools, users are added and deleted from workgroups. In the same manner, policies of operation and security filters can be applied. In a sense, the virtual network accomplishes the goal of managing the individual users and individual conversations, rather than the devices that make up the network.

VIRTUAL NETWORKING DEFINED

The ideal virtual network does not restrict access to a particular topology or protocol. A virtual network that can only support Ethernet users with Transmission Control Protocol/Internet Protocol (TCP/IP) applications is limited. The ultimate virtual network allows any-to-any connectivity between Ethernet, Token Ring, Fiber Distributed Data Interface (FDDI), Asynchronous Transfer Mode (ATM), Internet Protocol (IP), Internetwork Packet Exchange (IPX), AppleTalk, or Systems Network Architecture (SNA) networks. A single virtual network infrastructure under a single management architecture is the goal.

Network management software becomes a key enabling requirement for the construction of switched virtual networks. The greatest challenge network designers face is the separation of the physical network connectivity from the logical connection services it can provide. Many of the design issues associated with networks can be attributed to the physical parameters of protocols and the routers used as the interconnection device. A challenge for any manager is to remain compatible with existing layer 3 protocols and routers and still preserve the investment in existing local area network (LAN) equipment to the greatest extent possible.

Using Telephony as a Model

The principles of operation for switched virtual networks are concretely founded in the success of the global communications systems. Without doubt, the phone system is the world's largest and most reliable network. Built using advanced digital switches controlled by software, extensive accounting and management tools ensure the success of this highly effective means of communication. The connection-oriented switch is the key. End-to-end connections across multiple switches and various transmission types ranging from copper to fiber optics to microwave to satellites allow millions of calls per day to be successfully completed, regardless of the type of phone or from where the user is calling. The telephony model is used throughout this chapter to help illustrate the workings of a virtual network.

SWITCHING DEFINED

One of the more confusing terms in the networking industry today is the word *switch*. For the purpose of this chapter, switching can be broken down into three fundamental areas:

1. configuration switching
2. packet switching
3. cell switching

The earliest form of switching enabled the network manager to assign an individual port or an entire group of ports to a particular backplane segment within an intelligent hub device. This port configuration switching allowed the logical grouping of users onto a particular segment without the need to physically travel to the wiring closet to move cables or connectors. In a sense, this offers an electronic patch panel function. Although the benefit is a reduction of moves, adds, and change costs, this advantage can only be realized within the confines of a single hub. The application of this type of switching is limited because it cannot extend beyond one intelligent concentrator. Although beneficial in the work group, the enterprise needs cannot be met.

Phone system operators in the 1940s manually patched user connections through to destinations and recorded call time and duration. Using configuration switching is similar to patching phone lines together. Just as the phone network grew at a pace that required the switching to be performed automatically without operator intervention, so too have data networks outgrown the limitations of configuration switching.

Packet switching isolates each port to deliver dedicated bandwidth to each user in the network. Fundamentally, a packet switch is any device that accepts an incoming packet on one port and then makes a decision whether to filter or forward the packet out another interface. There are two types of packet switch transports: connectionless and connection-oriented.

Connectionless Packet Switching

Connectionless devices are probably more familiar to IS professionals when described as bridges or routers. A bridge is a layer 2 (of the Open Systems Interconnection [OSI] reference model) switch that bases its decisions on the media access control (MAC) address of attached workstations. What many vendors describe as a switch is actually a wire-speed MAC layer bridge. Three methods of decision making in these types of devices are cut-through, modified cut-through, and store-and-forward.

The Cut-Through Switch. This switch reads a packet only until the destination address before it starts forwarding to the outbound interface. The benefit is an extremely low latency or delay in the forwarding of packets. The penalty is the propagation of errors, because the frame is being forwarded before it can be verified as valid, and the inability to support interfaces of different speeds that prevent high-bandwidth uplinks of FDDI or ATM on these type of devices.

The Modified Cut-Through Switch. This switch reads the first 64 bytes of a frame and then starts forwarding to the outbound interface, which greatly reduces the chances of propagating errored frames throughout the network. However, this method still requires all ports to be of the same type and speed.

Store-and-Forward Switch. The most flexible switch design uses a store-and-forward methodology that reads the entire frame before any filtering or forwarding decisions are made, thus ensuring that only packets that are error free are forwarded on the network. This method also allows packets to be buffered when transferring data between networks of different types, such as Ethernet to FDDI or ATM.

Bridges and Routers. A router is a layer 3 switch that bases its decisions on the network protocol address of attached work stations. Bridges and routers are considered connectionless because they forward and forget, requiring a decision to be made on every single inbound packet. The performance implications are that even though two communicating nodes on opposite sides of a bridge or router may be the only devices on their respective networks, the bridge or router must continuously make filter or forward decisions on every packet sent between the two nodes.

A connectionless transport is not capable of defining which path its payload will take, cannot guarantee delivery, and is generally slower than a connection-oriented system. When a node sends a packet through a bridged or routed network, it is analogous to dropping a letter into a mailbox. It is not apparent how the letter got to its destination. The arrival of a letter cannot be guaranteed (protocol prioritization techniques are comparable to sending a letter by express mail). If a letter is lost (or a packet dropped), determining where it was lost is often difficult. The only way the sender knows that the letter was received is if the recipient sends another letter back to the sender (i.e., frame acknowledgment).

In a sense, today's shared-access networks are like the party lines of the early telephone network. But just as the phone network evolved from party lines to dedicated lines as usage and deployment grew, so too must the data networks offer this same level of service guarantee and broad adoption.

Connection-Oriented Switches

The connection-oriented switch that the phone systems use offers immediate acknowledgment of communications when the person picks up at the other end. The exact path the call took as well as its time and duration can be logged. The destination needs to be dialed only once and information is exchanged until both parties hang up.

The idea of connection-oriented communications is not new. This type of switching provides a high degree of reliability and reduces operational costs. Multiple classes of service can be defined to support voice, video, and data transfer. Excellent bandwidth management through congestion control techniques is possible and security and access control are greatly improved. Connection-oriented switching, along with easy-to-implement policy-based management and accounting facilities, have enabled the phone system to become universally accessible.

Frame relay technology is centered around connection-oriented communications, as is the most promising future networking technology — ATM. ATM is the most desirable networking technology because it offers dedicated, scalable bandwidth solutions for voice, video, and data.

ATM Switching. ATM switching is connection-oriented. Communications in an ATM network can be broken down into three phases: call setup (analogous to dialing a phone), data transfer (talking on the phone), and call teardown (hanging up the phone). The use of fixed-length 53-byte cells for data transfer delivers fixed latency transfer times for constant bit rate applications such as voice and video. ATM addressing schemes are similar to a telephone number. In fact, the original designers of ATM technology had their roots in the telephony arena, so many analogies to the operation of the phone system can be made when referring to an ATM network.

Although the benefits of ATM networking are attractive, there are currently nearly 100 million networked personal computers that do not have ATM interfaces. Few organizations can afford to replace all of their existing desktop and server interfaces, not to mention network analyzers and troubleshooting equipment.

Through the preservation of existing interface technology, by merely changing the internetworking devices from being connectionless to connection oriented, many of the benefits of ATM may be realized without requiring the investment in all new ATM equipment. If LANs were designed to operate using the same principles as ATM, rather than making ATM compatible with LANs, users would benefit without significant capital investments in new equipment. By adding switching technology to the middle of the network, network administrators can be spared the trouble of upgrading numerous user devices, and users can be spared the inconvenience of rewiring and disruptions at their work site during an upgrade.

FEATURES OF SWITCHING SOFTWARE

The software that runs on switches is just as important as the switches themselves. A salesperson from Lucent Technologies, Fujitsu, or Northern Telecom does not focus the potential customer on the hardware aspects of the telephone switches. On the contrary, the salesperson conveys the benefits of the call management software, accounting, and automatic call distributor (ACD) functions. Switched virtual networks should also be evaluated for their ability to deliver value because of the software features.

The Virtual Network Server

Network management software has traditionally been thought of as software that passively reports the status and operation of devices in the network. In the switched virtual network, the network management software takes on a new role as an active participant in operations as well as configuration and reporting. A new middleware component known as the virtual network server (VNS) enforces the policies of operation defined by the network administrator through management software applications. The switches provide the data transport for the users of the network.

Directory Service. One of the software features in the VNS is the directory service. The directory service allows the identification of a device by logical name, MAC address, network protocol address, and ATM address, along with the switch and port that the user is connected to within the virtual network domain. The directory listing could be populated manually or dynamically as addresses are discovered. To fully realize the benefits of switched virtual networking, automatic configuration is absolutely essential. The directory service allows end nodes to be located and identified.

Security Service. The VNS security service will be used during call setup phases to determine whether users or groups of users were allowed to connect to each other. On a user-by-user and conversation-by-conversation basis, the network manager would have control. This communications policy management is analogous to call management on a telephone private branch exchange (PBX) where 900 numbers, long-distance, or international calls can be blocked. Users could be grouped together to form policy groups in which rules could be applied to individual users, groups, or even nested groups. Policies could be defined as open or secure, inclusive or exclusive.

A sample default policy can ensure that all communications are specifically defined to the VNS in order to be authorized. Policy groups can be manipulated either through drag-and-drop graphical user interfaces or programatically through simple network management protocol (SNMP) commands.

Finally, and most important, the directory service can work in conjunction with the security service to ensure that policies follow the users as they move throughout the network. This feature alone could save time spent maintaining a router access list, as occurs when a user changes location in the traditional network. However, it is important to realize that switched virtual networks ease administrative chores, they do not eliminate them.

Connection Management Service. The VNS connection management service is used to define the path communications would take through the switch fabric. A site may be linked by a relatively high-speed ATM link and a parallel but relatively low-speed Ethernet link. Network connections with a defined high quality of service (QoS) could traverse the ATM link and lower QoS connections could traverse the Ethernet. This connection management service allows for the transparent rerouting of calls in the event of a network fault. Connection management could also provide ongoing network monitoring in which individual user conversations could be tapped or traced for easy troubleshooting.

Bandwidth Service. The VNS bandwidth service is used during the call setup when a connection request is made. Video teleconferencing users may require a committed information rate (CIR) of 10 Mbps whereas the terminal emulation users may only require 1 Mbps. This is where ATM end stations and ATM switches negotiate the amount of bandwidth dedicated to a particular virtual circuit using user-to-network interface (UNI) signaling. Ethernet, Token Ring, and FDDI nodes do not recognize UNI signaling, but the switches they attach to could proxy the signal for the end station, thus allowing a single bandwidth manager for the entire network, not just the ATM portion.

Broadcast Service. The VNS broadcast service uses as its base the concept of the broadcast unknown server (BUS) that is part of the ATM Forum's LAN emulation draft standard. This is how broadcasts are flooded through the network to remain compatible with the operation of many of today's protocols and network operating systems. A degree of intelligence can be assigned to the VNS that would allow for broadcasts or multicasts based on protocol type or even policy group.

Virtual Routing Service. The VNS virtual routing service is one of the most critical components of a virtual network. Just as traditional networks required traditional routers for interconnection, virtual LANs will require virtual routers for internetworking between virtual LANs. In other words, routing is required, but routers may not be. Some protocols such as TCP/IP actually require a router for users on two different subnetworks to speak with each other. In addition, most networks today are logically divided based on network layer protocol addresses with routers acting as the building block between segments.

The difference in operation between a virtual router and a traditional router goes back to the connection-oriented vs. connectionless distinction. Routing allows for address resolution between the layer 3 protocol address and the layer 2 MAC address just as it happens through the address resolution protocol (ARP) process in TCP/IP networks. The VNS virtual routing service performs the address resolution function, but once the end station addresses are resolved, establishes a virtual connection between the two users. Two users separated by a traditional router would always have the router intervening on every single packet because the router would have resolved the protocol addresses to its own MAC address rather than the actual end station's MAC address. This VNS routing service allows the network to route once for connection setup and switch all successive packets.

Accounting Service. The VNS accounting service is beneficial because it allows the creation of the network bill. Similar to the way a telephone bill is broken down, the accounting service details connection duration with date and time stamp along with bandwidth consumption details. This is most directly applicable in the WAN. For many managers, WAN usage is never really accounted for on an individual user basis, yet it can consume up to 40 percent of the operations budget.

As usage-based WAN service options such as integrated services digital network (ISDN) gain popularity, accounting becomes that much more critical. Interexchange carriers (IXCs), competitive access providers, and the regional Bell operating companies (RBOCs) continue to deliver higher-bandwidth links with usage-based tariffs. In the future, they could install a 155 Mbps synchronous optical network (SONET) OC-3 link and only charge for the actual bandwidth used. Unless managers have tools to control access to and account for usage of WAN links, WAN costs will continue to rise. This service lets IS managers know who is using the WAN.

VIRTUAL NETWORKS VS. VIRTUAL LANS

Throughout this discussion, words have been carefully chosen to describe the operation of switched virtual networks. Many of the current vendor offerings on the market have as their goal the construction of a switched virtual LAN. These virtual LANs are interconnected using a traditional router device. However, the router has been viewed as the performance bottleneck. Routers should be deployed when segmentation or separation is the need; switches should be used to deliver more bandwidth.

The virtual LAN (VLAN) concept is merely an interim step along the way to realizing the fully virtual network.

The ATM Forum's draft LAN emulation standard allows ATM devices to internetwork with traditional LAN networks such as Ethernet and Token Ring. However, it seems ironic that it essentially tries to make ATM networks operate like a traditional shared-access LAN segment. Although it is required for near-term deployment of ATM solutions into existing LAN architectures, its position as an end-all solution is questionable. A more logical approach uses ATM as the model that LANs must emulate.

CONCLUSION

Each vendor's approach to virtual networking features will vary slightly in implementation. Most vendors have agreed, however, that the router is moving to the periphery of the network and the core will be based on switching technologies with virtual network capabilities. The three critical success factors that a virtual network vendor must display to effectively deliver on all the promise of virtual networks are connectivity, internetworking, and network management.

Connectivity expertise through a demonstrated leadership in the intelligent hub industry ensures the user a broad product line with numerous options with regard to topology and media types. The product should fit the network, rather than the network design being dictated by the capability of the product. This indicates a vendor's willingness to embrace standards-based connectivity solutions as well as SNMP management and remote monitoring (RMON) analyzer capabilities.

Internetworking expertise ensures that the vendor is fully equipped to deal with layer 2 as well as layer 3 switching issues through an understanding of protocols and their operation. This is not something that can be learned overnight. The integration of these technologies is still unattainable.

Network management software is crucial — virtual networks do not exist or operate without it. The virtual network services provide all the value to the switch fabric. Users should look for a vendor that has delivered distributed management capabilities. Just as the telephone network relies on a distributed software intelligence for its operations, so too must the switched virtual network provide the same degree of redundancy and fault tolerance. Users also should consider whether the vendor embraces all of the popular network management platforms (e.g., SunNet Manager, HP OpenView, Cabletron SPECTRUM, and IBM NetView for AIX) or only one. Finally, users should make sure the vendor has experience managing multiple types of devices from vendors other than itself. It would be naive to think that all the components that make up a network are of one type from one vendor.

Chapter 23
Putting VPNs to Work for Small Businesses and Offices

Joy Pinsky
Michael Kennedy

MODERN BUSINESS PROCESSES DEMAND TIGHT LINKS between mobile users, customers, and third parties on both a temporary basis (project-based) and permanent basis. Virtual Private Networks (VPNs) can provide significant business benefits by overcoming the barriers to achieving widely available and secure communication. VPNs provide the appearance of a single network connecting corporate offices, telecommuters, customers, and even competitors, while using separate public and private networks. A company retains control of user access and the privacy and integrity of its data even though the data travel on the public Internet. VPNs can provide as much as 60 percent cost savings over private leased lines and significantly reduce telecommuter dial-up charges.

VPNs and their many benefits, however, have traditionally been the domain of larger organizations. These huge companies enjoy access to the capital and scale necessary to build VPNs and have the technical staff to maintain them. They are able to use VPNs to enhance and sustain their competitive advantage over their smaller and less technically sophisticated competitors. In practical terms, the benefits of VPNs have been off limits to small- and medium-sized businesses. And, even larger organizations have had difficulty deploying VPNs in branch offices because they are often too small to justify on-site IT staff.

The barriers to creating and maintaining a VPN include the need to construct and maintain a secure physical infrastructure and administer a wide range of data communications services. The infrastructure challenges include setting up access equipment, firewalls, servers, telecommunications services, and maintaining connections to multiple Internet Service Providers (ISPs) at hundreds or even thousands of enterprise locations.

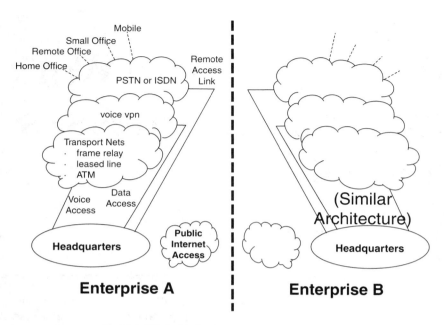

Exhibit 23-1. Today's enterprise networks.

Administrative challenges include maintenance of servers, synchronization of software upgrades, replication of Web servers, and sophisticated policy management spanning the whole network. Services that must be supported include e-mail, directory, internal and external Web, firewall, FTP, and access control.

Virtual Services Management (VSM) technology and secure VPN transports are making VPNs realistically deployable for smaller organizations and branch offices. VSM solves the service-related headaches of multiple points of administration required when setting up multiple sites, users, devices, and Internet Service Providers (ISPs). Through use of low-cost, easily managed, and secure VPNs, the benefits of improved business management practices can be realized by even medium and small companies.

EMERGENCE OF THE VIRTUAL PRIVATE NETWORK

Today's private networks resemble the network in Exhibit 23-1. Basic connectivity is provided to a wide variety of locations, but the overhead costs are severe. The functionality includes the following services.

Remote Access

Remote access has matured from a "nice-to-have" option to a business-critical requirement to support a mobile workforce and telecommuters.

For example, utility companies are increasing the productivity of their field service workers and eliminating the cost of maintaining distribution centers by applying remote access technologies. Line crews take their vehicles home with them and receive their day's work orders through either telephone or wireless dispatching systems. This setup eliminates the time it takes to report to the service center, pick up the service vehicle, and drive to the first job site. Remote access creates a win-win-win situation for the company, worker, and customer. The utility company realizes increased worker productivity, reduced transportation costs, and reduced building and land costs. The worker eliminates commuting time and expense, while customers obtain faster, more responsive service, and lower rates.

Sales and marketing organizations are especially reliant on remote access capabilities. The use of remote access capabilities and laptop computers enables salespeople to complete contracts and obtain real-time technical sales support while being face-to-face with customers — meeting customer needs and resolving buyer objections through a single sales call and resulting in more successful sales and shorter sales cycles.

Intracorporate Core Connectivity

Business process reengineering programs and application of Enterprise Resource Planning (ERP), such as SAP, succeed by eliminating barriers to communications across departmental boundaries and by replacing slow paperwork procedures with shared electronic databases. These management practices and the associated computer software require reliable, high-speed, and secure communications among all employees. The same high level of communications connectivity is required at all of the enterprise's establishments. This setup typically requires that small offices and branch offices be upgraded to the higher standards more commonplace at large headquarters locations. The payoff for successful ERP implementation is an order of magnitude reduction in cycle times, increased flexibility and responsiveness, and sharp reductions in IT overhead costs.

Closed User Groups with Partners, Customers, and Suppliers

Some of the most dramatic improvements in business processes are obtained by eliminating certain subprocesses entirely. The supply chain is one business process where big improvements are being realized. For example, Boeing suppliers are required to participate in its supply network. This enables Boeing to eliminate stores and parts costs entirely by moving those functions back into the supplier's operation. Similar successes have been achieved in sales and marketing. In another example, Saturn customers can step through the entire sales process online. Saturn reduces selling costs and provides prospective customers with full and accurate examination of options and features, independent of high-pressure salespeople.

Saturn also offers prospective buyers direct access to engineers and product experts at its headquarters.

Highly technical sales organizations can create lock-in relationships with their customers through creation of closed user groups. For example, semiconductor manufacturers provide online engineering design tools so that circuit designers can incorporate the manufacturer's chips directly into finished designs. Closed user groups not only assure product loyalty, they also provide value to circuit designers by reducing cycle times.

Public Internet Access

Essentially all functional areas can benefit from public Internet access. Accounting organizations retrieve forms and advice from federal, state, and local revenue offices. Human resources organizations use the Monster Board for recruiting. Mechanical designers can peruse online parts catalogs and download CAD/CAM drawings directly into their blue prints. Energy marketers buy and sell natural gas through Internet-based trading systems and retrieve weather data from government and private sources. Pension fund managers follow the financial markets and retrieve stockholder information from company Web pages. IT professionals stay ahead of industry developments and product releases by studying computer and software vendors' online product literature. The business benefit of most of this activity is faster and better-informed decisionmaking.

Internet-Based Customer Interaction

Retail sales and service companies operate on thin operating margins. Their success depends on executing transactions rapidly and at low cost while giving the customer the appearance of custom-tailored service — this is sometimes referred to as mass customization. Industries such as airlines, utilities, banks, brokerage, insurance, and mail-order retailers know that market segmentation, customer loyalty, and low transaction costs are the keys to their success (or survival). Of course, the more time customer service representatives spend with customers and the more they can learn about customers, the better the market segmentation and the customer relationship. Unfortunately, this tender loving care costs money and drives up transaction costs.

Well-designed Internet-based customer interaction systems resolve this dilemma by eliminating customer service staffing costs and simultaneously providing customers with many custom choices. Information provided by the customer during these online sessions flows directly to the enterprise's data warehouse and is used by data-mining tools to further refine the market segmentation models. Brokerage and financial services firms are especially effective at using the Internet to drive down small-lot trading fees and eliminate the cost of account representatives. For example, a trade of 100 shares that once cost several hundred dollars can be done on the Internet for $10. As another example, airlines, including United Airlines, provide Web pages where customers can shop for the best price and schedule, and book their travel over the Internet.

Web Presence

The public Internet is rapidly replacing mass media, including television, radio, and print, as the vehicle for certain product and institutional advertising. While practically all businesses feel compelled to have a Web page, it is essential in many industry segments. Use of Web pages is firmly entrenched in the IT industry itself, financial services, education, and government services. The key item these enterprises share in common is a need for dissemination of large quantities of time-sensitive information to millions of people.

While these enterprises gain high value from rapid and cheap dissemination of information through Internet Web pages, they also face large risks. Incorrect or false information could destroy the public trust that was built up over decades. Slow information access or unreliable access could create an image of ineptitude or unresponsiveness, damaging institutional loyalty and trust. Failure to safeguard customer data and protect privacy could, at best, destroy trust and, at worst, cause financial ruin. Thus, a Web presence can be effective in reaching the mass market, but security and reliability must be assured.

GETTING REAL BUSINESS VALUE FROM VIRTUAL PRIVATE NETWORKS

The preceding section describes six ways data communications can be used to produce business value. However, today's data communications networks are failing to deliver the value, because they are too complex and costly. VPNs provide more efficient and secure data communications at a fraction of the cost of today's network architectures. In particular, VPNs reduce the administrative effort and costs of building and operating private networks. This is particularly true as customers, suppliers, and third parties are added to the network. Exhibit 23-2 shows the emerging VPN architecture.

One difference between the VPN architecture and today's private network architecture is that the VPN architecture is seamless. Users in each enterprise, regardless of whether their location is at headquarters or on a wireless link, obtain the same access and logical view of services, despite being served by a number of ISPs and through different physical media. Another difference between the private data communications network and the VPN is that business users never see the network complexity, and network administrators are freed from complex network engineering tasks.

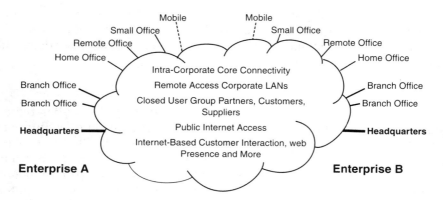

Exhibit 23-2. Emerging VPN architecture.

VIRTUAL SERVICE MANAGEMENT

Many of today's VPNs have focused only on providing a secure transport, the network "plumbing." But in practical terms, the benefits of VPN have been off limits to smaller businesses and organizations with limited IT staff and resources, because of the technical complexity of setting up and administering a VPN. Virtual Services Management (VSM) is critical to making a VPN easy to administer and manage across multiple locations and services.

The administrative challenge of creating and maintaining a VPN is formidable. A single enterprise often must accommodate headquarters, campuses, branch offices to home offices, and users who want to use a range of applications and services, and have specific accessing privileges and options. In addition, modern management practice requires many additional links to suppliers, customers, and third parties, as well as access to the public Internet with its 100 million computers.

Through a single point of administration anywhere on the network (local or remote), VSM technology simplifies the administrative burden of setting up multiple branch office e-mail, Web, firewall, and other user services; multiple domain and user names; and coordination among multiple ISPs. It also simplifies the administrative burden through automatic synchronization of software upgrades, replication of Web servers, and sophisticated policy management. VSM overcomes the barrier to private network implementation and VPN that could previously be addressed by only a handful of the largest, more technically sophisticated enterprises.

VSM can help resellers by making it easy for them to add services without raising the level of technical support they will need to provide. This can by done with service providers or as a stand-alone value-added feature.

Similarly, service providers can take advantage of VSM and VPNs to provide a value-added network feature to their customers. VPN services are typically provided on a monthly fee basis and often require customers to perform the network configuration and route determination for their VPN. Where the customer is doing much of the work already, customers often acquire the lines and build a VPN network using CPE products such as an all-in-one Internet system (described below). Many enterprises are finding if they partner with their service provider to produce a VPN solution, it can be a very effective way to take development costs out of the equation.

SECURE AND RELIABLE NETWORKING TRANSPORT

To provide secure and reliable transport across the network, three main issues must be resolved:

1. Overall network security
2. Wide-area network tunneling
3. Class of service and quality of service

Products and standards are in place to provide overall network security while emerging standards will soon resolve the other two issues.

Four functions are key to overall network security:

1. Authentication — verify the identity of the user
2. Authorization — verify which services the user is allowed to access
3. Accounting — create an audit trail of the user's network activity
4. Encryption — protect data privacy

These four functions are typically provided by access control lists in routers that restrict access to data packets and network segments in both directions. Firewalls provide more sophisticated control of incoming and outgoing packets at the network's edge. Authentication and authorization is provided by services such as PAP or CHAP and by security servers. Proxy application servers and the network operating system provide additional network security. These necessary services and products are now widely deployed in ISPs and private networks.

Wide-area network tunneling is a technique that establishes a secure network connection across the public Internet. Trade press articles sometimes equate VPNs to tunneling. Our view is that tunneling, while an essential ingredient of the VPN solution, is but one element of the VPN and that administrative and reliability issues are at least as important to successful VPN adoption. Major networking vendors have advanced proposed tunneling standards such as Point-to-Point Tunneling Protocol and L2F. Much marketplace confusion has resulted from these competing standards. Happily, it appears that a compromise approach called L2TP will resolve the differences between these competing standards and will soon emerge from the IETF standards-setting process.

IMPLEMENTING THE VPN

The key to deploying a VPN is to give the appearance of a seamless network with identical user services at all locations — headquarters, branch offices, home offices, and those of partners, suppliers, and customers. One approach to VPN implementation for small- and medium-sized organizations is to deploy all-in-one Internet systems, sometimes called "Internet edge servers," at the network edge between each enterprise site and the local ISP. The all-in-one Internet system integrates Internet server, firewall, and networking functionality for organizations that want to take greater advantage of the Internet without adding a complex and costly assembly of boxes and IT staff.

VSM capabilities supported by the system can then provide single-point administration of VPN services. Exhibit 23-3 shows how the three versions of VSM technology — in-branch, remote, and extranet applications — can be used.

A multibranch VPN can be used to connect a company's remotely located, LAN-attached offices. An all-in-one Internet system will be required at each office, in this case. Class of Service policies, such as access privileges and priorities, can be applied as if the branch users were physically located at headquarters. Security can be implemented through the emerging industry-standard IP Security (IPSec) protocol, which will provide DES encryption, authentication, and key management.

A remote VPN can enable mobile workers and telecommuters to dial into a local ISP to access corporate information and service, making it appear as if they were sitting at their desks in the main office. An all-in-one Internet system will be required at headquarters and Microsoft's Point-to-Point Protocol (PPTP), available with MS Windows clients, will be required on the remote user's desktop or laptop system. A Point-to-Point Protocol server in the system can authenticate the remote user, then open an encrypted path through which traffic flows as if through the LAN.

An extranet VPN opens a corporate network selectively to suppliers, customers, strategic business partners, and users having access to a limited set of information behind the corporate firewall. An extranet VPN implementation differs from branch and remote VPN implementations in that its use is likely to involve temporary virtual networks which may be set up for specific projects and dismantled as the project's end.

It is important that all necessary service management, security, and Quality of Service functions are combined in the system so that multiple

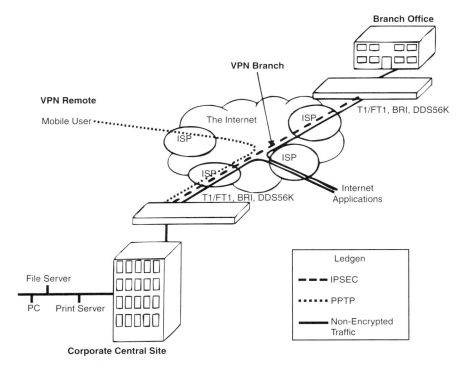

Exhibit 23-3. The three versions of VSM technology.

---

systems can be administered as though they are on a single local network. The supported services should include all of the administrative, security, and reliability requirements of the VPN:

- IP router
- Web server
- firewall
- e-mail
- file transfer (FTP)
- Domain Name Service (DNS)
- Dynamic Host Configuration Protocol (DHCP)
- remote management

Hardware costs can also be minimized because all the necessary administrative, security, and reliable transport functionalities are combined in a single unit. Administrative and operating expenses can be controlled through VSM, which permits management of all sites from a single point — minimizing the need for costly data communications experts.

CONCLUSION

The VPN supports the business needs of a company by eliminating the technical and administrative obstacles to rapid electronic information flows within a company and with partners, customers, and suppliers. The VPN delivers the same networking services to all parties, whether at large or small sites, and across multiple ISP networks. Virtual Services Management makes it economical for small- and medium-sized enterprises to build VPNs and permits delivery of corporate networking services out to even the most remote corporate outpost. The VPN's low cost and uniform networking environment supports the implementation of business strategies necessary to achieving and maintaining a sustainable competitive advantage.

Chapter 24
Virtual Private Networks: Secure Remote Access over the Internet

John R. Vacca

THE COMPONENTS AND RESOURCES OF ONE NETWORK OVER ANOTHER NETWORK are connected via a Virtual Private Network (VPN). As shown in Exhibit 24-1, VPNs accomplish this by allowing the user to tunnel through the Internet or another public network in a manner that lets the tunnel participants enjoy the same security and features formerly available only in private networks.

Using the routing infrastructure provided by a public internetwork (such as the Internet), VPNs allow telecommuters, remote employees like salespeople, or even branch offices to connect in a secure fashion to an enterprise server located at the edge of the enterprise local area network (LAN). The VPN is a point-to-point connection between the user's computer and an enterprise server from the user's perspective. It also appears as if the data is being sent over a dedicated private link because the nature of the intermediate internetwork is irrelevant to the user. As previously mentioned, while maintaining secure communications, VPN technology also allows an enterprise to connect to branch offices or to other enterprises (extranets) over a public internetwork (such as the Internet). The VPN connection across the Internet logically operates as a wide area network (WAN) link between the sites. In both cases, the secure connection across the internetwork appears to the user as a private network communication (despite the fact that this communication occurs over a public internetwork); hence the name Virtual Private Network.

VPN technology is designed to address issues surrounding the current enterprise trend toward increased telecommuting, widely distributed global

0-8493-0859-3/00/$0.00+$.50
© 2000 by CRC Press LLC

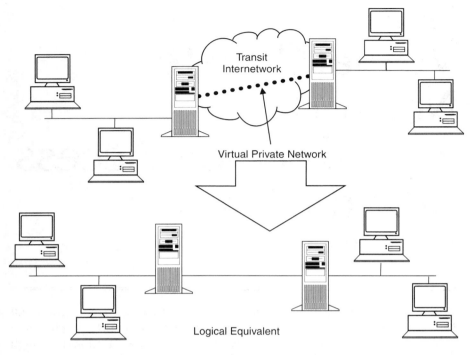

Virtual Private Network

Logical Equivalent

Exhibit 24-1. Virtual Private Network.

operations, and highly interdependent partner operations. Here, workers must be able to connect to central resources and communicate with each other. And, enterprises need to efficiently manage inventories for just-in-time production.

An enterprise must deploy a reliable and scalable remote access solution to provide employees with the ability to connect to enterprise computing resources regardless of their location. Enterprises typically choose one of the following:

- an IT department-driven solution, where an internal information systems department is charged with buying, installing, and maintaining enterprise modem pools and a private network infrastructure
- value-added network (VAN) solutions, where an enterprise pays an outsourced enterprise to buy, install, and maintain modem pools and a Telco infrastructure

The optimum solution in terms of cost, reliability, scalability, flexible administration and management, and demand for connections is provided by neither of these traditional solutions. Therefore, it makes sense to find a middle ground where the enterprise either supplements or replaces its current investments in modem pools and its private network infrastructure with a less-expensive solution based on Internet technology. In this manner, the enterprise can focus on its core competencies with the assurance that accessibility will never be compromised, and that the most economical solution will be deployed. The availability of an Internet solution enables a few Internet connections (via Internet service providers, or ISPs) and deployment of several edge-of-network VPN server computers to serve the remote networking needs of thousands or even tens of thousands of remote clients and branch offices, as described next.

VPN Common Uses

The next few subsections of this chapter describe in more detail common VPN situations.

Secure Remote User Access over the Internet. While maintaining privacy of information, VPNs provide remote access to enterprise resources over the public Internet. A VPN that is used to connect a remote user to an enterprise intranet is shown in Exhibit 24-2. The user first calls a local ISP Network Access Server (NAS) phone number, rather than making a leased-line, long-distance (or 1-800) call to an enterprise or outsourced NAS. The VPN software creates a virtual private network between the dial-up user and the enterprise VPN server across the Internet using the local connection to the ISP.

Connecting Networks over the Internet. To connect local area networks at remote sites, there exist two methods for using VPNs: using dedicated lines to connect a branch office to an enterprise LAN, or a dial-up line to connect a branch office to an enterprise LAN.

Using Dedicated Lines to Connect a Branch Office to an Enterprise LAN. Both the branch office and the enterprise hub routers can use a local dedicated circuit and local ISP to connect to the Internet, rather than using an expensive long-haul dedicated circuit between the branch office and the enterprise hub. The local ISP connections and the public Internet are used by the VPN software to create a virtual private network between the branch office router and the enterprise hub router.

Using a Dial-Up Line to Connect a Branch Office to an Enterprise LAN. The router at the branch office can call the local ISP, rather than having a router at the branch office make a leased-line, long-distance or (1-800) call to an enterprise or outsourced NAS. Also, in order to create a VPN between the branch office router and the enterprise hub router across the Internet, the VPN software uses the connection to the local ISP as shown in Exhibit 24-3.

VPN traffic

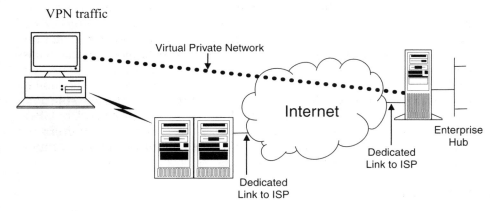

Exhibit 24-2. Using a VPN to connect a remote client to a private LAN.

The facilities that connect the branch office and enterprise offices to the Internet are local in both cases. To make a connection, both client/server, and server/server VPN cost savings are largely predicated on the use of a local access phone number. It is recommended that the enterprise hub router that acts as a VPN server be connected to a local ISP with a dedicated line. This VPN server must be listening 24 hours per day for incoming VPN traffic.

Connecting Computers over an Intranet

The departmental data is so sensitive that the department's LAN is physically disconnected from the rest of the enterprise internetwork in some enterprise internetworks. All of this creates information accessibility problems for those users not physically connected to the separate LAN, although the department's confidential information is protected.

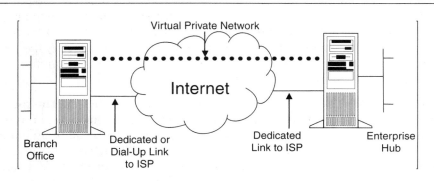

Exhibit 24-3. Using a VPN to connect two remote sites.

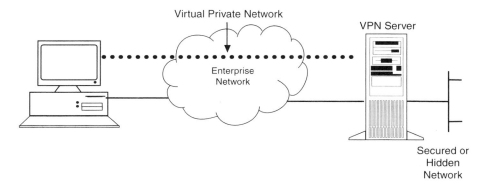

Exhibit 24-4. Using a VPN to Connect to two computers on the same LAN.

VPNs allow the department's LAN to be separated by a VPN server (see Exhibit 24-4), but physically connected to the enterprise internetwork. One should note that the VPN server is not acting as a router between the enterprise internetwork and the department LAN. A router would interconnect the two networks, thus allowing everyone access to the sensitive LAN. The network administrator can ensure that only those users on the enterprise internetwork who have appropriate credentials (based on a need-to-know policy within the enterprise) can establish a VPN with the VPN server and gain access to the protected resources of the department by using a VPN. Additionally, all communication across the VPN can be encrypted for data confidentiality. Thus, the department LAN cannot be viewed by those users who do not have the proper credentials.

BASIC VPN REQUIREMENTS

Normally, an enterprise desires to facilitate controlled access to enterprise resources and information when deploying a remote networking solution. In order to easily connect to enterprise local area network (LAN) resources, the solution must allow freedom for authorized remote clients. And, in order to share resources and information (LAN-to-LAN connections), the solution must also allow remote offices to connect to each other. Finally, as the data traverses the public Internet, the solution must ensure the privacy and integrity of data. Also, in the case of sensitive data traversing an enterprise internetwork, the same concerns apply. A VPN solution should therefore provide all of the following at a minimum:

- *Address management:* the solution must assign a client's address on the private net, and must ensure that private addresses are kept private
- *Data encryption:* data carried on the public network must be rendered unreadable to unauthorized clients on the network

VPNs, INTERNETS, AND EXTRANETS

- *Key management:* the solution must generate and refresh encryption keys for the client and server
- *Multiprotocol support:* the solution must be able to handle common protocols used in the public network; these include Internet Protocol (IP), Internet Packet Exchange (IPX), etc.
- *User authentication:* the solution must verify a user's identity and restrict VPN access to authorized users; in addition, the solution must provide audit and accounting records to show who accessed what information and when

Furthermore, all of these basic requirements are met by an Internet VPN solution based on the Point-to-Point Tunneling Protocol (PPTP) or Layer 2 Tunneling Protocol (L2TP). The solution also takes advantage of the broad availability of the worldwide Internet. Other solutions meet some of these requirements, but remain useful for specific situations, including the new IP Security Protocol (IPSec).

Point-to-Point Tunneling Protocol (PPTP)

PPTP is a Layer 2 protocol that encapsulates PPP frames in IP datagrams for transmission over an IP internetwork, such as the Internet. PPTP can also be used in private LAN-to-LAN networking.

PPTP is documented in the draft RFC, "Point-to-Point Tunneling Protocol."[1] This draft was submitted to the IETF in June 1996 by the member enterprises of the PPTP Forum, including Microsoft Corporation, Ascend Communications, 3Com/Primary Access, ECI Telematics, and U.S. Robotics (now 3Com).

The Point-to-Point Tunneling Protocol (PPTP) uses Generic Routing Encapsulation (GRE) encapsulated Point-to-Point Protocol (PPP) frames for tunneled data and a TCP connection for tunnel maintenance. The payloads of the encapsulated PPP frames can be compressed as well as encrypted. How a PPTP packet is assembled prior to transmission is shown in Exhibit 24-5. The illustration shows a dial-up client creating a tunnel across an internetwork. The encapsulation for a dial-up client (PPP device driver) is shown in the final frame layout.

Layer 2 Forwarding (L2F)

L2F (a technology proposed by Cisco Systems, Inc.) is a transmission protocol that allows dial-up access servers to frame dial-up traffic in PPP and transmit it over WAN links to an L2F server (a router). The L2F server then unwraps the packets and injects them into the network. Unlike PPTP and L2TP, L2F has no defined client.[2]

328

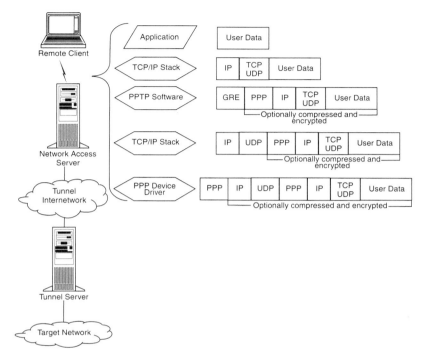

Exhibit 24-5. Construction of a PPTP packet.

Layer 2 Tunneling Protocol (L2TP)

A combination of PPTP and L2F makes up L2TP. In other words, the best features of PPTP and L2F are incorporated into L2TP.

L2TP is a network protocol that encapsulates PPP frames to be sent over Asynchronous Transfer Mode (ATM), IP, X.25, or frame relay networks. L2TP can be used as a tunneling protocol over the Internet when configured to use IP as its datagram transport. Without an IP transport layer, L2TP can also be used directly over various WAN media (such as Frame Relay). L2TP is documented in the draft RFC, Layer 2 Tunneling Protocol "L2TP" (draft-ietf-pppext-l2tp-09.txt). This draft document was submitted to the IETF.

For tunnel maintenance, L2TP over IP internetworks uses UDP and a series of L2TP messages. As the tunneled data, L2TP also uses UDP to send L2TP-encapsulated PPP frames. The payloads of encapsulated PPP frames can be compressed as well as encrypted. How an L2TP packet is assembled prior to transmission is shown in Exhibit 24-6. A dial-up client creating a

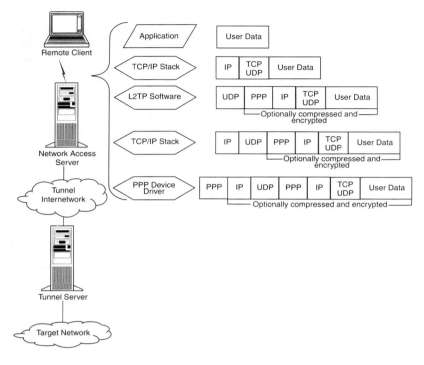

Exhibit 24-6. Construction of an L2TP packet.

tunnel across an internetwork is shown in the exhibit. The encapsulation for a dial-up client (PPP device driver) is shown in the final frame layout. L2TP over IP is assumed in the encapsulation.

L2TP Compared to PPTP. PPP is used to provide an initial envelope for the data for both PPTP and L2TP. Then, it appends additional headers for transport through the internetwork. The two protocols are very similar. There are differences between PPTP and L2TP, however. For example,

- L2TP provides for header compression. When header compression is enabled, L2TP operates with four bytes of overhead, as compared to six bytes for PPTP.
- L2TP provides for tunnel authentication, while PPTP does not. However, when either protocol is used over IPSec, tunnel authentication is provided by IPSec so that Layer 2 tunnel authentication is not necessary.
- PPTP can only support a single tunnel between endpoints. L2TP allows for the use of multiple tunnels between endpoints. With L2TP, one can create different tunnels for different qualities of service.

- PPTP requires that the internetwork be an IP internetwork. L2TP requires only that the tunnel media provide packet-oriented point-to-point connectivity. L2TP can be used over IP (using UDP), Frame Relay permanent virtual circuits (PVCs), X.25 virtual circuits (VCs), or ATM VCs.

Internet Protocol Security (IPSec) Tunnel Mode

The secured transfer of information across an IP internetwork is supported by IPSec (a Layer 3 protocol standard). Nevertheless, in the context of tunneling protocols, one aspect of IPSec is discussed here. IPSec defines the packet format for an IP over an IP tunnel mode (generally referred to as IPSec Tunnel Mode), in addition to its definition of encryption mechanisms for IP traffic. An IPSec tunnel consists of a tunnel server and tunnel client. These are both configured to use a negotiated encryption mechanism and IPSec tunneling.

For secure transfer across a private or public IP internetwork, IPSec Tunnel Mode uses the negotiated security method (if any) to encapsulate and encrypt entire IP packets. The encrypted payload is then encapsulated again with a plaintext IP header. It is then sent on the internetwork for delivery to the tunnel server. The tunnel server processes and discards the plaintext IP header and then decrypts its contents to retrieve the original payload IP packet. Upon receipt of this datagram, the payload IP packet is then processed normally and routed to its destination on the target network. The following features and limitations are contained within the IPSec Tunnel Mode:

- It is controlled by a security policy: a set of filter-matching rules. This security policy establishes the encryption and tunneling mechanisms available in order of preference and the authentication methods available, also in order of preference. As soon as there is traffic, the two machines perform mutual authentication, and then negotiate the encryption methods to be used. Thereafter, all traffic is encrypted using the negotiated encryption mechanism and then wrapped in a tunnel header.
- It functions at the bottom of the IP stack; therefore, applications and higher-level protocols inherit its behavior.
- It supports IP traffic only.

The remainder of this article discusses VPNs and the use of these technologies by enterprises to do secure remote access (e.g., by traveling employees and sales reps) over the Internet in greater detail.

EASY TO MANAGE AND USE

While squeezing the maximum possible from budget and support staffs, today's enterprises are asking their information technology groups (ITGs) to deliver an increasing array of communication and networking services. It appears that the situation is no different at Microsoft Corporation (Redmond, Washington). The Microsoft ITG needed to provide secure, Internet-based remote access for its more than 35,000 mobile sales personnel, telecommuters, and consultants around the world.

Microsoft's ITG is currently using and deploying a custom Windows-based remote dial-up and virtual private networking (VPN) solution by using Windows-based clients and enhanced Windows 2000® RAS (Remote Access Server) technology available in the Windows 2000 Option Pack (formerly named Windows NT 5.0). Users are given quick, easy, and low-cost network access. Additional user services are provided with new Windows-based network services from UUnet Technologies, Inc.[3]

Integrated RAS-VPN Clients

According to Microsoft, its ITG has learned that the widespread adoption and use of technology largely depends on how easy and transparent the experience is for the end user. Likewise, Microsoft's ITG has learned not to deploy technologies for which complexity results in an increased support burden on its limited support staff. Microsoft's ITG provided a single client interface with central management to simultaneously make the remote access solution easy to use and manage.

Single Client. A single client is used for both the direct dial-up and virtual private network connections. Users utilize the same client interface for secure transparent access, whether dialing directly to the enterprise network or connecting via a VPN, by using Windows integrated dial-up networking technology (DUN) and Microsoft Connection Manager. In fact, users do not need to concern themselves with which method is employed.

Central Management. Central management is used for remote dial-up and VPN access phone numbers. According to Microsoft, its ITG has found that one of the most common support problems traveling users face is determining and managing local access phone numbers. This problem translates into one of the principal reasons for support calls to Microsoft's user support centers. Using the Connection Manager Administration Kit (CMAK) wizard (which is part of Microsoft's remote access solution), Microsoft's ITG preloads each client PC with an electronic phone book that includes every dial-up remote access phone number for Microsoft's network. The Windows solution also allows phone books to be centrally integrated and managed from a single remote location, and clients to be updated automatically.

WINDOWS COMMUNICATION PLATFORM

In order to provide a flexible and comprehensive network solution, the open extensibility of the Windows 2000 allows Microsoft's ITG to preserve its current hardware network investments while partnering with UUnet Technologies, Inc. According to Microsoft, the Windows platform enabled its ITG to integrate the best-of-breed network services and applications to best meet its client and network administration needs.

High-Speed Internet Access on the Road

Microsoft employees can also connect to high-speed Internet access by plugging into public IPORT[4] jacks in hotels, airports, cafes, and remote locations. The Microsoft ITG integrates the IPORT[5] pay-per-use Internet access features into its custom remote access solution. According to Microsoft, this high-bandwidth, easily available connection helps Microsoft employees be more productive and have a better online experience while on the road.

Secure Internet Access and VPN

Microsoft's ITG, like its counterparts at every enterprise, must ensure that the edge of its network is secure while still providing all employees with the freedom needed to access information worldwide. Microsoft's ITG has also deployed Microsoft Proxy Server to securely separate the LAN from the Internet to meet this need.

To ensure that no intruders compromise the edge of network, the Microsoft Proxy Server firewall capabilities protect Microsoft's network from unauthorized access from the Internet by providing network address translation and dynamic IP-level filtering. Microsoft's ITG uses the powerful caching services in Microsoft Proxy Server to expedite the delivery of information at the same time.

The Proxy Server is able to service subsequent user requests of already-requested information without having to generate additional network traffic by reusing relevant cached information. In addition, in order to operate at peak efficiency with the utmost security, ITG uses Microsoft Proxy Server to enable the Microsoft intranet and remote employees.

RAS Reporting and Internal Usage Chargeback (Billing)

Microsoft pays a substantial amount for remote access fees due to the need to maintain private leased lines and dedicated 800 numbers like many large enterprises with a multitude of branch offices and remote employees. In addition, according to Microsoft, the sheer number of LAN entry points and autonomy afforded its international divisions made centralized accounting and retail reporting for remote access use and roaming users important.

Microsoft's ITG is deploying a VPN solution — bolstered with centralized accounting and reporting of enterprisewide remote access and VPN use — by using Windows 2000, integrated user domain directory, and RADIUS services. As part of this solution, Microsoft is also deploying TRU RADIUS Accountant™ for Windows 2000 from Telco-Research.[6]

Furthermore, Microsoft's ITG is also able to generate detailed reporting of remote access and VPN network use for internal cost-accounting purposes while using familiar Windows 2000 management tools by using Telco Research's product. In addition, Microsoft's ITG is able to quickly and easily deploy a turnkey reporting solution built on the intrinsic communication services of Windows 2000 in this manner. According to Microsoft, while maintaining the flexibility to accommodate future change, they receive better security as a result, reduced implementation costs, and enhanced reporting to improve remote access management and charge-back service.

VIP Services: Economical Internet Access and VPN

By working with UUnet Technologies, Inc. (the largest Internet service provider in the world), the Microsoft ITG supplemented its private data network infrastructure and RAS with VPN services. Microsoft's VPN solution is integrated with the UUnet Radius Proxy servers through the Windows 2000 native support for RADIUS under this relationship.

Through the Windows 2000 Remote Access Service integrated RADIUS support, Microsoft's ITG made reliable and secure local access to UUnet Technologies IP network available to all Microsoft mobile employees. This resulted in the delivery of high-quality VPN services over the UUnet Technologies, Inc. infrastructure at a reduced cost. The ITG conservatively estimates that this use of VPN service as an alternative to traditional remote access will save Microsoft more than $7 million per year in remote access fees alone. Additional savings are expected from the elimination of call requests for RAS phone numbers and greatly reduced remote access configuration support.

The ITG utilized the integrated support for RADIUS-based authentication available from the Windows Directory in Windows 2000. This allowed them to retain all existing authentication rights for both Internet and LAN access, avoiding change or redundant replication of directory, and provided for enhanced network security.

According to Microsoft, their ITG was able to instantly extend network access to its more than 50,000 employees in more than 100 countries through its relationship with UUnet Technologies. So that Microsoft employees can access information locally anywhere with reliability guarantees and the support of UUnet, UUnet Technologies' transcontinental backbone provides access throughout North America, Europe, and the Asia–Pacific region.

PLANNING FOR THE FUTURE

Finally, Microsoft's ITG wanted to ensure that its current investment in the remote access infrastructure would not only be able to meet today's needs, but also enable it to make the most of opportunities provided by the digital convergence of network-aware applications in the near future. Evidence of an increased need for higher degrees of client/server network application integration is found in the momentum of Windows 2000 as a platform for IP telephony, media-streaming technologies, and the migration to PBX systems based on Windows 2000.

The flexibility needed to economically address current and future needs of Microsoft's ITG is provided through the use of Windows 2000 as the backbone of the remote access solution. Through partnerships with multiple service providers such as UUnet Technologies, the selection of a Windows-based solution allows ITG the freedom to both centrally manage and incrementally extend the Microsoft direct-dial and VPN infrastructure at a controlled pace and in an open manner.

In order to connect Microsoft subsidiaries, branch offices, and extranet partners securely to the enterprise network over private and public networks, Windows 2000 Routing, RAS, and VPN services — along with tight integration with Microsoft Proxy Server — are already enabling Microsoft's ITG to seamlessly extend its RAS–VPN infrastructure. Furthermore, to meet Microsoft's enterprise needs into the future, the broad application support enjoyed by the Windows communication platform ensures that ITG will continue to have access to a host of rich application services made available by developers and service providers, such as ATCOM, Inc., Telco-Research, and UUnet Technologies, Inc.

CONCLUSION AND SUMMARY

As explained in this chapter, Windows 2000 native VPN services allow users or enterprises to reliably and securely connect to remote servers, branch offices, or other enterprises over public and private networks. Despite the fact that this communication occurs over a public internetwork in all of these cases, the secure connection appears to the user as a private network communication. Windows VPN technology is designed to address issues surrounding the current enterprise trend toward increased telecommuting and widely distributed global operations, where workers must be able to connect to central resources and where enterprises must be able to efficiently communicate with each other.

VPNs, INTERNETS, AND EXTRANETS

This chapter provided an in-depth discussion of virtual private networking, and described the basic requirements of useful VPN technologies — user authentication, address management, data encryption, key management, and multiprotocol support. It discussed how Layer 2 protocols, specifically PPTP and L2TP, meet these requirements, and how IPSec (a Layer 3 protocol) will meet these requirements in the future.

Every VPN solution needs to address the technological issues cited in the preceding text and provide the flexibility to address enterprise issues such as network interoperability, rich application integration, and infrastructure transparency. Enterprise infrastructure decisions need to be made in a manner that empowers client access to local connections and client utilization of the network in a transparent manner to bolster economy and productivity.

Furthermore, escalating remote access and telecommuting needs and an increase in the use of distributed enterprise models like extranets require pragmatic remote access solutions that are easy to use, economical, and flexible enough to meet the changing needs of every enterprise. To support its 50,000+ employees worldwide with best-of-breed remote access and virtual private networking (VPN) services, Microsoft capitalizes on the built-in communication services included in Windows®, integrated VPN firewall and caching support from Microsoft® Proxy Server, and complementary services from partners such as UUnet Technologies, Inc., Telco-Research, and ATCOM, Inc.

The remote access infrastructure that Microsoft's Redmond, WA, headquarters uses for its 15,000 HQ employees consists of four dedicated VPN server computers running the Windows 2000 network operating system. Each machine runs three 400-MHz new Pentium III processors, with 204MB of RAM, 3×3 GB of local storage, and three 200-Mbps network interface cards.

The UUnet Technologies, Inc. network that supports Microsoft's wholesale remote access and VPN services provides access to one of the largest IP networks in the world. UUnet's backbone infrastructure features a fully meshed network that extends across both the Atlantic and Pacific and includes direct fiber optic connections between Europe, North America, and Asia. UUnet also provides satellite access services for remote areas that lack Internet connections.

Telco-Research's TRU RADIUS Accountant™ for Windows 2000 provides Microsoft's ITG with a single source for reporting internal usage and chargeback (billing) information required to control remote access costs. TRU RADIUS easy-to-use applications provide a turnkey analysis of remote access usage and the data needed to proactively manage Microsoft's remote employee costs across its enterprise.

Microsoft's use of UUnet infrastructure to provision its VPN services to its sales force and mobile users is a testament to the quality and reliability of UUnet's multinational IP network. Using Windows 2000 integrated communication services, both UUnet and Microsoft ITG can centrally update Microsoft remote users with the latest local points of presence (POPs) and RAS connection points as soon they become available around the world.

Notes

1. Internet draft documents should be considered works in progress. See http://www.ietf.org for copies of Internet drafts.
2. L2F functions in compulsory tunnels only.
3. For more information on UUnet Technologies, Inc. integrated VIP Services for enterprises using Windows, see http://www.uunet.net.
4. For more information on ATCOM Inc. IPORT solutions, see http://www.atcominfo.com/IPORT or http://www.microsoft.com/industry/hospitality/IPORT/default.htm.
5. IPORT is a trademark of ATCOM, Inc.
6. For information on Telco-Research's TRU RADIUS Accountant™ for Windows NT, see http://www.telcoresearch.com.

Chapter 25
IPSec VPNs
James S. Tiller

INTRODUCTION

VPNS ARE MAKING A HUGE IMPACT ON THE WAY COMMUNICATIONS ARE VIEWED. They are also providing ample fodder for administrators and managers to have seemingly endless discussions about various applications. On one side are the possible money savings, and the other are implementation issues. There are several areas of serious concern:

- performance
- interoperability
- scalability
- flexibility

Performance

Performance of data flow is typically the most common concern, and IPSec is very processor intensive. The performance costs of IPSec are the encryption being performed, integrity checking, packet handling based on policies, and forwarding, all of which become apparent in the form of latency and reduced throughput. IPSec VPNs over the Internet increase the latency in the communication that conspires with the processing costs to discourage VPN as a solution for transport-sensitive applications. Process time for authentication, key management, and integrity verification will produce delay issues with SA establishment, authentication, and IPSec SA maintenance. Each of these results in poor initialization response and, ultimately, disgruntled users.

The application of existing hardware encryption technology to IPSec vendor products has allowed these solutions to be considered more closely by prospective clients wishing to seize the monetary savings associated with the technology. The creation of a key and its subsequent use in the encryption process can be offloaded onto a dedicated processor that is designed specifically for these operations. Until the application of hardware encryption for IPSec, all data was managed through software computation that was also responsible for many other operations that may be running on the gateway.

0-8493-0859-3/00/$0.00+$.50
© 2000 by CRC Press LLC

Hardware encryption has released IPSec VPN technology into the realm of viable communication solutions. Unfortunately, the client operating system participating in a VPN is still responsible for the IPSec process. Publicly available mobile systems that provide hardware-based encryption for IPSec communications are becoming available, but are sometime away from being standard issue for remote users.

Interoperability

Interoperability is a current issue that will soon become antiquated as vendors recognize the need to become fully IPSec compliant — or consumers will not implement their product based simply on its incompatibility. Shared secret and ISAKMP key management protocol are typically allowing multi-vendor interoperability. As Certificate Authorities and the technology that supports them become fully adopted technology, they will only add to the cross-platform integration. However, complex and large VPNs will not be manageable using different vendor products in the near future. Given the complexity, recentness of the IPSec standard, the and the various interpretations of that standard, time to complete interoperability seems great.

Scalability

Scalability is obtained by the addition of equipment and bandwidth. Some vendors have created products focused on remote access for roaming users, while others have concentrated on network-to-network connectivity without much attention to remote users. The current ability to scale the solution will be directly related to the service required. The standard supporting the technology allows for great flexibility in the addition of services. It will be more common to find limitations in equipment configurations than in the standard as it pertains to growth capabilities. Scalability ushers in a wave of varying issues, including:

- authentication
- management
- performance

Authentication can be provided by a number of processes, although the primary focus has been on RADIUS (Remote Access Dial-In User Security), Certificates, and forms of two factor authentication. Each of these can be applied to several supporting databases. RADIUS is supported by nearly every common authenticating system from Microsoft Windows NT to NetWare's NDS. Authentication, when implemented properly, should not become a scalability issue for many implementations, because the goal is to integrate the process with existing or planned enterprise authenticating services.

A more interesting aspect of IPSec vendor implementations and the scalability issues that might arise is management. As detailed earlier, certain implementations do not scale, due to the shear physics of shared secrets and manual key management. In the event of the addition of equipment or increased bandwidth to support remote applications, the management will need to take multiplicity into consideration. Currently, VPN management of remote users and networks leaves a great deal to be desired. As vendors and organizations become more acquainted with what can be accomplished, sophisticated management capabilities will become increasingly available.

Performance is an obvious issue when considering the increase of an implementation. Typically, performance is the driving reason, followed by support for increased numbers. Both of these issues are volatile and interrelated with the hardware technology driving the implementation. Performance capabilities can be controlled by the limitation of supported SAs on a particular system — a direct limitation in scalability. A type of requested encryption might not be available on the encryption processor currently available. Forcing the calculation of encryption onto the operating system ultimately limits the performance. A limitation may resonate in the form of added equipment to accomplish the link between the IPSec equipment and the authenticating database. When users authenticate, the granularity of control over the capabilities of that user may be directly related to the form of authentication. The desired form of authentication may have limitations in various environments due to restrictions in various types of authenticating databases. Upgrade issues, service pack variations, user limitations, and protocol requirements also combine to limit growth of the solution.

THE MARKET FOR VPN

Several distinct qualities of VPN are driving the investigation by many organizations to implement VPN as a business interchange technology. VPNs attempt to resolve a variety of current technological limitations that represent themselves as costs in equipment and support or solutions where none had existed prior. Three areas that can be improved by VPNs are:

- remote user access and remote office connectivity
- extranet partner connectivity
- internal departmental security

Remote Access

Providing remote users access via a dial-up connection can become a costly service for any organization to provide. Organizations must consider costs for:

- telephone lines
- terminating equipment
- long-distance
- calling card
- 800/877 number support

Telephone connections must be increased to support the number of proposed simultaneous users that will be dialing in for connectivity to the network. Another cost that is rolled up into the telephone line charge is the possible need for equipment to allow the addition of telephone lines to an existing system. Terminating equipment, such as modem pools, can become expenses that are immediate savings once VPN is utilized. Long-distance charges, calling cards that are supplied to roaming users, and toll-free lines require initial capital and continuous financial support. In reality, an organization employing conventional remote access services is nothing more than a service provider for their employees. Taking this into consideration, many organizations tend to overlook the use of the Internet connection by the remote users. As the number of simultaneous users access the network, the more bandwidth is utilized for the existing Internet service.

The cost savings are realized by redirecting funds, originally to support telephone communications, in an Internet service provider (ISP) and its ability to support a greater area of access points and technology. This allows an organization to eliminate support for all direct connectivity and focus on a single connection and technology for all data exchange — ultimately saving money. With the company access point becoming a single point of entry, access controls, authenticating mechanisms, security policies, and system redundancy is focused and common among all types of access regardless of the originator's communication technology.

The advent of high-speed Internet connectivity by means of cable-modems and ADSL (Asynchronous Digital Subscriber Line) is an example of how VPN becomes an enabler to facilitate the need for high-speed, individual remote access where none existed before. Existing remote access technologies are generally limited to 128K ISDN (Integrated Services Digital Network), or more typically, 56K modem access. Given the inherent properties of the Internet and IPSec functioning at the network layer, the communication technology utilized to access the Internet only needs to be supported at the immediate connection point to establish an IP session with the ISP. Using the Internet as a backbone for encrypted communications allows for equal IP functionality with increased performance and security over conventional remote access technology.

Currently, cable-modem and ADSL services are expanding from the home-user market into the business industry for remote office support. A typical remote office will have a small frame relay connection to the home office. Any Internet traffic from the remote office is usually forwarded to the home office's Internet connection, where access controls can be centrally managed and Internet connection costs are eliminated at the remote office. However, as the number of remote offices and the distances increase, so does the financial investment. Each frame relay connection, PVC (Permanent Virtual Circuit), has costs associated with it. Committed Information Rate (CIR), port speed (e.g., 128K), and sometimes a connection fee add to the overall investment. A PVC is required for any connection; so as remote offices demand direct communication to their peers, a PVC will need to be added to support this decentralized communication. Currently within the United States, the cost of frame relay is very low and typically outweighs the cost of an ISP and Internet connectivity. As the distance increases and moves beyond the United States, the costs can increase exponentially and will typically call for more than one telecommunications vendor. With VPN technology, a local connection to the Internet can be established. Adding connectivity to peers is accomplished by configuration modifications; this allows the customer to control communications without the inclusion of the carrier in the transformation.

The current stability of remote, tier three and lower ISPs is an unknown variable. The arguable service associated with multiple and international ISP connectivity has become the Achilles' heel for VPN acceptance for business-critical and time-critical services. As the reach of tier one and tier two ISPs increases, they will be able to provide contiguous connectivity over the Internet to remote locations using an arsenal of available technologies.

Extranet Access

The single, most advantageous characteristic of VPNs is to provide protected and controlled communication with partnering organizations. Years ago, prior to VPN becoming a catchword, corporations were beginning to feel the need for dedicated Internet access. The dedicated access is becoming utilized for business purposes, whereas before it was viewed as a service for employees and research requirements.

The Internet provides the ultimate bridge between networks that was relatively nonexistent before VPN technology. Preceding VPNs, a corporation needing to access a partner's site was typically provided a frame relay connection to a common frame relay cloud where all the partners claimed access. Other options were ISDN and dial-on-demand routing. As this requirement grows, several limitations begin to surface. Security issues, partner support, controlling access, disallowing unwanted interchange between partners, and connectivity support for partners without supported access technologies all conspire to expose the huge advantages of VPNs over the Internet. Utilizing VPNs, an organization can maintain a high granularity of control over the connectivity per partner or per user on a partner network.

Internal Protection

As firewalls became more predominant as protection against the Internet, they were increasingly being utilized for internal segmentation of departmental entities. The need for protecting vital departments within an organization originally spawned this concept of using firewalls internally. As the number of departments increase, the management, complexity, and cost of the firewalls increase as well. Also, any attacker with access to the protected network can easily obtain sensitive information due to the fact that the firewall applies only perimeter security.

VLANs (Virtual Local Area Networks) with access control lists became a minimized replacement for conventional firewalls. However, the same security issue remained, in that the perimeter security was controlled and left the internal network open for attack.

As IPSec became accepted as a viable secure communication technology and applied in MAC environments, it also became the replacement for other protection technologies. Combined with strategically placed firewalls, VPN over internal networks allows secure connectivity between hosts. IPSec encryption, authentication, and access control provide protection for data between departments and within a department.

CONSIDERATION FOR VPN IMPLEMENTATION

The benefits of VPN technology can be realized in varying degrees depending on the application and the requirements it has been applied to. Considering the incredible growth in technology, the advantages will only increase. Nevertheless, the understandable concerns with performance, reliability, scalability, and implementation issues must be investigated.

System Requirements

The first step is determining the foreseeable amount of traffic and its patterns to ascertain the adjacent system requirements or augmentations. In the event that existing equipment is providing all or a portion of the service the VPN is replacing, the costs can be compared to discover initial savings in the framework of money, performance, or functionality.

Security Policy

It will be necessary to determine if the VPN technology and how it is planned to be implemented meets the current security policy. In case the security policy does not address the area of remote access, or in the event a policy or remote access does not exist, a policy must address the security requirements of the organization and its relationship with the service provided by VPN technology.

Application Performance

As previously discussed, performance is the primary reason VPN technology is not the solution for many organizations. It will be necessary to determine the speed at which an application can execute the essential processes. This is related to the type of data within the VPN. Live traffic or user sessions are incredibly sensitive to any latency in the communication. Pilot tests and load simulation should be considered strongly prior to large-scale VPN deployment or replacement of exiting services and equipment.

Data replication or transient activity that is not associated with human or application time sensitivity is a candidate for VPN connectivity. The application's resistance to latency must be measured to determine the minimum requirements for the VPN. This is not to convey that VPNs are only good for replication traffic and cannot support user applications. It is necessary to determine the application needs and verify the requirements to properly gauge the performance provisioning of the VPN. The performance "window" will allow the proper selection of equipment to meet the needs of the proposed solution; otherwise, the equipment and application may present poor results compared to the expected or planned results. Or, more importantly, the acquired equipment is underworked or does not scale in the direction needed for a particular organization's growth path. Each of these results in poor investment realization and make it much more difficult to persuade management to use VPN again.

Training

User and administrator training are an important part of the implementation process. It is necessary to evaluate a vendor's product from the point of the users, as well as evaluating the other attributes of the product. In the event the user experience is poor, it will reach management and ultimately weigh heavily on the administrators and security practitioners. It is necessary to understand the user intervention that is required in the everyday process of application use. Comprehending the user knowledge requirements will allow for the creation of a training curriculum that best represents what the users are required to accomplish to operate the VPN as per the security policy.

FUTURE OF IPSec VPNs

Like it or not, VPN is here to stay. IP version 6 (IPv6) has the IPSec entrenched in its very foundation; and as the Internet grows, Ipv6 will become more prevalent. The current technological direction of typical networks will become the next goals for IPSec; specifically, Quality of Service (QoS). ATM was practically invented to accommodate the vast array of communication technologies at high speeds; but to do it efficiently, it must control who gets in and out of the network.

Ethernet Type of Service (ToS) (802.1p) allows for three bits of data in the frame to be used to add ToS information and then be mapped into ATM cells. IP version 4, currently applied, has support for a ToS field in the IP Header similar to Ethernet 802.1p; it provides three bits for extended information. Currently, techniques are being applied to map QoS information from one medium to another. This is very exciting for service organizations that will be able sell end-to-end QoS. As the IPSec standard grows and current TCP/IP applications and networks begin to support the existing IP ToS field, IPSec will quickly conform to the requirements.

The IETF and other participants, in the form of RFCs, are continually addressing the issues that currently exist with IPSec. Packet sizes are typically increased due to the added headers and sometimes trailer information associated with IPSec. The result is increased possibility of packet fragmentation. IPSec addresses fragmentation and packet loss; the overhead of these processes are the largest concern.

IPSec can only be applied to the TCP/IP protocol. Therefore, multi-protocol networks and environments that employ IPX/SPX, NetBEUI, and others will not take direct advantage of the IPSec VPN. To allow non-TCP/IP protocols to communicate over a an IPSec VPN, an IP gateway must be implemented to encapsulate the original protocol into an IP packet and then be forwarded to the IPSec gateway. IP gateways have been in use for some time and are proven technology. For several organizations that cannot eliminate non-TCP/IP protocols and wish to implement IPSec as the VPN of choice, a protocol gateway is imminent.

As is obvious, performance is crucial to IPSec VPN capabilities and cost. As encryption algorithms become increasingly sophisticated and hardware support for those algorithms become readily available, this current limitation will be surpassed.

Another perceived limitation of IPSec is the encryption export and import restrictions of encryption. There are countries that the United States places restrictions on to hinder the ability of those countries to encrypt possibly harmful information into the United States. In 1996, the International Traffic in Arms Regulation (ITAR) governing the export of cryptography was reconditioned. Responsibility for cryptography exports was transferred to the Department of Commerce from the Department of State. However, the Department of Justice is now part of the export review process. In addition, the National Security Agency (NSA) remains the final arbiter of whether to grant encryption products export licenses.

The NSA staff is assigned to the Commerce Department and many other federal agencies that deal with encryption policy and standards. This includes the State Department, Justice Department, National Institute for Standards and Technology (NIST), and the Federal Communications

Commission. As one can imagine, the laws governing the export of encryption are complicated and are under constant revision. Several countries are completely denied access to encrypted communications to the United States; other countries have limitations due to government relationships and political posture. The current list of (as of this writing) embargoed countries include:

- Syria
- Iran
- Iraq
- North Korea
- Libya
- Cuba
- Sudan
- Serbia

As one reads the list of countries, it is easy to determine why the United States is reluctant to allow encrypted communications with these countries. Past wars, conflict of interests, and terrorism are the primary ingredients to become exiled by the United States.

Similar rosters exist for other countries that have the United States listed as "unfriendly," due to their perception of communication with the United States.

As one can certainly see, the concept of encryption export and import laws is vague, complex, and constantly in litigation. In the event a VPN is required for international communication, it will be necessary to obtain the latest information available to properly implement the communication as per the current laws.

CONCLUSION

VPN technology, based on IPSec, will become more prevalent in our every day existence. The technology is in its infancy; the standards and support for them are growing everyday. Security engineers will see an interesting change in how security is implemented and maintained on a daily basis. It will generate new types of policies and firewall solutions — router support for VPN will skyrocket.

This technology will finally confront encryption export and import laws forcing the hand of many countries. Currently, there are several issues with export and import restrictions that affect how organizations deploy VPN technology. As VPNs become more prevalent in international communications, governments will be forced to expedite the process. With organizations sharing information, services, and product, the global economy will force computer security to become the primary focus for many companies.

For VPNs, latency is the center for concern and, once hardware solutions and algorithms collaborate to enhance overall system performance, the technology will become truly accepted. Once this point is reached, every packet on every network will be encrypted. Browsers, e-mail clients, and the like will have VPN software embedded, and only authenticated communications will be allowed. Clear Internet traffic will be material for campfire stories. It is a good time to be in security.

Chapter 26
Integrating Data Centers with Intranets
Anura Gurugé

NEARLY ALL ENTERPRISES THAT HAVE MAINFRAMES or large, networked AS/400s now have an intranet. Most, in addition, already have a presence on the Internet in the form of a home page, and many are actively exploring the possibilities of using the Internet for electronic commerce, customer support, and as an ultra cost-effective means of global remote access. In parallel, intranet-to-intranet communication via extranets is being viewed as the means of streamlining and expediting enterprise transactions. There is, however, a beguiling disconnect vis-à-vis these new strategic and burgeoning TCP/IP-centric networks and the traditional data center functions that continue to be imperative for the day-to-day operations of these enterprises. Very few enterprises at present have tightly integrated their intranets with their data centers. This is despite the fact that up to 70 percent of the vital data, and many of the mission-critical applications required by these enterprises, are still likely to reside on their mainframes or AS/400s. That is akin to baking an apple pie with no apple filling.

Integrating an intranet with a data center is not simply a matter of implementing TCP/IP on a mainframe or AS/400 along with a Web server. Many of the host resident, mission-critical applications still required were developed, typically 15 years ago, such that they only work in Systems Network Architecture mode. The nearest that one can come to making theses applications TCP/IP compatible is to use them in conjunction with a host resident or "Off-Board" tn3270(E) (or tn5250, in the case of AS/400s) server which will perform standards-based SNA-to-TCP/IP protocol conversion. Otherwise, the applications will have to be rewritten to work in TCP/IP mode. This is not feasible since the cost and effort of doing so for the $20 trillion installed base of SNA mission-critical applications would make all the tribulations associated with the Y2K challenge appear trivial!

0-8493-0859-3/00/$0.00+$.50
© 2000 by CRC Press LLC

While some of the data center resident data could be accessed using an Open Database Connectivity type scheme, this is certainly not true for all of the data center resources. Some data, especially if stored on "flat files" or nonrelational databases (such as IBM's still widely used Information Management System), can only be accessed via SNA applications. In other instances, the data make sense only when combined with the "business logic" embedded within an SNA mission-critical application. In addition to these crucial SNA applications, there is inevitably a large installed base of SNA-only "legacy" devices such as IBM 4700 Financial Systems, automated teller machines, and control units that still need to be supported. Thus, there is a need for explicit SNA-related technologies in order to get the most from your host vis-à-vis your intranet.

The good news is that highly proven and stable technology from more than 40 credible vendors including IBM, Cisco, Attachmate, OpenConnect Systems, Wall Data, Eicon, Novell, WRQ, Farabi, Client/Server Technology, Sterling Software, Blue Lobster, etc., is now readily available to facilitate data-center-to-intranet integration in a seamless and synergistic manner. Enterprises around the world such as GM, FedEx, Ohio State University, Royal Jordanian Airlines, Nestles, The Chickering Group, National Van Lines, the State of Idaho, Al Rajhi Banking & Investment Corp. (Saudi Arabia's largest bank), and Gazprom (a $30 billion natural gas company in Russia) are already gainfully using this intranet-to-data center integration technology on a daily basis for business-critical production use. Al Rajhi Bank, for example, uses browser-based access to SNA to provide home banking, while GM, National Van Lines, Royal Jordanian Airlines, and The Chickering Group use it to permit agents to access applications or databases resident on mainframes or AS/400s over the Internet.

INTRANET TO DATA CENTER INTEGRATION TECHNOLOGIES

To be viable, integration technologies need to be able to accommodate an extremely broad and disparate population of client equipment and functionality including PCs, UNIX workstations, coax-attached 3270/5250 terminals, printers, minicomputers, SNA applications that communicate program-to-program using LU 6.2 or LU-LU Session Type 0-based protocols, SNA-only devices, SNA-LAN gateways (e.g., NetWare for SAA), and legacy control units. The PCs, workstations, and printers may work in either SNA or TCP/IP mode. Consequently, you will need SNA Access technologies to deal with TCP/IP clients, particularly PCs and workstations, and SNA Transport technologies to deal with SNA-only clients. The most pertinent technologies are:

- SNA Access technologies that permit non-SNA clients to gain access to SNA applications
  - *ip3270/ip5250* — the use of existing PC/workstation SNA emulators (e.g., Attachmate EXTRA!Personal Client) and existing SNA-LAN

gateways (e.g., Microsoft's SNA server) with proprietary encapsulation schemes for conveying a 3270/5250 data stream within TCP/IP

— *tn3270(E)/tn5250* — IETF standard that enables TCP/IP clients (e.g., Attachmate EXTRA!Personal Client) to access SNA applications via tn3270(E) (e.g., IBM 2216) or tn5250 servers

— *Browser-based Access with 3270/5250-to-HTML Conversion* — thin client solution where a server resident SNA-Web gateway performs 3270/5250 data stream to HTML conversion replete with some amount of user interface rejuvenation so that SNA applications can be accessed directly from a browser.

— *Browser-invoked Java or ActiveX applets* — dynamically downloadable applets, which can optionally be cached on a PC/workstation hard disk, that provide 3270/5250 emulation either directly or in conjunction with an intermediate SNA-Web gateway

— *Browser-invoked applets as "4" above,* but with user interface rejuvenation

— *Application-specific web-to-data-center gateways,* e.g., IBM's CICS Web Interface or Interlink's ActiveCICX

— *Programmatic (or Middleware) Servers,* e.g., IBM's MQSeries, Blue Stone's Sapphire/Web, or Blue Lobster's Stingray SDK

• SNA end-to-end transport

— *Data Link Switching* — ubiquitous, standards-based encapsulation scheme performed by bridge/routers that permits any kind of SNA/APPN traffic, independent of session type, to be transported end-to-end across a TCP/IP WAN. Desktop DLSw (DDLSw) is also available where SNA traffic can be encapsulated within TPC/IP at the source PC

— *High Performance Routing-over-IP* — alternative to the DLSw championed by IBM, whereby SNA-oriented routing is performed across IP

— *AnyNet* — IBM protocol conversion technology, integrated within IBM server software including Comm. Server/NT and OS/390 as well as within some SNA/3270 emulation packages, that converts SNA message units into corresponding TCP/IP packets

The three transport technologies ensure that the still large installed base of SNA devices and control units are able to communicate with mainframe- or AS/400-resident SNA/APPN applications across an intranet using SNA on an end-to-end basis. Of the three, standards-based DLSw, which is available on nearly all major brands of bridge/routers, is by far the most widely used and the most strategic. AnyNet, in marked contrast, is not available on bridge/routers or within SNA devices such as 3174s, 4700s, etc. Consequently, it cannot be used easily as a universal scheme for supporting any and all SNA devices and control units as can DLSw. Thus, AnyNet is not as strategic or useful as DLSw. High Performance Routing (HPR) is IBM's follow-on architecture to APPN and SNA. HPR-over-IP, now available on IBM 2216 and CS/NT, has irrefutable advantages over DLSw: it can support native, data-center-to-data-center SNA/APPN routing over TCP/IP; SNA LU 6.2 Class-of-Service (COS)-based path selection; and traffic prioritization. If and when this technology is more readily available, corporations that require SNA/APPN routing to obtain optimum traffic routing in multi-data center networks, or those that have LU 6.2-based applications that rely on COS, may want to consider HPR-over-IP as an alternative to DLSw.

DLSw's ability to support any and all types of SNA/APPN traffic effortlessly could be easily abused when trying to integrate intranets with data centers. DLSw could be used all by itself to realize the integration by grafting the existing SNA/APPN network, totally unchanged, onto the intranet through the extensive deployment of DLSw all around the periphery of the intranet. This brute force, "no SNA-reengineering whatsoever" approach has been used in the past to integrate SNA networks into TCP/IP networks. With this type of DLSw-only network you would find SNA-LAN gateways being used downstream of the intranet, and then DLSw being used to transport the SNA output of these gateways across the intranet. While such networks indubitably work, there are other strategic techniques such as a 3270-to-HTML and applet-based 3270/5250 emulation that should typically be used in conjunction with DLSw to achieve the necessary integration. Exhibit 26-1 summarizes how the various SNA Transport and SNA Access integration techniques can be gainfully synthesized to integrate data centers with intranets.

Exhibit 26-1. Synthesizing SNA transport and SNA access integration techniques.

PCs, Macs, workstations	• Browser-based • tn3270/tn5250 • ip3270/ip5250 • Programmatic	If a "full-stack" SNA/3270 emulator is currently installed: • DLSw • DDLSw • AnyNet • HPR-over-IP
Network Computers	• Browser-based • Programmatic	
SNA-Only Devices	• DLSw • HPR-over-IP	
Remote SNA-LAN Gateways	Eliminate the remote gateway and opt for ip3230/ip5250, tn3270/tn5250, or browser-based access	Prior to gateway elimination: • DLSw • HPR-over-IP
Devices that work in SNA or TCP/IP Mode	• Convert to IP and then use TCP/IP-based access schemes • tn5250/tn3270 • Programmatic	If the device cannot be converted to TCP/IP: • DLSw • AnyNet • HPR-over-IP

TOO MUCH CHOICE IS THE BIGGEST HURDLE

The availability of seven very different SNA access solutions is indeed one of major distractions in the intranet-to-data-center integration process. However, having such a wide range of solutions is also beneficial and should be gainfully exploited. With the solutions at hand you can tailor highly effective and pragmatic configurations where different access solutions are employed depending on both the requirements of the end user, and whether the access is across an intranet or the Internet. Exhibit 26-2 provides guidelines as to how the various access solutions may be best deployed.

The following is a comprehensive list of all the SNA access-related components that may be required to integrate an intranet to a data center, grouped, where appropriate, into "functional" classes:

- Web Server — to download applets or HTML-converted 3270 screens
- Web Browser — for browser-based access
- Client software other than the web browser:
  - full-function, 3270/5250 emulator for ip3270 or ip5250
  - tn3270(E) or tn5250 client
  - terminal (and printer) emulation applet, with or without interface rejuvenation capability
  - programmatic client which could be in the form of an applet
  - optional, very small (e.g., 5K) "keyboard support" applet used by some 3270-to-HTML conversion solutions (e.g., Novell's HostPublisher) to overcome the problem that browsers currently do not support all the function keys found on a PC/workstation keyboard
- TCP/IP-to-SNA Gateway:
  - SNA-LAN gateway for ip3270/ip5250, such as Microsoft's SNA Server, located on a PC server or a channel-attached controller such as Bus-Tech's NetShuttle
  - tn3270(E) or tn5250 Server, located on a PC server, bridge/router, channel-attached bridge/router, channel-attached controller, or mainframe
- SNA-Web Gateway — for applet-based solutions either to augment the applet's functionality, provide security features, or both. Examples include Attachmate's HostView Server and OCS's OC://WebConnect Pro. Typically resident on an NT or UNIX server, though OCS has a version, it has an integrated TCP/IP-to-SNA gateway functionality that runs on a mainframe
- 3270-to-HTML or 5250-to-HTML Gateway
- Application-Specific Web Gateway — for example, IBM's CICS Internet Gateway or CICS Gateway for Java
- Programmatic Server — an external, server-resident component required for certain programmatic access schemes

Exhibit 26-2. Deploying the best access solution.

	Intranet		The Internet	
	Interim	**Mid-term**	**Interim**	**Mid-term**
Employees:				
• Data Entry	tn3270(E)	Browser: tn3270(E) emulation		
• Power User (e.g., programmer)	ip3270	ip3270		
• Senior Management; queries, e-mail, calendar …	ip3270	Browser: with rejuvenation, or programmatic		
• Professional: < 2 hours/day mainframe access	tn3270(E)	Browser: some rejuvenation, or programmatic		
• Professional: > 2 hours/day mainframe access	ip3270	Browser: some rejuvenation, possibly programmatic		
• Telecommuter			Browser-based access	
• Mobile User			Browser-based access	
• "Agent" working for the company; e.g., dealership, travel agent			Browser: tn3270(E) emulation- cached applet	Browser: rejuvenation either with applet or 3270-to-HTML
Public:				
• Simple Query			Browser: 3270-to-HTML	
• Insecure, Multistep Query			Browser: 3270-to-HTML with some form of screen sequencing	
• Secure, Multistep Transaction			Browser: applet with rejuvenation	

Of the seven access techniques, ip3270/ip5250 and tn3270(E)/tn5250 represent the "old guard," well-known and widely deployed schemes employed by over 20 million users. The best way to put these two techniques in context is to look at their pros and cons as shown in Exhibit 26-3.

Exhibit 26-3. Pros and cons of traditional emulation approaches.

	ip3270/ip5250	tn3270(E)/tn5250
Pros	• In most cases works with existing 3270 emulators and SNA-LAN gateway configuration, in which case a good tactical solution • Total support for all terminal emulation and workstation customization features • Extensive support for printing • Support for LU 6.2 • Support for other emulator-provided application APIs • Availability of channel-attached SNA-LAN gateways, e.g., Bus-Tech NetShuttle • Wall Data plans to have an applet that talks ip3270	• Widely adopted industry standard • Highly scalable tn3270(E) servers available on mainframes and channel-attached routers (e.g., Cisco 7xxx/CIP) • tn3270/tn5250 is the underlying "applet-to-gateway" protocol used by many browser-based access solutions including IBM's "Host-on-Demand" and WRQ's Reflection EnterView • Efficient, nonverbose protocol • Deemed by all to be a strategic technology for building SNA-Capable i•nets • Enjoys both vendor and customer mind-share
Cons	• Proprietary protocol • No mainframe-resident gateways • Not promoted by any vendors — even though this is probably an oversight because many forget the distinction between tn3270 and ip3270 • Client emulator may be more expensive than a tn3270 client • Most customers do not understand that this is an option open to them • No standard encryption schemes	• No support for LU 6.2 as yet • Printing options not as extensive or flexible as that potentially possible with ip3270/ip5250 • Cannot match ip3270 when it comes to the esoteric, power-user-oriented terminal emulation and customization features • Unlikely to support the application APIs supported by ip3270 emulators • Any end-to-end encryption available is going to be vendor specific or realized through the use of Virtual Private Networks (VPNs)

Browser-Based Access via 3270-to-HTML Conversion

Browser-based access to SNA applications was initially made possible in late 1995 by 3270-to-HTML conversion. With HTML being the native language for creating web pages, converting 3270 data stream to HTML and vice versa was the obvious, logical, and most straightforward way to web-enable SNA applications. Alluding to the fact that web site and web page creation is often referred to as "Web Publishing," 3270-to-HTML conversion came to be known as "Host Publishing," with many product names such as Attachmate's HostPublishing System, Farabi's HostFront Publishing, Novell's HostPublisher, and IBM's Host Publisher feature in Ver. 6.0 of CS/NT amplifying this theme of how host (i.e., SNA) data can now be readily published on the Web. Exhibit 26-4 shows the general architecture of a 3270-to-HTML scheme.

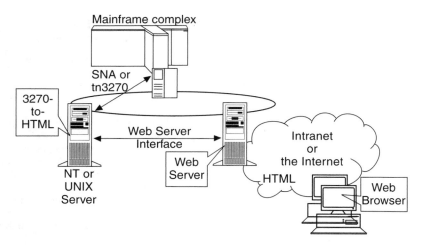

Exhibit 26-4. Typical architecture of 3270-to-HTML conversion.

3270-to-HTML has two incontrovertible advantages over that of an applet-based, "green-on-black" emulation approach:

1. *It only requires a browser at the client end.* This obviates any and all issues related to applet download time and the time taken to establish a persistent end-to-end connection between the applet and the pertinent data center component. Eliminating the need for an applet also makes 3270-to-HTML essentially browser-agnostic.
2. *It always delivers at least a "default" amount of user interface rejuvenation.* It is referred to as "Auto GUI," e.g., background and web page-like "trench" input fields. Extensive rejuvenation is possible, usually with the aid of visual programming tools such as JavaScript, Jscript, or Microsoft's Active Server Page technology.

3270-to-HTML is, thus, ideally suited for Internet-based SNA access, particularly to permit the public casual access (e.g., querying the delivery status of a package) to mainframe or AS/400 applications. Not having to download an applet will expedite the access process, while the rejuvenation capabilities will protect the innocent from the brutalities of the "green-on-black" screens. 3270-to-HTML used to get short shrift because the early implementations did not have good, cogent answers to issues such as session integrity, end-to-end persistence, file transfer, function key support, light pen support, etc. Some of these limitations were due to shortcomings of the browser or the HTTP protocol. The good news, however, is that some of today's implementations, for example Novell's intraNetWare HostPublisher and Eicon's Aviva Server, have gone to great lengths to come up with innovative but pragmatic solutions to nearly all of these previous limitations.

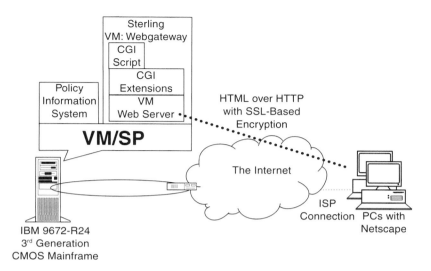

Exhibit 26-5. The Sterling Software VM:Webgateway-based architecture of the 3270-to-HTML solution used by Lafayette Life Insurance.

Take the sacrosanct session integrity and "persistence" issue. HostPublisher, through the use of session IDs, screen sequence numbers, timeouts, and unique "session name" validation (as opposed to IP-address-based correlation) can persuasively circumvent most, if not all, of the "horror" scenarios that could potentially occur given that 3270-to-HTML solutions do not maintain an end-to-end persistent connection à la applet-based solutions. Exhibit 26-5 shows the actual architecture of a mainframe-centric 3270-to-HTML solution actively used by Lafayette Life Insurance (Lafayette, Indiana) to provide 1,000+ field agents, as well as corporate staff in Indiana, real-time, online access to policy information via the Internet. Exhibit 26-6 weighs the pros and cons of such a solution.

Browser-Based Access Using Applets for 3270/5250 Emulation

Applet-based access schemes have the inalienable advantage that they provide a near complete "green-on-black" tn3270(E)/tn5250 emulation scheme, replete with TCP-based, end-to-end persistent connections in the form of a dynamically downloadable "thin-client." Distributing and, moreover, maintaining 3270/5250 emulation and tn3270(E)/tn5250 clients, especially given the incessant barrage of updates for such software, had become a costly and time-sapping endeavor for most SNA shops. Once host printing, IND$FILE-based file transfer, and cut-and-paste between windows was in place by Spring 1998, applet-based emulation was a tempting proposition. It delivered tn3270(E)/tn5250 functionality, albeit by some

357

Exhibit 26-6. Pros and cons of Lafayette Life Insurance 3270-to-HTML solution.

Pros
• Only requires a browser at the client side
• Works with "any" browser given that there are no applets or JVMs involved
• A client platform-agnostic solution in that this access scheme will work on any platform that can run a web browser
• Facilitates and forces user interface rejuvenation
• Able to automatically exploit any standard, server-to-browser security schemes, including end-to-end encryption à la SSL V. 3.0
• Relatively simple, cost-effective solution that can be easily implemented on a PC server
• Ideal for enabling Internet users to gain casual access to SNA applications

Cons
• Most solutions do not support function keys and light pens since browsers do not currently recognize those items
• No SNA-specific printing or file transfer — with printing typically limited to screen printing functions provided by a browser
• Cannot deal with unsolicited screens from an application
• Schemes to ensure data integrity and session security in the absence of end-to-end persistent connections are implementation-specific, with some implementations being significantly better than others
• Rejuvenation schemes, though typically using off-the-shelf products such as JavaScript, are implementation-specific with no real commonality between the various products
• Corporate users, who require access to SNA applications and other web information concurrently, need to open multiple browser windows
• Some solutions may only support a few hundred concurrent SNA sessions per server

esoteric and little used 3270 graphical capabilities, in the form of a browser-invoked "thin client." In addition, it promised the possibility of user interface rejuvenation via drag-and-drop tools, Java-based APIs, rules-based systems, or Visual Café-type applet programming.

Versions 4 or greater of Netscape and Microsoft Internet Explorer permit both Java and ActiveX applets to be cached on the hard disk of a PC/workstation. Caching eliminates the need for an applet to be downloaded from a Web server each time it is invoked. Caching, however, does not compromise the version control and automatic software update advantages of downloaded applets. With cached applets, a Web server is still automatically queried each time the applet is invoked to determine if there is a newer version of the applet. If there is, the user is given the option of dynamically downloading it. Cached applets, thus, provide users as well as Network Administrators with the best of all worlds — automatic version control without the continual wait for an applet to be downloaded.

A browser user invokes a terminal emulation applet by clicking on a "button" on a pre-designated Web page in much the same way that 3270-to-HTML conversion is invoked. A key difference, however, is that there is no "script" per se, as is the case with 3270-to-HTML. Instead, the applet is embedded within the Web page. Invoking the applet causes it to be activated. The applet may either be downloaded from the Web server hosting the "mother" page that has the applet embedded, or be started up from a cached version following a quick version validation. Today, most of the applets perform a tn3270(E) or tn5250 client emulation, with Wall Data's Cyberprise Host Pro and Farabi being in the minority in that they work with SNA-LAN gateways rather than just tn3270(E) servers. Nearly all of the SNA access applets were Java-based at the beginning. Now, however, some vendors, such as Attachmate, Wall Data, and Farabi, are offering both ActiveX and Java applets.

Most of the applet solutions open up a separate emulation window alongside the browser window rather than having the emulation screen appearing as a "pane" inside the browser window. The advantage of keeping the applet emulation window separate is that it does not block the browser from being used for other purposes. Thus, the browser is not locked into an SNA session, as is the case with 3270-to-HTML conversion. Note, however, that regardless of whether the applet window runs alongside or within the browser, today's SNA access solutions invariably rely on a virtual machine provided by the browser, as opposed to the operating system, on which to run the applet. This means that the applet window will be abruptly and unceremoniously terminated if the browser hosting that applet is closed. An SNA access applet could, in theory, be converted and made to run as an application on a virtual machine provided by the operating system if one really wanted to eliminate dependence on the browser.

Quite a few of the applet-based emulation schemes require an intermediate SNA-Web gateway between the applet and the tn3270(E)/tn5250 server. Providing security, both in terms of authentication and encryption, is the overriding rationale for these intermediary SNA-Web gateways, so much so that, if an applet-based access scheme does not use an intermediary server component, you need to start thinking immediately of auxiliary security measures such as VPN. (See Exhibit 26-7) This will, however, change in the future when native end-to-end encryption is added to the tn3270(E) standard.

Exhibit 26-7. Pros and cons of the Applet-based emulation scheme.

Pros
• Powerful terminal emulation comparable to tn3270(E)/tn5250 clients
• "Thin-client" solution that minimizes software distribution and maintenance cost and effort — with the added attraction of cache-able applets
• Support for host printing à la tn3270(E), IND$FILE file-transfer, and cut-and-paste between windows
• Applet window can run alongside browser, thus leaving the browser window free for other interactions
• End-to-end persistent connections ensure data integrity and session security
• Encryption possible when an SNA-Web gateway is used
• Java applets facilitate cross-platform portability
Cons
• Rejuvenation only possible with certain solutions
• Encryption contingent on the presence of an SNA-Web gateway
• Potential delays when the applet is being downloaded, when caching is not used
• Most solutions currently only support Java applets
• May not work with "older," e.g., Ver. 3, browsers

The Bottom Line

Proven technologies now abound to facilitate intranet-to-data-center integration. Some of these technologies, such as DLSw and tn3270(E)/tn5250, are standards-based, mature, and very widely used. Even newer technologies such as browser-based access are now field tested and increasingly heavily deployed. Technology is not a barrier when it comes to intranet-to-data-center integration. The one distraction could be that there is too much choice, but that should not be used as an excuse; it is more an opportunity. You will require multiple access options and at least one transport scheme to satisfactorily meet all your needs. The technology and the products are here today to ensure that you have plenty of flexibility and variety in choosing that solution set.

Chapter 27
Implementing and Supporting Extranets

Phillip Q. Maier

EXTRANETS HAVE BEEN AROUND as long as the first rudimentary LAN-to-LAN networks began connecting two different business entities together to form WANs. In its basic form, an extranet is the interconnection of two previous separate LANs or WANs with origins from different business entities. This term emerged to differentiate between the previous definitions of external "Internet" connection and a company's internal intranet. Exhibit 27-1 depicts an extranet as a Venn diagram, where the intersection of two (or more) nets form the extranet. The network in this intersection was previously part of the "intranet" and has now been made accessible to external parties.

Under this design, one of the simplest definitions comes from R.H. Baker,[1] "An extranet is an intranet that is open to selective access by outside parties." The critical security concept of the extranet is the new network area that was previously excluded from external access now being made available to some external party or group. The critical security issue evolves from the potential vulnerability of allowing more than the intended party, or allowing more access than was intended originally for the extranet. These critical areas will be addressed in this article, from basic extranet setup to more complex methods and some of the ongoing support issues.

The rapid adoption of the extranet will change how a business looks at its security practices, as the old paradigm of a hard outer security shell for a business LAN environment has now been disassembled or breached with a hole to support the need for extranets. In many cases, the age-old firewall will remain in place, but it will have to be modified to allow this "hole" for the extranet to enable access to some degree to internal resources that have now been deemed part of the extranet.

0-8493-0859-3/00/$0.00+$.50
© 2000 by CRC Press LLC

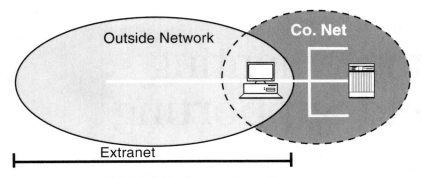

Exhibit 27-1. Extranet Venn diagram.

Recognizing the growth of extranets as a common part of doing business today is important, and therefore the business enterprise must be ready with architectures, policy, and approaches to handle the introduction of extranets into its environment. A few of the considerations are the requirements-versus-security balance, policy considerations, risk assessments, and implementation and maintenance costs.

From a requirements-versus-security balance standpoint, the issue is the initial claim by business that extranets are an immediate need and absolutely must be established "if we are to remain competitive." But from a security standpoint, such a drastic change to the environment, which may not have had any form of an extranet in place, may well be throwing their financial data assets out the door with the first implementation of an extranet. Therefore, care must be taken from a security perspective and put in balance with the claimed business need for an extranet implementation.

One of the first areas of review and (possibly) update is the inner company's security policy. This policy most likely was not written with extranets in mind and thus may need modification if a common security philosophy is to be established regarding how a company can securely implement extranets. However, the policy review does not stop with one company's review of its own policy, but also includes connecting the company or companies on the outside. In the case of strategic business relationships that will be ongoing, it is important that both parties fully understand each other's responsibilities for the extranet, what traffic they will and will not pass over the joined link — what degree of access, and by whom, will occur over this link.

Part of any company's policy on extranets must include an initial requirement for a security risk assessment, the main question being: what additional levels of risk or network vulnerability will be introduced with the implementation of the proposed extranet? As well as vulnerability assessment, a performance assessment should be conducted to assist in the design of the extranet to ensure that the proposed architecture not only addresses the security risk, but that it also will meet performance expectations. Some of the questions to be asked in a combined security and performance assessment should be:

- data classification/value of data
- data location(s) in the network
- internal users' access requirements to extranet components (internal access design)
- data accessibility by time of day (for estimating support costs)
- protocol, access services used to enter extranet (network design implications)
- degree of exposure by transmission mechanism (Internet, private net, wireless transmission)
- end-user environment (dial-up, Internet)
- number of users, total/expectation for concurrent users access (line sizing)
- growth rate of user base (for estimating administrative costs)
- CONUS (continental U.S.), international access (encryption implications)

The risk and performance assessment would, of course, be followed by a risk mitigation plan, which comes in the form of selecting an acceptable extranet architecture and identifying the costs. The cost aspect of this plan is, of course, one of the critical drivers in the business decision to implement an extranet. Is the cost of implementing and maintaining the extranet (in a secure manner) less than the benefit gained by putting the extranet in place? This cost must include the costs associated with implementing it securely; otherwise, the full costs will not be realistically reflected.

Finally, the company implementing the extranet must have a clear set of architectures that best mitigate the identified vulnerabilities, at the least cost, without introducing an unacceptable degree of risk into its computing environment. The following section reviews various extranet architectures, each with differing costs and degrees of risk to the environment.

EXTRANET ARCHITECTURES

Router-Based Extranet Architecture

The earliest extranet implementations were created with network routers that have the capability to be programmed with rudimentary "access control lists" or rules. These rules were implemented based solely on TCP/IP addresses. A rule could be written to allow External User A access to a given computer B, where B may have been previously unreachable due to some form of private enterprise network firewall (and in the early days, this firewall may have been a router also). Exhibit 27-2 depicts this very basic extranet. A more realistic rule can be written where all computers in

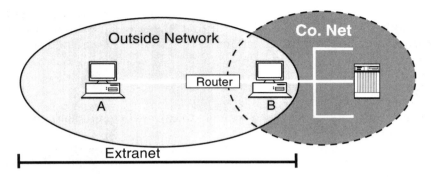

Exhibit 27-2. Basic extranet with router.

an "outside network" are allowed to access computer B in a company network, thus forming an extranet. This is depicted in Exhibit 27-3.

As network security architectures matured, routers as the sole network access control device were replaced by more specific security mechanisms. Routers were originally intended as network devices — and not as security mechanisms — and lost functionality as more and more security rules were placed in them. Additionally, the security rules that were put into them were based on TCP/IP addresses, which were found to be subject to spoofing/masquerading and thus deemed ineffective in positively identifying the real external device being granted access. Therefore, routers alone do not provide an entirely secure extranet implementation; but when used in conjunction with one of the following extranet architectures, routers can be a component to add some degree of security, but only when used in conjunction with other network security devices.

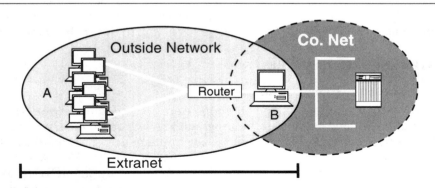

Exhibit 27-3. More realistic extranet.

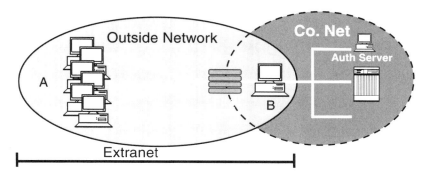

Exhibit 27-4. Extranet using an application layer gateway firewall.

Application Gateway Firewalls

As network security architectures matured, the introduction of application layer gateway firewalls, software tools on dedicated machines, usually dual-homed (two network interfaces, one internal, one external), became the more accepted external protection tool. These software tools have the ability to not only perform router-type functions with access control rules, but also provide user authentication services on a per-user basis. This user authentication can take the form of an internal user authentication list, or an external authentication call to token-based authentication services, such as the ACE SecureID™ system. Exhibit 27-4 depicts this type of architecture setup to support an extranet using an a application layer gateway firewall to enable authenticated users inward access to an enterprise in a controlled manner.

In addition to supporting access control by IP address and user, some gateways have the further capability to restrict access by specific TCP/IP service port, such as Port 80, HTTP, so the extranet users can only access the internal resource on the specific application port and not expose the internal machine to any greater vulnerability than necessary.

Follow-on application layer gateway implementations have since emerged to provide varying additional degrees of extranet connectivity and security. One such method is the implementation of a proxy mechanism from an outside network to a portion of an internal company network. Normally, a proxy performs control and address translation for access from an intranet to the external Internet. These types of proxies normally reside on the firewall, and all user access to the Internet is directed through the proxy. The proxy has the ability to exert access control over who in the intranet is allowed external access, as well as where they can go on the Internet. The proxy also provides address translation such that the access packet going

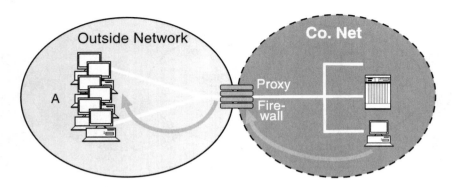

Exhibit 27-5. Outbound proxy architecture.

to the Internet is stripped of the user's original internal address, and only the external gateway address of the enterprise is seen on the packet as it traverses the Internet. Exhibit 27-5 depicts these proxy functions.

The proxy provides both security and network address functions, although the entire process can be used in its reverse to provide an extranet architecture because of its ability to provide access rules over who can use the proxy, where these proxy users are allowed to go, and what resources they can access. Exhibit 27-6 depicts a *reverse proxy* extranet architecture.

Today, most proxies are set up for HTTP or HTTP-S access, although application layer gateway proxies exist for most popular Internet access services (Telnet, FTP, SQL, etc.). One of the major issues with proxy servers, however, is the amount of cycle time or machine overhead it takes to manage many concurrent proxy sessions through a single gateway. With highly scalable hardware and optimized proxy software, it can be carried

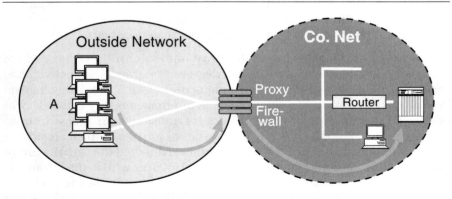

Exhibit 27-6. Reverse proxy extranet architecture.

to potentially handle high user demands, but the system architecture must be specifically designed for high loads to be able to meet user response expectations while still providing the security of an authenticated proxy architecture. On the *inward* proxy depicted in Exhibit 27-6, the proxy can be configured to only allow access to a single internal resource on a given TCP/IP port. Further protection can be added to this reverse proxy architecture by putting the target internal resource behind a router with specific access control rules, limiting the portion on the company intranet that inbound proxies can reach, which can ensure limited access on the intranet; should the internal machine ever be compromised, it cannot be used as a "jumping off point" into the rest of company intranet.

A somewhat *hybrid* architecture extranet, where some firewall controls are put in place but the external user is not granted direct inward access to an enterprise's internal domain, has been evolving and put in place as a more popular extranet implementation. In this architecture, the external user is granted access to an external resource (something outside of the enterprise firewall), but still on the property of the enterprise. Then, this external resource is granted access to one or more internal resources through the enterprise firewall. This architecture is based on minimizing the full external access to the intranet, but still makes intranet-based data available to external users. The most popular implementation is to place an authenticating Web server outside the firewall and program it to make the data queries to an internal resource on the enterprise intranet, over a specific port and via a specific firewall rule, allowing only that one external resource to have access to the one internal resource, thus reducing the external exposure of the intranet. Exhibit 27-7 depicts this type of extranet.

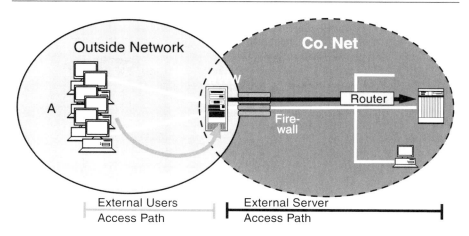

Exhibit 27-7. Extranet with athenticating Web server.

Issues with this type of architecture include reliance on a single user interface that can be safely placed outside the enterprise firewall, which makes it vulnerable to attack. Additionally, there is the issue of whether tight enough access rules can be placed on the access method between the external user interface resource (the Web server, in this example) and the internal resources that it needs access to on the protected enterprise intranet. If these two issues can be safely addressed, then this form of extranet can be very useful for an enterprise extranet with a high volume or varied user base and a large intranet-based data repository.

The user front end has been deployed as a Web server, usually SSL-enabled to ensure data integrity and protection by encrypting the data as it passes over an external SSL link. Access to this external server is also associated with some form of user authentication, either a static ID and password over the SSL link, and more recently with client digital certificates where each individual accessing the SSL-enabled site is issued his own unique digital certificate from an acknowledged certificate authority, thereby validating his identity. Each client maintains its own digital certificate, with the Web server having some record of the public-key portion of the client's digital certificate, either directly in the Web server internally, or accessible from a stand-alone directory server (usually LDAP reachable).

The most recent entrant in the extranet architecture arena is the Virtual Private Network (VPN). This architecture is based on a *software tunnel* established between some external entity, either client or external network, and a gateway VPN server. Exhibit 27-8 depicts both types of VPN architectures. External Network A has a VPN server at its border which encrypts all traffic targeted for Company Network C; this is a gateway-to-gateway VPN. Or, External Client B may have client VPN software on his workstation which would enable him to establish a single VPN tunnel from his workstation over the external network to Company C's VPN server.

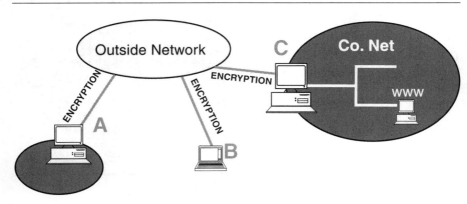

Exhibit 27-8. VPN architectures.

Although both server-to-server VPN and client-to-server VPN architectures are offered in the industry today, it is this author's experience that the more popular extranet architect is the client-to-server VPN architecture, as it offers the most flexibility for the most diverse audience of external users. This flexibility does add to the complexity of the implementation, as it can involve a potentially large number of external desktops, all with differing configurations. The benefits of VPNs include the ability to safely traverse external public networks with some assurance of data integrity and authentication as part of the VPN implementation. This architecture shows the most promise to meet the needs of extranets and cost savings for a world hungry for connectivity over public/external networks, although it still has some growing pains to go through to reach full product maturity.

An emerging standard for VPNs is coming out of the ITEF IPSec implementation, which draws a roadmap for the next-generation TCP/IP security protocol. Under this protocol, standards are being drafted that will enable differing devices to securely communicate under an agreed-upon security protocol, including key exchange for encryption and standardized authentication. Today, there are IPSec-compliant products on the market; however, the standard is still evolving and tests are being conducted to evaluate differing vendor compatibilities with each under the IPSec standard. One of the leading initiatives to evaluate this compliance is the Automotive Network Exchange (ANX) test, which is intended to establish a large extranet environment between the core automotive manufacturers and their vendors.

In the meantime, there are a wide variety of VPN product vendors on the market — some touting IPSec compliance and others, with proprietary implementations with IPSec in their future product roadmaps, choosing to wait until the standard stabilizes. The recommendation is to either select a vendor offering IPSec if it has some degree of maturity within its own product line, or one that is planning on adopting the standard; IPSec appears to be a viable standard once it fully matures.

Regardless of what VPN solution is being considered for implementing secure extranets, a few technical considerations must be understood and planned for before selecting and implementing a VPN extranet architecture.

Scalability. Similar to proxy servers, VPN servers incur a fair amount of processing overhead that consumes processing resources as high levels of concurrent VPN sessions pass through a single server. It is important to attempt to estimate one's projected user base and current access to appropriately size a VPN server. Some servers are on established lower-level processors for smaller environments and should not be implemented where high concurrent access rates are expected, although there is some benefit to physical load balancing spreading the access among multiple servers. However, there is also concern about implementing too many servers to manage easily. A balance between installing a single large server and creating a single point of failure — versus implementing many smaller servers — creates an administrative nightmare.

Multi-homed Intranets and Address Translation. In large intranet environments, many operate under a *split DNS* (domain naming structure) where intranet addresses are not "advertised" to the external networks, and external addresses are kept external so as not to flood the internal network. Additionally, many larger intranet environments have multiple gateways to external networks. If one of the gateways is established with a VPN gateway and an external client makes a connection to the internal intranet, it is important that the tunnel comes in through the appropriate VPN gateway, but also that the return traffic goes back out through that same gateway so that it gets re-encrypted and properly returned to the external VPN client. Exhibit 27-9 depicts the correct traffic patterns for a multihomed intranet with a single VPN gateway and an external VPN client.

VPN-Based Access Control. Many forms of gateway VPN servers offer the ability to restrict user access to a company intranet based on access groupings. This is especially important when intranets are being established for a diverse set of external users and it is important to minimize user access to the intranet. This type of access control is, of course, critical in establishing secure extranets, which further highlights the importance of understanding VPN access control capabilities.

User Authentication. Multiple options exist for user authentication, although the recommended option is to select a high-level authentication

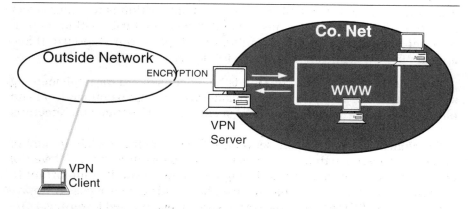

Exhibit 27-9. Traffic patterns for multi-homed intranet with a single VPN gateway and an external VPN client.

method (e.g., one-time passwords) or a time-synchronized password method. Under the IPSec standard, client-side digital certificates are evolving as a standard for high-level authentication. Unfortunately, initial implementations of client-side digital certificates for user authentication are entirely software based, eliminating the second-factor authentication, the "something the user physically has" in their possession. The return to true two-factor authentication under digital certificates will not really occur until physical smart cards become part of the authentication architecture. (Smart cards are credit card-type tokens that have a physically embedded chip which can be read electronically and written to, either with a portion of the client's digital certificate or the encryption algorithm used to unlock the digital certificate.)

IPSec Interoperability. Ultimately, the IPSec standard will stabilize, and all vendors following the established standard will allow different vendors' VPN products to interoperate. Under this environment, a company can implement a vendor's VPN server, and their acknowledged clients can purchase and use an IPSec-compliant client to gain access to the company intranet once they are authorized.

SUMMARY

Secure extranets are becoming the external network of choice in today's business world. There are multiple implementation options, as discussed in this article, each with varying degrees of risk and implementation complexity. Each implementation must be evaluated against a business case using the recommended risk and performance analysis outline. The basic router-controlled extranets are only recommended for the least valuable data environments, while the more sophisticated VPN extranet architectures appear to be the future for extranets, especially when the IPSec standard matures and gains industry adoption.

Section IV
Traffic Analysis and Performance

THE ABILITY TO REDESIGN OR RESTRUCTURE AN EXISTING NETWORK depends upon knowledge of the use of the network. In addition, many times the analysis of an existing network can provide a very useful foundation of knowledge that can be applied to the design of a new network.

A second important area of networking is the analysis of the level of network performance. If a network provides a reasonable level of performance, the need to modify the network will be minimal. Conversely, an unacceptable level of performance will more than likely require either the redesign or replacement of an existing network.

This section focuses on the dynamic duo of network design and traffic analysis and performance. In this section, the reader will find nine chapters that cover one or both topics. In Chapter 28, **Enterprise Network Monitoring and Analysis in a Mission-Critical Environment,** author Colin Wynd describes the role that network monitoring and analysis takes in administrating networks. Commencing with the concept of serial level management (SLM), this chapter discusses the range of functionality that network monitoring provides. This chapter is followed by a more specific chapter on traffic analysis. In Chapter 29, **Web Traffic Analysis: Analyzing What Is Happening on Your Site,** author Michael McClure describes how one can use Web server log files to obtain a variety of traffic reports. In addition to providing information useful for network design, this chapter provides detailed information on log file formats and the interpretation of data in such files. This information can be valuable for other data mining activities, with the author providing several examples of the use of log file data.

For network managers and LAN administrators creating a new network, the available bandwidth and cost per port can be important considerations in the design process. Chapter 30, author Duane Sharp's chapter on **Network Architectures and Performance,** provides the previously mentioned information in a review of available network architectures and their ability to handle increased user demand.

The next two chapters in this section also focus on performance-related topics. In Chapter 31, **Performance Engineering in Client/Server Environments,** author Scott T. Smith first defines the field of performance engineering. Once this is accomplished, Smith reviews several approaches to performance engineering and their application to client/server environments. This chapter is followed by a more specific performance-related chapter; in Chapter 32, author Gilbert Held introduces the reason why the performance of one type of a Gigabit Ethernet network may only produce a very slight level of performance increase over Fast Ethernet. This chapter, which is titled **Understanding Gigabit Ethernet Performance**, commences with a detailed examination of the Ethernet frame. Using this information as a base, Held computes the maximum frame rates and information transfer capability for Ethernet, Fast Ethernet, and Gigabit Ethernet. In addition to providing insight into the performance of Gigabit Ethernet, information in this chapter can be very valuable in selecting bridges and routers to interconnect different types of Ethernet LANs.

Because there are many factors one must consider when connecting LANs and WANs, Chapter 33 provides timely information in this area. In the chapter titled **LAN/WAN Interconnection Requirements and Implementation Considerations,** author Duane E. Sharp first reviews several network design issues prior to focusing attention on hardware and software. Concerning the latter, Sharp describes the use of NetWare as a tool for building networked communities.

In Chapter 34, author Howard C. Berkowitz provides a simple but effective method for describing and improving network performance. Berkowitz's chapter, titled **Demystifying Network Performance,** introduces the components of network delay and the role of service level agreements (SLAs) as well as methods one can consider for drafting SLAs.

In Chapter 35, Roshan L. Sharma's chapter titled **Planning, Designing, and Optimization of Enterprise Networks** provides information on the critical elements of a network manager's job. Included in this chapter are descriptions of an effective network planning effort, modeling and performance issues, and tools for network design and optimization. Concluding this section is a chapter that this editor considered for placement as the first or the last chapter in this section. This chapter, authored by Tim Clarke and titled **Proactive Performance Management**, provides critical information concerning how end users can use performance management tools as a mechanism to ensure SLAs are being met. This chapter also serves as a tool to note network problems before the problems actually reach a level where users complain. After considerable thought, it was felt that the topics discussed in Chapter 36 is more appropriate for concluding this section than for introducing the topic covered in this section.

Chapter 28
Enterprise Network Monitoring and Analysis in a Mission-Critical Environment
Colin Wynd

NETWORKS AND HOW PEOPLE USE NETWORKS HAVE CHANGED considerably over the years. Network environments have also evolved and matured to the point where the focus has shifted from technology adoption and implementation issues to management activities needed to support business end users in a mission-critical environment. As a result, the strategic role that information technology (IT) plays in delivering business continuity across the company has been elevated from an afterthought to the group that adds a competitive edge to the corporation. The role of the chief information officer (CIO) (and therefore all IT personnel) has reflected this change. CIOs used to report to the chief financial officer (CFO) and were thought of as a facilities-type of people, whereas now CIOs now usually report directly to the chief executive officer (CEO) and can bring about changes to the entire corporation.

Business end users are also starting to expect error-free network connectivity with guaranteed uptime and response time. These users also expect network services to be delivered regardless of the underlying technology. This increase in reliance on client/server applications as a fundamental part of conducting business means that end users need to rely on the network as much as the phone. The combination of the maturing of the underlying technology and the end users' expectations means that the monitoring and analyzing of the network is a critical function of any IT group.

0-8493-0859-3/00/$0.00+$.50
© 2000 by CRC Press LLC

This chapter discuses the role that network monitoring and analysis takes in administrating networks. It starts by explaining the concept of service-level management (SLM) and where network monitoring fits into that "framework." We then show the range of functionality that network monitoring brings to the IT manager's arsenal.

SERVICE-LEVEL MANAGEMENT

A common misconception of IT managers is that it is the *technology* that provides the correct level of service to the business, but actually it is the correct *implementation* of a technology. IT managers (and engineers) must make the transition from the latest technology provider to providing the best service for the business. In many cases, applying the latest technology will not improve the service that is being provided. What is required is a strategy and a methodology for providing the correct service to the business.

IT service management is based on *defining*, *achieving*, and *maintaining* required levels of IT service to the business user population with the company. At this point in time, few client server IT organizations have realized that IT service management is the only strategy that allows them to meet the business end users' needs. Another way of looking at IT service management is that it is the "glue" that allows IT to align itself with the businesses that it supports. The language that IT and business groups communicate through is service-level agreements.

By implementing service-level agreements between IT and the business groups, one can increase the efficiency of IT staff and further automate and control the process of meeting service-level agreements. Because service-level management helps align multiple IT management processes to meet service objectives, it becomes increasingly important to coordinate the work of the IT staff toward that end.

IT organizations are typically very tactical. This stems primarily from the reactive "firefighting" mentality that historically IT has needed when implementing new technologies. A reactive approach to IT management is very tactical, not strategic. IT should aim to move to a proactive approach, and that requires planning. Planning requires setting objectives based on a clear vision. Objectives stem from a clearly defined set of strategies that can be expanded into implementation tactics to support the objectives defined in the planning process. Much can be learned from this methodology when tackling the problem of managing the distributed IT environment.

SERVICE-LEVEL AGREEMENTS

The "language" that can bind IT organization to the business is the service-level agreement (SLA). SLAs are documents that define the various levels of service that IT must deliver to end users. SLAs are written for individual applications from end to end. A business can have multiple SLAs for each application (i.e., Web, E-commerce, order entry). One of the challenges IT organizations face is proper decomposition of the problem into manageable parts. This can be especially difficult in today's client/server environment. Although there are many components to the SLA, not all are required. Many elements an SLA may contain include the following:

- **Service volume.** IT needs to quantify the volume of the service to be provided, such as average and peak rates and the time of day the demand is expected to occur. The business may also be provided with the incentive to receive better service, or a reduced cost for service, by avoiding peak resource usage periods (similar to discount phone rates at night). Being able to determine the volume of service allows IT to determine the infrastructure needed to support that service (i.e., do we need a two-lane road or a six-lane expressway).
- **Service timeliness.** IT needs a qualitative measure for most applications to be able to measure performance of the application. For some applications (i.e., an automated teller machine) it should be "90 percent of transactions processed within two seconds."
- **Service availability.** When will the service be available to the user? IT must be able to account for both planned and unplanned downtime. The business must be able to specify when they expect the system to be available to achieve their specified levels of work.
- **Service limitations.** It is too costly to normally supply a service without some form of limitation. The limitations to the service are documented here.
- **Service compensation.** This is the penalty clause area. If the service is not provided, then some form of remuneration should be documented. Also, there is a cost to providing the service. This cost can be recovered with a chargeback system, for example.
- **Measurement of service.** This section describes the monitoring process by which service levels will be compared against the agreed-upon service levels. IT must define how the service levels will be monitored and the frequency with which normal monitoring will take place.

SERVICE-LEVEL OBJECTIVES

For IT managers, being able to define service-level objectives (SLOs) from the SLA is the critical aspect of IT service management. SLOs are solely the domain of the IT manager and his or her staff. They are derived from what the stated business user service levels need to be based upon the development of the SLA. From the SLOs, IT can define the metrics (system, network, database, and application) that it needs to collect, monitor, measure, and report on. Some examples of metrics in a SLO include the following:

- **Application availability:** This metric reflects the application availability from the end users' standpoint. This metric can be different depending on the implementation of the application (i.e., client/server versus stand-alone).
- **Application performance:** Monitoring and measuring the applications to determine if user response time meets the service level specified in the SLA against specific business transactions. A volume metric can also be defined if defined in the SLA.
- **Application security:** Mechanisms must be put in place to insure secure access to certain applications due to company confidentiality or competitive threats. Measures to the effectiveness of this system must be put in place and monitored against service objectives (e.g., no unauthorized access, different levels of access to certain parts of an application, etc.).
- **Application reliability:** Measurements need to be established and collected to determine the accuracy of an application. This may require periodic sampling of the work accomplished by the application or may require the application to be instrumented to provide those measures in real time.

SLOs are defined from SLAs. An important aspect is defining the proper metrics to measure service objective compliance. This is especially true in the distributed environment where the components of the infrastructure that need to be measured are many (network, system, application, and database) and geographically dispersed. Using this method to refine the metrics needed means increased focus can be given to the quality of the metrics rather than the quantity. It also allows for a phased implementation of service-level monitoring and what it means.

The bottom line is this: *Focus on getting the right metric for the management task at hand.* This implies the task is understood and the desired solution has been well-defined. Ignore the urge to implement all management tools and collect every piece of data all the time with the thought that someday it may be needed.

One resource for finding more detail on service management processes and procedures is the IT Information Library. This is the ultimate guideline on IT service management. It has information on all aspects of implementing IT service management, including recommendations for managing people, processes, and tools. The Information Technology Service Management Forum (IT SMF) is a global consortium of more than 400 international corporations responsible for advancing the IT Information Library.

Service management is important to the network manager, as it allows the correct resources to be allocated to the correct business. Service management allows the IT manager to decide where to allocate resources, what level of support is needed.

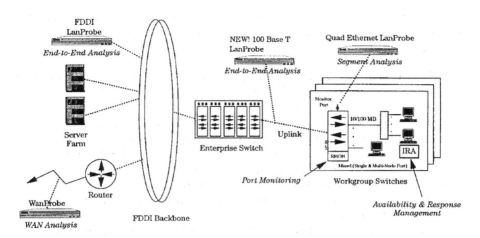

Exhibit 28-1. Remote monitoring agents installed on a large enterprise network.

NETWORK MONITORING AND ANALYSIS DEFINED

Distributed network monitoring is the ability to view a remote network and perform monitoring and analysis on that remote network as if it were local. In the past, portable devices were carried to remote sites and placed onto the network when problems occurred on that segment. Having a network monitoring device on a segment only when there are problems means that the segment is not monitored 99 percent of the time. Monitoring devices permanently placed on mission-critical segments can constantly monitor traffic. That means analysis can be performed over and above fault management.

The Exhibit 28-1 shows an example of remote monitoring agents installed on a large enterprise network with a variety of media types such as WAN's, Switches and Media types such as FDDI and Ethernet.

The agents, or "probes," reside on the remote segments and collect information of the traffic that it sees. The segments can be of any media type from various local-area nework (LAN) media types, such as Ethernet, FDDI, Token Ring, or some WAN protocol such as frame relay. The segments can be geographically dispersed, but in general must be interconnected. The network management console contains a suite of applications that collect the network information from these remote agents and interprets them using power graphical user interfaces. Interestingly, the network management console communicates with agents using the same network that the agents are monitoring. (Out-of-band communication between the manager and agents is also possible.)

With this configuration, network administrators can use monitoring tools to manage the whole network. Some functions a network administrator can perform are as follows:

- **Network performance management:** The ability to continuously monitor certain network statistics to ensure adherence to the SLA. Setting network thresholds to identify anomalies and creating baselines to aid in determining "normal" network performance.
- **Network security monitoring:** Ensuring that only authorized users access the network. This includes monitoring the effectiveness of firewalls as well as internal security monitoring.
- **Fault management and availability:** Being able to troubleshoot network problems in a timely fashion and monitor the availability of servers from end users' perspective.
- **Network service simulation:** Traffic profile modeling allows a network manager to do a quick "what-if" analysis before reconfiguring network resources. Having the appropriate data of past network trends determines what changes need to be made to handle the ever-growing network growth.
- **Policy-based management:** Being able to control who gets the limited amount of network bandwidth has always been a goal of network administrators, but until now some of the recent standards have been almost impossible to implement. By implementing some of the recent standards, true policy-based management is at the network manager's fingertips.

NETWORK MONITORING AND ANALYSIS IN THE IT ENVIRONMENT

The IT management environment covers the whole range of devices that reside on the network as well as the network that enable business end users to function. We can break this down into four components:

- **Systems management:** This is concerned with the performance of the computers on the network and usually deals with issues such as database performance and disk use on file servers.
- **Element management:** This is concerned with managing the various networking devices, such as bridges, routers, and hubs. Typical management issues deal with configuration tables, throughput, link states, and port partitioning. A device management application usually shows a picture of the device on your screen, complete with installed cards and indicator lights.
- **Desktop management:** This is concerned with the end-user workstations and PCs. The management issues are PC configuration files, disk use, application support, etc.

- **Network monitoring and analysis:** This is primarily concerned with the activity on the wire. It looks at the flow of data across the network in an effort to understand network performance and capacity and to resolve problems related to networking protocols.

Network monitoring and analysis allows the IT department to manage one part of the end-to-end management picture. System, database, and application management issues are not discussed in this chapter.

STANDARDS OVERVIEW

Network monitoring has benefited from several standards. The main standard in use for network monitoring is the remote monitoring (RMON) standard, which defines a method of monitoring traffic up to the DataLink layer (Layer 2) in the Open Systems Internet (OSI) stack. The RMON2 standard, which has not yet been ratified by the Internet Engineering Task Force (IETF) defines how to monitor traffic at the network layer (OSI Layer 3) and some portions of the application layer (Layer 7).

- Simple Network Management Protocol (SNMP)
- Simple Network Management Protocol version 2 (SNMPv2)
- Remote Monitoring (RMON) standard
- Remote Monitoring version 2 (RMON2) standard

Why Do Network Monitoring?

As part of an IT departments SLA with its business end users, IT must maintain a certain level of network service. To be able to do this, the network must be monitored to ensure error-free connectivity, responsiveness, and level of throughput. If the network is not monitored, it would be impossible for the IT department to guarantee any level of service.

In today's competitive environment, new client/server applications are quickly appearing in business environments; some examples are the World Wide Web and Lotus Development Corp.'s Notes. If the network is not being monitored, then the effect of adding one of these network-intensive applications is unknown and eventually one will bring the network to its knees. If the environment is being monitored, network bandwidth can be monitored and traffic trends analyzed to ensure that network bandwidth will always exceed future growth.

The ability to monitor trends changes IT from being reactive — waiting until something breaks before resolving the problem — to being proactive — resolving potential issues before they break. The IT department should now blend into the background, allowing business end users to focus on their functions.

Traffic Analysis and Performance

Who Does Network Monitoring?

Because there are many parts to network monitoring, many people are involved. Here are some generic descriptions:

- **Network manager:** Responsible for long-term strategic decisions regarding the network. Involved in looking at new technologies, such as 100Base-X or asynchronous transfer mode (ATM), deciding where and when to modify bandwidth. This person tends to look at network trends, performing forecasting and capacity planning.
- **Network engineer:** Responsible for day-to-day operations of the network. Upgrades network devices, adds capacity. Also acts as a second line of support for problems that the operations center engineer cannot resolve.
- **Operations center engineer:** Most large corporations have a centralized monitoring center that is staffed with "level 1" engineers that attempt basic troubleshooting on problems. These engineers monitor for events that are triggered by servers, workstations, or network devices that can alert the operations center on potential problems. These engineers are the first line of support and are constantly in reactive mode.

What Data Is Provided?

Monitoring the network means that information on every packet on every segment can be gathered. Network monitoring really means deciding which data is important and should be gathered and which data is redundant. Corporations with many segments need to decide on only a few critical pieces of information, otherwise they are inundated with data. The cost of analyzing the network would exceed the actual cost of the network. Some of the most critical measurements that should be gathered are as follows:

- Utilization: Segment utilization information should be gathered to generate trends for capacity planning purposes, baselining purposes, performance information.
- Error rates: Total error rate information can give performance indicators; baselining the error rate of the network, correlated with utilization, can give indicators of physical layer network problems.
- Protocol distribution: This can generate trends for changing application mixes; monitoring the usage of new applications and the effect of new applications on the network.
- Top talkers: These can also give indications on the performance of the network, performance of machines, load of application, and services on the network. Top talkers can also indicate potential new applications

382

that are unknown to the network department (new Internet applications such as PointCast have been discovered using this method).
- Latency measurements (echo tests): These lead to trends in performance.

How Does Network Monitoring Work?

Network monitoring is a large subject, and there are many proprietary protocols involved. This chapter covers only standards based protocols, plus the most widespread proprietary protocols.

The Simple Network Management Protocol (SNMP)

The Simple Network Management Protocol (SNMP) was a draft standard in 1988 and was finally ratified in April 1989. SNMP is described by Request For Comments (RFC) 1098. SNMP has three basic components:

- **Agent:** A software program that resides in managed element of the network such as a hub, router, or specialized device.
- **Manager:** This communicates with the agent using the SNMP commands.
- **Management information base (MIB):** A database that resides with the agent and holds relevant management information.

Exhibit 28-2 shows the relationship between those three components.

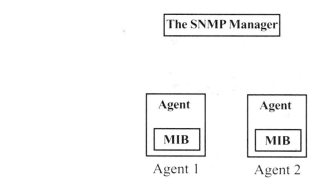

Exhibit 28-2. Relationship between Agent, MIB, and Manager.

There are five types of SNMP commands, which are called protocol data units (PDUs):

1. **Get request:** A manager requests (from the agent) the value of a variable stored in the MIB.

2. **Get-Next request:** The manager uses this to request information on multiple variables. Used to reduce network traffic. If one variable is not available, no values are returned. It is also used to retrieve unknown rows if available.
3. **Set request:** The manager instructs the agent to set a MIB variable to the desired value.
4. **Get-Response:** This is sent by the agent as a response to a secure electronic transaction (SET) or Get-Next command as either an error or identical to the SET to show it was accepted, or to a Get-Next with the value portions of the request filled in. The manager checks its list of previously sent requests to locate the one that matches this response. If none is found, the response is discarded, otherwise it is handled.
5. **Trap:** One of two unsolicited messages sent from the agent to the manager, often used for event notification.

THE MANAGEMENT INFORMATION BASE TREE

MIBs are hierarchical in nature (see Exhibit 28-3). This allows unique identifiers for each MIB variable (or Object). Some MIBs of interest are as follows:

- RFC1213 – MIBII — basic system information and basic level statistics
- RFC1757 – RMON (Remote Monitoring)
- RFC1513 – RMON (Remote Monitoring) extension for Token Ring

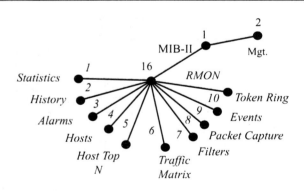

Exhibit 28-3. The hierarchical nature of MIBs.

There are several advantages that network management applications have with SNMP:

- The protocol is easy to implement.
- The protocol requires few resources to operate.

- The protocol is mature, stable, and well-understood.
- The protocol is widely available (on most computers), and most network devices have some form of agent/MIB embedded within them.

However, as networks have grown and the need for network management has become more imperative several disadvantages with SNMP have become apparent. Some of these disadvantages include the following:

- limited security
- lack of a block transfer
- polling-based protocol
- trap limitations

SNMPv2

SNMPv2 is a proposed standard that attempts to address these issues. Some of the proposed extensions to the standard include the following:

- Manager-to-manager communication capability
- Additional SNMP commands (PDUs):
  — Get BulkRequest — for getting whole tables
  — InformRequest — A manager-to-manager PDU
- Reliable traps

The last area of contention with SNMPv2 is security. Two proposed drafts attempt to address the security issue.

THE REMOTE MONITORING PROTOCOL (RMON)

The RMON standard is a specific standard for performing remote monitoring on networks. The RMON standard is defined by two standards RFC 1757 and RFC 1513. The standard defines a MIB that is broken down into ten groups, the first nine define monitoring of Ethernet networks and the tenth defines extensions for Token Ring. There are no standards for monitoring FDDI, 100Base-X, or WAN networks. RMON vendors have added their own proprietary extensions for these additional media types. RMON is limited, as it gives visibility only up to the data link layer (Layer 2) in the OSI stack.

- **Statistics group:** This group contains many segment statistics in 32-bit counters, such as packets, dropped packets, broadcasts, and multicasts. These are just counters, not studies.
- **History group:** This group contains segment history statistics for various counters such as broadcasts, errors, multicasts, packets, and octets. These numbers are for certain time periods. RMON defines two default time periods — 5 seconds and 1800 seconds.
- **Alarms group:** This covers threshold monitoring and trap generation when that threshold has been reached. It allows alarms to be set of various counters and patch match. Traps can start and stop packet capture.

- **Host group:** This contains host table and traffic statistic counters, plus a time table of discovery.
- **Host top N:** This contains studies for X time and X hosts, listing top talker for the study group.
- **Traffic matrix group:** This group contains matrix of Medium Access Control (MAC) layer (Layer 2) conversations. Information such as error, packets, and octets sorted by MAC address.
- **Packet capture/filter group:** These two groups are used together. Packet capture group contains the packets that have been captured. Multiple instances can be created.
- **Token Ring group:** Contains specific information about Token Ring, such as ring order, ring station table, and packet size distribution for history studies.

Remote Monitoring version 2 (RMON2) Protocol

The RMON standard brought many benefits to the network monitoring community, but it also left out many features. The RMON2 standard tries to address this (see Exhibit 28-4) by allowing the monitoring of Layer 3 (Network Layer) information as well as protocol distribution up to Layer 7 (Application Layer).

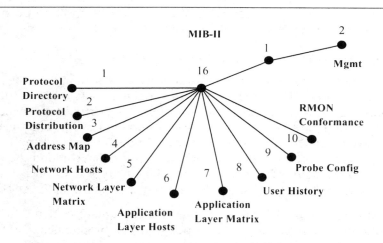

Exhibit 28-4. RMON2 new standards.

NETWORK PERFORMANCE MANAGEMENT

Performance management means being able to monitor segment activity as well as intrasegment traffic analysis. Network managers must be able to examine traffic patterns by source, destination, conversations, protocol/application type, and segment statistics such as utilization and error rates. Network managers must define the performance goals and how notification of performance problems should happen and with what tolerances. Some objectives that network managers are faced with are as follows:

- Baselining and network trending: How to determine the true operating envelope for the network by defining certain measurements such as segment utilization, error rate, and network latency, to check SLOs and irregular conditions that, if gone unchecked, may have drastic consequences on networked business users productivity.
- Application usage and analysis: This helps managers answer questions such as "What is the overall load of your WWW traffic?" and "What times of the day do certain applications load the network?" This allows network managers to discover important performance information (either real-time or historic) that will help define performance SLOs for applications in the client/server environment.
- Internetwork perspective: Is traffic between remote sites and interconnect devices critical to the business? With internetwork perspective capabilities one can discover traffic rates between subnets and find out which nodes use WAN links to communicate. It can also help one define "typical" rates between interconnect devices. Internetwork perspective can show how certain applications use the critical interconnect paths and define "normal" WAN use for applications.
- Data correlation: This allows one to select peak network usage points throughout the day and discover which nodes contributed to the network load at that peak point in time, which nodes they were sending traffic to, and which applications were running between them.

Exhibit 28-5 shows and example of traffic flow between several segments. The thickness of the line indicates the volume of traffic. With this information it is easy to identify potential WAN bottlenecks.

Exhibit 28-6 shows clients and servers correlated with a time graph. Being able to determine how much a particular sever affects the network can help in the positioning of that server and again improve performance.

Network Security Monitoring

Security management encompasses a broad set of access control policies that span network hosts, network elements, and network access points (firewalls). Consistent policies are the key here; the objective is to support access and connectivity that is appropriate to the business need while restricting clearly inappropriate network-based access. As in other activities, constant monitoring for specific violations is critical, as is a notification mechanism. For certain conditions, immediate, automatic action maybe

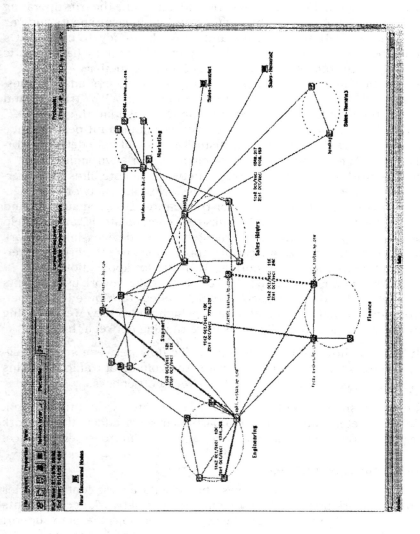

Exhibit 28-5. Traffic flow between several segments.

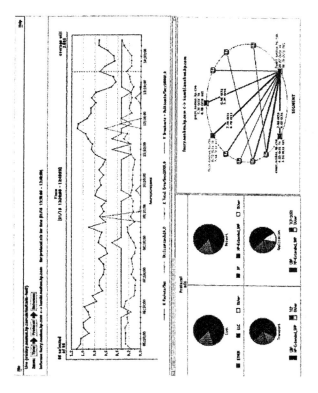

Exhibit 28-6. Clients and servers correlated with a time graph.

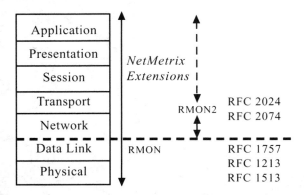

Exhibit 28-7. RMON, RMON2, and Hewlett–Packard NetMetrix Extensions.

required (i.e., "Shut down this connection" or "Shut down the firewall"). Monitoring should include both passive and active monitoring (probing).

Access level monitoring ensures that the controls and security that are in place actually perform to expectations. Monitoring the traffic flow to a firewall for instance, ensures that no intruders access it internally. Access level monitoring polices the "police" and ensures that nothing has been overlooked by the security. (See Exhibit 28-7.)

Management and Availability

Fault. Fault management is the continuous monitoring of the network and its elements and the detection of failures within the network environment. When a failure is detected, notification of the failure must occur in a timely fashion. The failure must be qualified with respect to other failures and prioritized.

Fault management systems include software to detect and notify a centralized system of these failures. The centralized system normally includes some form of discover and mapping software that allows the network manager to have a graphical view of the network. These notifications must be correlated so that event storms are eliminated. A trouble ticketing system can also be incorporated so that a document trail is kept of the problem and a mechanism can communicate the status of the problem to the end users.

Another aspect to fault management is availability. This is the monitoring of servers from business end users' perspectives to ensure that the machine is available to the end users. Tracking and notification of any interruption of client/server access is a critical part of the IT department's function.

Capacity Planning. Network demand is growing at unprecedented rates. New applications, such as SAP and the World Wide Web (WWW), are encouraging extensive use of the network. Graphics are now sent regularly over the network (either through a corporation's intranet or over the Internet). As network managers increase bandwidth, new applications for the network (such as voice-over-IP or multimedia) become viable. This causes another spurt of demand for the network.

Capacity planning allows the network manager to look forward by looking at the past and helps the manager to forecast what the demand will be. This means the IT department can keep one step ahead of demand.

Network Reporting. Part of the IT department's function is to demonstrate that members perform their functions to the prescribed level. Being able to document that the network runs at the level agreed to in the SLA is an important justification tool.

It is critical that reports are generated automatically, otherwise reports will not be generated or the effort to generate them will be too substantial to make it worthwhile.

NETWORK SERVICE SIMULATION

Being able to move from reactive troubleshooting to a proactive approach is critical to the success of IT. Part of this is being able to predict accurately the impact of network and application changes in a dynamic network environment. By simulating the effect of network and network-centric application changes, IT can intelligently provide the quality of service for its end users. By being able to simulate the network, it will be able to do the following:

- deploy network-centric applications with confidence
- choose and implement new technologies with assurance
- prepare the network for an increasing number of users
- create attainable network SLOs
- reduce the risk of service disruptions and SLA violations

Replication of the Network

One issue with simulation is that it must model the network. A bad model will lead to bad simulation. The best simulators will take network topology as well as network performance data gathered from your own network. Creating network topology and network traffic from scratch is a fruitless exercise. The closer the representation of your existing network, the more accurately you can simulate your network.

Test-Driving New Technologies

Most simulation tools have a library of modeled network devices and media based on real-world characteristics. When testing new devices (such as the latest switch) or new technologies (such as Gigabit Ethernet), one should be able to place these devices/technologies within your simulated environment to see the changes. Using a high-fidelity model library allows network managers to test-drive products and new technologies, such as moving from Ethernet to Fast Ethernet, moving to ATM, adding a FDDI backbone, or creating completely new network segments. This reduces the risk in implementing a new technology and determines the best combination of technologies that will provide the service your business demands.

New Application Load Simulation

Simulation can reduce the impact of deploying network-centric applications by simulating the result of the load on your network. Being able to simulate new applications (i.e., SAPR/3) or adding demand to existing applications (i.e., the Web) allows the network manager to determine if the current network infrastructure will be sufficient for the new load. This is critical to ensuring that any changes will not cause problems to the existing SLAs the IT manager already has in place.

Simulating Organizational Scaling

Organizational restructuring is common in today's business. These changes can significantly affect the performance of the network and business. Simulation allows one to test the impact of adding new users and their applications to the network before a network change is even made. If the simulation contains both accurate network topology and traffic data, the simulation can anticipate end-user response times under differing scenarios, allowing you to plan for a smooth transition while maintaining acceptable network service levels for all users.

POLICY-BASED MANAGEMENT

Policy-based network management allows IT administrators to control who gets which network services when. This allows IT to manage a network to provide services according to business needs. For example, one user wants to surf the Web, one wants to process SAPR/3 transactions, and the last wants to submit an order. This means that three levels of service are needed to ensure that mission-critical traffic requirements are met while providing adequate services for less-critical traffic. Another aspect is that there are now more uses for the same network (voice, video, data). Voice-over-IP, videoconferencing, and E-commerce are now being merged onto the same network infrastructure. Policy-based network management allows network managers to set and configure policies to control their network environment to ensure that various SLAs are met. Many vendors (i.e., 3Com, Cisco Systems, etc.) now offer equipment (i.e., switches, routers, etc.) that understand policy-based management. Critical to the success of policy-based management is central management of these policies.

What is a Policy?

A policy is an association between a service and the rules that govern the use of or access to the service. Policies consist of two distinct elements:

1. The service, such as "priority bandwidth access," "security actions," or "access control."
2. The rules describing the conditions under which the service is available, such as "application SAP has access to 10M bytes of bandwidth between 8 a.m. and 6 p.m." A resource is the network element of software that provides the service.

Components of Policy-Based Network Management

Most policy-based network management implementations consists of a console, where the IT manager defines, edits, administers, and distributes the policies, and a set of agents that enforces the policies. In many cases the console is broken into two distinct components, a GUI and a policy server.

There are three generic types of agents:

1. **Outsourcing agent.** This runs on a network component (router, switch, etc.) and controls the resources on that device (i.e., bandwidth). For example, when an element receives a Resource Reservation Protocol (RSVP) request, that request is sent to the policy server using the Common Open Policy Service (COPS). The policy server decides how the request should be handled and sends that information back to the agent for enforcement.
2. **Configuration agent.** This normally runs on servers or machines with dedicated CPUs. This combines the policy server with the agent. An example is a policy-based software firewall that will make changes to its configuration as policies change.
3. **Proxy agent.** This agent takes the policy information and makes changes to the clients it manages (i.e., switches that are not "policy-aware") on behalf of the policy server. For example, using voice/IP, a port associated with a voice application can be given a higher priority than a port associated with a data transfer, thereby avoiding the latency and jitter often associated with voice transmission over IP.

Policy-based management is still in the early stages of its life cycle. Few corporations have widely implemented policy-based management strategies. Fast adoption will come as more corporations implement service level management and as voice, video, and data start to converge on the same network infrastructure over the coming months (and years). Many vendors claim policy-based management "aware" components, but in reality it is extremely difficult to implement policy-based management in a heterogeneous environment.

LIMITATIONS OF NETWORK MONITORING AND ANALYSIS

Monitoring the network with the RMON standard means that only data link layer (Layer 2) information is collected. This is not high enough in the OSI stack to gather information about traffic trends of client/server applications. RMON has reached a point where it is widely deployed within switches, but it is not at the level in the stack to add much value from an application monitoring viewpoint.

The RMON2 standard defines a method of monitoring up to Layer 7 at certain times. RMON2 does not define continuous monitoring of all Layer 7 traffic, nor does RMON2 define any metrics for performance management.

As more types of traffic (i.e., voice, video) are mixed into the network, current monitoring tools will lag behind in being able to diagnose problems with these types of traffic. This is where implementing SLAs and some form of policy-based management becomes critical to the success of the organization to ensure that mission-critical data is processed.

SUMMARY

Enterprise network management is a fast-changing environment. From the early days of monitoring the physical layer of the networks to the future of application-layer service-level management, the whole arena is helping IT management take control of the distributed environment that it spans.

Network management will always have several aspects that have been described in this chapter, and the tools for implementing SLAs between business end users and IT departments are quickly maturing.

However, network management is only part of the total end-to-end solution that must include the whole environment that business end users operate. This means systems, databases, and application monitoring tools must be deployed in conjunction with the network monitoring tools so that the whole environment can be viewed. Tools such as Hewlett–Packard's PerfView are being released that for the first time and can integrate seamlessly database, application, network, and system information on a single pane of glass for the end-to-end view that is necessary in this complex environment that IT must now work.

References

1. *LAN Traffic Management*, Peter Phaal, Prentice Hall ISBN: 0-13-124207-5.
2. *Network Monitoring Explained*, Dah Ming Chiu and Ram Sudama, Ellis Horwood, ISBN 0-13-614-710-0.
3. *Focus On OpenView*, Nathan Muller, CBM Books, ISBN 1-878956-48-5.
4. *The Simple Book*, Marshall T. Rose, Prentice Hall, 0-13-812611-9.

Chapter 29
Web Traffic Analysis: Analyzing What Is Happening on Your Site

Michael McClure

THE WEB TRAFFIC ANALYSIS MARKET BARELY EXISTED A FEW SHORT YEARS AGO and is already a multimillion dollar segment of the E-business industry. Web traffic analysis growth is being driven by the growth of the World Wide Web and the desire to know as much as possible about visitors through self-identification, registration, and Web server logs. According to a recent report by International Data Corporation, the Web traffic analysis market will break $100 million by the year 2002.

Web traffic analysis tools take Web server traffic information and try to make sense of it so intelligent business conclusions can be drawn. Simple things like how many total files were requested can be easily calculated and reported. By looking for multiple requests from the same computer during the same timeframe, more complex things can be calculated, like the number of total visitors and visits that were made to a site. By adding other information to the analysis, such as advertising information, ad impressions, and click-through rates also can be calculated.

Two types of Web traffic analysis are described below, namely Web log analysis and Web mining.

WEB LOG ANALYSIS — TRADITIONAL WEB TRAFFIC ANALYSIS

Web log analysis software reports basic traffic information based on Web server log files. Tools in this category use calculations and assumptions to create a maximum amount of log data relationships for inclusion in reports.

The main purpose for Web log analysis has traditionally been to gain a general understanding of what is happening on the site. Webmasters and system administrators who are responsible for keeping the site up and running often want to know how much traffic they are getting, how many requests fail, and what kinds of errors are being generated. This information is typically used for Web site management purposes.

Recently, Web log analysis has become more popular with Web marketers. By adding information such as advertisement names, filters, and virtual server information, log data can be further analyzed to track the results of specific marketing campaigns. Product managers and marketers who are responsible for allocating budgets in the most efficient manner require this type of information to make intelligent business decisions. Web log analysis can be used to answer questions like:

- What companies are visiting your site?
- What pages are the most and least popular?
- What sites are your visitors coming from?
- How much bandwidth does your site utilize?

WEB MINING — ADVANCED WEB TRAFFIC ANALYSIS

Rather than look at Web traffic data as its own island of information (Exhibit 29-1), Web mining integrates Web traffic information with other databases in the corporation such as customer, accounting, profile, and e-commerce databases. The resulting reports not only use advanced relationships between log data, but also draw from these external databases as well.

The main purpose of Web mining is to analyze online investments of the entire enterprise, in an effort to maximize return. Executive management and chief information officers are typical candidates for this type of information.

Many Web miners base their offers on visitor profiles and, more importantly, create new products that match the results of their analysis. Web mining is typically used to answer more complex Web-related questions like:

- How do visitors' demographic and psychographic information correlate with their Web site browsing behavior?
- What is your Web site's return on investment?
- Which advertising banners are bringing the most qualified visitors to your site?
- Which sites refer the highest number of visitors who actually purchase?

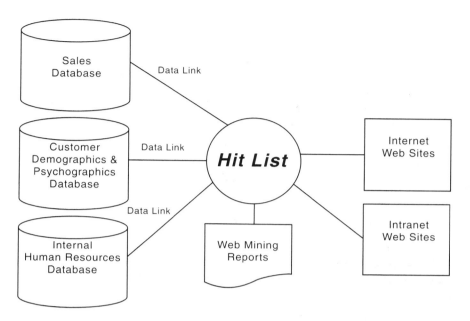

Exhibit 29-1. Web mining tools integrate Web traffic data with other corporate data from sales, customer, and human resources databases.

An Overview of Web Traffic Analysis Software

To accomplish its goal, Web traffic analysis software must be able to collect Web traffic data from multiple Web sites, store it into a data warehouse, integrate it with other sources of information, and then analyze and report the results quickly and accurately. The ideal Web traffic analysis system is also both completely programmable and extensible to support customization and scalability with the enterprise. This section goes through an overview of the technology typically used to accomplish each of these tasks. Good Web traffic analysis software is available today and ranges in price from free to over $20,000. The most popular packages are priced at around $300.

DATA COLLECTION

Web traffic analysis tools must first be able to collect Web traffic information, often from multiple Websites deployed throughout the world. This can be accomplished through reading Web server log files or more recently through TCP/IP packet sniffing techniques.

Web Server Log Files

Web server log files are undoubtedly the most common source for Web traffic information. Behind every Web site is a Web server, whose purpose in life is to respond to visitors by locating and sending the requested files. After each request, the Web server logs the results of the exchange in a "log file." A typical log file is ASCII-based and contains information about which computer made the request, for which file and on which date.

These log files contain useful Web traffic information. By looking for multiple requests from the same computer during the same time frame, conclusions can be drawn about the total number of visitors and visits that were made to a site.

Data Collection through Packet Sniffing Technology

Packet sniffing technology has recently been introduced into the traffic analysis market which eliminates the need to collect and centralize log file data entirely. This technology gets its information directly from the TCP/IP packets that are sent to and from the Web server.

The advantages here are

- Data are collected in real-time rather than being read in from a log file after the fact. This keeps the data warehouse up-to-date on a continuous basis.
- Data are continuously being read into the data warehouse rather than being collected from huge log files. This increases the data warehouse capacity.
- Companies with distributed Web servers can easily and automatically collect information in a centralized data warehouse. This solves the problem of collecting all the latest log files from sites located throughout the world.

Packet sniffing technology (Exhibit 29-2) watches network traffic going to and from the Web server and extracts information directly from the TCP/IP packets. The data collector must be installed on a computer located on the same network segment as the Web server that it is supposed to monitor, in order to "see" the network traffic as it goes by. Most packet sniffing tools are priced over $10,000.

DATA INTEGRATION

For Web mining applications, Web traffic data must be linked to other traditional business and marketing databases within the company. These databases might include E-commerce, profile, accounting, and customer registration databases, for example.

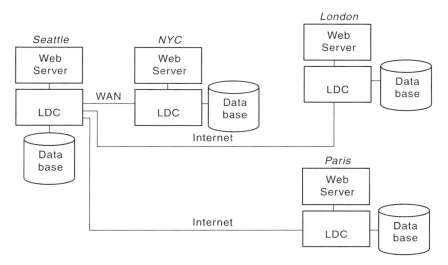

Exhibit 29-2. **Packet sniffing allows for multiple distributed Web servers to send traffic information over the Internet to a centralized data warehouse. Here, Live Data Collectors (LDCs) are used in New York, London, and Paris to form a data warehouse in Seattle.**

A typical way to perform this is through the computer IP address, as all requests to your Web server will include this information. Once you link an IP address to a particular company or person, you will be able to correlate future visits from the same IP address. This method is not perfect, however, as it is common for IP addresses to be shared among multiple users. This is done by larger organizations, such as Microsoft, as well as by Internet service providers such as America Online.

A more accurate method of creating this link is through the use of "cookie" technology. This ensures that the same computer is connected to your site, independent of the IP address that is used to make the connection. Both cookies and computer IP addresses are covered in more detail in the next sections.

DATA REPORTING AND ANALYSIS

This is a typical area that Web traffic analysis tools overlook. It is important to keep in mind that the end goal of Web traffic analysis is to allow for online investments to be quickly analyzed and business decisions to be made. These reports, therefore, must include real data that can be acted on, rather than just reams of detailed technical information. If you can't easily analyze this information, put it in a presentation-quality format, and quickly get it to the right decision maker, then there is not much purpose to collecting the information in the first place.

A quality Web traffic analysis package will include features like multi-level filtering, remote reporting, and will support multiple output formats. These features make Web traffic information easy to obtain for everyone in the organization.

EXTENSIBLE AND PROGRAMMABLE

The final essential feature for Web traffic analysis tools is the ability to easily program the tool to integrate it with other Web applications you may have, or extend its capabilities. This is a key requirement for any organization that has had to wrestle with a tool that could not grow with the organization's needs and eventually needed to be replaced — an extremely painful and expensive process.

The ability to program a tool, through a standard scripting language, makes it easy to add custom functions. This might be used, for example, to remotely administer advertisements through user-created ASP pages.

Beyond programmability, the ability to add plug-ins is a requirement if you need to purchase or integrate your own custom functions. This can be used to extend data collection capabilities to other file types such as advertising servers and streaming-media logs, for example. It can also be used to create custom output types that might be necessary for proprietary data analysis systems.

Some Important Web Traffic Analysis Concepts

To better understand Web traffic analysis software and what visitor information can be obtained from a Web site server, it is useful to have a basic understanding of how a Web server collects and logs visitor data.

To illustrate this, we will use the Marketwave Web server as an example. When visitors enters the URL "http://www.marketwave.com/default.htm" into a Web browser, they are asking the Marketwave Web server to send a file to them called default.htm that is located in the root directory. The Marketwave server responds to this request by sending the file and logging the results of the exchange in a server "log file."

In Marketwave's case, the default.htm file has references to two other HTML files and 23 other graphic files, which are needed to fully display the page. These files will also be automatically sent by the Marketwave Web server to the computer making the request and will be logged by adding lines to the Marketwave Web server log file. This means that a visit to the Marketwave home page will result in 26 total files (three HTML files and 23 graphic files) being transferred and 26 lines being added to the server log files.

This example illustrates some key definitions that are imperative to understand when analyzing Web sites:

- *Hit or Request.* A "Hit" or "Request" refers to an individual file request made to the Web server. This can be measured very precisely by simply counting the number of lines contained in the Web server log file. Measuring requests, however, is not a very accurate measure of Web site popularity, as each visit to a site can generate large numbers of file requests. The way a Web site is designed and the number of graphics it has will both significantly affect the number of file requests a site receives. In the example above, there are 26 requests.
- *Page View.* A better measurement of site traffic can be found by counting page views. A page view is simply the transfer of a specific HTML file. Page views can also be measured precisely by simply counting the number of requests for HTML files. Page views are a better measurement of Web site popularity, but are still imprecise when multiple HTML files are required to display a page (when using frames on a site, for example). In the example above, there are three page views, due to the use of frames on the Marketwave home page.
- *Visitor.* A visitor is defined simply as a unique computer "IP address." This measurement is less precise, due to the fact that IP address are sometimes shared by many people, as is the case with large corporations and online service organizations. This precision can be improved by using other information as well, such as the browser type or a persistent cookie (more on this technology later). Visitors are a much better measurement of gross Web site traffic than page views or requests. In the above example, there is only one visitor.
- *Visit.* A visit is a collection of requests that represent all the pages and graphics seen by a particular visitor at one time. The total number of visits is usually more than the total number of visitors because each visitor can visit the site more than once. Visits are more difficult to measure precisely, because there is no way to be certain that a series of requests actually belongs to the same person, or, for that matter, to the same person during the same visit. Measuring visits is also a good measure of gross Web site traffic popularity. In the example above, there is only one visit.

It is important to realize that measuring Web site popularity is an imperfect science. The art of good Web traffic analysis includes the ability to draw business conclusions using data that are imperfect. Having an understanding of the data, how they are collected, and what limitations exist, is key to drawing the proper business conclusions. As demonstrated in our example, one must understand and trade off between PRECISION (Requests and Page Views are precise but less accurate) and ACCURACY (Visits and Visitors are more accurate, but less precise) before drawing conclusions.

MORE DETAILS ON LOG FILES

This section is included to give you the detailed background needed to understand how Web traffic data are collected and analyzed. A typical Web server log file is ASCII based and contains information about which computer made the request, for which file. Additional information can be recorded including the date, the browser type, the requesting computer's IP address, any error codes, and the referring site, to name a few.

LOG FILE FORMATS

Different Web servers record this information in different log file formats. Most formats have similar information — they simply store it in different ways. Common log file formats include NCSA, W3C, Microsoft IIS, and O'Reilly. Here is a portion of a log file from the Marketwave Web site. This file was created by Microsoft's Internet Information Server, Version 4.0, which stores its log output in W3C format.

This log file shows 54 log files entries (requests), 10 HTML file request (page views), and one unique IP address (visitor). Lets analyze it in more detail and explain each piece of the data to demonstrate what can be learned from this information.

The first thing to notice is that there are 18 unique fields (columns) in this log file, each representing a different piece of the Web traffic puzzle. In this respect, Web log analysis is a lot like music composition — there are only a few basic pieces of information (notes) to build from, yet by putting this information together in different ways, it is amazing what can be derived.

LOG FILE FIELD DEFINITIONS

The definitions of these fields are as follows:

- *Request date.* This is the date that the request was made of the server.
- *Request time.* This is the time the request was made of the server. Some Web servers will include the time, as well as the offset from Greenwich Mean Time. If you are analyzing data from multiple Web sites located around the world, you will want to account for date and time-zone changes.
- *Request IP address.* This is the IP address of the computer that made the request. Every computer on the internet has a unique IP address so that other computers can find and connect to it. An IP address is made up of a series of four numbers separated by dots (206.129.192.10). Because humans have a difficult time remembering long strings of numbers, the Internet Domain Name System (DNS) was created, allowing these IP address to be associated with more readable domain names (e.g., marketwave.com).

- *Authenticated user name.* This is for sites that require a user to fill in a name and password before accessing a page. Whatever the visitor types in as their username is added to this field in the log file. This is typically used to restrict content on your site to only a few select users who know the password.
- *Server name.* This is the name of the server that responded to the request. It is useful for individually tracking multiple sites that are hosted on one computer (called virtual servers). For example, a publishing company might have a different Web site for each of its magazines, but host them all through one computer and one Webmaster. The term virtual server comes from the fact that there is only one computer behind the scenes, but to the outside world there appears to be multiple "virtual" Web sites, one for each magazine. This field allows the publishing company to analyze each site individually, as well as create aggregate statistics for the entire Web operation.
- *Computer name.* This is the name of the computer that responded to the request. It is useful for larger sites that require more than one computer to handle the number of requests being made (sites like Netscape, Microsoft, and Yahoo). This field could be used to calculate the "load" on each of the Web server computers and help determine when it is time to add additional resources or perform "load balancing" among the computers.
- *Server IP address.* This is the IP address of the server that responded to the request. In Marketwave's case, the Web server's IP address is 206.129.192.10, which is the computer hosting the Marketwave Web site.
- *Method.* This is the method that was used to respond to the request. GET is the most common command to retrieve HTML documents. Another commands you may see include HEAD, which is used to retrieve just the header portion of a file, and POST, which passes data to the server directly without being displayed in the URL (usually for security reasons).
- *Requested file name.* This is the path and file name that was requested relative to its root directory location on the Web server.
- *Query string.* This field includes any "query" text that was entered along with the URL. For example, in the URL "http://www.marketwave.com/default.htm?MWUID=info@marketwave.com" the text after the ? (MWUID=info@marketwave.com) is referred to as a query string. You will notice these strings being used on dynamically generated sites like search engines and may sometimes see them embedded in hyperlinks to better track marketing campaigns. By intelligently using query strings, you can improve the trackability of your site.
- *Error code.* This is the Web server error response code. A "successful" request (meaning the visitor's browser loaded the entire HTML/GIF/JPEG, etc.) generates a response code of 200. Codes in the 200 and 300

range are generally okay, while codes in the 400 range are bad, and in the 500 range are really bad. Server codes are grouped into ranges as follows:

- 200 Range — successful delivery of the requested file
- 300 Range — successful re-direct to another file
- 400 Range — failure to deliver the file
- 500 Range — server error

- *Bytes received.* This is the number of bytes of data that were received by the Web server.
- *Bytes sent.* This is the number of bytes of data that were transferred to the client during the visit.
- *Time taken.* This is the time the server took to respond to this request.
- *Version.* This is the format and version number of the request protocol, in this case HTTP, version 1.0. A protocol is simply the "language" that computers use to communicate with one another. HTTP is the standard protocol of the Web and stands for HyperText Transfer Protocol. Another protocol you may run into is FTP, which stands for File Transfer Protocol.
- *Agent.* This is a code that identifies which browser and operating system made the request. "Mozilla/4.04" refers to the Netscape browser, and Win95 refers to the operating system, which in this case is Windows 95.
- *Cookie.* This is any cookie information from the browser (more on this later).
- *Referring page.* This is the page and site our visitor was on immediately prior to making this request. This is very useful information if we want to determine how visitors are finding our site.

INTERPRETING THE LOG FILE

Looking at our example log file tells us quite a bit about what is happening with our Web site. The first line is a request for the Marketwave home page (default.htm). We notice a couple of useful pieces of information in this line, including the referring site (www.uu.se) and the referring page /software/analyzers/access-analyzers.html. This immediately tells us that this visitor came from a site based in Sweden (from the .se extension) and indicates that this site probably has a link to the Marketwave site on the /software/analyzers/access-analyzers.html page. If we go to this site ourselves, we find out that this is a university and the page in question has lots of links to different Web traffic analysis software packages.

The error code of 304 is also interesting. It tells us that this visitor already had access to cached version of our home page. Rather than send the file again, the Marketwave Web server responds with a status 304, indicating to the visitor's browser that it should go ahead and use the version of the page it already has.

The next 25 requests are all related to the home page. These are the additional two HTML frames and 23 graphics files (GIFs) that make up the remainder of the Marketwave home page. Notice that all of these requests resulted in an error code of 304, meaning that this visitor already had up-to-date copies of these files available. No files needed to be exchanged to display the Marketwave home page, frames, and graphics, as this computer has been to our site before and has our pages cached locally.

The next request is for a file called hitlist/live/default.htm. Odds are, this visitor clicked on a link to the Hit List Live page. This resulted in an error code 200, meaning the file was transferred and received successfully. The next 21 lines are the frames and graphics associated with the Hit List Live page. Notice that all of them were transferred successfully (error code 200) and the file sizes range from a few hundred Kbytes to almost 5000 Kbytes.

The next request was for a file called /downloads/frames-default, which is the Marketwave download page. Great! This prospect hit our home page, then hit our Hit List Live page, and then went right to the download page. You can't ask for much more than that from a Web site!

As can be seen, a lot of information is available in the log file. Understanding how your Web site is designed will really help with interpreting these data. If you didn't know that the Marketwave home page used frames, for example, you might think that the first three lines of the log file referenced three separate pages on the site. By knowing how the site is designed and looking at the data in the Web server log file, we can start to draw conclusions about visitors who can to the site.

Don't Waste Your Time Manually Interpreting Log Files!

Don't misinterpret the intent of the previous section! I highly recommend that you DON'T waste your time manually trying to interpret your log files. There are plenty of good software packages on the market that will do this job for you, including many of them that are offered free of charge. You can get a reasonably complete list by going to any search engine and looking for "Web traffic analysis" or "log file analysis."

The intent of the last section was to give you enough of an understanding of what is happening in the background of this process so that you can better interpret the results you get from these packages. As with any type of data analysis, understanding what is behind the data is a key part of interpreting the results. The more details you understand, the better choice you'll make when buying Web traffic analysis software and the better job you will do interpreting the results.

Getting Fancy with Web Traffic Information

The last section shows how simple conclusions can be drawn directly from the information in the log file. With this information alone we could easily calculate things like:

- which browsers and operating systems are the most common (through the agent field)
- how many bytes are being transferred by the server (through the bytes sent field)
- which files and directories are the most popular (through the requested file names)
- what sites are visitors coming from (through the referring pages)

But wait! With a little more work, there is still more information we can add to this analysis.

CONVERTING IP ADDRESSES BACK TO DOMAIN NAMES

We know this particular visitor was using a computer connected to the internet with IP address 193.237.55.144. Remember that every IP address has a corresponding domain name associated with it and these are linked through the Domain Name System (DNS). When a visitor entered www.marketwave.com into their browser, it was the DNS system that converted this name into the appropriate IP address (206.129.192.10) so that the computers could connect with each other. We can use the DNS system in reverse (called a reverse DNS lookup) to convert our mystery visitor's IP address back into a domain name. In this case, after doing a reverse DNS lookup, we find that the IP address 193.237.55.144 belongs to the domain issel.demon.co.uk. With this information we surmise that our visitor was using a computer owned by a company name Issel (due to the first part of the domain name) which is based in the United Kingdom (due to the .uk extension in the domain name).

You can either have your Web server perform this DNS conversion for you, or have your Web traffic analysis software do it. I generally recommend that you have your Web traffic analysis software do it, so you do not slow your Web server with this task. In addition, if someone else hosts your site, you may not have a choice in the matter, as most service providers don't want to slow their servers down to perform reverse DNS lookups. That's okay, simply get the log files from your provider and have your Web traffic analysis software do it for you.

CONVERTING FILE NAMES TO PAGE TITLES

A well-designed site will have a title (using the TITLE HTML keyword) for every page on the site. Rather than simply report the file names that were requested, we can easily look at these files and determine the corresponding page names. In general, page names are much more human-friendly in terms of communicating information. By simply extracting the page names from the files that are listed in our Web server logs, we can end up with a report that contains actual page names, rather than simply the file names themselves.

CALCULATING VISITORS AND VISITS

If we make a simple assumption that any log file entry with same IP address and same browser is probably the same visitor, we can easily calculate the number of visitors on our site. Note that this assumption is not perfect, as it is certainly possible that two different visitors happen to have the same IP address and browser type (from an online service provider for example). In general, however, this is unlikely to happen enough to significantly change the results of your analysis.

We can also calculate the number of visits to the site by assuming that if we do not see any more requests from that same visitor in 30 minutes, that the visit has ended. If we then see that same IP address and browser sometime in the future, we can assume that the same visitor is back for a second visit.

PATH ANALYSIS

By linking log file entries and then sorting by time and date, we can also start to see the path that a visitor took through the site. This is what we did in our example above. The log file shown only included requests from IP address 193.237.55.144 on 7/19/98. If we did this for each individual visitor, we would be able to calculate the most popular paths taken through the site as a whole.

GROUPING INFORMATION

By grouping information together, we can start to draw conclusions. For example, if we group all Netscape Browser and all Microsoft Browser information together we could calculate which company's browser was the more popular on our site. Using this same technique with referrer information, and looking for any referring URL with the word "Yahoo" in it, we could see how many of our visitors came from Yahoo as a whole.

COUNTRIES

By looking at the extensions on our visitors domain names, we can also estimate where in the world our visitors are coming from. Example extensions include:

.ca — Canada
.au — Australia
.se — Sweden
.uk — United Kingdom

FILTERING INFORMATION

By filtering information, we can answer very specific questions about the site. For example, to calculate how many visitors we got from Microsoft this week, we would only look at information from this week, and only look at visitors that have the word "Microsoft" contained in their domain name. This could be compared to our overall traffic to determine what percentage of our visitors presumably work for Microsoft.

CORRELATING INFORMATION

By correlating and cross-tabbing information, we can answer questions like, "Of the visitors I get from Germany, how many of them use Microsoft Windows 98 as their operating system?" This kind of detailed information can be useful for both site management and marketing segmentation purposes.

QUERY STRING PARSING

A piece of information we have glossed over is the query string field, which was blank in our example above. Query strings are typically used on database-driven sites and consist of all of the data at the end of a URL (usually delimited with a "?"). For example, the following referring URL is from Yahoo: http://search.yahoo.com/bin/search?p=Web+Traffic+Analysis.

By looking at the data after the "?" we see that this visitor searched for "Web Traffic Analysis" on Yahoo before coming to our site. Yahoo encodes this information with a query parameter called "p" and separates each search keyword with the "+" character. In this example, "p" is called the query parameter and "Web," "Traffic," and "Analysis" are each referred to as parameter values.

This information would normally be stored via the query field in the log file, and by looking at it in detail we can draw conclusions about what our visitors was searching for before hitting our site. This is useful information when trying to design the site to come up higher on the list of search engines, or when trying to determine what visitors are looking for before coming to our site.

VIRTUAL SERVERS

If you host multiple sites, another useful piece of information is contained in the site name field. By using this information intelligently, we could perform a separate analysis for each of the sites that you host. This would tell you which of your sites is responsible for the most traffic.

ADDING COOKIES INTO THE PICTURE

Another field we glossed over was the cookie field, which is a topic that has received much attention and debate in the press. Up to this point, we have not actually been tracking people, but are instead tracking Internet (IP) addresses as they come to our site. Cookies were invented to attempt to do a better job of tracking people, rather than simply IP addresses.

This technology was developed by Netscape and is really pretty ingenious. A cookie is merely a unique identifying code that the Web server gives to the browser to store locally on the hard drive during the first visit to the site. The intent of a cookie is to uniquely identify visitors as they come to the site.

Cookies benefit Web site developers by making individual "requests" much more trackable, which results in a greater understanding on how the site is being used and, therefore, a better Web site design. Cookies also benefit visitors by allowing Web sites to "recognize" repeat visitors. For example, Amazon.com uses cookies to enable their "one-click" book ordering. Because the company already has your mailing address and credit card on file, they don't make you reenter all of this information to complete the transaction. It is important to note that the cookie did not obtain this mailing or credit card information. This information was collected in some other way, typically by the visitor entering it directly into a form contained on the site. The cookie merely confirms that the same computer is back during the next visit to the site.

Unfortunately, cookies remain a misunderstood and controversial topic. Contrary to many beliefs, a cookie is not an executable program, so it can not format your hard drive or steal private information from you (note that languages like Java CAN do either of these things, but for some reason Java doesn't get the negative "security" press that cookies do). The second objection regarding cookies is that some people feel that it is a violation of their resources to be forced to store information on their computers for the benefit of the Web site's owner. In reality, the amount of disk space that a cookie takes up is trivial. Regardless of how you feel about cookies, modern browsers all have the ability to turn this feature off and not accept cookies.

If your site uses cookies, this information will show up in the cookie field of the log file and can be used by your Web traffic analysis software to do a better job of tracking repeat visitors.

Now comes the time to put all this log file information together into a readable report that we can draw conclusions from. Next is an example report showing the types of information that can be obtained from simply running your log files through a typical Web traffic analysis program.

WEB MINING — GOING BEYOND WEB SERVER LOG FILES

As mentioned at the beginning of this chapter, Web mining can be used to incorporate other information along with Web server log files into your analysis. This allows for information to be correlated to Web browsing behavior, such as accounting, profile, demographic, and psychographic information. Complex questions like the following, therefore, can be addressed:

- Of the people that hit our Web site, how many purchased something?
- Which advertising campaigns resulted in the most purchases (not just "hits")?
- Do my Web visitors fit a certain profile? Can I use this for segmenting my market?

As an example of this technology in action, we will again use the Marketwave Web site (www.marketwave.com). When you download a Hit List product from our Web site, we ask you to register it. During this registration process we ask you for information including your name, company, phone number, e-mail address, and state/country. This information (along with your IP address, the date, and the product you downloaded) is automatically stored in a contact management software package. All Marketwave personnel use this centralized database to handle any interactions we have with you. This includes our sales, marketing, public relations, and support departments.

Our contact management database is linked to the Hit List Web traffic database through "data link" technology using your computer's IP address as the key field. Combining Hit List information with sales and marketing data opens up a whole realm of one-to-one marketing possibilities. In our case, every time we see your computer (the same IP address) on our site, we can pull up your registration information and take appropriate action. Often, this action is personalized to your particular situation.

One of the first things we do with the information we collect from you is to sort it by territory and send it to our worldwide distribution network (Exhibit 29-3). On a daily basis, we automatically e-mail a report to the appropriate Marketwave personnel. This report shows Web activity for the previous day, as well as product downloads. We sort these by territory to make it easy for our territory managers to personally follow up on the leads in their area. We also link our database of actual contact names and phone numbers into the report, rather than only including domain names which, by themselves, aren't as useful to our distribution channel.

TRACKING E-BUSINESS SALES

Marketwave recently added the ability to order Hit List directly from our Website using a credit card. Our marketing department and management staff now receive a daily report with E-business information in DOLLARS (not just hits, page views, or visits). This is accomplished by linking to our E-business database. The report shows how many online sales were made

Exhibit 29-3. A worldwide distribution report of top sales prospects who hit the Web site yesterday (Jana Winslow — VP, Domestic Sales).

Company	Contact	E-mail	Telephone	Visits
Microsoft	Seth Longo	Sethl@microsoft.com	206-962-1200	3
Tango Designs	Suzanne Gayaldo	Sgayaldo@dirk.tango.net	509-323-6027	3
Intel	Sanford Arnold	Sa@intel.com	212-865-8584	2
Lucent	Larry Rubin	Larry_rubin@lucent.com	201-386-4200	2
Volvo	Yasim Kinneer	Ykinner@vd.volvo.se	206-765-1008	2
ESPN	Michael Louis	Orioles@espn.com	203-585-2000	1
USDA	Tom Bianchi	Tommyb@dc.usda.gov	202-548-2435	1
Apple	Mark Sojic	Mark@apple.com	301-255-7500	1

Note: This information has been generated by matching Web traffic data stored in the Hit List database with information stored in the Marketwave customer registration database.

the previous day and how many dollars were involved. More importantly, we also report on the number of sales that were not completed and who they were. This helps us track down prospects who had trouble with the online ordering process, as well as those who simply need a bit more information before making a purchase decision.

The Way We Manage Our E-Mail Campaigns

When we release new product versions, we first go back and market to our existing installed base of users. Generally, this is done through e-mail. In this e-mail, we add a link that looks something like: http://www.marketwave.com/default.htm?CAMPAIGN=date&MWUID=email.

The query string characters you see in this URL after the "?" are for tracking purposes. In this case, the campaign you are responding to (CAMPAIGN) is filled in with today's date and your Marketwave User ID (MWUID) is your e-mail address. When people click on this URL, these parameters end up in the query field of the log file. This means that we cannot only find out how many visitors we got as a result of our marketing efforts (through the CAMPAIGN parameter), but we can also tell who those visitors were (through the MWUID parameter).

Measuring Marketwave Print Advertising

In addition, Marketwave directs visitors to our site through print advertising campaigns. These ads point people to our Web site for more information on our product and free evaluation software. The URLs we give in our print ads usually look something like: http://www.marketwave.com/adname.

413

This allows us to measure how many people responded to the campaign, by simply looking for how many people came from this URL. For example, by adding an entry page filter set to "adname*" to any of our reports, we would be able to see how many visitors we had to the site that clicked on the above URL.

I suggest keeping "adname" to just a few characters, as many people won't type long strings of text into their browsers. Also, like most marketing information, the data we get are not perfect. Many of our visitors will not type the "/adname" portion of the URL into their browser, so your actual response rate is probably higher than what is reported through your Web traffic analysis software.

Measuring Marketwave Banner Advertising

Marketwave also is currently running multiple banner advertising campaigns. We also use query strings to track these. When we submit the ads to the sites we want to run them on, we also submit click-through URLs for each ad that look something like these:

http://www.marketwave.com/default.htm?AdName=ad1&AdSource=sitename1
http://www.marketwave.com/default.htm?AdName=ad2&AdSource=sitename1
http://www.marketwave.com/default.htm?AdName=ad2&AdSource=sitename2

We then run reports filtering on AdName as the query parameter when we want to know how each ad is doing relative to the other (ad1 vs. ad2). To compare our ad sites, we use filters that look for different AdSource as the query parameter (sitename1 vs. sitename2). These data not only are used to make future advertising decisions, but also to check the validity of the data we get from the sites we choose to do business with.

Measuring Return on Investment

The ultimate measure of an advertising campaign is return on investment. On a periodic basis, we report the cost of each of our ad campaigns and impressions. This is then compared to our E-business database to calculate a total return for any particular campaign.

We then shift our promotional budget towards those ad campaigns that perform the best for us — in dollars returned, not visitors returned. As you may already suspect, it is not always true that the least advertising CPM (cost per thousand impressions) is the best value.

OTHER EXAMPLES OF WEB MINING TECHNOLOGY

This section demonstrates some other real-world applications that Web mining technology is currently being used for within other major corporations.

Qualifying Leads

Web mining can be used to not only collect and distribute leads, but also qualify them as well. For example, imagine using the Dun and Bradstreet SIC database to integrate corporate information along with your Web traffic information. Leads could be sorted by territory, then by company size, and distributed worldwide to the proper sales territory. This process can be completely automated, distributing Web leads as often as you would like.

In addition, these data can be used in a marketing report showing what pages are the most popular by industry (SIC code), as shown in Exhibit 29-4. This information could then be used to better target site information to particular industries.

Exhibit 29-4. Most popular pages by SIC code.

Page Name	SIC Code	Total Requests
Home Page.htm	3454 — Manufacturing	4090
	5466 — Software	3000
	8745 — Real Estate	3500
Pricing Page.htm	0343 — Construction	10,057
	2354 — Insurance	1300
Ordering Page.htm	6404 — Banking	3700
	2111 — Manufacturing	2300
Reseller Page.htm	9999 — Financial Services	3516
	6854 — Telecommunication	5400

Note: Shows which pages are most commonly requested by companies with the following SIC codes and SIC descriptions.

Performing Marketing Segmentation

When combined with a profiling system, Web mining can be used to perform marketing segmentation. This allows Web marketers to better target campaigns and messages to each target group.

For example, an online music company using a profiling system could easily create reports detailing the differences in browsing behavior based on age ranges. They might find that most of their actual purchasers are in their twenties (Exhibit 29-5). An understanding of what information was attractive to other visitors would be invaluable in designing the Website to appeal to a wider audience. This information could then be used to expand content and quickly direct visitors to the right place.

**Exhibit 29-5. Report showing browsing
profiles by age range per page.**

Page Name	Age Range	Requests
Home Page	0:9	1
	10:19	3
	20:29	23
	30:39	13
	40:49	11
	50:59	8
	60:69	3
Product Page	0:9	1
	10:19	4

Note: Shows the age ranges, in 10-year increments, of visitors to each page.

FEATURES USERS LOOK FOR IN WEB TRAFFIC ANALYSIS TOOLS

If you are in the market for a good Web traffic analysis software package, this section covers specific features you should consider when comparing tools.

Basic Log Analysis Features (The Basic Stuff)

Product Architecture. We start with product architecture, as it is probably the single biggest difference in the leading Web traffic analysis tools and significantly impacts what can be done with the product. Some tools parse log file information directly into memory and then produce reports, all in one step. Others, first create a database of Web traffic information, then use this database to create Web traffic reports.

The main advantage of the "parsing" approach is speed for the *first* report, as writing data to a database is a step that is completely avoided. The main disadvantage of this approach is flexibility. Every change you need to make to a report (like a simple filter or query) will require that you reread all the log files and recreate a report from scratch. Not only does this take time, but it also eliminates the possibility of using the product with extremely high-traffic sites.

The main advantage to the database approach is that once a database has been formed, detailed reports can be generated by making simple queries to this database. In addition, having these data available is *fundamental* to the ability to perform one-to-one marketing and Web mining. Using a standard database opens up a realm of possibilities to effectively data mine your Web traffic information. This allows Web visitation information to be integrated into the rest of your organization, rather than having Web traffic analysis be its own island of information within your company.

Reporting Speed. When comparing Web traffic analysis tools for speed, I have two suggestions:

1. Make sure you are comparing "apples to apples." Some products don't store their results in a database and do not perform IP address lookups. For an "apples-to-apples" comparison, make sure you store the results and turn on IP-lookup capability, if it is available.
2. Make sure you compare multiple reporting sessions rather than simply running one report. Products that parse log files into memory will be faster on the first pass, as they do not store any data, so save the time of this step. The downside to this is that a *second* report with a simple change (like a filter or query) will require that you reread all the log files and recreate the report from scratch.

Predefined Reports/Elements. This is the number one requested feature by users — predefined reports that already perform the most common analysis tasks. Look for products that already include reports on advertising, marketing, technical analysis, proxy server, long-term trends, virtual server, and management summaries.

Flexible Filtering. Look for products that make it easy to get more detailed information, usually through the use of filters. Overview reports are fine, but you will soon find yourself asking for more detailed data, like how many visitors am I getting from each of the search engines? Sophisticated filtering includes the ability to apply filters to individual reports and individual reporting elements.

Easy Creation of New Reports and Customization of Existing Reports. Look for products that are easy to use and are intuitive, especially when creating your own reports. You want to spend your time analyzing the data, not creating the report.

Report Output in Common Formats Like HTML, ASCII, CSV, Word Processor, and Spreadsheet Formats. Look for a product that produces reports in the formats you need and use. Another nice feature is the ability to automatically post reports on a network or Web site.

Support for Multiple Web Servers. Make sure the product reads and understands all of the Web server formats you use in your organization. Often companies will have multiple formats around the world that will need to be combined for reporting purposes.

Automated Event Scheduling. Look for a solution that lets you automate the creation and distribution of reports. For example, you may want a daily report to be created every night and automatically e-mailed to your sales force

Automatic LAN and FTP Retrieval of Compressed Log Files. If you have Web site located remotely, look for a product that can automatically retrieve compressed log files from any FTP site or LAN.

Language Manager for Customization. Look for support for foreign language as well as support for company-specific terminology.

Advanced Log Analysis Features (The Fancy Stuff)

Search-Engine Keyword Reporting. Look for software that intelligently uses the query string information. This is useful for tracking marketing campaigns, as well as understanding what visitors are searching for both on and off your site.

Advertising Banner Campaign Analysis

If you run advertising campaigns, look for the ability to track them through measurement of impressions and click-through rates. In addition, you may consider a package that can link to your accounting database, so that results can be measured in terms of expenses and revenues generated, as opposed to just "Hits."

Virtual Server Reporting. If you run multiple sites, look for a package that can report on individual (real or virtual) servers separately. This allows you to understand how each server and site is doing.

Detailed Visitor Path Analysis. Some packages include the ability to analyze the most common paths that visitors take through the site. This is useful for optimizing the site to direct visitors towards certain areas, such as the ordering page or the technical support page.

Link Checking Capability. Web traffic analysis can highlight any error or broken links that visitors are encountering. This is useful for Webmasters to understand the details of what errors users are encountering on the site.

Remote Reporting with Security Manager. Remote reporting allows any authorized user to obtain Web traffic information with nothing more than an Internet connection and browser. This makes it easy to get data to the people who need it, without having to install custom software or design individual reports for them. Making Web traffic data easily accessible to the nontechnical business specialists will improve an organization's efficiency in a distributed decision-making environment.

Database-Driven Site/Query Reporting. If you run a database-driven site, you will need the ability to parse your query strings into the parameters and values that are called from the integrated database. When combined with data link, query parsing results of dynamic site activity can be linked back to tables within the actual dynamic site generator to provide more meaningful information, such as a page title or content description.

Custom Columns and Calculations Including User-Defined Variables and Formatting. Much like a spreadsheet, look for the ability to add a column to any report table with custom calculations and formatting. This could be used by an ISP, for example, to calculate customer bills based on bytes transferred and display the result in dollars. When combined with data link, billing rates could even be read from another database.

Web Mining Features (The Really Fancy Stuff)

Plug-In Architecture for Extendibility. If you have custom needs, you should look for the ability to extend the software to perform the tasks you wish.

Web Mining for Combining Web Log Data with Information from Other E-Business Databases. This means that Web traffic information does not have to be yet another island of data within your organization. For example, reports can incorporate detailed customer information like real names, e-mail addresses, and phone numbers. For complex users, look for SQL statement support for ultimate information flexibility. This allows more complex questions to be answered based on dollars and ROI, rather than just hits and visits.

Integrated Programming Language and Editor. Many companies will need the ability to customize their Web traffic analysis tool to meet specific needs or integrate with other E-business applications. Look for extendability through a standard programming language such as Visual Basic and Visual C++.

Remote Administration from Any Connected Computer. If you work for a larger organization, consider the ability to administer your software from any network connection. This makes maintenance and administration in distributed environments extremely easy from any location.

Real-time Data Collection Via TCP/IP Packet Sniffing and Web Server Plug-ins Packet sniffing eliminates the need to collect and manage multiple distributed server log files by automatically collecting traffic information in real time directly from the TCP/IP network packets. The resulting database is always up-to-date and available for reporting. The benefit here is not only the real-time aspects of data reporting, but also the complete elimination of log file administration. This feature is especially useful for companies with multiple Web sites located throughout the world. Packet sniffing allows data to be collected and stored in a centralized data warehouse, completely automatically and in the background.

CONCLUSION

The Internet is the most significant technology the world has seen since the computer and has the potential to revolutionize business and marketing techniques. If you are serious about your online investment, the first step is to get a better understanding about who is visiting your site and what they are looking for.

Knowing this information allows you to make better business decisions by catering to your best customers and delivering the information they are looking for. With today's powerful Web traffic analysis software, this analysis can be performed easily and inexpensively.

Chapter 30
Network Architectures and Performance

Duane E. Sharp

IN TODAY'S FAST-PACED BUSINESS ENVIRONMENT, immediate access to critical data is an important element in the day-to-day operation of many organizations. One of the technologies that has evolved over the past two decades and is being used extensively to ensure the flow of critical data among organizations is networking.

International Data Corp. (IDC) estimates that, on a worldwide basis, more than 180 million PCs will have been networked in local area networks (LANs) by the year 2000. This number represents a 360 percent increase in just five years.

Critical applications that require more bandwidth, more powerful PCs and servers, and downloading large files from intranets and the Internet are all contributors to increasing LAN traffic and the requirement for greater network capacity and high utilization.

The growing need for standardization in the design and development of networks, as well as the need to interconnect networks with different protocols, led to the development of the Open Systems Interconnection (OSI) reference model in 1978. The OSI was developed by the International Organization for Standardization (ISO), in response to user demand for an open system architecture that would adhere to published standards with defined interfaces. The OSI has formed a background of standardization for all the architectures referenced in this chapter (see Exhibit 30-1).

NETWORK PERFORMANCE

The capability of networks to handle various forms of communications traffic and to interconnect is based on a number of network characteristics. Each of these network characteristics needs to be considered by network

0-8493-0859-3/00/$0.00+$.50
© 2000 by CRC Press LLC

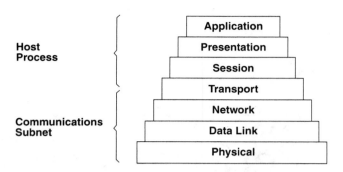

Exhibit 30-1. The Open System Interconnection (OSI) reference model.

---

designers and administrators when developing a new network, modifying existing networks, and interconnecting networks.

The traffic that flows among various network locations and the performance levels required for the various types of traffic, in terms of data volumes the network can handle and response times, form part of the specifications network designers use to develop a network. These specifications determine which network architecture and transmission medium will be used as well as define hardware components and the choice of network operating system.

The two primary characteristics that define network performance are network capacity and network utilization.

1. Network Capacity

Network capacity is a function of bandwidth, a scarce resource required to exchange information between computers over a LAN, WAN (wide area network), or serial connections. The maximum capacity of a network, or the amount of data that can be carried on the network, is determined by its bandwidth, measured in bits per second or, more commonly, megabits per second (Mbps). In a LAN, the greater the bandwidth of the transmission medium, the larger the volumes of data that can be handled.

In addition, the higher the bandwidth, the greater the capability of the network to handle traffic with high bandwidth requirements (e.g., video) as well as voice and data.

2. Network Utilization

Network utilization, another measure of network performance, is an instantaneous measurement of the ratio between the number of bits transmitted in a given period, such as one second, divided by the network capacity. Typical network utilization factors range from 20 percent to 30 percent.

The major network architectures described in the sections that follow provide a range of characteristics for the network designer. These characteristics enable networks to handle a variety of multimedia transmissions: data, voice, and video.

ETHERNET: THE FIRST PROTOCOL

An interesting historical perspective that also indicates that advances in technology should never be underestimated is illustrated by the fact that when Robert Metcalfe invented Ethernet — the first LAN protocol — in 1973, he predicted a maximum LAN bandwidth requirement of 5 Mbps. As a safety factor, he doubled the speed to 10 Mbps to handle unforeseen bandwidth-intensive applications.

In the intervening years, increasing demands on network traffic led to the defelopment of network protocols to handle much higher bandwidths — 100 Mbps and above. Although many networks still operate in the 10 Mbps range, today's high-performance network architectures, typically backbones, or networks which connect other networks, operate at 100 Mbps or higher to handle a range of different forms of traffic and provide faster response times.

Ethernet is a good vehicle for distributed computing; however, high-powered UNIX clients, Pentium-powered PCs, and new network-based applications are causing congestion on the 10-Mbps Ethernet pipe.

One factor that could extend the life of Ethernet is the current development of standards, expected to be ready this year, for an enhanced architecture called gigabit Ethernet. This architecture would allow Ethernet to be carried over fiber-optic cable. Although some vendors propose the same protocol over copper cabling, this protocol is limited to distances of about 100 feet.

Several other protocol choices, incompatible with each other, were competing to replace Ethernet as the LAN architecture of choice in the late 1990s and into the twenty-first century. They include the following:

- *Ethernet Switching (Ether-switch)*. Adds capacity to an Ethernet network by lowering the number of devices per network segment
- *FDDI*. A 100-Mbps network developed by the American National Standards Institute (ANSI), FDDI (Fiber-Distributed Data Interface) uses fiber-optic token passing ring and a frame format
- *Fast Ethernet*. 100-Mbps bandwidth, based on Ethernet technology, and offering high speeds at affordable prices; it is a forerunner of Gigabit Ethernet
- *ATM*. The most sophisticated network protocol and the preferred architecture for corporate backbones, ATM (Asynchronous Transmission

Mode) cell-based, expensive, and subject to a number of different standards

The following sections describe the characteristics of these protocols from several perspectives: standards, performance (capacity and bandwidth), technical characteristics, and cost implications. Exhibit 30-2 compares the bandwidths of these network architectures, and Exhibit 30-3 is a comparison of per-port costs.

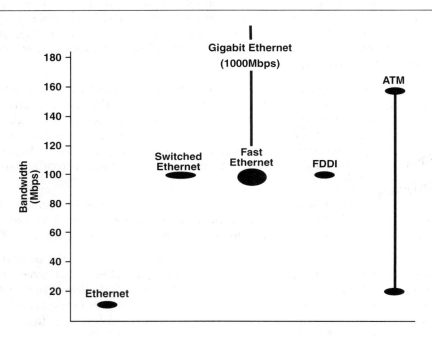

Exhibit 30-2. Bandwidth ranges for major network architectures.

ETHERNET SWITCHING (ETHER-SWITCH)

As noted previously, Ethernet was the earliest network protocol and is still one of the most popular LAN network protocols. Ethernet can transmit information among computers at speeds of 10 Mbps over a range of different transmission media, from twisted pair to fiber-optic cable. Standards for Ethernet have been developed for the past two or more decades and continue to be developed by the Institute of Electrical and Electronics Engineers (IEEE), under the Ethernet standards committee (802.3).

The Ether-switch protocol adds capacity to the network by reducing the number of devices in each network segment. Several configurations of Ether-switch protocols each offer alternative features and characteristics a

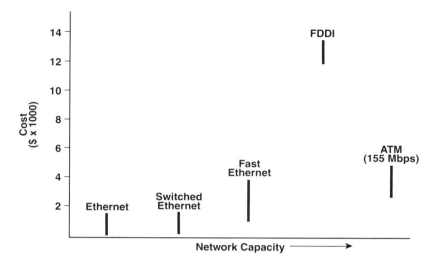

Exhibit 30-3. Typical cost per port for major network architectures (maximum and minimum).

user can match to a particular network requirement. The network-layer Ether-switch protocol offers some speed advantages, although it still relies on Ethernet's 10 Mbps capacity.

FDDI

FDDI (Fiber Distributed Data Interface) has been a popular network architecture since the early 1990s as a high-speed backbone for conventional router-based networks (see appendix for a glossary of terms). However, it was slow to be accepted because of its high cost. Typically, LANs are connected to the FDDI by routers that are attached to the primary ring. The secondary ring is for backup and provides high reliability for this protocol.

Many consultants were reluctant to recommend FDDI in its early stages, and users were reluctant to install it, largely because of its initial high cost. This reluctance is still evident, even though FDDI has become less expensive, because of its lack of support for multimedia transmissions. It is still a strong contender for corporate backbones, because there is a wide selection of hardware/software available for this protocol, and it can be operated over distances up to 100 km.

Two disadvantages of FDDI are the still high cost of hardware components compared to other network architectures and a potentially complex implementation. Some industry consultants consider FDDI to be an obsolete limited-life technology; however, statistics indicate that about 75 percent of

U.S. *Fortune* 500 companies have FDDI deployed. One recent U.S. study indicates that of 200 FDDI users surveyed, 50 percent indicated they would be migrating to a different network architecture within the next three years.

FAST ETHERNET

Two alternative Fast Ethernet specifications are on the market today. The first, the 100 Base-X specification, has strong ties to its Ethernet roots and maintains many of the same technical characteristics. The major, limiting factors of this technology are a 210-meter total distance network limit, the lack of availability of protocol drivers, and an access mechanism that will not allow network segments with multiple stations to reach full 100 Mbps capacity.

The second specification, 100-VG AnyLAN protocol, supports both Ethernet and token ring framing formats, but it is not really an Ethernet protocol. It is based on a new access mechanism and offers total network distance in excess of 2000 meters.

ATM

The most advanced of network protocols is ATM. ATM's high-speed, short, fixed-cell structure enables this network architecture to carry all types of traffic payloads, including voice, video, and data, over connection-oriented or connectionless circuits at speeds up to 155 Mbps. Since its introduction to the user marketplace, ATM has undergone a continual evolution, in the development of interface solutions with other network protocols and to simplify implementation, network management, and reduce costs. ATM is a multiplexing technology combining the features of circuit switching (constant transmission delay and guaranteed capacity) with those of packet switching, which offer flexibility and efficiency for intermittent traffic. The cell concept differs from other high-speed networking alternatives because it deviates from the shared media model. It also contrasts with variable-size LAN data units.

Recent developments on the ATM standards scene have improved the capabilities of this protocol and enhanced its application to networking requirements in a variety of environments. It now also has the capability to interconnect with other network protocols. ATM is acknowledged as a more mature architecture than some of its high-performance competitors previously referenced — particularly Gigabit Ethernet — because its basic standards are in place and the other protocol standards are still in the development and committee stages.

The three new ATM specifications approved by the ATM Forum in mid-1997, Multiprotocol over ATM (MPOA), LAN Emulation (LANE), and Inverse Multiplexing over ATM (IMA), have opened additional networking areas to this sophisticated protocol. MOPA will enable ATM to interface with other network technologies in a heterogeneous network environment. LANE provides a data encapsulation scheme for ATM which adds the capability to multiplex multiple data streams over the same virtual circuit. IMA will allow data to be transmitted over a broader range of transmission media with bandwidths ranging from 1.5 Mbps to 45 Mbps.

Although ATM will not meet the requirements of every network environment and does not readily interconnect with other network protocols, it is a continually evolving technology. Of all of the high-performance network protocols referenced in this article, its performance characteristics offer the best compromise of network solutions for many applications.

CONCLUSION

In the fast-paced world of networking, change is the only constant, as the vendor community and standards committees address changes in standards and enhancements to their network protocols. User communities have an exciting if somewhat frustating maze of choices. These choices are made more difficult by the complexity of the technology, which is characteristic of network architectures and the hardware and software elements that form part of the network environment.

As is the case for technology-oriented project, the selection of a network protocol in the network design stages must be made with due consideration for increasing demands of the user community for faster, more reliable networks to carry corporate data.

APPENDIX: GLOSSARY OF NETWORKING FACTS AND TERMINOLOGY

ATM (Asynchronous Transfer Mode). ATM is a transfer mode in which all types of information are organized into fixed-form cells for delivery on an asynchronous or nonperiodic basis over a range of media. It is often the preferred network architecture for corporate backbone networks. The ATM Forum, an international consortium of vendors and end users, is responsible for developing ATM standards to ensure the highest degree of interoperability and utility.

Backbone or Backbone Network. A network connecting other networks. Backbone networks are the eight-lane superhighways of the Internet. Generally, the term refers to a high-performance network of thick Ethernet or fiber-optic cable, enabling data transmission among lower-level networks. The terms may also be applied to the system of cables in a specific physical environment.

Bandwidth. The time required, measured in bits per second, to exchange information between computers over a LAN, WAN, or even serial connection.

Ethernet. Ethernet is the most popular LAN for transmitting information between computers at speeds of 10 Mbps over a range of media, including twisted pair and fiber optics. Ethernet standards are developed under the direction of the IEEE 802.3 standards committee.

Fast Ethernet. This is quickly becoming the next most popular LAN technology for connecting power workstations and servers at 10 times the speed of Ethernet over a similar range of media.

FDDI (Fiber-Distributed Data Interface). A popular backbone technology for transmitting information at high speed with a high level of fault tolerance. FDDI standards are developed under the direction of ANSI (the American National Standards Institute).

Gigabit Ethernet. Gigabit Ethernet has rapidly emerged as the next-generation LAN technology for connecting high-speed devices and switches at 100 times the speed of Ethernet. Gigabit Ethernet standards have been developed by the IEEE 802.3 working committee.

Hub. A networking device that provides LAN connectivity on one or more shared segments. There are two main types of hubs: stackable and modular. Stackable hubs usually support only one media type, such as twisted pair copper, and a single interface, such as Ethernet.

Internetworking: LAN, MAN (metropolitan area network), and WAN. The collection of interfaces and protocols required to interconnect computers locally and externally including the Internet. Most LAN standards are overseen by IEEE 802.3 committees. MAN and WAN standards are developed and coordinated by international organizations and related industry consortia including the International Telegraph Union (ITU) and ATM Forum.

IP (Internet Protocol). The collection of protocols used to interconnect computers locally and exteranlly over the Internet or a private intranet. Their development is coordinated by the Internet Engineering Task Force (IETF).

LAN (Local Area Network). A collection of interfaces and protocols that enable the exchange of information between local computers. Most LAN standards are governed by the IEEE 802 committee and its working groups.

MAC (Media Access Control). The six-byte OSI layer 2 address which is burned into every networking device that provides its unique identity for point-to-point communication. Internet working devices (switches, routers, bridges) use these addresses for forwarding and filtering decisions.

MAN (Metropolitan Area Network). A collection of interfaces and protocols that enables the exchange of information between computers on a metropolitan or wide-area basis.

Network Management. The mechanism by which the central functions of the network are managed and controlled. These functions include isolation of faults, configuration, performance measurement, and security. Network management components include intelligent agents, standard protocols such as SNMP/RMON, and a suite of applications for access, reporting, and analysis.

Router. A network layer device that supports multiple LAN interfaces and segments LANs into smaller collision and broadcast domains. As a network layer device, routers maintain a hierarchical network and service the interconnection of computers on different networks in that hierarchy.

Token Ring. The second most popular LAN for transmitting information between computers at speeds of 16 Mbps over a range of media including twisted pair and fiber optics. Token ring standards are developed under the direction of the IEEE 802.5 committee.

WAN (Wide Area Network). A collection of interfaces and protocols that enable the exchange of information between computers on a wide-area basis. WAN examples include frame relay, ISDN, T1-T3, and ATM. Standards governing these technologies are developed by organizations such as the ITU.

Chapter 31
Performance Engineering in Client/Server Environments
Scott T. Smith

AS PART OF AN OVERALL STRATEGY TO LOWER ITS IT COSTS, an oil and gas company considered deploying its database management system within a client/server environment, thus cutting both hardware expenditures and software licensing fees. The organization was skeptical, however, of the network's ability to support 150 concurrent users at an acceptable response rate. Long transaction times would reduce the level of customer service yet increase organizational costs for customer service representatives.

To evaluate the proposed system environment, the company devised and conducted a benchmark test to emulate its anticipated workload. This proof-of-concept benchmark demonstrated that the architecture could indeed handle the requisite load within acceptable performance parameters. The company could confidently install the new system without compromising customer service or incurring unexpected expenditures. By incorporating performance engineering at an early stage of the decision and design process, the company achieved its goals with minimal disruption and maximum economy.

WHAT IS PERFORMANCE ENGINEERING?

Performance engineering models the computing resource consumption of alternative technical architectures and measures their ability to perform business functions. Its aim is to design acceptable levels of performance into an installation's hardware configuration, network design, online and batch architecture, and data design.

Performance engineering's two approaches — benchmarking and predictive modeling — allow IT organizations to systematically anticipate component interaction rather than respond to it after installation. Performance engineering is particularly important for large transaction-processing, decision support, and executive information systems. In these large-scale and complex applications, performance problems after roll-out are more likely, more troublesome, and more expensive than in simpler settings.

Approaches to Performance Engineering

Benchmarking and predictive modeling are two closely related approaches to performance engineering in both the mainframe and client/server environments. Both may be done at various points in the systems development process. The later they are done, the more the results will reflect real design information as opposed to conjecture and approximation — but the cost of change will be greater. Both approaches also require approximations of application transactions volumes, database use by each transaction, and database structures.

Benchmarking. Benchmarking is the process of executing a set of test transactions against a test database on an actual computer system or network. After running the benchmark, results are measured in terms of average response time or elapsed time to determine whether performance falls within acceptable parameters.

Predictive Modeling. Predictive modeling — which is possible only as a result of prior benchmarking — generates estimates of system performance. The performance factors include quantitative models of application transaction volumes and resource use, database volumes and structure, and processor capabilities. Unlike benchmarking, predictive modeling cannot accurately estimate competition for shared resources.

In the mainframe environment, the few technical options available changed slowly. It was possible to do benchmarking as a research and development activity, and then use the knowledge gained to build quantitative models that would support predictive modeling for years. The situation is very different in client/server environments.

Predictive modeling is quicker, easier, and less costly to do than benchmarking, but it requires an accurate set of performance factors for the target hardware and software. In the current environment, products and technology change so quickly that assembling all the information needed to build a predictive model for target technologies is difficult. In many cases, benchmarking is the only option if performance engineering is to be undertaken.

Performance Engineering versus Hardware Expenditures

Some organizations try to accomplish performance engineering through post-implementation tuning or by buying more hardware. Usually, such attempts are unsuccessful. When they do work, these measures are expensive, with operating costs disproportionate to the service levels provided. At the same time, as hardware prices fall, companies must balance the cost of performance engineering against the amount saved in hardware costs and possible implementation delays.

Several trade-offs must thus be evaluated when considering the merits of performance engineering versus hardware expenditures. Before making a decision to invest in hardware rather than performance engineering, companies should take into account three key factors:

1. **Performance engineering for an application is a one-time investment.** Hardware and operating costs are ongoing for the life of the application.
2. **Numerous performance problems cannot be solved by increased hardware.** For example, many availability requirements and service levels can only be met through performance-oriented design.
3. **Scalability should be engineered into an application during the design phase.** If not, the cost of scaling an application later may be prohibitive.

More than ever before, a company's competitiveness depends on how well it builds new applications and uses advanced technology. Development costs are usually high, and if new applications do not perform to expected levels, that investment is substantially misspent. Fixing a poorly designed or badly installed application can delay its implementation by months or even years. Performance engineering can reduce the risk of unplanned costs.

BENEFITS AND CHALLENGES IN CLIENT/SERVER ENVIRONMENTS

Although most organizations are familiar with performance engineering in mainframe environments, they are far less familiar with its implementation in client/server environments. Client/server technologies are essential for most business process redesign and reengineering initiatives, and have been deployed in every functional area. Often, an organization will move toward a client/server architecture simply to make use of current technology or to take advantage of falling hardware prices.

The client/server environment is emerging so quickly that no consensus on its definition has yet been reached. What is clear, however, is that the technologies being applied differ from the ones that companies have come to know so well during the past 20 years in the mainframe environment. This fundamental change poses new and different challenges in applications that must perform at required levels with acceptable availability.

At the same time that they offer distinct advantages, client/server systems introduce several issues that were either nonexistent or easier to address in mainframe environments.

Large Numbers of Components. The sheer number of components is greatly increased by the size and complexity of the systems being built, and by the tendency to create smaller, more modular components. As a result, there are more rocks to look under to uncover performance problems. Where performance efforts once focused on database design and application data access, they must now be increasingly sensitive to network load and design, desktop performance issues, middleware bottlenecks, and the new challenges created by shortcomings in database management system (DBMS) software available on the midrange platforms.

Multiple Environments and Configurations. Client/server technology enables and encourages the creation of heterogeneous environments comprising many different hardware and software components. Because each of these components is becoming a commodity, it is almost inevitable that an architecture will have components from many different vendors. The large number of possible configurations makes it difficult to judge the practicality of an architecture by comparing one system to another. Even if comparable architectures can be found, it is likely that some of the components will be from different hardware vendors, so performance metrics will vary. Performance engineering thus must address large numbers of possible component synergies.

Object Orientation. Both client/server systems and object orientation represent dramatic changes in applications architecture, and many companies attempt to implement them simultaneously. To date, there have been few, if any, instances of object orientation implementation for large transaction-processing applications in client/server environments. Companies must strive to understand how these applications can accommodate good performance design and how to integrate object-oriented design and implementation with relational databases.

Accelerated Application Development (X/AD) and Prototyping. The union of X/AD, prototyping, and performance engineering is not always a happy one. X/AD and prototyping emphasize small, decentralized activities; performance engineering is a centralized activity. X/AD and prototyping techniques encourage developers to "go fast." Performance engineering's message is to "be careful." X/AD and prototyping do not tolerate bottlenecks. Performance engineering must sometimes be a bottleneck.

The important thing to remember is that the overall business objective is the same: to deliver business benefits through technology.

Service Levels. Client/server technologies — and the types of business applications being implemented with these technologies — change the way organizations define service levels. IT organizations face complicated decisions about acceptable response time and batch versus online processing. Even the definition of a transaction has become less clear. As a result, IT managers must tie service levels more closely to business transactions than to technical ones. If the average phone call to customer service now takes two minutes instead of three minutes, it should be counted as a success even if the technical processes take longer to complete.

MEETING THE CHALLENGES OF CLIENT/SERVER ENVIRONMENTS

The new challenges presented to performance engineering by client/server environments are not insurmountable. At one time, performance engineering was new to the mainframe environment. It is now pervasive.

Similarly, as client/server environments evolve, the importance of engineering performance in the applications development process is increasing. Despite the abundance of inexpensive processing power on the desktop and server platforms, client/server systems have several characteristics that make performance engineering critical.

First of all, the hardware and architectural choices within a given client/server profile — such as the location of application logic and Structured Query Language, tiers in the architecture, use of stored procedures and triggers, and network topology — greatly affect system performance. In addition, with the system spread over several processors, the network — especially the wide area network — can be a substantial bottleneck. Data distribution decisions can profoundly affect system performance and scalability.

Second, new products or releases that have yet to be proven in actual use, especially with substantial volumes, are frequently necessary to implement new architectures. While the resistance to using unproved products has eased by necessity, too many product choices are based on the promises of vendors rather than on track records. Even if it has been proven, the software used in nonmainframe client/server systems has shortcomings that make it difficult to implement the very large databases that can be accommodated by a mainframe database management system.

Despite the shift in environments from mainframe to client/server, the objective of performance engineering remains the same: building applications that meet business requirements. Regardless of the environment, performance engineering is still a requisite for optimal system design.

IMPLEMENTATION PHASES

As in the mainframe environment, performance engineering for client/server environments is implemented through a clearly defined development life cycle (see Exhibit 31-1). A brief outline of the specific tasks and deliverables involved in each phase of the project follows.

Exhibit 31-1. Phases, tasks, and deliverables of performance engineering in client/server environments.

Phases	Tasks	Deliverables
Vision and strategy	Begin planning Identify resources Collect data	PE components of project plan PE personnel requirements Key estimating factors
Architecture	Review methodology Conduct PE review of architecture Define service levels Plan training Refine key estimating numbers	Add PE deliverables to methodology Performance-oriented system architecture Service-level definitions (response time, availability, processing windows, report turnaround) Training curriculum for performance engineers, programmers, database designers, architects
Business requirements	Influence data model Influence technical architecture Construct predictive models Conduct initial benchmark Refine technical architecture	Data model with statistics for performance modeling Initial models for peak processing period, key batch processes, key online processes, utility schedule, daily/weekly/monthly processing schedules, network load Proof-of-concept benchmark for technical architecture
Detailed specifications	Influence physical database design Perform capacity planning Execute detailed benchmark Enhance performance models Complete performance-oriented training	Performance-oriented physical database design Capacity estimates (CPU, disk, network, desktop) Detailed performance models Precise benchmark for application to support capacity planning effort Trained development personnel
Coding and unit testing	Conduct stress test Perform response time capabilities tests Conduct code reviews Execute benchmark against alternative technical architectures Provide additional training	Established performance monitoring capabilities Refined technical architecture Improved code, especially SQL or other data access Refined capacity plan Performance monitoring capability
Installation and support	Perform tuning	Performance improvement, cost reduction

Vision and Strategy. During this initial phase, data collection commences and key estimating factors are determined.

Architecture. Data collection continues to ensure that the methodology being assembled contains components that will provide the information necessary for performance engineering. Service levels are defined for transaction response time, query response expectations, data and system availability, processing windows, and key processing deadlines. Vendor software products are identified for both application processing and performance monitoring.

Business Requirements. Data collection continues, and a first-level benchmark is conducted as a technical proof of concept. Predictive models are set up to provide initial estimates and to serve as the basis for expansion in subsequent steps.

Detailed Specifications. The project team enhances the models established in the previous phase, completes physical data design, and conducts any additional benchmarking. Next, the tools and procedures needed to monitor performance in production are defined and procured.

Coding and Unit Testing. Unit testing is performed to check response time and to isolate and correct performance issues at any level, but particularly in the data access or desktop architecture. As part of the system and integration testing phase, the system is subjected to stress testing, and code is reviewed — especially database access code.

Installation and Support. During and shortly after installation, heavy performance monitoring and tuning occur. In addition, databases that begin with little or no data and grow and fragment with the use of the system will require careful monitoring.

CONCLUSION

Performance engineering has repeatedly demonstrated its value in mainframe environments. As many organizations migrate to client/server environments, performance engineering projects are producing similarly dramatic results in a new environment. The challenges are different, but the lesson remains the same: realizing the benefits of client/server technology is probable only when performance is engineered into large applications from the earliest stage of development.

Chapter 32
Understanding Gigabit Ethernet Performance
Gilbert Held

GIGABIT ETHERNET represents the latest Institute of Electrical and Electronic Engineers (IEEE) Carrier Sense Multiple Access with Collision Detection (CSMA/CD) 802.3 standard. In developing the Gigabit Ethernet standard, the IEEE decided that it was important to retain the CSMA/CD access protocol and frame format to provide a truly scalable technology, ranging from Ethernet's 10Mbps operating rate to the 100Mbps operating rate of Fast Ethernet, and to the 1Gbps operating rate of Gigabit Ethernet. Retaining the same media access and frame format simplifies equipment design as the difference between each version of Ethernet becomes primarily speed adaptation on clocking. Unfortunately, retaining the frame structure of Ethernet and Fast Ethernet introduced a new problem in the form of a collision domain.

Both Ethernet and Fast Ethernet provide sufficient time between the next-to-last bit in a frame being placed on a network and the receipt of a propagated collision signal to enable a cabling length of 100 meters from a workstation to a hub port. In a Gigabit Ethernet environment, the higher operating rate restricts the diameter of a network to approximately ten meters, as cabling beyond that distance closes the collision window and makes it possible for a station to transmit every bit in a frame when a collision has occurred on some prior bits and the collision signal is still propagating toward the transmitting station. Because a ten-meter diameter would be overly restrictive, the IEEE standardized a technique referred to as "carrier extension technology" that adds special symbols to the end of relatively short frames on a Gigabit network. While the resulting technique literally opens the collision window and permits a much more practical 200-meter network diameter, the carrier symbols occupy bandwidth and adversely affect the ability of Gigabit Ethernet to transport information per

0-8493-0859-3/00/$0.00+$.50
© 2000 by CRC Press LLC

unit of time under certain conditions. Thus, the trade-off was between obtaining a reasonable network cabling diameter and lowering the ability of the network to transport information under certain network situations.

It should be noted that carrier extension technology is only applicable to half-duplex, shared-media Gigabit Ethernet. This is because full-duplex, non-shared media Gigabit Ethernet uses separate paths for the transmission and reception of data, precluding the possibility of collisions. However, because shared-media Gigabit Ethernet is copper based and costs significantly less per port than full-duplex, nonshared media, it is reasonable to expect that many network managers and LAN administrators will focus their attention on the less expensive technology. After all, 1Gbps of shared media bandwidth represents a considerable improvement over 100Mbps Fast Ethernet. Or does it? To answer this question, one must first examine the potential frame flow on different types of Ethernet networks.

ETHERNET FRAME FLOW

Exhibit 32-1 illustrates the composition of an Ethernet frame. Note that the "Data" field must be a minimum of 46 bytes in length and is filled with pad characters if the number of bytes to be transported is less than 46. Thus, the minimum length of an Ethernet frame is 72 bytes.

In some literature one may have read that the minimum length of an Ethernet frame is 64 bytes. That metric references the IEEE standard that defines the frame prior to its placement on the network at the physical layer. Because network adapter cards automatically add the "Preamble" and "Start of Frame Delimiter" fields that add eight bytes to the frame for synchronization, the minimum length of the frame as it flows on the network is 72 bytes.

Returning to the Ethernet frame's "Data" field, its maximum value is 1500 bytes. When one considers the 26 overhead bytes in each frame, this means that the maximum frame length on the network is 1526 bytes. Many publications reference a maximum frame length of 1518 bytes. Once again, such publications are referencing the length of the frame prior to its placement on the network and do not consider the additional eight bytes added by the network adapter card.

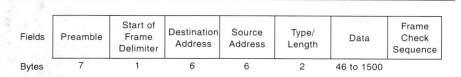

Fields	Preamble	Start of Frame Delimiter	Destination Address	Source Address	Type/ Length	Data	Frame Check Sequence
Bytes	7	1	6	6	2	46 to 1500	

Exhibit 32-1. The Ethernet frame format.

By understanding that the minimum length of an Ethernet frame is 72 bytes and its maximum length is 1526 bytes, one can compute the maximum number of minimum length and maximum length frames that can flow on an Ethernet network. Because many readers may be from the "Show Me" state of Missouri, the computations are given here.

At a 10Mbps operating rate, the Ethernet standard requires a "dead time" of 9.6 µs between frames, while the bit duration is 100 ns. Thus, the time required to transmit a 72-byte minimum length Ethernet frame becomes:

$$9.6 \text{ µs} + 72 \text{ bytes} \times 8 \text{ bits/byte} \times 100 \text{ ns/bit}$$

or 67.2×10^{-6} s. Thus, in one second, there can be a maximum of $1/67.2 \times 10^{-6}$, or 14,880, minimum size 72-byte frames flowing on an Ethernet 10Mbps network.

Similar to the manner by which the maximum number of minimum length frames that can flow on a 10Mbps Ethernet network was calculated, one can also compute the maximum number of maximum length frames that can flow on that network. To do so, first compute the time per frame as follows:

$$9.6 \text{ µs} + 1526 \text{ bytes} \times 8 \text{ bits/byte} \times 100 \text{ ns/bit}$$

or 1.23 ns. Then, in one second, there can be a maximum of 1/1.23 ns, or 812, maximum length frames that can flow on a 10Mbps Ethernet network.

In examining Fast Ethernet technology, one notes that the dead times between frames and bit duration are one tenth of 10Mbps and that both technologies use the same frame format with the same minimum frame length of 72 bytes and maximum frame length of 1526 bytes. Due to this, the maximum frame rate obtainable on Fast Ethernet is ten times the frame rate of 10Mbps Ethernet.

In addition to determining the maximum frame rate on Ethernet and Fast Ethernet, one can also compute their information transfer capability. To do so, multiply their maximum and minimum frame rates by the number of bytes capable of being transported in maximum length and minimum length frames. For example, consider the maximum frame rate when minimum length frames are transported on an Ethernet network. Because a minimum length 72-byte frame is capable of transporting 46 bytes and 14,880 minimum length frames per second can flow on an Ethernet network, the data transfer rate becomes:

$$14,880 \text{ frames/s} \times 46 \text{ bytes/frame} \times 8 \text{ bits/byte} = 5.476\text{Mbps}$$

Similarly, one can also compute the information transfer capability of 10Mbps Ethernet for maximum length 1526-byte frames. Because a maximum of 812 frames per second can flow on that network and each maximum

Exhibit 32-2. Ethernet frame and information transfer capability.

Average Frame Size (Bytes)	Maximum Frame Rate	Maximum Information Transfer
Ethernet		
72	14880	5.476 Mbps
1526	812	9.744 Mbps
Fast Ethernet		
72	14880	54.76 Mbps
1526	8120	97.44 Mbps

length field can transport 1500 bytes, then the maximum data transfer rate for maximum length frames becomes:

$$812 \text{ frames/s} \times 1500 \text{ bytes/frame} \times 8 \text{ bits/byte} = 9.744 \text{Mbps}$$

Exhibit 32-2 summarizes the maximum frame rates and information transfer capability for minimum length and maximum length frames flowing on Ethernet and Fast Ethernet networks. Because Fast Ethernet uses the same frame format and only differs from Ethernet by placing bits on the network faster by an order of ten, its transfer rate is ten times that of Ethernet. Thus, although one could compute the information transfer of Fast Ethernet in the same manner as for the information transfer for Ethernet, this will not be done. Instead, note that because the maximum frame rate on Fast Ethernet is ten times that of Ethernet, this results in the information transfer capability also being ten times that of Ethernet.

Returning to the examination of the entries in Exhibit 32-2, one can now focus on the maximum information transfer capability of Ethernet and Fast Ethernet. Note that when the minimum frame length occurs that corresponds to the transmission of frames carrying interactive traffic, the maximum information transfer on Ethernet and Fast Ethernet is slightly more than half of the operating rate of each network. At the opposite end of the range of frame lengths, the transmission of maximum length frames that corresponds to file transfers results in the information transfer rate approaching the operating rate of each network. Thus, the average frame length flowing on a network has a significant effect on the information transfer rate obtainable on an Ethernet network. With this in mind, one can focus on Gigabit Ethernet by first examining the extension of the Ethernet frame via the use of carrier extension technology.

THE GIGABIT ETHERNET FRAME

As previously mentioned, the higher operating rate of Gigabit Ethernet resulted in the IEEE extending its frame through the use of carrier extension technology for shared-media, half-duplex operations. This frame

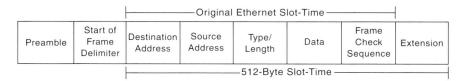

Exhibit 32-3. Half-duplex Gigabit Ethernet using carrier extension to extend timing.

extension occurs by the addition of carrier extension symbols to ensure all frames have a minimum length of 512 bytes in the adapter and 520 bytes when placed onto the network. Through the use of carrier extension technology, a 200-meter network diameter can be supported. Otherwise, the need to ensure that a station could hear a collision propagate on the network between transmitting the next-to-last bit in a short frame and the last bit in the frame would have significantly reduced the allowable cabling distance to 10 meters (or approximately 33 feet).

Exhibit 32-3 illustrates the Gigabit Ethernet frame format. Note that the carrier extension extends the frame timing to guarantee at least a 512-byte slot time (520 bytes on the network) for half-duplex, shared-media operations. The increase in the minimum length frame does not change the frame size and only alters the time the frame is on the network. This enables compatibility to be maintained between Ethernet, Fast Ethernet, and Gigabit Ethernet.

Although the carrier extension scheme permits the support of a more reasonable and practical network diameter, that extension is not without a price. That price is one of additional network bandwidth utilization by carrier extension symbols, which reduces the information transfer capability of Gigabit Ethernet when carrier extension symbols are required.

One can determine the frame rate for Gigabit Ethernet in the same manner as for Ethernet; that is, first compute the transmission time required for placing a Gigabit Ethernet frame on the network. Once this is accomplished, divide that time into one second to determine the number of frames per second that can flow on the network. Because Gigabit Ethernet also has minimum length and maximum length frames, perform two computations to determine the maximum number of minimum length frames and maximum length frames that can flow on a Gigabit network. Once this is accomplished, multiply the frame rates by the number of bytes in the "Data" field of each frame to compute the information transfer rate for minimum length and maximum length frames. Obtaining this information will illustrate the effect of transporting certain types of data on the performance of Gigabit Ethernet, which will in turn illustrate the importance of throughput above the operating rate of a network.

To compute the frame rate on Gigabit Ethernet, note that the minimum length frame is now 520 bytes when placed on the network. Because carrier extension symbols are added to the end of an Ethernet frame, the actual composition of the frame is not altered. This means that the "Data" field will vary between 46 and 1500 bytes. Thus, the minimum number of bytes that can be transported in a minimum length Gigabit Ethernet frame is 46, which is the same as Ethernet and Fast Ethernet. However, instead of being 72 bytes in length, the minimum frame is 520 bytes on the network to include 448 carrier extension symbols.

To compute the maximum number of minimum length frames that can flow on a Gigabit Ethernet network, use a dead time between frames of 0.096 µs, a frame length of 520 bytes, and a bit duration of 1 ns. Thus, the time per minimum length frame becomes:

$$0.096 \times 10^{-6} + 520 \text{ bytes} \times 8 \text{ bits/byte} \times 1 \text{ ns/bit} = 4.256 \times 10^{-6} \text{ s}$$

Then, in one second, there can be a maximum of $1/4.256 \times 10^{-6}$, or 234,962, frames per second. Because each frame can transport up to 46 bytes of data, the maximum information transfer capability for minimum length Gigabit Ethernet frames becomes:

$$234,962 \text{ frames/s} \times 46 \text{ bytes/frame} \times 8 \text{ bits/byte} = 86.46 \text{Mbps}$$

In comparing the value just computed to the entries in Exhibit 32-2, note that the ratio of Gigabit Ethernet's Information transfer to that of Fast Ethernet for minimum length frames is 86.46/54.76, or approximately 1.58 to 1. Thus, although Gigabit Ethernet's operating rate is ten times the operating rate of Fast Ethernet, when used to transport relatively short interactive queries its information transfer capability is only slightly better than Fast Ethernet.

A similar computation for the maximum length Gigabit frame shows that Gigabit Ethernet indeed provides ten times the information transfer capability of Fast Ethernet. This results from the fact that as the "Data" field increases, the number of carrier extensions decreases until a "Data" field transporting 494 or more bytes of data requires no carrier extension symbols and provides exactly ten times the information transfer capability of Fast Ethernet. Thus, for all frames with "Data" fields between 494 and 1500 bytes, half-duplex, shared-media Gigabit Ethernet provides what one would normally expect from the technology — an information transfer rate ten times that of Fast Ethernet and 100 times that of Ethernet.

RECOMMENDED COURSE OF ACTION

While Gigabit Ethernet provides an operating rate ten times that of Fast Ethernet, its information transfer rate can be much lower. This means it is important to examine the type of data being transmitted on a network prior to considering the use of a shared-media, half-duplex Gigabit Ethernet backbone. If the organization's average frame length is relatively low, one may need to consider installing a more expensive, full-duplex Gigabit Ethernet backbone, or consider an alternate technology such as ATM.

Chapter 33
LAN-WAN Interconnection Requirements and Implementation Considerations
Duane E. Sharp

Networkologist: one who professionally practices the art and business of networkology ... an industry mover and shaker ... network technology driver ... one who designs enterprisewide networks and applications, evaluates today's network products and tomorrow's networking technologies; and understands that the network is the application that provides the competitive edge.

Courtesy of *Network World*

THE INTERNET, DOUBLING IN SIZE EVERY YEAR SINCE 1988, is an excellent example of the need to interconnect. Analysts estimate that over 50 million people worldwide are logging on to the Internet, with growth expected to continue exponentially. IDC estimates that by the year 2000, more than 180 million PCs worldwide will be networked via in-building LANs worldwide, a 360 percent increase in just five years. Today, more and more businesses are being interconnected in a networked community of interconnected WANs, as seamless as a LAN workgroup, and interconnectivity among local and wide area networks is one of the fundamental requirements of most network installations.

Standards and Protocols

The International Organization for Standardization (ISO) has defined a Reference Model for internetworking that has become a worldwide standard

0-8493-0859-3/00/$0.00+$.50
© 2000 by CRC Press LLC

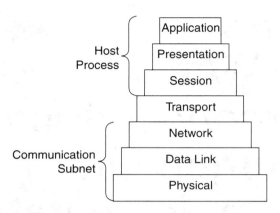

Exhibit 33-1. The Open System Interconnection (OSI) reference model.

---

or high-level protocol for designers of network products and for network designers. The reference model in Exhibit 33-1 defines the computer communications function in terms of seven distinct layers, and is designed to enable open systems to communicate with one another. In the world of standards, open systems are defined under the OSI reference model as those that comply with protocols for communication with other open systems, protocols which are common to both systems.

Design Issues

There are several significant technological developments and societal phenomena that have impacted the network designer's world over the past few years. PCs have proliferated and LANs have become as common and as essential as telephone networks. A growth rate of 100 to 200 percent per year of workstations per network is not uncommon. Rapid and sometimes instantaneous growth of businesses through acquisitions and mergers has resulted in a dramatic increase in the requirement to interconnect — often among widely dispersed geographical areas.

As a result of these changes in the requirements of businesses to communicate, frequently over considerable distances, today's network designer is usually required to include LAN-WAN interconnectivity in a network design.

LAN-WAN interconnectivity and the type of transmission facility required for a particular application are key design issues in interconnecting networks, as well as being essential components in determining network performance.

Once the functional goals for the internetwork are defined, they can be used as a statement of objectives. The primary features to be considered in designing a LAN-WAN internetwork are not dissimilar to those for a LAN, which are:

- cost
- performance
- maintenance and support
- reliability
- redundancy
- robustness

Robustness is especially critical to the LAN-WAN integration because a robust integration architecture will enable the internetwork to handle periods of heavy usage or peak activity.

Understanding Applications

A number of different networking applications may be required in the internetworking environment — file transfer, electronic messaging, electronic commerce, or multimedia transmission, to name a few. If there are common elements among these applications, the design job will be easier. It is important for enterprise managers to clearly understand the applications that will run on the LAN-WAN internetwork and their requirements in terms of the network characteristics.

Analyzing Network Traffic

This function will require a determination of the internetwork traffic that will flow among various network locations and the performance levels required by users at the remote sites.

Forecasting Traffic Growth

An analysis of the traffic growth over the next year, three years, and five years will ensure that the network capacity and components will be able to handle the increased traffic that will occur as the network matures.

Identifying and Selecting Network Components

The LAN-WAN interconnection will require hardware and software components at every location. The network designer will determine which LAN architecture — Ethernet, Token Ring, Fast Ethernet, FDDI, ATM — is implemented, and then ensure that the LAN-WAN internetwork provides a seamless interface, by appropriate selection of components.

The LAN operating system in existence at each location — Banyan VINES, Novell NetWare, 3COM 3 + Open, Windows NT, for example — will also be an important consideration in the interconnection process. It is much easier to interconnect operating systems with a degree of commonality in hardware or software, even if they have different architectures and protocols.

Exhibit 33-2. Characteristics of network components.

Router
• Operates at OSI network layer
• Depends on network layer protocol
• Uses network topology
• Separates subnetworks into logical elements
• Internetwork communication applications
Repeater
• Operates at OSI physical layer
• Extends LAN range
• Regenerates/repeates physical signals
Brouter
• Operates at OSI data link and network layers
• Combines the protocol transparency of a bridge with the ability to route certain protocols
• Used for networks with mixed-protocol traffic
Bridge
• Operates at OSI data link layer
• Logically separates network segments
• Independent of higher layer protocols
• Used for LAN traffic management
Gateway
• Operates at OSI higher levels
• Dependent on user application
• Used for application-to-application communication

Internetworking Hardware and Software

There are five different types of hardware devices used in internetworking design, as depicted in Exhibit 33-2:

1. Routers
2. Repeaters
3. Brouters
4. Bridges
5. Gateways

One or more of these devices will be selected by the designer to handle LAN-WAN interconnection requirements involving multimedia, dissimilar LAN architectures, several different protocols, or compatible application programs to be accessed across the network.

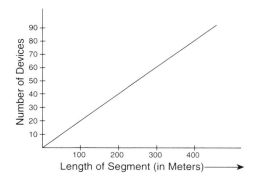

Exhibit 33-3. Ethernet network: Devices per meter of cable length.

---

1. Routers. Routers separate network traffic based on the network layer protocol (Exhibit 33-1), and are commonly used for internetwork communications. These devices control network traffic by filtering according to protocol, dividing networks logically instead of physically. Routers can divide networks into various subnets so that only traffic destined for particular addresses passes between segments. This form of intelligent forwarding and filtering usually results in reduced network speed because the process takes more time than required by a switch or bridge that looks at access to the shared transmission medium.

2. Repeaters. Repeaters are the building blocks of complex networks and are an important element in LAN-WAN internetworks, extending the physical length of a cable by amplifying signals and allowing additional workstations to be connected in each network segment. For example, in a thin Ethernet/IEEE 802.3 LAN, 30 devices can be supported for each 185-meter segment. Repeaters can be inserted to accommodate more devices per segment or an increase in the length of a segment. All network architectures have constraints that dictate how many devices can be attached per segment. Exhibit 33-3 illustrates these constraints for a typical Ethernet architecture. Other networks — ARCNET, Token Ring, and FDDI — have similar limitations on number of devices and distance between segments.

Repeaters also monitor all connected segments in a network to ensure that the basic characteristics are present for the network to perform correctly. When a network becomes inoperable — for example, when a break occurs — all segments in a network may become inoperable. Repeaters limit the effect of these problems to the faulty section of cable by segmenting the network, disconnecting the problem segment, and allowing unaffected segments to function normally.

451

3. Bridge. A bridge is a "traffic manager" used to divide the network into logical subsets, and to direct traffic away from workstations that frequently communicate on a common LAN. Most bridges are multiport devices that connect one network to another, using store-and-forward filtering techniques and handling potential bridging loops between networks. Bridges enable redundancy to be built into a network by providing multiple pathways between network segments.

4. Brouters. Brouters are hybrids of the bridge and router, are also referred to as routing bridges, and are designed to provide the processing speed of a bridge with the internetworking capabilities of a router. They are protocol-independent devices that direct traffic based on the OSI data link access (Exhibit 33-1). However, they are more sophisticated devices, designed to logically segment the network based on the routing algorithm, higher layer protocol, or the WAN architecture that has been implemented.

5. Gateways. Gateways are devices that have been designed to handle specific applications, such as the interconnection between different classes of hardware or network architectures — mainframes, Token Rings, workstations, or midrange systems. They may operate at all seven OSI layers (Exhibit 33-1) and are often used to interconnect incompatible e-mail systems, to convert and transfer files from one system to another, or to enable interoperability between dissimilar operating systems.

BUILDING NETWORKED COMMUNITIES WITH NETWARE

Over the years, Novell, Inc. has played a leading role in perfecting the foundation technology resulting in networked communities of PC users and business workgroups. Workgroup networks enable individuals to share documents and expensive hardware resources such as printers and disk drives.

These workgroup networks can be expanded to support communication and collaboration in enterprisewide WANs, leading to a variety of LAN-WAN interconnection options. Novell and other networking companies anticipated that the original concept of building communities of PC users by connecting workgroups into enterprise networks was the way of the future (Exhibit 33-4).

The latest version of Novell's network operating system provides the full range of distributed services required to enable networking enterprisewide WANs. NetWare products now run on more than 2.5 million networks; therefore, a sound knowledge of Novell's networking products is important for the network designer.

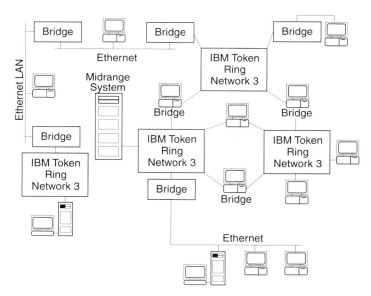

Exhibit 33-4. Typical bridge interconnections among multiple LANs.

FUNDAMENTAL PRINCIPLES OF LAN-WAN INTERNETWORKING

Novell's strategy for forging the future of networking provides a guideline for network designers, and rests on three basic principles: (1) smart networks; (2) anytime, anywhere access; (3) and network heterogeneity.

1. The Smart Network

The first principle maintains that making networks smarter can relieve users of the arcane world of operating systems, applications, and tools. Without a smart network that identifies the user, knows what information is required, and how to provide it to the user, connections to a global network will be a difficult task.

2. Network Access: Anytime, Anywhere

This principle is based on the premise that a simple, single log-in procedure will enable access to these smart networks anytime, from anywhere, by anyone. Such access would, among other things, transform work from a place into an activity. For many, the concept of the virtual office is already here, and with it, enormous new demands for accessing information, resources, and other people. In the current thinking on networks, "the network has become the computer."

3. The Heterogeneous Network

The final principle recognizes that the network will always be heterogeneous, with several different operating systems and many different applications and services, designed with a variety of tools, and capable of being accessed from a wide variety of intelligent devices.

Interweaving disparate business units of international organizations, located at different physical sites into a single network presents real issues of hardware and software compatibility. On a global scale, the complexities of integration increase exponentially. Network designers need to establish corporate computing standards that will remain in effect with changes in business requirements and applications. Through each stage of the evolution of networking — first building workgroup communities of PC users, then building enterprise communities of workgroups and a single community linking them all together — the challenge is for the network to present a simple homogeneous view of its entire heterogeneous resources for users, administrators, and developers.

TRANSMISSION ALTERNATIVES IN LAN-WAN NETWORKS: SEEKING A PATH THROUGH A WAN TECHNOLOGY JUNGLE

The choices available to users today in the selection of a LAN-WAN interconnection are wide ranging. While previous services usually offered minimal bandwidth and were unreliable and overpriced, they did the job. WAN services available today are cheaper, offer greater bandwidth, and are far more reliable.

These services are available in a variety of shapes and sizes, as standard telephone lines, digital communications lines, switched or permanent links, and packet- or circuit-switched connections, depending on the particular needs of the network.

For an existing LAN, the LAN characteristics will have been previously determined. If the LAN is in the design stages, the WAN media can be selected once the LAN specifications have been defined.

The following considerations will assist in determining which media to select.

- Will the network connections be used for LAN connections and to connect telecommuters to the corporate information system?
- What level of traffic will the WAN handle? And how often?
- What are the forecast traffic patterns for the LAN-WAN internetwork? Constant bit rate video, file transfer, or multimedia?
- Will the traffic cross regional, national, or global boundaries, requiring special considerations for regulatory provisions?

- What level of reliability is needed? Is a backup required?
- What level of service will WAN communications require? Round-the-clock? Intermittent?

Answers to these questions will provide direction to the network designer in determining which transmission technologies will fit the specification for the LAN-WAN interconnection. The following paragraphs provide some of the pros and cons of the various common transmission technologies available to the network designer:

POTS (Plain Old Telephone System)

The traditional telephone system (Plain Old Telephone System, or POTS) is useful in situations where only a limited amount of bandwidth (up to 28.8Kbps) is required for periodic connections. Telecommuting applications and low backup of WAN links fall into this category, where the analog connection provided by the POTS is of sufficient bandwidth.

However, POTS cannot meet the requirements of high bandwidth applications, such a multimedia transmissions, or other high-performance requirements of most modern networks.

The key to using this medium is to understand its limitations in terms of long-distance reliability, and to use it mainly for local connections to minimize the costs incurred by distance-sensitive pricing.

ISDN

One of the communication technologies that has gained prominence and will prove useful in many LAN-WAN internetworks, is ISDN (Integrated Services Digital Networks). This technology is an evolution of POTS, enabling faster, more reliable digital connections on existing telephony infrastructures.

The increased speed, low latency, and reliability extends the range of applications to which ISDN can be applied, to the extent that it is useful for constant bit-rate applications such as videoconferencing. Like POTS, it is useful for telecommuting applications, and at much higher speeds, as well as such applications as direct or backup LAN-to-LAN connectivity.

A major aspect of ISDN that will undoubtedly ensure a long life for this technology is that in North America, ISDN is widely deployed and available in most dialing areas. By comparison, other technologies such as ASDL (Asymmetric Digital Subscriber Line) and cable have relatively sparse geographical coverage. On the other hand, although it is capable of much higher speed connections (between 128Kbps and 2.048Mbps) than POTS, its cost effectiveness is limited to intermittent local transmissions, due to its distance and usage-sensitive tariffs.

Leased Lines

Leased lines have been the foundation of corporate internetworks in North America, although their permanence limits their use to LAN-to-LAN connections. In terms of performance for corporate communications, they can provide suitable network solutions because they offer a range of speeds from 19.2Kbps and T3, and provide 99.99 percent uptime (in North America). They are dedicated permanent links; however, they are more secure than other WAN alternatives and suitable for a variety of different types of network traffic (including video).

A disadvantage of leased lines is their cost. Leased line connections are costly because pricing is distance sensitive, an important consideration in evaluating leased lines over equivalent-bandwidth alternatives.

X.25

Packet-switched networks are an alternative to direct connections, with X.25 as the most advanced, established international protocol. With packet-switched services, a communications link is a virtual connection that does not exist physically.

An advantage of X.25 services is that the protocol is available on a universal basis, offering bandwidths ranging from 9.2Kbps to 256Kbps. The service is so well established that it supports a number of access technologies, including POTS, ISDN, and leased line connections. This capability makes X.25 ideally suited for global LAN-WAN internetworks.

However, X.25 is not suited for high-bandwidth applications (such as video), which cannot tolerate the latency introduced by a packet-switched network.

Frame Relay

Frame relay is a packet-switched service that will replace leased lines. Dial-up access into frame relay networks via POTS and ISDN has made this a viable remote user solution in many network environments. It is a simplified version of the X.25 protocol, without the error correction facilities that guarantee reliable data delivery. The cost of frame relay is usually less than an equivalent-bandwidth leased line, with the price differential growing as the distance between sites increases.

One downside to frame relay is that it is only available where digital communications facilities are in place. Further maturation of this technology should provide frame relay with the same degree of flexibility as X.25.

ATM

Asynchronous Transfer Mode (ATM), the most sophisticated of transmission technologies, is a cell-switching, multiplexing technology that combines the features of circuit switching (constant transmission delay and guaranteed capacity) with those of packet switching (flexibility and efficiency for intermittent traffic). It is particularly suitable for the simultaneous transmission of voice, video, and data, and is finding wide application in multimedia environments.

The ATM Forum, a standards organization with over 700 members formed in the early 1990s to promote ATM interoperability, has developed a range of standards for ATM to meet a variety of network management, interface, and transmission requirements, while product vendors have been developing products to meet these standards.

ATM was originally developed as a WAN technology for broadband ISDN. Using ATM as a WAN aggregate link extends of the use of ATM as a backbone in a campus environment and to larger LAN-WAN environments, where design decisions are influenced by the progress of tariffs and service rollouts by carriers.

ATM is a natural successor to FDDI at the enterprise level, offering scalability and fault tolerance, as well as providing an integration point for other networking technologies such as Ethernet, Token Ring, and frame relay. Over the past few years, ATM has grown in popularity in those applications where multimedia capability is a fundamental requirement and where cost and complexity are not inhibiting factors.

The basic transmission unit in ATM is defined to be a fixed-length cell with the following characteristics:

- Switching is performed in silicon, providing much lower switch latencies and much higher switch throughputs.
- Fixed length cells allow the switch to operate isochronously with fixed and predictable delays.

ATM is asynchronous in nature — there are no fixed arrival rates of cells — and operates in a constant bit rate mode for video or voice applications because it is carried electronically on an asynchronous transport system. ATM is tightly coupled with this underlying transmission media.

For LAN-WAN internetworking, the potential applications of ATM are:

- as a replacement for broadcast LAN media (Ethernet, Token Ring, or FDDI)

- as a LAN backbone technology in a campus or metropolitan area environment
- as a WAN aggregate link technology

For a LAN backbone, ATM has been described as better than FDDI architecture. ATM backbones scale well because the technology is nonbroadcast, providing dedicated, nonblocking, 155Mbps, bidirectional, point-to-point virtual circuits between routers. This means that there is no contention for bandwidth as there is in FDDI, thus allowing for more devices to be added to the backbone without compromising effective throughput of existing devices. This important characteristic of ATM makes it a key transmission architecture for consideration in LAN-WAN internetworks where it can meet the required specifications.

Unfortunately for the network designer, current ATM offerings do not provide a viable means to emulate the broadcast nature of LAN media. In many network environments, ATM is used primarily as a permanent virtual circuit.

While ATM is gradually evolving into a standard building block for network backbones, its growth in some networking environments has been inhibited by three factors:

1. relative complexity of implementation compared to other protocols
2. the high cost of interface products for desktop applications
3. limited availability of ATM products for various computer types

Addressing and dynamic signaling are two issues with ATM that need to be resolved. For example, a network administrator needs to do significant network configuration analysis to perform simple network modifications, such as adding a new user to an ATM LAN.

Current assessments of ATM, the most advanced of the transmission technologies available today, indicate that it will be at least another year before this technology penetrates the WAN market significantly, and it will be two or more years before it makes a significant impact on the LAN environment.

SUMMARY

Each of the LAN-WAN internetworking transmission media described has certain strengths and weaknesses that make them best suited to specific applications. Some industry forecasters predict that Ethernet will continue to be the technology of choice for most corporations, in both LAN and LAN-WAN environments, for several reasons: its pervasiveness in current networks; the wide availability of products; the relatively painless growth for bandwidth; and price.

However, the technologies available for interconnecting LANs and WANs — hardware, software, network operating systems, transmission media — are rapidly evolving, along with standards for implementation and reduced costs. It is important that the network designer retains flexibility within the network architecture, continually assessing vendor offerings, to take advantage of new, proven technologies that will enhance network performance.

Chapter 34
Demystifying Network Performance
Howard C. Berkowitz

In PRACTICE, THE SOLUTION OF NETWORK PERFORMANCE PROBLEMS begins the same way as the solution to any business problem: the customer's expectations and objectives must be defined. Technical analysis then follows; this involves a comparison of the user's performance requirements with the internal network and host components that influence the performance factors that are visible to the user.

The network manager's next task is to define the simplest practical methods for measuring performance. This can be accomplished by the following steps:

- Set service level goals (both at internal and external system interfaces) with the appropriate customer.
- With favorable response time as a goal, identify the components whose cumulative delays — from user input or user output — make up the response time.
- Formalize the service level agreement. If the system is new, performance goals must be set as part of component design, and the components must be built. A continuing monitoring program must also be planned.
- Look for, and correct, simple problems first. The system must be kept on track with short-term tuning and long-term capacity planning and enhancement.

SETTING GOALS

A useful approach to performance specification, applicable both externally (e.g., to service level agreements) and internally (e.g., to component design goals), relies on the architecture of American National Standards

Institute X3.102. That architecture assumes that all data communications performance can be specified in terms of the performance of a measured communications facility that connects a service user with a service provider. (Network users may be either human end users or computers. A packet switch uses a high-speed trunk to connect it with another switch, much as a human terminal user connects a dumb terminal and a timesharing host.)

Whether human or computer, only three performance factors are experienced by a user: the probability that the network is available to do work, the probability that it will do the work incorrectly, and the time it will take to do that work. Parameters dealing with the first factor include percent availability and mean time between failure (MTBF).

The most general approach to measuring the last performance factor (i.e., time) is to examine the statistical duration of network activity to perform some meaningful service for the user. Because there are both human and automated users, it is helpful to think of users as end users or intermediate systems: end users either originate traffic and expect a response, or receive traffic and generate a response (an example of the former would be terminal users; of the latter, hosts). Intermediate systems receive data and pass it along, possibly with no concern for the response. End users perceive the time component as response time, while intermediate systems perceive it as transit delay.

For intermediate systems in particular, it is better to report cumulative delay statistics than to report individual transaction measurements. The time component should be represented as a threshold (e.g., 95 percent of transactions complete in less than six seconds) rather than an average response time. Threshold specifications of this type can be used with simple statistical decision models.

Poor performance involves quantifiable costs, expressed as losses to the user and as penalties to the service provider. In each of these cases, a risk-to-reward trade-off exists. For example, if a service provider guarantees a given service level, inaccuracies in the provider's measurement tools can lead to an inability to defend against a user's accusation of poor performance. At some point, risk avoidance using better (but more expensive) measurement becomes more costly than paying occasional penalties on marginal measurements. Variability of performance time can be even more important than its absolute value. Users are more likely to complain of a steadily increasing, or wildly fluctuating, response time than they are of a response time that is slower but remains constant.

IDENTIFYING RESPONSE TIME COMPONENTS

The American National Standards Institute X3.102 measurement model divides complex communications systems into sets of one-way paths through a measured network. Using this model, paths connect a source user and a destination user. These users may be any arbitrary users of a system: they may be two people, they may be a terminal and a host, or they may be two local area networks (LANs) connected through a Media Access Control bridge. X3.102 does not define response time measurement, but response times can be calculated accurately by combining the one-way performance on each path from originating user input to originating user output. Using this model, the host becomes a measured network between communications input and communications output; processing time becomes network delay.

The communications process, in X3.102 terms, has three phases: access, user information transfer, and disengagement. Access and disengagement are null in connectionless protocols. Each phase begins with a protocol-dependent interface event that maps into an abstract reference event, which starts a performance trial. Performance trials have an outcome, which reflects either successful performance of the phase, misperformance of the phase, or nonperformance of the phase. Success means that the desired purpose of the phase occurred in a specific period. Misperformance means that an undesirable outcome resulted from the starting event (e.g., a wrong number when dialing a telephone). Nonperformance means that no response resulted from the starting event (e.g., no dial tone in response to lifting a telephone from its hook).

Successful performance is measured in units of time, from the starting event to the event that denotes success. The probabilities of the occurrence of different error types are the parameters for misperformance and nonperformance. These error types include delivery to incorrect destination, delivery of data containing errors, or duplication or loss of data.

End users of interactive applications are concerned with response time, not one-way delays. X3.102 is applicable to response time measurement, by defining response time as a series of one-way delays from input to output. The actual one-way delays used are specific to the architecture and application, and selecting these delays is the process of defining network components.

Interface Responsibility and User Fractions

User actions can bias response time measurements. A measurement strategy must consider interface responsibility. Interface responsibility is the binary state that indicates whether or not a measured unit of information has reached the system under measurement. If a network interface is ready to accept or deliver data, the network transfers responsibility to the user. For example, if a measured network delivers data — a line of print — to a terminal, the network is not responsible if delivery to its ultimate destination — the printer — is delayed because the printer must be refilled with paper.

463

If the user starting a service trial is not ready to complete the process, or the receiving user is not ready to receive, the transferring network between source and sink cannot be blamed for additional user-associated delay. Because this type of delay is part of the performance measurement, X3.102 has a set of user fractions that qualify various performance times. User fractions are dimensionless numbers that define the ratio of user-associated delay to the total time needed to complete a phase of communications. For example, the user fraction of access time in the telephone network is the additional time needed by the caller to dial, in comparison to the shortest dialing time that is possible.

Network Delay

The round-trip set of delays that compose response time occurs over several paths. Formulas exist for calculating the minimum time a message (and its protocol overhead) takes to cross a line that operates at a given maximum bit rate. Rules of thumb exist for estimating delay in network switching elements (e.g., 100 msec in front-end processors or concentrating computers that use conventional technology, and smaller, but vendor-dependent times for new switching elements, like frame relay and fast packet switches).

Inside the network, it is rarely useful to track individual transaction delays. Response time is more easily estimated using statistics for characteristic information units on specific paths. In addition, there may be different numbers of service trials in each one-way path. These numbers may differ because a user-perceived message can be split into smaller pieces, or can be joined with other transactions' messages into a larger block, by an intelligent communications network.

For example, a user input might consist of a screen of data containing 4096 bytes. When this message flows through an X.25 network with a maximum data packet size of 1024 bytes, the original message is segmented into four 1024-byte packets. Each 1024-byte packet experiences a statistically independent delay in transmission, which must be added to calculate the transmission time of the original message. The latter transmission time must also include the time needed for segmentation and reassembly.

Host Delay Component

An important component of response time is host (or server) delay, which is the time required to process an incoming transaction (incoming to the host) and return it to the network. Host delay can be calculated from the processing times of multiple messages, and may or may not include time in a communications processing routine (e.g., a front-end processor).

Host delay can be treated as a measured network in the X3.102 sense. In finding the start and end of the host delay phase, the start and end of host responsibility for the transaction must be identified. Host processing begins when the last byte of information in a given inbound transaction arrives at the host. It is not useful to start timing host delay when the first byte of an incoming message arrives at the host, because the delivery delay between start byte and ending byte is often paced by the network, not the host.

Allocating Delays

Response time objectives set a budget, measured in units of time, which must be allocated among the various components that can cause delay. Each component, including transmission lines, must be examined and a maximum delay allowed for each component must be allocated. This allocation process may show that the desired response time cannot be provided by the set of components selected. For example, a subsecond response time for a complex transaction is not possible when using satellite communications because of the speed-of-light delay implicit in sending signals to and from the satellite. When a goal cannot be realized, either the goal must be renegotiated or the network design must change.

A series of node components (e.g., switches) and transmission media make up end-to-end connections, even in a single direction. Delay is not described as something that occurs at a node; rather, it is something that is described as occurring through a node. For planning (not tuning), other measures complement nodal delay. Some measure of capacity (e.g., throughput) is useful in gross planning. When dealing with components operating above the link control level, measures (e.g., messages or Protocol Data Unit per unit time) are more useful than traditional bits or bytes per second.

Packet switching equipment, for example, often spends much more time processing packet headers than processing the body of the packet. Packet count limits the capacity of packet switches more than the absolute number of bytes received by the switch. Packet switch vendors sometimes inflate their capacity claims by citing a packet per second throughput based on packets of maximum length; such a throughput may not be realizable with short packets (e.g., those used in credit authorization).

DRAFTING THE SERVICE LEVEL AGREEMENT

The next step in solving a performance problem is to draft the service level agreement. This is accomplished by first describing the application and then establishing parameters and measures of their variability. Next, the terms and conditions of measurement (e.g., times during which the service level agreement applies and rules for assessing the effects of downtime) need to be defined. Finally, values for the service level parameters must be specified.

Characterizing Workload and Refining the Service Level Agreement

Service level agreements need to have workload definitions under which they are valid. Service providers have an unfair advantage when allowed to prove they meet the service level agreement under conditions of little or no load; service users are unfair to providers if they expect performance to remain acceptable given an infinitely increasing workload. The following represents a basic list of questions to answer when defining communications workload.

- How many users will be served? If various users have various use patterns, all parameters should be specified.
- Who or what is responsible for the service accessed through the measured communications network? Are there different hosts to service different user requests?
- At what times is service available? Are there designated periods of unavailability? Is the network provider responsible for repair downtime?
- How many transactions do users initiate per unit of time?
- What is the rate at which users start transactions? A distinction should be drawn between simple query-and-response transactions and those involving multiple interactions.
- What is the size distribution of responses?
- What is the length distribution of user transactions?

Often, there are factors, not obvious and frequently system dependent, that affect the provision of a given service level. For example, IBM TSO has a time parameter called system logical wait time. When a user is inactive for more than this time value, the user process may be swapped from RAM to disk, so the next user transaction is delayed not only by network and host processing, but by time needed to load the user environment from the disk. System logical wait time trains users to increase their transaction interarrival rates, sometimes by pressing the Enter key. Service level agreements in this environment must include a transaction interarrival time that can be validated with measurements; failure to maintain an adequately high rate will guarantee slower response time because of disk overhead.

Measurements of the host portion of response time vary significantly, depending on whether the response measurement starts at the first, or the last, byte exiting the host. In measuring availability, service level agreements should specify that downtime extends from a problem report to its correction. Alternatively, time periods without maintenance coverage should be subtracted from the total.

COMMON PROBLEMS AND SOLUTIONS

Although it is possible to come up with many components of performance, in practice it is important to identify the most common contributors to poor performance and correct them before taking performance measurements.

Simple observation reveals many problems, but others will be detected only with formal monitoring. Measurement can be simple or complex. It may be done in hardware or in software. In many user environments, simulation or modeling tools may complement or even replace instrumentation. One approach may be to avoid direct measurement of end-user response time, except as a check on calculated end-user delay. In networks of practical complexity, the insertion of response time measurement capability in end systems often adds needless cost and complexity and a burden of returning measured data to an analysis point. Several common contributors to delay are easy to identify, if not to measure precisely.

Eliminating Errors

Data error rates are a major determinant of communications performance. If, in a protocol that corrects errors by retransmission, discovering 30 percent to 50 percent errors means the line is effectively doing nothing but retransmitting errors, no useful work is being accomplished. If monitoring of the error log or other facilities available in such an environment proves that the error rate is inordinately high, no further performance measurement should be made until the source of errors is found and fixed; not to do so would bias measurements.

Isolating Host Delay

Another area that is simple to examine is the distinction between host and network problems. There are different views of performance: that of the end user, that of the systems developer on the host, and that of the network developer. From the perspective of the end user, any problems are due to the computer. There is a natural tendency for the host people to blame the network people for problems, and vice versa. Unfortunately for the egos of the host and network people, a simple method of finding the cause of delay exists. This approach involves measuring the application host delay from the perspective of a simulated user in the host, or alternatively at a local connection to the host (e.g., a Systems Network Architecture channel-attached controller). This measurement is compared to the delay measured from a network-attached terminal.

If the delay for the internal or local connection is roughly equal to that for the network connection, the problem is not in the network; user response time is limited by host delay. If there is a major difference, it must be determined whether the larger component delay is in the host or in the network. Only if the network delay portion is a significant fraction of the total delay can the network be suspected as the primary fault.

Evaluating Traffic Loading

Any network's performance will degrade when handling excessive traffic. Simple observations can be helpful in finding problems caused by excessive loading. If minimizing response time is the goal, and interactive users complain of poor response time, checks should be made to see if any noninteractive users are loading the network. Typical sources of noninteractive loads are large print jobs and file transfers. Backups can often present unusual loads, as can software maintenance involving sizable software downloading.

Loading from noninteractive sources can often be managed by assigning this traffic a lower priority than interactive traffic, if the network supports multiple priorities. Forcing large transfers to intersperse with interactive traffic and deferring the transfers to interactive traffic can often maintain throughput without degrading response time.

APPLICATION EXAMPLES

Specific tuning recommendations are protocol and implementation specific. This section offers some rules of thumb for the more frequently encountered environments. The network user must distinguish between short-term tuning and longer-term capacity planning.

X.25

Factors that can be controlled by a public packet switched network user are: virtual calls per trunk, access line speed, and packet size versus window size. Host delay, of course, influences response time but is not a network responsibility. If the application under study uses terminals connected by a packet asembler-disassembler (PAD) — a protocol converter — the PAD can introduce significant delays. Response time can be intolerably slow if the terminal expects local echoing of entered characters, and the remote host does this echoing. When echoing is needed, it should be done by the PAD. In polled protocol applications, the PAD should emulate the polling master station; polling overhead should not be sent across a packet network.

PADs can have parameters that control how quickly packets, or parts of packets, are assembled and transmitted. A trade-off can exist between maximizing throughput by waiting for full packets to form, and minimizing delay by sending packet-encapsulated user data quickly. Transmission errors are a problem on the access line — not throughout the network.

Error statistics on the line are often available, and until errors on the access link are minimized, other network measurements are not useful.

The number of virtual calls on a single link is often a major factor. Although the decision is always implementation specific, performance may be better on two 9600-bps lines, each with half the virtual circuit, than with one 19.2-Kbps line. This observation applies to two lines each using the single-link procedure for link control, not two lines using the multilink procedure.

Maximum data packet length and window size are strong determinants of performance. In general, a longer packet length leads to better performance. Small window sizes are best for interactive applications; long window sizes work better for file transfer.

When X.25 service is being provided through Public Data Network, network performance information available to the end user is limited. This is not a practical limitation when performance requirements are specified at the network interface. It is the provider's responsibility to tune the network internals to meet contracted requirements.

SNA 3270

Because polled 3270 terminals often coexist with printers, noninteractive devices must not monopolize the line. Fifty percent use is a desirable maximum if noninteractive devices are not present. Use can be much higher if noninteractive devices have a lower priority (i.e., are serviced less often), and the size of their transmissions — when they have permission to transmit — is limited.

Problems common to multiple devices need to be identified. Excessive delay affecting all devices on a line suggests a line problem (e.g., excessive errors or traffic). If the excessive delay is restricted to one cluster, there may be too many devices in that cluster. Solutions here include adding a new controller for some of the devices, increasing the speed of the line servicing the controller, or, where the physical situation permits, moving terminals to less busy positions.

When excessive delay is restricted to specific terminals, possibly on different clusters, unusual use patterns should be suspect. Those users may be entering transactions with unusual host processing needs or with unusually large volumes of data. The latter problem may be traced to an intelligent emulator doing uploads and downloads. 3270 emulation on intelligent workstations is common. Such emulation may be used for file transfers, and file transfers defeat the algorithms used to properly configure 3270 systems. Many of these algorithms assume typical, bursty rates of human input, not the continuous input of a file transfer. Emulators doing

469

file transfer can be recognized in traffic statistics because they will have a higher transaction interarrival rate than true interactive terminals.

Systems network architecture (SNA) interconnects intelligent switching nodes with transmission groups, which can be built from one or more lines. They allow multiple priorities. Multiline transmission groups impose much higher overhead than a single-line transmission group, so they should be used only when increased availability is necessary, or if no single line of sufficient bandwidth is available.

Response Time with Ethernet-Type LANs

Several simple rules of thumb may be used to tune response time on LANs. The first rule is to decide whether the network performance is actually a significant part of response time. The second rule is to measure whether the LAN is overloaded. To determine whether network performance is causing the slow response time, a transaction can be run on two identical workstations and the response time measured. A statistically significant number of performance trials of the same transaction are run with one workstation connected to the LAN and one connected directly to the server. Approximate network delay is calculated by subtracting the mean response time at the directly connected workstation from the response time at the network-connected workstation.

To measure whether a LAN is overloaded, a protocol analyzer is used. If busy hour use is 50 percent or greater, the network will soon need to be split into subnetworks. If use is 70 percent or greater, it must be split immediately. The network should not be split on the basis of measurements of maintenance activity (e.g., backups) during times in which end users do not access the network.

Diskless workstations present a special challenge. Although keeping data files on a file server is generally wise, and a reasonable number of system files can be kept there, significant increases in workstation performance often result from equipping the workstation with a small local disk. On this disk are kept read-only operating systems and scratch or swap files that do not need periodic backups.

CONCLUSION

Although performance optimization is an integral part of the day-to-day maintenance of any network, the problems that arise are not insurmountable. The network manager trying to solve these problems and increase efficiency at the same time does not need a specialized degree in queuing theory. By following a routine set of steps, like those detailed in this chapter, and by allocating a specific amount of time for unavoidable delays, the network manager can systematically locate the root of any performance problem.

470

Chapter 35
Planning, Designing, and Optimization of Enterprise Networks
Roshan L. Sharma

INTRODUCTION

NETWORK PLANNING, DESIGN, AND OPTIMIZATION should be an important
component of a network management process despite its benign neglect
by most network managers. Such a benign neglect resulted from the fact
that network design was traditionally accomplished through the use of
powerful mainframe computers. Because these computers required the
use of large tariff-related databases, a great deal of time was spent in entering input data. A great deal of time was also spent on interpreting the output data that invariably came in the form of a thick stack of computer printouts. Lack of graphics provided no illustration of network topologies.
Furthermore, the user was always kept out of the computer room. This
made the network design process a mysterious effort, scaring even the
most experienced network manager. Most of the modern network design
tools still employ the old philosophy, which prevents the network managers from deriving the full benefits of new innovations in computer hardware and software.

The VLSI (Very Large Scale Integration) technology has now made the
availability of very powerful personal computers, desktop or laptop variety, within reach of every network designer and planner. However, the lack
of a user-friendly software for network design and planning had prevented
the network managers from making use of the latest desktop hardware.
Several new software packages have been created to make use of the new
PC hardware platforms. The author has developed one such package called
EcoNets as fully described in Reference 1. We will make use of EcoNets later
and show how the network planning, design, and optimization process can
be simplified to a level unimagined before. In fact, EcoNets can now be

treated as a new type of scientific calculator bringing simplicity and ease of use to every networking specialist.

Any network planning and design effort can be broken into the following distinct tasks:

1. Creating a database for all locations and types of dumb terminals (e.g., telephones), intelligent workstations (WSs), customer premise equipment (CPE such as PABX or data LAN), and communication facilities serving those locations
2. Modeling all types of end-to-end multi-hour traffic flows between all locations
3. Modeling traffic growth during a life cycle of the network system
4. Defining end-to-end performance requirements for all forms of communications
5. Designing strategic and tactical network alternatives using available technologies
6. Selecting the best alternative based on cost, cutover, and performance
7. Testing the performance of a post-cutover network implementation
8. Updating the analytical tools and getting ready for next design cycle
9. Documenting the results

A cursory look at the above tasks will suggest that any network manager must accomplish these tasks in an iterative and a clear fashion. One will need a judicial combination of just plain old perseverance (for Tasks 1 and 9), traffic engineering practices (for Tasks 2 and 3), defining performance requirements (for Task 4), availability of a user-friendly and highly interactive design tools (for Tasks 5 and 8), systems engineering skills (for Task 7), and marketing savvy for selling the final solution to the upper management (for Task 6). Such capability requirement for a typical network manager is not that formidable if the right traffic analysis and network design tools are available. We will now describe each of the capabilities that must be controlled by the network manager.

THE ENTERPRISE DATABASE (EDB)

The first task is by far the most time-consuming. An enterprise database (EDB) should at least list the exact mailing address; ten-digit telephone numbers; associated Vertical and Horizontal (V&H) coordinates; all CPEs with vendor's name, date of installation, single point-of-contact for maintenance, the utilization level of each CPE, and type and number of communication facilities serving each location; and associated point-of-presence (POP) central offices of local exchange carriers (LECs) and interexchange carriers (IECs) with their V&H coordinates. The list can grow into a very large one when the database must also classify the users at each location with their interlocation communications needs. Despite the difficulty of creating the EDB, many network managers and top company officials have already discovered the importance of such a database. In any case, *the task of network planning, design, and optimization is impossible without the availability of such an EDB.*

TRAFFIC ENGINEERING TECHNIQUES AND TOOLS

The next three tasks demand a capability for traffic modeling and traffic analysis. Before we define the traffic engineering efforts, we must first introduce some basic traffic-related concepts.

Basic Traffic Concepts

There are two types of traffic encountered in enterprise networks:

1. well-behaved voice and video traffic
2. bursty data traffic

It always is assumed that connection-oriented voice traffic behaves in a predictable fashion which implies that (1) the call holding times can be expressed by at least first two moments (i.e., an average and a variance), and (2) the finer structure of traffic flows do not require rapid changes in network resource deployment. But a close observation of speech energy over the duration of a talk will show that there are many pauses. Furthermore, two of the four-wire access lines (ALs) and trunks are always idle because only one party can talk at a time. These facts have helped long-distance carriers send more calls over expensive ocean cables than are possible over available trunks using pure circuit switching by using the time asynchronous speech interpolator (TASI) technology. Such a technology was never cost-effective over cheaper, land-based leased line. With the availability of Asynchronous Transfer Mode (ATM) or Broadband ISDN, one will be able to get the same benefit through the use of Variable Bit Rate (VBR) capability. The connection-oriented video traffic should not yield this benefit because intelligent WSs can maintain a full-duplex connection.

The data traffic between two CPEs is always bursty. This is caused by the complex rules of data communication protocols. Very small control messages may be involved in both directions before user information can flow. Although a full-duplex connection can be maintained, shared transmission lines in a packet-switched network can carry variable-length packets from many sources concurrently, thus muddying the picture in a hurry. The faster the transmission lines, the burstier the transmission will appear. It becomes clear that a notion of an average message length over a transmission line becomes rather vague.

One can now devise ways to measure traffic intensity considering the above aspects of two major types of traffic encountered in enterprise networks.

Circuit-switched (CS) voice and video traffic intensity is measured in *erlangs,* which is equal to the average number of circuits busy during a so-called busy hour (BHR) between two network nodes. We will define such a BHR later. To illustrate, if 15.5 conversations are observed concurrently between two network nodes (e.g., between a PABX and a voice switch or over an access line bundle) during a BHR, then the voice traffic intensity is 15.5 erlangs. The older measure of CS traffic intensity was *hundred call seconds (CCS).* But such a measure was almost useless since it did not represent any physical truth, such as the number of conversations observed.

Packet-switched data traffic intensity can be measured as the traffic rate in bits per second (bps) during a so-called busy hour. Only data rate in bps can describe the bursty nature of data traffic. Experienced network specialists have been using the concept of data erlangs for many years for defining the average data traffic intensity between two network nodes. This is obtained by dividing the observed BHR data rate (R) by the capacity (C) of each separate transmission line. For example, if the BHR data rate between two nodes is 392,000 bps and the capacity of a transmission line is 56,000 bps, then the data traffic intensity is 7 erlangs.

Modeling Traffic Flows in an Enterprise Network

Basically there are two kinds of network systems that present unique situations for modeling traffic flows within an enterprise network: (1) a *brand new* network system, and (2) an *existing* network system.

Modeling Traffic Flows in a Brand-New Enterprise Network.
Many network specialists feel helpless in modeling traffic flows for a brand-new system. Many approximate methods have been devised over the years for predicting traffic intensities (TIs) between all major CPEs. To illustrate, a voice LAN (or PABX) generates about $0.1*N_s$ erlangs of BHR traffic where N_s is the number of active subscribers served by the PABX. Similarly, a data LAN generates about $(2/3)(WSC)*N_s$ where WSC is the BHR traffic intensity (in bps) generated by each *active* station on the LAN. A breakdown of these traffic expressions into intranodal and internodal traffic should be determined by the known pattern observed at each enterprise. Some network designers employ the 70/30 breakdown that implies that 70 percent of the traffic remains within the site (voice/data LAN) and 30 percent of the traffic goes to other CPEs as internodal flows. These TI values can then be entered into an input file that defines each site ID, the related V&H coordinates, and the total traffic (in and out) intensity handled by the site. The EcoNets tool calls such a file the VHD file.

The next task is to model the internodal traffic flows (i.e., exact traffic intensities handled by all the nodes and links in the path of a CPE-CPE connection). These computations are generally performed by the network planning/design software package for each assumed network topology (i.e., number of network switches and the link types employed at each network hierarchy). Some tools employ some critical design parameters to determine the fraction of traffic handled by ALs (connecting CPE and a switch) and trunks (connecting two switches). Eventually, the tool provides the total traffic intensity handled by each resource (node or link) of each network topology considered during a typical busy hour.

Modeling Traffic Flows in an Existing Enterprise Network. One can model exact traffic flows by using the detailed traffic data gathered by intelligent network nodes (e.g., PABX or LAN). The source ID, the destination ID, the call originating time, and the call duration for each connection is recorded in Station Message Data Recording (SMDR) tapes of voice network. Similar data is recorded by the data LAN for the packetized traffic. Simple traffic analysis packages are obtainable for analyzing the exact internodal traffic patterns between all pairs of CPEs. Such data can then be entered in a From-To-Data File (FTF) to define CPE traffic as simple vectors (From-Node ID, To-Node ID, and the BHR traffic intensity) for each CPE-nodal pair. This effort eventually provides actual traffic flows (i.e., the actual traffic intensity handled by all resource, nodes, and links) of each network topology studied during a typical BHR.

Modeling Time-Consistent Averages (TCAs) of Traffic Flows. Choosing a busy hour can be a very important task. No network can be economical if one selects the hour with the highest traffic. It may provide the required grade-of-service (GOS) during the busiest hour, but at all other hours of the day (especially during the evening and night hours) it becomes overkill. Nobody can afford such a network. If one selects an hour with the least traffic during the day, the network manager will hear complaints all day long. Therefore, one needs a proven methodology to select the so-called TCA traffic intensity for network design. There are two methodologies — one used in North America and one used by the other countries.

The first methodology requires the selection of a typical month and creating a matrix (30×24) of traffic intensities (TIs) for each network resource for that month. Next, it computes the average traffic intensity for each hour of the day over all 30 days of the month. This process is repeated for each of the 24 hours. The TCA traffic is the maximum value of all 24 TCA values. This value, as it will shown later, determines the size of the resource (number of AL and trunks in the bundle connecting two nodes or the computing power of an intelligent node). Again, one needs either the use of a software package for computing TCA traffic intensity (TI) values or a simple approach for approximating the TCA TI values.

The second methodology requires the observation of the 36 highest TI values over an entire year and then computing the average of these values to get a TCA value. This must be done for all resources.

Both of these methodologies are known to yield economical networks. It should be emphasized that no single methodology can predict an exact traffic pattern for the future. Traffic values behave like the stock market fluctuations. A single catastrophe, such as an earthquake or a major terrorist-bomb explosion somewhere, can also change the traffic patterns drastically. The objective of a good traffic engineering practice is to synthesize a cost-effective enterprise network using a consistent approach.

Modeling Traffic Growths during a Life Cycle of a Network System. In order to estimate the total costs incurred during the life cycle of a network system, one must first model the traffic intensities for each of the life cycle year. Experience shows that the so-called Delphi Approach (based on Socratic approach) works the best. Through interviews of all general managers, one can build good models of traffic growth during every year of the life cycle. There are times when one may find that some division may disappear altogether, either through divestiture or pure attrition. The data from all of the interviews must be collected, weighed, and processed to create a meaningful model.

PERFORMANCE ISSUES

Before one can define performance requirements for all the communication needs of an enterprise, one must first study the available concepts of performance and then study the exact enterprise needs in each of their business areas.

Concepts of Network System Performance

It is a commonly known fact that most of the existing network systems were implemented without any regard to their performance. As long as they satisfy the basic needs for communications, everyone is happy. No effort is expended in (1) predicting or measuring the actual performance of the system and (2) making any measured systemwide improvements after the system is operational. The lack of any concerted effort in defining and measuring performance of network system may lie in ignorance of concepts related to system performance. One can define the performance of a network system in four ways:

1. Total system costs computed on a monthly basis
2. System throughputs in terms of all types of transactions handled during a unit time
3. Systemwide quality-of-service (QoS)
4. Systemwide grade-of-service (GoS)

476

Total Monthly Costs. Transmission facilities determine the majority of total monthly costs of MANs and WANs. Because such costs are always paid on a monthly basis (just like our utility bills) to Local Exchange Carrier (LEC), Interexchange Carriers (IECs), and Other Common Carriers (OCCs), it simplifies matters a great deal. The other major items are one-time hardware costs and recurring costs of network management and control (NMC). It is a simple matter to convert the one-time hardware costs into equivalent monthly costs considering the life cycle duration (7 or 10 years depending on the enterprise) and cost of loaning money. It is similar to computing the monthly payment for a mortgage. The NMC costs related to spares can be handled just like one-time hardware costs. The remaining NMC costs on a monthly basis can be the same as either the monthly salaries paid to the NMC specialists or the monthly bills paid to an outsourcing company. It is therefore a simple task to compute the total monthly cost of a network system.

System Throughput. System throughput is measured at the rate at which the various types of transactions are handled per unit time (usually second or minute). It is equal to the number of call attempts or calls completed per second for a voice network. It is equal to the number of packets handled per second or total bits (in and out) per second handled during a second. The throughput capability of each node is generally defined by the vendor of the equipment. The challenge lies in measuring the system throughput. By enumerating the exact paths of each transaction, one can estimate the system throughput. Consult Reference 1 for additional insight.

System Quality of Service (QoS). Performance aspects dealing with transmission quality, perceived voice quality, error-free seconds, data security, and network reliability (mean time between system failures) fall into the QoS criterion. Most of these are very hard to compute for the entire system. One can measure these performance aspects for some critical resource to get a feel. See Reference 1 for greater insight.

System Grade of Service (GoS). The GoS criterion deals with end-to-end blocking for a voice network and average response time (measured as the elapsed time between the moment the send key is pressed and the moment the return reply is discerned by the user) for a data communication. Analytical tools are available (Reference 1) for estimating such GoS parameters for voice, data, and integrated networks.

Defining Performance Goals for an Enterprise

Performance goals of a enterprise network should be developed by the corporate strategic planners. A typical strategic planning cycle lasts several years and it entails the following activities:

1. Continuous evaluation of the needs of the enterprise and its competitors. This activity defines the relationship of system response times to information workers' productivity for each of the transactions.
2. Studying the evolving new technologies, CPEs, and networking standards and finding ways to deploy these to achieve cost-effective enterprise networks and enhancing the productivity of its workers. This activity provides the cost and performance attributes of new hardware (e.g., ATM switches and LAN switches).

In order to perform its duties successfully, a strategic planning group should be properly structured to act in close cooperation with the corporate Information Technology (IT) department, and it should be provided with all the necessary resources and tools. Furthermore, a mechanism should be in place to properly reward all the members of this important group.

All future enterprise networks will have to deal with the ever-increasing demand for (1) voice, video, image, and data communications; (2) multiplexing of digitized voice, image, and video signals with regular data traffic at all hierarchies of enterprise locations through modern switches (e.g., ATM switches); and (3) unscheduled or varying demands for digital bandwidth at all hours of a day on a dynamic basis.

In order to design such an integrated enterprise network, the strategic planning group needs a user-friendly tool for evaluating alternative solutions very quickly. Such an approach should be an extension of the so-called "back-of-the-envelope" method employed by network managers of yesterday. They were generally concerned with designing only voice networks. The older "back-of-the-envelope" approach is no longer useful due to the complexity of modern integrated, hybrid, multilevel enterprise networks. It has been found that most of the hunches based on the so-called "common sense" are generally wrong when predicting the performance of an integrated network system. A user-friendly tool should help the strategic planning group to get "ball-park" solutions iteratively and interactively in order to fulfill its charter. See page 587 in *An Example of Planning and Design of an Integrated Enterprise Network Using Econets*, for an illustration of a "what if" approach required for rapid planning and designing or obtaining quick conceptual solutions by both the strategic and tactical planning teams.

NETWORK PLANNING AND DESIGN TOOL

Before we review the old and the new network design technologies, it should also be useful to discuss some major network design issues.

Major Network Design Issues

The current published literature dealing with networking is very confusing, at best. Most of the published articles are generally characterized by buzz words, a good deal of hype, lots of possible solutions, and no single recommendation. Although a part of the problem may lie in the fact that no single approach is ideally suited for all enterprises, no one can defend a lack of clarity that characterizes most published articles. While some articles recommend all virtual lines for enterprise voice networks, other articles emphasize the need for an integrated network management technique. While some articles recommend full freedom in designing departmental LANs and interconnections of these LANs through bridges and routers, other articles show the need for frame relay, SMDS and B-ISDN, or ATM in order to realize economies-of-scale in integrated enterprise networks. Most of the articles attempt only to expound a new type of switch technology or hardware. They rightfully leave up to the reader to assess the usefulness of the new technology or networking hardware to his or her enterprise.

Network design process is basically concerned with two issues: (1) topological optimization, which determines the way network nodes are connected to one another (including the type of connections) while satisfying a set of critical design and performance constraints, and (2) system performance dealing with end-to-end response times, path congestion, and availabilities.

Recurring network cost is generally the most important performance criterion and it is mainly determined by its topology. Network topology also determines the remaining performance issues such as response times and availability. Each network design package analyzes these performance issues in only an approximate manner.

Closed-form solutions for end-to-end system performance have been getting harder and harder to obtain ever since the first day a network was installed. Some of the current excitement about the interconnections of data LANs ignores the tribulations involved during the 1970s when voice LANs (i.e., PABXs) were being interconnected to create enterprise networks with consistent topologies. Unfortunately, data internetworks encourage point-to-point type connections between LANs. This approach creates an undue network complexity for large networks. This in turn increases costs of NMC. The new ATM technology should eventually reduces this complexity by enforcing a consistent network topology and architecture.

The Old Network Design Technology

The many older network design tools handled only voice or multidrop data networks. Some of the tools that came later handled only interconnections of data LANs to achieve an enterprise data WAN. Furthermore, most of these tools required mainframes. The use of a mainframe introduced an unnecessary curtain between the network designer and the host processor. The network design jobs were entered invariably via the "batch" approach, and the outputs came in the form of large printouts after a good deal of delay. Each change of a design parameter or study of a new technology required a new noninteractive, unfriendly delay. The absence of network-related graphics from outputs caused additional delays in interpreting the significance of results.

The old design technology also required the use of an extensive database of tariffs. These tariffs have been increasing in number and changing quite rapidly since the divestiture in 1984. The complexity of the tariff database was probably the main reason behind the need for mainframes. If such a database is incorporated into a desktop minicomputer or a PC-based workstation, one will experience sizable processing delays. In any case, one will be prevented from getting a truly interactive tool.

Because enterprise networks are planned and designed for a future period, this preoccupation with utmost accuracy in tariffs is uncalled for. Furthermore, since network topologies do not change with perturbations in any given tariff (they change only with varying design parameters and technologies), using a simplified set of existing or new tariffs will yield optimized networks in rapid succession even on a user-friendly desktop workstation. These topologies can be studied for a detailed cost analysis at a later period using one of the many available PC-Line Pricer (PCLP) units. This two-step approach should create a separation between the network design algorithms and the ever-changing tariffs. There should be no need to update the network design package just because a tariff changed slightly.

Network design tools based on the older technology were not only noninteractive, but they also were unfriendly to use. A lack of a good graphical user interface (GUI) required lengthy training and a prolonged hands-on design experience to become familiar with the tool. A good design package should be an intuitive tool in the hands of an expert network designer and no more. A good hammer and a chisel alone will never guarantee beautiful furniture — one also needs a good carpenter. It should not be hard to understand why the vendors of network design tools have always had a hard time marketing these unfriendly network design tools. Most vendors have gone in and out of business several times under different names.

Some vendors (Reference 2) market software packages based on computer simulation for evaluating system performance. LANs (voice or data) and WANs consisting of interconnected data LANs can be evaluated for performance through computer simulation. A good deal of time must be spent on (1) writing the simulation program based upon the exact network topology and the underlying communication protocols, and (2) debugging the software before one can evaluate all of the performance metrics such as throughput and end-to-end response times. Because typical enterprise networks require exhorbitant runtimes, a simulation tool is no longer an ideal way for synthesizing an optimum network topology. A network topology optimization package based on analytical tools is always the best approach. The resulting topology can be evaluated for studying detailed system response times and availabilities using an expensive simulation tool.

The New Network Design Technology

The new desktop workstation technology now provides several platforms for a user-friendly, interactive tool for optimizing network topology in an iterative fashion while varying the values of critical design parameters rapidly. Some well-known tools for network design also provide special menus for computing end-to-end response times for unusual operational conditions. Some packages even provide special tools for analyzing subsystem security and reliability.

Many new tools based on the graphical-user-interface (GUI) can evaluate any mix of CPEs, transmission facilities, and network topologies very rapidly in an intuitive manner. But in no way can this new technology eliminate the need for an expert network designer or an architect. Since the expert designer is always involved with "what-if" type analyses at all times through the graphical-user-interface, the solutions remain always meaningful and topical only if the network design tool provides such solutions rapidly. This approach is becoming an ideal one since the tariffs as we have known them are about to disappear. The modern tools allow the entry of approximate tariffs quickly. Next, we will describe one network planning and design package called EcoNets, and we will describe an example illustrating the network planning and design process associated with EcoNets.

Capability Highlights of the EcoNets Network Planning and Design Package

Inputs are in the form of flat, sequential files. Results are provided in the form of (1) graphics illustrating network topology with summary costs of communications facilities and response times (if applicable), and (2) output files containing detailed cost distributions and critical performance data.

The most important input file is called the VHD file listing the site/node ID, Vertical and Horizontal (V&H) coordinates, and total busy hour (BHR), time-consistent traffic intensities in bits per second (for data) or millier-langs (for voice) for each location of the enterprise. A from-to-data (FTD) file can also be used to represent exact traffic flows. Another file called the daily traffic profile relates the BHR intensities to the other 24 hours of the day for computing the costs on a daily/monthly basis. For an enterprise with many time zones, several BHR models can be used. The second most important LINK file defines the link-type that serves each location.

The third most important input file, called the NLT file, defines the link type, capacity (C), allowed maximum data rate (W_m), multiplexing factor (MF defining the equivalent number of voice conversations carried by the link), corresponding tariff number, and the multiplying factor for a privately owned facility (F_{pf}), if applicable. Up to ten link types and corresponding C, W_m, MF, tariff number and F_{pf} can be defined by the NLT file. The Tariff file can define up to ten manually entered tariffs, each modeled by 17 parameters. Several Link, NLT, and Tariff files can be prepared to model many combinations of links and tariffs at all levels of network hierarchy. An input file called the system design file (SDF) defines the design parameters required to model/design the network.

The input file called the FTF defines the BHR from-to traffic for all significant pairs if such data is known. Other input files define the LATA numbers and names associated with each location. Several specialized input files are also employed for modeling/designing ACD networks employing a mix of virtual facilities and leased FX lines.

The File Menu allows the creation and viewing/updating of all input/output files. The Networking Menu allows the modeling/designing of multilevel voice, data, and IV/D network using the appropriate star data, directed link and multidrop data network topologies, and voice networks based on star topology. One can also model, design, and optimize backbone networks on an iterative manner. The Networking Menu also allows the designer to find optimum locations for concentrators/switches by starting with good solutions and improving these through a fast iterative process. By specifying the design parameters, one can model and design traditional data networks based on IBM's SNA (System Network Architecture); traditional packet-switched networks based on CCITT's X.25 standard; and fast packet-switched networks based on frame relay and ATM technology.

By specifying the design parameters, one can model hybrid voice networks using all types of leased and virtual facilities with or without multiplexing. One can also optimize a backbone network topology and model any given topology (for cost and routes). The Analysis Menu allows the designer to model/analyze any point-to-point and several multilink paths for congestion/queuing delays, LAN performance, and reliability. An Analysis Menu item also allows the computation of equivalent monthly cost of hardware and payoff periods for privately owned hardware and transmission facilities.

AN EXAMPLE OF PLANNING AND DESIGN OF AN INTEGRATED ENTERPRISE NETWORK USING ECONETS

An enterprise has 17 sites scattered throughout the United States. Its headquarters are in Las Colinas, Texas. It is engaged in the manufacture, distribution, marketing, and maintenance of highly specialized intelligent workstations. Two separate networks serve the enterprise. A voice network connects all its 17 locations (or PABXs) to a voice switch located at Las Colinas with leased voice-gradelines (VGLs). A separate data network connects workstations located at all of its locations to a host using the

SNA-BSC protocol and 9600 bps lines. The newly appointed network manager wants to study the feasibility of a new network architecture. A consultant is engaged to study the problem.

A database (a subset of the EDB) for network design was created. It is illustrated in Exhibit 35-1. The 17 sites, their V&H coordinates, and BHR TCA of traffic intensities are shown for both voice (in millierlangs) and data (in bps). Also shown are their names according to a six-symbol city-state (CCCCST) code. Next, a Node-Link-Type (NLT) file is defined for four link types: VGL, 56Kbps line, T1 line, and T3 line. The simplified tariffs are defined for these links types next.

The consultant first modeled the existing voice and data networks. The monthly costs for these two separate networks were computed to be as $60,930 and $10,017, respectively. For a comparison, the EcoNets tool was then employed to study various topologies consisting of 1,2,3,4,5 switches and three links types for voice, and only the 9600 bps line for data (higher-speed lines resulted in no improvements).

The results are shown in Exhibit 35-2. The optimum voice-network topology (Exhibit 35-3) consisted of two switches (as determined by the Eco-Nets' center-of-gravity [COG] finding item of Networking Menu) and 56Kbps lines, each of which carries eight digitally encoded voice conversations. The one-time cost of 17 special hardware boxes that perform voice encoding and multiplexing in the same box did not influence the optimum network topology. The optimum data network topology (Exhibit 35-4) also consisted of the same two switches as for the voice network and 9600bps lines. The cost of these optimum networks was found to be $37,546 and $9,147, respectively. This represented a monthly saving of $23,254 (or about 32.8 percent of existing costs). No matter which way one looks at this figure, it is a substantial saving.

Additional saving can be achieved by computing the total data rate (in bps) of voice conversations from each site and adding the regular data traffic and constructing a new VHD file. One can achieve an optimum star-data topology consisting of two switches and 56Kbps lines. Its topology is identical to that for the optimum voice network (Exhibit 35-2) and its monthly cost is about the same as for the optimum voice network. The cost of the separate data network disappears completely. The new monthly saving of $33,392 savings represents 47.1 percent of the existing costs. These additional savings resulted from the fact that the 56K bps lines used in the integrated voice/data (IVD) network had enough excess capacity to handle the data traffic. Such a phenomenon is similar to the one experienced by network managers working with the larger T1 networks of the 1980s. Those enterprise voice networks had enough excess capacities (in the T1 trunks) to handle the data traffic. The broadband data networks of the future should have enough excess capacity to handle the voice and image traffic.

Exhibit 35-1. Enterprise database (EDB) 17-node network design (voice/data applications).

				Lata		
N#	-V-	-H-	Load	(BPS/MEs)	Link	Name
1	8438	4061	40000	552	0	LCLNTX
2	8436	4034	5000	552	0	DALLTX
3	8296	1094	1300	952	0	SRSTFL
4	8360	906	1300	939	0	FTMYFL
5	6421	8907	1300	674	0	TACMWA
6	6336	8596	1300	676	0	BELVWA
7	4410	1248	1300	128	0	DANVMA
8	6479	2598	1300	466	0	VERSKY
9	9258	7896	1300	730	0	TOAKCA
10	9233	7841	1400	730	0	NORWCA
11	9210	7885	1400	730	0	WLAXCA
12	7292	5925	1400	656	0	DENVCO
13	7731	4025	1300	538	0	TULSOK
14	7235	2069	1300	438	0	NORCGA
15	5972	2555	2500	324	0	COLMOH
16	9228	7920	2500	730	0	STMNCA
17	8173	1147	2500	952	0	TMPAFL

Nodal Definition Data

Total BHR Traffic = 68500

Node-Link Type

Link Type	Link Capacity	MaxLink Rate
1	9,600 bps	6,300 bps
2	56,000	48,000
3	1,544,000	1,440,000

Tariff No. 1

Average Local Loops Charge ($)=294

Milage Bands	50	100	500	1000	10000
Fixed Cost ($)	72.98	149.28	229.28	324.24	324.24
Cost per Mile ($)	2.84	1.31	0.51	0.32	0.32

Exhibit 35-1. *(Continued)*

Tariff No. 2

Average Local Loops Charge (\$)=492					
Milage Bands	50	100	500	1000	10000
Fixed Cost (\$)	232	435	571	1081	1081
Cost per Mile (\$)	7.74	3.68	2.32	1.3	1.3

Tariff No. 3

Average Local Loops Charge (\$)=2800					
Milage Bands	50	100	500	1000	10000
Fixed Cost (\$)	1770	1808	2008	2500	2500
Cost per Mile (\$)	10	9.25	7.25	7.25	7.25

Tariff No. 4

Average Local Loops Charge (\$)=8000					
Milage Bands	10000	10000	10000	10000	100000
Fixed Cost (\$)	16600	16600	16600	16600	16600
Cost per Mile (\$)	47	47	47	47	47

Daily Traffic Profile

Hour Numbers and Corresponding Fractions of Daily Traffic are as Fallows:					
1-0	2-0	3-0	4-0	5-0	6-0
7-0.05	8-0.1	9-0.1	10-0.1	11-0.1	12-0.1
13-0.1	14-0.1	15-0.1	16-0.1	17-0.05	18-0
19-0	20-0	21-0	22-0	23-0	24-0

The preceding examples illustrate only small enterprise networks. Bigger savings can be expected through optimization of larger enterprise networks. Basically, savings result from two facts: (1) integrated networks make use of excess capacity, and (2) aggregation of many separate applications allows the deployment of transmission facilities with higher capacities that generally cost less on a per-transaction basis. Now every network manager has unlimited opportunities to provide a cost-effective integrated network to the enterprise. There is no excuse for not attempting to save big bucks for any strategically minded enterprise.

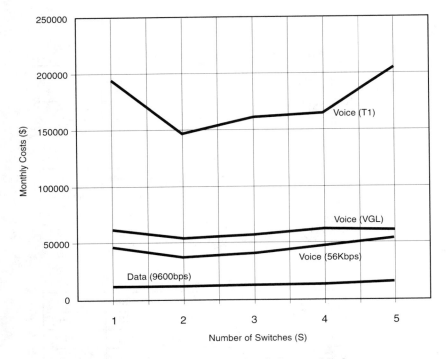

Exhibit 35-2. Cost vs. number of switches and link types.

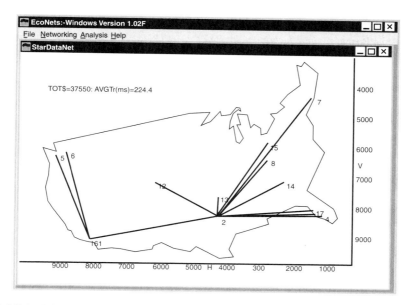

Exhibit 35-3. Optimum star-data network topology for IVD application.

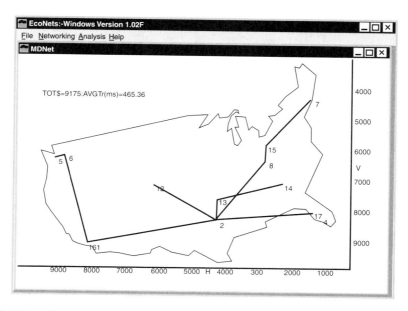

Exhibit 35-4. Optimum MD-data network topology with two switches.

References

1. Sharma, Roshan L. *Introduction to Network Design Using EcoNets Software*, International Thomson Computer Press, Boston, 1997.
2. Fike, J. L and H. D. Jacobsen. *Applying Modeling Techniques in Network Design*, Paper presented at the June 3, 1991 Session M13 at the ICA Conference.
3. Van Norman, H. J. "WAN Design Tools: the New Generation," *Data Communications*, October 1990.
4. Axner, David. "New Tools for Predicting Network Performance," *Business Communications Review*, November 1995.

Chapter 36
Proactive Performance Management

Tim Clark

ONCE VIEWED AS INTERNAL UTILITIES for interorganization communication, the networks of today are being built to deliver essential business processes to partners and to customers. It is critical for organizations to be able to proactively manage the available bandwidth and systems for effective overall performance management.

Network management is a term that encompasses many complex, interrelated disciplines. Many organizations define the elements of network management as FCAPS — fault management, configuration management, accounting/billing, performance management, and security management — and try to address each element. However, the primary emphasis in many organizations is on fault determination and event isolation and correlation. These are critical elements, obviously, but the changing nature and complexity of the network are elevating the importance of performance management.

Enterprise networks are increasingly becoming a critical delivery mechanism for the products and services of a company. Corporate intranets are being accessed by business partners and even the public to perform basic business transactions. The purchase of books, the tracking of packages, and home banking are just a few examples of goods and services being delivered over the Internet.

With this trend, the enterprise network is both more critical to the day-to-day business operations of an entity and under more stress. The bandwidth demands are skyrocketing as the usage of the new Web-based applications grows. The potential for bottlenecks grows. To meet these increasing demands, LAN and WAN switches are being deployed. Service providers are augmenting the private network. The performance of this new network

0-8493-0859-3/00/$0.00+$.50
© 2000 by CRC Press LLC

is much more complex to manage than its relatively static and stable, in-house, router-based predecessor.

THE CURRENT STATE OF PERFORMANCE MANAGEMENT

Organizations today often have a variety of different tools to help manage the performance of the network. Those that have mainframes deployed are running a version of TME 10 NetView. SNMP (Simple Network Management Protocol) management applications by HP, IBM, Sun, Cabletron, and others are being widely deployed. Applications from router and switch vendors help to manage those elements and devices. A wide range of specific point tools provide information limited to a particular facet of performance management.

These tools are utilized to conduct many different types of network performance analysis:

- monitor real-time network performance
- network performance threshold alarms
- historical network performance reports
- network performance service level agreements (SLAs)
- LAN capacity planning
- WAN capacity planning
- server capacity planning
- network modeling
- baselining
- benchmarking

The analysis is performed using performance reports from a very wide range of network components:

- routers
- serial links
- frame relay CIR
- Ethernet segments
- Token Ring segments
- hubs
- LAN switches
- WAN switches
- servers
- workstations
- applications

Despite the plethora of tools and the variety of tasks that are undertaken in the typical enterprise network, comprehensive and proactive performance management still eludes many organizations. The barriers are numerous. In many cases, there is insufficient staff available that have the experience and training necessary to configure and administer the system,

Exhibit 36-1. Performance management checklist.

1. Do you know the exact state of the network across the enterprise at any given time?	Yes___ No___
2. Do you know the demand on network resources?	Yes___ No___
3. Do you know how and where things have changed on the network?	Yes___ No___
4. Do you know where problems are emerging — or are about to emerge?	Yes___ No___
5. Do you know who is using the network?	Yes___ No___
6. Do you have instant accessibility of real-time performance data?	Yes___ No___
7. Do you have real-time trending statistics from across the enterprise?	Yes___ No___
8. Do you have reliable access to critical information for making business decisions?	Yes___ No___
9. Are you able to identify over/underutilized resources?	Yes___ No___
10. Can you spot trouble before it starts?	Yes___ No___
11. Are you able to plan your network's growth with accurate useable information?	Yes___ No___
12. Can you see, analyze, and baseline all ports on all routers, hubs, and switches?	Yes___ No___
13. Can you provide management with the network reports it wants?	Yes___ No___

write applications to enhance the system, and maintain the system. As a result, organizations often resort to reacting to network performance problems rather than proactively managing the network's performance.

Exhibit 36-1 should be used to evaluate the current state of performance management within an organization.

PROACTIVE PERFORMANCE MANAGEMENT

The goal of proactive performance management is to ensure that SLAs are being met and will continue to be met. To accomplish this goal, it is necessary to identify current and potential bottlenecks, inefficient or poorly performing components, and potential failures. Proactive performance management is the gathering of statistical data for monitoring and correcting the operation and measuring the overall effectiveness of the network, as well as aiding in the network planning and analysis process. Performance management is not performed in a vacuum, however. It must be integrated with other network management functions, like fault management and event correlation, to be maximally effective. Performance and fault management should be tightly integrated to ensure NMS and operations staff are aware of potential errors or trends that could impact client services.

Performance management involves establishing a set of performance objectives for resources and addressing the following steps:

1. *Monitoring:* tracks resource and communication activities in order to gather the appropriate data for determining performance.
2. *Thresholding:* sets and modifies the operational standards (e.g., threshold values) by which the system performance is monitored and judged.
3. *Reporting:* involves the presentation of gathered data.
4. *Analyzing and trending:* consists of trending and statistical analysis, which *was* performed by network operators and planners to assess the results of performance measures. New software systems now do this for you.
5. *Modeling:* imports performance data to predict where additional resources will be required to meet SLAs, and to understand what impact a new application will have on current resources.
6. *Tuning:* focuses on the adjustment or reconfiguration of resources and communications activities to improve performance.

Exhibit 36-2 illustrates the relationships between these various activities, and the key interaction between performance management steps and fault management.

Exhibit 36-3 lists the required elements of a proactive performance management system or set of systems.

DEVELOPING A BASELINE

In order to begin a process of enhancing the performance management capabilities of an organization, one must begin with a baseline. With today's technology, few problems are caused by equipment failure. Most are caused by the increasing demands being placed on large and complex networks. To get a jump on these problems, one needs a comprehensive picture of the network that can be used for the analysis and modeling efforts that are part of any ongoing network design task.

One must have a baseline of past activity by which to judge present and future performance. With a baseline established, network hot spots can be acted on quickly or can be predicted and prevented altogether. Developing a baseline requires the focus on the first three activities in performance management: monitoring, thresholding, and reporting.

Most organizations have implemented products and systems that are already gathering information about network performance. SNMP MIB performance metrics represent specific performance characteristics of network elements. SNMP MIB attributes are periodically polled and trend data is collected over a period of time. Some metrics are requested on a demand-only basis, while others are collected only when an alarm condition exists on the network. Networks contain a wealth of information in their SNMP MIBs and Remote Monitoring (RMON) data. However, collecting and

Proactive Performance Management

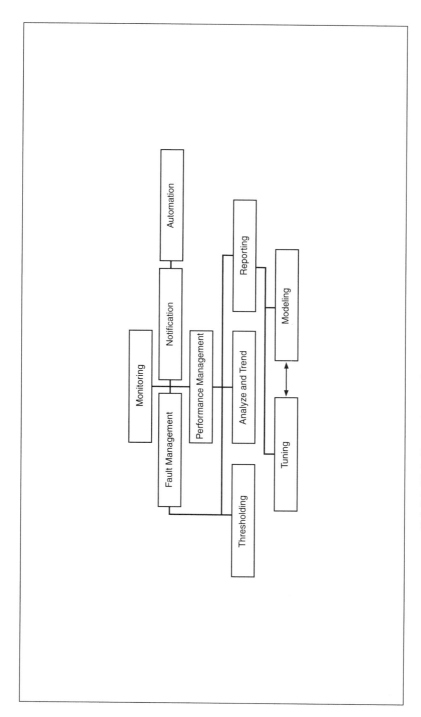

Exhibit 36-2. Proactive performance management activities.

493

Exhibit 36-3. Required elements of a proactive performance management system.

Required Elements	Benefits
Monitor hardware, software, remote links, and systems	Enables shift from reactive to *proactive* network performance management
24 × 7 collection of SNMP and RMON statistics	Enables staff to quantify network performance; improves understanding of network health and performance
Automatic notification of performance alerts	Increases end-user satisfaction and productivity; avoids additional headcount and capital expenditures
Predictive trend analysis	Predicts when next trouble spots will occur and identifies cause; solves problems before they impact network service levels
Daily reports and reviews of network performance trends and capacity trends	Enables true proactive management; provides necessary factual data and frees up IT personnel to focus on more strategic objectives

analyzing the data can be an arduous, resource-intensive process. The development of a network baseline should pull together the relevant SNMP and RMON data that are indicators of network performance. Exhibit 36-4 illustrates these indicators.

Resource availability statistics, derived from the fault management system, are the actual measure of the accessibility of a network resource when compared to the time the resource should be available. It must be noted that there is a clear distinction between reliability and availability. Reliability is the measure of the network's ability to function without failure. Availability is the measure of the network's ability to serve the purpose for which it was installed (from the user perspective). Availability depends on the reliability of the network, as well as the efficiency of the network control staff to restore services after a failure. As noted previously, clients will primarily be concerned with service availability, whereas the network control center will also be concerned with actual component reliability.

Exhibit 36-4. Indicators of network performance.

Network	Resource Availability	Quality of Service	Capacity	Utilization
Physical	Link status	Disrupted seconds %	Bandwidth	Bandwidth usage %
Routing	Device/interface status	Packets dropped %	Packets per second	Packet per second %
LAN (Ethernet, Token Ring)	Status	Error packets	Bandwidth	Bandwidth usage %

- *Quality of service* is the measure of service delivery in terms of number of errors, packets or circuits dropped, etc.
- *Capacity* or *throughput* is the measure of the network size and can be measured in terms of bandwidth, number of WAN links in the physical layer, or packet processing speed in the routing layer.
- *Utilization* is the measure of the actual use of a resource when compared to its theoretical throughput.

Once the appropriate monitoring is set in place, thresholding allows network technicians to monitor, identify, analyze, and react to changes in system and network performance. When conditions occur that cause monitored parameters to fall outside of predetermined thresholds, the management system can be set to trigger alarms or monitor and report changes in system status. For each indicator of interest, thresholds must be carefully selected. Thresholds that are too rigid will result in frequent alarms, while thresholds that are too relaxed can result in performance degradation that may be overlooked by support personnel. In the development of a baseline, thresholds can identify current hot spots and potential problems.

The final step in developing a network baseline is the development of pertinent reports for communication to various constituents. This then becomes an ongoing process, particularly with new tools that allow the easy publishing of the information via corporate intranets. Performance and capacity reports can be generated using a variety of reporting tools. These tools provide an automated process to easily summarize SNMP MIB element data that has been collected from network objects. The reporting features of these tools allow for report generation as well as immediate online viewing of the data.

Performance reports are useful to clients, the network operations staff, and the network systems planning group. These reports will provide the vehicle to assist network planners in preventing future outages and drops below the minimum service level agreements (SLAs), as well as allowing sufficient time for the network system planning to provide necessary network resources for the future. An excellent medium for providing personnel with reports is via HTML Web pages over the corporate intranet. Performance problems may be due to inadequate resources (e.g., bandwidth), inefficient processes (e.g., unnecessary encapsulation of protocols), or an inefficiently used resource (e.g., excessive noise on a circuit requiring retransmission). Some sample performance and capacity reports are described below.

- *Resource availability report:* The minimum/average/maximum availability of the network resource reported for a day/week/month; 99.91 percent availability over a period of time

- *Resource maintainability report:* the mean time to repair (MTTR) for the network resource
- *Resource failure report:* the number of resources reported to be unavailable for more than "n" time

Online Utilization Reports

The following reports can be provided online to the user community:

- LAN utilization
- interface utilization statistics
- environmental reporting

Automated Trend Analysis

A statistical analysis is needed for graphs of collected data. The analysis could contain a description of the data's behavior, including any trends. It may contain an opinion with a recommendation to change. It can provide the statistics derived from the data for those who like such numbers. The enclosed statistics should include data set minimum, maximum, average, standard deviation, and linear regression parameters. For example, the bandwidth utilization graph with an analysis tells one if the usage trend is increasing to the point of degraded performance. If so, it will predict a theoretical date that performance will hit 100 percent and it will advise one to upgrade the bandwidth speed. Separate advice should be provided to accommodate serial links, Ethernet, and Token Ring. However, if bandwidth utilization is normal, it should tell one that. All this information allows one to predict when upgrades will be required, if needed, rather than passively wait for some device to fail due to saturation.

Trouble Ticket Reports

Clients need to have confidence that their trouble ticket report is seriously considered as a source of identifying and attacking the problems that they are encountering. They also need to know who is handling their problem, that the problem is understood from their perspective, some projected time frame when can it be resolved, and when the problem is considered resolved by the management system. Some trouble ticket reports will be generated by conditions within the network system itself and routed to operations prior to client reports. In many cases, problems will be resolved automatically as they occur or prior to client reporting.

Reports issued for user feedback should include the following:

- number of complaints by region, system, and user group
- number of trouble tickets generated by region, system, and user group
- number of trouble tickets resolved daily, weekly, and monthly
- average time to resolve trouble ticket per category

- ratio of trouble tickets per category
- ratio of resolution per category
- types and numbers of recurring trouble tickets by region, system, and user group

A PROACTIVE PLAN

Network systems planning is the process of using historical operating data, as well as estimated future resource requirements, to determine the optimal design of the network. The ultimate goal of network systems planning is to make optimal use of network resources to ensure network services are provided at a level necessary to meet client demands and SLAs while maintaining cost-effectiveness.

An extremely important aspect of network system planning is network optimization. Optimization involves balancing the efficient use of network resources, client requirements, and costs. Effective network optimization requires a detailed understanding of the following areas:

- client business requirements
- client priorities (i.e., response time vs. availability)
- disaster recovery requirements
- network protocols (WIN NT, TCP/IP, AppleTalk)
- transmission methods and media (analog, digital, fiber, copper, microwave)
- comparison of vendor-provided services vs. in-house supported services
- application design and implementation
- component capacity and throughput (client systems as well as switches)
- component compatibility
- industry trends
- available technology and future directions
- standards efforts
- network metrics/indicators and their interpretation
- network modeling
- costs and return on investment (ROI)

The importance of having a planning group that understands all of the above items and their interrelationships cannot be overstated. A network design omitting even one of these items could result in undesirable consequences.

Input to the planning process can come from any area of network management. Specifically, these can include, but are not limited to:

- performance reports
- trouble ticket reports

- component configuration
- client resource usage estimates
- security requirements
- costs

Component configuration refers to understanding the limitations of each component in the network with regard to capacity as well as physical limitations (number of available slots, power requirements, environmental limitations, etc.). In addition, planners must be aware of future changes to vendor-supplied components such as incompatible hardware upgrades or software that will no longer be supported.

The most difficult piece of planning data to gather is an accurate list of future client resource requirements. In many cases, end users may not have the technical skills or tools to estimate network resource requirements.

This process of optimizing the network design as performed in the network systems planning function is a key to turning the performance management function from being reactive to being proactive. This is the critical function that will allow organizations to prevent problems from occurring. By utilizing the reports generated from the monitoring and thresholding activities, potential bottlenecks can be identified and the resolution of those bottlenecks can be set in place before they hamper network performance.

SUMMARY

Today's networks are becoming very critical and very visible elements in the day-to-day operation of a business. The complexity of these networks will continue to grow as the demands on them increase over time. Network performance management is an essential component of an overall strategy for these new networks. If you are a bank and your customers become frustrated with your home banking service because of network bottlenecks and long response times, they will find somewhere else to bank. It is that easy.

Today, many organizations are forced into reacting to performance issues rather than anticipating them. Often, they simply throw bandwidth at the problem although a bottleneck is caused by overutilization of a device, system, or component. Putting in place a proactive performance management system that assists in identifying current and future trouble spots will be key to the organization's ability to respond to new demands on the network.

Section V
Migration Considerations

ONE OF THE MORE OFTEN OVERLOOKED AREAS in the network design process is the manner by which one transitions one network environment to another. Often referred to as migration, this important topic is the focus of this section.

In this section are chapters covering both general and specific migration topics. In Chapter 37, author Eileen Birge's chapter titled **Moving the IT Workforce to a Client/Server Environment** examines the issues involved in transforming a current mainframe environment and operations staff to a client/server environment. In this chapter, Birge reviews such important areas as position descriptions of employees, skill and performance levels, mapping of positions, and the development of training plans. Although many readers represent organizations that long ago moved from a mainframe environment, the information presented in this chapter can be extremely useful in developing a checklist of items to consider when migrating to a new environment.

Chapter 38 focuses on a specific area of migration. In this chapter, titled **Selecting and Deploying E-mail Migration Tools and Utilities,** author Sven James first describes in detail the planning process for a successful migration. Once this is accomplished, James discusses the features one should consider in using e-mail migration tools and includes a list of vendors to consider to include the legacy e-mail systems they can transfer.

Chapters 39 through 41 focus on the migration of System Network Architecture (SNA) to IP and frame relay. Because IBM and IBM-compatible mainframe networks currently operate 60,000 SNA networks, the migration process can be expected to continue for many years. Thus, although these chapters are very specific, their usefulness can be expected to continue well into the future.

In Chapter 39, **Gracefully Transitioning from SNA to IP: Why, How, and When?** author Anura Gurugé covers how an organization can retain its mainframe as a participant on a TCP/IP network. In this chapter, Gurugé reviews the rationale for upgrading IBM mainframes to a TCP/IP environment and discusses the technology to do so. Chapters 40 and 41 focus on migrating SNA to frame relay. In Chapter 40, titled **Transporting Legacy SNA Traffic over Frame Relay,** author Andres Llana first provides the rationale for migrating to frame relay. In this chapter, the author briefly describes the rationale for using frame relay as a transport mechanism for SNA. Once this is accomplished, the author describes how SNA traffic is carried across frame relay. In doing so, Llana examines the efficiencies frame relay provides when transporting SNA and includes coverage of the use of frame relay for accessing an AS/400 network. In Chapter 41, author Dick Thunen provides additional information concerning the use of frame relay to transport SNA. In this chapter, titled **SNA over Frame Relay,** Thunen adds coverage of network management issues to include frame relay's Local Management Interface (LMI) and the Single Network Management Protocol (SNMP).

The concluding chapter in this section was selected for inclusion due to its comprehensive list of planning items that are critical for a successful migration. In Chapter 42, author Thomas Osha's chapter **Planning a Cutover to a New Voice System** provides a most comprehensive list of functions to consider. Although this chapter is oriented toward the cutover to a new voice system, the author provides an extensive list of tasks that illustrate that any cutover represents a considerable planning process. In addition, Osha includes a timeline that illustrates the use of this planning tool, which is applicable for any cutover one may plan. Other items listed in this chapter include sizing equipment locations, determining electrical requirements, flooring requirements, and even consideration of environmental concerns. This extensive list of items to consider makes this a valuable chapter to read regardless of the type of cutover one's organization is planning.

Chapter 37
Moving the IT Workforce to a Client/Server Environment

Eileen Birge

TRANSFORMING CURRENT MAINFRAME DEVELOPMENT and operations staff to a client/server environment is an intensive process. During the first year of the move to client/server technology, the IS department makes critical decisions — decisions that will affect the systems development and operating environments for years to come.

GAINING COMMITMENT FOR STAFF RETRAINING

Companies have taken several approaches to acquiring client/server skills:

- laying off existing resources and hiring personnel with the new skills
- using systems integrators to develop the initial applications and transferring knowledge to the current staff
- independently retraining the current staff and hiring (or contracting for) a minimum number of new skill resources

Recruiting fees, reduced productivity while learning the organization's structure, culture and products, management time to recruit and interview, and high turnover from a workforce with limited company loyalty are just a few of the costs associated with replacing current employees.

Most companies moving to client/server have looked at the costs and the benefits of transforming their current staff and elected to retrain and retain. What are the benefits of retaining?

- *Employee loyalty.* Systems work often requires extra effort. Employees who recognize the investment the company has made in them will respond appropriately.
- *Retention of knowledge.* This includes retention of knowledge about the company and its values.
- *Knowledge of systems development process, audit trails, security, and controls.* Many of the skills associated with good development are not specifically technology related. It is usually less expensive to retain these skills and add the technology component than to buy pure technology knowledge and build development skills.

One research company has estimated the cost of retraining for a standard 200-person department at $5.5 million. Management must thoroughly understand that transformation is a process and that not all benefits of the new technology will be realized in the first few months. This whole project should be treated as a major capital expenditure with the same types of approvals and reviews that a company would give to a capital project of this magnitude.

MAKING THE PARTNERING DECISION

Early in the transformation process, the organization must determine the extent of involvement of outside resources. At one end of the spectrum is a partnership arrangement where the experienced outside resource has a long-term commitment throughout the process and provides or contracts for nearly all services. At the other extreme, an organization uses outside resources only in a limited manner, with an internal commitment to do it themselves, rather than use outsiders (i.e., make rather than buy) whenever possible. Regardless of the choice, the approach to a partnering decision should be articulated at the beginning. If the organization chooses significant partner involvement, time and effort should be spent in choosing the partner carefully. Key items to look for include the following:

- *Depth of commitment.* Does the prospect practice internally the methods, technologies, and organizational behavior of interest to the organization?
- *Corporate culture.* Is the prospect's culture one with which the organization feels comfortable?
- *Flexibility.* Will the prospect truly study the organization, or is the prospect wedded to one approach and ready to advocate that solution? For example, do they sell one particular vendor's products or only sell their own proprietary approach?
- *Track record.* How has the prospect performed in assisting other companies?
- *Risk acceptance.* Is the prospect willing to tie financial reward to successful outcomes?

CREATING AN ATMOSPHERE OF CHANGE

There is an anecdote on change. The chair of a meeting says: "Change is good. Change is exciting. Let the change begin." Meanwhile all the meeting participants are thinking: "Who's getting fired?" If this anecdote represents thinking of the organization to be transformed, attitudes must be adjusted before proceeding.

The process of creating the right atmosphere for change is a major project in itself and beyond the scope of this chapter. Key points for creating this atmosphere, however, include the following:

- allowing room for participation
- leaving choices
- providing a clear picture
- sharing information
- taking a small step first
- minimizing surprises
- allowing for digestion
- demonstrating IS management commitment repeatedly
- making standards and requirements clear
- offering positive reinforcement
- looking for and rewarding pioneers
- compensating extra time and energy
- avoiding creating obvious losers
- creating excitement about the future

ESTABLISHING THE VISION OF THE IS GROUP OF THE FUTURE

The Vision Statement

What will be the role of IS in the future of the organization? How will success be measured? Are the mission and strategy of the IS department in concert with that of the organization as a whole? Regardless of how client/server technology is implemented, it will be a major financial commitment. Before that commitment is made, the role of IS should be reexamined and optimal use of financial resources ensured.

A Functional Organization Chart for the IS Department

The current organization probably reflects many assumptions from mainframe technology roots, with offshoots reflective of the growth of LAN technology. For the transition to client/server to be effective, an organization must do more than merely layer technology onto the existing organization. A sample new functional client/server-legacy organization chart is shown in Exhibit 37-1.

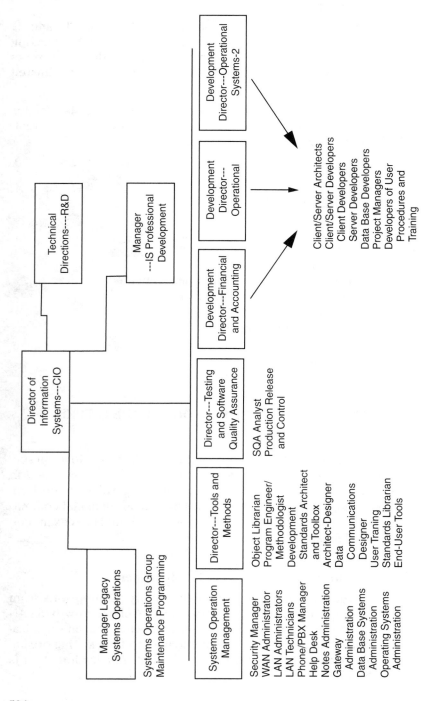

Exhibit 37-1. Sample functional client/server legacy organization chart.

The sample organization emphasizes tools and methods. The client/ server environment can be an intensively productive environment — some companies have reported throughput improvements of two to four times in the effort to design and implement systems, with similar increases in user satisfaction. Companies can only realize these gains when the developers have an understanding of the tools they are to use, the design guidelines to follow, database standards, and version control procedures, among other issues. It is also important to note the position of Manager, IS Professional Development, in the exhibit. Transitioning the staff, updating the plan, tracking progress, and managing a multimillion dollar budget requires full-time commitment.

Position Descriptions for the Future Department

IS managers should create a picture of what their staff will be doing in the not-so-distant future. To create the transformation plan, they must know where they are going. They should write descriptions that are as clear as possible, giving serious thought to how performance will be measured for each item on the position description (a sample is included in Exhibit 37-2). Managers should make a preliminary estimate of how many of each type of skill set they will need. They should focus on what the person in the position will be doing as opposed to the place in the organizational hierarchy.

In developing position descriptions and estimated staffing quantities, IS managers should consider the following:

- Client/server development teams should be kept as small as possible. Teams of five to seven are optimal, eight to ten are manageable.
- A development team requires a full-time manager, three to four developers, a part-time or full-time database analyst, a part-time or full-time client/server architect, and (in the later stages of the project) a full-time user procedure analyst/training specialist. (If the project affects a large number of users and has a significant training component, these metrics do not apply. The project to design and deliver the training material may dwarf the systems project.) One architect and one database analyst can be assumed for eight developers.
- Client/server developers work with users to identify requirements, reengineer processes, design, code, and test. Development methodologies in this environment are most effective when they stress iterative prototyping and refinement. For optimal efficiency, the roles of analyst and programmer should not be separated.
- A client/server architect works with members of the tools and methods group to set up development environments and to identify components of production environments. If a production environment will involve use of previously untested products or new releases of products, the

Exhibit 37-2. Sample position description: Client/Server Developer.

COMPANY ABC
POSITION DESCRIPTION

Date: 8/1/98   Position Title: Client/Server Developer

Primary Function

Develop and maintain ABC business applications.

General Description of Work Performed

1. Design logical databases using ABC development platforms.
2. Work with data administration staff to implement and tune databases.
3. Conduct and record facilitated joint application sessions.
4. Lead prototyping sessions and implement user requests.
5. Interview users and document user requirements.
6. Create detailed program specification packages and test plans.
7. Code and unit test programs.
8. Create and implement systems test plans.
9. Implement conversion plans.
10. Provide quality assurance testing of programs coded by others.
11. Create systems documentation.
12. Design and implement user interfaces in compliance with CUA and ABC standards.
13. Provide user support on ABC business applications.
14. Provide assistance to user procedure/training analysts in the development of user training and documentation manuals.
15. Interview and assist in the recruiting of S professional staff.
16. Participate in staff and status meetings.

Key Measures of Success

1. Customer satisfaction with usability and quality of delivered software.
2. Programming accuracy and completeness.
3. Timely completion of assigned tasks.
4. Compliance with ABC design and development standards.
5. Customer and project manager assessment of ability to function successfully as a member of a team.

Education and Experience

BA or BS in Computer Science or Business Degree with IS minor
2 years development experience
ABC's Client/Server Technology Series
Organizational development training (as specified by Human Resources)

---

architect tests the technical architecture before significant development efforts are expended.

- The tools and methods group can be highly leveraged. One tool builder-designer should be assumed for each 50 developers-architects-analysts.

- If software is being developed for internal use only, one tester should be assumed for every two developers.
- One LAN administrator should be assumed for every 200 users and one groupware administrator for every 400 users. Growth in management tools should reduce staffing requirements over time.

This is an area where most organizations look to consultants for assistance — both for identifying the responsibilities and to work with human resources to determine the impact on pay scales and incentive plans.

Skills and Performance Needed

In the preceding step, responsibilities and work performed were defined by each position. In this step, they are translated into the types of skills and levels of proficiency required. For example, a client/server developer position description may include some of the following responsibilities:

- interviewing users and documenting user requirements
- preparing logical data models
- preparing unit-test plans and executing plans
- managing own time against task deadlines

Those responsibilities can then be translated into skills. Interviewing users requires the following:

- interviewing techniques
- effective listening
- interview planning

Documenting user requirements requires:

- effective writing skills
- understanding of the selected methodology and associated documentation techniques

It is tempting to declare that all staff be expert in all skills required for their positions, but that is both unrealistic and unaffordable. It is necessary to identify the minimal skill level needed to perform in the position in a satisfactory manner.

The translation of job responsibilities into skills requirements is difficult. Doing this job well, however, has a tremendous payoff. It affects the evaluation process and has a dramatic effect on explaining the role of training and staff development to senior management. It focuses the workforce. Setting the expected skill levels assists staff in planning their own self-study activities.

Hiring and Arranging for Skills from the Outside

At this stage, IS managers should have an initial feel for the skills that are likely candidates for acquisition from new hires or consultants. They should start the process for acquiring these skills now so that the candidates will be on board when they are ready to start implementing the plan. The hiring and acquisition process will continue at the same time as the next seven steps.

CREATING THE PLAN

After establishing the environment needed for success and also establishing the vision of the IS group of the future, companies are ready to tackle the nuts and bolts of the transformation to a client/server environment.

Mapping Current Staff to Future Positions

For this task, managers must look at their current organization and personnel and attempt to fit the individuals and positions into their future roles. During the mapping operation, interests and individuals should be matched rather than it being assumed that programmers will become client/server developers. All staff members should have access to materials developed so far. The position descriptions help staff identify what roles they believe are most suited to their own abilities.

How do managers decide who is best suited to be a client/server developer? A client/server architect? No fixed rules exist, but there are some guidelines. The client/server architect will typically be more technical than his or her developer counterparts. The architect usually has less user involvement and interacts more with the development team. Managers should look for persons and development positions that focus on the technical vs. the functional aspects of the work.

Aptitude should be considered. One report concluded that 26 percent of existing mainframe personnel could not be converted to client/server. In other experiences, this figure has been closer to 35 percent. These persons are clearly the candidates to maintain legacy systems during a transition period.

Skills Analysis

The positions of the future and the skills they require have been identified. The probable candidates for each position have also been identified. In this step, managers identify what skills the candidates already have to avoid wasting training dollars.

A skills assessment document should be prepared. The document asks individuals to rate themselves as 0 (no knowledge), 1 (conceptual), and so forth. Guidelines are given so that the staff understands the indicators for these levels. Guidelines are not meant to be all-inclusive (i.e., the guidelines should help individuals assess themselves, not delineate the total knowledge requirements for that level).

First, each staff member should self-assess without knowledge of the suggested skill levels for the proposed positions. Next, an independent party should assess each individual. Managers should meet with the staff member to discuss any significant variations between the self-assessment and the independent assessment. The final, agreed-upon skill level should be documented.

The manager responsible for implementing the transition plan now has a picture of each individual: current skills, current skill levels, and the target skills and levels needed to perform in the future. Managers must analyze and summarize to develop the profile of the typical staff person slotted for any position for which six or more staff will be assigned. These positions may include: project managers, client/server developers, database administrators, client/server architects, LAN administrators, and software quality assurance testers. For such positions as WAN administrator or object librarian, plans can be tailored to individual needs. Little benefit will be gained from summarization because there will be only a few candidates for each position.

The Training or Job Assignment Plan

Armed with the profile of typical current skill levels and the target skill levels, a training assignment plan designed to raise skill levels to the targets can be created. The following rules apply:

- Training alone cannot create level 3 (works independently) or level 4 (expert) personnel. Although training often only creates a level 1 (conceptual understanding) rating, effective training can create a level 2 (works under supervision) rating. Training also helps level 3 and 4 performers maintain currency in their skills.
- Within two months after training and using a major new tool on a daily basis, productivity should be at 50 percent of target. By six months, productivity should be at 100 percent (and skill level should be at 3).
- Training not followed quickly by job-reinforcing experience is wasted.

Given these rules, it is helpful to look at a sample training or assignment plan for an organization's first group of client/server developers.

1. *Form a team of six to eight people.* Provide a high-level description of the system to be implemented (people learn best when they can relate the knowledge to what they need to know — so as they take classes, they can relate the concepts taught to the system they will work on). Plan on training the team together.

2. *Provide initial technology awareness training and needed soft skills training in the following areas:*
   - client/server and LAN basics (e.g., terminology and theory)
   - client and server operating systems
   - office suite productivity training (e.g., for word processors, spreadsheets, and graphics tools — tailored to the documentation and probable uses)
   - data analysis and documentation tool (relational or object oriented)
   - effective listening and writing
   - methodology orientation
   - facilitation (developers only)
   - LAN administration (LAN administrators only)

3. *Assign the first job.* The first job assignment within the department should not be a mission-critical system nor have a deadline that is critical to success. One company elected to make its first client/server implementation a companywide budgeting system, to be delivered in September to coincide with the beginning of the annual budget cycle. Not surprisingly, the system failed to make the deadline: everyone in the company knew and IS's judgment was seriously questioned. Preferably, the project should have some kind of high impact when delivered so that the first client/server application helps fuel the excitement about the change to this architecture. The assignment should be sufficiently complex to test most aspects of the technical architecture and reinforce the needed technical skills.

   Plan to have this team conduct the initial user-requirements definition — using the data design tool, methodology, and writing techniques. The LAN administrators should set up the development environment and productivity tools.

4. *Provide second-level training after the requirements.* Typically, the developers and architects will need training in user-interface design, the specific development tool, and prototyping. The architect may require additional training on the components of the technical architecture assumed for use in this application. Other members of the team may require training in database administration and performance tuning.

5. *Build prototypes and the technical architecture.* Plan to have the team return to the project and conduct prototyping sessions with the user. Critical functional ability and performance features should be developed to the point where the technical architecture can be tested and modified, if necessary.

6. *Complete the system.* Integrate the completion with methodology training appropriate for the project phase.

An Infrastructure to Manage the Plan

With a 200+ person department, a three-year plan, dozens of vendors, more than 2,500 person-skill combinations, as much as $2 million in hard costs to budget, classrooms to equip and schedule, and as many as 300 official and unofficial training courses to track, management is a challenge. For the typical Fortune 1,000 company, executing this plan requires a full-time commitment and appropriate systems support.

TESTING AND EXECUTING THE PLAN

Testing and Refining the Plan

A plan has already been developed for the first team. Now, the plan must be executed. The manager responsible for all professional development should participate in as much of the training as possible to observe the participants and the material. Participants should be debriefed after each training session to determine strengths and weaknesses. Participants should also be interviewed at intervals after the training to find out what worked and what did not. The project managers can help determine how job-ready the participants were after returning from training. The suggestions from the first project team should be incorporated into the training plan.

Executing the Plan with the Remaining Staff

The remaining staff should be scheduled into the refined training plan. Again, the mode of training development teams together should be followed once a project has been identified. It should be assumed that a new group can be started through the process every four to eight weeks. The schedule should be modified to reflect current assignments.

Refining the Training Plan

Feedback should be collected from system users regarding satisfaction levels. Additional feedback can be obtained from staff going through the plan and incorporated into the plan on a continuing basis. Staff who went through the training earlier may need refresher or catch-up topics to reflect new thinking or new technology. The plan should be verified at least quarterly with the group responsible for technology to update tools and architecture information.

Incorporating Continuing Change and Development into the Culture

The environment will continue to change. Business and strategies will change faster. It is important for the IS staff to realize that the transformation process will never end. At least semi-annually, each staff member should reassess current skill levels, create new targets for performance, and identify the combinations of job experience, self-development, and formal training needed to achieve those skills. Preferably, achievement of skill development goals should be a component of the bonus or raise process.

CONCLUSION

As can be seen, moving a staff to client/server is just like most systems projects: Managers must determine what they want, refine the requirements, create a plan to implement the requirements, and then test and refine the plan. What seems to be a monumental task can be broken down into manageable and measurable steps; see Exhibit 37-3 for a review of the steps and Exhibit 37-4 for a Gantt chart depicting their timeline.

Exhibit 37-3. Major tasks in moving to a client/server environment.

1. Establishing the environment needed for success, including
   - Making the partnering decision.
   - Establishing the technical architecture and operating environment.
   - Gaining management commitment to the staff transformation approach. Creating an atmosphere of change.
2. Establishing the vision of the IS group of the future, including
   - Creating a vision statement for IS.
   - Creating an organization chart for the EUC department in the future.
   - Creating position descriptions for the future department.
   - Identifying the skills and performance levels that will be needed.
3. Creating the plan, including
   - Making a preliminary cap of current personnel to future positions.
   - Performing a skills analysis
   - Determining which skills must be acquired vs. built.
   - Creating a training and job assignment plan.
   - Creating an infrastructure to help manage the plan.
   - Initiating hiring or arranging for skills from the outside.
4. Testing and executing the plan, including
   - Testing the plan.
   - Executing the plan with the remaining staff.
   - Evaluating and refining the training plan.
   - Incorporating continuing change and development into the culture.

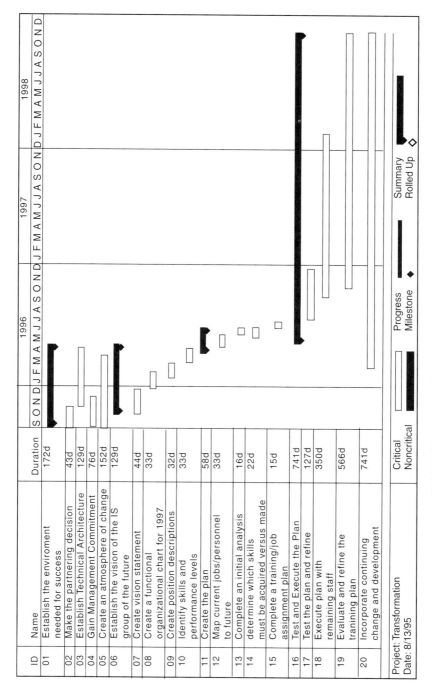

Exhibit 37-4. Gantt Chart for transformation process.

Chapter 38
Selecting and Deploying E-Mail Migration Tools and Utilities

Sven James

DURING THE PAST THREE YEARS, a revolution within the corporate world has taken place. Companies started implementing Lotus Notes and Microsoft Exchange. Due to the sheer marketshare that these two products have captured, new companies have been born, or reinvented, and have dedicated themselves to creating products and services specifically geared toward automating the process of migrating from any other e-mail system to Notes or Exchange. This chapter discusses customer requirements for e-mail migration tools and utilities and goes on to describe features and functionality of products currently available on the market.

The marketplace for e-mail migration tools and utilities is young even compared to today's quickly evolving e-mail systems. E-mail migration tools have only been around a couple of years; however, these tools are having an impact far beyond what has, up to this point, been the definition of tools and utilities. E-mail migration has seen the birth of full-blown migration and coexistence applications that can be integrated into today's most popular messaging systems.

CUSTOMER REQUIREMENTS FOR MIGRATION AND COEXISTENCE

Customer requirements for migration and coexistence are simple: "Move my user data, synchronize my directories and data, allow everyone to send and receive from and to all other systems, and yes, automate it so that it requires no additional personnel or resources."

Migration tools and utilities can be configured to do all of the above. However, before starting to think about the tool, it is very important to consider what you want to do and the order in which you want to do it. Small shops (less than 1,000 users) may be in the position of being able to migrate their mail over a weekend. However, the rest of the corporate world must function with "e-mail system coexistence." Coexistence is the act of two or more e-mail systems exchanging data in a manner seamless to the user. Since most shops will be in coexistence mode, this chapter is written for them. Users that have the luxury of a straight migration can ignore all the coexistence steps and just move their users. Aren't they lucky!

MIGRATION AND COEXISTENCE PLANNING — BEFORE THE TOOLS AND UTILITIES

Before describing the various data-types, functions, and features of migration tools and utilities it is very important that your company have a migration and coexistence plan. Entire books are becoming available on enterprise migration planning and the reason is simple. Migration and coexistence needs to be carefully planned and implemented.

The following is an overview of just some of the issues, and answers that your company should address prior to actually implementing the migration and coexistence process:

- Create a messaging topology that reflects your e-mail system:
    - Today — as it really exists today
    - Tomorrow — a picture of the e-mail environment to which you are migrating
    - Reality/Interim — a picture of what your e-mail environment will really look like during the coexistence period
- Moving the data is a necessity: would you really move offices without taking your filing cabinet?
- Prepare for user migration and use migration as a training aid.
- Who is going to move? In what order? Who moves first?
- Determine the data-types that are business critical (i.e., directory, in-baskets, file folders, archives, bulletin boards, etc.).
- Determine what data you can migrate and what data must be synchronized.
- Determine migration schedule.
- Determine which tools and utilities can automate the process to fulfill your plan.

THE DIRECTORY

The prerequisite for any migration tool or utility is the directory. A directory must exist on the legacy e-mail system, and a directory must be created or synchronized with on the new e-mail system.

Your company will be in one of two positions:

1. You will either have a messaging switch (hub) with directory syn-chronization already in place, which means that you have a great head start on the rest of the corporate world, or,
2. You will need to build the directory on the new e-mail system.

An issue to consider when looking for tools is the ability to build names for the new e-mail system based on their rules, yet at the same time using the legacy e-mail addresses as the source for the new directory. It is impor-tant to have a reliable cross-reference of names in each e-mail system. In addition, you will need to match a unique identifier on names across the e-mail systems and the ability of the directory synchronization process to run automatically without manual intervention. Other useful tools include the ability to do a "one-way load" and the ability to load mailing lists from the legacy system into the new e-mail system.

Heads Up! Resolve Duplicate IDs Today!

The number one issue in migrating the directory from the legacy system to Notes or Exchange is resolving duplicate IDs. If you have duplicates now, stop creating them. Go to management and get their buy-in on this as soon as you can. If you have the people-power, start resolving duplicate IDs today so that you can build toward your new corporate directory in the future. Suffice it to say that this one paragraph cannot even begin to resolve your directory issues; however, for migration purposes, most tools and utilities on the market, not to mention your help desk, will have a much easier time if you resolve this issue.

Directory synchronization tools are generally available for migration to Lotus Notes, Microsoft Exchange, and Novell GroupWise from the following legacy e-mail systems. A complete list of migration vendors is contained in Exhibit 38-1.

- OV/400
- OV/VM
- OV/MVS
- Emc2/TAO
- MEMO
- SYSM
- Netscape
- Exchange
- Notes
- CC: Mail
- MS Mail
- All-In-1

Exhibit 38-1. Chart of Migration Tool and Utility Vendors

Company/URL	Legacy E-mail Systems	Destination E-mail System
Altis Limited www.altisltd.com	All-In-1	Notes
Binary Tree www.binarytree.com	MS Mail, Exchange, cc:mail, Schedule+, Organizer	Notes
CompuSven, Inc. www.compusven.com	Emc2/TAO, SYSM, MEMO	Notes, Exchange
www.iga.com	All-In-1	Notes, Exchange
Lotus Development Corp. www.lotus.com	OV/VM, OV/400	Notes
Microsoft Corp. www.microsoft.com	MEMO, AllIn-1, GroupWise, OV/VM, CC:mail	Exchange
Toronto Business Systems www.tbssoft.com	OV/MVS	Notes, Exchange

PRIVATE AND PUBLIC MAIL MIGRATION AND COEXISTENCE

Private mail is usually defined by an individual's in-basket and file folders. Public mail is usually defined as letters in bulletin boards, conferences, and newsgroups.

Private data is usually migrated and public data can both be migrated and then synchronized if the tool or utility is up to the task.

When evaluating e-mail migration tools, look for applications that can be easily integrated into a company's directory synchronization and administrative processes. The reason for this is that one should be able to let the e-mail system know that one wants to migrate a user in a single location. From specifying this in one location, the process should run from there. Lotus Notes R5 has done a superlative job of integrating the migration process in with the administrative interface. Other tools interface with Exchange so that one can define various levels of migration.

Levels of migration might include the ability to migrate mail once a user has his forwarding address changed in the new e-mail system, or it may mean that a user has his mail migrated to the new e-mail system, but still has the ability to logon and use the legacy e-mail system.

Private data features and functions to look for should include:

- Retain "from address:"
  - This ensures that recipients can reply to migrated mail.
  - This is the major advantage of using a migration tool over each user manually forwarding mail.

- Retain original date/time stamp.
- Migration filter (do not migrate) mail older than a specified date. This allows for e-mail system cleanup.

Public data migration is very similar to private data migration, with the only difference being that public data is usually migrated to public databases in Notes, or public folders in Exchange. Again, look for the same features and functions as for private mail.

Public data synchronization can be the key to making migration and coexistence a success. Public data synchronization allows one to migrate a bulletin board, conference, or newsgroup and then keeps them all synchronized. If a user adds a letter to the legacy system, it is automatically (and, ideally, real-time) copied to the new e-mail system. Conversely, should a message be added to a Notes database or Exchange public folder, then that message should be copied to the legacy e-mail system.

One of the world's largest banks uses a legacy e-mail system bulletin board to post daily foreign currency exchange rates. In order for management to buy-in to user migration, they had to get beyond the real business issue of providing the functionality of the new e-mail system without removing access to the data on the legacy system.

GATEWAYS BETWEEN E-MAIL SYSTEMS

One of the very basic needs of coexistence is for mail to flow from the legacy system to Notes, Exchange, the Internet, GroupWise, etc. The past year has seen vendor-specific gateways move from old SNADS-based addressing to open standard SMTP-based gateways. Another phenomenon is the availability of a new type of gateway called a Point-to-Point Gateway.

Gateways do more than just deliver mail from one system to another. They also determine addressing standards and ease of addressing mail from the local e-mail system. For example, e-mail systems that support SMTP addresses may have the SMTP address of firstname.lastname, wherein the firstname.lastname corresponds to a specific Notes Address Book (NAB) or Exchange Global Address List (GAL) entry.

Look for a gateway that will satisfy your needs. Gateways typically interface with your specific e-mail systems and then interface to SMTP, SNADS, or directly to Notes or Exchange. Notes and Exchange now have the ability to become the Messaging Switch. This enhancement (or set of enhancements) will allow customers to move from the older Softwswitch Central, LMS, Linkage, and legacy Exchange type of solutions to gateways that connect directly from one e-mail system to another. This then allows Notes and Exchange to become the hub and the central directory.

Another very important component of a gateway for coexistence is performance. A company may have an e-mail policy or specific service level agreements in place that the gateway needs to meet.

Finally, a gateway, more than any other application, will determine the success or failure of the migration and coexistence process. A migration for a user can be re-run. However, a gateway is an important part of an e-mail system and must be dependable and robust. The support organization behind the vendor is often the key for a gateway's stability since gateways usually have a number of points of failure and the ability, or the support organizations ability, to reduce the points of failure can often make the difference.

FORMS MIGRATION AND CROSS-PLATFORM DISTRIBUTION

Forms migration products come in many shapes and sizes. Most migration products base their ability on what the legacy system forms supported. For those e-mail systems (3270 — green screen) that support limited functionality forms, one will end up with forms that look more like legacy forms rather than the forms in the new e-mail system. The good news here is that there are migration and coexistence utilities that allow cross-platform forms distribution; however, do not look for forms to look exactly as they did in the legacy system. One may find utilities that convert 90 percent of forms. However, forms may require manual updates once they have been migrated.

Look for products that provide the company with the ability to find the forms, convert the forms, distribute forms cross platform, and maintain the basic look and feel of each form.

Forms migration applications are usually limited to flat forms and do not support intelligent workflow style forms. The reason for this is that most intelligent forms contain proprietary (or interpretive) language that would really require a compiler converter, much like converting an application from COBOL to "C."

MIGRATION IS NOT JUST FOR USERS! DO NOT FORGET MAIL ENABLED APPLICATIONS OR APPLICATION PROGRAM INTERFACE (API)

Once one has moved the users, set up directory and data synchronization, and has the gateways working, then one will be on the way to a complete migration. Once the last user is moved, turn off directory synchronization, some of the gateways, and then ... Wait ... Do you have any applications that send mail or access your legacy e-mail systems? If not, go ahead, you can now turn off your legacy e-mail system. Otherwise, you need to look at tools and applications that either re-route the legacy API programs, can be substituted for the legacy API programs, or have the

Exhibit 38-2. Legacy and new e-mail systems.

	Legacy						
	OV/400	OV/VM	OV/MVS	Emc2	SYSM	Exchange	Notes
New: Notes	X	X	X	X		X	
New: Exchange			X	X			X

legacy API programs manually moved from the legacy platform to the new e-mail platform.

Look to the large migration product vendors for this type of product. A prerequisite for this type of application is a good cross-reference of legacy mail IDs and mail IDs in your new e-mail system. Then, depending on the platform (MVS, for example), one can find specific vendors who have the ability to help either re-route the mail from the legacy e-mail system to the new one, or have the ability to actually port the entire application from the legacy platform to the new one.

CALENDAR MIGRATION AND COEXISTENCE

A number of utilities are available for migration and limited cross-platform scheduling. However, of all the data-types, calendaring migration tools have been the last to be developed. There are some migration tools available; however, functionality is limited. Exhibit 38-2 contains a chart of known, generally available calendar migration and cross-platform scheduling products and a list of the legacy and new e-mail systems.

PUTTING IT ALL TOGETHER

Once one has identified all the data-types and components that are required for the company, one is ready to start the migration. There are tools and utilities available that "do it all" and are completely integrated, with service offerings and end-to-end message system expertise. The ideal coexistence application is one that has directory synchronization, a gateway, built-in migration tools, built-in data synchronization, and cross-platform forms ability. Such an application will allow one to install one application and provide a single point of administration. If running more than two or three legacy e-mail systems, one may have to run multiple migration tools and utilities from various vendors.

Chapter 39
Gracefully Transitioning from SNA to IP: Why, How, and When?

Anura Gurugé

WHEN EVALUATING THE MERITS AND IMPLICATIONS OF TRANSITIONING to a TCP/IP-centric IT infrastructure, it helps to reflect on the tale of the Great King Canute of England and Denmark (ca. 1016) who tried to demonstrate to his adoring subjects that there were powers that even he could not control by showing them that he was powerless to stop the tide from coming ashore. Just as was the case with PCs and LANs, TCP/IP is now an unstemmable technological tide; possibly even a tidal wave. Whether one likes it or not, relishes it or fears it, TCP/IP is here to stay — and will dominate worldwide computing for at least the next two decades, thanks to the endorsement and kudos it gets on a daily basis as the sustaining force behind the Internet miracle.

Mainframe shops today cannot claim unfamiliarity with TCP/IP. Without exception, corporations that use mainframes for their MIS now have a TCP/IP-based intranet in addition to their traditional SNA/APPN or multi-protocol-oriented enterprise network. Most, furthermore, already have a presence on the Internet in the form of a home page, and many are actively exploring the possibilities of using the Internet for electronic commerce, customer support, public relations, product promotions, and global remote access. Not missing out on the tantalizing potential of E-commerce over the Internet, next to that of Y2K concerns, is indubitably the most pressing MIS issue that is being discussed at the highest levels of corporations, starting at the board room. In parallel, intranet-to-intranet communications via extranets are being viewed as the most effective means of streamlining and expediting enterprise-to-enterprise transactions. All of this intranet and Internet (i.e., i·net) activity means that TCP/IP is already being widely used alongside mainframe-based computing systems.

Installing TCP/IP on a mainframe these days is not a difficult, nerve-racking, or laborious undertaking. Extensively proven, extremely efficient, highly scalable, and extremely reliable TCP/IP stacks for mainframes are readily available. IBM claims that more than half of the mainframes running MVS or OS/390 already have TCP/IP installed. Installing TCP/IP on a mainframe facilitates its integration with intranets or the Internet; permits fast, high-speed bulk data transfers with TCP/IP clients or other systems; and, moreover, positions it as a data server for Web-based applications. Once TCP/IP is installed, one could, if required, even have the mainframe acting as a high-capacity Web server. There are companies, such as $9.5B Lafayette Life Insurance (Lafayette, Indiana), that already have Web servers running on their mainframes — which in the case of Lafayette happens to be an IBM 9672-R24, 3rd generation CMOS-based S/390 Parallel Enterprise Server.

There are significant strategic and tactical advantages to going ahead and installing TCP/IP on a mainframe and moving toward a TCP/IP-centric computing environment. For a start, it provides a solid basis for any and all E-commerce-related initiatives. It can also reduce, sometimes quite significantly, overall capital and operational costs. For example, the browser-based access to SNA solutions that are now readily available from over 40-odd credible vendors for providing unrestricted SNA terminal access across i·nets, totally eliminate the considerable cost associated with installing, managing, and periodically upgrading SNA/3270 emulation software on each and every PC/workstation that needs access to SNA applications.

Using TCP/IP all the way into the mainframe, and then performing SNA conversion at the mainframe per the tn3270(E) standard, also ensures that one no longer needs highly expensive, SNA-oriented communications controllers like the 3745 or the 3746-950. Instead, one can profitably utilize high-performance, low-cost, channel-attached routers such as the IBM 2216-400, Cisco 7500/CIP, or Cisco 7200/CPA as the means of interconnecting the mainframe to the network. Then there are networking-related cost savings. With a TCP/IP-centric infrastructure, one can, albeit with the appropriate security measures (e.g., firewalls), gainfully use the Internet as a way to realize extremely cost-effective remote access for far-flung remote offices, agents, telecommuters, and overseas distributors. Intranets, given that they are based on widely available commodity technology, are also invariably less costly to implement than comparable SNA/APPN or multiprotocol networks. Exhibit 39-1 illustrates a TCP/IP-centric environment.

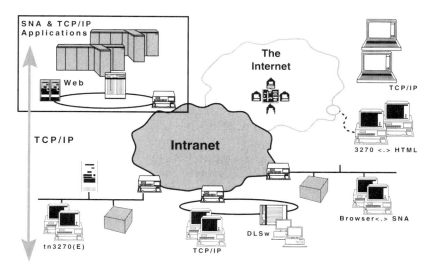

Exhibit 39-1. TCP/IP-Centric Environment. Clients have access to both TCP/IP and SNA resources across an intranet as well as the Internet.

DISPELLING YOUR CONCERNS

Before the advantages of moving to a TCP/IP-centric infrastructure with TCP/IP on the mainframe are articulated any further, it is best to allay any concerns one may have about moving away from SNA.

- Security is no longer the roadblock it used to be with highly proven, bulletproof TCP/IP-specific security solutions for mission-critical commercial computing systems.
- Total unencumbered access to mission-critical SNA/APPN applications running on mainframes or AS/400s is in no way compromised, jeopardized, or even inconvenienced by the installation of TCP/IP on a mainframe and the standardization on a TCP/IP-centric infrastructure. There are a plethora of well-established, standards-based SNA-to-TCP/IP integration technologies, such as tn3270(E) and Data Link Switching (DLSw), that ensure unrestricted SNA access and end-to-end SNA transport across TCP/IP networks.
- Installing TCP/IP on a mainframe and using a TCP/IP-centric i·net for all mainframe access does not prevent one from having ACF/VTAM on that same machine as well. Therefore, one can continue to have the same level of APPN/HPR support that is on one's mainframe today to guarantee that mission-critical SNA/APPN applications will continue to work without any problems.

525

- Today's TCP/IP stacks for mainframes deliver exceptional throughput and are highly optimized to maximize efficiency and scale easily to support tens of thousands of concurrent users. TCP/IP is not the CPU hog that it was portrayed to be a few years ago. Mainframe TCP/IP is so efficient these days that some corporations run, without any difficulty or degradation in overall performance, multiple stacks on the same mainframe to gain added throughput and ensure that different applications (e.g., FTP and tn3270(E)) can each have their own dedicated stack.

- Incisive, sophisticated, and comprehensive TCP/IP-based network, application, TCP/IP-stack, and system management is now possible with mainframe-resident management systems such as Interlink's e-Control. E-Control provides TCP/IP-centric management tools and facilities for problem determination, performance management, change management (i.e., the configuration and administration of mainframe TCP/IP resources), and capacity planning.

- With today's mature router technology, it is now possible to realize TCP/IP-based networks that are sufficiently resilient and robust to provide high-availability networking with uptimes in excess of 98(+) percent. Today's TCP/IP-centric networks are significantly more reliable and stable than the bridge/router-based multiprotocol networks currently used for transporting SNA/APPN traffic.

- Traffic prioritization between different classes of applications vis-à-vis the TCP/IP network is no longer an issue with today's router software offering functions such as Quality of Service (QoS), Bandwidth Reservation Protocol (RSVP), and highly customizable queuing schemes (e.g., Cisco's Custom Queuing). For those few situations where there is a need to support SNA LU 6.2 Class-of-Service (COS) prioritization on an end-to-end basis, IBM offers a scheme known as Enterprise Extender that permits APPN/HPR routing across IP.

- The continued presence of ACF/VTAM on the mainframe alongside TCP/IP ensures total, uncompromised support for parallel sysplex operation — including multi-node persistent sessions (MNPS), workload balancing, and generic resources.

- High-performance, highly efficient, full-duplex TCP/IP transfers across ESCON channels is not a problem with the TCP/IP-specific CLAW protocol that permits two subchannels to be grouped together for high-throughput and simultaneous bidirectional communications. If anything, TCP/IP channel transfers are significantly faster than SNA/APPN transfers with both IBM or Cisco channel-attached solutions such as the IBM 2216-400 and the Cisco 7500/CIP.

- Mainframe-based TCP/IP printing is not an impediment with tn3270(E) now supporting host print, and with products such as Interlink's very comprehensive Enterprise Print Services (EPS).

CASE AGAINST A LAST-MINUTE SNA REVIVAL

Despite the daily mounting evidence to the contrary, there are still some who believe that IBM will not allow SNA/APPN to succumb to IP, and that there will be a concerted attempt to reestablish SNA/APPN-based networking. IBM recognizes that the role SNA/APPN plays in the future will be restricted to the mainframe in the context of mission-critical applications, and that TCP/IP, unassailably, will be the networking fabric of the future. The following four examples alone should convince the reader that IBM is not just reconciled to, but is in reality one of the greatest advocates of, TCP/IP-centric networking.

- In June 1998, IBM announced an ESCON channel-attachment capability for its flagship 12.8Gbps throughput 8265-17S Nways ATM Switch, which can support 622Mbps ATM uplinks. The only protocol supported across this channel attachment is IP.
- In March 1998, IBM discontinued the 2217 Nways Multiprotocol Concentrator, which was an APPN/HPR-based router that permitted TCP/IP, IPX/SPX, and NetBIOS to be routed end-to-end across an SNA network. The 2217 was the antithesis of a conventional TCP/IP-based router. By discontinuing the 2217, IBM tacitly admitted that there was no call or future for IP-over-SNA routing.
- IBM is avidly promoting the notion of APPN/HPR-over-IP routing with its Enterprise Extender technology, which is now available on the IBM 2216, 2212, and 2210. Cisco, Bay/NT, and others are expected to also support this capability. By promoting the notion of routing APPN/HPR-over-IP, which is the exact opposite of the routing scheme employed by the 2217 that IBM discontinued, IBM is making it very clear that the only WAN networking role it sees for APPN/HPR in the future is within the context of it being used on top of IP.
- The IBM 2216-400 can be attached to an IBM 3746 via an expansion chassis known as the Multi-Access Enclosure (MAE). If one only wants to transfer IP traffic into the mainframe, MAE offers a native, high-speed coupling facility between the 2216-400 and the 3746. If one insists on wanting support for SNA, the best that IBM can offer is a dual Token Ring connection between the 2216-400 and the 3746. When factoring this in with the 8265 IP-only channel-attachment scheme discussed above, it becomes clear that IBM is already positioning itself for an era when most of the mainframe channel traffic is IP based.

THE PRIMARY ADVANTAGES OF MOVING TO MAINFRAME IP

- Enables seamless integration of one's fast-growing intranet with one's mainframe, given that at least 70 percent of the corporate data that one's in-house intranet users require is still on a mainframe rather than on a Web server, NT server, or UNIX system.

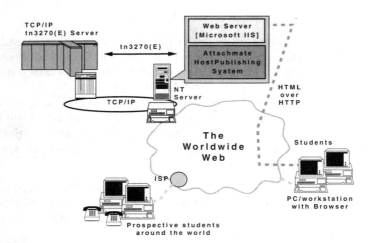

Exhibit 39-2. Ohio State University diagram. Existing and prospective students are provided with access to mainframe-resident SNA applications over the Web using a totally TCP/IP-centric infrastructure, including TCP/IP and tn3270(E) server on the mainframe.

- Decisively positions one to exploit all the rich potential of E-commerce over the Internet by ensuring that all of the applications and data one may require to enable such commerce is now TCP/IP-ready and can be easily integrated with the necessary Web technology. Business-to-business E-commerce over the Internet is expected to be in excess of $30B by the year 2002.

- Permits one to exploit the Internet as an extremely low-cost means of realizing global remote access to mainframe applications including all mission-critical SNA applications, as shown in Exhibits 39-2 and 39-3. In addition to browser-based access, extremely secure Virtual Private Networking (VPN) solutions — such as those provided by Interlink's NetLOCK V.2.0 — can be used to realize enterprise-specific remote access over the Internet.

- Facilitates and expedites the File Transfer Protocol (FTP)-based file downloads and uploads that one is likely now doing on a daily basis with all of one's distributed servers.

- Allows one to quickly open up mainframe applications for new, Internet-based services such as home banking, online investment, personal travel reservation, and Web-based status checking (e.g., querying the status of an expedited mail item or a cargo shipment), as demonstrated in Exhibit 39-4.

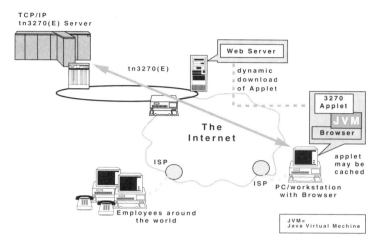

Exhibit 39-3. **A totally TCP/IP-Based system. This system is currently being tried out by a $18B U.S. conglomerate to ensure that telecommuters and mobil users around the world have access to mainframe-resident SNA applications across the Internet.**

Exhibit 39-4. **Actual screen shot of a rejuvenated 3270 user interface. This was used by a mainframe-centric, Internet-based home banking system realized using browser-based access in the form of 3270-to-HTML conversion.**

- Greatly minimizes the cost of SNA access by being able to use tn3270(E) or browser-based access to SNA solution. The browser-based access solutions will eliminate the considerable costs associated with installing, managing, and regularly updating SNA/3270 emulation software on individual PCs/workstations by using either an applet-based scheme, where the applet is dynamically downloaded from a Web server, or a 3270-to-HTML conversion scheme, as shown in Exhibit 39-4, which only requires a browser to be present within the client PC/workstation.
- Enables one to quickly phase out the very expensive, SNA-oriented IBM 3745 or IBM 3746 communications controllers in favor of high-performance, low-cost channel gateways such as the IBM 2216-400, Cisco 7500/CIP, or Cisco 7200/CPA.
- Permits one to use the mainframe as a high-capacity, very low-cost-per-user Web server for intranet, extranet, or even Internet applications.
- Greatly simplifies the integration of mainframe data with the new Web applications that are being developed using tools such as NetDynamics 4.0, Bluestone Sapphire/Web, and ColdFusion.
- Eliminates the need for external, low-capacity tn3270(E) gateways such as Microsoft's SNA server by using integrated, highly scalable, mainframe-resident tn3270(E) servers such as the one included within Interlink's e-Access TCPaccess TCP/IP software.
- Gain better channel throughput by using TCP/IP across the channel to a mainframe-resident tn3270(E) server. Phase out the cost and complexity of doing business-to-business transactions using SNA Network Interconnection (SNI) by moving toward a secure, low-cost extranet scheme.

PROVEN TECHNOLOGY TO FACILITATE THE TRANSITION FROM SNA TO IP

The good news is that highly proven and stable technology, from over 40 credible vendors including Interlink, Cisco, OpenConnect Systems, IBM, Attachmate, Wall Data, Eicon Technology, Novell, Farabi Technology, Client/Server Technology, Blue Lobster, etc., is now readily available to facilitate TCP/IP on the mainframe and the standardization on a TCP/IP-centric networking infrastructure — although one still relies on quite a few mainframe-resident, mission-critical SNA applications. The technologies available will enable one to integrate the current SNA/APPN-based environment with the new TCP/IP-centric world in a seamless and synergistic manner.

Athough it may feel like it, one will not be a lone pioneer beating across hitherto uncharted territory. The move from SNA to IP is happening with accelerating pace around the world. In reality, this transition has been happening for the last few years. Enterprises around the world — such as GM, FedEx, Sabre/American Airlines, The Library of Congress, Ohio State

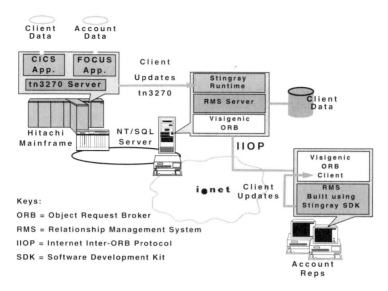

Keys:

ORB = Object Request Broker

RMS = Relationship Management System

IIOP = Internet Inter-ORB Protocol

SDK = Software Development Kit

Exhibit 39-5. Mainframe TCP/IP-based system. This system is being used by Lincoln National Reinsurance Companies, one of the largest reinsurers in the world, to provide its account reps with up-to-date client information across the Web.

University, Royal Jordanian Airlines, Nestles, The Chickering Group, National Van Lines, the State of Idaho, Lafayette Life, Lincoln National Reinsurance, Swiss Air, Al Rajhi Banking & Investment Corp. (Saudi Arabia's largest bank), and Gazprom (a $30B natural gas company in Russia), to name but just a few — have already started to integrate their data center resources with TCP/IP-centric i·nets. Exhibit 39-5 illustrates the solution deployed by Lincoln National Reinsurance.

To be of use, the technology that enables the transition from SNA to IP needs to be able to accommodate an extremely broad and disparate population of client equipment and functionality. Just some of the entities that need to be dealt with vis-à-vis this transition include PCs; UNIX workstations; coax-attached 3270/5250 terminals; printers; minicomputers; SNA applications that communicate program-to-program using LU 6.2 or LU-LU Session Type 0-based protocols; SNA-only devices (e.g., IBM 4700 Financial Systems); and legacy control units. The PCs, workstations, and printers at remote sites may work in either SNA or TCP/IP mode. Consequently, one will need SNA access technologies to deal with TCP/IP clients, in particular PCs and workstations, and SNA transport technologies to deal with SNA-only clients. This is not a problem. Today, there is a wealth of solid, well-established, field-tested technologies to realize both SNA access and SNA transport in the context of mainframe TCP/IP — and a totally TCP/IP-based network.

531

Some of the key technologies that will permit an easy transition from SNA to IP include:

- *tn3270(E):* widely used, ten-year-old IETF standard-based access scheme that enables low-cost TCP/IP clients to access SNA applications via a mainframe-resident tn3270(E) server. Today, tn3270(E) is being used by over ten million SNA users. tn3270(E) clients are ubiquitously available from all of the traditional SNA/3270 emulation vendors. All examples shown in Exhibits 39-2, 39-3, and 39-5 utilize tn3270(E) in some form.
- *Browser-based access with 3270-to-HTML conversion:* a thin-client solution (as shown in Exhibit 39-2) where a server-resident SNA-Web gateway performs 3270 datastream-to-HTML conversion, replete with some amount of user interface rejuvenation, so that mainframe SNA applications can be accessed directly from a browser across an i·net. The rejuvenated user interface for home banking (shown in Exhibit 39-4) was realized using 3270-to-HTML conversion. Secure Sockets Layer (SSL)-based authentication and encryption, as available with contemporary browsers, is used with this scheme to provide end-to-end data encryption.
- *Browser-invoked Java or ActiveX applets:* dynamically downloadable applets that can optionally be cached on a PC/workstation hard disk, and that provide tn3270(E) client emulation. This was the technique used in the system shown in Exhibit 39-3. User interface rejuvenation, as well as end-to-end data encryption, is also possible with this technique.
- *Application-specific Web solutions:* such as Interlink ActiveCICX, IBM CICS Web Interface, Interlink ActiveIMX, and Interlink OPEN-IMS, that expeditiously integrate mainframe-resident applications with the Web.
- *Programmatic (or middleware) solutions:* such as IBM MQSeries, Blue Stone Sapphire/Web, or Blue Lobster Stingray SDK, etc., that permit mainframe applications to be interfaced with TCP/IP or Web applications.
- *Data link switching:* like tn3270(E), is a ubiquitous, IETF standards-based encapsulation scheme performed by bridge/routers that permits any kind of SNA/APPN traffic, independent of session type, to be transported end-to-end across a TCP/IP WAN. DLSw ensures that any kind of legacy SNA device or application can be nondisruptively and gracefully accommodated within a TCP/IP-based infrastructure
- *High-performance routing-over-IP:* an alternative to DLSw championed by IBM whereby APPN/HPR-oriented routing is performed across IP. This scheme has the advantage over DLSw in that it can permit APPN-based routing between multiple data centers, and is capable of supporting LU 6.2 COS prioritization on an end-to-end basis over an IP network.

By using one or more of the above technologies, one can gracefully transition from SNA to IP without losing the services of any current mission-critical SNA/APPN applications, sacrificing any functionality, or compromising security or reliability.

THE BOTTOM LINE

With the rapid growth of intranets and the daily increasing significance of the Internet as the next frontier for commerce, the hold that TCP/IP has on commercial sector networking continues to solidify. Even IBM has acknowledged that the role of SNA, APPN, and HPR is going to be relegated to the mainframe as the basis for mission-critical applications. Many of the concerns that MIS professionals had in the past about TCP/IP — such as its security, reliability, and efficiency — are no longer germane. Solid and highly proven TCP/IP solutions are now available from multiple vendors for all aspects of mainframe-oriented computing — whether it be TCP/IP stacks, tn3270(E) servers, security packages, management platforms, applications, channel gateways, or network infrastructures. There really are no impediments to transitioning from SNA to IP. Thousands of companies around the world have already started to standardize on an end-to-end, mainframe-to-PC, TCP/IP fabric. Increasing numbers have already started to use the Internet for remote access and information dissemination. The technology required to successfully and gracefully transition from SNA to IP — such as tn3270(E), browser-based access, and DLSw — is here, is widely available, is cost-effective, and is remarkably solid. E-commerce beckons. What are you waiting for?

Chapter 40
Transporting Legacy SNA Traffic over Frame Relay

Andres Llana, Jr.

FOR YEARS, IBM MAINFRAME INSTALLATIONS the world over have formed the basis for host-centric networks. These networks support many of the world's largest business enterprises (e.g., airlines, financial firms, government agencies, transportation companies, and utilities). All of those networks share communications with remote locations.

Early networks, for the most part, were composed of slow, asynchronous, analog point-to-point or multidrop lines. To guarantee the quality of data transmission, IBM developed a telecommunications protocol known as Systems Network Architecture (SNA).

Although SNA is a successful and reliable transmission solution, users must still manage with a multitude of low-speed lines, each of which represents a single point of failure. However, because of its reliability, network managers still use SNA to support mission-critical applications while they consider other alternatives.

SNA TRANSPORT STRATEGIES

Some mainframe users have attempted to upgrade their front-end processors and remote controllers to support frame relay access, but have found the process to be costly. Furthermore, this upgrade may not represent a long-term solution as IBM migrates its mainframe product line toward distributed client/server environments. In keeping with this trend toward mixed networks — which must support multiple protocols including Token Ring, Ethernet, and Novell (IPX) — routers have become the solution of choice because of their ability to encapsulate SNA traffic in the IP.

0-8493-0859-3/00/$0.00+$.50
© 2000 by CRC Press LLC

Devices built around IP-based architectures use one of two basic methods:

1. SDLC to LLC conversion combined with TCP/IP encapsulation
2. Direct TCP/IP encapsulation of the SDLC frame to carry native SDLC traffic from a 3270 SDLC-type device through the network

The name for these processes may vary by vendor and the protocol overhead may also vary with each device. Overhead approaching 70 bytes per packet is the mean, while data link switching (DLSw) can add as much as 50 bytes per packet.

Once these SNA packets have been encapsulated, they can be encapsulated into frame relay packets. This is not true of frame relay switches, which eliminate the IP overhead by placing SNA frames directly into frame relay frames.

IP routing has not proven to be satisfactory for some users because running SNA through routers has resulted in unpredictable performance in some networks. Another problem is that the cost levels for routers have been higher than some frame relay switches, which also integrate voice traffic.

WHY FRAME RELAY?

Frame relay, which can trace its origins to ISDN, has matured into a practical and affordable replacement for low-speed, dedicated, private-line networks. For example, typical frame relay service is provisioned at 56 Kbps as compared with 4.8 or 9.6 Kbps for an SDLC multidrop line. In some cases frame relay service can be provisioned at T1/E1 levels ranging in channel speeds from 128 Kbps to 1.53 Mbps (fractional to full T1).

Frame relay for the user is a straightforward service in which there are logically defined data link connection identifiers (DLCIs). In addition, permanent virtual circuits (PVCs) or permanent logical links (PLLs) provide for a virtual permanent connection. Frame relay transparently passes most protocols if the endpoint frame relay access device (FRAD) supports encapsulation (DLSw or RFC 1490).

Guaranteed Bandwidth

Frame relay networks provide a guaranteed bandwidth to each PVC, however, any unused bandwidth can be shared among several active users. The guaranteed bandwidth of a PVC is specified as the committed information rate (CIR). A user's traffic may exceed the CIR rate and is referred to as the "burst rate" of the PVC. Traffic that exceeds the CIR rate may be eligible for discard.

Frame Relay Switching for More Efficient Network Operation

A FRAD located at the user's node is required to transform data into frame relay packets. A frame consists of a flag, which indicates the beginning and end of a data packet. A frame header contains the destination of the data in the packet. The user data is the data to be transmitted. An FCS validates the integrity of the data. Frames may be variable in length.

The frame relay network is composed of a group of interconnected switches that relay data across the network. The DCLI information contained in the header is used to forward the data across the network to its destination. The frame relay switch uses a two-step process to forward a frame of information. First, the network management tool checks the integrity of the frame using the frame check sequence (FCS). If the network manager finds an error, the frame is discarded. Second, the network manager validates the DLCI destination address. If the address is invalid, the packet is discarded. Any frame that is not discarded is forwarded to its destination. Because the network manager makes no attempt to correct a frame or request a retransmission, the network can operate more efficiently, leaving error recovery to the end stations.

More Performance for Less Money

FRADs are a more cost-effective approach for SNA networks because they simply convert SNA traffic into a frame relay packet, leaving the SNA data intact. Because the FRADs do not have to support multiprotocol routing (as do routers), they are more efficient and cost less. Furthermore, packet-based transport mechanisms offer a predictable performance for SNA networks. For example, in an IP network, packets containing time-sensitive information could get delayed behind a router queue while waiting to get transferred across the network. Frame relay transport mechanisms, on the other hand, offer a predictable performance by providing a connection-oriented session between devices in a remote site and the mainframe host. Furthermore, prioritizing mechanisms ensure that priority packets get through.

HOW SNA TRAFFIC IS CARRIED ACROSS FRAME RELAY

A frame relay network frames native SNA packets and sends them on their way. This is accomplished by a well-defined encapsulation process. Two possible encapsulation technologies for transporting information across a frame relay network are DSLw and RFC 1490.

DSLw

DSLw only supports the encapsulation of SNA, APPN, and NetBIOS traffic across a frame relay network. DSLw is an effective solution in an IP-based backbone supporting SNA and APPN multiprotocol environments. This is particularly true when a network has some native TCP/IP traffic.

The strength in the DSLw technology is its ability to dynamically locate SNA, APPN, or NetBIOS destinations using the destination's Layer 2 MAC address. DLSw conducts the destination location process using a search protocol. This protocol is an optimized version of source-route bridging's (SRB) broadcast search mechanism across a wide area network (WAN) using TCP/IP.

The DSLw technology involves the administration and management of 32-bit IP addresses, which requires defining the IP and the address at all remote local area network (LAN) bridge/routers, as well as at each source DSLw bridge/router. In addition to defining DSLw-specific IP addresses, it is necessary to specify all SRB-related parameters such as LAN segment numbers, bridge numbers, and MAC addresses at all destinations. This is definitely not a "plug-and-play" process.

DSLw does not support SNA or advanced peer-to-peer networking (APPN) routing or any kind of session layer switching between mainframes or APPN nodes. DSLw does support virtual point-to-point connections between pairs of MAC addresses across a TCP/IP WAN.

RFC 1490

RFC 1490 is the industry standard and an enhancement to the original RFC 1294 standard for frame relay encapsulation. RFC 1490 provides a low-overhead, highly optimized means for transporting SNA and APPN traffic. It also supports other multiprotocol traffic across a WAN. RFC 1490 is best suited for packet-switched networks, particularly when a network is totally frame relay-oriented.

RFC 1490 does not require the same amount of predefinition as DSLw. For example, in contrast to DSLw, RFC 1490 administration only involves Layer 2 PVC setup and definition to begin operation over a frame relay network. In contrast to DSLw, an RFC 1490 solution provides a greater level of service (e.g., bandwidth allocation and traffic prioritization). Some RFC routers can complement the inherent transparent alternate routing within a frame relay network by serving as frame relay switches. These switches also support dialback, which provides a vital disaster recovery resource.

RFC 1490 encapsulates SNA/APPN traffic directly within a frame relay with just a 10-byte-type control and logical link control Type 2 (LLC2) header prefixing the SNA message units (with no other protocols or headers involved). RFC 1490 is a Layer 2 minimum overhead, with an ultralight encapsulation technique including frame relay flags, two-byte address fields, and frame relay sequence. The total overhead for any SNA/APPN message unit is 16 bytes. Therefore, RFC 1490's overhead is minimal compared with that of DSLw, as DSLw relies on TCP/IP and requires two TCP connections between every remote bridge and router and the central site bridges and routers. Thus, a network with 250 remote sites would need 500 TCP connections at the central site. For this reason, if a network manager was to use frame relay to support the WAN fabric of a network with SNA or APPN traffic, RCF 1490 would be more efficient for integrating it with other multiprotocol traffic.

FRAME RELAY EFFICIENCIES FOR SNA

The technology of frame relay devices has gone through several developmental evolutions that have made it possible for the end user to realize an expanded application of frame relay. In comparing traditional SNA WAN technology, it is easy to see the advantages of transporting SNA traffic over frame relay. For example, because frame relay uses the same framing and CRC bits as SDLC, all FEP SDLC line interface couplers (LICs), data service unit/channel service units (DSU/CSUs), and modems can be used with frame relay.

Improved Throughput

With typical network access ranging from 56/64 Kbps to T1/E1 (1.55 Mbps), network throughput is greatly improved over the more traditional 4.8 to 9.6 Kbps line speeds associated with SNA networks. Because SDLC and frame relay are software implementations on an FEP, no hardware changes are required to support frame relay transport. In addition, migrating SDLC host applications to frame relay requires no software changes. Unlike SNA, frame relay can transport multiple protocols providing support for mixed or hybrid client/server networks. Frame relay also supports point-to-point or many-to-many connectivity.

Increased Bandwidth

Guaranteed bandwidth is ensured through the PVC's established committed information rate with the ability to support a burst mode above the CIR rate. Traffic such as voice or video can be prioritized over regular data traffic to ensure that it reaches its destination. Some carriers provide high-priority PVCs (priority PVC services) which can be dedicated to mission-critical SNA, voice, or video applications. In this scenario, a high-priority PVC might be sampled four times as often as a low-priority PVC.

Interoperability

Newer releases of IBM's Network Control Program (NCP) software provide an SNA boundary network node with connectivity between a PU4 to a PU2 device across a frame relay network. It is possible to establish connectivity across a frame relay network between an SNA node (PU2) and a front-end processor (FEP). This software also allows connectivity between a 3174 and an FEP.

SNA Network Interconnect (SNI) provides for the interconnection of two SNA networks over frame relay via an SNA link. This capability allows users on one SNA network to access resources on another SNA network.

With IBM's incorporation of the RFC 1490 standard across its current product line, interoperability between IBM and other IBM frame relay products can be established. In this scenario, interoperability requires SDLC to be converted to LLC2.

Unlike a dedicated network, meshed frame relay networks provide the user with a number of alternate routes, guaranteeing that all traffic that is not discard-eligible can reach its destination.

Better Functional Support

Although not all FRADs are the same, more advanced frame relay switches provide a much higher level of functional support. For example, if a PVC is experiencing high levels of traffic, the originating terminal can invoke flow control or metering to ensure that all traffic stays under the CIR level for the PVC being accessed. In addition, the network can send a backward explicit notification (BECN) bit to inform the endpoint device of a potential problem. In this instance, the endpoint device can regulate the flow of data to ensure that high-priority data can get through.

Network Backup

Frame relay provides fault tolerance with the inherent ability to reroute in the event of a failed route. Frame relay networks also tend to be more robust and less prone to error as opposed to more traditional network arrangements. However, outages can occur on the local loop that supports a remote location's access to the frame relay network. To meet this contingency, dial backup circuits may be used to restore service if the dedicated 56 Kbps link goes out of service. Dial-up ISDN with one B channel can support 64 Kbps service, which can be used to access an open port on the network. Regardless of the type of restoration that is in place, dial backup, address security, flexibility, and ease of installation are all important issues that network managers must address.

PRACTICAL APPLICATIONS OF FRAME RELAY

Frame relay provides a less expensive alternative than leased-line services while providing bandwidth for such added services as LAN, voice, and fax traffic. For example, if the right equipment is used to interface the

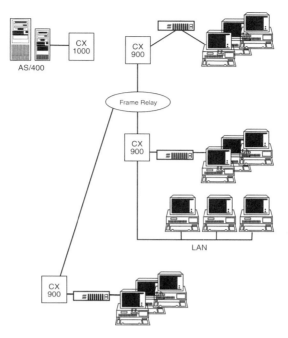

Exhibit 40-1. Star-configured network.

network, the network planner can integrate voice, data, and fax. This strategy makes it possible to aggregate all information traffic across the frame relay network.

AS/400 Networks

Exhibit 40-1 shows a typical AS/400 network arrangement. The network links form a star topology, radiating from the hub to the outer periphery. In this example, CX 900 switches are at the periphery with a CX 1000 switch at the central site (mainframe). At each of the customer's remote locations there will be either an IBM 5394 or a third-party controller, as well as a LAN running NetWare for SAA. The CX 900s located at these sites convert the SDLC link protocol running from the cluster controller to frame relay protocol using the RFC 1490 encapsulation protocol. The central site CX 1000 converts the RFC 1490 protocol back to SDLC for presentation to the AS/400. The CX 1000 also "spoofs" the SDLC polling, appearing as a cluster controller.

In this solution, only the CX 1000 and CX 900 were added to establish a corporate network across a public frame relay network. No changes were required to the cluster controller parameters or other network equipment.

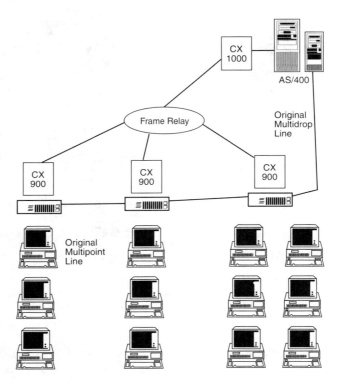

Exhibit 40-2. Multipoint, multidrop network.

Exhibit 40-2 illustrates a multidrop or multipoint network architecture, possibly the most popular of all AS/400 network designs. Converting this type of network requires virtual multipoint mapping, which requires the CX 1000/900s to map the controllers from a point-to-point line to a multipoint line. This remapping allows the AS/400 to think it is operating over a multipoint line when in fact it is running over public frame relay.

Support for Voice Traffic

Exhibit 40-3 shows another AS/400-based network in which a mix of IP/IPX/SNA and AppleTalk protocols is to be transported over frame relay. LANs as well as legacy nodes in several of the remote locations require integration into the network. In these locations, servers are running SNA emulators that allow them to appear as SDLC-attached controllers. TCP/IP and IPX traffic also comes from other servers in the same remote offices.

In this arrangement, the CX 900 was able to function as a router sending traffic over the frame relay network back to its ultimate destination. In this network, the CX 900 may also have to transport a mix of SNA, IP, and IPX

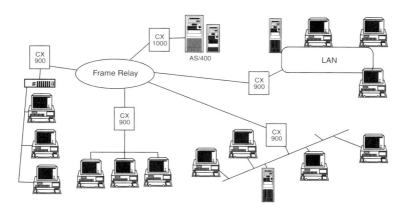

Exhibit 40-3. Hybrid network with IP, IPX, and SNA.

over a single communications link (DCLI). It should also be noted that in Exhibit 40-2, voice traffic is integrated over the frame relay network. In this scenario, each of the remote locations has two voice channels configured on the CX 900. These voice channels are attached to the local telephone system and appear as off-premise, extension-type connections. At the host, the CX 1000 provides support for each of the channels coming back from the remote locations. These appear as separate extensions on the PBX at the host site. This allows the remote offices to make calls to other locations or to the corporate headquarters. Companies using this strategy have saved a great deal of money on their voice traffic by piping it over the data network. Some users have reported tremendous savings in overseas calls by riding over their international frame relay network.

Special Application Servers

AS/400s are frequently used to support LANs as special application servers. In this scenario, the clients might access the AS/400 over an Ethernet. The CX 900 can be linked directly to the Ethernet via an LLC2 interface. The CX 900 can link to other remote CX 900s that interface with a remote cluster controller via an SDLC interface. A transparent Token Ring-to-Ethernet bridge might be used to link a Token Ring to an Ethernet backbone. Again, the CX 900 would be used to indirectly link traffic between the Token Ring and any of the other remote locations over the frame relay network.

CONCLUSION

In these times of belt tightening, network managers are under pressure to protect their investments in existing network infrastructures. As SNA network managers strive to improve their networks' performance, they must do so without any risk to the core business.

MIGRATION CONSIDERATIONS

SNA over frame relay has obvious cost benefits. The application of frame relay to transport native SNA directly allows network administrators to continue the application of their SNA devices without reconfiguring their network devices. Eliminating the overhead associated with polling minimizes congestion and provides more available bandwidth for actual data transportation. This strategy allows the end user to realize greater network performance without buying more bandwidth. Furthermore, reducing local polling removes an overhead burden from the FEP, freeing processing cycles for other tasks. This reduces expensive FEP upgrades while providing much better network throughput. The key here is the selection of the right level of FRAD equipment to provide the maximum advantage of frame relay service. Not all frame relay access devices are created equal. When provisioning a frame relay network, terminals should provide the following capabilities:

- termination of an SDLC protocol
- SDLC mapping to eliminate tasks from the AS/400
- supporting the AS/400 SDLC host
- supporting RFC 1490
- supporting Annex G
- supporting data compression for bursty LAN traffic
- supporting IPX and AppleTalk routing
- supporting LAN routing
- supporting voice/fax
- supporting international connections

Using these criteria as a guide, migrating to frame relay need not be done on a wholesale basis. Selecting a frame relay switch that provides a flexible platform is a key to upward expansion. This strategy allows network managers to plan for the future as their application mix begins to expand requiring such high-priority services as video and voice integration.

Chapter 41
SNA over Frame Relay
Dick Thunen

TODAY, MOST TELECOMMUNICATIONS CARRIERS PROVIDE FRAME RELAY SERVICES that allow the IBM Systems Network Architecture (SNA) user to reap a number of benefits, including:

- investment protection in SNA devices
- lower line costs compared to dedicated links
- up to 40 percent increases in network utilization through frame relay's multi-protocol support
- sustained integrity and control of the SNA network with NetView and Simple Network Management Protocol (SNMP) management
- integration of SNA and multi-protocol LANs
- high-performance access networking for Advanced Peer-to-Peer Networking (APPN) and a migration path to Asynchronous Transfer Mode (ATM) backbones

Traditional IBM host networks connect users to mainframes via SNA or bisynchronous multidrop lines. These are usually low-speed analog lines that represent a single point-of-failure between user and host. Although these networks subject network managers to the complexities of dealing with a multitude of leased lines, many organizations continue to maintain their IBM host networks because of the mission-critical applications they support.

IBM Corp. introduced X.25 as a cost-effective alternative to private lines. Many network planners have chosen not to implement it, however, because of higher user-response times from network overhead delays caused by every node in the X.25 network performing error detection/correction, message sequencing, and flow control. Frame relay, however, performs these functions only at the network access points using an end-to-end protocol; thus, frame relay uses the network more efficiently.

IBM has developed a set of SNA frame relay products for packet-based wide area networks (WANs). Frame relay is an integral element of the evolution of SNA networks into the future with full support for APPN and ATM.

FRAME RELAY TECHNOLOGY: AN OVERVIEW

Frame relay is a relatively new technology offering virtual private-line replacement. As a network interface, it traces its origins to Integrated Services Digital Network.

When integrated services digital network (ISDN) was being developed, two transport services were envisioned: circuit-mode services for voice and transparent data, and packet (i.e., X.25 and frame relay) mode for data. Frame relay has since evolved into a network interface in its own right, independent of ISDN. It is now specified as a set of American National Standards Institute (ANSI) and International Telecommunications Union (ITU) standards.

The User Perspective

Although services are typically available with transmission rates from 64 Kbps to T1/E1 (1.53/2.05 Mbps), frame relay is defined as an access interface up to T3 or 45 Mbps. By contrast, the typical Synchronous Data Link Control multidrop line is a 4.8- or 9.6-Kbps analog line. The transmission of a typical two-page text document on a frame relay network takes 1/4 second at 64 Kbps and 1/100 second at 1.53 Mbps. Transmission of the same two-page text document on an SDLC multidrop line takes 3 1/3 seconds at 4.8 Kbps and 1 1/6 seconds at 9.6 Kbps.

To the user, a frame relay network appears simple and straightforward. Users connect directly to destinations on the far side of the network. Frame relay provides logically defined links — commonly called data link connection identifiers (DLCIs), permanent virtual circuits (PVCs), or permanent logical links (PLLs) — for a permanent virtual connection.

For example, user A is connected across the frame relay network through separate permanent virtual circuits to both user B and user C. The permanent virtual circuits are multiplexed across user A's frame relay interface. Frame relay networks guarantee bandwidth to each permanent virtual circuit, but allow unused bandwidth to be shared by all active users. The guaranteed bandwidth of a permanent virtual circuit is specified as the committed information rate (CIR) of the permanent virtual circuit. A user's traffic can have transmission data rates in excess of the committed information rates, referred to as the burst rate of the permanent virtual circuits.

User B appears to user A with frame relay address data link connection identifier 100, and user A appears to user B with data link connection identifier 80. A permanent virtual circuit connects user A's frame relay interface through the Frame Relay network to user B's frame relay interface. Each

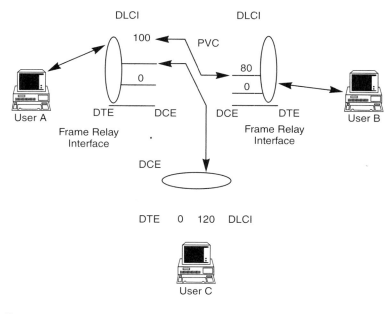

Key:
DCE   data communications equipment
DLCI data link connection identifier
DTE   data terminal equipment

Exhibit 41-1. Frame relay permanent virtual circuit (PVC).

user's data link connection identifier numbers have local significance only. User A has a second permanent virtual circuit with its own data link connection identifier number connecting to user C. In addition, each user has a local management interface, typically on data link connection identifier 0 (see Exhibit 41-1).

The Frame Relay Frame

Each frame relay access station is responsible for transforming the data into frame relay packets for transport (i.e., relay) over the network. Each frame contains the following elements:

- **Flag:** indicates the start and end of a frame relay packet.
- **Frame relay header:** contains the destination of the user data packet and management information.
- **User data:** contains the data to be transported across the frame relay network.
- **Frame check sequence:** allows the integrity of the data to be validated.

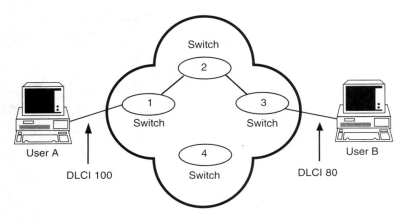

Key:
DLCI data link connection identifier

Exhibit 41-2. Frame relay network showing PVC connecting User A and User B.

The frame relay network receives, transports, and delivers variable-length frames. The frame relay network consists of a group of interconnected nodes (i.e., switches) that relay the data across the network on the appropriate permanent virtual circuits. A frame relay switch uses only the data link connection identifier information contained in the frame relay header to forward the frame across the network to its destination (see Exhibit 41-2).

The path through the network is transparent to the user. The data link connection identifier does not include any description of how the connection transverses the network or the routing topology of the network. A frame relay network operates an Open Systems Interconnection (OSI) layer 2 router network. Each frame relay access node puts the routing information (destination data link connection identifier) in the data link layer (i.e., frame relay header) of the frame. The frame relay network uses only this information to relay the frame across the network (see Exhibit 41-3.) In other words, the frame relay network nodes look only at the Frame Relay header and the frame sequence check.

The frame relay switch, or node, uses the following two-step review process to forward frames across the network:

1. The integrity of the frame is checked using the frame check sequence; if an error is indicated, the frame is discarded.

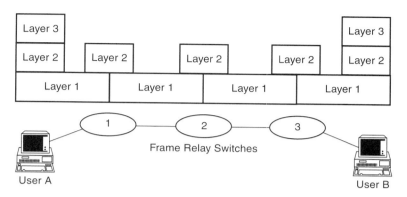

Exhibit 41-3. Layer 2 router network.

2. The destination data link connection identifier address is validated, and if it is invalid, the frame is discarded. The data link connection identifier destination address is contained in the frame relay header of the frame.

All frames that are not discarded as a result of the frame check sequence or data link connection identifier checks are forwarded. The frame relay node makes no attempt to correct the frame or to request a retransmission of the frame. This results in an efficient network, but requires that the user end-stations assume responsibility for error recovery, message sequencing, and flow control.

Thus, frame relay switches do not look at the user data packets, which makes the network transparent to all protocols operating at levels above OSI level 2.

RFC 1490

Because frame relay networks do not look at the contents of the user data, any format can be used to packetize the data, such as X.25 or high-level data link control. IBM uses logical link control type 2 (LLC2) as its frame relay SNA data format.

The IBM format is based on ANSI T1.617a Annex F, which covers encapsulating protocol traffic in frame relay. This process has been approved by the Frame Relay Forum and is included in its Multiprotocol Encapsulation Agreement. IBM's treatment of a frame relay network is based on standards and promotes interoperability with third-party implementations. IBM uses the LLC2 frame format and protocol for transporting SNA across Token Ring and Ethernet LANs.

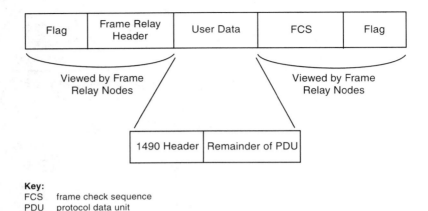

Key:
FCS   frame check sequence
PDU   protocol data unit

Exhibit 41-4. RFC 1490 frame relay frame format.

For SNA data, the Regional Financial Center 1490 (RFC 1490) header designates that it is 802.2 (LLC2) data, whether it is SNA subarea, peripheral, or Advanced Peer-to-Peer Networking data, and the LLC2 destination and source addresses. This format, illustrated in Exhibit 41-4, is also used for NetBIOS data.

Users connected to the network using RFC 1490 frame relay data terminal equipment have a logical view of the frame relay network as a virtual LAN. IBM's use of RFC 1490 for its frame relay equipment provides a familiar metaphor to SNA users.

Because the frame relay network does not look at the contents of user data, it allows the multiplexing of multiple protocols across a single frame relay interface. Frame relay network access nodes are responsible for converting the user data into the appropriate RFC 1490 format for SNA and LAN traffic. In summary, a frame relay WAN:

- provides packet-mode technology
- does not utilize store-and-forward
- relies on intelligent endpoints and high-integrity lines
- results in low transit delay
- is transparent above layer 2

As a result, frame relay provides a cost-effective alternative to dedicated-line networks.

FRAME RELAY AS A REPLACEMENT FOR SDLC

Frame relay delivers enhanced services compared to alternative SNA WAN techniques such as SDLC. Frame relay:

- Uses the same framing and cyclic redundancy checking bits as SDLC. This means that all front-end processor (FEP) SDLC line interface couplers (LICs), modems, and DSUs/CSUs can be used with frame relay.
- Usually allows for frames up to 2106 bytes in a frame relay network, but IBM's Network Control Program allows for the configuration of up to 8250-byte frames for use on high-quality, private frame relay networks. Large packets reduce network overhead and improve network performance.
- Allows network access connections from 56/64 Kbps to T1/E1 speeds, whereas the typical multidrop connection is 4.8/9.6 Kbps. User response times are directly improved by efficient network backbone connectivity.
- Is implemented in software (like SDLC), which means that no hardware changes in either the front-end processor or remote devices are required to move to frame relay.
- Can be managed by NetView management by network control program (NCP) for both SDLC and frame relay connections. Therefore, familiar network management tools and practices can be used on the frame relay network.
- Adds multiple protocol transport. All protocols can be transported across the frame relay network; SDLC supports only SNA traffic.
- Provides SNA guaranteed bandwidth through the PVC's committed information rate.
- Requires no host application changes to migrate from SDLC to frame relay.
- Supports point-to-point connections, like SDLC. Frame relay also provides many-to-many connections; SDLC requires a multidrop line to provide one-to-many connections.
- Provides for transparent network routing. SDLC is a single physical path connection.
- Supports burst mode, which lets users exceed their committed information rates of the link.

SNA FRAME RELAY NETWORKS

IBM provides connections for frame relay networks on all its current networking products, including the 3745 communication controller, 3172 interconnect controller, OS/2 RouteXpander/2, 3174 network server, AS/400, and the 6611 network processor. Users can evolve their current SNA networks from an SDLC multidrop backbone to a Frame relay WAN. IBM supports all SNA topologies: Intermediate Network Node, Boundary Network Node, SNA Network Interconnect, and Advanced Peer-to-Peer Networking across a frame relay network.

IBM's frame relay products are configured as Frame Relay Data Terminal Equipment devices, except the Front-End Processor (3745 communication controller), which can also be configured as a frame relay data communications equipment (DCE) device and can act as a frame relay switch.

Intermediate Network Node (INN)

IBM's Network Control Program software provides an INN connection — PU4-to-PU4 — between front-end processors (FEPs) over a frame relay network. This support was first announced for Network Control Program (NCP) Version 6, Release 1 (V6R1) in 1992. IBM supports mixed-media, multiple-link transmission groups that can include frame relay, SDLC, and Token Ring links. Thus, frame relay can be incorporated with other data link types in a transmission group to give users flexibility in network design.

Because frame relay is an Open Systems Interconnection level 2 routing protocol, it provides fast INN routing, which is an efficient means of interconnecting multiple FEPs. Level 2 frame relay eliminates SNA processing on intermediate FEPs. Furthermore, as each pair of FEPs appears to be directly linked, the intermediate network configuration is transparent to SNA routing algorithms.

SNA Network Interconnect (SNI)

NCP Release 6, Version 1 also introduced SNA over frame relay for interconnecting multiple SNA networks. Two traditional SNA networks can be connected using a System Network Interconnect (SNI) link over frame relay so the users of one SNA network can access the resources or applications of another across a frame relay network.

Boundary Network Node (BNN)

NCP Version 7, Release 1 fully expands the role of the network control program (NCP) to that of providing System Network Architecture Boundary Network Node — PU4-to-PU2 — connectivity between an NCP and an SNA node (PU2/2.1). The FEP can establish an SNA/BNN connection across a frame relay network with users on a 3174 network processor or users connected through an IBM 6611 network server or RouteXpander/2.

AS/400

IBM's AS/400 supports direct frame relay connectivity to another AS/400, or through a frame relay bridge to a 5494 remote controller or PC workstation. SNA nodes connected to an AS/400 across a frame relay network must be SNA Type 2.1 nodes, such as an IBM 5494 remote controller.

APPN

IBM's APPN Network Node products, 6611 IBM Network Processor, AS/400, and OS/2 Communication Manager (RouteXpander/2) can be configured to establish an APPN network across a frame relay WAN.

APPN end-node applications can thus take advantage of the combined frame relay and APPN network.

IBM Legacy Devices

Many IBM networks include legacy devices that are incapable of supporting frame relay network access, such as 3274 controllers, System 3X computers, and 5394 controllers. A frame relay assembler/disassembler (FRAD) provides connection to a frame relay network for a non-frame relay capable device.

A FRAD translates the SNA controller's SDLC data stream into frame relay frames for transport over the network. FRADs based on Regional Financial Center 1490 can interoperate across a frame relay network with IBM's frame relay products. Interoperability with IBM requires that the SDLC be converted to LLC2 for encapsulation in frame relay.

In addition to basic framing functions, a FRAD usually concentrates a number of low- or medium-speed SDLC lines into a single, high-speed frame relay link. By combining data from multiple, low-speed controllers onto one or more high-speed lines, FRADs reduce overall network costs.

Private Frame Relay Network

NCP Version 6, Release 2 (V6R2) adds Data Circuit-terminating Equipment support to the front-end processor. The FEP functions as a frame relay switch (i.e., DCE) for frame relay data terminal equipment (DTE) such as an OS/2 RouteXpander, so users can create private frame relay networks based on the IBM FEP. Private frame relay networks support both SNA and LAN protocols. In summary,

- All current IBM SNA products provide frame relay network access.
- All SNA topologies are supported across a frame relay network.
- FRADs can be used to provide high-performance connectivity for legacy IBM SDLC and binary synchronous communications devices.

IBM MULTI-PROTOCOL SUPPORT

IBM's frame relay access products use the Regional Financial Center 1490 standard, which specifies the frame format and characteristics for multiplexing multiple protocols across a frame relay network on a single frame relay link.

Treatment of LAN protocols is similar to that described for SNA-over-frame relay. The Regional Financial Center 1490 header for LAN protocols indicates whether the packet is being bridged or routed. A bridged frame header includes what media it is originating on — 802.3, 802.4, 802.5, FDDI, or 802.6 — whether it is being source routed or transparently bridged, and its destination medium access control (MAC) address.

Some routed protocols have an assigned Direct Network Layer Protocol Identifier, or NLPID, such as IP. For these protocols, the NLPID is used to identify the frame. Otherwise, the Subnetwork Access Protocol (SNAP) header for the frame is used to identify frame contents.

RFC 1490 specifies the transport of both bridged and routed LAN protocols across a common frame relay interface and provides a standard format for the frame relay packets. RFC 1490 specifies for bridged data the protocol being used — source route or transparent — and thus facilitates multi-vendor networking based on industry standard implementations. For routed data, however, there is currently no means of specifying the routing protocol being used for a given LAN protocol, so interoperability of routed protocols is more complicated.

All of IBM's frame relay products provide for multi-protocol support over frame relay. This support is available over public and private frame relay networks and includes both the bridging and routing of LAN protocols. The IBM 6611 also allows SNA/SDLC traffic to be transported across a frame relay WAN.

NETWORK MANAGEMENT

With the addition of frame relay as a packet-mode WAN supported by IBM's Network Control Program software, IBM incorporates support for frame relay WAN in NetView network management software, including NPM, NTune, and NetView/6000, its Simple Network Management Protocol manager. IBM provides a complete picture of the SNA and frame relay internetwork, including both SNA and non-SNA traffic and DTE devices. Exhibit 41-5 shows the SNA network management topology.

NetView Management Services

Although simple network management protocol and other open network management standards continue to evolve, NetView remains the only way to provide comprehensive network management, control, and diagnosis of an SNA network. All SNA network nodes are inherently commandable from NetView and report all network management-related activities directly to NetView for processing by one of its function-specific applications.

IBM's NetView support extends NetView management of the SNA network across the frame relay network to the end user's controller. This support allows complete SNA network visibility and control with no remote-line and physical unit black holes, compatibility with existing NetView tools and applications, and virtually no operator retraining.

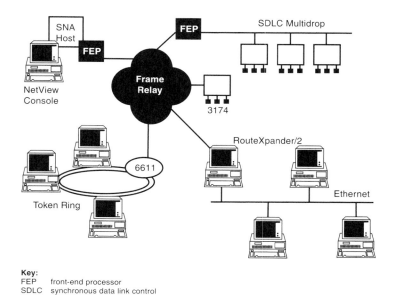

Key:
FEP   front-end processor
SDLC   synchronous data link control

Exhibit 41-5. SNA network management topology.

Virtual Telecommunications Access Method (VTAM)
Network Control Program (NCP)

The Virtual Telecommunications Access Method Dynamic Reconfiguration (DR) facility supports the addition of network control program (NCP) frame relay data link connection identifiers. A permanent virtual circuit can be created or deleted without interrupting the frame relay network or regenerating network control program (NCP).

Alternative Routing

NCP provides alternative automatic routing by a private frame relay network if a primary (i.e., public) frame relay network becomes unavailable.

Local Management Interface (LMI)

A reserved link address (local data link connection identifiers) is used for communication between the FRAD and the frame relay network. The management interfaces are defined by American National Standards Institute T1.617-1991 Annex D and ITT Q.933 Annex A for data link connection identifier 0. Users are able to specify either the ANSI or ITT Local Management Interface implementation as part of the configuration. This data link connection identifier is used for communicating network resources (i.e.,

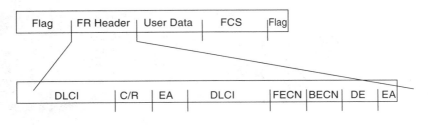

Key:
BECN   backward explicit congestion notification
C/R   committed information rate
DE   discard eligibility
DLCI   data link connection identifier
FECN   forward explicit congestion notification

Exhibit 41-6. Frame relay header.

the list of valid data link connection identifiers), determining the link status of each data link connection identifier, and determining network status.

The local management interface data link connection identifiers cannot be used for data traffic. A status-inquiry message is used to query the status of the network. The status message is either a keep-alive message or a full-network status report. The status update message reports an unsolicited status change in a network component.

Frame Relay Network Congestion

The frame relay network provides notification of network congestion to end-user devices. Upon encountering congestion, a frame relay switch provides forward notification of network congestion along the data route by setting the Forward Explicit Congestion Notification bit in the frame relay header, as shown in Exhibit 41-6.

The network also notifies the sending node of congestion along the PVC by setting the Backward Explicit Congestion Notification bit of packets going to the sender along the permanent virtual circuit. The bit is changed from 0 to 1 to indicate the presence of congestion. Network congestion is determined by a switch using the switch's queue length or buffer utilization (see Exhibit 41-7.)

It is the function of the frame relay access node, or data terminal equipment (DTE) device, to respond to the Forward Explicit Congestion Notification (FECN) and Backward Explicit Congestion Notification (BECN) bits. IBM's frame relay devices respond by controlling the transmit window size of devices transmitting on the congested data link connection identifier. When frame relay data terminal equipment (DTE) receives notification of network congestion, it reduces its transmit window to 1. Once a network has indicated that it is returning to a normal state, the transmit windows

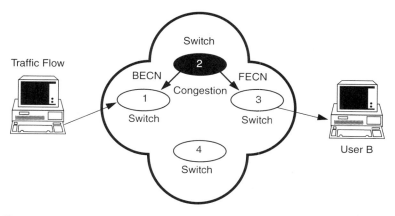

Key:
BECN backward explicit congestion notification
FECN forward explicit congestion notification

Exhibit 41-7. Congestion notification.

are increased a frame at a time until they return to their normal transmit windows.

Consolidate Link Layer Message (CLLM)

If there are no frames returning to the sender, the end node can determine the presence of congestion over a data link connection identifier through the CLLM information on the next query. The network is otherwise prohibited from notifying the sender of congestion on the data link connection identifier.

Discard Eligibility Bit

Frame relay access nodes can mark frames for discard eligibility by the network as a means of reducing congestion during moderate traffic congestion periods. When the Discard Eligibility bit in a frame is set to 1, the user has indicated that the frame can be discarded if it encounters network congestion.

The network sets the Discard Eligibility bit to 1 on data that follows on a physical link in excess of the committed information rate (CIR). Thus, the network can be divided into the following three zones:

- *Guaranteed transmission:* the dataflow is less than the CIR.
- *Transmit if possible:* the dataflow is above the CIR but less than the maximum rate.

557

- *Discard excess frames:* the dataflow is above the maximum rate. The frame relay network does not notify a user of frames being discarded. It is the responsibility of the FRADs to monitor the integrity of the data flow.

SNMP Management

Proliferation of LAN internetworks often leads to a separate management organization seeking a common management platform for multi-vendor equipment. Often, the solution is Simple Network Management Protocol. Most of IBM's frame relay products can be configured with a Simple Network Management Protocol (SNMP) agent for management by IBM's NetView/6000 Simple Network Management Protocol Manager.

Support of concurrent Simple Network Management Protocol and NetView enables each functional operations group, System Network Architecture, and LAN internetwork, to execute their respective network management and control responsibilities through their management platform of choice.

FRAME RELAY COMPARED WITH ROUTER NETWORKS

IBM's products transmit LAN, System Network Architecture, and Advanced Peer-to-Peer Networking traffic across a frame relay WAN. This section compares IBM's treatment of a frame relay WAN and the router approach. The major issues include:

- *Backbone:* frame relay network is compared with a meshed-router backbone network.
- *WAN protocol:* IP encapsulation is compared with native-protocol frame relay transport.
- *SNA support:* support for all SNA interconnects is compared with data link switching (DLSw).
- *Network management:* native NetView and Simple Network Management Protocol are compared with Simple Network Management Protocol.

Backbone

The typical router backbone is a mesh of point-to-point links. In these networks, the router backbone is the network. The router is responsible for routing between end-user clients and application servers. Thus, routers are responsible for the definition and maintenance of network topology and the appropriate routing path for applications. Router networks may be referred to as administratively rich.

In a frame relay backbone, by contrast, the network services are inherent in the frame relay service. Each frame relay access device provides application-transparent communication directly with its corresponding node across the network. This simplifies the configuration and administration of frame relay compared to a router-based network.

WAN Protocol

The router solution to this issue is to encapsulate all traffic in IP packets for transmission over the frame relay (or other) network in conjunction with a proprietary routing protocol. Thus, the router solution is based on adding IP framing overhead to all data prior to adding frame relay framing for transmission over the network. Because most router protocols are proprietary and noninteroperable, a single vendor's product must reside on both sides of the network.

SNA Support

The router solution is to use data link switching (DLSw) to terminate SDLC and LLC2 traffic in the router and encapsulate the SNA data in IP using the DLSw routing protocol over the WAN. This provides a single backbone protocol for SNA and non-SNA traffic over the WAN. Once the SNA data is encapsulated in IP, the WAN treats it as any other IP traffic. The router solution requires a second DLSw-compatible router on the destination side of the frame relay network to remove the SNA data from the IP packet. However, DLSw only covers SNA/BNN PU2 data on SDLC lines and Token Ring LANs and NetBIOS traffic.

IBM uses Regional Financial Center 1490 for the transmission of SNA data over a frame relay WAN network. RFC 1490 provides for the transport of SNA/BNN PU 2 and Type 2.1, but also SNA Intermediate Network, Advanced Peer-to-Peer Networking, and SNA Network Interconnect traffic across a frame relay network. Therefore, RFC 1490 covers all SNA traffic without encapsulation in IP, and DLSw covers only SNA/BNN PU2 traffic and adds the IP overhead.

Network Management

SNMP is the principal network management tool used with routers, whereas NetView is the network management tool of choice for SNA networks. The SNMP management stations are not usually located in corporate data centers, which necessitates a separate set of data link connection identifiers for SNMP management to each remote location.

Such a scheme creates a redundant tier of network overhead that reduces bandwidth availability for data, impedes SNA session responsiveness and reliability, obstructs NetView visibility, and complicates network design and problem-solving. This results in poor SNA network performance in terms of efficiency and cost.

MIGRATION CONSIDERATIONS

When SNA is internetworked using routers that do not provide NetView support, a "black hole" is created in the network, preventing the NetView operator from viewing, managing, or monitoring the frame relay DTE devices. In particular, routers usually do not support SDLC LL2, LPDA-2, or NPM statistic collection.

IBM provides an integral NetView connection in all its frame relay products. NetView connections share the same permanent virtual circuit as SNA data, thereby eliminating the need for a separate management network for communication with NetView and its component applications.

CONCLUSION

Frame relay — multiplexing multiple protocols over a common link — is an efficient solution for unifying LAN and System Network Architecture networks. Frame relay is the WAN of choice for organizations moving to Advanced Peer-to-Peer Networking. The wide-scale deployment of APPN networks will soon be served by IBM's High-Performance Routing technology to deliver connectionless routing, and frame relay will be supported by IBM's initial implementations of High-Performance Routing (HPR). Exhibit 41-8 illustrates frame relay as the unifying network for LAN and SNA.

Current frame relay network specifications and service-provider implementations are designed for permanent virtual circuits (PVCs). PVCs provide a direct replacement for leased-line SNA connections, but SNA networks often include switched, dial-up SDLC connections for casual SNA host access. This capability is being added to frame relay. A number of vendors have initiated standardization of switched virtual circuits (SVCs).

Frame relay is also being positioned as the access network for Asynchronous Transfer Mode. A Regional Financial Center that specifies a frame relay interface to Asynchronous Transfer Mode networks is currently being worked through the standards process. This interface, referred to as Data eXchange Interface, covers Asynchronous Transfer Mode adaptation layer 1 (AAL 1).

Frame relay provides users with short-term payback and long-term preparedness — immediate economic benefits and a migration path to future, high-performance routing (HPR) and networking.

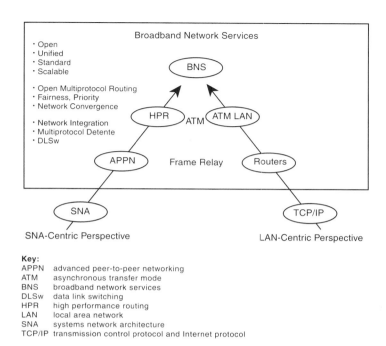

Key:
APPN   advanced peer-to-peer networking
ATM   asynchronous transfer mode
BNS   broadband network services
DLSw   data link switching
HPR   high performance routing
LAN   local area network
SNA   systems network architecture
TCP/IP transmission control protocol and Internet protocol

Exhibit 41-8. Frame relay as the unifying network for LAN and SNA networks.

Chapter 42
Planning a Cutover to a New Voice System
Thomas Osha

INTRODUCTION

DID YOU KNOW THAT TODAY, ROUGHLY 80 PERCENT of a company's business is conducted using some form of telecommunications?

Your business communications systems are among your company's most vital tools for success. They are the critical link to your customers, suppliers, and employees. The companies that will succeed in the future marketplace are those that can take charge of existing and emerging technologies to gain a competitive advantage in their respective fields.

Because we rely so heavily on telecommunications for the majority of our business communications, it is imperative that our business communications systems be as productive as possible. The better the telecommunications system operates, the greater its ability to support the success of your business.

In many organizations, it is the network manager who is responsible for the operation, maintenance, and administration of the telecommunications systems and peripherals. And, because a company's telecommunications systems are such a crucial element of its operations, this position takes on increased significance and visibility any time critical changes such as a major upgrade, addition, or the cutover to an entirely new system are undertaken.

This chapter will provide you with the insight and methodology necessary to plan and execute the cutover to a new voice communications system in a smooth and seamless manner without causing communications interruption or confusion in your organization.

Although this chapter focuses primarily on large-scale voice systems, the planning elements and implementation checklist can be modified and applied to many types of communications installations.

0-8493-0859-3/00/$0.00+$.50
© 2000 by CRC Press LLC

IMPLEMENTATION BEGINS BEFORE THE SALE

Large-scale voice systems are not impulse purchases. They are purchased for a reason, usually to satisfy a need, provide an application, or enable a company to communicate with its customers in a new way. In short, at the heart of the buying decision lies the business problem which prompted the need for a new voice system in the first place. Whatever the need: to interface with a voice mail or voice response system, to establish a call center, or just to handle routine calls in a more efficient manner, a successful implementation depends upon solving this underlying business problem as well as having a smooth cutover.

To ensure success, you should be as much a part of the buying cycle as possible. Even if you do not have the authority to specify, recommend, or approve the vendor or the model selected, as the future administrator, your input is valuable, but more importantly, the more you know about the system and its reasons for being purchased, the better equipped you are to smoothly implement the system.

For large-scale telephone systems such as PBXs (private branch exchange), the purchase cycle is usually governed by an RFP (request for proposals). This document acts as a guide for fair comparisons among systems from different vendors. At its heart is a set of questions and conditions that represent the buyer's business problems and communications requirements. The vendor must answer these questions in the body of their proposal. Thus, in many ways, a well-written RFP can function as a blueprint for your early implementation efforts.

Contained within the RFP response from your vendor of choice will be answers to many of the technical questions we will consider later in the chapter as well as descriptions of the system's features and design. The RFP and its corresponding response can be very useful in developing timelines and checklists for the project as well as serving as a guide to the original business problems and communications solutions.

IMPLEMENTATION KICKOFF

Once your organization signs a contract to purchase a new telecommunications system, the clock starts ticking. The contract generates a due date, which is normally 30 to 120 days (depending on system complexity) from the date of the contract. In this time, you must coordinate and direct the activities of a myriad of players, including: voice system vendor, local phone company, long distance vendor, building management, and system peripherals vendor.

In many cases you might also have to deal with: wiring contractors, electricians, architects, and software applications vendors. And, all of this coordination must be accomplished with great diligence. If even one detail is forgotten or late, the entire process can fall like a row of dominoes.

The best way to ensure that the hundreds of steps and details necessary to implement a new voice system are completed on time and in the proper order, is to hold an implementation kick-off meeting as soon as possible after the contract is signed. This meeting should bring together every vendor who will have a part, no matter how small, in the implementation as well as any employees of your company critical to the process.

As the project manager, you will lead the group in the two most crucial tasks to a successful cutover — the development of an implementation timeline and the assignment of roles and responsibilities to each of the participants. The Implementation Checklist (Exhibit 42-1) represents the four common phases of a voice system implementation and the required elements in each phase. This checklist is the focal point of the implementation kick-off meeting. With each of the vital participants present, all of the critical tasks can be assigned, from ordering and provisioning the network to the day of the cut activities.

As each task is assigned to a vendor or to a member of your staff, the number of days needed to complete the task should be estimated. Since many tasks can affect subsequent events, the order and timing of completion is important. For example, the long distance vendor is unable to test their service until the local telephone company finishes installing the trunks. But the local phone company cannot terminate the local trunks until the wiring contractor has finished installation of the cross connect field. However, the wiring vendor cannot finish the cross-connect until the building management has completed the equipment room. Looked at in this light, it is easy to see how bottlenecks can occur and how projects can get behind schedule.

By developing an implementation timeline (Exhibit 42-2), all participants know their role and where their tasks fit into the implementation plan. Each person is now responsible for keeping their tasks on time so as not to jeopardize the timely completion of the project. In fact, many organizations include in their purchase agreements with vendors severe penalties for missing crucial deadlines.

After the initial meeting, you should hold weekly status meetings until the final week when they are held daily. These meetings serve to keep you informed of everyone's progress toward meeting their deadlines, as well as exposing any difficulties early enough to be dealt with before becoming major obstacles.

Let us look at the critical elements of the Implementation Checklist more closely and examine their importance to the voice system cutover.

Exhibit 42-1. System cutover implementation checklist.

TASK	RESPONSIBILITY
Contract accepted	Vendor/Customer
Floor plans obtained and marked	Vendor/Customer
System order transmitted and scheduled	Voice System Vendor
Network orders placed	Local Telephone Company
Customer kick-off meeting	Customer/All Vendors/Others
Equipment room requirements to customer	Voice System Vendor
Customer switch admin. training scheduled	Voice System Vendor
Customer adjunct training scheduled	Voice System Vendor
Software kick-off meeting	Customer/Voice System Vendor
Department coordinators training	Customer/Voice System Vendor
Station reviews	Customer/Voice System Vendor
System network trunking reviews	Customer/Voice System Vendor
Develop revised order (if required)	Customer/Voice System Vendor
Install wire	Wire Vendor
Equipment room preparation	Customer
Voice System materials arrive/inventory	Customer/Voice System Technicians
Install and test switch	Voice System Technicians
Install and test adjuncts	Peripheral Equipment Technicians
Initialize adjuncts	Peripheral Equipment Technicians
Install cross-connects	Wire Vendor/Voice System Techs
Print button labels	Voice System Vendor
Install and test sets	Voice System Technicians
Build System Master Disk	Voice System Vendor
Set-up Users training room	Voice System Vendor
End-user training	Voice System Trainer
Install trunks	Local Telephone Company
Integrated system test	Voice System Technicians
Cutover meeting	Customer/All Equipment Vendors
Cutover system	Voice System Technicians
Help desk	Customer/Voice System Vendor
Trouble resolution	Customer/Voice System Technicians
Remove old system	Voice System Technicians
Security review	Customer/Voice System Vendor
Post-cut meeting, if required	Customer/All

Exhibit 42-2. System cutover implementation timeline.

Task	Duration
Contract Signed	0 days
Kick-off Meeting	1 day
Order & Provision Network	28 days
Equipment Room Preparation	10 days
Equipment Room Ready	3 days
Customer Switch Administration Training	10 days
Peripheral Administration Training	10 days
Station Reviews	1 day
System Ordered	0 days
Build and Ship	15 days
Install and Test PBX	5 days
Install and Test Peripherals	5 days
Install Cross-connects	1 day
Install and Test Sets	1 day
Install Trunks	5 days
End-User Training	3 days
Cutover	1 day
In Service	1 day
Help Desk	1 day

ORDER AND PROVISION NETWORK

As soon as the contract for the new voice system is executed (which will result in an order for the system's various hardware components), you should begin working with your local telephone company account executive and long distance carrier account executive to start the network design and provisioning process.

Network trunks are your voice system's link to the outside world. Local trunks deliver dial tone and allow you to make and receive local calls. Interexchange trunks carry long-distance traffic and inbound 800 number calls. There are also trunk lines which carry high speed data communications, link multiple voice systems together, or enable video applications. The number, type, and design of your system's trunking facilities will depend upon your organization's communications needs and business goals.

Your local telephone and long-distance account representatives have methods for studying your organization, determining the proper network elements, and engineering trunking and routing plans that fit your applications and communications needs.

Properly designing and provisioning network trunks for a PBX can be a complicated and time consuming process. Beyond just studying and analyzing your calling patterns and volumes, the local phone company will need to ensure that it has sufficient facilities running from its central office to your premises; and in the event that it does not, creating them.

On average, you should allow at least one month for trunk facilities to be designed, engineered, and installed. In certain cases (i.e., moving into a newly constructed building where no previous trunk facilities existed), you may want to allow up to three months for this process. Even if you are staying in your present location, the cutover to a new voice system presents an excellent opportunity to review your current network resources, call volumes, and calling patterns.

EQUIPMENT ROOM PREPARATION

One of the keys to a successful cutover and an easy to administer, maintain, and expand, voice system is the timely completion of a well-designed equipment room. Design and construction of a suitable equipment room is usually handled by the customer and can be your organization's most important contribution to a successful implementation.

Beyond just providing floor space for the PBX hardware, there are other factors which must be considered and will have an impact on the future operation of your system. While it is true that telecommunications equipment has gotten smaller and more forgiving in terms of its environmental requirements, smart planning is still required to prevent cutover delays and allow the equipment to perform to its fullest capacity.

Talk to any voice system vendor and you will learn that the majority of horror stories about installations gone awry revolve around the equipment room dimensions and environmental factors. Stories abound about rooms that are too small to hold the hardware or doorways too narrow to fit equipment through. One vendor showed up for a cutover and found a well-designed equipment room — on the third floor of a building with no elevator. Another installed a PBX only to find that every day at 11:30 a.m., the PBX would shut down. It turns out the equipment room shared an electrical circuit with the lunch room. At lunchtime employees would begin using all six of the cafeteria's microwave ovens, causing electrical overload to the PBX.

Carefully researching the PBX's technical requirements contained in the RFP response and working closely with your vendor's technical support staff can prevent these types of costly and embarrassing mistakes. Following are some common technical considerations when constructing an equipment room.

ROOM DIMENSION

Besides just housing the PBX, your equipment room will probably need to serve other functions like providing system administrator workspace, room for storage of extra phones, and housing peripheral equipment. Plus, at some point, you may need to expand, upgrade, or add other application hardware to your system. All of this will require additional space.

Most typical PBXs are housed in cabinets the size of a common refrigerator. The number of cabinets is determined by the size and complexity of the system. The RFP response or your vendor will be able to tell you how many cabinets your system will have. But unlike refrigerators, PBX cabinets have doors on the front and back. Therefore, the cabinets must be positioned to allow for a clearance of about four feet front and back to enable access from both sides.

Basically, the equipment room should be large enough to hold twice the number of cabinets in your system, which leaves room for expansion; large enough to provide four feet of clearance front and back, which gives technicians access to the hardware; plus large enough to provide extra storage space for equipment, manuals, and other necessities. The room should also be large enough to comfortably accommodate three to four people working simultaneously.

ELECTRICAL REQUIREMENTS

As a sensitive piece of electronic equipment, your PBX will need a dedicated, reliable, clean source of power. Most PBXs require a dedicated 120 volt, 208 volt, 220 volt, or 240 volt circuit. The type of service is determined by your cabinet size and configuration. This circuit cannot be shared by any other equipment, cannot be controlled by a wall switch, and must be properly grounded. In addition to the PBX cabinet, are system administration terminals, remote access modems, and other miscellaneous pieces of equipment that will require common 110 volt circuits. It is advisable to install double the number of required outlets, and two additional 20 amp circuits to give you flexibility and expansion capacity.

Again, the RFP response and your vendor will be able to provide details about the power requirements of the telecommunications system and associated equipment. It is a good idea to check with every vendor, including your local telephone and long distance vendors, to ask about their power requirements. Many times data equipment, trunking equipment, and monitoring equipment have their own specific electrical requirements.

In critical installations (hospitals, public safety, call centers), uninterrupted power supplies (UPS) and battery backup units are commonly installed. These units provide constant power levels to critical equipment in the event of a brown-out or total power failure. If a UPS system is part of your installation, remember to plan room to house the batteries which, depending on size and configuration, can be substantial.

Finally, be aware most PBXs and even some peripheral equipment do not use standard three-pronged electrical connectors. Most PBXs require special connectors and matched wall receptacles. It is advisable to have a professional electrician review your power requirements to ensure that you have the proper type and number of circuits, outlets, and connectors.

FLOORING REQUIREMENTS

Fortunately, as telecommunications systems have become smaller and lighter, the load distribution element of equipment room planning has largely become obsolete. Gone are the horror stories told of some unfortunate network manager who would install a four cabinet PBX on the first floor on Friday and come to work on Monday to find it sitting in the basement.

But, the one flooring issue that must be taken into consideration is electrostatic discharge (ESD). A PBX, like any piece of sensitive electronic equipment, is very susceptible to static electricity. Sudden discharges can frequently overload and burnout circuit cards in the PBX. Since circuit cards can cost from $1000 to $5000, depending on the type of card, ESD is a serious concern for network managers.

Fortunately, with some basic equipment room planning, ESD can be neutralized. The major cause of ESD is carpeted floors. Therefore, equipment rooms should be designed with concrete or linoleum floors to reduce the buildup of static electricity. Additionally, many equipment rooms will have static discharge mats inside each door. These mats pull the static electricity out of your body as you step from a carpeted surface onto them. With a little planning, an equipment room can safely be located in a variety of office locations providing that they have proper freight elevator service and meet the other room conditions discussed in this chapter.

SECURITY CONCERNS

For network managers, security became a watchword of the 1990s. As telecommunications have become increasingly vital to an organization's operations, they must also be vigilantly protected from deliberate and accidental tampering.

Tightly controlling access to your equipment room is the most effective way of preventing physical security problems. Studies have shown that over half of system security violations are perpetrated by employees or others working inside the organization.

One of the more common security concerns stems from the ability of PBXs to transfer calls from an incoming set of trunks to an outgoing set of trunks. This feature can be useful in specialized remote access applications. But because of the danger of having outsiders use this feature to call into your system, then transfer to an outside line, which in effect becomes an unlimited "free" long distance line for the hacker, this feature is rarely enabled in most PBX installations.

However, there have been numerous reports of malevolent employees who, unbeknownst to the network manager, gain access to their company's equipment room and activate this feature for their own purposes; thus putting the PBX in danger of major toll-fraud abuse. Unfortunately, this behavior is more common than one might think and instructions for enabling this feature on most models of PBX can be found on almost any Internet site devoted to hacking. Restricting access to your PBX and peripheral equipment drastically reduces your exposure to malicious acts by insiders.

Another reason for limiting room access to only selected individuals is to maintain control over changes to your system or its components. These kinds of problems are usually caused by well-meaning vendors whose technicians may make changes to the system during repairs or routine maintenance, then leave without telling the network manager what work was done.

This can result in problems in resolving cases of trouble or making feature changes. In most PBXs there are features which can counteract other features. If a technician activates one set of features, and the network manager unknowingly activates a different set of features the resulting compatibility error can take time to identify and correct.

To prevent this situation, establish a clear procedure for gaining access to the equipment room with all persons affected: your staff, facilities management, security, and each of your vendors. It is best to have the technician gain access to the room through the network manager. That way work to be performed can be discussed and the technician can be made aware of any special applications or unusual configurations in your PBX.

However, if there is such a room access arrangement, there should be two backup points of contact in addition to the network manager, such as a facilities manager, or a security manager. These individuals can give technicians room access to make important or emergency repairs in your absence. But they should always instruct the technician to leave you a note or voice mail describing the repairs or changes made.

Another physical security concern to take into consideration when designing an equipment room is handling fire suppression. A fire in your equipment room can destroy your PBX, cripple your business, and, of course, put your employees in danger. Therefore, the smallest hint of fire needs to be dealt with immediately and effectively.

Unfortunately, the sprinkler systems in use by most organizations today can do almost as much damage to a PBX as fire and are less effective against electrical fires. Therefore, most large equipment rooms install fire suppression systems that use halon gas instead of water to extinguish the fire. A halon system uses halon gas to displace the oxygen in the room, effectively smothering the fire. Once the fire has been extinguished, fresh air is pumped into the room and restoration work on the system can begin.

Halon systems are very effective, but because they are designed to remove all of the breathable air in a room, there are strict rules and codes regulating their installation and use. In some systems, warning lights and sirens are used to alert employees working inside the room to a fire condition, giving them a certain amount of time to leave the room before the gas discharges. Also, safety switches can be installed allowing employees to shutdown the system and prevent the gas discharge if necessary. These measures prevent employees from becoming trapped in the room and suffocating when the breathable air is removed by the halon gas. There are also regulations governing the airtightness of the equipment room, periodic inspection of the system, and the procedures for aerating the room after the system has been activated.

Most smaller equipment rooms with only one or two PBX cabinets may not need such a sophisticated fire fighting system. In this case, several fire extinguishers rated for electrical fires and placed in the proper positions around the room will suffice. Always be sure to check with your local fire marshall regarding the correct fire suppression system for your municipality and building category.

ENVIRONMENTAL CONCERNS

Although we have stated that today's PBXs are more forgiving in terms of environmental factors, there are still some factors to take into consideration when designing your equipment room. As in the other parts of the building, heating, ventilation, and air conditioning (HVAC) also are important in the equipment room. Even though most PBXs have their own cooling fans, they are still susceptible to heat buildup in certain circumstances. The temperature threshold of a modern PBX can range from 50 to 85 degrees. Once the room temperature exceeds these thresholds, abnormalities may occur in the operation of the PBX or its adjuncts.

These "gremlins" sometimes can be extremely hard to locate and diagnose. Most telecommunications technicians cite examples of a PBX that misroutes or loses calls occasionally. The customer calls the repair center and the technician is dispatched. He arrives to find the network manager in the equipment room trying to find the problem.

They work for several hours trying to locate the problem. Meanwhile, the PBX is operating normally. This situation is repeated several times, until one day the technician happens to be in the area and drops by to check the problem. He or she and the network manager enter the equipment room together, and find the temperature over 95 degrees. The technician realizes that whenever the network manager would enter the room, he or she would prop the door open to relieve the stuffiness. By the time the technician arrived, the room had cooled and the temperature had returned to within the threshold and the "gremlins" had disappeared.

To avoid this type of problem, install adequate heating, ventilation, and air conditioning to keep room temperatures at the same levels as the remainder of the building.

Another environmental element that can cause problems for telecommunications systems is dust. As dust is pulled into the PBX cabinets by the cooling fans, it settles on circuit boards and can interfere with connection points between circuit boards.

Equipment rooms should be kept as dust-free as possible. If possible, the room should be constructed without windows, without carpeting, and the air filters on the ventilation ducts supplying the room should be changed frequently. These measures should greatly reduce the amount of dust buildup. If you do notice dust in your system, do not use rags or dusters to clean electronic equipment. A can of compressed air can rid your equipment of dust without damaging fragile components or subjecting you to the risk of electrical shock.

One final environmental element that can easily be overlooked is lighting. Because the room is designed to hold equipment, architects usually do not spend much time planning lighting beyond a few fluorescent or incandescent fixtures. However, a PBX is composed of hundreds of very small circuit boards, cable connectors, and other components. When the network manager or system technicians are working on the cabinets, they often will need to be able to see in some very small spaces. For this reason, it is recommended that your equipment room be as well lighted as possible. A good equipment room lighting plan will include numerous fixtures, well placed to provide bright and even lighting throughout the room as well as moveable spot lights, used to see inside of cabinets and other small spaces.

BUILDING WIRING

Once the equipment room is completed, your wiring contractor will need to complete the plan for connecting each user's telephone to the PBX. This is usually accomplished through the use of a cross connect field between the PBX and the in-building wiring scheme. Generally, a cross-connect has two sides, the port side and the station side. The port side represents each of the telephone ports in the PBX, and the station side represents each jack in the building. A phone is then connected to the system by a wire jumper running from the station side of the cross-connect to the port side.

The type of wiring from the station side to each telephone will depend on several factors such as the distance from cross-connect to telephone jack, the type and function of the telephone set being used, and the type of wire needed. Early in the implementation process, you should arrange a meeting between your PBX vendor and your wiring contractor to discuss the system wiring requirements, size of the cross-connect field, number of wire runs, quality, pairs of wires in each run, and jack type (RJ11, RJ45, etc.). They should also determine the number of port side cables that will run from the cross connect to the PBX cabinet.

Many successful network managers use the following guidelines when designing a wiring scheme.

- To allow for future growth and flexibility of your voice system, you should design a cross-connect field at least 30 percent larger than what you currently require.
- When calculating the number of wire runs, be sure to include several for the equipment room for phones and for testing purposes.
- When it comes to wire quality, always buy the best you can afford. Most PBXs require category three, four, or five wire. The better the wire, the more resistant it is to interference and the more flexibility you will have in the future.
- The same theory also holds true for the pairs of wires in each run. The more pairs in each run, the more flexibility you have for connecting phones.
- For instance, analog phones require a one pair wire run and digital phones require two or four pairs depending on the model. If you install one pair wherever you plan to place analog phones, those jacks will never be able to be used for any other type of phone.
- But if you install four pair runs everywhere, you can plug any type of phone into any jack and be assured of it working. A slightly larger investment up front can pay huge dividends later on when you upgrade phone sets, add new capabilities, such as voice over data or video to phone sets, or reconfigure your office environment.
- Also, work with your wiring contractor to determine if the present wire can be reused in an existing building or in a new construction, require wire to be installed before the drywall work is completed. These two steps can drastically reduce wiring costs.
- Finally, require that the cross-connect field and each jack be clearly and understandably marked. This simple step can save time and money when future changes are needed or equipment is added.

SYSTEM ADMINISTRATOR TRAINING AND SUPPORT

Because it is so powerful, a PBX is also a very complicated piece of equipment. In most large organizations, one person is identified as the system administrator — the person with day-to-day responsibility for managing the telecommunications system. Several organizations also see this job as an extension of the network manager. Familiarity with personal computer interfaces and being comfortable with technology are two keys to being a successful system administrator. For this reason, network managers make good system administrators.

The most crucial tool for success for whomever fills the position of system administrator is solid training on the voice system and all associated adjuncts. All major PBX vendors offer system administrator courses for their customers, covering the entire range of system capabilities, programming options, and maintenance and troubleshooting. The perfect time to attend this training is before the cutover, not after.

The more knowledgeable a system administrator is about the system, its design, features, and capabilities, the more valuable they are to the implementation project and especially the cutover day activities. A system administrator who is trained and "up to speed" prior to the cutover can be proactive, recognizing and heading off problems before they arise and can threaten a smooth cutover. A system administrator who is not trained can only rely on the knowledge of others and is purely in a reactive mode as problems arise and resources must be diverted from cutover activities to deal with them.

Beyond PBX training, you should attend training classes on as many of the system's adjuncts and peripherals as possible before the cutover. Depending on your system configuration, you may also need to attend training classes on the voicemail system, voice response system, call management system and software platforms like call accounting and contact management. Your equipment vendors can help you identify and register for the proper classes.

After you have been to the necessary training classes, you should meet with your equipment vendors to plan the ongoing administration of the voice system. Duties such as routine maintenance, programming changes, moving users, running system reports, and simple troubleshooting are all commonly handled by the system administrator. The vendor provides technical support, advanced troubleshooting and repair, and upgrade and enhancement notification and installation.

You and your vendor should create a schedule of administrative activities to keep the system running smoothly, a set of escalation procedures that provide the system administrator vendor support for complicated maintenance and repair functions, and a vendor point of contact for receiving information about future upgrades and enhancements. Finally, both the vendor and the system administrator should identify an individual to serve as backup in their absence. This ensures that important activities and emergency repairs can take place when you are on vacation, at a conference, or otherwise unavailable.

STATION REVIEWS/SYSTEM PROGRAMMING

At the same time as the hardware elements are being planned, you should begin working with your voice system vendor to plan the software programming of the system. The system programming controls how the PBX handles calls, provides features to the users, and performs other functions.

In all but the smallest PBXs, the system programming and user setup are actually completed before the hardware is installed. This is accomplished by compiling all of the user profile and system programming information in a database, and using it to create a system configuration master disk. The process of creating this master disk is informally called conducting station reviews.

The station review is your opportunity to gather the information needed to program the system to meet each user's individual needs as well as setting overall system attributes. The station review is conducted by the system administrator and the PBX vendor. Using a station review form, (Exhibit 42-3), each user is interviewed to determine their communications needs and establish the features and functionality that will form their profile.

Exhibit 42-3. System cutover station review information required.

• User name
• Voice terminal type
• Extension number
• Call Pickup Groups
• Coverage Paths
• Fax/Modem/Off premises extension requirements
• Hunt Group information
• Voice terminal configurations (i.e., button assignments)
• Night service requirements
• Speed calling list information (i.e., who gets personal lists, who gets group lists, numbers for system list)
• Provide information on long distance network requirements (i.e., 800 numbers to be tested, configuration and specifications of long distance and local trunks)
• System parameters information (i.e., trunk-to-trunk transfer, call forwarding off-net, preferred feature access codes)
• Marked floor plans including extension number, set type, jack location
• ARS pattern information (call handling and routing information)

For each user, the following comprises their profile:

- Personal information — user name, office location, telephone set location, extension number, and telephone set type. In situations where the new voice system is replacing an older one, the previous extension numbers can usually be retained. Telephone set type is usually determined by a corporate standard determined by level in the organization or functional needs.
- Call answering information — call pickup groups, coverage paths, night service. Today's sophisticated PBXs have the ability to deliver calls to users in a variety of ways. Call pickup groups allow several users to answer each others calls from any phone. They are useful for sales and support functions where several users cover for each other. Call coverage paths are the instructions which dictate where a call will go when it is not answered at the called station. When the called station is busy or does not answer, the call will ring at other selected stations. For instance, if a user is not at their desk, then a call for them would next ring at their secretary's phone, and if he or she was unavailable, the call would be directed to voicemail. Each user can have their own coverage path depending on their needs and personal preference. For systems where calls are first answered by a receptionist, night service enables calls to be delivered in another manner after hours or when the receptionist is unavailable.
- Button assignments — buttons can be customized for a user's individual preference. Combinations of call appearances, features buttons (redial, call forwarding, etc.), speed dial, or user programmable buttons can be set. Speed dial buttons can be set by the administrator for system wide use (branch offices, security, other commonly used numbers), or left to be programmed by the user.

The system profile comprises the following:

- Call routing — calls can be delivered over trunks in a variety of ways. Different long distance carriers have different rates at different times of the day. Intelligent routing in the PBX can deliver long distance calls over the most economical service depending on call type. There is also routing information that needs to be programmed to deliver 800 number calls to the proper destinations; sales, service, etc. If your PBX is part of a larger network of PBXs or uses private lines dedicated to your company, these need to be identified in the system programming. In short, the PBX must be told the number and kinds of trunks it has and what to do with incoming or outgoing calls on those trunks.
- System security — in the same manner that physical security in the equipment room is important, it is also necessary to safeguard the

system software from unauthorized use. Password protection should always be enabled on every system administration terminal and the password should be strictly guarded. Many PBXs have a password aging feature which forces the system administrator to change the password regularly, thus adding another level of protection. Toll restriction is another useful security feature. With the explosion of toll fraud committed against organizations, any ability that you have to limit your exposure to abuse should be utilized. Toll restriction features enable you to limit long distance calling access on a station by station basis. You may not want reception room phones to have any long distance access; you may limit conference rooms, break rooms, and other public areas to only 800 number access; and you may limit still other phones to only pre-approved toll numbers (which can be programmed on a system wide speed dial list). For employees who may gain access to the system remotely, either from home or the road, the monitoring and reporting features governing remote access should always be used. Regular reading of the remote access reports can discover abuse or hacking attempts. Some PBXs also have the ability to deny ports to certain phone numbers that originate unsuccessful or suspicious access attempts.

- System parameters — governs system wide features, report generation, and peripheral integration. A modern PBX is capable of delivering more than 200 features, a fraction of which appear on the users' phones. The remainder dictate how the system functions in different situations. Some features such as message waiting indication and send to coverage, provide added functionality to all phones. Other features, such as dial plan definition and attendant routing define system operations. Still other features such as hospitality service and shared tenant service are industry specific. And finally, features such as trunk to trunk transfer and call forwarding outside the system pose some risks and should never be activated unless necessary and then only with security precautions in place. Because of the enormous flexibility of a PBX, you, with the help of your voice system vendor, have a broad range of systemwide features to choose from to solve your business problems and meet your communications goals. System parameters is also where you select criteria for the system to conduct measurements and generate reports. In system administrator training you will learn the usefulness of traffic and threshold reports and how to use their data to keep your system running at peak efficiency. Finally, when adjuncts or other peripherals like voice mail or computer-telephony integrated workstations are present, the PBX must be told how to send and receive information from them. This allows several components from different manufacturers to operate as one seamless communication system.

INSTALLATION AND TESTING

Completion of the system master disk usually coincides with the arrival of the PBX hardware about one week before the cutover date. Once the equipment room is ready, technicians will begin installing the PBX hardware and any associated peripherals such as voicemail or a call management system.

Once the hardware installation is complete, each component is rigorously tested to ensure everything has been installed correctly, is working properly, and is communicating accurately. When the voice system technicians are satisfied the hardware installation and testing are complete, they will connect the PBX to the port side of the cross connect field and test those connections.

Next, phones will be placed on users' desks and in other specified locations. If there is a phone system already in place, the new phones will be placed next to the old ones. Tests are now run from the telephone sets to the station side of the cross connect field. Finally, when all connections are made and satisfactorily tested, the PBX is connected to the telephone company's line of demarcation, the point at which trunk service enters your building. Once these connections are established and tested, the voice system will be ready for the final cutover.

END USER TRAINING

At the same time that the hardware installation and testing is occurring, training sessions should be held for all employees on operating the new phone system. These sessions should last about 30 minutes and should deal with the basics of placing and receiving calls, what their new phone will look like and how it will work, simple features like hold, transfer, conference, send calls, and any specialized features specific to their workgroup or job.

Cutover day activities should be explained and all users should be given clear instructions on getting questions answered, problems resolved, and additional assistance in the first few days with the new system. It is also a good idea to give each user a booklet on how their model of phone works along with system wide information such as dialing instructions, group speed dial numbers, and how their coverage path works. These steps should alleviate noncritical calls to the help desk during and immediately after the cutover.

CUTOVER DAY

Once all of the hardware testing, trunk testing, and user training is complete, it is time to cutover the PBX. In many instances, this is done on a Friday evening after business hours to provide the maximum time for cutover and last minute modifications without affecting your business operations or inconveniencing your employees.

One set of technicians will begin to terminate the new trunks or redirect the old trunks on the line of demarcation and connect them to the PBX. The technicians then begin placing and receiving calls on all trunks, testing the lines and the PBX's call handling configuration.

Simultaneously, another set of technicians is activating each of the phones on the system. When each phone is connected, the technicians will restart the system using the system programming master disk. The system is now operating according to the information provided in the station review process. The user profile database also produces button labels for each phone set. These labels are installed and each extension is tested to ensure that its features match its station review profile.

The advantage of cutting a voice system at night or on a weekend is if any problems are encountered, they can be taken care of without affecting your business operations. And, the old phone system can be left in place for a few days, so that if a major service affecting problem surfaces, the trunks can be reattached to the old system preserving phone service until the problem is corrected.

When all technicians and the system administrator are satisfied that each segment of the new voice system is operating correctly and as designed, the local telephone central office releases the trunks and your new PBX is officially in service.

FIRST DAY ACTIVITIES

The first day of business operations under the new voice system is always a busy and exciting day for the system administrator and employees alike. As users begin to use the new system and their new phone, small problems invariably surface. In most cases they are caused by mislabeled buttons on the phone, a user who has forgotten how to use a particular feature, or business needs that have changed since the station review.

To handle these problems and ensure that each one is corrected to the user's satisfaction, you should establish a help desk on your premises for the first few days under the new system. This help desk should be staffed by yourself, your backup system administrator, and technical support staff from each of your equipment vendors.

This group will be able to answer most questions that users have about how to use features in the system and on their phone. Programming changes and more complicated problems are placed on a "punch list."

Technicians and the system administrator prioritize items in the list, (even in a midsize implementation the punch list can run several hundred, mostly minor items) and make the changes necessary to clear items from the list.

After a few days, or when help desk call volumes drop to almost zero, the help desk is closed and future questions are referred to the system administrator. Once the punch list has been cleared, the vendor support staff and technicians leave and the voice system is officially turned over to the system administrator.

GOING FORWARD

After you have officially taken charge of the voice communication system, you should immediately perform a system audit and backup. In a system audit you catalog every piece of equipment in your telecommunications system by recording the type of equipment, date of purchase, model and serial numbers, and vendor contact. You also record each system administration login ID and password for each system. Next record the circuit number of every trunk, remote access line, and the account codes of your long distance service. When you are finished, you have a document containing the specifications of each component of your telecommunications system. Now, anytime you need to troubleshoot a problem, talk with your vendor's technical support, or check for billing accuracy, you have all of the vital information in one place.

One copy of this document, minus the administration logins and passwords (which should be kept locked up when not in use), should be kept in a book next to the system administration terminal in your equipment room. Another copy, with the administration logins and passwords, should be kept in a secure place offsite or kept in a fireproof safe at your location. With this set of documents should be a full backup of the PBX translations. This is your disaster recovery kit.

As you have learned, installing the voice system hardware is only a small portion of a new system implementation. In the event of a major catastrophe — fire, flood, hurricane, destroying your entire system, the hardware can be replaced fairly quickly. But without the configuration and system translation information, reprogramming the system is a monumental task. Some vendors store your initial system master disk for use in such an emergency. But remember, the system master disk was made before the punch list changes were made, so you will still have some work to do before all system functionality is restored. Keeping a full set of system audit and backup information in a secure location can help you quickly recover from a major outage as well as more easily administer the system on a daily basis.

SUMMARY

The job of implementing and administering a PBX voice communications system is challenging and wide ranging. But, it helps to know that you are not in it alone. In many cities user groups have been established where system administrators can share information and ideas with each other, learn about enhancements and upgrades to their systems, and develop their network communications management skills.

During the implementation process, have your vendor register you for your local users group chapter and attend their meetings. You will probably gain valuable insight and learn how to avoid some problems that others have encountered, helping you to a successful implementation of your new voice communications system.

Section VI
Networking Tools and Techniques

THE FIELD OF NETWORK DESIGN HAS EVOLVED CONSIDERABLY since the use of communications to link remote users to mainframes began during the early 1960s. Today, the control unit-based, mainframe-centric network has evolved into workstations on LANs accessing mainframes in a client/server environment via bridges, routers, and gateways. Instead of only having to consider text-based applications, network managers and LAN administrators must now consider the effect of different types of multimedia applications on current and planned networks. To facilitate the network design process, a number of tools and techniques have evolved over the past few years that facilitate the design process and are the subject of this section.

In this section are three chapters focused on providing detailed information concerning the use of different networking tools and techniques which, when used, can considerably facilitate the network design process. In Chapter 43, author G. Thomas des Jardin's **A Simulation Method for the Design of Multimedia Networks** introduces three basic phases of the simulation method used for multimedia network design. In the preparation phase, the author describes how to define goals in measurable terms. Next, in the baseline phase, information concerning data capture and the validation of such data are presented. The third phase of the design process is referred to by the author as the delta phase. During this phase, changes are applied to the baselined network, after which the results are analyzed and summarized through information presented in the three phases. This chapter provides a methodology one can use to simulate a wide variety of networks.

The second chapter in this section focuses attention on techniques one can use to determine a number of quantitative metrics involved in client/server computing via bridges and routers. In Gilbert Held's chapter, titled **Determining Remote Bridge and Router Delays**, the author uses queuing theory to illustrate various performance metrics associated with interconnection geographically separated LANs via remote bridges or routers. Although the author illustrates how to project queuing delays, of far more importance is the presentation of how one can use queuing theory to answer a classic network design problem. That problem is the appropriate selection of a WAN operating rate to interconnect two geographically separated LANs.

In concluding this section, author Gilbert Held adds a second chapter. In Chapter 45, titled **Network Baselining as a Planning Tool**, Held reviews a core set of popular communications tools one can consider using to facilitate the network design process. Examples of planning tools covered in this chapter include Triticom, Inc.'s SimpleView, an easy-to-use SNMP management platform; NetManage's Newt, a program that provides statistics on network activity associated with individual users; Ethervision, a program from Triticom that provides statistical information on individual Ethernet network users as well as information concerning the overall activity of the network; and Foundation Manager, a product of Network General Corporation, which is now part of Network Associates, and which provides information on both local and remote networks via SNMP. Through the use of the products covered in this chapter or similar products, one can develop a baseline of network activity that is extremely valuable for planning network upgrades or for considering the replacement of a current network by a new network.

Chapter 43
A Simulation Method for the Design of Multimedia Networks

G. Thomas des Jardins

VENDORS OF NETWORK DESIGN TOOLS usually provide ample documentation and examples concerning the use of the tool. What is often lacking, however, is a methodology for applying simulation techniques in general.

Multimedia networks and the tools that represent them are complex, and simple examples are often insufficient to impart an understanding of the process or methodology that a network designer needs to use to achieve accurate simulation results. This chapter describes one such methodology, which is applicable to the use of tools for the design and analysis of multimedia networks that carry voice, video, and data. The chapter provides the structure and approach that are missing from the user manuals.

Furthermore, the information is intended to be helpful regardless of the simulation tool chosen. The chapter also discusses approaches to solving particular modeling problems that arise in multimedia networks.

THE MODELING PROCESS

Networks that are complicated enough to have multimedia segments are frequently too complex and too large for simple rule-of-thumb calculations. Simulation is the best means of collecting performance data on networks that are in the planning and design stages.

Complexity requires a great deal of organization in data collection, model validation, and analysis of results. A defined process increases confidence in the results by increasing organization and thereby managing complexity.

0-8493-0859-3/00/$0.00+$.50
© 2000 by CRC Press LLC

This chapter specifically draws to the reader's attention the following aspects of simulation:

- important data that will be required
- means for obtaining this data
- suggestions for modeling the data
- possible interpretations of results
- how the modeling procedure might be segmented into tractable units

Simulation results are highly dependent on the quality of data being input. The large amount of detailed data being handled increases the margin for error. By paying attention to the process, the network manager can maintain the data in an organized fashion, track the validation of the model, and increase the confidence in the results.

There is no such thing as being too organized. The corollary is that if there is any confusion about the results, the procedure should be interrupted and investigated until there is no longer any confusion. Bad data and bugs are the worst enemies of accurate simulations.

The process described in this chapter contains the following three basic phases:

- Phase I: Preparation
- Phase II: Baseline
- Phase III: Delta

The tasks for each phase are outlined briefly here, then discussed in detail:

- Phase I tasks include:
  - *Goals.* These must be stated in measurable and clear terms.
  - *Data collection.* The topology and traffic of the existing network is captured.
- Phase II tasks include:
  - *Capture.* The collected data is captured in the model.
  - *Validation.* The captured model is validated.
- Phase III tasks include:
  - *Delta.* Changes are applied to the baselined network.
  - *Analysis.* The results are analyzed and summarized.

PHASE I: PREPARATION

This phase includes the definition of goals and the collection of topology and traffic data for the baseline network. The first task is identifying the goals.

Identifying Goals

A simulation should have clearly defined goals. For the hypothetical case discussed in this chapter, there are two principal goals: The first is to develop a validated baseline model of the network in its current configuration; the second is to model the introduction of an asynchronous transfer mode (ATM) backbone.

A brief summary of the modeling strategy entails the following actions:

1. Decide if modeling is appropriate.
2. Determine simulation goals.
3. Describe the network in one or two slides.
4. Combine each goal and its network description into a series of scenarios, each with a simple, testable model description and a clearly defined goal.
5. For each model description, define the data to be collected, the results expected, and how the model will be validated.
6. Combine these individual documents into a simulation notebook.
7. After the individual models have been validated, repeat the process by combining the models into more complex models and validating each in a stepwise, iterative fashion.

Sample Goals of a Modeling Project. Frequently, network managers embark on projects without ensuring that they have defined achievable goals, although they may have an intuitive idea of what problem they seek to resolve and what steps might be useful to take. The difficulty is in translating these qualitative statements to quantitative goals based on known metrics. Without these goals, even beginning a modeling project is a waste of time.

Problem. Users are experiencing delays of 1.5 seconds running application X (problem could also be expressed in terms of low throughput).

Goal. The goals of a modeling project can often be stated simply. For example, the goal in solving the previous problem may be to "run application X, reducing delay to 0.5 seconds."

Experiments to consider to solve the problem include:

- *Segmentation.* Can further segmentation of the existing Ethernet LAN improve the performance to the desired level?
- *Backbone increase.* Can upgrading the backbone improve the performance to the desired level?
- *Segment upgrade.* Will upgrading the network improve the performance to the desired level?

Projecting Costs. Next, a spreadsheet for anticipated costs should be created. For example:

Experiments Considered	*Cost of Experimental Upgrade*
Segmentation	Bridges = $
	Routers = $
	Switching hubs = $
Backbone increase	New backbone hardware = $
	Plant (e.g., cabling) upgrade = $
Segment upgrade	Adapter cards = $

This step is usually followed by some qualitative analysis as to the amount of room for future growth, improvements in supportability, and so on.

Preparing a spreadsheet is relatively easy; however, it is not that easy to decide what precise changes are required to give needed quality of service. In addition, it is difficult to set parameters for wide area network interfaces because the answers to request for proposals for WAN services may use different sets of metrics.

Figures of Merit. The key is to define what measurements are important; these are often called figures of merit.

For example, is end-to-end delay the figure of merit that must be improved to provide users with the required quality of service? Are hardware costs more important than recurring costs? Is on-line transaction processing running across some segments? Voice? Video? For each set of users, there must be some number that can be extracted from the analysis that can quantitatively define the quality of service (QoS) being provided for each group.

To begin, a spreadsheet should be created for each group of supported users, showing the applications they are using currently or will be using in the future. For each of these applications, the metrics that describe the desired QoS should be defined (the network manager should already, to a large extent, be familiar with these).

Next, the available tools should be examined in light of the following questions:

- Can the modeling tool provide these measurements?
- Can these measurements be extracted from the network (for validation)?
- Do these measurements provide insight into users' satisfaction?

If the answer to any question is no, the tools, metrics, or decision to model should be reevaluated. If the modeling tool does not provide the desired reports, perhaps the manufacturer will modify the tool. If the network monitoring tools are inadequate, it may be necessary to add instrumentation to the network. The network manager may need to identify additional network monitoring hardware for acquisition or lease — or perhaps simulation is not the answer to the problem. Once these criteria are satisfied, the baseline should be defined by collecting the topology and traffic of the network.

Performance Metrics

In order to manage a network, its performance must be measurable and network goals must be specified in measurable metrics. Some of the more important metrics include:

- queue buildup
- end-to-end delay
- throughput
- jitter
- goodput

Models must be instrumented according to the data collection requirements, by placing probes or turning on data collection routines in certain modules. The way that data collection is performed is unique to each simulation tool, but most tools will allow the collection of much of this information. The following paragraphs describe these metrics.

Buffer/Queue Size. Queue buildup is an important indicator of potential congestion points. Queue size is one of the largest factors in delays on ATM LANs. It is also the largest contributing factor to jitter.

Large queues always add to end-to-end delay and can indicate possible packet loss, which could adversely affect throughput by causing retransmission. When a network device such as an ATM switch has more traffic than it can send out on a given link, it is faced with two choices: either discard the traffic or save it in a buffer.

Assuming an infinite supply of buffers, frequently buffering is the optimal choice because it improves throughput. Buffering, however, creates queue buildup, and cells of a given quality of service must wait in turn to exit, in order to maintain first in, first out ordering. This means that the cell that arrives at the back of the line must wait for all of the cells in front of it to exit the switch before it can exit, increasing its latency.

Latency or End-to-End Delay. Latency is the amount of delay introduced by a particular device or link; end-to-end delay is the sum of all latencies experienced from source to destination. End-to-end delay is important because many applications require a specific quality of service.

While buffering cells, rather than dropping them, can certainly improve throughput, this waiting increases latency and contributes to jitter. In ATM networks, latency is one of the QoS metrics that a committed bit rate (CBR) or variable bit rate (VBR) traffic stream may negotiate, and therefore may seek to minimize. In other types of networks it may simply be a design goal. In other words, some applications would rather have the data right away or not at all.

Jitter. Jitter is also an ATM QoS metric for which some CBR and VBR applications desire to negotiate a low value. If a cell arrives at a switch when it has a large number of cells in its buffer, and another cell arrives when the switch has a small number of cells in its buffer, the difference between the buffer sizes in these cases is that particular switch's contribution to a cell's total end-to-end jitter.

Jitter is minimized by maintaining constant buffer queue sizes. In general, ATM available bit rate (ABR) traffic expects to have a very low cell loss probability and higher latencies and jitter. Some switches address this problem by having multiple queues.

Utilization, Throughput, and Goodput. Utilization is the amount of time a link is idle, versus the amount of time it is in use. This calculation does not necessarily show how much data is reaching the end system.

Throughput defines how much data is delivered to the end system. Throughput needs to be determined to ensure that components and links are sized correctly.

The calculation of raw bandwidth is trivial, but does not include any bandwidth lost because of retransmission or other protocol and hardware interactions. Thus, throughput is important to measure because it allows the manager to estimate reserve capacity; it also reveals those interactions in the network that may lower overall throughput.

Goodput includes the actual upper-layer contributions to performance, such as whether TCP received the packets in a usable amount of time. In some instances, goodput is a preferred metric if it can be obtained. Some simulation tools, such as CACI's COMNET III, can measure goodput, throughput, and utilization.

Data Collection

Once metrics are defined, the actual characteristics of the network as it exists currently must be collected. This is the first step in baselining the network.

First, a topology data collection sheet is created. A sample is shown in Exhibit 43.1. Using the topology data collection spreadsheet, each hardware

Exhibit 43-1. Example of a topology data collection sheet.

Network Type	Node Description	ID		
Data	10Base-T hub	DH1		

Link Name	Link Type	Speed	From	To
WAN	Coaxial	DS-3	DH1	AT&T
Backbone	Fiber	SONET	DH1	DR1

device in the network and the links that connect them are documented. The number and rate of each link are identified.

This is also a good time to note all network costs. The cost of a link consists of the local component as well as the long-distance charges; some simulation tools are integrated with tariff data bases to some extent.

Most simulation tool manufacturers have or are planning interfaces to network management tools, which will simplify information collection on the data portions of the network. Tools have different levels of integration with network management. Some tools can collect topology information; others can also collect traffic information. There are three categories of traffic: voice, video, and data.

Traffic collection is the more difficult activity, especially for data and voice. Once again, a very careful, systematic approach yields the best results.

Some useful numbers for calculating propagation delay times in various media are:

Medium	*Propagation Delay*
Coaxial cable	4 µs/km
Fiber	5 µs/km

Voice Network Information. To collect the topology and traffic information for the voice portion of the network, here are some recommendations as to how the information might be represented in the model.

Topology. All segments of the voice network have to be described, including trunks, PBXs, and additional analog lines used by fax and data equipment for each location that is serviced by the network. Links to remote users also should be documented by listing the closest points of presence (POP) of any services that remote users will be calling. Quality of service and bandwidth required for each link should be noted.

Traffic. Billing information for any voice lines should be helpful in providing usage patterns for voice links. Most PBXs collect this information.

Any simple network management protocol (SNMP)-managed devices in the voice network may deliver usage information to the management tool.

This information may be expressed in several forms, but for the simulation a probability distribution function is needed to drive the traffic sources in the models. Because voice traffic exhibits a high degree of randomness, it is frequently viewed as a Poisson distribution. Depending on the modeling tool, there should be several distributions for voice traffic:

- the distribution of addresses (i.e., who is calling whom)
- the distribution of the length of the message (i.e., call holding time)
- the distribution of the number of calls (i.e., call attempts)
- the desired quality of service

Modeling Recommendations. Typically, voice traffic is represented as a Poisson distribution. This method specifies the number of events that will occur over time. The exponential distribution is what is actually used to produce a Poisson distribution of traffic arrival because the exponential distribution determines the amount of time to the next event (i.e., the call to be generated).

Another method to simulate voice traffic is to use an interrupted Markov process to generate spurts of digitized speech packets. If the traffic is to be carried over a CBR circuit, it is entirely valid to use a constant source at the defined rate. Typical data rates for voice lines are as follows (because faxes are also essentially voice traffic, they are included in the table):

Traffic on Voice Circuit	Rate
Voice	64K bps
Group 3 fax	14.4K bps
Group 4 fax	64K bps

In ATM networks, voice traffic is usually represented as CBR traffic. Because it is CBR, it is tempting to subtract CBR traffic from the model in an attempt to speed it up; however, it is not recommended unless the manager is extremely familiar with the way the switch handles buffer allocation. Even though the CBR traffic is always there, some jitter may occur in the competition for buffer space, which will affect queue buildup.

Video Network Information. To collect the topology and traffic information for the video portion of the network, here are some recommendations as to how it might be represented in the model.

Topology. All video segments should be described, in the same fashion as the voice network, noting areas of overlap.

Traffic. Again, billing information may be of great assistance when determining the usage pattern for video links. Many video codecs (e.g., PictureTel's) use two switched 56K-bps lines. It can be safely assumed that current usage for such a link is at least 2x56K-bps multiplied by the holding time of the call in this case. The manufacturer of the video codec equipment should be able to provide a more accurate idea of the traffic the device generates. The holding times of the video sessions may be derived from billing or from equipment checkout logs.

For each video source there should be the following information:

- maximum bit rate generated by the codec
- holding time for each session
- number of sessions for the sample period
- address distribution of sessions (i.e., who is calling whom)

The character of these sessions may vary a great deal; if so, developing several scenarios for the model may be appropriate. One scenario might be supporting a worst-case video session during the worst-case data session and worst-case voice; another scenario could show a more normal video session.

With improved network services, users may alter their habits and begin using the service at worst-case times. Because the network manager is usually interested in the worst-case behavior, maximum usage should be assumed for the video portion of the model.

If a model is a discrete event simulation of an ATM network, long periods will not be simulated. ATM simulations take a large amount of computer time. Therefore it is generally safe to simply presume that all of the video sessions are already established and in use for the length of the worst-case scenario. This is simpler than attempting to capture any periodic qualities they may have.

Modeling Recommendations. The data rate for a video codec can vary. Some produce constant bit rate traffic while others generate traffic with a bit rate that changes as the amount of data that can be compressed changes. Because all of the data is important, these can either be represented as a worst-case constant video source at the bit rate desired, or as "bursts of bursts."

Generally, Poisson distributions are extremely poor at representing this sort of traffic. If an ATM or frame relay network is to be the carrier for this data, one important consideration is what sort of QoS is anticipated. If this traffic will be sent over a CBR connection, then it would be appropriate to model it as a constant source. Some typical video data rates are shown in Exhibit 43.2.

Exhibit 43-2. Data rates for several types of video traffic.

Video Type	Uncompressed	Compressed
Real tlme, 30 fps ($128 \times 240 \times 9$)	8,294	2,000
Studio 30 fps ($640 \times 480 \times 24$)	221,184	4,000
MPEG	N/A	>1.86M b/s
H.261	N/A	> = 128K b/s

Data Network Information. To collect topology and traffic information for the data portion of the network, here are recommendations as to how it might be represented in the model.

Topology. Describe the network's topology, including virtual (e.g., source and destination of traffic) as well as physical aspects.

Traffic. The hardest type of traffic for which to get an accurate probability distribution is often data. To get a profile of the distribution of data, several techniques can be used. For the subnets that make up the WAN, one technique is to place a sniffer or similar device at each of the subnetwork WAN interface points and to measure the actual loading.

This method yields the most accurate and fastest-running simulation, because the actual LANs are not modeled, only the load they offer to the WAN. Many network managers only have equipment suitable for monitoring the LAN side of their interconnecting device. In this case, the capacity of the current link can be used with estimates of current user activities to derive profiles of the data traffic.

In addition, many devices have SNMP information bases that provide some useful information. Network management tools may also be useful. If frame relay or ATM is currently being used, information may be available from the provider regarding traffic patterns. For each interface (i.e., traffic source) to the WAN, the following traffic details are necessary:

- the data rate of sources
- the size of the packets
- the quality of service desired (as for voice channels)
- the distribution of the addresses

Modeling Recommendations. The best way to model data sources is to think of them as bursts with some space between them. An example would be to have fixed burst sizes with some distribution of random delay between.

However, most tools (including COMNET III, BONeS, and Opnet) can drive the simulation to some extent from sniffer-collected traces. If there is a large amount of query-and-response type data, it may be better to define

Exhibit 43-3. Representative packet sizes for use in simulations.

Network Type	Most Common Packet Size	Next Most Common Packet Size
Ethernet	64 bytes (50% of traffic)	1,500 bytes (50% of traffic)
Token Ring	64 bytes (75% of traffic)	
ATM	9,180 bytes (default for ATM)	
FDDI	4,352 bytes (default for FDDI)	

the applications' query response in the model, with the guidance of the sniffer-acquired data.

On ATM networks, data is generally sent as ABR or perhaps even as uncommitted bit rate (UBR). Ethernet packets are generally either the largest or the smallest that the Ethernet can handle; Token Ring packets are almost always small. Some packet size data for use in simulations is shown in Exhibit 43.3.

PHASE II: BASELINE MODEL POPULATION AND VALIDATION

After capturing the data required to construct the baseline, model design can begin. The goal now is to transform the collected information into a valid baseline.

Simple small steps, gradually increasing the complexity as each step has been validated, should be used. This way, data collection efforts can be validated, establishing confidence in the tool and modeling methodology.

Guidelines for Building Models

Creating Subnets. Preliminary steps should be modeling a portion of the network that the network manager understands very well — for instance, the simple case of determining the loading of the video portion of the Net. Although it may not prove to be a very interesting model, it will give confidence in the use of the tool. Later, smaller separate models for portions of each type of traffic in the network (e.g., voice, video, and data) can be built. By keeping the problems simple and only gradually adding complexity, the overall quality of the work is greatly improved.

The following paragraphs provide more detailed, step-by-step guidelines. Vendors of network design tools provide considerable support for their products that can be of additional assistance.

Step 1: Tool Use and Data Collection Validation. During this step, the goal is to learn how to use the tool and to validate the data collection techniques.

It is likely that some data requirements of the problem or model will have been overlooked. A small representative of the network should be modeled, preferably using portions that are fairly well understood.

By validating knowledge of the tool and the manager's ability to capture raw data in a model, much work will be saved. Putting off gaining this intuitive understanding of how the modeling tool represents the network's components only postpones difficulties. Later, when the model has more data in it and more processes running, it will not be possible to see what happens with the very simple cases. The idea is to conduct simple experiments until the tool is completely understood.

Some suggestions for these early experiments are video only (this is probably the simplest part of the problem), a simple WAN link, or a very simple voice link. Most networks, when lightly loaded, are of little interest so it is a good idea to experiment by reducing the bandwidth at a random bottleneck point.

Validating Subnets

Once a subnet is built, it must be validated. The process of validation requires running the model and comparing the results against data collected for the real subnet. Validation should be in three steps:

- *Topology.* The topology of the subnetwork or network should be checked. For example, are all of the links connected to the correct devices? Are they of the correct type and bandwidth? Is each traffic source connected correctly?
- *Routing.* Are the router tables set up correctly? For the path of a packet traveling through the network, does it go where it should (and on the reverse path as well)?
- *Load.* Run the simulation with only one source turned on at a time. Is the correct amount of traffic sent to each destination? Is the delay close to what the network really experiences?

Step 2: Beginning to Validate the Data Network. At this point subnets (which later will be collected into a larger model) should be created. Start with subnets that can operate independently. Rather than spending time encoding large amounts of routing or other information for larger future networks, it is better to model a small subnet correctly. In doing so, tools and models will be built up for future use in other areas.

For instance, using COMNET III, application profiles (including message response pairs) may be built, which will be very useful when building up other models. At first, entries should have depth as opposed to breadth. Once a working subnet is created, it may be copied in its entirety. In brief, the steps are to build a subnet, validate it, and repeat.

All of the subnets that may possibly be built should be built and validated before moving on. Validation can have multiple meanings. A simple validation might be a data check: Was the correct information entered for the model? Next might be a sanity check: Does it make sense? A logical check might be next: Does it behave as expected? Do all sources reach their destinations? Are source message pairs coded correctly?

Only proceed when all of this work has been done. The more time spent testing the pieces, the easier the job will be when putting them together.

Integrating and Validating Subnets. When the subnets have been validated, they must be integrated and validated in a stepwise fashion. An example might be considering replacing a collapsed Ethernet backbone with a distributed ATM backbone that also carries video and contiguous portions of the voice network. First the data is integrated, then the video, and finally the voice.

Once again, there are three tips to successfully building an accurate simulation of a network:

1. *Never proceed if there are any doubts about a result.* Stop immediately and investigate the problem until it is resolved. If the problem is not resolved, numerous bugs will creep in. This practice cannot be overemphasized.
2. *Be organized.* There is a lot of data to compile. The spreadsheet can be the biggest asset.
3. *Understand the network.* To this end, a good network analyzer is invaluable. If the expense of buying one cannot be justified, many leasing agencies and sometimes even the manufacturers rent them out.

The key to successful integration and validation is taking small steps, testing the results each time, and never proceeding if there are any doubts about a result. It is best to work up in complexity by beginning with the portions of the network that are best understood.

PHASE III: ALTERATION OF BASELINE TO ACQUIRE DATA

When a baseline with which to compare is completed and validated, alterations can be introduced. The alterations should be introduced with the same care that the baseline was constructed.

An example might be to compare the performance of both 100Base-T Ethernet and ATM backbone links. (Both should be able to handle the offered data load easily, but video traffic may be too much for the Ethernet backbone.) Loss and delay experienced by each traffic source should be measured, as well as the throughput on the backbone, to determine if these meet the required quality of service.

There are limits as to how much accuracy can be achieved by modeling. Efforts should focus on those areas that yield the highest return. Focusing on describing the offered load accurately will yield a more accurate simulation.

The goal is to have a model that yields valid information to guide decisions when doing experimentation on the network.

SUMMARY

This chapter has offered a brief description of a methodology that may be used to simulate a wide variety of networks using network design tools such as COMNET III. Because of the complexity of networks and the tools that represent them, simple examples are often insufficient to impart an understanding of the process or methodology that a network designer needs to use to achieve accurate simulation results.

Many steps described in this chapter are a necessary part of network analysis and design, yet they are often not found in the manuals of network design tools themselves. By focusing on the methodology rather than a particular tool's implementation, this chapter has attempted to provide the structure and approach that are missing from the users' manuals and to give readers insight into approaches they can use to solve some of the particular modeling problems that are expected in modeling multimedia networks.

There are many issues still untouched. Examples include parameter sensitivity analysis, confidence intervals, and length of time to run a simulation. Unfortunately, these issues are beyond the scope of this chapter. However, an excellent text on simulation that covers these issues is Dr. Raj Jam's book *The Art of Computer Systems Performance Analysis* (New York: Wiley, 1991).

Chapter 44
Determining Remote Bridge and Router Delays
Gilbert Held

THIS CHAPTER EXAMINES THE USE OF QUEUING THEORY to determine the delays associated with remote bridges and routers. In addition, it investigates the effects of modifying the operating rate of the WAN links — in particular, the effects of various communications circuit operating rates on equipment delays. There is a point beyond which increasing the operating rate of a communications circuit has an insignificant effect on equipment and network performance.

WAITING LINE ANALYSIS

Queuing theory, the formal term for waiting line analysis, can be traced to the work of A.K. Erlang, a Danish mathematician. His pioneering work spanned several areas of mathematics, including the dimensioning or sizing of trunk lines to accommodate long-distance calls between telephone company exchanges. This chapter bypasses Erlang's sizing work to concentrate on the analysis of waiting lines.

BASIC COMPONENTS

Exhibit 44-1 illustrates the basic components of a simple waiting line system. The input process can be considered the arrival of people, objects, or frames of data. The service facility performs some predefined operation on arrivals, such as collecting tolls from passengers in cars arriving at a toll booth or the conversion of a LAN data frame into a synchronous data link connection (SDLC) frame by a bridge or router for transmission over a WAN transmission facility. If the arrival rate temporarily exceeds the service rate of the service facility, a waiting line known as a queue forms. If a waiting line never exists, the server is idle or there is too much service capacity.

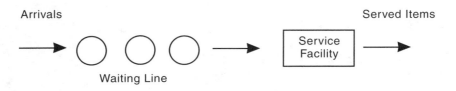

Exhibit 44-1. Basic components of a simple waiting line system.

The waiting line system illustrated in Exhibit 44-1 is more formally known as a single-channel, single-phase waiting line system — single channel because there is one waiting line, and single phase because the process performed by the service facility occurs at one location. One toll booth on a highway or a single-port bridge connected to a LAN are two examples of single-channel, single-phase waiting line systems.

Exhibit 44-2 illustrates three additional types of waiting line systems. On multichannel systems, arrivals are serviced by more than one service facility, which results in multiple paths or channels to those service facilities. On multiphase systems, arriving entities are processed by multiple service facilities.

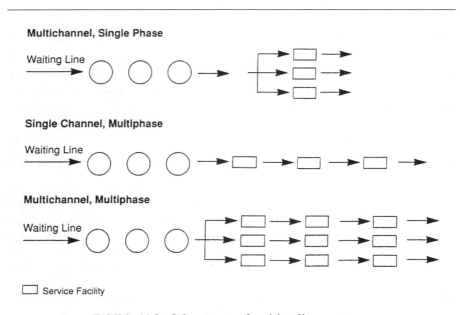

Exhibit 44-2. Other types of waiting line systems.

One example of a multiphase service facility is a toll road in which drivers of automobiles are serviced by several series of toll booths; for example, a turnpike that has toll plazas every few miles. Another example of a multiphase system is the routing of data through a series of bridges and routers. The computations associated with multiphase systems can become quite complex, and because most networks can be analyzed on a point-to-point basis as a single-phase system, this chapter restricts its examination of queuing models to single-phase systems.

ASSUMPTIONS

Queuing theory is similar to other types of theory in that it is based on a series of assumptions. Those assumptions primarily have to do with the distribution of arriving entities and the time required to service each arrival.

Both the distribution of arrivals and the time to service them are usually represented as random variables. The most common distribution used to represent arrivals is the Poisson distribution:

$$P(n) = \frac{\lambda^n e^{-\lambda}}{n!}$$

where: $P(n)$ = Probability of n arrivals

λ = Mean arrival time

e = 2.71828

$n!$ = n factorial

= $n(n-1)(n-2)\ldots 1$

One of the more interesting features of the Poisson process concerns the relationship between the arrival rate and the time between arrivals. If the number of arrivals per unit time is Poisson distributed with a mean of λ, the time between arrivals is a negative exponential probability distribution with a mean of $1/\lambda$. For example, if the mean arrival rate per 10-minute period is 3, the mean time between arrivals is 10/3, or 3.3 minutes.

NETWORK APPLICATIONS

Through the use of queuing theory or waiting time analysis, it is possible to examine the effect of different WAN circuit operating rates on the ability of remote bridges and routers to transfer data between LANs. This answers questions about the average delay associated with the use of a remote bridge or router, the effect on those delays of increasing the operating rate of the WAN circuit, and when an increase in the WAN circuit's operating rate results in an insignificant improvement in bridge or router performance.

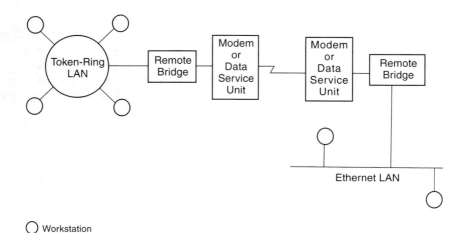

◯ Workstation

Exhibit 44-3. Internet consisting of two LANs connected through remote bridges.

The following example illustrates the application and value of queuing theory to network problems.

Two geographically distant LANs are to be connected through a pair of remote bridges as illustrated in Exhibit 44-3. Today, most remote bridges support both RS-232 and V.35 interfaces, permitting the bridge to be connected to modems, or to higher-speed data service units (DSUs) for digital transmission. This means that there are a wide variety of circuits that can be used to connect a pair of remote bridges, both analog and digital, and at different operating rates.

This example assumes that, on the basis of prior knowledge obtained from monitoring the transmission between locally interconnected LANs, the data communications manager has determined that approximately 10,000 frames per day can be expected to flow from one network to the other. The average length of a frame is 1250 bytes.

QUEUING THEORY CALCULATIONS

The 10,000-frame-per-day rate must be converted into an arrival rate. In this case, the next assumption is that each network is active only eight hours per day and both networks are in the same time zone. A transaction rate of 10,000 frames per eight-hour day is equivalent to an average arrival rate of 10,000/(8 * 60 * 60), or 0.347222 frames per second. In queuing theory, this average arrival rate (AR) is the average rate at which frames arrive at the service facility for forwarding across the WAN communications circuit.

Monitoring has determined that the average frame length is 1250 bytes. Because a LAN frame must be converted into a WAN frame or packet for transmission over a WAN transmission facility, whatever header and trailer information is required by the WAN protocol is added to the frame or packet. Thus, the actual length of the WAN frame or packet exceeds the length of the LAN frame. This example assumes that 25 bytes are added to each LAN frame, resulting in the average transmission of 1275 bytes per frame.

To compute an expected service time requires knowing the operating rate. If the WAN communications circuit illustrated in Exhibit 44-3 operates at 9600 bps, the time required to transmit one 1275-byte frame or packet becomes 1275 * 8/9600, or 1.0625 seconds. This time is more formally known as the expected service time and represents the time required to transmit a frame whose average length is 1250 bytes on the LAN and 1275 bytes when converted for transmission over the WAN transmission facility. Given that the expected service time is 1.0625 seconds, the mean service rate (MSR) can be computed easily. That rate is the rate at which frames entering the bridge destined for the other LAN are serviced and is 1/1.0625, or 0.9411765 frames per second.

Two key queuing theory variables — the arrival rate and the mean service rate — have now been computed. The service rate computation was dependent on the initial selection of a WAN circuit operating at 9600 bps.

Exhibit 44-4 illustrates the results of the initial set of computations for one portion of this Internet. In this case, 10,000 frames per eight-hour day flow in each direction, so only one-half of the Internet has to be analyzed. If this had not been true, each half could be analyzed and a circuit operating rate selected based on the highest arrival rate's effect on LAN performance.

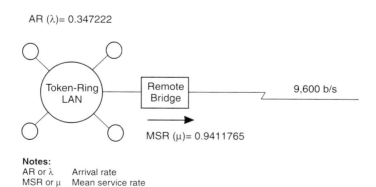

AR (λ)= 0.347222

Token-Ring LAN — Remote Bridge — 9,600 b/s

MSR (μ)= 0.9411765

Notes:
AR or λ Arrival rate
MSR or μ Mean service rate

Exhibit 44-4. Initial computational results.

In Exhibit 44-4, the queuing theory designators are indicated in parentheses. Thus, in a queuing theory book, the average arrival rate of 0.347222 transactions or frames per second would be indicated by the expression $\lambda = 0.347222$.

Although the mean service rate exceeds the average arrival rate, on occasion the arrival rate results in a burst of data that exceeds the capacity of the bridge. When this occurs, queues are created as the bridge accepts frames and places those frames into buffers or temporary storage areas. Through the use of queuing theory, the expected time for frames to flow through the bridge can be examined and the circuit operating rate adjusted accordingly.

A communications network that uses remote bridges or routers corresponds to a single-channel, single-phase queuing model. The utilization of the service facility (P) is obtained by dividing the average arrival rate by the mean service rate. That is,

$$P = AR/MSR$$
$$= 0.347222/0.9411765$$
$$= 0.3689$$

Use of a circuit operating at 9600 bps results in an average utilization level of approximately 37 percent. In queuing theory texts, the preceding equation is replaced by $P = \lambda/\mu$, where λ is the average arrival rate and μ is the mean service rate.

The utilization level of the service facility (remote bridge) is AR/MSR, so the probability that there are no frames in the bridge, Po, becomes:

$$Po = 1 - AR/MSR = 1 - \lambda/\mu$$

For the remote bridge connected to a 9600-bps circuit:

$$Po = 1 - 0.37 = 0.63$$

Thus, 63 percent of the time there will be no frames in the bridge's buffers awaiting transmission to the distant network.

For a single-channel, single-phase system, the mean number of units expected to be in the system is equivalent to the average arrival rate divided by the difference between the mean service rate and the arrival rate. In queuing theory, the mean or expected number of units in a system is designated by the letter L. Thus,

$$L = AR/(MSR - AR) = \lambda/(\mu - \lambda)$$

Returning to the network example, the mean or expected number of frames that will be in the system, including frames residing in the bridge's buffer area or flowing down the WAN transmission facility, can be determined:

$$L = 0.347/(0.941 - 0.347) = 0.585$$

Thus, on the average, approximately 6/10 of a frame resides in the bridge's buffer and on the transmission line.

By multiplying the utilization of the service facility by the expected number of units in a system, the mean number of units in the queue or, in common English, the queue length, is obtained. The queue length is denoted by Lq and thus becomes:

$$Lq = PL = \left(\frac{AR}{MSR} \right) \left(\frac{AR}{MSR - AR} \right)$$

$$= \left(\frac{\lambda}{\mu} \right) \left(\frac{\lambda}{\mu - \lambda} \right)$$

$$= \frac{\lambda^2}{\mu(\mu - \lambda)}$$

Again returning to the network example

$$Lq = \frac{(0.347)^2}{0.941(0.941 - 0.347)}$$

$$= 0.216$$

On the average, 0.216 frames are queued in the bridge for transmission when the operating rate of the WAN is 9600 bps and 10,000 frames per eight-hour day require remote bridging. There were 0.585 frames in the system, so the difference, $0.585 - 0.216$, or 0.369 frames, is flowing on the transmission line at any particular time.

TIME COMPUTATIONS

In addition to computing information concerning the expected number of frames in queues and in the system, queuing theory furnishes tools to determine the mean time in the system and the mean waiting time. In queuing theory, the mean waiting time is designated as the variable W, whereas the mean waiting time in the queue is designated as the variabe Wq.

The mean time in the system, W, is

$$W = 1/(MSR - AR = 1/(4 - \lambda)$$

For the bridged network example, the mean time a frame can be expected to reside in the system can be computed:

$$W = 1/(0.941 - 0.347) = 1.68 \text{ seconds}$$

By itself, this tells us that an average response time of approximately 1.7 seconds can be expected for frames that must be bridged if the WAN transmission facility operates at 9600 bps. Whether this is good or bad depends on the acceptability of the 1.7-second delay.

The last queuing item is the waiting time associated with a frame being queued. That time, Wq, is equivalent to the waiting time system multiplied by the use of the service facility. That is,

$$Wq = PW = \left(\frac{AR}{MSR} \right)\left(\frac{1}{MSR - AR} \right)$$

$$= \frac{AR}{MSR(MSR - AR)}$$

In terms of queuing theory, Wq is

$$Wq = \frac{\lambda}{\mu(\mu - \lambda)}$$

Returning to the bridged network example, the waiting time for a queued frame is

$$Wq = \frac{0.347}{0.941(0.941 - 0.347)} = 0.621 \text{ seconds}$$

Previously, it had been determined that a frame can be expected to reside for 1.68 seconds in the bridged system, including queue waiting time and transmission time. The computed queue waiting time is 0.621 seconds. The difference between the two, $1.68 - 0.621$, or approximately 1.06 seconds, is the time required to transmit a frame over the 9600-bps WAN transmission facility.

DETERMINING AN OPTIMUM LINE OPERATING RATE

Each of the variables could be recomputed for different line operating rates, but it is simple to write a small computer program to perform this operation. Exhibit 44-5 lists the statements of a Beginner's All-Purpose Symbolic Instruction Code language program named QUEUE.BAS. The execution of this program is shown in Exhibit 44-6, which displays the values

Exhibit 44-5. QUEUE.BAS program listing.

```
REM PROGRAM QUEUE.BAS
CLS
REM AR = arrival rate
REM MSR = mean service rate
REM L = mean (expected) number of frames in system
REM Lq = mean number of frames in queue
REM W = mean time (s) in system
REM Wq = mean waiting time (s)
REM EST = expected service time
transactions = 10000            'transactions per day
avgframe = 1275                 'average frame size
hrsperday = 8
AR = transactions/(8*60*60)
DATA 4800,9600,19200,56000,64000,128000,256000,384000,768000,1536000
FOR i = 1 TO 10
READ linespeed(i)
est(i) = avgframe * 8/linespeed(i)
msr(i) = 1/est(i)
utilization(i) = AR/msr(i)
prob0(i) = 1-(AR/msr(i))
L(i) = AR/(msr(i)-AR)
Lq(i) = AR^2/(msr(i)*(msr(i)-AR))
W(i) = 1/(msr(i)-AR)
Wq(i) = AR/(MSR(i)*(msr(i)-AR))
NEXT i
PRINT "Line Speed    EST    MSR    Po    p    L    Lq    W    Wq"
FOR i = 1 TO 10
PRINT USING " ######  #.#### ###.## "; linespeed(i); est(i); msr(i);
PRINT USING " #.#####   .#####"; prob0(i); utilization(i);
PRINT USING "  #.#####  #.##### #.##### #.#####"; L(i)l Lq(i); W(i); Wq(i)
NEXT i
PRINT
PRINT "where:"
PRINT
PRINT "EST = expected service time  MSR = mean service rate"
PRINT "Po = probability of zero frames in the system p = utilization"
PRINT "L = mean number of frames in system  Lq = mean number in queue"
PRINT "W = mean waiting time in system  Wq = mean waiting time in queue"
```

for eight queuing theory parameters for line speeds ranging from 4,800 bps to 1.536 Mbps. The 536-Mbps line speed is the effective operating rate of a T1 circuit because 8000 bps of the 1.544 Mbps operating rate of that circuit is used for framing and is not available for the actual transmission of data.

The utilization level P and the mean waiting time in the queue, $W(q)$, in Exhibit 44-6, should be examined. At 4800 bps, the utilization level is approximately 74 percent, and the waiting time in the queue is almost 6 seconds. Clearly, linking the two LANs with remote bridges operating at 4800 bps provides an unacceptable waiting time due to the high utilization level of the remote bridge.

Exhibit 44-6. QUEUE.BAS execution results.

Line Speed	EST	MSR	Po	P	L
4800	2.1250	0.47	0.26215	.73785	2.81457
9600	1.0625	0.94	0.63108	.36892	0.58459
19200	0.5313	1.88	0.81554	.18446	0.22618
56000	0.1821	5.49	0.93676	.06324	0.06751
64000	0.1594	6.27	0.94466	.05534	0.05858
128000	0.0797	12.55	0.97233	.02767	0.02846
256000	0.0398	25.10	0.98617	.01383	0.01403
384000	0.0266	37.65	0.99078	.00922	0.00931
768000	0.0133	75.29	0.99539	.00461	0.00463
1536000	0.0066	150.59	0.00769	.00231	0.00231

Lq	W	Wq
2.07672	8.10596	5.98096
0.21567	1.68363	0.62113
0.04172	0.65141	0.12016
0.00427	0.19444	0.01230
0.00324	0.16871	0.00934
0.00079	0.08196	0.00227
0.00019	0.04040	0.00056
0.00009	0.02681	0.00025
0.00002	0.01334	0.00006
0.00001	0.00666	0.00002

Note:

EST = Expected service time

PO = Probability of zero frames in the system

L = Mean number of frames in system

W = Mean waiting time in system

MSR = Mean service rate

P = Utilization

Lq = Mean number in queue

Wq = Mean waiting time in queue

Press any key to continue

As the line speed is increased, each bridge can service frames at a higher processing rate. The average arrival rate is fixed, so increasing the line operating rate should lower the utilization level of the bridge as well as the time a frame resides in the queue. This expectation is verified by the results of the execution of QUEUE.BAS (Exhibit 44-6). Note that, as expected, both the utilization level and mean waiting time in the queue decrease as the line speed increases.

Queuing theory can be used to determine the operating rate of transmission lines for linking remote bridges and routers. In actuality, such use will not produce a magic number. Instead, queuing theory returns a range of values that can be used to make a logical decision. As shown in Exhibit 44-6, a line operating rate of 4800 bps is clearly unacceptable. But operating rates of 9600 bps, 19,200 bps, and 56,000 bps must be evaluated.

Exhibit 44-7 graphs the probability of a bridge containing zero frames (e.g., having empty buffers) and the utilization level of the bridge based on the 10 line operating rates. At line rates above 56 Kbps or 64 Kbps, the reduction in the utilization level of the bridge and increase in the probability of zero frames occurring in the system are insignificant. Thus, the line operating rate could safely be restricted to the maximum of 56 Kbps or 64 bps. Exhibit 44-6 shows that increasing the line rate from 19,200 bps to 64 Kbps only marginally decreases the waiting time in the queue from 0.12 seconds to 0.009 seconds. If the application is not likely to grow, a 19,200-bps analog leased line would be a good choice as the cost of that line is usually less than the cost of a digital line. If greater use of remote bridges is expected, the more expensive 56-Kbps or 64-Kbps digital l line is an appropriate choice.

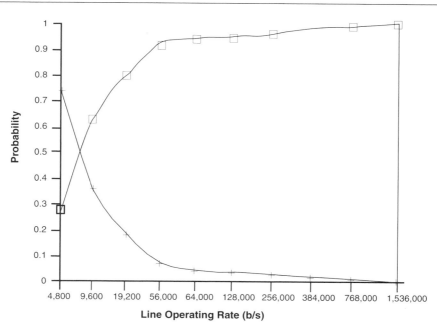

☐ Probability of zero frames

+ Utilization

Exhibit 44-7. Bridge performance at different line operating rates.

CONCLUSION

To correctly apply queuing theory to the interconnection of LANs, the number of transactions and the average frame size of each transaction that will flow to the other network must be determined. Once this is accomplished, an allowance must be made for the increase in the average frame size when WAN protocol header and trailer information is added. The average arrival rate of frames as well as the mean service rate of the bridge or router can then be calculated, as well as the additional queuing parameters discussed in this chapter. By recalculating those parameters for different transmission line operating rates, the network manager can select an appropriate operating rate.

Note

For specific information concerning the application of A. K. Erlang's work to the sizing of parts of multiplexers and concentrators, readers are referred to *Network Design Techniques* (Gilbert Held, Wiley, New York).

Chapter 45
Network Baselining as a Planning Tool
Gilbert Held

BASELINING PROVIDES A MECHANISM FOR DETERMINING THE LEVEL OF UTILIZA-
TION OF A NETWORK, including its computational and transmission facilities. As such, it plays a central role in a network manager's capacity planning effort because the baseline shows whether or not there is sufficient
capacity available, as well as providing a foundation for future network
measurements that can be compared to the baseline to indicate the direction of network utilization. Thus, the network baselining effort represents
the first major step in the capacity planning effort.

In addition, baselining enables network managers and administrators to
identify and respond to network capacity requirements before they
become an issue, in effect providing a mechanism to head off network-
related problems.

BASELINING TOOLS AND TECHNIQUES

There are a variety of network baseline tools and techniques that can be
used to facilitte an organization's capacity planning effort. The actual techniques employed are commonly based on the type of tool used. This chapter focuses on a number of commercially available network baselining
tools, and discusses appropriate techniques concerning their use.

SimpleView

SimpleView is an easy to use and relatively inexpensive Simple Network
Management Protocol (SNMP) management platform from Triticom, Inc., of
Eden Prairie, Minnesota. Through the use of SimpleView, users can retrieve
statistical information maintained by Remote Monitoring (RMON) network
probes. SimpleView supports a Management Information Base (MIB) walk
capability, shown in the MIB Walk window, that lets a user click on an MIB
group to select the group starting point, or double-click on the group to
explode its elements, enabling a specific element from the group to be
selected for retrieval.

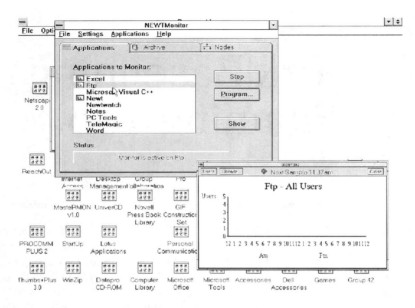

Exhibit 45-1. The NetManage NEWTMonitor program provides the capability to examine the activity on a network based upon certain types of predifined applications.

NEWT

NetManage of Cupertino, California, well known for its Chameleon suite of Internet applications, also markets a program called NEWT that can be used to monitor the use of desktop applications as well as to provide statistics on network activity associated with individual users. Exhibit 45-1 illustrates the use of NEWTMonitor on the author's computer to monitor the number of simultaneous FTP sessions occurring over a period of time. Doing so can be extremely important, especially when used in conjunction with normal RMON traffic statistics that do not look beyond the data link layer. NEWTMonitor enables the use of specific types of TCP/IP applications. In comparison, if the network probes and network management system support RMONv2, or can be upgraded to this new version of RMON, it can be used to obtain a distribution of traffic through the application layer.

Exhibit 45-2 illustrates the use of NEWTGraph to display different TCP/IP statistics by node. In the example shown in Exhibit 45-2, the author displayed Interface Errors for his node.

EtherVision

When checking the activity associated with an individual network, users can choose from a variety of network monitoring programs. One such program is EtherVision, also from Triticom, Inc., of Eden Prairie, Minnesota.

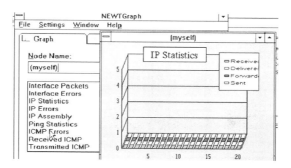

Exhibit 45-2. Through the use of the NetManage NEWTGraph program, graphs of different types of TCP/IP statistical information can be displayed.

Exhibit 45-3 illustrates the statistics summary display based on the monitoring of frames using their source address for constructing a statistical baseline. EtherVision supports monitoring by either Source or Destination address, enabling users to build two baselines. In examining Exhibit 45-3, note that the statistics summary presented indicates the frame count over the monitored period of time, current network utilization in the form of a horizontal bar graph, and a summary of "average," "now" or current, and "peak" utilization displayed as a percentage, as well as the time peak utilization occurred. The latter can be extremely handy as it allows a user to run the program on a workstation connected to an Ethernet LAN and return at the end of the day to determine the peak percentage of network use as well as when the peak occurred.

Although not shown in Exhibit 45-3, an EtherVision user can also set the program to generate a report that will log each period of activity over a certain percentage of network activity. Then, using the logged report, a network manager or LAN administrator can easily determine the distribution of network utilization throughout the monitoring period.

In the upper right corner of Exhibit 45-3, note that EtherVision maintains a distribution of frames transmitted on the network based on their size or length, falling into five predefined intervals. By examining the distribution of frames based on their length, users can determine the general type of traffic flowing on a network. This is possible because interactive query-response applications are generally transported in relatively short frames. In comparison, file transfers, such as Web browser pages containing one or more images, commonly fill frames to their full length. In examining the distribution of frame sizes shown in Exhibit 45-3, note that there are relatively few full-sized Ethernet frames in comparison to the total number of frames

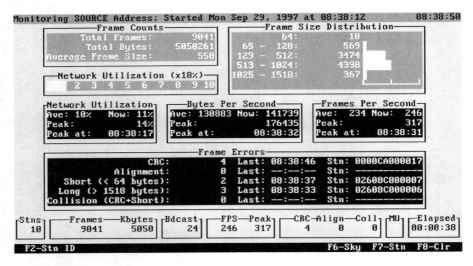

Exhibit 45-3. The Triticom EtherVision statistics summary display can be used to obtain information about network utilization and frame distribution.

encountered during the period of monitoring. This indicates a low level of file transfer and Web browser activity occurring on the monitored network.

Although EtherVision provides numeric information concerning network utilization, many users prefer to work with charts that note trends at a glance. To accommodate such users, EtherVision includes a number of built-in displays such as the one shown in Exhibit 45-4, which plots network utilization over a period of time. By examining a visual display, users can immediately note any potential capacity-related problems. In the example shown in Exhibit 45-4, the maximum level of network utilization is slightly above 46 percent. However, based on the monitored period, network traffic rose from 22 to 46 percent numerous times during the monitoring period. Because an Ethernet LAN gets congested at utilization levels above 50 percent due to its CSMA/CD access protocol, and the effect of the delay associated with the use of a random exponential back-off algorithm after a collision occurs, Exhibit 45-4 indicates a baseline of network utilization that justifies careful attention and a scheduled remonitoring effort to ensure traffic on the network does not turn into a bottleneck.

Foundation Manager

Foundation Manager, a product of Network General Corporation, is a sophisticated SNMP Network Management System (NMS) platform that

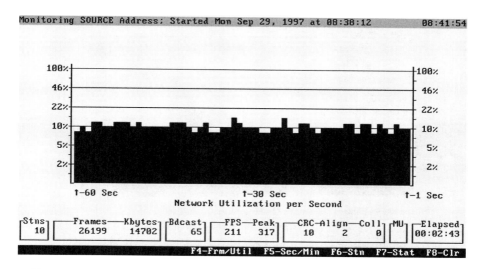

Monitoring SOURCE Address: Started Mon Sep 29, 1997 at 08:38:12   08:41:54

Exhibit 45-4. EtherVision supports the display of network utilization over a period of time, which facilitates observing the changing state of this important baseline metric.

operates on Intel-based computers using different versions of Microsoft's Windows operating system.

Foundation Manager was upgraded to support the emerging RMONv2 standard. When used to gather statistics from an RMON v2-compatible probe, it can provide a summary of statistics through the application layer, allowing it to replace the use of multiple products to obtain equivalent information.

Exhibit 45-5 illustrates the use of Foundation Manager to monitor a local Token Ring network. In the example, two buttons under the Local Token Ring Monitoring bar were pressed to initiate two displays of information from the Token Ring Statistics Group that an RMON probe on the locat network accumulates. The first button clicked on is the bar chart icon to the right of the icon with the upraised hand in the form of a stop sign. Clicking on the bar chart icon results in the display of the top row of eight bar charts that indicate the total number of different types of frames and level of network utilization.

For example, the second bar chart located on the left side of the top display indicates that network utilization is at three percent on a 100 percent basis. Other bar charts on the top row indicate the current number of logical link control (LLC) bytes and frames, multicast frames, broadcast frames, beaconing frames, purge events, and claim events. The second row

615

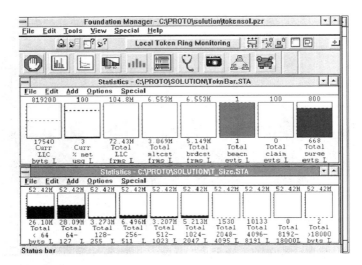

Exhibit 45-5. Using Network General's Foundation Manager to monitor the distribution of frames by length and type on a Token Ring network.

of bar charts resulted from clicking on the third icon to the right of the raised hand icon. This sequence of ten bar charts indicates the distribution of Token Ring frames in a manner similar to the method that EtherVision used to summarize Ethernet frame sizes. Foundation Manager follows the RMON standard and provides a more detailed breakdown of the distribution of Token Ring frames by their length.

Similarly, when using Foundation Manager to monitor Ethernet networks, the program retrieves RMON probe-kept frame distribution information that is more detailed than that kept by EtherVision. However, it is important to note that the retail price of EtherVision is under $500 and it can operate by itself. In comparison, the retail price of Foundation Manager is approximately $5000 and a single probe can cost approximately $1000, requiring an investment of an additional $5500 to obtain an enhanced level of frame size distributions as well as some additional features.

Two of the more interesting features of Foundation Manager are its QuickStats and discovery, and baselining capabilities. Exhibit 45-6 illustrates the use of the Foundation Manager Quick Stats feature to display a quick set of statistics for a remotely monitored network. In the example, statistics for an RMON probe connected to a network located in San Diego are displayed.

Foundation Manager is capable of displaying up to eight Quick Stats graphical reports at one time, with each report generated by clicking on an

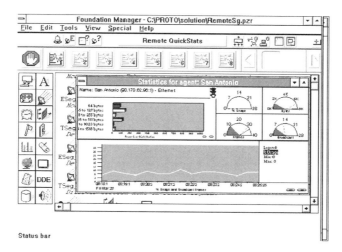

Exhibit 45-6. The Foundation Manager QuickStats display provides users with the ability to visually note important network baseline parameters both in real-time and over a period of time.

appropriate icon to the right of the icon with the raised hand in the form of a stop sign.

Each Quick Stats display presents summary information about a monitored network in a similar manner. In examining the statistics display for the network located in San Diego, the upper left display presents a distribution of frame length for the monitored LAN as a horizontal bar chart. The upper right portion of the display contains four gauges that provide a real-time view of network utilization, bytes transmitted, broadcast traffic, and frame rate. The lower half of the display shows a real-time plot over a period of predefined length for any two of the gauge values. Thus, the use of the Foundation Monitor Quick Stats display provides users with the ability to visually note important network baseline parameters both in real-time and over a period of time.

A second interesting feature built into Foundation Manager is its discovery and baselining capability. This capability is available for both local and remotely located networks being monitored, and provides the ability to gather pattern flow information that can be extremely valuable when attempting to determine if the cause of a high level of network utilization results from the activity of one or a few stations on the network.

Exhibit 45-7 illustrates the Foundation Manager local discovery and baselining display as a matrix map of network activity. The first portion of the title of the display, "Discovery," results from the fact that the probe

Foundation Manager - C:\PROTO\solution\dscvrsol.pzr

File Edit Tools View Special Help

Local Discovery and Baselining

Map - C:\PROTO\solution\PMatrix.map

File Edit Action Level Options Special

From \ To	10005ae0fa21	08005ac0e7a1	680019c8420d	0001c84d376d
10005ae0fa21		1		
08005ac0e7a1	1			
680019c8420d				14
0001c84d376d			27	
0004acfc09de		2		
100090a49895				
c000ffffffff				
100090899a8a				
10005af51080				
0000f62e2401				
400037451000	1			58
000098923d20				
c00099000080				
0004acfc09e6				
005500230d17		5		
10005a992d15				
c00000002000				
0000f62e60d1		96		
10005a726504				
000098623880				
000038348ed0				

Display Map Matrix of network

Exhibit 45-7. **The local discovery and baselining capability of Foundation Manager enables the flow of data between stations to be identified.**

examines each frame flowing on the monitored network and discovers its source and destination by examining the source and destination addresses contained in the frame. The second portion of the title of the display, "Baselining," results from the fact that Foundation Manager extracts information from a matrix table maintained by the probe that denotes the number of frames transmitted from one address to another. Thus, in examining Exhibit 45-7, such numerics as 1, 2, 27, 14, 58, 5, and 96 represent the number of frames transmitted from the address located in the row in the table to the address in the column portion of the table.

When baselining a network, matrix information should be considered as a mechanism to identify the cause of high network utilization. If Quick Stats or a similar display denotes a low level of network utilization, there is no need to use the matrix capability of Foundation Manager or a similar product to identify the actual flow of data between network stations. This is because even if the user can locate a station using too much bandwidth, a modification of the operation of the station will, at best, have a negligible effect upon improving network performance if the network already has a low level of utilization.

CONCLUSION

Baselining is an important process that enables the communications manager and LAN administrator to quantify the status and activities of a network. In doing so, it provides a base of information that enables network trends to be identified, which can allow changes to be made to a network infrastructure prior to network capacity becoming an issue. Thus, network managers and administrators should consider using the tools and techniques described in this chapter as a mechanism to baseline their network infrastructures.

Section VII
Security

ONE OF THE MOST IMPORTANT ASPECTS OF THE NETWORK DESIGN PROCESS is considering appropriate hardware, software, and operational techniques to enhance security. While security was a minor concern in the era of closed, hierarchical-structured, mainframe-based networks, it cannot be overlooked in a modern communications environment. Today, any network connected to the Internet or an organization with employees who access the Internet at home can be attacked. Common attack methods include denial-of-service attacks from hackers attempting to adversely affect a Web site to various virus attacks that could occur if an employee brings in a disk with an infected file downloaded from the Internet. Thus, in this modem era of communications, the network designer must consider both hardware and software protection measures as well as the formulation of organizational policies and procedures, which are the focus of this section.

Because routers represent the first line of defense for a network, author Gilbert Held has three router-related chapters that begin this section. Chapter 46, titled **Working with Cisco Access Lists,** first acquaints the reader with the different types of access lists supported by Cisco routers. Once this is accomplished, Held covers the syntax or format associated with each type of access list and provides a series of practical examples of their use. Because access lists are used to filter packets, they represent the first line of defense for a network, and this chapter illustrates the coding necessary to implement router-based network security.

In Chapter 47, author Gilbert Held continues his trilogy of router security chapters. In the chapter titled **Securing Your Router,** Held covers methods one can use to protect a router's operating system from misconfiguration. This chapter is a logical follow-on to the previous chapter since a common method of network attack is to connect to a router's control port, break into the router via a dictionary attack, and modify its access list to open a hole to attack the protected network.

The third router-related chapter in this section authored by Held is contained in Chapter 48, entitled **Protecting a Network from Spoofing and Denial of Service Attacks.** Held continues his presentation of router-related security by illustrating how Cisco routers can be programmed to block commonly employed attacks that use spoofed IP addresses. In this chapter, one learns how to block directed broadcast and ping attacks as

SECURITY

well as how to throw packets with improper source IP addresses into the great bit bucket in the sky.

Chapter 49 focuses on additional aspects of the TCP/IP protocol. Author Douglas G. Conorich's chapter, **Internet Security: Securing the Perimeter,** discusses the role of firewalls and proxy servers as well as describes methods to test one's perimeter connection to the Internet.

As networks grow in importance, usage from employees traveling or working at home becomes common. Because allowing such employees to access network services could open a security hole, it is important to be able to authenticate remote users. This topic is covered by author Ellen Bonsall in Chapter 50. In this chapter, **Remote Access Authentication,** Bonsall covers different types of remote access controls and authentication methods.

Another important security-related area involves insuring private communications remain private through the use of cryptography. In Chapter 51, **An Overview of Cryptographic Methods,** author Gary C. Kessler introduces the reader to different cryptographic techniques. In a second cryptographic-related chapter, author Andrew Csinger introduces the use of public key cryptography. In Chapter 52, titled **Public Key Infrastructure: Using the Internet as a Virtual Private Network,** Csinger focuses attention on public key certificates and how they can be applied to secure VPNs established through the Internet.

Two common security areas of growing concern to network managers and LAN administrators are Web servers and applets downloaded by users surfing the Internet. Both of these topics are examined in Chapters 53 and 54. In Chapter 53, **Making Your Web Site Hacker Safe: Internet Security,** Jim Hewitt first provides a series of steps one should consider to secure a Web site. Once this is accomplished, Hewitt describes a series of preventative measures one organization implemented to secure its Web site as well as describes internal security policies and procedures that can enhance the security of an organization's Internet server. Chapter 54 focuses on network-based programs that run on client systems and are referred to as applets. In the chapter titled **Applets and Network Security: A Management Overview**, author Al Berg describes how applets work, the threats they present, and what security precautions one can take to minimize the security exposures presented by applets.

In concluding this section on security, author Dave Schneider's chapter, titled **Security Management,** provides information concerning the use of Internet service providers (ISPs), Web server placement options, and different VPN configurations. This chapter, which concludes this section, also discusses the configuration of firewalls and their use to limit user access at a number of distinct levels. In addition, Chapter 55 describes the problems of scale, which can add new problems for growing organizations.

Chapter 46
Working with Cisco Access Lists

Gilbert Held

AN ACCESS LIST REPRESENTS A SEQUENTIAL COLLECTION OF PERMIT AND DENY CONDITIONS that are applied to certain field values in packets that attempt to flow through a router interface. Once an access list is configured, it is applied to one or more router interfaces, resulting in the implementation of a security policy. As packets attempt to flow through a router's interface, the device compares data in one or more fields in the packet to the statements in the access list associated with the interface. Data in selected fields in the packet are compared against each statement in the access list in the order in which the statements were entered to form the list. The first match between the contents or conditions of a statement in the access list and one or more data elements in specific fields in each packet determines whether or not the router permits the packet to flow through the interface or sends the packet to the great bit bucket in the sky via a filtering operation.

At a minimum, router access lists control the flow of data at the network layer. Because there are numerous types of network layer protocols, there are also numerous types of access lists, such as Novell NetWare IPX access lists, IP access lists, and Decnet access lists. Due to the important role of IP in accessing the Internet and in the construction of intranets and extranets, this article focuses on the examination of access lists that support the Transmission Control Protocol/Internet Protocol (TCP/IP) protocol suite.

THE TCP/IP PROTOCOL SUITE

To obtain an appreciation for the manner by which IP access lists operate, a brief review of a portion of the TCP/IP protocol suite is in order. At the application layer, the contents of a data stream representing a particular application in the protocol suite, such as a file transfer, remote terminal session, or an electronic mail message, are passed to one of two transport layer protocols supported by the TCP/IP protocol suite — the Transmission Control Protocol (TCP) and the User Datagram Protocol (UDP).

0-8493-0859-3/00/$0.00+$.50
© 2000 by CRC Press LLC

Both TCP and UDP are layer 4 protocols that operate at the transport layer of the International Standards Organization (ISO) Open Systems Interconnection (OSI) Reference Model. Because a host computer operating the TCP/IP protocol stack can support the operation of multiple concurrent applications, a mechanism is required to distinguish one application from another as application data is formed into either TCP or UDP datagrams. The mechanism used to distinguish one application from another is the port number, with each application supported by the TCP/IP protocol suite having an associated numeric port number. For example, a host might transmit a packet containing an e-mail message followed by a packet containing a portion of a file transfer, with different port numbers in each packet identifying the type of data contained in each packet. Through the use of port numbers, different applications can be transmitted to a common address, with the destination address using the port numbers in each packet as a mechanism to demultiplex one application from another in a data stream received from a common source address. Port numbers are assigned by the Internet Assigned Numbers Authority (IANA), which maintains a list of assigned port numbers that anyone with access to the Internet can obtain.

TCP is a connection-oriented protocol that provides a guaranteed delivery mechanism. Because a short period of time is required to establish a TCP connection prior to obtaining the ability to exchange data, it is not extremely efficient for transporting applications that only require small quantities of data to be exchanged, such as a management query that might simply retrieve a parameter stored in a remote probe. Recognizing that this type of networking situation required a speedier transmission method resulted in the development of UDP. UDP was developed as a connectionless, best-effort delivery mechanism. This means that when a UDP session is initiated, data transmission begins immediately instead of having to wait until a session connection is established. This also means that the upper-layer application becomes responsible for having to set a timer to permit a period of time to expire without the receipt of a reply to determine that a connection either was not established or was lost.

Although both TCP and UDP differentiate one application from another by the use of numeric port values, actual device addressing is the responsibility of IP, a network-layer protocol that operates at layer 3 of the ISO OSI Reference Model. As application data flows down the TCP/IP protocol stack, either a TCP or a UDP header is added to the data, with the resulting segment of data containing an appropriate port number that identifies the application being transported. Next, as data flows down the protocol stack, layer 3 operations result in an IP header being prefixed to the TCP or the UDP header. The IP header contains the IP destination and IP source addresses as 32-bit numbers, which are frequently coded when configuring the protocol stack as four numerics separated by decimal points, resulting in the term "dotted decimal notation" used to reference an IP address in this format. Here, the destination IP address represents the recipient of the packet, while the source IP address identifies the originator of the packet.

Based on the preceding, there are three addresses that can be used in an IP access list for enabling or disabling the flow of packets through a router's interface: the source IP address, the destination IP address, and port number that identifies the application data in the packet. In actuality, Cisco Systems and other router manufacturers also support other IP-related protocols — such as the Internet Control Message Protocol (ICMP) and Open Shortest Path First (OSPF) protocol — as a mechanism to enable or disable the flow of predefined types of error messages and queries; an example of the latter is an ICMP echo packet request and echo packet response.

USING ACCESS LISTS

In a Cisco router environment, there are two types of IP access lists one can configure: standard or basic access lists and extended access lists.

A standard (basic) access list permits filtering by source address only. This means one can only permit or deny the flow of packets through an interface based on the source IP address in the packet. Thus, this type of access list is limited in its functionality. In comparison, an extended access list permits filtering by source address, destination address and various parameters associated with upper layers in the protocol stack, such as TCP and UDP port numbers.

Configuration Principles

When developing a Cisco router access list, there are several important principles to note. First, Cisco access lists are evaluated in a sequential manner, beginning with the first entry in the list. Once a match occurs, access list processing terminates and no further comparisons occur. Thus, it is important to place more specific entries toward the top of the access list.

A second important access list development principle to note is the fact that there is always an implicit deny at the end of the access list. This means that the contents of a packet that do not explicitly match one of the access list entries will automatically be denied. One can override the implicit deny by placing an explicit "permit all" as the last entry in the list.

A third principle regarding the configuration of access lists concerns additions to the list. Any new access list entries are automatically added to the bottom of the list. This fact is important to note, especially when attempting to make one or more modifications to an existing access list. This is because the addition of statements to the bottom of an access list might not result in obtaining the ability of the list to satisfy organizational requirements. Many times, it may be necessary to delete and recreate an access list instead of adding entries to the bottom of the list.

A fourth principle concerning access lists is that they must be applied to an interface. One common mistake some people make is to create an appropriate access list and forget to apply it to an interface. In such situations, the access list simply resides in the router's configuration memory area but will not be used to check the flow of data packets through the router, an effect similar to leaving the barn door ajar after spending time to construct a fine structure. Now having an appreciation for key access list configuration principles, one can focus on the creation (basic) of standard and extended Cisco router access lists.

STANDARD ACCESS LISTS

The basic format of a standard access list is:

```
access list number {permit|deny} [ip address] [mask]
```

Each access list is assigned a unique number that both identifies the specific list, as well as informs the router's operating system of the type of the access list. Standard Cisco IP access lists are assigned an integer number between 1 and 99. A new release of Cisco's router operating system permits access list names to be defined. However, because named access lists are not backward-compatible with earlier versions of router operating system, numbered lists are used in the examples presented in this article.

Because standard access lists only support filtering by source address, the IP address in the above access list format is restricted to representing the originator of the packet. The mask that follows the IP address is specified in a manner similar to the way in which a network mask is specified when subnetting an IP address. However, when used in an access list, the binary 0 in the mask is used as a "compare" while a binary 1 is used as an "unconditional" match. This is exactly the opposite of the use of binary 1s and binary 0s in a network mask to subnet an IP address. Another difference is that, in Cisco router terminology, the mask used with an access list is referred to as a wildcard mask and not as a network mask or a subnet mask.

To illustrate the use of a Cisco router wildcard mask, assume that the organization's router is to be connected to the Internet. Further assume that a World Wide Web server will be located behind the router and one wants to allow all hosts on the Class C network whose IP address is 205.131.176.0 access to the server. If using a traditional network mask, its composition would be 255.255.255.0. Writing the network and mask in binary would result in the following, where the letter 'x' represents a "don't care" condition in which either a binary 1 or binary 0 can occur in the appropriate bit position.

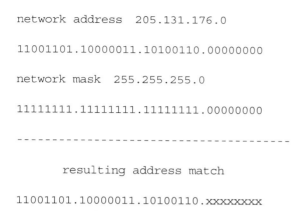

```
network address  205.131.176.0

11001101.10000011.10100110.00000000

network mask  255.255.255.0

11111111.11111111.11111111.00000000

----------------------------------------

     resulting address match

11001101.10000011.10100110.xxxxxxxx
```

Note that a binary 1 in the network mask represents a compare, while a binary 0 represents an unconditional match. When working with Cisco access lists, the use of binary 1s and 0s in the wildcard mask is reversed. That is, a binary 1 specifies an unconditional match, while a binary 0 specifies a compare condition. However, if one attempts to use the same mask composition instead of reversing its composition, one will more than likely obtain a result that does not meet operational requirements. This is illustrated by the following example, where a wildcard mask is used instead of a network mask.

```
network address  205.131.176.0

11001101.10000011.10100110.00000000

wildcard mask  255.255.255.0

11111111.11111111.11111111.00000000

----------------------------------------

     resulting address match

xxxxxxxx.xxxxxxxx.xxxxxxxx.00000000
```

In the above example, any value in the first three octet positions are allowed as long as the value in the last octet was all 0s. This is obviously not a satisfactory solution to the previously assumed Web server requirement. However, if 0s are placed in the wildcard mask where one would normally place binary 1s in the network mask, and vice versa, then one properly defines the wildcard mask. Modifying the masking operation one more time obtains:

```
network address   205.131.176.0

11001101.10000011.10100110.00000000

wildcard mask   0.0.0.255

00000000.00000000.00000000.11111111

----------------------------------------

    resulting address match

11001101.10000011.10100110.xxxxxxxx
```

Note that the creation of the above mask results in specifying any host on the 205.131.176.0 network, which is the requirement one was attempting to satisfy. The use of Cisco wildcard masks can be a bit confusing at first (especially if one has a considerable amount of experience in using subnet masks); but once the concept is grasped, it is easy to apply to an access list as a subnet mask to a network address. However, it is extremely important to remember that the wildcard mask is a reverse of the network mask to include the function of binary 1s and 0s and their positioning in the mask and to apply it accordingly. With an understanding of the creation and use of Cisco wildcard masks, one can now return to the example and complete the creation of a standard access list. That access list would be constructed as follows:

```
access list 77 permit 205.131.176.0 0.0.0.255
```

In this example, the list number 77, being between 1 and 99, identifies the access list as a standard access-list to the router's operating system. Also note that the network address of 205.131.176.0 and a wildcard mask of 0.0.0.255 results in a "don't care" condition for any value in the last octet of the network address, permitting any host on the 205.131.176.0 network to have its packets flow through the router without being filtered.

A few additional items concerning access lists warrant attention. First, if one omits a mask from an associated IP address, an implicit mask of 0.0.0.0 is assumed, which then requires an exact match between the specified IP address in the access list and the packet to occur for the permit or deny condition in the access list statement to take effect. Second, as previously mentioned, an access list implicitly denies all other accesses. This is equivalent to terminating an access list with the following statement:

```
access list 77 deny 0.0.0.0 255.255.255.255
```

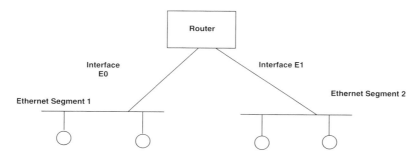

Exhibit 46-1. Using a router to interconnect two Ethernet segments.

To provide another example of the use of a standard access list assume that an organization uses a router to connect two Ethernet segments together, as illustrated in Exhibit 46-1. In examining the use of the router illustrated, let us assume that Segment 1 has the network address 198.78.46.0 and one wants to enable clients with the host addresses .16 and .18 on Segment 1 to access any server located on Segment 2. To do so, the initial router configuration to include applying the access list to the outgoing interface on Ethernet 1 (E1) would consist of the following statements:

```
Interface ethernet 1
access-group 23 out
access list 23 permit 198.78.46.16 0.0.0.0
access list 23 permit 198.78.46.18 0.0.0.0
```

In the preceding example, note that the access group statement is used to define the dataflow direction that is associated with an access list. Also note that the access list was applied to the outgoing interface on Ethernet 1 instead of the inbound interface on Ethernet 0 (E0) toward the router from Segment 1 as an inbound access list. While either method would work, the latter method would have the potentially undesirable effect of blocking all other traffic from leaving Segment 1. Thus, in this example this author elected to apply the access list to the outgoing interface on E1.

With an appreciation for standard IP access lists, one can now focus attention on their extended cousin.

EXTENDED ACCESS LISTS

A standard access list is limited to specifying a filter via the use of a source IP address. In comparison, an extended access list provides the ability to filter by source address, destination address, and upper-layer protocol information, such as TCP and UDP port values. In fact, extended access lists provide the ability to create very complex packet filters with capabilities that can significantly extend beyond the capabilities of a standard access list.

Extended access lists have the following format:

```
access-list number {permit|deny} protocol source IP address
source-mask destination IP address destination-mask /
[operator operand] [established]
```

Similar to standard access lists, extended access lists are numbered. Extended access lists are numbered between 100 and 199 to distinguish them from standard IP access lists. The protocol parameter identifies a specific TCP/IP protocol, such as ip, tcp, udp, icmp, and several routing protocols that can be filtered. Examples of the latter include the Interior Gateway Routing Protocol (IGRP) and the Open Shortest Path First (OSPF) routing protocol. The arguments source IP address and destination IP address represent the source and destination IP addresses expressed in dotted decimal notation. The arguments source-mask and destination-mask represent router wildcards used in the same manner as previously described when examining the operation of standard access lists. To obtain the ability to specify additional information about packets for filtering, one can include the optional arguments operator and operand in the extended access list. When used, the operator and operand can be employed to compare tcp and udp port values. Concerning tcp and udp, the argument operators can be one of the following four keywords:

lt	less than
gt	greater than
eq	equal
neq not	equal

In comparison, the argument operand represents the integer value of the destination port for the specified protocol. For the TCP, the additional optional keyword "established" is supported. When specified, a match occurs if a TCP datagram has its ACK or RST field bits set, indicating that an established connection has occurred.

To illustrate an example of the use of an extended access list, assume that the router illustrated in Exhibit 46-1 will be connected to the Internet. Further assume that one wants to enable any host on the network behind the router whose IP address is 198.78.46.0 to establish TCP connections to any host on the Internet. However, also assume that, with the exception of accepting electronic mail via the Simple Mail Transport Protocol (SMTP), it is organizational policy to bar any host on the Internet from establishing TCP connections to hosts on the 198.78.46.0 network.

To accomplish this, one must ensure that the initial request for an SMTP connection, which is made on TCP destination port 25, occurs from a port number greater than 1023. The originator should always use destination port 25 to access the mail exchanger on the organization's network and that host using a port number greater than 1023 to respond. Based on the preceding and assuming that the address of the mail exchanger on the 198.78.46.0 network is 198.78.46.07, the following two access lists would be employed:

```
access-list 101 permit tcp 198.78.46.0 0.0.0.255 0.0.0.0
255.255.255.255
access-list 102 permit tcp 0.0.0.0 255.255.255.255
 198.78.46.0
0.0.0.255 established
access-list 102 permit tcp 0.0.0.0 255.255.255.255
 198.78.46.07
eq 25
interface serial 0
ip access-group 101
interface ethernet 0
ip access-group 102
```

In the preceding example, note that access list 101 is applied to the router's serial port and is constructed to enable any host on the 198.78.46.0 network to establish a TCP connection to the Internet. The second access list (numbered 102) in the above example is applied to the Ethernet 0 (E0) interface illustrated in Exhibit 46-1. The first statement in the 102 access list permits any TCP packet that represents an established connection to occur, while the second statement in the access list permits TCP packets from any source address flowing to the specific network address 198.78.46.77 with a port value of 25 to flow through the interface. Thus, an inbound connection via port 25 must occur in order for the first statement in the 102 access list to permit succeeding packets with port numbers greater than 1023 to flow through the router.

LIMITATIONS

Although access lists provide a significant capability to filter packets, they are far from a comprehensive security mechanism. Thus, in concluding this examination of Cisco access lists, a few words of caution are in order concerning their limitations.

In examining access lists, one notes that they are constructed to filter based on network addresses. This means that they are vulnerable to address impersonation or spoofing. Another key limitation associated with the use of access lists is the fact that they cannot note whether or not a packet is part of an existing upper-layer conversation or what the conversation is about. This means that a person could run a dictionary attack through the packet filtering capability of a router if that person's address was not barred. Similarly, a host that is allowed FTP access could issue an `mget *.*` command and retrieve several gigabytes of data from a server, in effect creating a denial of service attack. Due to the preceding limitations, most organizations supplement router access lists through proxy services incorporated into a firewall.

Chapter 47
Securing Your Router
Gilbert Held

A ROUTER REPRESENTS AN ENTRY POINT INTO MOST NETWORKS as well as the primary communications device used to move data between networks. As such, it represents a very strategic communications networking device because the inadvertent or intentional change in its configuration could have a major bearing on the ability of an organization to maintain its network in a desired state of operation. In addition, if routing tables or other parameters are altered, it becomes possible for organizational data to be directed to locations where such information could be recorded and read by third parties. Thus, it is important to understand how one can access and take control of a router and steps one can employ to secure this communications networking device.

This chapter examines and discusses methods of router access in both general and specific terms. The discussion of router access in general terms will be applicable to products manufactured by different vendors. However, for specific methods of access and methods one can use to secure access to a router, specific details applicable to routers manufactured by Cisco Systems will be used to supplement the generalizations. The selection of the use of examples specific to routers manufactured by Cisco Systems is based on this vendor currently having approximately a 75 percent share of the market for routers. Although specific examples of methods to protect access to routers in this chapter will be oriented toward Cisco routers, most routers manufactured by other vendors include similar capabilities. If an organization uses routers manufactured by another vendor, one should check the vendor's router manual for the access security functionality of that router. One should also check the specific commands supported by the router to facilitate one or more access security features for enabling, disabling, and protecting access to the device.

NEED FOR ACCESS SECURITY

When considering router security, most people automatically think of router access lists. Router access lists are used to establish restrictions on the transfer of data through router ports and are considered by many to represent the first line of defense of a network. Although router access lists are an extremely important aspect of network security, this author considers them to actually represent the second line of defense of a network. This is because the ability to access and configure a router represents the first line of defense of a network. If other than designated personnel obtain the ability to access and change the configuration of organizational routers, this means that any previously developed access lists can be altered or removed — in effect, stripping away any previously developed network protection. Similar to the farmer who constructs a solid henhouse but inadvertently goes home at the end of the day and leaves the door ajar, failure to secure access to organizational routers permits predators of the two-legged variety to gain access to valuable resources.

Probing deeper into router access, one will note that there are several methods to bar the proverbial door to this communications device. In fact, one method to be discussed involves the use of an access lists as a mechanism to control access to the router to certain predefined IP addresses. However, prior to doing so, one must lock the door, which should be accomplished prior to the use of the access list capability of the router. Thus, the use of access lists should be viewed as a second line of defense.

ROUTER ACCESS

For the purposes of this chapter, the term "router access" represents the ability of a person to connect to a router and gain access to its operating system. Most routers include one or more serial ports built into the device that permits terminals or personal computers operating a specific type of terminal emulator to gain access to the router. This terminal access can occur directly via a direct cable connection or remotely via a communications path that results in a modem or DSU connected to a router's serial port. Although the use of a serial port connection is the primary method used by most organizations to provide access to a router's operating system to enable the device to be configured, it is not the only method of access. Additional methods supported by many routers include Telnet access and the use of the trival file transfer protocol (TFTP) to store and transmit system images and configurations files to and from routers and workstations.

Telnet Access

Telnet provides the ability to access a remote device to include a router as if the terminal device operating a Telnet client program was directly connected to the remote device. Telnet access to a router can occur from in front or behind a router, with the term "in front" used to reference access to a router via a wide area network connection from a station located on another network not directly connected to a specific router, while the term "behind" references a station located on a network directly connected to a routers local area network port. This means that Telnet access to a router can occur from a device located on a local organizational network or, if the router is connected to the Internet, from virtually any terminal device in the world that has Internet access. This also means that regardless of the location of the client operating the Telnet program, the operator of the program only needs to know the IP address of the network interface of the router to attempt to initiate a Telnet session to the router and gain access to the device. If the operator of the Telnet client makes a connection to the router, the operator will receive a prompt, such as routername (where routername represents the name an organization assigned to the router).

It should be noted that many organizations have an IP addressing policy where they assign low addresses to router interfaces. For example, if an organization's Class C IP network address was 205.123.124.0, it might assign 205.123.456.1 as the address of the interface from the 205 network to the router. Due to this common scheme of addressing used by many organizations, it is often easy to determine the address of a router for subsequent telnetting attempts. At this point in time, a Telnet client operator may be able to directly access all of the router's configuration capabilities and in effect take over control of the router. As an alternative, the Telnet client operator may be prompted to enter a password to gain access to the router. Concerning the latter, many routers are configured at the factory to have a default password for Telnet access. Unfortunately for many organizations that should know better, one should never use a default password. This is because such passwords are listed in the vendor's router manual, which may be available for purchase for $29.95 or available for access via the World Wide Web for free. This means that a virtually unlimited number of persons have the ability to discover the default password needed to access a router via a Telnet connection.

If the router administrator fails to change the default Telnet password or does not place any additional restrictions on Telnet access, anyone with knowledge of the IP address of the router interface can gain access to the device. As noted later in this chapter, if the router administrator overlooks another aspect of device access control, a security hole big enough to literally move a truck full of hackers will be opened, enabling literally millions of remote users to obtain the ability to take control of an organization's router.

TFTP Access

Most routers have two types of memory: conventional random access memory (RAM) and nonvolatile memory. Unlike conventional RAM wherein contents are erased upon the removal of power, the contents of nonvolatile memory remain in place. When configuring a router, nonvolatile memory is commonly used to store an image of router memory as well as backup or alternative router configurations. Because routers do not contain diskettes nor do they have hard drives, their ability to store more than one or perhaps a few alternative configurations is severely limited. This means that administrators that require the ability to store backup or alternative router configurations beyond the capacity of the limited amount of router nonvolatile memory typically do so on a workstation and use the trivial file transfer program (TFTP) to load and save router system images and configuration files. This also means that if TFTP access is enabled, depending on how the router supports TFTP access, it may be possible for unauthorized persons to create configuration data that, when used by the router results in a breach of security or an unintended operational environment.

Now that one has an appreciation for the main methods that can be used to gain access to a router, one can focus on the methods that can be used to either protect such access or literally lock the door on the access method, making it extremely difficult for nonauthorized persons to gain access to a router and obtain the ability to view and possibly change the configuration of the device. In doing so, this chapter will also, when applicable, discuss certain Cisco Systems router commands.

SECURING CONSOLE AND VIRTUAL TERMINALS

After unpacking a router and initiating its installation process, it is extremely important to consider the manner by which access to configuring the device will occur. If one only plans to enable configuration changes to occur from a directly connected terminal device, then one should ensure that Telnet and TFTP access are disabled. In a Cisco router environment, one can configure access from the console and virtual terminals via the use of the *line* command. That command has the following format:

```
line [type-keyword] first-line [last-line]
```

where information in brackets represent options. The type-keyword entry can be either *console*, *aux*, or *vty*.

The *console* entry is used to represent a console terminal line, representing a device directly cabled to a port on the router. In comparison *aux* is used to indicate an auxiliary line and allows one to specify access via a port on the router connected to a CSU, DSU, or modem, permitting serial communications from afar. The third option, *vty*, represents a virtual terminal connection for remote console access. Note that when entering the line command, the first and last lines represent a number of contiguous entries that are applicable to a specific device and can be represented and associated with a line number.

When configuring access through the use of the *line* command, it is also important to consider associating a password with the device that one enables for access. Even if one only plans to allow access to a router via a directly cabled terminal device located in a secure technical control center, every once in awhile a situation can occur that would justify password protection. In one event this author is familiar with, a tour of the technical control center of a government network by a group of Boy Scouts resulted in one extremely inquisitive individual inadvertently causing great havoc. As the rest of the grouped moved to an area of the technical control center to view a graphical display of the status of the network, this inquisitive individual started playing with a terminal that was directly cabled to a router and that functioned as the router console. Not knowing what to enter, the Boy Scout entered a question mark (?), which resulted in the display of router commands. Within a short period of time, this Boy Scout managed to misconfigure the router while the rest of the group were on the other side of the center listening to a briefing given by the manager of the center. Needless to say, if a password was previously associated with terminal access, the unintentional misconfiguration of the router and the resulting havoc it created would not have been possible.

In a Cisco router environment, one can associate a password with a remote access method. To do so, one would use the password command? For example, the line console password "bugs4bny" would block console access until the console operator responded with the password "bugs4bny" to a prompt generated by the router for a password.

The password associated with the Cisco password command can be up to 80 characters in length. The password is case-sensitive and can contain any combination of alphanumeric characters to include spaces. While this capability provides the router administrator with the ability to be innovative, it also provides the ability to make it extremely difficult for authorized users to gain access to the router. This is because selecting a password based on a large number of varying upper- and lower-case letters mixed with numerics makes it subject to erroneous entry. While this type of password will certainly be difficult to guess and should avoid the possibility of a successful dictionary attack, it is also easy for an authorized router administrator to enter incorrectly. If incorrectly entered three times, a Cisco router will return the terminal attempting access to the idle state of operation. Thus, when selecting a password, it is important to remember several password principles. First, use a mixture of alphabetic and numeric characters to alleviate the potential of a dictionary attack being successful. Second, when structuring a password, remember that as one extends the length of the password, one also increases the possibility of password entry error. In general, passwords that are between six and eight characters in length should be sufficient if they are structured to join a few abbreviated words with a sequence of numerics.

FILE TRANSFER

As previously noted, TFTP is commonly supported by routers as a mechanism to permit system image and configuration files to be stored on workstations. In a Cisco router environment, to enable the loading of network configuration files at router reboot time, one must specify the *service config* command, as fortunately the default is the disabling of this capability. If this capability is enabled, the router will broadcast a TFTP read request message and the first station to respond will have the file with a specific name based on the router's configuration loaded into the router across the network. Because a standardized file-naming scheme is used, this author believes it is best to consider leaving this feature in its disabled state instead of opening the ability for inquisitive employees with a bit of knowledge to "see what would happen" if they create a configuration file.

INTERNAL ROUTER SECURITY

Once access is gained into a router, the operating system of the device can provide a further level of protection capability that one can use for additional router access security. In a Cisco router environment, the command interpreter included in the operating system is referred to as the EXEC. The EXEC has two levels of access: user and privileged.

The user level of access allows a person to use a small subset of all router commands, such as commands that enable the listing of open router connections, commands for providing a name to a logical connection and displaying certain statistic concerning router operations. In comparison, the privileged level of access includes all user access commands as well as commands that govern the operation of the router, such as the configure command that allows a router administrator to configure the router, the reload command, that halts the operation of the device and reloads its configuration, and similar commands that have an active effect on the operational state of the device.

Due to the ability of a person gaining access to the privileged mode of operation of a Cisco router obtaining the ability to directly control the operation of the router, this level of access can also be password protected. Thus, when installing a Cisco router, it is important to use the *enable-password* configuration command to protect access to the privileged level of router access. For example, to assign the password "power4you" for the privileged command level, one would use the *enable password* command as follows:

```
enable password power4you
```

Similar to the password associated with a serial terminal line, the password assigned to the privileged command level is case sensitive, can contain any mixture of alphanumeric characters to include spaces, and can consist of up to 80 characters. Thus, by placing a password on the serial port or on any allowed virtual terminal connections as well as on the privileged command level of the router, one protects both access into the router as well as the use of privileged commands once access is obtained.

ADDITIONAL PROTECTIVE MEASURES

If one needs to provide one or more persons on a network with the ability to configure one or more routers, one can add an additional layer of protection beyond passwords. To do so, one can program one or more router access lists. One notes that router access lists represent a sequential collection of permit and deny conditions that can be applied to Internet addresses. This means that if one can determine the IP addresses of stations that will require the ability to have operators configure one or more routers via a network connection, then one can use the access list capability of each router to restrict Telnet access to each router to one or more specific IP addresses. This means that not only does the terminal operator need to know the correct passwords to gain access to an appropriate router, but in addition, the operator can only perform such access from predefined locations. By combining password protection into a router with password protection to its privileged mode of operation and restricting configuration access to predefined locations via the use of one or more access lists, one can, in effect, close the proverbial door to the router.

Chapter 48
Protecting a Network from Spoofing and Denial of Service Attacks

Gilbert Held

ALONG WITH THE EVOLUTION OF TECHNOLOGY, we have witnessed an unfortunate increase in random violence in society. While it is doubtful if the two are related, it is a matter of fact that some violence is directed at computers operated by federal, state, and local governments, universities, and commercial organizations. That violence typically occurs in the form of attempts to break into computers via a remote communications link or to deny other persons the use of computational facilities by transmitting a sequence of bogus requests to the network to which a computer is connected. Because either situation can adversely affect the operational capability of an organization's computational facilities, any steps one can initiate to enhance the security of a network and networked computers may alleviate such attacks.

This chapter examines several common types of hacker attacks against networks and networked computers. In doing so, it first examines how the attack occurs. Once an appreciation for the method associated with an attack is obtained, attention can focus on techniques that can be used to prevent such attacks. Because the vast majority of routers used for Internet and intranet communications are manufactured by Cisco Systems, examples illustrating the use of the Cisco Systems' Internetwork Operation System (IOS) will be used when applicable to denote different methods to enhance network security. By examining the information presented in this article, one will note practical methods that can be implemented to add additional protection to an organization's network. Thus, this chapter serves both as a tutorial concerning spoofing and denial of service attacks, as well as a practical guide to prevent such activities.

SECURITY

SPOOFING

According to Mr. Webster, the term "spoof" means to "deceive or hide."
In communications, the term "spoofing" is typically associated with a person attempting to perform an illegal operation. That person, commonly
referred to as a hacker, spoofs or hides the source address contained in the
packets he or she transmits. The rationale for hiding the hacker's source
address is to make it difficult, if not impossible, for the true source of the
attack to be identified. Because spoofing is employed by most hackers that
spend the time to develop different types of network attacks, one should
first examine how spoofing occurs. This is followed by a discussion of
methods one can employ to prevent certain types of spoofed packets from
flowing into a network.

SPOOFING METHODS

There are several methods hackers can use to spoof their source
addresses. The easiest method is to configure their protocol stack with a
bogus address. In a TCP/IP environment, this can be easily accomplished
by a person coding a bogus IP address in the network address configuration
screen displayed by the operating system supported by their computer.
Because only the destination address is normally checked by networking
devices (such as routers and gateways), it is relatively easy to hide one's
identity by configuring a bogus source IP address in one's protocol stack.

When configuring a bogus IP address, hackers, for some unknown reason, commonly use either an address associated with the attacked network or with an RFC 1918 address. Concerning the latter, RFC 1918 defines
three blocks of IP addresses for use on private IP networks. Because the
use of RFC 1918 addresses on networks directly connected to the Internet
would result in duplicated IP addresses, they are barred from direct use on
the Internet. Instead, they are commonly used by organizations that have
more computers than assigned IP addresses. For example, assume an organization originally requested one Class C IP address from their Internet Service Provider (ISP). A Class C IP address is capable of supporting up to 254
hosts, because host addresses 0 and 255 cannot be used. Now suppose the
organization grew and required more than 254 workstations to be connected to the Internet. While the organization could request another Class
C network address from its ISP, such addresses are becoming difficult to
obtain and the organization might have to wait weeks or months to obtain
the requested address. As an alternative, the organization could use RFC
1918 addresses and use its router to perform network address translation
as illustrated in Exhibit 48-1.

In examining Exhibit 48-1, note that two Ethernet segments are shown
behind the router. Each segment could represent an individual Class C network using RFC 1918 addresses. The router would translate those RFC 1918

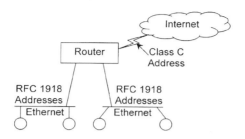

Exhibit 48-1. Using RFC 1918 addresses and network address translation to support internet connectivity for many workstations.

addresses to either a group of pooled Class C addresses or one Class C address, with the method of translation based on the manner in which the router's translation facility was configured.

If a pooled Class C address is used, the number of simultaneous sessions is limited to 254. If one Class C address is used, the router uses TCP and UDP port numbers to translate from RFC 1918 addresses to a common Class C address, with port numbers used to keep track of each address translation. Because there are thousands of unused port numbers, this method provides a greater translation capability as it limits or avoids potential contention between users behind the router requesting access to the Internet and available IP addresses.

Perhaps because RFC 1918 addresses are popularly used by many organizations, yet hidden by network address translation, they are commonly used as a source address when a hacker configures his or her protocol stack. Exhibit 48-2 lists the three address blocks reserved for private IP networks under RFC 1918.

Exhibit 48-2. RFC 1018 address blocks.

10.0.0.0	10.255.255.255
172.16.0.0	172.31.255.255
192.168.0.0	192.168.255.255

The use of an RFC 1918 address or the selection of an address from the target network results in a static source address. While this is by far the most common method of IP address spoofing, on occasion a sophisticated hacker will write a program that randomly generates source addresses. As will be noted shortly, only when those randomly generated source addresses represent an address on the target network or an RFC 1918 address are they relatively easy to block.

BLOCKING SPOOFED ADDRESSES

Because a router represents the point of entry into a network, it also represents one's first line of defense. Most routers support packet filtering, allowing the network administrator to configure the router to either permit or deny the flow of packets, based on the contents of one or more fields in a packet.

Cisco routers use access lists as a mechanism to perform packet filtering. A Cisco router supports two basic types of access lists: standard and extended. A Cisco standard IP access list performs filtering based on the source address in each packet. The format of a standard IP access list statement is shown below:

```
access-list list# [permit/deny] [ip address] [mask] [log]
```

The list# is a number between 1 and 99 and identifies the access list as a standard access list. Each access list statement contains either the keyword "permit" or "deny," which results in the packet with the indicated IP address either being permitted to flow through a router or sent to the great bit bucket in the sky. The mask represents a wildcard mask that functions in a reverse manner to a subnet mask. That is, a binary 0 is used to represent a "don't-care" condition. Note this is the opposite of the use of binary 0s and 1s in a subnet mask. In fact, the wildcard mask used by a Cisco router is the inverse of a subnet mask, and each position in the wildcard mask can be obtained by subtracting the value of the subnet mask for that position from 255.

The keyword "log" is optional and when included results in each match against a packet being displayed on the router's console. Logging can facilitate the development of access lists as well as serve as a mechanism to display activity that the access list was constructed to permit or deny. Thus, on occasion, it can be used to see if one's router is under attack or if suspicious activity is occurring.

In a Cisco router environment, access lists are applied to an interface in the inbound or outbound direction. To do so, one would use an interface command and an ip access-group command. Because spoofed IP addresses represent packets with bogus source addresses, one can use either standard or extended access lists to block such packets from entering a network. Because extended access lists will be discussed and described later in this chapter, we first illustrate the use of a standard access list to block packets with spoofed IP addresses. In doing so, assume an organization uses a Cisco router as illustrated in Exhibit 48-3 to connect a single Ethernet segment with a Web server and conventional workstations to the Internet. In examining Exhibit 48-3, note that it is assumed that the network address is 198.78.46.0 and the server has the IP address of 198.78.46.8.

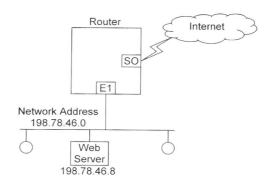

Exhibit 48-3. Connecting an Ethernet segment to the Ethernet.

ANTI-SPOOFING STATEMENTS

Because statements in a Cisco access list are operated upon in their sequence, top down, one should place anti-spoofing statements at the beginning of the access list. Because one wants to protect the network from persons attempting to remotely access the network via the Internet, one would apply the anti-spoofing statements in the access list to be created to the serial interface of the router. The access list will be applied in the inbound direction since one wants to examine packets flowing from the Internet toward the organization's Ethernet segment for bogus IP addresses.

The example shown in Exhibit 48-4 illustrates the configuration and application of a Cisco standard IP access list to effect anti-spoofing operations. In this example, four deny statements at the beginning of the access list preclude packets with a source address of any possible host on the organization's network, as well as any RFC 1918 address from flowing through the router.

The first deny statement checks each packet for a source address associated with the 198.78.46.0 network. Note that the wildcard mask of

Exhibit 48-4. An access list that performs anti-spoofing operations.

interface serial 0
ip access-group1 in
!
ip access-list1 deny 198.78.46.0 0.0.0.255
ip access-list1 deny 10.0.0.0 0.255.255.255
ip access-list1 deny 172.16.0.0 0.31.255.255
ip access-list1 deny 192.168.0.0. 0.0.255.255   ip access-list1 permit 0.0.0.0 255.255.255.255

0.0.0.255 results in the router matching the first three positions of each dotted decimal address but not caring about the fourth position. Thus, any packet with a source address associated with the internal network will be tossed into the great bit bucket in the sky. The next three deny statements in effect bar packets that use any RFC 1918 address as their source address. Because an access list denies all packets unless explicitly permitted, the access list just created would support anti-spoofing but disallow all other packets. Thus, a permit statement was added at the end of the access list. That statement uses a wildcard mask of 255.255.255.255, which in effect is a complete don't-care and represents the keyword "any" that one can use synonymously in a Cisco access list to represent an address and mask value of 0.0.0.0 255.255.255.255. Because statements are evaluated in their order in the list, if a packet does not have a source address on the 198.78.46.0 network or an RFC 1918 address, it is permitted to flow through the router. Also note that the command "interface serial 0" defines serial port 0 as the interface the access list will be applied to, while the command "ip access-group 1 in" defines that access-list1 will be applied to the serial 0 port in the inbound direction.

Now that there is an appreciation for how one can prevent packets with spoofed IP addresses from flowing into a network, attention can be turned to the manner by which one can prevent several types of denial of service attacks.

PING ATTACKS

One of the more common methods of creating a denial of service attack occurs when a person in a computer laboratory goes from workstation to workstation and configures each computer to ping a target using the -t option supported by most versions of Windows. The -t option results in the computer continuously pinging the target IP address. While one or a few workstations continuously pinging a Web server will only slightly impact the performance of the server, setting 50 or 100 or more workstations to continuously ping a server can result in the server spending most of its time responding to pings instead of user queries.

One method that can be used to prevent a ping attack is to block pings from entering the network. If the organization uses a Cisco router, one can block pings through the use of an extended IP access list. The format of a Cisco extended IP access list is shown below.

```
access-list list# [permit/deny] protocol [source address]
  [source-wildcard] [source port] [destination address]
  [destination-wildcard] [destination port] [options]
```

Unlike a standard IP access list that is limited to filtering based on the source address in a packet, an extended access list permits filtering based on several fields. Those fields include the type of protocol transported in the packet, its source address and destination address, and upper layer protocol information. Concerning the latter, one can use extended IP access lists to filter packets based on the value in their source and destination port fields. In addition to the preceding, an extended access list supports a range of options (such as "log"), as well as other keywords to enable specific types of access-list functions.

Returning to the problem at hand, how can one bar pings into an organization's network? The answer to this question is to use an extended IP access list. To do so, one would configure an access list statement that uses the ICMP protocol, since pings are transported by ICMP echo-request packets. The following Cisco extended IP access list statement could be used to block pings:

```
access-list 101 deny icmp any any echo-request
```

In the above extended IP access list statement, one will block echo-requests (pings) from any source address flowing to any destination address. Because one would apply the access list to the serial interface in the inbound direction, it would block pings from any address on the Internet destined to any address on the organization's Ethernet network. Knowing how to block pings, one can focus attention on another type of hacker denial of service attack — as directed broadcasts.

DIRECTED BROADCASTS

Refocusing on Exhibit 48-3, one notes that the network address of 198.78.46.0 represents a Class C network. A Class C network uses 3 bytes of its 4-byte address for the network address and 1 byte for the host address. Although an 8-bit byte can support 256 distinct numbers (0 to 255), an address of 0 is used to represent "this network," while an address of 255 is used to represent a "broadcast" address. Thus, a maximum of 254 hosts can be connected to a Class C network.

A directed broadcast occurs when a user on one network addresses a packet to the broadcast address of another network. In this example, that would be accomplished by sending a packet to the destination address of 198.78.46.255. The arrival of this packet results in the router converting the layer 3 packet into a layer 2 Ethernet frame addressed to everyone on the network as a layer 2 broadcast. This means that each host on the Ethernet network will respond to the frame and results in a heavy load of traffic flowing on the LAN.

One of the first types of directed broadcast attacks is referred to as a Smurf attack. Under this denial of service attack method, a hacker created a program that transmitted thousands of echo-request packets to the broadcast address of a target network. To provide an even more insidious attack, the hacker spoofed his or her IP address to that of a host on another network that he or she also desired to attack. The result of this directed broadcast attack was to deny service to *two* networks through a *single* attack.

Each host on the target network that is attacked with a directed broadcast responds to each echo-request with an echo-response. Thus, each ping flowing onto the target network can result in up to 254 responses. When multiplied by a continuous sequence of echo-requests flowing to the target network, this will literally flood the target network, denying bandwidth to other applications. Because the source IP address is spoofed, responses are directed to the spoofed address. If the hacker used an IP address of a host on another network that the hacker wishes to harm, the effect of the attack is a secondary attack. The secondary attack results in tens of thousands to millions of echo-responses flowing to the spoofed IP address, clogging the Internet access connection to the secondary network.

Although the original Smurf attack used ICMP echo-requests that could be blocked by an access list constructed to block inbound pings, hackers soon turned to the directed broadcast of other types of packets in an attempt to deny service by using a large amount of network bandwidth. Recognizing the problem of directed broadcasts, Cisco Systems and other router manufacturers soon added the capability to block directed broadcasts on each router interface. On a Cisco router, one would use the following IOS command to turn off the ability for packets containing a directed broadcast address to flow through the router:

```
no ip directed-broadcast
```

SUMMARY

This chapter focused on methods that can be used to prevent packets containing commonly used spoofed IP addresses from flowing into an organization's network. In addition, it also examined how several popular denial of service attacks operate and methods one can employ to block such attacks.

When considering measures that one can employ to secure a network, it is important to note that there is no such thing as a totally secure network. Unfortunately for society, many hackers are very smart and view the disruption of the operational status of a network as a challenge, periodically developing new methods to disrupt network activity. To keep up with the latest threats in network security, one should subscribe to security bulletins issued by the Computer Emergency Response Team (CERT) as well as periodically review release notes issued by the manufacturer of your organization's routers and firewalls. Doing so will alert one to new threats, as well as potential methods one can use to alleviate or minimize the effect of such threats.

Chapter 49
Internet Security: Securing the Perimeter
Douglas G. Conorich

THE CORPORATE COMMUNITY HAS, IN PART, CREATED THIS PROBLEM FOR ITSELF. The rapid growth of the Internet with all the utilities now available to Web surf, combined with the number of users who now have easy access through all the various Internet providers, make every desktop — including those in homes, schools, and libraries — places where an intruder can launch an attack. Surfing the Internet began as a novelty. Users were seduced by the vast amounts of information they could find. In many cases, it has become addictive.

Much of the public concern with the Internet has focused on the inappropriate access to Web sites by children from their homes or schools. A business is concerned with the bottom line. How profitable a business is can be directly related to the productivity of its employees. Inappropriate use of the Internet in the business world can decrease that productivity in many ways. The network bandwidth — how much data can flow across a network segment at any time — is costly to increase because of the time involved and the technology issues. Inappropriate use of the Internet can slow the flow of data and create the network approximation of a log jam.

There are also potential legal and public relations implications of inappropriate employee usage. One such issue is the increasing prevalence of "sin surfing" — browsing the pornographic Web sites. One company reported that 37 percent of its Internet bandwidth was taken up by "sin surfing." Lawsuits can be generated and, more importantly, the organization's image can be damaged by employees using the Internet to distribute inappropriate materials. To legally curtail the inappropriate use of the Internet, an organization must have a policy that defines what is acceptable, what is not, and what can happen if an employee is caught.

As part of the price of doing business, companies continue to span the bridge between the Internet and their own intranets with mission-critical applications. This makes them more vulnerable to new and unanticipated

0-8493-0859-3/00/$0.00+$.50
© 2000 by CRC Press LLC

security threats. Such exposures can place organizations at risk at every level — down to the very credibility upon which they build their reputations.

Making the Internet safe and secure for business requires careful management by the organization. Companies will have to use existing and new, emerging technologies, security policies tailored to the business needs of the organization, and training of the employees in order to accomplish this goal. IBM has defined four phases of Internet adoption by companies as they do business on the Internet: access, presence, integration, and E-business. Each of these phases has risks involved.

1. *Access.* In this first phase of adoption, a company has just begun to explore the Internet and learn about its potential benefits. A few employees are using modems connected to their desktop PCs, to dial into either a local Internet service provider, or a national service such as America Online. In this phase, the company is using the Internet as a resource for getting information only; all requests for access are in the outbound direction, and all information flow is in the inbound direction. Exchanging electronic mail and browsing the Web make up the majority of activities in this phase.

2. *Presence.* In this phase, the company has begun to make use of the Internet not only as a resource for getting information, but also as a means of providing information to others. Direct connection of the company's internal network means that now all employees have the ability to access the Internet (although this may be restricted by policy), allowing them to use it as an information resource, and also enabling processes such as customer support via e-mail. The creation of a Web server, either by the company's own staff or through a content hosting service, allows the company to provide static information such as product catalogs and data sheets, company background information, software updates, etc., to its customers and prospects.

3. *Integration.* In this phase, the company has begun to integrate the Internet into its day-to-day business processes by connecting its Web server directly (through a firewall or other protection system) to its back-office systems. In the previous phase, updates to the Web server's data were made manually, via tape or other means. In this phase, the Web server can obtain information on demand, as users request it. To use banking as an example, this phase enables the bank's customers to obtain their account balances, find out when checks cleared, and other information retrieval functions.

4. *E-business.* In the final phase, the company has enabled bi-directional access requests and information flow. This means that not only can customers on the Internet retrieve information from the company's back-office systems, but they can also add to or change information stored on those systems. At this stage, the company is

conducting business electronically; customers can place orders, transfer money (via credit cards or other means), check on shipments, etc; business partners can update inventories, make notes in customer records, etc. In short, the entire company has become accessible via the Internet.

While a company can follow this road to the end, as described by IBM, they are most likely somewhere on it — either in one of the phases or in transition between them.

INTERNET PROTOCOLS

Communication between two people is made possible by their mutual agreement to a common mode of transferring ideas from one person to the other. Each person must know exactly how to communicate with the other if this is to be successful. The communication can be in the form of a verbal or written language, such as English, Spanish, or German. It can also take the form of physical gestures like sign language. It can even be done through pictures or music. Regardless of the form of the communication, it is paramount that the meaning of an element, say a word, has the same meaning to both parties involved. The medium used for communication is also important. Both parties must have access to the same communication medium. One cannot talk to someone else via telephone if only one person has a telephone.

With computers, communications over networks is made possible by what are known as protocols. A protocol is a well-defined message format. The message format defines what each position in the message means. One possible message format could define the first four bits as the version number, the next four bits as the length of the header, and then eight bits for the service being used. As long as both computers agree on this format, communication can take place.

Network communications use more than one protocol. Sets of protocols used together are known as protocol suites or layered protocols. One well-known protocol suite is the Transport Control Protocol/ Internet Protocol (TCP/IP) suite. It is based on the International Standards Organization (ISO) Open Systems Interconnection (OSI) Reference Model (see Exhibit 49-1).

The ISO Reference Model is divided into seven layers:

1. The **Physical layer** is the lowest layer in the protocol stack. It consists of the "physical" connection. This may be copper wire or fiber optic cables and the associated connection hardware. The sole responsibility of the physical layer is to transfer the bits from one location to another.

2. The second layer is the **Data-Link layer.** It provides for the reliable delivery of data across the physical link. The data-link layer creates a checksum of the message that can be used by the receiving host to ensure that the entire message was received.

3. The **Network layer** manages the connections across the network for the upper four layers and isolates them from the details of addressing and delivery of data.

4. The **Transport layer** provides the end-to-end error detection and correction function between communicating applications.

5. The **Session layer** manages the sessions between communicating applications.

6. The **Preparation layer** standardizes the data presentation to the application level.

7. The **Application layer** consists of application programs that communicate across the network. This is the layer with which most users interact.

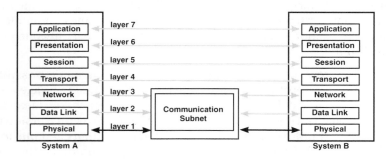

Exhibit 49-1. The ISO model.

Network devices can provide different levels of security, depending on how far up the stack they can read. Repeaters are used to connect two Ethernet segments. The repeater simply copies the electrical transmission and sends it on to the next segment of the network. Because the repeater only reads up through the data-link layer, no security can be added by its use.

The bridge is a computer that is used to connect two or more networks. The bridge differs from the repeater in that it can store and forward entire packets, instead of just repeating electrical signals. Because it reads up through the network layer of the packet, the bridge can add some security.

Application Layer consists of applications and processes that use the network
Host-to-Host Transport Layer provides end-to-end data delivery service.
Internet Layer Defines the datagram and handles the routing of data.
Network Access Layer consists of routines for accessing physical networks.

Exhibit 49-2. The TCP/IP protocol architecture.

It could allow the transfer of only packets with local addresses. A bridge uses physical addresses — not IP addresses. The physical address, also know as the Ethernet address, is the actual address of the Ethernet hardware. It is a 48-bit number.

Routers and gateways are computers that determine which of the many possible paths a packet will take to get to the destination device. These devices read up through the transport layer and can read IP addresses, including port numbers. They can be programmed to allow, disallow, and reroute IP datagrams determined by the IP address of the packet.

As previously mentioned, TCP/IP is based on the ISO model, but it groups the seven layers of the ISO model into four layers, as displayed in Exhibit 49-2.

The network access layer is the lowest layer of the TCP/IP protocol stack. It provides the means of delivery and has to understand how the network transmits data from one IP address to another. The network access layer basically provides the functionality of the first three layers of the ISO model.

TCP/IP provides a scheme of IP addressing that uniquely defines every host connected to the Internet. The network access layer provides the functions that encapsulate the datagrams and maps the IP addresses to the physical addresses used by the network.

The Internet layer has at its core the Internet Protocol (RFC791). IP provides the basic building blocks of the Internet. It provides:

- the datagram definition scheme
- the Internet addressing scheme
- the means of moving data between the network access layer and the host-to-host layer

- the means for datagrams to be routed to remote hosts
- the function of breaking apart and reassembling packets for transmission

IP is a connectionless protocol. This means that it relies on other protocols within the TCP/IP stack to provide the connection-oriented services. The connection-oriented services (i.e., TCP) take care of the handshake — the exchange of control information. The IP layer contains the Internet Control Message Protocol (ICMP).

The host-to-host transport layer houses two protocols: the Transport Control Protocol (TCP) and the User Datagram Protocol (UDP). Its primary function is to deliver messages between the Application Layer and the Internet Layer. TCP is a reliable protocol. This means that it guarantees that the message will arrive as sent. It contains error detection and correction features. UDP does not have these features and is, therefore, unreliable. For shorter messages, where it is easier to resend the message than worry about the overhead involved with TCP, UDP is used.

The application layer contains the various services that users will use to send data. The application layer contains such user programs as the Network Terminal Protocol (Telnet), File Transfer Protocol (FTP), and Simple Mail Transport Protocol (SMTP). It also contains protocols not directly used by users, but required for system use — for example, Domain Name Service (DNS), Routing Information Protocol (RIP), and Network File System (NFS).

ATTACKS

As previously noted, TCP is a reliable messaging protocol. This means that TCP is a connection-oriented protocol. TCP uses what is known as a three-way handshake. A handshake is simply the exchange of control information between the two computers. This information enables the computers to determine which packets go where and ensure that all the information in the message has been received.

When a connection is desired between two systems, Host A and Host B, using TCP/IP, a three-way handshake must occur. The initiating host, Host A (the client), sends the receiving host, Host B (the server), a message with the SYN (synchronize sequence number) bit set. The SYN contains information needed by Host B to set up the connection. This message contains the IP address of the both Host A and Host B and the port numbers they will talk on. The SYN tells Host B what sequence number the client will start with, seq = x. This number is important to keep all the data transmitted in the proper order and can be used to notify Host B that a piece of data is missing. The sequence number is found starting at bit 32 to 63 of the header.

When Host B receives the SYN, it sends the client an ACK (acknowledgment message). This message contains the sequence number that Host B will start with, SYN, seq = y, and the sequence number of Host A incremented, the ACK, x + 1. The acknowledgment number is bits 64 through 95 of the header.

The three-way handshake is completed when Host A receives the ACK from Host B and sends an ACK, y + 1, in return. Now data can flow back and forth between the two hosts. This connection is now known as a socket. A socket is usually identified as Host_A_IP:Port_Number, Host_B_IP:Port_Number.

There are two attacks that use this technology: SYN Flood and Sequence Predictability.

SYN Flood Attack

The SYN Flood attack uses a TCP connection request (SYN). The SYN is sent to the target computer with the source IP address in the packet "spoofed," or replaced with an address that is not in use on the Internet or that belongs to another computer. When the target computer receives the connection request, it allocates resources to handle and track the new connection. A SYN_RECEIVED state is stored in a buffer register awaiting the return response (ACK) from the initiating computer, which would complete the three-way handshake. It then sends out an SYN-ACK. If the response is sent to the "spoofed," nonexistent IP address, there will never be a response. If the SYN-ACK is sent to a real computer, it checks to see if it has a SYN in the buffer to that IP address. Since it does not, it ignores the request. The target computer retransmits the SYN-ACK a number of times. After a finite amount of wait time, the original SYN request is purged from the buffer of the target computer. This condition is known as a half-open socket.

As an example, the default configuration for a Windows NT 3.5x or 4.0 computer is to retransmit the SYN-ACK five times, doubling the time-out value after each retransmission. The initial time-out value is three seconds, so retries are attempted at 3, 6, 12, 24, and 48 seconds. After the last retransmission, 96 seconds are allowed to pass before the computer gives up on receiving a response and deallocates the resources that were set aside earlier for the connection. The total elapsed time that resources are in use is 189 seconds.

An attacker will send many of these TCP SYNs to tie up as many resources as possible on the target computer. Since the buffer size for the storage of SYNs is a finite size, numerous attempts can cause a buffer overflow. The effect of tying up connection resources varies, depending on the TCP/IP stack and applications listening on the TCP port. For most stacks, there is a limit on the number of connections that can be in the half-open

SYN_RECEIVED state. Once the limit is reached for a given TCP port, the target computer responds with a reset to all further connection requests until resources are freed. Using this method, an attacker can cause a denial-of-services on several ports.

Finding the source of a SYN Flood attack can be very difficult. A network analyzer can be used to try to track the problem down, and it may be necessary to contact the Internet Service Provider for assistance in attempting to trace the source. Firewalls should be set up to reject packets from the external network with any IP address from the internal network.

Sequence Predictability

The ability to guess sequence numbers is very useful to intruders because they can create a short-lived connection to a host without having to see the reply packets. This ability, taken in combination with the fact that many hosts have trust relationships that use IP addresses as authentication; that packets are easily spoofed; and that individuals can mount denial of service attacks, means one can impersonate the trusted systems to break into such machines without using source routing.

If an intruder wants to spoof a connection between two computers so that the connection seems as if it is coming from B to A, using your computer C, it works like this:

1. First, the intruder uses computer C to mount a SYN Flood attack on the ports on computer B where the impersonating will take place.
2. Then, computer C sends a normal SYN to a port on A.
3. Computer A returns a SYN-ACK to computer C containing computer A's current Initial Sequence Number (ISN).
4. Computer A internally increments the ISN. This incrementation is done differently in different operating systems (OSs). Operating systems such as BSD, HPUX, Irix, SunOS (not Solaris), and others usually increment by $FA00 for each connection and double each second.

   With this information, the intruder can now guess the ISN that computer A will pick for the next connection. Now comes the spoof.
5. Computer C sends a SYN to computer A using the source IP spoofed as computer B.
6. Computer A sends a SYN-ACK back to computer B, containing the ISN. The intruder on computer C does not see this, but the intruder has guessed the ISN.
7. At this point, computer B would respond to computer A with an RST. This occurs because computer B does not have a SYN_RECEIVED

from computer A. Since the intruder used a SYN Flood attack on computer B, it will not respond.

8. The intruder on computer C sends an ACK to computer A, using the source IP spoofed as computer B, containing the guessed ISN+1.

   If the guess was correct, computer A now thinks there has been a successful three-way handshake and the TCP connection between computer A and computer B is fully set up. Now the spoof is complete. The intruder on computer C can do anything, but blindly.

9. Computer C sends `echo + + >>/.rhosts` to port 514 on computer A.

10. If root on computer A had computer B in its /.rhosts file, the intruder has root.

11. Computer C now sends a FIN to computer A.

12. Computer C could be brutal and send an RST to computer A just to clean up things.

13. Computer C could also send an RST to the synflooded port on B, leaving no traces.

To prevent such attacks, one should NEVER trust anything from the Internet. Routers and firewalls should filter out any packets that are coming from the external (sometimes known as the red) side of the firewall that has an IP address of a computer on the internal (sometimes known as the blue) side. This only stops Internet trust exploits; it will not stop spoofs that build on intranet trusts. Companies should avoid using rhosts files wherever possible.

ICMP

A major component of the TCP/IP Internet layer is the Internet Control Message Protocol (ICMP). ICMP is used for flow control, detecting unreachable destinations, redirection routes, and checking remote hosts. Most users are interested in the last of these functions. Checking a remote host is accomplished by sending an ICMP Echo Message. The PING command is used to send these messages.

When a system receives one of these ICMP Echo Messages, it places the message in a buffer, then re-transmits the message from the buffer back to the source. Due to the buffer size, the ICMP Echo Message size cannot exceed 64K. UNIX hosts, by default, will send an ICMP Echo Message that is 64 bytes long. They will not allow a message of over 64K. With the advent of Microsoft Windows NT, longer messages can be sent. The Windows NT hosts do not place an upper limit on these messages. Intruders have been sending messages of 1MB and larger. When these messages are received, they cause a buffer overflow on the target host. Different operating systems will react differently to this buffer overflow. The reactions range from rebooting to a total system crash.

FIREWALLS

The first line of defense between the Internet and an intranet should be a firewall. A firewall is a multi-homed host that is placed in the Internet route, such that it stops and can make decisions about each packet that wants to get through. A firewall performs a different function from a router. A router can be used to filter out certain packets that meet a specific criteria (i.e., an IP address). A router processes the packets up through the IP layer. A firewall stops all packets. All packets are processed up through the application layer. Routers cannot perform all the functions of a firewall. A firewall should meet, at least, the following criteria:

- In order for an internal or external host to connect to the other network, it must log in on the firewall host.
- All electronic mail is sent to the firewall, which in turn distributes it.
- Firewalls should not mount file systems via NFS, nor should any of its file systems be mounted.
- Firewalls should not run NIS (Network Information Systems).
- Only required users should have accounts on the firewall host.
- The firewall host should not be trusted, nor trust any other host.
- The firewall host is the only machine with anonymous FTP.
- Only the minimum service should be enabled on the firewall in the file `inetd.conf`.
- All system logs on the firewall should log to a separate host.
- Compilers and loaders should be deleted on the firewall.
- System directories permissions on the firewall host should be 711 or 511.

THE DMZ

Most companies today are finding that it is imperative to have an Internet presence. This Internet presence takes on the form of anonymous FTP sites and a World Wide Web (WWW) site. In addition to these, companies are setting up hosts to act as a proxy server for Internet mail and a Domain Name Server (DNS). The host that sponsors these functions cannot be on the inside of the firewall. Therefore, companies are creating what has become known as the DeMilitarized Zone (DMZ) or Perimeter Network, a segment between the router that connects to the Internet and the firewall.

Proxy Servers

A proxy host is a dual-homed host that is dedicated to a particular service or set of services, such as mail. All external requests to that service directed toward the internal network are routed to the proxy. The proxy host then evaluates the request and either passes the request on to the internal service server or discards it. The reverse is also true. Internal requests are passed to the proxy from the service server before they are passed on to the Internet.

One of the functions of the proxy hosts is to protect the company from advertising its internal network scheme. Most proxy software packages contain Network Address Translation (NAT). Take, for example, a mail server. The mail from Albert_Smith@starwars.abc.com would be translated to smith@proxy.abc.com as it went out to the Internet. Mail sent to smith@proxy.abc.com would be sent to the mail proxy. Here it would be readdressed to Albert_Smith@starwars.abc.com and sent to the internal mail server for final delivery.

TESTING THE PERIMETER

A company cannot use the Internet without taking risks. It is important to recognize these risks and it is important not to exaggerate them. One cannot cross the street without taking a risk. But by recognizing the dangers, and taking the proper precautions (such as looking both ways before stepping off the curb), millions of people cross the street safely every day.

The Internet and intranets are in a state of constant change — new protocols, new applications, and new technologies — and a company's security practices must be able to adapt to these changes. To adapt, the security process should be viewed as forming a circle. The first step is to assess the current state of security within one's intranet and along the perimeter. Once one understands where one is, then one can deploy a security solution. If one does not monitor that solution by enabling some detection and devising a response plan, the solution is useless. It would be like putting an alarm on a car, but never checking it when the alarm goes off. As the solution is monitored and tested, there will be further weaknesses — which brings us back to the assessment stage and the process is repeated. Those new weaknesses are then learned about and dealt with, and a third round begins. This continuous improvement ensures that corporate assets are always protected.

As part of this process, a company must perform some sort of vulnerability checking on a regular basis. This can be done by the company, or it may choose to have an independent group do the testing. The company's security policy should state how the firewall and the other hosts in the DMZ are to be configured. These configurations need to be validated and then periodically checked to ensure that the configurations have not changed. The vulnerability test may find additional weaknesses with the configurations and then the policy needs to be changed.

Security is achieved through the combination of technology and policy. The technology must be kept up to date and the policy must outline the procedures. An important part of a good security policy is to ensure that there are as few information leaks as possible.

One source of information can be DNS records. There are two basic DNS services: lookups and zone transfers. Lookup activities are used to resolve IP addresses into host names or to do the reverse. A zone transfer happens when one DNS server (a secondary server) asks another DNS server (the primary server) for all the information that it knows about a particular part of the DNS tree (a zone). These zone transfers only happen between DNS servers that are supposed to be providing the same information. Users can also request a zone transfer.

A zone transfer is accomplished using the `nslookup` command in interactive mode. The zone transfer can be used to check for information leaks. This procedure can show hosts, their IP addresses, and operating systems. A good security policy is to disallow zone transfers on external DNS servers. This information can be used by an intruder to attack or spoof other hosts. If this is not operationally possible, as a general rule, DNS servers outside of the firewall (on the red side) should not list hosts within the firewall (on the blue side). Listing internal hosts only helps intruders gain network mapping information and gives them an idea of the internal IP addressing scheme.

In addition to trying to do a zone transfer, the DNS records should be checked to ensure that they are correct and that they have not changed. Domain Information Gofer (DIG) is a flexible command-line tool that is used to gather information from the Domain Name System servers.

The `PING` command, as previously mentioned, has the ability to determine the status of a remote host using the ICMP ECHO Message. If a host is running and is reachable by the message, the PING program will return an "alive" message. If the host is not reachable and the host name can be resolved by DNS, the program returns a "host not responding" message; otherwise, an "unknown host" message is obtained. An intruder can use the PING program to set up a "war dialer." This is a program that systematically goes through the IP addresses one after another, looking for "alive" or "not responding" hosts. To prevent intruders from mapping internal networks, the firewall should screen out ICMP messages. This can be done by not allowing ICMP messages to go through to the internal network or go out from the internal network. The former is the preferred method. This would keep intruders from using ICMP attacks, such as the Ping 'O Death or Loki tunneling.

The TRACEROUTE program is another useful tool one can use to test the corporate perimeter. Because the Internet is a large aggregate of networks and hardware connected by various gateways, TRACEROUTE is used to check the "time-to-live" (ttl) parameter and routes. TRACEROUTE sends a series of three UDP packets with an ICMP packet incorporated during its check. The ttl of each packet is similar. As the ttl expires, it sends the ICMP packet back to the originating host with the IP address of the host where it expired. Each successive broadcast uses a longer ttl. By continuing to send longer ttls, TRACEROUTE pieces together the successive jumps. Checking the various jumps not only shows the routes, but it can show possible problems that may give an intruder information or leads. This information might show a place where an intruder might successfully launch an attack. A "*" return shows that a particular hop has exceeded the three-second timeout. These are hops that could be used by intruders to create DoSs. Duplicate entries for successive hops are indications of bugs in the kernel of that gateway or looping within the routing table.

Checking the open ports and services available is another important aspect of firewall and proxy server testing. There are a number of programs — like the freeware program STROBE, IBM Network Services Auditor (NSA), ISS Internet Scanner™, and AXENT Technologies NetRecon™ — that can perform a selective probe of the target UNIX or Windows NT network communication services, operating systems and key applications. These programs use a comprehensive set of penetration tests. The software searches for weaknesses most often exploited by intruders to gain access to a network, analyzes security risks, and provides a series of highly informative reports and recommended corrective actions.

There have been numerous attacks in the past year that have been directed at specific ports. The teardrop, newtear, oob, and land.c are only a few of the recent attacks. Firewalls and proxy hosts should have only the minimum number of ports open. By default, the following ports are open as shipped by the vendor, and should be closed:

- echo on TCP port 7
- echo on UDP port 7
- discard on TCP port 9
- daytime on TCP port 13
- daytime on UDP port 13
- chargen on TCP port 19
- chargen on UDP port 19
- NetBIOS-NS on UDP port 137
- NetBIOS-ssn on TCP port 139

Other sources of information leaks include Telnet, FTP, and Sendmail programs. They all, by default, advertise the operating system or service type and version. They also may advertise the host name. This feature can be turned off and a more appropriate warning messages should be put in its place.

661

SECURITY

Sendmail has a feature that will allow the administrator to expand or verify users. This feature should not be turned on on any host in the DMZ. An intruder would only have to Telnet to the Sendmail port to obtain user account names. There are a number of well-known user accounts that an intruder would test. This method works even if the `finger` command is disabled.

VRFY and EXPN allow an intruder to determine if an account exists on a system and can provide a significant aid to a brute-force attack on user accounts. If you are running Sendmail, add the lines `Opnovrfy` and `Opnoexpn` to your Sendmail configuration file, usually located in /etc/sendmail.cf. With other mail servers, contact the vendor for information on how to disable the verify command.

```
# telnet xxx.xxx.xx.xxx
Trying xxx.xxx.xx.xxx...
Connected to xxx.xxx.xx.xxx.
Escape character is '^]'.
220 proxy.abc.com Sendmail 4.1/SMI-4.1 ready at Thu,
    26 Feb 98 12:50:05 CST
expn root
250- John Doe <jdoe>
250 Jane User <juser>
vrfy root
250- John Doe <jdoe>
250 Jane User <juser>
vrfy jdoe
250 John Doe <john_doe@mailserver.internal.abc.com>
vrfy juser
250 John User <jane_user@mailserver.internal.abc.com>
^]
```

Another important check that needs to be run on these hosts in the DMZ is a validation that the system and important application files are valid and not hacked. This is done by running a checksum or a cyclic redundancy check (CRC) on the files. Because these values are not stored anywhere on the host, external applications need to be used for this function. Some suggested security products are freeware applications such as COPS and Tripwire, or third-party commercial products like AXENT Technologies Enterprise Security Manager™ (ESM), ISS RealSecure™ or Kane Security Analyst™.

662

SUMMARY

The assumption must be made that one is not going to be able to stop everyone from getting in to a computers. An intruder only has to succeed once. Security practitioners, on the other hand, have to succeed every time. Once one comes to this conclusion, then the only strategy left is to secure the perimeter as best one can while allowing business to continue, and have some means to detect the intrusions as they happen. If one can do this, then one limits what the intruder can do.

Chapter 50
Remote Access Authentication

Ellen Bonsall

THE COMPUTING WORLD HAS EVOLVED FROM A CENTRALIZED ENVIRONMENT consisting of single mainframes and multiple dumb terminals to a distributed client/server networking environment. Given this global change in information systems (IS), networking industry experts around the world agree that the management of information systems — particularly network security — is an increasingly difficult task for executives of today. IS managers live with the fear that a great financial loss due to an unforeseen network security breach will be blamed solely on the IS team.

Complex distributed networks have made security a critical component of network architecture. Client/server technology is delivering sensitive data and mission-critical applications directly to the desktop. Most of security products of today are designed to do one specific job, without regard to their roles in the larger security scheme. Without appropriate protection on both the Internet and enterprise sides of the network, an organization is vulnerable to even the simplest of attacks. To protect information assets of an organization, IS teams must establish security policies, procedures, and systems to support these assets.

USER AND CLIENT AUTHENTICATION

IS security professionals must combine the task of integrating worldwide authentication services across multiple networking platforms with that of securing information in the burgeoning distributed and mobile computing environment. User and client authentication must be the foundation of any viable network security plan. To compete in the global economy of today, CEOs, CIOs, and IS professionals are seeking ways to seamlessly tie employees, business and technology partners, suppliers, and customers together for information sharing — while simultaneously protecting sensitive data.

SECURITY

The market for remote access security and authentication products boils down to one fact: people want to know with whom they are dealing. However, as advancing technology makes complex distributed networks the norm, rather than the exception, it becomes increasingly difficult to guarantee that information will be protected from unauthorized users. It can be devastating for individuals and organizations when sensitive information falls into the wrong hands. IS professionals should track patterns of information crime, study the ways in which other organizations have dealt with network security breaches, and keep abreast of the latest products designed to protect information assets.

The specter of unauthorized local area network (LAN) remote access has caused many IS departments to consider an authentication complement for their network security schemes. Even with added protection, however, systems are vulnerable. IS security is not just about protecting electronic communications from Internet criminals. Moreover, a new range of access points in current open systems has made it possible to hack into systems from sites located anywhere in the world. To establish easy-to-use, cost-effective safeguards, IS security professionals must coordinate with CEOs, CIOs, IS staff, and users to address basic security fundamentals. Optimum solutions cannot be achieved without user cooperation and participation. Regardless of how fail-safe a system may appear, if users can disable it or gain access to information without having to comply with established security standards, the safeguard is useless. Finally, many organizations put the cart before the horse by installing the latest security panacea (e.g., an internal or external firewall) without first establishing an overall security policy. It is essential to effective access and user authentication strategies to pinpoint exactly what is being protected and from whom.

DEFINING THE SECURITY PROCESS

If an organization does not already have an official security policy that is endorsed at all levels of management, it is essential that the IS team gather the necessary parties and create one. Some departments may already have policies; the basic elements of these may be relevant to an organizational policy. The policy should be implemented as soon as possible and should, above all, mandate an enterprisewide user authentication solution that can be scaled to differing security requirements.

The IS team should develop a code of conduct for employees, and should require that employees sign a compliance document once they have read and understood the code. To further ensure compliance, the team should plan to educate employees about the importance of security and the value of information to the organization. Employee awareness programs are useful for this purpose.

Making Enterprise-Specific Security Choices

Myriad solutions exist to combat security problems of today, some of which cost more than others both in time and monetary investment. Vendors of firewalls, routers, and communications servers are continually integrating the latest technology to make their security products more reliable. IS staff who are responsible for choosing and implementing such products should carefully compare products before purchasing and implementing them. The best security solutions for an organization are not necessarily those used by other organizations in the same industry. Primary in importance is that the IS team begins the process and establishes safeguards, with the assumption that products will require constant review and updating. Before addressing specific strategies for securing servers with either native options or third-party systems, IS staff should take special care to secure any server that can be accessed remotely or that can be accessed from other remotely accessed servers on the wide area network.

When evaluating security tools, it is useful to establish the goals of the organization security system, including the user authentication facet of security. IS staff should establish exactly what the security and remote access authentication system will protect, who will be permitted access, and, relatedly, who will be denied specific access. The more specific the outline of user access requirements is, the more comprehensive remote access security will be. The success of these access objectives can be measured when the system is implemented, and the objectives can be changed as personnel, networks, and organizational goals change.

IS staff should draw up written procedures that detail how and when the security systems will be audited. In addition, an independent, internal or external audit team should look over the systems at least quarterly, and the members should be fully aware of all of the security and access objectives of the organization. When the independent audit team submits a report, any noncompliance should be addressed by the IS team immediately.

Establishing Basic Controls

A number of fundamental controls should be implemented in any organization to secure Internet and dial-up remote access.

Management Controls. Technical personnel within the organization should be trained before they are permitted to cruise the Internet or to dial in to the LAN through a remote connection. If the organization is connected to external networks, IS staff must understand the risks and manage these connections properly. In addition, a policy on the acceptable use of the Internet should be distributed to all employees. Internet access can negatively affect productivity unless reasonable limits are set and enforced.

IS staff should also establish and execute procedures for reporting and resolving detected breaches of remote access security. Procedures should include reporting breaches to management or to external organizations such as the Computer Emergency Response Team (CERT). Monitoring programs that scan the system regularly for Trojan horses, sniffers, and other undesirable programs and data are also fundamental security tools.

Inbound Traffic Controls. Inbound traffic controls include the implementation of network and node application restrictions through a firewall to limit access by remote connection to applications. Additional application controls should be installed, such as restrictions on certain types of transactions that a remote user may process. IS staff should maintain logs of all activity originating through remote access and review the logs for anomalies.

Authorization and authentication of employees must be required to view or modify internal application data. Users requesting access through an external network or remote access must also be authenticated. Proxy log-ins should be prohibited; allowing one user to act for another invites unauthorized access.

Outbound Traffic Controls. Systems security is often designed to protect an organization's networks from those who would attempt to break in. It is just as critical, however, that outbound traffic controls be established to monitor the information that leaves the organization. Implementing such controls can be very difficult, as the legal tangle of personal privacy and e-mail vs. corporate liability demonstrates. At a minimum, IS staff should maintain logs of all external network activity originated by internal users and identify and communicate to users any risks or potential threats (e.g., viruses).

File Transfer Controls. To ensure that records are transmitted and that data is received, IS staff should implement manual or automated controls to monitor file transfers. Executable code should be transmitted by only systems and applications designed to prevent unauthorized or inadvertent execution. It is usually difficult to protect against data-driven attacks, or attacks in which something is mailed or copied to an internal host and then executed. All attempts at unsolicited distribution of executable files should be called to the attention of management. Executable files are a popular way to spread viruses.

IS staff should control the use of the file transfer protocol site through a proxy server. If this is not possible, another way of restricting incoming connections to the network must be explored.

Defining Remote Access: Establishing a Common Vocabulary

Once an organizational policy has been written and fundamental controls implemented, remote access and authentication can be targeted. The security team must ensure that everyone in the organization shares a common, remote access vocabulary, so that all of the security provisions will be fully understood and complied with.

In most organizations, IS departments struggle to maintain control of information in the midst of rapidly changing strategic business and communications issues. Healthcare systems are an effective example of this. Instead of having users dial in to three or four different platforms and use different equipment for applications that might include claims entry, individual eligibility, and claim status verification, an IS team could purchase an integrating access server to centralize remote connections. A single dial-in access connection would allow users to access multiple hosts across diverse platforms.

AUTHENTICATION

Authentication should not be confused with identification or authorization. The IS team must agree on the definition of remote access user authentication and the tools associated with it before it makes decisions about specific technologies or products.

- **Identification.** User identification is the process by which people identify themselves to the system as valid users. The log on process is an example of a simple user identification. Identification is not the same process as authentication, which establishes that the person logging on to the network is indeed that user.
- **Authentication.** Authentication is the process of determining the true identity of a user or an object (e.g., a communications server) attempting to access a system. It is the confirmation of the claimed identity.
- **Authorization.** Authorization is the process of determining what types of activities are permitted. In the context of authentication, once the system has authenticated a user, he may be authorized for various levels of access or different activities.
- **Authentication token.** This is a portable device (or software loaded directly on a PC) that is used for authentication. Authentication tokens use a variety of techniques, including challenge-response asynchronous, event-time-based synchronous, and time-only-based synchronous technologies.
- **Authentication tool.** An authentication tool is a software or handheld hardware "key" or "token" used during the authentication process.

Remote Access

The generic term "remote access" is commonly applied to terminal emulation, file transfer and network management. Remote access software (such as Symantec Corp.'s PCAnywhere) makes PC drives or peripherals available to other computers. It can dial up another PC through a modem, query the hard drive of that computer, and give commands to print or to transfer files. Basic remote access software does not give as high a level of power as remote control products, which establish the PC as a node on the LAN. In using remote access software only, the access control measures provided by it are not robust enough to protect against unauthorized intrusion.

Remote Control

Remote control is the taking over of a host system with a PC keyboard and mouse and viewing its screen from anywhere in the world. The user can run programs, edit and transfer files, read e-mail, or browse a distant database. The user can dial up with a modem or a node-to-node LAN connection and take complete charge of the screen, keyboard, and mouse of another computer. The simplest remote-control scheme is a synchronous, one-to-one, dial-up connection between modems attached to two PC. Whatever mode, or combination of modes, the user's network employs, user and client authentication are vital to protecting information assets.

When a remote node connection is established, the PC is actually sitting on the LAN with which it has been connected. The PC or workstation is connected to all of the network services of the remote PC. The user has access to any services or information for which it has been authorized. Therefore, if the remote network does not have an authorization, identification, and authentication system in place, the user may roam at will.

A limited, secure connection can be established first through the use of a remote control software package and the use of any security features native to the operating system or communications hardware. If levels of security are required that are not provided by native security, third-party authentication technology should be added.

SIX COMPONENTS THAT SECURE REMOTE ACCESS

Authenticating LAN dial-up users is a starting point in evaluating user authentication technology. A variety of reasons for controlling access to the LAN and to office network workstations exist, but not all of them are about protecting the organization. Protecting the privacy of personal information is a top priority for many companies or users. Most users create personal information on their computers. No one wants such personal information made public. By controlling access, business plans and proposals, pricing figures, payroll information, and other sensitive information can be kept from prying eyes. Controlling access also reduces the chances of virus infection and slows the spread of an infection, should one occur.

Authenticating users preserves the integrity of information. By locking out unauthorized users, the chances that someone will make unwanted (or unintentional) changes to critical files are reduced. Six components are critical to secure remote access:

1. Authorization
2. Authentication
3. Confidentiality
4. Auditing
5. Control
6. Nonrepudiation

Authorization

The key to secure remote access is to understand and integrate the critical components without leaving anything out. Network managers must be able to authorize users (i.e., control who on the network may access which resources). Properly implemented, authorization systems prohibit the engineering department, for example, from reading the CEO's business projections. Authorization systems should provide secure, single sign-on, which allows users to log on to a network once and to gain access to all the resources that they require (but none of the ones that they are unauthorized to have).

In most cases, authorization systems are comprised of complex software packages with code that executes on specifically secured computers on the network. Some examples are: IBM's, Cygnus Support's, and Cyber-SAFE's Kerberos-based systems, and ICL Enterprises North America's SES-AME-based system. However, such security is limited by the specific platforms on which they work.

User Authentication

Authentication is the process of verifying the identity of end users (and clients). It should be considered a basic building block of secure remote access. A critical component of any network architecture, user authentication employs passwords — the most common method of authenticating users. Virtually all network operating systems offer limited password protection, as do most communications servers and other applications that allow access to a network. The reusable (i.e., static) passwords that are employed are easy to use, but they offer an extremely limited degree of security. User authentication takes place after entry into the system with common ID and resuable passwords. Security is very lax. Reusable passwords have been shown over a lengthy period of time to be the least successful way to protect networks.

Why are static, reusable passwords so easy to steal or guess? Several intrinsic weaknesses are found in reusable passwords. First, most people have a difficult time remembering passwords, especially if they must remember many different passwords that are unique to each network or application that they use. Typically, they give the passwords to co-workers or paste them in visible areas for easy reference, especially if the IS staff requires them to change the passwords on a regular basis. Second, if permitted to choose their own passwords, they often pick trivial ones that are easy to remember. These may include permutations of their names, their children's names, or personal information, such as date of birth. Trivial passwords are common words that are subject to "dictionary attacks" or simply educated guesses, which is not a very secure form of authentication. Third, static passwords are vulnerable because it is possible to steal them electronically. This can be done either by unauthorized insiders or by outsiders (i.e., hackers) through a "password sniffer" or similar program designed to monitor and record the names and passwords of authorized users as they log onto a network. Because of these basic weaknesses, reusable passwords seriously jeopardize overall communications security. It is too easy to impersonate authorized users by logging on with passwords that actually are legitimate to access restricted information.

To solve this problem, network security experts are now choosing from a variety of authentication systems that generate one-time-use-only (i.e., dynamic) passwords for a greater degree of user authentication and, therefore, information security. Handheld authentication devices (e.g., tokens) employ encryption and public or proprietary algorithms to calculate these one-time-use-only passwords (or responses) to random challenges issued by authentication servers residing on the network. More specifically, there are stand-alone devices (i.e., hardware boxes) placed in front of a communications server or router to provide authentication prior to network entry; and software security servers (i.e., software running on a dedicated machine designed to operate directly on the network), for example, on a Windows NT or UNIX box. Server-based authentication software responds to requests originating from network access control points, such as firewalls, remote access servers, or O/S security software.

An Authentication Security Server. An authentication security server is not a communications server. In many cases, third-party vendors work with the manufacturers of firewalls, communications servers, and routers to integrate user authentication technology so that users may be authenticated before they pass through gateways to the LAN. Types of communications servers that integrate third-party user authentication technology include: Shiva Corp.'s LANRover; Microsoft Corp.'s NT Remote Access Service (RAS) Server; Attachmate's Remote LAN Node Server (RLN), a Cisco Systems, Inc. router operating as a communications server; Checkpoint

Systems, Inc.'s firewall; and Atlantic Systems Group's TurnStyle firewall. The entire authentication process is dependent on the use of tokens (either hardware or software) so that one-time-use passwords used for authentication can be generated on both ends of the authentication process and then compared before access is granted. (Passwords are generated on the user's end, by the token, and at the network server end, by the authentication server.)

Authentication Tokens

Some of the tokens that work with the previously mentioned authentication servers may be used to verify dial-up users, users already on LANs, or users seeking access to a LAN through the Internet. Different tokens have different capabilities. Some products even authenticate users connecting through fax machines or telephones. Tokens can be small, handheld hardware devices, a connector-size device that sits between a computer and a modem, or software that runs on the user's PC. Some have more complex features and are considered more secure than others. However, all challenge–response tokens serve the same purpose. They generate passwords that a user's PC transmits to an authentication server that resides at an access point on a network. Alternatively, they transmit them to authentication software residing on, for example, a Microsoft NT Remote Access Server. The authentication servers (or the software residing on a PC or workstation located directly on the network) verify that the users are who they say they are when they first identify themselves.

Challenge–Response, Asynchronous Authentication

In a secure, challenge–response, asynchronous authentication process, network managers typically configure the tokens themselves — a definite benefit over factory-issued secret keys. No one except the network manager or administrator has access to the database of user secret keys and other pertinent user information. A LAN dial-up remote access can provide an example on how this works. A user dials up remotely, and before the network allows the user access, the call is intercepted by a master authentication device (or a software authentication server), which prompts the user for an ID. When the user is identified as one of the individuals allowed access to the network, the server issues a random, alphanumeric challenge to begin the process of authenticating (i.e., determining that the user is who he says he is).

That random challenge is used by both the token and the server to calculate a one-time-use password based on a secret key value stored in both the token and the server. The process typically involves the use of an encryption algorithm. The reliability of the algorithm used in the authentication solution of an organization should be carefully evaluated.

Solutions that employ the challenge–response process, secret user keys, and encryption algorithms to generate passwords result in a very high level of authentication security. The one-time-use passwords are issued only once, can be used only once, and even if stolen or captured, can never be used again. The mathematics involved in the encryption process to calculate the passwords makes it essentially impossible to reuse them.

Synchronous-Only-Based Authentication

Time-only, synchronous authentication is based on time clocks and secret keys that reside in two places: on the network (i.e., protected) side and on the user side (i.e., the side to be authenticated). On the network side, a time clock and database of secret keys operate in either a dedicated authentication hardware box or in a software authentication server. On the user side of the authentication equation, a clock, which is synchronized to the authentication server, and a secret key (corresponding to a secret key in the server) operate inside the token.

Several implementations are possible of time-only, synchronous authentication. In one specific, time-synchronous scheme, a proprietary algorithm continually executes in the token to generate access codes based on the time clock and the secret key of the token. In this case, the time is the "variable." A new access code is generated by the token approximately once a minute. The token is always activated. When the user dials in to the authentication server, the server issues a prompt to the user for an access code. The user simply attaches his or her secret Personal Identification Number (PIN) to the code currently displayed on his token at the moment access is required, and then the user transmits the combined PIN and code (which become the "one-time password"). This code is transmitted over telephone lines to the authentication server. The server uses the PIN to identify the user to compare the transmitted access code with its own current version for that user.

In a different implementation of time-synchronous authentication, the user enters his secret PIN to activate the token, which then generates a true, one-time-use password based on the token time clock and a secret key value stored inside the token. This system is more secure because the password generated does not include the PIN when it is transmitted over public telephone lines or networks. PINs should always remain secret to be considered a viable part of the "two-factor" authentication process. "Two factor" refers to something secret that only the user knows (i.e., his PIN) and something held in the user's possession (i.e., his token). For secret information to remain secret, it should not be transmitted in any way that allows unauthorized individuals to hack the information and use it at a later date. If someone captures a PIN as it is being transmitted over public telephone lines, it would be relatively easy to steal the token and use it to gain unauthorized access. It does not matter if the access code is considered a one-time-use password: if a thief has the PIN and the token, he has what is needed for unauthorized access to confidential information.

Window of Time

Time-only synchronous authentication systems are based on making available a "window of time" within which the password match must occur. The time clocks in the server and the token must remain "in sync" because the time is the variable on which the calculation depends. If the clocks are too far off, the user is denied access.

At this point, the technologies differ. When the token becomes out of sync with the server, there must be an efficient, cost-effective, user-transparent way to resynchronize the token. The user would be frustrated if he had to return his token for reprogramming before the information being requested is accessed. Centralized and remote token resetting capabilities should be considered, as well as the conditions under which tokens must be replaced. Replacing tokens or having to return them to a system administrator for resetting can be time-consuming and expensive. Authentication tokens should be "unlocked" remotely, preferably with some prearranged signal or code that only the user and the network administrator know.

Finally, the time on the token clocks gradually drifts, resulting in a lack of synchronization. If there are no provisions for unlocking or resetting, or for automatic switching of modes of operation (e.g., from synchronous to asynchronous) to back up the synchronous token, the authentication server, by necessity, will have to provide a larger "window of time" during which a user can be authenticated. Otherwise, too many tokens would go out of sync too often. The larger the window of time, the greater the security risk that someone will intercept passwords or PINs (if they are part of the transmission).

Synchronous, Event-Plus-Time Authentication

In event-plus-time synchronous authentication, the token also uses an algorithm and a secret key to generate passwords. However, it is based on two dynamic variables, instead of one, which increases the level of password security. The two variables are an event counter (i.e., the primary variable) and a time clock (i.e., the secondary variable). In one particular implementation of synchronous, event-plus-time authentication, there is also a third variable — a unique secret key that is calculated each time a password is generated by the token. This key becomes the secret key used to generate the succeeding password the next time the user activates the token. The first variable, "event," refers to the number of times a password has been generated by the token. The second variable, "time," refers to the clock counter in the token. The third variable — the new, unique key generated each time a password is issued — makes these event-time-synchronous passwords the strongest on the market.

For all synchronization authentication systems, questions should be asked about overall system management and token secret parameter programming. For example, network administrators should be able to maintain control not only of locking–unlocking procedures, but also of the user database, the setting of security parameters, and token programming. To comply with internationally recognized computer security standards, there should always be a "barrier" between the factory, which produces the tokens, and the customer, who operates those tokens. Specifically, secret parameters should be set by the customer, not by the vendor. Tokens that are programmed at the factory (or by the vendor) should be viewed with caution. It is possible that such products may result in people outside the organization having access to secret key values, user databases, and other basic token operations. These functions form the basis of secure user authentication. Such operations should remain under the auspices of the network administrators at all times.

A final point to consider with synchronous authentication systems is system management. Managing sites with a large number of users can become a daunting task under certain conditions. Questions should be asked about how the technology is going to handle distributed or centralized authentication system and token management, and how many servers will be necessary for the variety of access points or geographical locations that be must secured. The answers to these should be compared with other solutions. In the case of some technologies, cost-effective, efficient authentication system management can be impossible to achieve, and it may be necessary to purchase a larger number of authentication servers with one technology than with another. The cost of the overall user authentication system should be considered, not just the cost of the tokens, whether they hardware or software. Finally, when considering the cost of tokens, the frequency of replacement should be considered.

CONCLUSION

This chapter has discussed several methods of authenticating users: time-based-only synchronous authentication; event-plus-time-based synchronous authentication; and challenge–response asynchronous authentication. Each offers a different level of security and reliability when it comes to user authentication. The choice depends on the overall security policy of the organization and the depth of user authentication required. The technology of the different types of user authentication tokens should be carefully compared. The authentication technology requirements may be quite simple if security requirements are limited. On the other hand, an organization may require more reliable technology, such as two-factor, challenge–response asynchronous, or event-plus-time-based synchronous authentication. In an Internet atmosphere headed toward universal standards, the scalability and reliability of authentication systems based on technology that is not standards-based, or authentication-based on a time clock only, should be considered highly suspect.

Chapter 51
An Overview of Cryptographic Methods
Gary C. Kessler

DOES INCREASED SECURITY PROVIDE COMFORT TO PARANOID PEOPLE? Or does security provide some very basic protections that we are naive to believe that we do not need? During this time when the Internet provides essential communication between tens of millions of people and is being increasingly used as a tool for commerce, security becomes a tremendously important issue with which to deal.

There are many aspects to security and many applications, ranging from secure commerce and payments to private communications and protecting passwords. One essential aspect for secure communications is that of cryptography, which is the focus of this chapter. But it is important to note that although cryptography is *necessary* for secure communications, it is not by itself *sufficient*. The reader is advised, then, that the topics covered in this chapter describe only the first of many steps necessary for better security in any number of situations.

This chapter has two major purposes. The first is to define some of the terms and concepts behind basic cryptographic methods, and to offer a way to compare the myriad cryptographic schemes in use today. The second is to provide some real examples of cryptography in use today.

THE PURPOSE OF CRYPTOGRAPHY

Cryptography is the science of writing in secret code, and it is an ancient art; the first documented use of cryptography in writing dates back to Egypt, circa 1900 B.C. In data and telecommunications, cryptography is necessary when communicating over any untrusted medium, which includes just about *any* network, particularly the Internet.

0-8493-0859-3/00/$0.00+$.50
© 2000 by CRC Press LLC

```
key                                key
plaintext ----------------> ciphertext ----------------> plaintext
```

Exhibit 51-1. Secret key (symmetric) cryptography.

Within the context of any application-to-application communication, there are some specific security requirements, including

- *Authentication*: The process of proving one's identity. (The primary forms of host-to-host authentication on the Internet today are name-based or address-based, both of which are notoriously weak.)
- *Privacy/confidentiality:* Ensuring that no one can read the message except the intended receiver.
- *Integrity:* Assuring the receiver that the received message has not been altered in any way from the original.
- *Nonrepudiation:* A mechanism to prove that the sender really sent this message.

Cryptography, then, not only protects data from theft or alteration, but it can also be used for user authentication. There are, in general, three types of cryptographic schemes typically used to accomplish these goals: secret key (or symmetric) cryptography, public key (or asymmetric) cryptography, and hash functions, each of which is described below. In all cases, the initial unencrypted data is referred to as *plaintext*. It is encrypted into *ciphertext*, which will in turn (usually) be decrypted into usable plaintext.

Secret Key Cryptography

In secret key cryptography, a single key is used for both encryption and decryption. As shown in Exhibit 51-1, the sender uses the key (or some set of rules) to encrypt the plaintext and sends the ciphertext to the receiver. The receiver applies the same key (or ruleset) to decode the message and recover the plaintext. Because a single key is used for both functions, secret key cryptography is also called *symmetric encryption*.

With this form of cryptography, it is obvious that the key must be known to both the sender and the receiver; that, in fact, is the secret. The biggest difficulty with this approach, of course, is the distribution of the key.

There are several widely used secret key cryptography schemes, and they are generally categorized as being either *block ciphers* or *stream ciphers*. A block cipher is so called because it encrypts blocks of data at a time; the same plaintext block will always be encrypted into the same ciphertext (when using the same key). Stream ciphers operate on a single bit, byte, or word at a time, and implement a feedback mechanism so that the same plaintext will yield different ciphertext every time it is encrypted.

The most commonly used secret-key encryption scheme used today is the Data Encryption Standard (DES), designed by IBM in the 1970s and adopted by the National Bureau of Standards in 1977 for commercial and unclassified government applications. DES is a block cipher employing a 56-bit key that operates on 64-bit blocks. DES has a complex set of rules and transformations that were designed specifically to yield fast hardware implementations and slow software implementations, although this latter point is becoming less significant today because the speed of computer processors (and, therefore, programs) is several orders of magnitude faster today than 20 years ago. IBM also proposed a 128-bit key for DES, which was rejected at the time by the government; the use of 128-bit keys is under consideration at this time, however, although the cost of conversion will be one of the major stumbling blocks.

There are a number of other secret key cryptography algorithms that are also in use today. Triple-DES, for example, is a variant of DES that uses either two or three different keys, coupled with three encryption steps. CAST-128 (described in Request for Comments, or RFC, 2144; CAST is not an acronym, but its name is derived from the initials of its inventors, Carlisle Adams and Stafford Tavares of Nortel) and the International Data Encryption Algorithm (IDEA) are conceptually similar to DES; both are 64-bit block ciphers using 128-bit keys. CAST and IDEA are also internationally available and, therefore, unencumbered for use by members of the Internet community. Rivest Cipher 4 (RC4), named for its inventor Ron Rivest, is a stream cipher using variable-sized keys; it is widely used in commercial cryptography products, although it can be exported using only keys that are 40 bits or less in length. RC5 is a block cipher that supports a variety of block sizes, key sizes, and number of encryption passes over the data.

Public Key Cryptography

Public key cryptography (PKC) was invented in 1976 by Martin Hellman and Whitfield Diffie of Stanford University to solve the key exchange problem with secret key cryptography. Their scheme requires two keys, where one key is used to encrypt the plaintext and the other key is used to decrypt the ciphertext. The important point here is that it does not matter which key is applied first, but both keys are required for the process to work (Exhibit 51-2). Because a pair of keys is required, this approach is also called asymmetric cryptography.

Exhibit 51-2. Public key (asymmetric) cryptography using two keys (one for encryption and the other for decryption).

In PKC, one of the keys is designated the public key and may be advertised as widely as the owner wants. The other key is designated the private key and is never revealed to another party. It is straightforward to send messages under this scheme. The sender, for example, encrypts some information using the intended receiver's public key; the receiver decrypts the ciphertext using his own private key. This method could also be used in both directions at the same time. For example, the sender could encrypt the plaintext first with his own private key and then encrypt again with the receiver's public key; this latter scheme might be used where it is important that the sender cannot deny sending the message (nonrepudiation).

The most common PKC scheme used today is RSA, named for its inventors Ronald Rivest, Adi Shamir, and Leonard Adleman, and used in hundreds of software products. The RSA scheme can be used for key exchange or encryption. RSA uses a variable size encryption block and a variable size key. The key pair is derived from a very large number, n, that is the product of two prime numbers chosen according to special rules; these primes may be 100 or more digits in length each, yielding an n with roughly twice as many digits as the prime factors. The public key information includes n and a derivative of one of the factors of n; an attacker cannot determine the prime factors of n (and, therefore, the private key) from this information alone and that is what makes the RSA algorithm so secure. (Some descriptions of PKC erroneously state that the safety of RSA is due to the difficulty in factoring large prime numbers. In fact, large prime numbers, like small prime numbers, have only two factors!) The ability for computers to factor large numbers, and therefore attack schemes such as RSA, is rapidly improving and systems today can find the prime factors of numbers with more than 140 digits. The presumed protection of RSA, however, is that users can easily increase the key size to always stay ahead of the computer processing curve.

An alternative to RSA was published by the National Institute for Standards and Technology (NIST) in 1991. The Digital Signature Algorithm is part of the NIST's proposed Digital Signature Standard (DSS), both part of the desire of the U.S. government to define a next-generation cryptography system.

Hash Functions

Hash functions, also called message digests and one-way encryption, are algorithms that, in some sense, use no key (Exhibit 51-3). Instead, they transform the plaintext mathematically so that the contents and length of the plaintext are not recoverable from the ciphertext. Furthermore, there is a very low probability that two different plaintext messages will yield the same hash value.

Exhibit 51-3. Hash functions using no key (plaintext is not recoverable from the ciphertext).

Hash algorithms are typically used to provide a digital fingerprint of the contents of a file, often used to ensure that the file has not been altered by an intruder or virus. Hash functions are also commonly employed by many operating systems to encrypt passwords.

Among the most common hash functions in use today in commercial cryptographic applications are a family of Message Digest (MD) algorithms, all of which are byte-oriented schemes that produce a 128-bit hash value from an arbitrary-length message. MD2 (RFC 1319) is well-suited for systems with limited memory, such as smart cards. MD4 (RFC 1320), developed by Rivest, is similar to MD2 but designed specifically for fast processing in software. MD5 (RFC 1321), also developed by Rivest, came about after potential weaknesses were reported in MD4; this scheme is similar to MD4 but is slower because more manipulation is made to the original data. MD5 has been implemented in a large number of products, although several weaknesses in the algorithm were demonstrated by German cryptographer Hans Dobbertin in 1996.

The Secure Hash Algorithm (SHA), proposed by NIST for its Secure Hash Standard (SHS), is seeing increased use in commercial products today. SHA produces a 160-bit hash value.

Why Three Encryption Techniques?

So, why are there so many different types of cryptographic schemes? Why are we unable to do everything we need with just one?

The answer is that each scheme is optimized for some specific application(s). Hash functions, for example, are well-suited for ensuring data integrity because any change made to the contents of a message will result in the receiver calculating a different hash value than the one placed in the transmission by the sender. Because it is highly unlikely that two different messages will yield the same hash value, data integrity is ensured to a high degree of confidence.

Secret key encryption, on the other hand, is ideally suited to encrypting messages. The sender can generate a session key on a per-message basis to encrypt the message; the receiver, of course, needs the same session key to decrypt the message.

SECURITY

Key exchange, of course, is a key application of public key cryptography. Asymmetric schemes can also be used for nonrepudiation; if the receiver can obtain the session key encrypted with the sender's private key, then only this sender could have sent the message. Public key cryptography could, theoretically, also be used to encrypt messages, although this is rarely done because secret key encryption operates at 100 to 1,000 times faster than public key encryption.

Public Key Certificates

As PKC becomes more commonplace, particularly for electronic commerce applications, it is important to discuss the tangential issue of repositories for public keys. Without such repositories, a sender has no way to find a receiver's public key and, therefore, cannot send encrypted messages.

Many, perhaps most, public key systems rely on repositories of public keys called certification authorities (CA). When a sender needs an intended receiver's public key, the sender must get that key from the receiver's CA. That works well if the sender and receiver have the same CA, but how does the sender know to trust the foreign CA? One industry wag has noted, about trust: "You are either born with it or have it granted upon you." Thus, some CA will be trusted because they are known to be reputable, such as the CA operated by BBN, CommerceNet, GTE Cybertrust Solutions Inc., the U.S. Postal Service, and VeriSign. CAs, in turn, form trust relationships with other CAs. Thus, if a user queries a foreign CA for information, the user may ask to see a list of CAs that establish a "chain of trust" back to the user.

As complicated as this may sound, it really is not in concept. Consider driver licenses. I have one issued by the state of Vermont. The license establishes my identity, indicates the type of vehicles I can operate and the fact that I must wear corrective lenses while doing so, identifies the issuing authority, and notes that I am an organ donor. When I drive outside of Vermont, the other jurisdictions throughout the United States, Canada, and many other countries recognize the authority of Vermont to issue this "certificate" and they trust the information it contains. Some other countries may not recognize the Vermont driver license as sufficient bona fides that I can drive.

Certificates for PKC systems are defined in International Telecommunication Union Telecommunication Standardization Sector (ITU-TSS) Recommendation X.509. X.509 certificates identify the holder, the holder's rights and privileges, the issuing authority, an expiration date, the public key data, and other information.

CRYPTOGRAPHIC ALGORITHMS IN ACTION

The paragraphs above have provided an overview of the different types of cryptographic algorithms, as well as some examples of some available protocols and schemes. Exhibit 51-4 provides an even longer list of some of the schemes employed today for a variety of functions, most notably electronic commerce. The paragraphs below will show several real cryptographic applications that many of us employ (knowingly or not) everyday for password protection and private communication.

Password Protection

Nearly all modern multiuser computer and network operating systems employ passwords at the very least to protect and authenticate users accessing computer or network resources. Passwords are not typically kept on a host or server in plaintext but are generally encoded using some sort of hash scheme. UNIX, for example, uses a well-known scheme via its crypt() function. Passwords are kept in the etc/passwd file (Exhibit 51-5); each record in the file contains the username, hashed password, user's individual and group numbers, user's name, home directory, and shell program. Note that each password results in a 13-byte hash.

Windows NT uses a similar scheme to store passwords in the Security Access Manager file. In the NT case, all passwords are hashed using the MD4 algorithm, resulting in a 128-bit (16-byte) hash value (they are then obscured using an undocumented mathematical transformation that was a secret until distributed on the Internet). Thus, the password might be stored as the hash value (in hexadecimal) 60771b22d73c34bd4a290a79c8b09f18.

Passwords are not saved in plaintext on computer systems precisely so they cannot be easily compromised. For similar reasons, we do not want passwords sent in plaintext across a network. But for remote logon applications, how does a client system identify itself or a user to the server? One mechanism is to send the password as a hash value. A weakness of that approach, however, is that an intruder can grab the password off of the network and use an offline attack (such as a dictionary attack in which an attacker takes every known word and encrypts it with the encryption algorithm of the network, hoping eventually to find a match with a purloined password hash). In some situations, an attacker only has to copy the hashed password value and use it later on to gain unauthorized entry without ever learning the actual password.

An even stronger authentication method uses the password to modify a shared secret between the client and server, but never allows the password in any form to go across the network. This is the basis for the Challenge Handshake Authentication Protocol (CHAP), the remote logon process supported by Windows NT.

SECURITY

Exhibit 51-4. Some secure communications protocols, cryptography systems, and their primary applications.

Capstone	U.S. National Institute of Standards and Technology (NIST) project for publicly available cryptography standards that can be implemented in one or more tamperproof computer chips (e.g., Clipper); comprises a bulk encryption algorithm (Skipjack), digital signature algorithm (DSA), and hash algorithm (SHA)
Clipper	The computer chip that will implement the Skipjack encryption scheme
CAST-128	A DES-like secret key cryptosystem using 128-bit keys
DES (Data Encryption Standard)	Secret key cryptosystem; provides message encryption for privacy; a variant, called Triple-DES, uses multiple keys and multiple encryption/decryption passes over the message
Diffie–Hellman	First public key cryptosystem, used for key exchange for secret-key (symmetric) cryptosystems
DSA (Digital Signature Algorithm)	Algorithm specified in the digital signature standard (DSS) proposed for Capstone; provides digital signature for the authentication of messages
IDEA (International Data Encryption algorithm)	Secret key cryptosystem; provides message encryption for privacy
Kerberos	A secret key encryption and authentication system, designed to authenticate requests for network resources within a user domain rather than to authenticate messages
MD2, MD4, MD5	Message Digest algorithms used for digital signature applications for message integrity
MOSS (MIME object security standard)	Designed as a successor to PEM to provide PEM-based security services to MIME messages
PCT (Private Communication Technology)	Developed by Microsoft and Visa for secure communication on the Internet; similar to SSL, PCT supports Diffie–Hellman, Fortezza, and RSA for key establishment; DES, RC2, RC4, and triple-DES for encryption; and DSA and RSA message signatures; a companion to SET.
PEM (Privacy Enhanced Mail)	Provides secure e-mail over the Internet and includes provisions for encryption (DES), authentication, and key management (DES, RSA); may be superseded by S/MIME and PEM-MIME
PEM-MIME	(See MOSS)
PGP (pretty good privacy)	Provides cryptographic routines for e-mail and file storage applications; uses Diffie–Hellman/DSS for key management and digital signatures (older versions use RSA); IDEA, CAST, or Triple-DES for message encryption; and MD5 or SHA for computing the hash value of the message
PKCS (public key cryptography standards)	A set of guidelines for coding various security-relayed messages, designed by RSA Data Security
RC2, RC4, RC5	Secret key cryptosystem; provides message encryption for privacy

686

Exhibit 51-4. *(Continued)*

RSA (Rivest, Shamir, Adleman)	Widely used public key cryptosystem for encryption, authentication, and key exchange (for secret key systems)
Secure IP (IPsec)	Comprises two mechanisms: the IP authentication header provides integrity and authentication for IP packets using MD5; while the IP encapsulating security payload provides integrity and confidentiality using DES-CBC
SET (secure electronic transactions)	A merging of two protocols: SEPP (secure electronic payment protocol), an open specification for secure bank card transactions over the Internet, developed by CyberCash, GTE, IBM, MasterCard, and Netscape; and STT (Secure Transaction Technology), a secure payment protocol developed by Microsoft and Visa; supports DES and RC4 for encryption, and RSA for signatures, key exchange, and public key encryption of bank card numbers; SET is a companion to PCT
S-HTTP (secure hypertext transfer protocol)	An extension to HTTP to provide secure exchange of documents over the Web; supported algorithms include RSA and Kerberos for key exchange, DES, IDEA, RC2, and Triple-DES for encryption
SHA (Secure Hash Algorithm)	The Message Digest (hash) algorithm in the Secure Hash Standard (SHS) proposed for Capstone
Skipjack	Secret-key (symmetric) encryption scheme proposed for Capstone
S/MIME (Secure Multipurpose Internet Mail Extension)	Adds digital signature and encryption capability to Internet MIME messages
SSL (secure sockets layer)	Developed by Netscape Communications to provide application-independent security and privacy over the Internet, allowing protocols such as HTTP, FTP (file transfer protocol), and Telnet to be layered on top of it transparently; RSA is used during negotiation to exchange keys and identify the actual cryptographic algorithm (DES, IDEA, RC2, RC4, or RSA) to use for the session; employs MD5 for message digests
TLS (transport layer security)	IETF specification intended to replace SSL; employs Triple-DES (secret key cryptography), SHA (hash), Diffie–Hellman (key exchange), and DSS (digital signatures)
ITU-T Recommendation X.509	Specification for format of certificates for public key cryptography systems; certificates map (bind) a user identity with a public key

```
carol:FM5ikbQt1K052:502:100:Carol Monaghan:/home/carol:/bin/bash
alex:LqAi7Mdyg/HcQ:503:100:Alex Insley:/home/alex:/bin/bash
gary:FkJXupRyFqY4s:501:100:Gary Kessler:/home/gary:/bin/bash
todd:edGqQUAaGv7g6:506:101:Todd Pritsky:/home/todd:/bin/bash
sarah:Jbw6BwE4XoUHo:504:101:Sarah Antone:/home/schedule:/bin/bash
josh:FiH0ONcjPut1g:505:101:Joshua Kessler:/home/webroot:/bin/bash
```

Exhibit 51-5. Sample entries in a UNIX password file.

As suggested above, Windows NT passwords are stored in a security file on a server as a 16-byte hash value. When a user logs on to a server from a remote workstation, the user is identified by the username sent across the network in plaintext (no worries here; it is not a secret anyway!). The server then generates a 64-bit random number and sends it to the client (also in plaintext). This number is the challenge.

The client system then encrypts the challenge using DES. Recall that DES employs a 56-bit key, acts on a 64-bit block of data, and produces a 64-bit output. In this case, the 64-bit data block is the random number. The client actually uses three different DES keys to encrypt the random number, producing three different 64-bit outputs. The first key is the first seven bytes (56 bits) of the hash value of the password, the second key is the next seven bytes in the password hash, and the third key is the remaining two bytes of the password hash concatenated with five zero-filled bytes. (So, for the example above, the three DES keys would be 60771b22d73c34, bd4a290a79c8b0, and 9f180000000000.) Each key is applied to the random number resulting in three 64-bit outputs, which comprise the response. Thus, the 8-byte challenge from the server yields a 24-byte response from the client and this is all that would be seen on the network. The server, for its part, does the same calculation to ensure that the values match.

Pretty Good Privacy (PGP)

PGP is one of the most widely used public key cryptography programs in use today. Developed by Philip Zimmermann and long the subject of controversy, PGP is commercially (http://www.pgp.com, San Mateo, California) available today and is also available as a plug-in for many e-mail clients, such as Microsoft Corp.'s Exchange and Outlook, and Qualcomm's Eudora.

PGP can be used to sign or encrypt e-mail messages with the mere click of the mouse. Depending upon the version of PGP, the software uses SHA or MD5 for calculating the message hash; CAST, Triple-DES, or IDEA for encryption; and RSA or DSS/Diffie–Hellman for key exchange and digital signatures.

PGP uses a different trust model than that described above with CA and X.509 certificates. In particular, PGP relies on a local keyring and a "web of trust." PGP users maintain their own list of known and trusted public keys. If I need a user's public key, I can ask him for it or, in many cases, download the public key from an advertised server. If you hold the public key of a user, I might get the key from you. How do I know that it is valid? Well, if I trust you and you think the key you gave me is valid, then I will trust that a key you give me is okay. But trust is not necessarily transitive, so I may not trust a third party merely because you do. In any case, encryption and signatures based on public keys can be used only when the appropriate public key is on the user's keyring.

```
-----BEGIN PGP SIGNED MESSAGE-----
Hash: SHA1

Hi Carol.

What was that pithy Groucho Marx quote?

/kess

-----BEGIN PGP SIGNATURE-----
Version: PGP for Personal Privacy 5.0
Charset: noconv

iQA/AwUBNFUdO5WOcz5SFtuEEQJx/ACaAgR97+vvDU6XWELV/GANjAAgBtUAnjG3
Sdfw2JgmZIOLNjFe7jPOY8/M
=jUAU
-----END PGP SIGNATURE-----
```

Exhibit 51-6. A PGP-signed message.

When PGP is first installed, the user has to create a key pair. One key, the public key, can be advertised and widely circulated. The private key is protected by use of a passphrase. The passphrase has to be entered every time the user accesses his private key.

Exhibit 51-6 shows a PGP-signed message. This message will not be kept secret from an eavesdropper, but a recipient can be assured that the message has not been altered from what the sender transmitted. In this instance, the sender signs the message using his own private key. The receiver uses the sender's public key to verify the signature; the public key is taken from the receiver's keyring based on the sender's e-mail address. Note that the signature process does not work unless the sender's public key is on the receiver's keyring.

Exhibit 51-7 shows a PGP-encrypted message (PGP compresses the file, where practical, prior to encryption because encrypted files cannot be compressed). In this case, public key methods are used to exchange the session key for the actual message encryption using secret-key cryptography. In this case, the receiver's e-mail address is the pointer to the public key in the sender's keyring; in fact, the same message can be sent to multiple recipients. When the destination side receives the message, the recipient must use their private key to successfully decrypt the message (Exhibit 51-8).

CONCLUSION ... OF SORTS

This chapter has briefly described how cryptography works. The reader must beware, however, that there are a number of ways to attack every one of these systems; cryptanalysis and attacks on cryptosystems, however,

```
-----BEGIN PGP MESSAGE-----
Version: PGP for Personal Privacy 5.0
MessageID: DAdVB3wzpBr3YRunZwYvhK5gBKBXOb/m

qANQR1DBwU4D/TlT68XXuiUQCADfj2o4b4aFYBcWumA7hR1Wvz9rbv2BR6WbEUsy
ZBIEFtjyqCd96qF38sp9IQiJIKlNaZfx2GLRWikPZwchUXxB+AA5+lqsG/ELBvRa
c9XefaYpbbAZ6z6LkOQ+eE0XASe7aEEPfdxvZZT37dVyiyxuBBRYNLN8Bphdr2zv
z/9Ak4/OLnLiJRk05/2UNE5Z0a+3lcvITMmfGajvRhkXqocavPOKiin3hv7+Vx88
uLLem2/fQHZhGcQvkqZVqXx8SmNw5gzuvwjV1WHj9muDGBYOMkjiZIRI7azWnoU9
3KCnmpR60VO4rDRAS5uGl9fioSvze+q8XqxubaNsgdKkoD+tB/4u4c4tznLfw1L2
YBS+dzFDw5desMFSo7JkecAS4NB9jAu9K+f7PTAsesCBNETDd49BTOFFTWWavAfE
gLYcPrcn4s3EriUgvL3OzPR4PlchNu6sa3ZJkTBbriDoA3VpnqG3hxqfNyOlqAka
mJJuQ53Ob9ThaFH8YcE/VqUFdw+bQtrAJ6NpjIxi/x0FfOInhC/bBw7pDLXBFNaX
HdlLQRPQdrmnWskKznOSarxq4GjpRTQo4hpCRJJ5aU7tZO9HPTZXFG6iRIT0wa47
AR5nvkEKoIAjW5HaDKiJriuWLdtN4OXecWvxFsjR32ebz76U8aLpAK87GZEyTzBx
dV+lH0hwyT/y1cZQ/E5USePP4oKWF4uqquPee1OPeFMBo4CvuGyhZXD/18Ft/53Y
WIebvdiCqsOoabK3jEfdGExce63zDI0=
=MpRf
-----END PGP MESSAGE-----
```

Exhibit 51-7. A PGP-encrypted message: The receiver's e-mail address is the pointer to the public key in the sender's keyring. At the destination side, the receiver uses his own private key.

---

are well beyond the scope of this chapter. In the words of Sherlock Holmes (okay, Arthur Conan Doyle, really), "What one man can invent, another can discover" (*The Adventure of the Dancing Men*).

Cryptography is a particularly interesting field because of the amount of work that is, by necessity, done in secret. The irony is that today, secrecy is not the key to the goodness of a cryptographic algorithm. Regardless of the mathematical theory behind an algorithm, the best algorithms are those that are well-known and well-documented because they are also well-tested and well-studied! In fact, time is the only true test of good cryptography; any cryptographic scheme that stays in use year after year is most likely a good one. The strength of cryptography is the choice of the keys; longer keys will resist attack better than shorter keys. A corollary to this is that consumers should be very wary of products that use a proprietary cryptography scheme, ostensibly because the secrecy of the algorithm is an advantage; this security through obscurity posture is doomed to fail.

```
Hi Gary,

"Outside of a dog, a book is man's best friend. Inside of a dog, it's
too dark to read."

Carol
```

Exhibit 51-8. The decrypted message from Exhibit 51-7.

REFERENCES AND FURTHER READING

Kahn, D., *The Codebreakers: the Story of Secret Writing*, revised ed., Scribner, New York, 1996.

Kaufman, C., Perlman, R. and Speciner, M., *Network Security: Private Communication in a Public World*, Prentice-Hall, Englewood Cliffs, NJ, 1995.

Schneier, B., *Applied Cryptography*, 2nd ed., John Wiley & Sons, New York, 1996.

Counterpane (Bruce Schneier). URL: http://www.counterpane.com.

Cypherpunks Web Page. URL: ftp://ftp.csua.berkeley.edu/pub/cypherpunks/Home.html.

International Computer Security Association Web Site. URL: http://www.icsa.com.

Pretty Good Privacy Web Site. URL: http://www.pgp.com.

RSA's Cryptography FAQ. URL: http://www.rsa.com/rsalabs/newfaq/home.html.

Yahoo! crypto pages. URL: http://www.yahoo.com/Computers_and_Internet/Security_and_Encryption/.

Chapter 52

Public Key Infrastructure: Using the Internet as a Virtual Private Network

Andrew Csinger

WHEN PEOPLE LOOK BACK ON THE BEGINNINGS OF THE INFORMATION AGE, they will remember not the networks, the affordances, the hype and gimmickry, and the technological window dressing that was all the talk of the times, but with the benefit of hindsight, they will talk about what made it possible for human activity to migrate into and then flourish in the new electronic medium.

They will remember the development that took the Internet from the realm of mere entertainment and curiosity — albeit on a mass scale — to a true virtual world. A world in which people meet people, and businesses do business. They will recall a development, now only poorly understood, quietly being evolved and enhanced in a few private labs around the world.

What is this technology? What are these developments of such import? What is the crucial development that enables people and businesses finally to project themselves out into the global network, to recognize each other there, and to engage each other in new ways as well as old?

Public Key Infrastructure (PKI) is what everyone will remember. Until you are part of the Global PKI (GPKI), you are not empowered, you are not a citizen of the global electronic community. You are not a citizen of your country unless you can prove your nationality. Likewise, you are not an agent to be reckoned with on the Internet unless you can prove who you are. This is what it means to be part of the GPKI.

VIRTUAL PRIVATE NETWORKS: ELECTRONIC COMMUNITIES

The GPKI is composed of Virtual Private Networks (VPNs). VPNs are like countries, or like country clubs. You are either a member or you are not. Members of a VPN are identified by their certificates — their passports, if you like, or their membership cards. Unlike countries, VPNs know no geopolitical boundaries. In fact, VPNs know no fixed boundaries at all. VPNs, being virtual, can be erected on a whim, and can disappear just as easily. On the other hand, the virtuality of a VPN is no hindrance to its vitality; it is a first-class legal entity and, as in the "real" world, membership can have its privileges. The fluid boundaries of a VPN can adapt quickly to change, respond to threats, and take advantage of new potentials much more effectively than the fossilized geopolitical entities we are leaving behind.

Examples of VPNs are easy to find. Consider your favorite magazine. The subscribership of the publication is a VPN. When this magazine makes the leap to the Internet, as many already have, and makes its editorial material available to its membership — and only to its membership — it becomes a true VPN. A library is a kind of virtual community, defined in large measure by the common interests of the readers who frequent it. A traditional library is limited by the geographical and political landscape it occupies: people from one side of the tracks may not be allowed to borrow books from a library on the other side of the tracks. Strange, but it happens all the time. A digital repository on the Internet, on the other hand, can "lend" material to a membership defined entirely independently of these geographical inconveniences, and need take no account of ancient conventionalizations. The butterfly collectors of the world, united by their common interest, can finally find each other and find strength in each other and speak to the world with a common voice. You get the picture.

The means it uses to identify its members and, hence, the means by which it controls access to its information, determines the extent to which a VPN participates in the GPKI.

INTERACTING VPNs: THE GLOBAL PKI

It's not enough for the VPN to just offer its information to whomever finds it interesting. This was the basis for the inception of the Internet in the first place. A common misperception today is that the Internet is ill-conceived because its computer protocols are insecure; although accurate in its assessment for current use, this diagnosis misses the historical mark. The Internet did not anticipate the need for security simply because it was initially designed not for global electronic commerce in the large, but for the communications purpose of a single VPN. The global, virtual community of researchers needed a vehicle to improve their communications, and a means by which to share information in a collegial forum. The Internet, far from being insecure, was a tightly controlled environment — a private network where membership was determined by a lofty technical wizardry requirement and affiliation with distinguished research and development organizations. As soon as the Internet became popular, the issue of security arose because of the need to establish boundaries between different VPNs with different interests, divergent philosophies, and widely ranging membership criteria. In effect, the growth of the Internet was an unwelcome incursion by other VPNs into the territory of the original, founding VPN of researchers.

It is also not enough for a VPN to restrict access to its information by locking it behind what is known today as a firewall. This metaphor is the death knell of the VPN, and anathema to global communications. Blinded by their security fixation, some information systems managers have run amuck and tried to strangle their information behind monolithic, vise-grip firewalls that make it more difficult for legitimate users to get the information they need, when they need it. No one is really sure whether these exaggerated efforts actually keep out determined hackers with lots of time on their hands. The metaphor is wrong: If information is the lifeblood of the organization, it needs to flow, to circulate, to be available to the right people at the right time, conveniently, easily. Rather than locking it up behind a barrier, we need the metaphor of a door, readily opened to those with the right key, solidly closed and bolted to those without.

Other systems in use today involve issuing "users" with passwords. Besides requiring people to remember a different password for each information service they use, the worst thing about this approach is that the ad hoc, usually locally implemented access control system does not make it possible for the individual or the organization to participate in the global network as a first-class citizen or first-class entity. Passwords do not really define a true VPN.

Giving someone a password is a little like giving them the key to the executive washroom. Giving someone a public key certificate is like giving them the keys to the kingdom.

PUBLIC KEY CERTIFICATES: THE KEYS TO THE VPN

A public key certificate is a digital document signifying membership of an individual in a VPN. A PKC is created by a certification authority (CA). A CA is a service run by or on behalf of a VPN that decides who should have membership privileges in the VPN. The PKC uniquely identifies the individual as a member of a VPN. It can be used by the individual as part of a process to sign digital documents in a legally binding manner, and it can be used to encrypt information to guarantee its communication only to intended parties. Most of all, a PKC gets the bearer access to the GPKI.

Of course, not all certificates are alike. Some VPNs are more important than others, in certain respects. For instance, although a certificate issued by the International Brotherhood of Butterfly Collectors is entirely meaningful to the Brothers, and may have well-understood consequences when presented as proof of membership at the IBBC's Website, it is not at all clear what value such a certificate has at the Expensive French Wine Internet Shop. Different certs for different folk? No doubt. But one side of the tracks on the Internet is just as clean and safe as the other.

Cross-Certification: PKCs from Unknown VPNs

However, life in the GPKI is not lived entirely behind VPN boundaries. One VPN can make ad hoc decisions about its relationships with other VPNs. Just like in the "real" world, where a business makes a business decision to transact with another business, a VPN can decide to honor the PKCs issued by the CA of another VPN. It can honor these other certs in any way it chooses, from complete equivalence with its own certs, to restricted, specialized access to a subset of its information space. It's entirely up to the VPN and its CA. Even if the VPN has never seen this user before, it can decide to grant access on the basis of the signature on the certificate presented by the user. The VPN is saying: "I do not know you, but I know and trust your CA. On the basis of that trust, I am willing to trust *you* enough to give you access to this information." These CAs have agreed to *cross-certify* (Exhibit 52-1) each other's certificates. (The term is used loosely here.)

What happens when someone with a certificate from a heretofore unknown CA approaches the boundary of a VPN? The local VPN has several choices. It can simply deny access, saying, in effect: "Go away. I do not

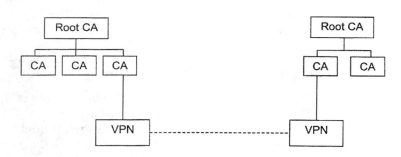

Exhibit 52-1. Cross-certification between disjoint hierarchies.

know you or the guy who signed your certificate. You are not part of the club." This is unfriendly, but makes perfect sense for some kinds of organizational VPNs.

Alternatively, the VPN's defenses can try to *authenticate* the user. Because it does not recognize the CA in question, it can try to find out more about the CA in order to decide whether to permit access or not. One way to do this is to search the GPKI for this CA, to see how it stands in relation to other CAs, which may be known to the VPN. If this unknown CA is subsidiary, for instance, to another CA that *is* known to the VPN, then the VPN has some basis for deciding to trust the certificate being presented. The specific means of achieving this objective are not important here. Suffice it to say that, in order to be able to search for an arbitrary signer with any reasonable chance of finding what we are looking for, there needs to be a fairly sophisticated and widespread directory service in place. Another way of addressing this issue is to have an implicit hierarchy of CAs (Exhibit 52-2), implied by the order of multiple signatures on the certificates of users. When presented at the gates of a VPN, the certificate's signatures can be checked one by one, in order, until the VPN finds a signature from a CA that it already knows.

The general goal of identifying the owner of the certificate that is presented *is* important, and is often referred to as *cross-authentication* between different domains, or realms. Note that in all cases, trust comes only *after* identification. Keeping this important detail in mind helps to avoid all kinds of confusion.

CERTIFICATE REVOCATION LISTS: THE VPN'S ELECTRONIC BLACKLIST

What happens when someone breaks a membership rule? Membership in a VPN, like in "real" organizations, is conditional and can be revoked. The CA of a VPN maintains a *Certificate Revocation List* (CRL). This is the list of revoked certificates, and is checked whenever someone tries to use

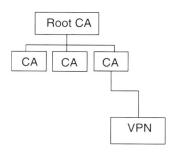

Exhibit 52-2. Hierarchy with a common root.

a certificate issued by that CA. In other words, it is not enough that someone's certificate be signed by a CA that is recognized by a VPN; the VPN will try not only to authenticate the user on the basis of the certificate presented, but will also try to *validate* the user by making sure that the certificate is not on the CA's CRL. To minimize delays and bandwidth usage, cooperating CAs can arrange to cache local copies of each other's CRLs, or more sophisticated cross-authentication protocols can be used to validate certificates on the fly.

APPLYING FOR MEMBERSHIP: THE VETTING PROCESS

How do you acquire a certificate? You apply for membership in a VPN. The people and processes at the VPN decide whether you should be in or out, and either approve or deny your request for a certificate. They put you through a *vetting* process.

CERTIFICATE POLICY STATEMENTS: THE VALUE OF MEMBERSHIP

What does the signature of a CA really mean? Good question. As we have already seen, not all certificates are alike, and there are many reasons for this. In addition to its certificate repository and its CRL, a CA should, by convention, maintain and offer for inspection to its peers a *Certification Policy Statement* (CPS). This is, as implied, a statement about the certification policies of the CA. It describes the vetting process in conventionalized terms, so that other VPNs can decide whether or not to accept certificates issued by this CA.

ONE CA OR MANY? BIG BROTHER VS. LITTLE SISTER

Most of the thinking about the GPKI until today has envisioned a strict hierarchy of CAs, where the root CA is the ultimate authority, and is the universally trusted third party to which all other CAs defer, and from where all trust relationships are derived. This model, on further analysis, simply does not appear realistic. Several unexamined assumptions underlie this vision of the future GPKI.

The first one is that everyone will trust, or even want to consider trusting, a single third party. This is fantasy. People can not agree on what to have for breakfast or on what constitutes a good book, let alone matters of trust in global hierarchies that will branch into all areas of commerce.

Second, although there may be a secure place for a Big Brother hierarchy in credit card clearance and other impersonal one-to-many transactions, and though this is indeed and will continue to be Big Business for Big Brother, it completely ignores the needs of business-to-business transactions. This, problem is *much* more interesting, and much more difficult to solve than the first. Or rather, the problem is very different.

In the Big Brother model of GPKI, the central issue appears to be *trust*, in the sense that there is a transitive commodity that somehow issues from an anointed source — the trusted third party Root CA. Big Brother wants to act as a *trust broker*.

In the Little Sister model, trust is outside the scope of the GPKI, and it is mere *identity* which is directly encoded by the relations between peer VPNs and their CAs. Two VPNs decide to do business with each other and reflect this agreement (tacitly or otherwise) in the access control rules with which they define the boundaries of their respective VPNs.

Of course, as in most things, there is a lot of middle ground between a rigid Big Brother hierarchy and the almost anarchic Little Sister philosophy. On the original Big Brother view, *all* certificates in the GPKI would be issued by a single CA. This perspective has softened, ostensibly in recognition of growing competition for the role of central CA, and in reaction to new and very flexible PKI technology being developed by companies who want to give every network device on the Internet its own unique certificate ID.

The picture of the GPKI as a strict hierarchy emerges from the Big Brother model: the Root CA certifies certificates issued by subsidiary CAs, or certifies the subsidiary CAs themselves (or certifies their CPSs …). If your CA is not part of The Hierarchy, your VPN is not part of the GPKI, and you are not *in*. This is bad. Your alternative is to beg (and pay) for certification by the Root CA. Or you can start your own PKI.

I strongly suspect that there is enough motivation in the business world for many organizations to seek to become VPNs under their own authority. The resulting volume of anarchic grassroots certification activity will seek to resolve itself via ad hoc cross-certification techniques of the sort that have already been described, leading to nonhierarchical constellations of VPNs. The topology of the GPKI does not *have* to be hierarchical, though it is difficult to conceive of a truly global alternative.

Big Brother can have a significant role to play, even in a democratic, distributed GPKI with lots of CAs cross-authenticating business-to-business relationships between disjoint VPNs. For instance, as part of an extended audit, Big Brother could study the practices of a VPN and certify the CPS of its CA. This way, cross-authenticating VPNs would have the word of one or more third parties as to whether or not the certificates are to be honored.

There are other intermediate positions. For instance, a large bank may wish to issue certificates for all of its employees, management, and each and every one of the banking customers of each of its many service branches. In the interests of name brand recognition, it insists that the signatures on all of the certificates be the same: that of the central office. However, even if the central office could generate the millions of signatures required, and perform the attendant logistics, it could never keep up: customers close accounts, overdraw, and die in alarming numbers. The branches themselves are in the best position to undertake the vetting processes, since they actually *know* their customers, can stare them in the face, and study their handwritten signatures. In this case, the branches can each run what is known as a *registration authority* (RA).

The function of an RA is to vet certificate requests and forward them to a CA for signing. The CA *knows* its RAs, of which there can be many, and rubber-stamps the requests with its signature, thereby generating a certificate, and returns this electronic document to the respective RA, who forwards it, in turn, to the customer, the end user of the certificate. Alternatively, the CA can send the certificate directly to the customer.

The GPKI will probably end up as a syncretic combination of a few Big Brother hierarchies and many subtly interconnected constellations of VPNs.

CERTIFICATES REVISITED

Certificates are just specially formatted electronic documents, with a specific intended interpretation (CA-*xyz* states that *Fred* is the bearer of this certificate). They are generally intended to be public documents; the security of the PKI is in no way compromised by publication of the certificate. In fact, most of the purpose of the PKI is to expedite widespread knowledge and availability of all certificates.

How does it work? The whole notion of a PKI is built from public key cryptography. A PKI is nothing more than an elaborate set of commonly accepted policies and procedures governing the application of public key cryptography. Luckily, you do not have to be a cryptographer to understand PKI. Here are the basics.

Public Key Cryptography: The Basics

Public key cryptography involves the use of two encryption keys called the *public key* and the *private key*. These keys are mathematically related in such a way that, in conjunction with certain cryptographic algorithms, a message encrypted with one key can be decrypted only with the other. Another important attribute of the keys is that it is extremely difficult, if not impossible, to determine the value of one key from the other. By convention, one of the keys (always the same one) is used to encrypt messages, and the other to decrypt.

The keys of the pair are named aptly. The public key is the encryption key. To send a message to Bob, so that only Bob can read it, I would use Bob's public key to encrypt it. Bob would use his private key to decrypt it. Were Bob to send me a reply, he would use my public key to encrypt the message, and I would use my private key to decrypt it. In this way, public key cryptography ensures the *privacy* of communications.

Senders can *sign* their messages as well. First, they create a unique fingerprint, or *digest,* of their message using a mathematical *hash function.* The result of encrypting this message digest *with their private key* is called a signature. The signature is sent along with the message. The receiver can decrypt the message and recreate the digest using the same hash function. Decrypting the signature with the sender's public key produces the original digest. If the digests match, the receiver can be certain that the message was actually sent by the signer, and is further certain that the message has not been tampered with in transit since the time it was signed. In this way, public key cryptography ensures the authenticity and the integrity of communications. Since the sender can not later deny having sent the message, nonrepudiability is also ensured.

That is all we need to know about cryptography in order to understand PKI. The remaining issues surround the mechanisms by which public keys are made public, and by which private keys remain private. This is the raison d'être of PKI. Out of so little is built so much. The entire GPKI emerges from the application of simple, well-understood, and commonly accepted policies and procedures to the key pairs of individual end users and organizations.

Joining the PKI: Getting a Certificate

To become part of a PKI, a user needs first to generate a public/private key pair (henceforth *key pair*). A VPN can perform this function on behalf of the user; for instance, a bank may create the key pair for a user, lodging the private key in a semiconductor device, perhaps a smart card, to thwart unauthorized use and increase security. The Butterfly Collector's club may let the user generate the key pair and might not care where the user stores the private component at all.

The user then needs to acquire a certificate from a VPN, as discussed. Technically, this involves sending the VPN's CA the user's public key, along with some relevant personal information, like the user's name, e-mail address, and so on. The CA vets the applicant as discussed, and then, if approved, signs the message consisting of the user's public key and associated information, producing a signed document called a certificate. The CA then publishes the certificate in its certificate repository, for all to see. How much *confidence* VPNs can place in the certificates issued by other CAs depends upon the level of *assurance* afforded by the vetting processes of these CAs.

CAs also have key pairs of their own, which they use for signing and other functions. The privacy of the CA's private key can be a serious

SECURITY

security concern, since compromise of the CA's private key can mean compromise of all of the certificates it has signed. Serious issues lurk just beneath the surface here, and we will tread lightly indeed, so as not to disturb them in our shallow overview of the subject. Suffice it to say that considerable care and attention has gone into specification and review of CA management policy and practice, and that specialized tamperproof hardware can be deployed for secure storage of CA private keys.

Notes

"Legislating Market Winners: Digital Signature Laws and the Electronic Commerce Marketplace," by C. Bradford Biddle (http://www.acusd.edu/~biddle/LMW.htm).

Chapter 53
Making Your Web Site Hacker Safe: Internet Security

Jim Hewitt

THE INTERNET SHOULD BE A BOON TO YOUR BUSINESS. Your customers and competitors are all there. It provides cheap, 24-hour global access, and makes it easy to link up with your partners and prospects.

But most users believe the Internet is unsafe and fear it for this reason. This lack of confidence is one of the greatest obstacles slowing the profitability of most Internet commerce. If you do business on the Internet, you are obliged to make sure your assets are adequately protected. If you participate as a user or a customer you should know what the risks are and how to manage them.

Opening your business to the Internet exposes it to a vast number of unseen potential attackers. Attackers are more numerous than ever and several trends favor them:

- The Internet has grown far ahead of the technical people and tools available to protect its users.
- Much of the technology is new and immature, with the unpredictability that entails.
- The business processes are new, too, without the safeguards of fully developed practices.

The problem is not software. The problem is people. With few exceptions, hackers exploit human errors, not core technical vulnerabilities.

You may be charged with convincing you company's management that risk to company assets is properly mitigated. The way to do that is by creating and implementing a security policy.

When data is sent from one computer to another on the Internet it makes dozens of "hops" from one intermediate machine to another. Every computer inbetween presents an opportunity for prying eyes to see what is being sent. This poses an obvious security problem. There are several solutions:

Prevention — Keep problems from occurring in the first place.
Vigilance — Keep on top of events at your site; do not assume that "all quiet" means you are safe.
Remediation — When problems come up, fix them immediately.

STEPS TO MAKING YOUR SITE SAFE

- Know what your assets are.
- Know what your risks are and how to mitigate each one.
- Educate your users.
- Lock down the superuser/administrative user IDs.
- Make sure your system is physically secure.
- Take "trust" out of your organization.
- Create a comprehensive security plan.
- Hire, train, and manage the best system administrator you can find.
- Minimize your system's exposure to the Internet.
- Find and fix all known security holes.
- Stay current on news about new ones.
- Create an ongoing defense plan.
- As you do more on the Internet, expand your security work to keep pace.

Computer Security Basics

A computer system is called "secure" when the following conditions are established:

- integrity
- access control
- authentication
- availability
- confidentiality
- nonrepudiation

There are two sources of vulnerability:

1. Outsiders — Barbarians at the Gate: "If you build it, they will come"
2. Insiders — The Enemy within the Walls

Your site may be used as a base for attacks on other sites.

Some hackers are criminals. Most are a mere nuisance, like vandals. Given the choice between the thief who steals your car and the vandal who scratches the paint, most car owners will choose to avoid them both. This chapter explains how to do that without keeping your wheels locked in the garage. It is for nontechnical people who need a practical approach to computer security.

DEFINITIONS

This chapter uses the term "hacker" to mean anyone who tries to get in where you, the system owner, do not want him or her to go. The following characteristics are not relevant:

- *Motivation.* It does not matter whether the hacker has illegal or malicious intentions, or is just curious
- *Success.* An attempt at illicit entry is not innocent just because it is unsuccessful
- *Stranger or insider.* Anyone who goes where he or she is not welcome

In computer industry terms, a "hacker" is anyone who delves into the inner workings of computer hardware or software, and a "cracker" is someone who uses this arcane knowledge in a malicious way. For the purpose of this chapter, a hacker is anyone who wants to get in where you do not want him or her to go.

GOALS FOR INTERNET SECURITY

No Internet site is perfectly safe. The best approach for a business-oriented Internet site owner is the following:

- Assess and understand what your risks are.
- Take a series of measured preventive steps to comprehensively manage this risk.
- Make site security an ongoing part of your organization's daily work.

Since "perfect safety" is not the goal, what is? The goals in securing your site is to:

- Raise the cost to potential attackers.
- Make sure the site manager can detect a violation and react to it quickly.
- Contain and minimize potential damage.
- Make recovery as easy as possible.
- Install strong security measures that enable you to present your site as "certified secure;" use this as a selling point privately with your customers; do not advertise it too loudly.

COMPUTER SECURITY FUNDAMENTALS

- Sooner or later someone will attack your site.
- An attack is defined as any attempt to get access to more system resources than the system owner intends the user to have.
- An unsuccessful attack is still an attack, and the attacker should be identified and held accountable for it.

- Your system has hundreds of features you do not know about, and will probably never care about. Many of these features make it vulnerable to attack.
- Most operating systems are insecure in their default configurations; they come out of the box with widely known default passwords and most of their security features turned off.
- Find out what the security features of your system are; turn them all on.
- Get all available patches for your operating system and applications, and install them; many of these patches close security holes, whether published or not.

Tips

- Most logging facilities are turned off by default. Turn them back on. Historically, logging was turned off because it consumes lots of disk space. In the late 1990s disk space became cheap, and dropping by 50 percent per year, so you can afford it.
- Back up your files thoroughly and often. It is an excellent low-cost way to limit the damage from a virus or malicious attacker.
- Do not store credit card numbers on any machine that is connected to the Internet. That goes for any other data that absolutely must not be accessed by unauthorized users.
- Most e-mail traffic is extremely insecure. Do not put anything in an e-mail message you would not want to be made public. If your e-mail must be kept confidential, use e-mail encryption.
- Limit the questions your staff put on Usenet, especially with regard to security and system configuration.

RISK

What are your risks?

- your firm's reputation, and the trust and confidence of your customers
- destruction of data and equipment crucial to the operation of your business
- loss of the investment in time spent on your Web site
- expense of the cleanup
- loss of business due to your site's downtime

Assessing risk

If your data are extremely sensitive, such that theft, loss, or tampering would cause loss of life or imperil the future of the company, it should not be on any machine that is directly or indirectly connected to the Internet. Store it on a machine that is accessible from your internal network only.

Identify your assets. Inventory all hardware components and software including third-party products, utilities, home-grown applications, driver programs, and operating systems. Identify all data — online, archives, backups, and even users.

If your Web site is a "brochure" site, with static pages of sales material, consider the cost of developing it and the expected sales benefits that would be lost if it were tampered with.

Assume there will always be holes and vulnerabilities you do not know about. This is all the more reason to close every single hole that *is* documented. No hole is too small

In the 1970s, security holes were allowed to remain open in the belief that they were accessible only to a tiny number of "experts." Today, the information is easy to find, and well-engineered "burglar's tools" obviate the need for a high level of technical talent.

Cost-Effective Risk Management

- Limit the assets you expose to the Internet.
- According to CERT (see *References*), the majority of breaches come from weak passwords. Weak passwords are 100 percent preventable (see *Password Guidelines*).

Types of Attack

Typical attackers' objectives include:

- deleting files from your site
- changing passwords so authorized users cannot log in
- stealing online assets, such as competitive information
- stealing files that can be used for commercial gain, such as credit card numbers

Hackers search for one weak point or pinhole in your site's security. Attacks are typically carried out by making a small, crucial changes to your system. For example, some remote login utilities may be secure in themselves, but are a little too verbose in that they tell outsiders what operating system and version you are using. Once a hacker knows that, he can research the security bugs in that OS, and he is off and running.

A good example is the German hacker detected and finally caught by Cliff Stoll in *The Cuckoo's Egg*. The hacker exploited an obscure bug in an e-mail program that allowed him to substitute his own version of a system executable file on the victim's system. This one change allowed him to make several other changes, each one small, and eventually run rampant through the victim's system. Stoll first detected the miscreant only by careful reading of system audit logs. He tracked the hacker's activity across many other systems. Virtually all of the other system managers were unaware of the hacker. Some of the systems were owned by the U.S. Department of Defense and thought to be impregnable. The hacker was competent and persistent, but no guru. Yet he was enormously successful in breaking into dozens of systems, and took part in a worldwide scheme to steal U.S. government secrets and sell them to the (then) Soviet Union. The e-mail bug that gave him a foothold was widely known and quickly fixed by the program's author.

Intrusion consists of either an unknown person gaining access to your system's resources or a known person accessing resources not intended for him or her. Results of intrusion are modification and also often loss of data, breach of confidentiality, and denial or disruption of service.

Note that many intrusions are carried out for the purpose of making your system the base for attacks on other systems.

THE SYSTEM ADMINISTRATOR: CARE AND FEEDING

To protect your site, you must manage, train, and motivate your system administrator (sysad). The sysad is charged with keeping hostile elements from damaging your system. The sysad's job objectives are

- establish confidence in the integrity of the system
- minimize risk to the company's system assets

The above objectives are accomplished by planning, designing, and implementing technical measures and organizational programs within the enterprise. If this sounds more demanding than setting up PCs and backing up files, it is.

- Invest in training to keep your sysad's skills up to date.
- If your sysad does not have time to pay adequate attention to security issues, restructure his or her duties.
- Establish a career path for system administrators; after two or three years a good sysad should be kicked upstairs; this works wonders as a motivational and recruiting tool.

There will always be new bugs and holes to take advantage of. Despite this, the hacker's best path into your system is by social engineering. This means getting to know the sysad, calling up posing as a user with a forgotten password, and watching the Usenet newsgroups for questions or problems that indicate vulnerabilities. An attacker may be able to get into your system, despite all its safeguards, by finding a "helpful" employee who gives away more than he or she should.

Vendors' notification of security fixes is usually limited. Announcements typically go to security-related newsgroups and mailing lists only. It is the sysad's job to monitor these actively and keep the system current.

Recruiting Your System Administrator

Hire the best sysad you can find. Get one with real experience in security, not only in system management.

When interviewing candidates, ask the following:

- if his or her previous sites have had explicit incident response procedures
- if he or she has handled a break-in, or break-in attempt, or other incident of unauthorized resource access, malicious or not
- which system services are typically turned off for Web servers

Here is a list of preventive measures from Farmer and Venema (see *Notes*). Your sysad candidate should be familiar with them.

- The *finger* service can reveal things about your system's OS and users that no one needs to know; disable it or replace the program it with a less "generous" version.
- Export read-write file systems only to specific, trusted clients
- Alternatively, export read-only file systems only.
- Restrict the *ftp* service, and disable *tftp*.
- Disable NIS.
- Get a list of machines that have "trust" relationships (see *Definitions*) with your own machines; a "trust" relationship means the machines mutually allow cross-logins without password verification; this means that the security of your machine is out of your control, never a good thing.
- Consider eliminating trust entirely.

The sysad weekly status reports should include the following:

- any relevant security advisories received and implemented — there are typically several new CERT advisories (see *References*) every month
- system monitoring and auditing work done
- maintenance work done to keep the site secure
- software patches made available by vendors
- software patches applied
- all user accounts added, deleted, or modified, with all privileges listed

Design your site to play to your sysad's strengths. If your staff does not have UNIX experience, get a Microsoft Windows NT box.

Ironically, hackers see the sysad as their primary pathway into the system. A common tactic is for a hacker to target a site after he makes a study of the sysad's habits, skills, and weaknesses. Your sysad must be mature and capable enough not to be vulnerable to these tactics.

MANAGEMENT STRATEGIES

If you engage an ISP, you are dependent on them for security. As a rule of thumb, the more things you run on your machine, the more security holes there likely will be, so your Internet server should run only the required minimum of services. Ask your Internet Service Provider if the same machine on which your data resides is running mail, POP3, NNTP, print serving, FTP, or login authentication. With each extra service, the likelihood of a security hole greatly increases.

SYSTEM AUDITING

A system audit lists all accounts and their privileges for every server and workstation, and all trust relationships.

In general, you should adopt several overlapping strategies and combine them at low cost.

1. Explicitly deny all services, file access, etc., except those specifically allowed.
2. Restrict, monitor, and audit access.
3. Establish your enterprise's acceptable risk level. If you can not tolerate any risk, you should not be on the Internet at all.
4. Connect only the required minimum of your network to the Internet, and assume it will come under attack by hackers. Put everything else behind the firewall.

SOURCES OF INTERNET MALFEASANCE

Your system is at much greater risk from your own employees than from hackers or computer criminals. Data security professionals at large companies typically spend 90 percent of their time making sure the internal staff are able to see and do only what their duties entail, and nothing else, and that they handle this responsibility professionally. They spend only small fraction of their time worrying about intruders, and so should you. In almost all cases, more valuable information walks out on floppy disks then will ever be taken by hackers.

Internal breaches are made by company staff who are supposed to have some access to the system, but contrive to get more. They may want to look in personnel files, pirate software, read the boss's mail, or just grab some extra disk space. Many fall into the "disgruntled employee" category.

An insider can see passwords taped to the front of terminals. Most company staff place assets at risk through carelessness and ignorance. As a manager, your time and budget will be very well spent working on these.

Internal staff who try to break into system resources they should not use have a variety of motivations: mischief, ego, boredom, or personal conflicts with other staff members. Some will say, "I have to break through system security to do my job." If this is true, then your business process is broken, not your Web site. Fix the process and close the hole your staffer used to hack it.

All of these indicate that the business process and your security policy are defective. Fixing these will do much more for your business than worrying about hackers.

More than 50 percent of vulnerabilities come from sheer carelessness. To test your own site's security, try this social engineering test: pretend to be a sales representative, and phone in from the field with an emergency system access problem. Tell the system administrator you just need a favor to get out of a jam — having a password reset to a known value, or access to a dial-in number.

Next, pretend to be a system administrator. Phone a field sales representative and say you need his or her password to "fix a system problem." If either of these scams succeed, you have a problem.

The bane of the system administrator's existence is the employee who asks for a favor in violation of the security policy and says the sysad had better accede to his or her request or the boss will get ticked off. If you are the boss, make it clear ahead of time that you will support the sysad in refusing requests of this kind.

In large organizations, a basic assumption is that most internal theft will occur in small amounts over long periods of time. For this reason, an employee who is found misappropriating even a tiny amount is immediately subject to firing and prosecution.

HACKERS

Most hackers are like vandals — a costly and damaging social nuisance; only a minority are in it for profit.

The most dangerous person is not the unknown outside attacker but the malicious insider with sanctioned business on your system. Much more valuable information leaves victims' sites by floppy disk and voice phone calls than by outside intruders.

A common tactic among hackers is to watch newsgroup messages and bulletin boards for messages signed, for example, "Richard Roe, System Administrator, XYZ Corporation." Let's say the newsgroup is devoted to baseball, and Mr. Roe says he is a Boston Red Sox fan. The hacker goes to the site and attempts to break in with passwords like "RedSox," "pennant," and so on.

A related tactic is to send Richard Roe an e-mail, claiming to be another Red Sox fan, and begin a long exchange of e-mail messages. In the course of online dialogue, the hacker learns Mr. Roe admires former Red Sox star Ted Williams. He goes to the site, tries "TedWilliams" or "400hitter" and bingo! Without using any technical skill the hacker comes in through the front door.

Never put anything important in an e-mail message. This especially applies to passwords and credit card numbers. The first thing most miscreants do is scan the mail directory for the words "password" and "Visa."

The scheme should be fail safe. If the system fails it should fail harmlessly. Just as the way a car's steering wheel lock makes the car more difficult to steal, the best approach is to deter hackers and make them move on to easier targets.

When Protection Is Not Protection

Several security schemes purport to protect your data, but in fact provide little or no protection. These may keep the honest people honest, but do not rely on them to provide any real security.

Security by Obscurity. Hackers' tools exist that will scan an entire site and show its complete directory structure. It will not work to put valuable files in an out-of-the-way directory and assume no one would bother to look there.

MS-Office and Zip File Password Protection. The encryption algorithms for both are known to be weak, and methods of defeating them have been widely circulated. If you must encrypt a file, use real encryption software such as PGP and F-Control.

SECURITY POLICY (INTERNAL)

There are two approaches to this, a "zero-based" approach and an "everything but" approach.

- Zero-based policy: the minimal, additive approach. Each user gets only what his or her day's work requires. Each system service is enabled with only the minimum required functionality. Explicitly deny all services not absolutely required and justified. The firewall stops everything except those few permitted services, such as e-mail.
- Everything-but policy: the services known to be vulnerable or dangerous are turned off, but most other services are left on. System security manages, monitors, and audits access more than restricting it.

To implement:

- Determine the resources needed for each business process and for each person involved in it.

- Based on this, decide which files and programs to make available.
- Lock down all other system facilities.
- Consider removing the restricted resources from the network entirely.

The key is not to take a reactive stance or wait for a problem to develop and try to play catchup.

User Education

Make sure each user is clear on the following:

- Each person is responsible for his or her own password and anything that is done while using it.
- Each person is responsible for the equipment, software, and login account resources entrusted to him or her.
- Each person is obligated to report untoward system behavior that may indicate an attack.

Computer misuse is just like any other type of crime, and the consequences are the same. Plug the holes in the dike. This approach entails creating a list of known security weaknesses, and takes steps to close each one.

Clearly, your site should use both approaches. You should take the zero-based approach first. Then start the "plug the holes" stage, which will be much smaller and simpler because of the first steps. Most sites start and finish with a "plug the holes" approach, or do nothing at all.

The job of the system administrator and the manager responsible for security is to find creative ways to reduce privileges to a minimum without creating undue complexity, hurting productivity, and making the users unhappy.

Finally, you should reassess your security policy at regular intervals, and whenever a major change occurs.

Incident Response Procedures

Formulate a series of steps to be taken:

- when a breach is discovered in progress
- when evidence of a past violation is discovered
- when a virus is suspected or positively determined to be present

Example: all security warnings/failure reports will be recorded and investigated, with their causes and actions taken forwarded to management. It is the employee's responsibility to:

- report possible security breaches
- know protocol for handling attacks

SECURITY

The CERT site is a gold mine of information on this topic. Go to http://www.cert.org/nav/securityimprovement.html.

System Configuration Standards

Keep in mind that most of the areas in which your system is vulnerable are caused by incorrect configuration settings.

Pay special attention to homegrown software. It is rarely built with security in mind. Connect only a limited segment of your network to the Internet. Expect that these machines will come under attack and that some attacks will succeed.

Consider making the file systems on the exposed machines read-only, thus by definition resistant to tampering.

SECURITY POLICY (EXTERNAL)

Your primary external defense is your firewall. A firewall is a group of system components whose job it is to enforce your system's security policy. Firewalls allow in some traffic and restrict everything else. The critical issue is that you must know what you want your firewall to do, what to allow, what to restrict. This is your security policy. Some firewalls are built using software alone, some use separate hardware components.

To keep out hackers, you need a comprehensive security program. The security policy should explicitly state rules for accessing the system via all available means. If there are dial-in modems attached, specify who is allowed to get in and what they may do. Management decides what will be visible from the Internet. Only those resources are made available and everything else is locked down.

Creating an Internet site means you want your system to be partially accessible to authorized users. "Partially" means that users get to the level of access you specify. If you have a static brochure site, readers may read some of your files, but only the ones you authorize, and they may not modify or destroy them. If your site is interactive, users can enter data where permitted, but cannot wreck or steal the resources the site presents.

PASSWORD GUIDELINES

CERT estimates that 80 percent of problems result from weak passwords. Educate staff on their obligation to maintain secure and unguessable passwords, and ensure they comply. Your site will become much more secure overnight. A "guessable" password is

- anything you can find in a dictionary — a word, name, place name, abbreviation, etc.

- the company name and the person's own name are used so often that intruders routinely guess them and frequently succeed

Hackers often attempt to break into to users' accounts by guessing passwords. This approach is very simple and staggeringly successful. Common passwords are used so much that this approach is often successful. According to a popular anecdote within the computer security industry, the second most common password is "love." The most common is a four-letter synonym for "love." *Hint*: If your site is dedicated to the study of orchids, the root password should not be "orchids."

One recommended guideline is that passwords contain a combination of numbers and uppercase and lowercase letters. A popular method is to take a phrase that is easy for the user to remember, such as a movie title, create a mixed-case acronym from it, and use that as a password. For example, "Titanic starring Leonardo DiCaprio and a big boat" would contract to "TsLDa2b2." This seems like a complex string to type, but it will become automatic within a day or two.

Password rules should be enforced by an automated utility. There are many of these on the market for every operating system. Typical password enforcement functions are

- require a reasonable minimum password length, usually eight character
- automatic password expiration parameters to force password changes quarterly; users generally find monthly password changes to be onerous
- check for and disallow use of already-used passwords
- disallow obviously weak passwords, such as the company name, or the user's name

A widely available hacker's tool wages a "dictionary attack" which repetitiously attempts automated logins using words in a large dictionary file. If a password is a word in the English dictionary, the program will discover it and so will the hacker.

An especially bad choice is the name of any family member. Working in data security for a large financial services firm, I would routinely see an employee's desk with a child's picture and perform the following:

- ask the name of the child
- with the employee looking on, log in as him and enter the child's name as the password

This works in an astonishing number of cases. Add the child's birth date to the name and the success rate climbs even higher. (Stranger still, I could visit the employee again a few weeks later, and log in again with the same unchanged password.)

SECURITY

Use a different password for each system you log into. If you subscribe to an online Website specializing in orchids, use a different password there from the one that protects your e-mail account or your Web site. Many hackers set up sham "promotion" sites, under the pretext of providing free software or special interest forums, for the purpose of collecting passwords.

I met a system administrator who uses the same password for the root accounts (see *Glossary*) on dozens of different machines. That password is an easily guessable word in English. I would like to borrow his ATM card!

PHYSICAL SECURITY

Anyone who can physically touch a machine can break into it. If you cannot restrict physical access to a machine that houses your system, it is not safe.

PROFESSIONAL HELP

Penetration-testing companies will attack your site to help your determine how vulnerable you are. These attacks simulate a real attack.

Consultants from penetration-testing companies provide the following services:

- check your system for technical compliance with security standards
- train your staff on how to find and fix holes
- provide ongoing strategic and technical advice to keep your site safe

These are consulting companies that field a penetration assessment team. Their methods are the same as those used by hackers. Their job is to identify your site's vulnerabilities, and train your IT staff on how to find and fix them.

Recommendations:

- Do not engage a penetration service company that only operates remotely. To do the job they will have to gauge social engineering and physical access vulnerabilities. This cannot be done effectively away from your site.
- The assessment team should be knowledgeable about security and about your business, not only about technical issues and security products.
- Many companies are concerned about penetration service companies learning too much and using the information against them. Select your vendor carefully, and talk with the customer references they supply.
- Costs are typically near the top of high-end IT consultancies.

Keep in mind that the best value is the knowledge retained by your own staff.

Notes

The U.S. General Accounting Office conducted a test break-in of the U.S. State Department's automated information system and found it prone to attack. The problems they found are present in many, if not most, companies' systems.

Most of the best information sources are academic or other noncommercial organizations, and are publicly available. Take advantage of this fact.

To get some insights on how hackers work and think, look into these two usergroups:

Alt.2600

Alt.2600.hackerz

"2600" refers to the frequency of a whistle used by a legendary phone system hacker to fool Ma Bell into providing free phone service.

Other good sources:

- Stoll, Clifford, *The Cuckoo's Egg,* Pocket Books, 1995, ISBN: 0671726889.
- Farmer, D. and Wietse, V., Improving Your Site by Breaking Into It, at www.best.com/~mld/unix/papers/improve_by_breakin.html. This is an excellent white paper, focused on UNIX but widely applicable.
- The mother lode of online security references: www.cs.purdue.edu/homes/spaf/hot-lists/csec-top.html.

GLOSSARY

Trust — A relationship among two or more computers, whereby users who are permitted to access one are automatically permitted on the others.

Firewall — A hardware or software component that restricts outside access to your system.

Service — A function performed by a computer. An example is a print service.

Hole — A defect in a computer program or operating system that allows a breach of security.

Social engineering — Nontechnical break-in methods that use information accidentally divulged by sanctioned system users. Typically this means tricking the victim into revealing a password, or providing clues that allow the hacker to guess it.

Hacker — A technical person who explores the inner workings of computer systems, usually without illegal intentions.

Cracker — A hacker who uses his or her technical skills to illegally break into other systems. "Crack" originally referred to the process of decoding passwords, something like cracking a code.

Root — The "superuser" login account that allows full access to every file and resource on the system, and can create other user accounts. The root password is the keys to the kingdom. Only the systems administration should know the root password.

Chapter 54
Applets and Network Security: A Management Overview
Al Berg

APPLETS ARE SMALL PROGRAMS THAT RESIDE ON A HOST COMPUTER and are downloaded to a client computer to be executed. This model makes it very easy to distribute and update software. Because the new version of an application only needs to be placed on the server, clients automatically receive and run the updated version the next time they access the application.

The use of applets is possible because of the increasing bandwidth available to Internet and intranet users. The time required to download the programs has been decreasing even as program complexity has been increasing. The development of cross-platform languages such as Sun Microsystems, Inc.'s Java, Microsoft Corp.'s ActiveX, and Netscape Communications Corp.'s JavaScript has made writing applets for many different computers simple — the same exact Java or JavaScript code can be run on a Windows-based PC, a Macintosh, or a UNIX-based system without any porting or recompiling of code. Microsoft is working to port ActiveX to UNIX and Macintosh platforms.

APPLETS AND THE WEB

The World Wide Web is the place that users are most likely to encounter applets today. Java (and to a lesser degree, JavaScript) has become the Webmaster's tool of choice to add interesting effects to Web sites or to deliver applications to end users. Most of the scrolling banners, animated icons, and other special effects found on today's Web pages depend on applets to work. Some Web pages use applets for more substantial applications. For example, MapQuest (http://www.mapquest.com) uses Java and ActiveX to deliver an interactive street atlas of the entire United States *Wired* magazine offers a Java-based chat site that, when accessed over the Web, allows users to download an applet that lets them participate in real-time conferencing.

THE SECURITY ISSUE

Every silver lining has a cloud, and applets are no exception. Applets can present a real security hazard for users and network managers. When Web pages use applets, the commands that tell the client's browser to download and execute the applets are embedded in the pages themselves. Users have no way of knowing whether or not the next page that they download will contain an applet, and most of the time, they do not care. The Internet offers an almost limitless source of applets for users to run; however, no one knows who wrote them, whether they were written with malicious intent, or whether they contain bugs that might cause them to crash a user's computer.

Applets and computer viruses have a lot in common. Both applets and viruses are self-replicating code that executes on the user's computer without the user's consent. Some security experts have gone as far as to say that the corporate network manager should prohibit users from running applets at all. However, applets are becoming an increasingly common part of how users interact with the Internet and corporate intranets, so learning to live safely with applets is important for network managers.

WHAT ARE THE RISKS?

According to Princeton University's Safe Internet Programming (SIP) research team, there have been no publicly reported, confirmed cases of security breaches involving Java, though there have been some suspicious events that may have involved Java security problems. The lack of reported cases is no guarantee that there have not been breaches that either were not discovered or were not reported. But it does indicate that breaches are rare.

As Web surfing increasingly becomes a way to spend money, and applets become the vehicle for shopping, attacks on applets will become more and more profitable, increasing the risk. Sun, Netscape, and Microsoft all designed their applet languages with security in mind.

JAVA: SECURE APPLETS

Java programs are developed in a language similar to C++ and stored as source code on a server. When a client, such as a Web browser, requests a page that references a Java program, the source code is retrieved from the server and sent to the browser, where an integrated interpreter translates the source code statements into machine-independent bytecodes, which are executed by a virtual machine implemented in software on the client. This virtual machine is designed to be incapable of operations that might be detrimental to security, thus providing a secure sandbox in which programs can execute without fear of crashing the client system. Java applets loaded over a network are not allowed to:

- read from files on the client system
- write to files on the client system
- make any network connections, except to the server from which they were downloaded
- start any client-based programs
- define native method calls, which would allow an applet to directly access the underlying computer

Java was designed to make applets inherently secure. Following are some of the underlying language security features offered by Java:

- All of an applet's array references are checked to make sure that programs will not crash because of a reference to an element that does not exist.
- Complex and troublesome pointer variables (found in some vendors' products) that provide direct access to memory locations in the computer do not exist in Java, removing another cause of crashes and potentially malicious code.
- Variables can be declared as unchangeable at runtime to prevent important program parameters from being modified accidentally or intentionally.

JAVA: HOLES AND BUGS

Although Sun has made every effort to make the Java virtual machine unable to run code that will negatively impact the underlying computer, researchers have already found bugs and design flaws that could open the door to malicious applets.

The fact that Sun has licensed Java to various browser vendors adds another level of complexity to the security picture. Not only can security be compromised by a flaw in the Java specification, but the vendor's implementation of the specification may contain its own flaws and bugs.

DENIAL-OF-SERVICE THREATS

Denial-of-service attacks involve causing the client's Web browser to run with degraded performance or crash. Java does not protect the client system from these types of attacks, which can be accomplished simply by putting the client system into a loop to consume processor cycles, creating new process threads until system memory is consumed, or placing locks on critical processes needed by the browser.

Because denial-of-service attacks can be programmed to occur after a time delay, it may be difficult for a user to determine which page the offending applet was downloaded from. If an attacker is subtle and sends an applet that degrades system performance, the user may not know that their computer is under attack, leading to time-consuming and expensive troubleshooting of a nonexistent hardware or software problem.

Java applets are not supposed to be able to establish network connections to machines other than the server they were loaded from. However, there are applets that exploit bugs and design flaws that allow it to establish a back-door communications link to a third machine (other than the client or server). This link could be used to send information that may be of interest to a hacker. Because many ready-to-use Java applets are available for download from the Internet, it would be possible for an attacker to write a useful applet, upload it to a site where Webmasters would download it, and then sit back and wait for information sent by the applet to reach their systems.

WHAT KIND OF INFORMATION CAN THE APPLET SEND BACK?

Due to another implementation problem found in August 1996 by the Safe Internet Programming research team at Princeton University, the possibilities are literally endless. A flaw found in Netscape Navigator versions 3.0 beta 5 and earlier versions, and Microsoft Internet Explorer 3.0 beta 2 and earlier versions, allows applets to gain full read and write access to the files on a Web surfer's machine. This bug means that the attacker can get copies of any files on the machine or replace existing data or program files with hacked versions.

Giving Java applets the ability to connect to an arbitrary host on the network or Internet opens the door to another type of attack. A malicious applet, downloaded to and running on a client inside of a firewalled system, could establish a connection to another host behind the firewall and access files and programs. Because the attacking host is actually inside the secured system, the firewall will not know that the access is actually originating from outside the network.

Another bug found in August 1996 by the Princeton team affects only Microsoft Internet Explorer version 3.0 and allows applets (which are not supposed to be allowed to start processes on the client machine) to execute any DOS command on the client. This allows the applet to delete or change files or programs or insert new or hacked program code such as viruses or backdoors. Microsoft has issued a patch (available on its Web site at http://www.microsoft.com/ie) to Internet Explorer that corrects the problem.

Princeton's SIP team also found a hole that would allow a malicious application to execute arbitrary strings of machine code, even though the

Java virtual machine is only supposed to be able to execute the limited set of Java bytecodes. The problem was fixed in Netscape Navigator 3.0 beta 6 and Microsoft Internet Explorer 3.0 beta 2.

JAVASCRIPT: A DIFFERENT GRIND

Netscape's JavaScript scripting language may be named Java, but it is distinct from Sun's applet platform. JavaScript is Netscape Navigator's built-in scripting language that allows Webmasters to do cross-platform development of applets that control browser events, objects such as tables and forms, and various activities that happen when users click on an object with their mouse.

Like Java, JavaScript runs applications in a virtual machine to prevent them from performing functions that would be detrimental to the operation of the client workstations. Also like Java, there are several flaws in the implementation of the security features of JavaScript. Some of the flaws found in JavaScript include the ability for malicious applets to:

- obtain users' e-mail addresses from their browser configuration
- track the pages that a user visits and mail the results back to the script author
- access the client's file system, reading and writing files

A list of JavaScript bugs and fixes can be found on John LoVerso's Web page at the Open Software Foundation (http://www.osf.org/~ loverso/javascript/).

ActiveX: Microsoft's Vision for Distributed Component Computing. Microsoft's entry in the applet development tool wars, ActiveX, is very different from Java and presents its own set of security challenges. ActiveX is made up of server and client components, including:

- Controls, which are applets that can be embedded in Web pages and executed at the client. Controls can be written in a number of languages, including Visual Basic and Visual C++.
- Documents that provide access to non-HTML content, such as word processing documents or spreadsheets, from a Web browser.
- The Java virtual machine, which allows standard Java applets to run at the client.
- Scripting, which allows the Web developer to control the integration of controls and Java applets on a Web page.
- The server framework, which provides a number of server-side functions such as database access and data security.

Java applets running in an ActiveX environment (e.g., Microsoft's Internet Explorer Web browser) use the same security features and have the same security issues associated with JavaScript. Microsoft offers a Java development environment (i.e., Visual J++) as well as other sandbox languages (i.e., VBScript, based on Visual Basic and JScript, Microsoft's implementation of Netscape's JavaScript) for the development of applications that are limited as to the functions they can perform.

When developers take advantage of ActiveX's ability to integrate programs written in Visual Basic or C++, the virtual machine model of Java no longer applies. In these cases, compiled binaries are transferred from the server to the Web client for execution. These compiled binaries have full access to the underlying computing platform, so there is no reason that the application could not read and write files on the client system, send information from the client to the server (or another machine), or perform a destructive act such as erasing a disk or leaving a virus behind.

USING AUTHENTICODE FOR ACCOUNTABILITY

Microsoft's approach to security for non-Java ActiveX applications is based on the concept of accountability — knowing with certainty the identity of the person or company that wrote a piece of software and that the software was not tampered with by a third party. Microsoft sees the issues related to downloading applets from the Web as similar to those involved in purchasing software; users need to know where the software is coming from and that it is intact. Accountability also means that writers of malicious code could be tracked down and would have to face consequences for their actions.

The mechanism that Microsoft offers to implement this accountability is called Authenticode. Authenticode uses a digital signature attached to each piece of software downloaded from the Internet. The signature is a cryptographic code attached by the software developer to an applet. Developers must enter a private key (known only to them) to sign their application, assuring their identity. The signature also includes an encrypted checksum of the application itself, which allows the client to determine if the applet has changed since the developer released it.

ACTIVEX: THE DOWNSIDE

This approach provides developers and users with access to feature-rich applications, but at a price. If an application destroys information on a user's computer, accountability will not help recover their data or repair damage done to their business. Once the culprit has been found, bringing them to justice may be difficult because new computer crimes are developing faster than methods for prosecuting them.

Microsoft acknowledges that Authenticode does not guarantee that end users will never download malicious code to their PCs and that it is a first step in the protection of information assets.

Further information on ActiveX can be found on Microsoft's Web site (http://www.microsoft.com/activex) and at the ActiveX Web site run by CNet Technology Corp. (http://www.activex.com).

AN OUNCE OF PREVENTION

So far, this chapter has discussed problems posed by applets. Following are some steps that can be taken to lessen the exposure faced by users.

Make Sure the Basics Are Covered

Users need to back up their data and programs consistently, and sensitive data should be stored on secure machines. The surest way to avoid applet security problems is to disable support for applet execution at the browser. If the code cannot execute, it cannot do damage.

Of course, the main downside of this approach is that the users will lose the benefits of being able to run applets. Because the ability to run applets is part of the client browser, turning off applets is usually accomplished at the desktop and a knowledgeable user could simply turn applet support back on. Firewall vendors are starting to provide support for filtering out applets, completely or selectively, before they enter the local network.

Users Should Run the Latest Available Versions of Their Web Browsers

Each new version corrects not only functional and feature issues, but security flaws. If an organization is planning to use applets on its Web pages, it is preferable to either write them internally or obtain them from trusted sources. If applets will be downloaded from unknown sources, a technical person with a good understanding of the applet language should review the code to be sure that it does only what it claims to.

Mark LaDue, a researcher at Georgia Tech, has a Web page (available at http://www.math.gatech.edu/~mladue/HostileApplets.html) containing a number of hostile applets available for download and testing. Seeing some real applications may help users recognize new problem applets that may be encountered.

CONCLUSION

IS personnel should monitor the Princeton University Safe Internet Programming group's home page (located at http://www.cs.princeton.edu/sip) for the latest information on security flaws and fixes (under News). It is also a good idea to keep an eye on browser vendors' home pages for news of new versions.

Applets offer users and network managers a whole new paradigm for delivering applications to the desktop. Although, like any new technology, applets present a new set of challenges and concerns, their benefits can be enjoyed while their risks can be managed.

Chapter 55
Security Management

Dave Schneider

NOW THAT WE HAVE MASTERED THE ART OF DEVELOPING AND DEPLOYING INTERNET APPLICATIONS, we need to ask how can we assure that:

- the intended audience will be able to access the applications
- all others will be unable to access the applications
- the applications are safe from modification by hackers
- the applications can be safely maintained and updated

These questions bring to light a basic conflict: encouraging proper access and use of our Internet applications, while discouraging inappropriate use and modification. The aim of security management is to make safe usage and maintenance possible, but to prevent modification and improper use.

THE HACKER THREAT

In order to understand the solutions available, first we need to discuss the mechanism by which Web applications are used and maintained. Exhibit 55-1 shows the salient parts of a computer that is used to support one or more Web applications.

The computer runs an operating system; the Web server — an application — runs under that operating system. One possible configuration would be an Intel Pentium-based system running Microsoft Windows NT operating system using the Microsoft's Internet Information Server (IIS) Web server.

Web applications usually consist of two types of files:

- Data files that contain text formatted according to the HTML specification.
- Support programs — executable code components — that conform to the CGI-BIN convention. These support programs may be written in a variety of programming languages, including Perl, C++, Basic, or Java.

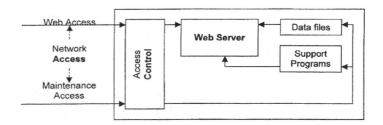

Exhibit 55-1. Components supporting a Web server.

Users access the Web applications via network connections, which go through the operating system's access control component. Similarly, company personnel who use network connections in order to update the data files and support programs go through the same operating system access control component. This component must allow a large user audience to access the Web applications, but a much restricted audience to perform application maintenance.

The root of the hacker problem is in the execution of support programs. If our application were only composed of data files that presented static information, it would not be vulnerable to hacking. The problem arises from the fact that the support programs are executable code that can, in principle, do anything to the files on the computer. The support programs can affect other running applications; and they can read, write, or transmit data from the disk.[1] Even if these programs are not intentionally malicious, they can do unintended damage.

For example, a popular attack is called *buffer overflow*: a very long string of characters is given to an application that is only expecting a short string. If the application does not check for this condition, the extra characters may be stored in memory and overwrite other data, most often resulting in the program's outright failure. However, a clever hacker may use the string as executable code! The famous *Internet worm* used this kind of attack. The code could cause unintentional data transmission or compromise the operating system's access control component, allowing the hacker to perform the same activities as legitimate maintenance personnel. The hacker could then damage, replace, or delete any of the application's data, support, or other disk files. The hacker could capture and export any data — including passwords.

Any interesting Web applications require the use of support programs. However, there is no way to absolutely guarantee that these support programs are not vulnerable to security compromise. You can take steps, however, to minimize this risk by performing these steps on a regular basis:

- Ensure that the operating system's access control component is configured to allow only the appropriate personnel to perform Web application maintenance. Do not provide more access to users than they need. For example, an application that provides users with access to their account information does not need to provide write access to the database itself — only read access.
- Review all support applications for proper operation. In particular, perform a separate review centering on security alone. Be paranoid!
- Review logs and audits. Both the operating system and the Web server keep logs of their operation. Review these logs for suspicious activity. A number of tools are available to analyze these logs, which are often voluminous. Don't be afraid to query users about any unusual accesses that the logs show.

WEB SERVERS

Web Server Placement — Use of ISPs

Now that we have paid attention to configuring, logging, and monitoring access, we should consider where within our networks we should attach the Web server computer. One answer is to make it someone else's problem! An Internet Service Provider (ISP) or other value-added network provider is willing to host your Website at their facilities and using their equipment for a nominal charge. Such providers generally have thought through the issues of security, and they have personnel available 24 hours a day, 7 days a week to deal with security issues.

The feasibility of having an ISP host your Web site depends on the nature of the data that users will access by means of your Web server. If primarily users from the Internet access your Web application and the data are not dynamic, that is, it can be copied to the ISP on an occasional basis, then this type of hosting may work well. ISPs generally have much faster Internet connections than you do, making for a happier user. If, however, the data change dynamically and are located at your site, having an ISP host your Web site may be inappropriate. You and your ISP should discuss such feasibility issues.

If contracting with an ISP to host your Web applications seems like the appropriate course of action to you, please do not stop reading! The remainder of this chapter acquaints you with the questions concerning the security of your Web site that you need to consider regardless of whether you contract with an ISP or host your own Web site.

Web Server Placement — In-House

If having an ISP host the Web site is not feasible, you need to consider the location of the computer running the Web server with respect to other

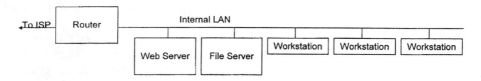

Exhibit 55-2. Simple direct LAN configuration.

computers on your LAN. One possible solution is to attach the server directly to the LAN. Exhibit 55-2 is a possible LAN configuration.

One side of the router[2] connects to your local phone company and hence to your ISP. The other side of the router is connected to your internal LAN, which connects employees' workstations, company file servers, and the Web server. This appears to provide everything needed — external and internal access to the Web server and local access to the Internet.

This is not a good configuration, however. Anyone, including users on the Internet, may try to access the internal file servers or workstations. Such access often succeeds due to a lack of knowledge or care on the part of your user community.

The most common solution to the problems exposed by this solution is the use of a *firewall*. Exhibit 55-3 shows the same configuration with the addition of a firewall.

A firewall is situated between the internal network (your LAN) and the external network (the Internet). The firewall allows network traffic to proceed only if the firewall is configured to allow it. You can configure a firewall to prohibit external users access to all internal resources except your Web server,[3] while allowing internal users to access resources on the Internet. This solves the main problem of attaching the LAN directly to the ISP: it prohibits outsiders from accessing internal resources other than those public resources managed by the Web server. However, hacking of the Web server may still open an indirect channel to other computers on your network. In addition, any internal workstation user may attempt to modify the Web application[4] where the operating system's access control component is the only line of defense.

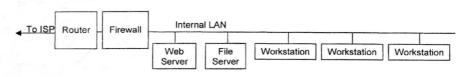

Exhibit 55-3. Firewall network placement.

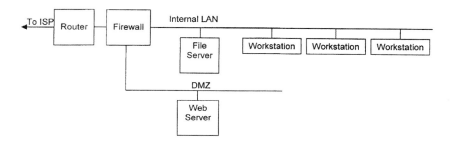

Exhibit 55-4. Use of a firewall with two internal networks.

Exhibit 55-4 shows another popular firewall configuration. This configuration features *two* internal networks.

The firewall in Exhibit 55-4 controls a separate LAN segment, often referred to as the *DMZ* — for demilitarized zone, to which the Web server is connected. Here you configure the firewall to control three major flows of traffic so that:

- no external traffic is allowed to reach the internal LAN
- only external Web traffic is allowed to reach the Web server on the DMZ
- Web and maintenance[5] traffic is allowed from the LAN to the Web server on the DMZ
- no traffic is allowed from the DMZ to the LAN

If a hacker breaks into the operating system on the Web server computer, the firewall isolates the hacker from the internal LAN.

Web Server Placement — It Is Not Always Simple

Things can get more complex than we have pictured here. Firewalls themselves are vulnerable. A hacker may break into the firewall's operating system and change the firewall's configuration. Doing so allows potential access to any DMZ or LAN server. Some companies employ two or more firewalls to minimize this risk. I should hasten to add that the vendors of firewall systems take this threat very seriously and provide very secure solutions, but *your* staff must install these solutions on *your* computers. Make sure to read and follow all of the vendor's instructions to ensure the safest possible installation.

In addition, the Web server often needs to access information contained in databases on other computers. You must consider these other computers with respect to normal and maintenance access as well. For these complex situations, it is best to engage a professional security consultant.

WEB APPLICATIONS DESIGNED FOR THE INTRANET/EXTRANET

The foregoing solutions work well for Web applications accessed primarily from the Internet. But what about Web applications designed to provide information to *selected* internal intranet users or to *selected* outsiders in an extranet?

Exhibits 55-3 and 55-4 show how a firewall can be used to protect Web applications that are intended to be accessed only from within the intranet, by prohibiting access from the Internet. This configuration limits the scope of such Web applications to those appropriate for access by everyone on the intranet — for example, company HR policies.

To achieve the best value out of our intranets, internal Web applications can and should provide more valuable, timely, confidential business information. To do so we must provide tools that can identify users and control their access to Web data more precisely. The most difficult problem is the identification of users who access the Web server. Web servers use either one of two techniques to identify users and control access to Web applications:

1. *Simple authentication.* The user provides a name and password to the Web server. The Web server checks the information against a list that is maintained by your security staff. The list specifies which applications are available to which users.
2. *Digital certificates.* In order to use this feature, each user installs a digital certificate on their own Web browser. This certificate contains the user's name and other validated information. When the user accesses the Web server, the Web server uses the information to allow access to a specific list of applications — again using information that your security staff maintains.

A number of vendors not associated with the primary Web browser and server developers — Microsoft and Netscape — offer software components for browsers and servers that augment the common identification and access controls included in the Web servers.

Alternatively, you can configure a firewall as shown in Exhibit 55-4 to identify intranet users and provide controlled access to Web applications. Most modern firewalls include a variety of identification techniques:

- *IP address or computer name.* This technique equates the user to the computer. This is not always appropriate; users may work on several different computers during the course of their normal work week. This is also a relatively insecure means of identification because users can configure their own workstation with the same IP address as another workstation.
- *Authentication tokens.* These handheld devices look like small calculators and uniquely identify the holder.

- *Network IDs.* Where LAN users log into their network, such as in Microsoft Windows NT, the firewall can identify users by their network ID.
- *Digital certificates.* A digital certificate is issued by a certificate authority and contains information that identifies the user. A digital certificate and a passport are analogous: they both identify you. An authority that validates those data issues both.

Using one or more of these techniques, the firewall can identify each user and control access by that user to Web applications and other network resources. Typically, firewalls can limit a user's access at a number of levels:

- To the server — The user is allowed, or denied, access to all information on the server.
- To the directory — The user is allowed access to a particular directory on the Web server and to all subdirectories.
- To the file — The user is allowed access to a particular file.

Although we have been talking about intranets, most of the identification techniques and all of the access control techniques are applicable to extranets as well.

THE PROBLEMS OF SCALE

Scaling any solution brings with it its own problem. All but the smallest organizations now have multiple locations that are connected through public or private networks. In addition, most have homeworkers or traveling employees that desire the same access to network resources as they have at the office. The growing size of an organization and the deployment of network connections can require a substantial amount of administrative effort.

If valuable information is to be shared among multiple company locations, it is essential that the locations communicate in a secure and private manner. Historically, this was accomplished with leased lines or frame relay connections. Today, in most cases, this can be accomplished by using the Internet as a communications backbone, and by using encryption to maintain privacy of the transmitted data. Such a configuration is called a *virtual private network (VPN)* because all of your LANs appear as a single network using common facilities.

Because anyone can author information for sharing on the intranet, information can originate from servers located anywhere in the VPN. Likewise, the information consumers are located throughout the VPN and include home and remote users. Exhibit 55-5 shows a network configuration that makes sense in this context.

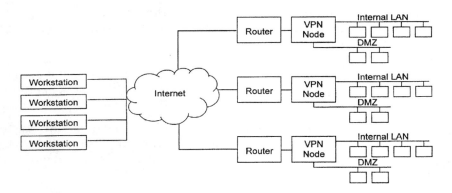

Exhibit 55-5. Virtual private network (VPN) configuration.

In Exhibit 55-5, the firewall from Exhibit 55-4 is replaced by a more sophisticated hardware/software device — a *VPN node*, whose responsibilities includes:

- All firewall functionality.
- Encryption and authentication of communications with other VPN nodes — The encryption enforces the privacy of communications between the nodes; it is the "P" in VPN. Authentication assures that encrypted communications is indeed coming from another node in the *same* VPN.
- Encryption and authentication of communications with home and remote users — This ensures privacy for users not housed within the various sites of the VPN.
- Access control — Enforcement of rules governing *who* is allowed to access *what* information.

With these capabilities and by virtue of the placement of the VPN nodes between information sources and information consumers, you can support enterprisewide sharing of information. Indeed, this is the very same structure that allows you to create an extranet to allow partners to access selected information resources.

When choosing such a VPN node product, be sure to consider its scalability — its ability to accommodate the growth in size and complexity of your intranet and extranet. Specifically:

- Make sure that the tools used to construct the VPN are all integrated into a central management interface. VPNs constructed out of a number of different products, each with its own administrative interface, can suffer increasing maintenance burdens and can hinder rather than facilitate expansion.

- Make sure that the product is of enterprise scope. That is, it must provide for information that originates anywhere and can be delivered to individuals anywhere — to intranet, Internet, and extranet partners.
- Make sure that the product has a way of safely distributing and delegating administrative responsibility. A product that must be administered centrally by one person will eventually limit growth. Multiple people must be able to perform administrative tasks simultaneously. Finally, it is wiser to use a system in which each administrator is delegated a specific sphere of authority rather than a system in which all administrators are allowed full and equal authority.
- Make sure that the product uses role-based user identification. Avoid products that require each and every user to be entered into a database. Doing so is an unnecessary administrative burden and can lead to security holes. Use a product that uses existing *role* information from network IDs, and plan to migrate toward the use of digital certificates in the future.

A product chosen using this set of rules will be capable of handling your current needs and future needs as well.

CONCLUSION

Let us summarize the recommendations made here:

- Carefully check all Web application support programs for accuracy and security.
- For Web applications that do not require constant access to database information, consider using an ISP to host your Web site.
- For Internet access to Web applications at a single site, install a reputable firewall system and utilize a DMZ to hold your Web server.
- For small intranets and extranets, look into user authentication and access control solutions based on the Web server itself or on third-party products that you can install with Web browsers and servers alike.
- For larger intranets and extranets, or for future growth, look into enterprise-scale VPN solutions that encompass firewall, VPN, and remote access capabilities.

Notes

1. Java programs operate in a restricted environment that makes them somewhat safer. Recently, however, bugs in Java language implementations have made them susceptible to abuse.
2. A box called a CSU/DSU often accompanies the router, but is not shown in the exhibit.
3. You can configure most routers to make these kinds of distinctions. Routers, however, lack the sophistication to operate in a strictly secure manner.

4. It has been well-documented that most security break-ins are attributed to employees working from the inside. This problem should not be minimized. In Microsoft networking terms, this would be accomplished through file sharing.
5. Although this chapter has concentrated on the issues surrounding Web application development and deployment, other applications play an important part in the Internet — FTP and News to name two. The VPN node product must include provisions for handling all Internet protocols.

Section VIII
Considering Evolving Technologies

ANY GOOD NETWORK DESIGN MUST INCLUDE FLEXIBILITY to potentially support one or more evolving technologies. While it is difficult, if not impossible, to accurately predict the possible use of evolving technologies by organizational employees, it is possible to note their potential effect on network bandwidth. Thus, knowledge of evolving technologies provides the ability to plan for the future as well as to consider the use of evolving technologies when implementing a new network or modifying an existing network.

The first chapter in this section examines developments in the communications infrastructure provided by different communications carriers. In Chapter 56, author Nathan J. Muller's chapter **Trends in Data Communications Services** first provides a review of the characteristics of evolving network access techniques to include different types of digital subscriber liens, cellular digital packet data, T1 and T3 circuits, and fractional T3. This is followed by a discussion of the use of different backbone technologies, which provides a summary of the operational characteristics of both existing and emerging communications technologies.

In Chapter 57, author Andres Llana expands on the first chapter in this section with his chapter titled **The Emerging Advantage of xDSL Technology.** In this chapter, Llana describes the various flavors of digital subscriber line technology as well as the use of different types of DSL technology to support different types of applications. Continuing our investigation of access technologies, Chapter 58 is focused upon the use of cable modems. In this chapter, **Preparing for Cable Modems**, author Gilbert Held acquaints the reader with the technology behind the use of cable modems and describes how their operation enables organizations to obtain an access technology that can provide support for data rates in the millions of bits per second range.

CONSIDERING EVOLVING TECHNOLOGIES

The following three chapters in this section focus on one of the most talked about emerging technologies that provides the potential to revolutionize the manner by which data networks are used. That technology involves the transmission of voice over networks originally designed to transmit data.

In Chapter 59, author Martin Taylor's chapter **Voice and Video on the LAN** describes and discusses voice and data convergence on the LAN, examining various technologies that make convergence possible. In Chapter 60, entitled **Internet Voice Applications,** author Frank J. Bourne first examines the state of Internet telephony. Once this is accomplished, Bourne provides a review of the characteristics of Internet voice and summarizes such important usage issues and impediments as IP addressing, interoperability standards, and multi-platform support prior to examining important infrastructure issues that make readers aware of the networking characteristics necessary to implement the technology.

Continuing our exploration of the use of voice over networks designed for data transmission, author John Fiske's chapter titled **Building an IP PBX Telephony Network** provides insight into the functions of a PBX and the methods necessary to develop an IP PBX. In Chapter 61, Fiske first describes the components of an IP PBX. Using this information as a base, Fiske reviews how an IP PBX can be configured and the variety of applications this type of PBX can support.

The concluding chapters in this section will examine two emerging IP applications that can provide significant cost savings to many organizations. In Chapter 62, titled **Fax over IP,** author John Fiske acquaints us with the technology required for facsimile to be transported via an IP network. Because fax is one of the most expensive communications applications employed by most organizations, the ability to send documents via an intranet or the Internet can considerably reduce networking costs. In this chapter, Fiske acquaints the reader with the advantages of fax over IP and then illustrates via a step-by-step methodology how one can create an Internet fax service.

Concluding this section, co-authors Christine Perey and Matthew Feldman's chapter titled **Videoconferencing over IP Networks** acquaints the reader with another emerging convergence area. In this chapter, one obtains information about the advantages of IP-based videoconferencing as well as the use of several products that can make this emerging technology a reality. By understanding the emerging technologies covered in this section, one will be better prepared for designing networks to support emerging applications. Similar to the Boy Scout motto, understanding these technologies provides one with the information to "be prepared" to support emerging customer applications.

Chapter 56
Trends in Data Communications Services

Nathan J. Muller

THE PAST FEW YEARS HAVE BEEN MARKED BY UNPRECEDENTED TECHNOLOGICAL INNOVATION in the communications field. Not only have new offerings such as frame relay and SMDS demonstrated their value, but older services such as X.25, T1/T3, and Integrated Services Digital Network are being revitalized. Making their debut are several new technologies that leverage the carrier's existing local loop infrastructure in support of high-speed data, including asymmetric digital subscriber line (ADSL) and high-bit-rate digital subscriber line (HDSL). Also being deployed are new wireless technologies, including Cellular Digital Packet Data, that connect mobile computer users to each other as well as to the data center. In addition, the country's entire communications infrastructure is poised for advancement with Synchronous Optical NETwork and Asynchronous Transfer Mode technologies for transmission and switching at multigigabit speeds. Long term, the combination of SONET and ATM paves the way for broadband ISDN (BISDN).

Communications at the customer premises is also undergoing rapid advancement. Fiber to the desktop and between LAN hubs is now a reality with the Fiber Distributed Data Interface, which offers transmission speeds of up to 100M bps. Several economical, albeit limited-distance, alternatives are offered over ubiquitous twisted-pair wiring, including 100Base-T and 100VG-AnyLAN. LAN hubs are also available that offer high-speed ATM switching enterprisewide. Another type of device, the bandwidth controller, is available for assembling low-speed 56K or 64K bps channels into economical high-speed pipes to support high-bandwidth applications over the public network.

Communications already plays an important role in the data center, and recent developments in this area will strengthen its role there. To aid the data center operations manager in keeping up with rapidly changing technologies, this chapter examines the key advances in communications in the context of corporate networking and applications requirements. In particular, this chapter examines developments in:

- optical fiber (e.g., line technologies, such as asymmetric and high-bit-rate digital subscriber line)
- cellular digital packet data
- T1 and T3
- X.25 frame relay
- integrated services digital network
- switched multimegabit data services
- asynchronous transfer mode
- synchronous optical network
- fiber-distributed data interface

OPTICAL FIBER

More computer and telephony applications are being developed that require the bandwidth that can only be provided by optical fiber. Carriers have been installing fiber-optic cable when it can be provided at a cost that is comparable to other transport modes, such as copper, or when competition from alternative access providers forces them to take counter measures. Thus, the carriers are committed to providing a fiber backbone as close to the point of service as is cost effective.

However, if the telephone companies are to offer advanced services in support of such bandwidth-intensive applications as multimedia, document imaging, and videoconferencing, they must increase as much as possible the transmission capacity of existing twisted-pair wiring in the local loop — and do so without further delay. Fiber to the customer premises would be best, but replacing existing arrangements could cost billions of dollars and will likely take 25 years to complete.

Asymmetric Digital Subscriber Line. One of the most promising local-loop upgrade technologies is asymmetric digital subscriber line (ADSL). This technology allows for the transmission of more than 6M bps over existing twisted-pair copper wiring. ADSL carves up the local loop bandwidth into several independent channels suitable for any combination of services, including LAN to LAN data transfers, ISDN, and plain old telephone service (POTS). The electronics at both ends of the ADSL compensate for line impairments, increasing the reliability of high-speed transmissions.

High-Bit-Rate Digital Subscriber Line. An alternative to ADSL is high bit-rate digital subscriber line technology (HDSL), which uses two full duplex pairs, each operating at 784K bps. This technology is an electronic technology for conditioning lines for heavy data usage without the use of repeaters over distances of up to 12,000 feet from the central office. Because approximately 85 percent of the local loops nationwide are within this distance, HDSL promises to have a significant impact on the embedded copper network. With the addition of a "doubler" technology, transmission distances can be increased even more, enabling HDSL to be used in all local loops and further easing the bottlenecks from fiber facilities.

Although HDSL was invented to solve telephone companies' T1 provisioning problems in the local loop, it is being extensively used in private networks as well. Universities, military bases, hospitals, corporate complexes, local governments, and other campus environments where multiple buildings require connections over relatively short distances, are ideal for HDSL solutions. Previously, campus applications, such as LAN-to-LAN, videoconferencing, CAD/CAM, and PBX networks were often restricted to 56K bps, due to cost and technical limitations.

CELLULAR DIGITAL PACKET DATA

Cellular digital packet data (CDPD) is a data-over-cellular standard for providing a LAN-like service over today's cellular voice networks. The CDPD infrastructure uses existing cellular systems to access a backbone router network, which uses the internet protocol (IP) to transport user data. PDAs, palmtops, and laptops running applications that use IP can connect to the CDPD service and gain access to other mobile computer users or to corporate computing resources that rely on wireline connections.

Because CDPD leverages the existing $20 billion investment in the cellular infrastructure, carriers can economically support data applications and avoid the cost of implementing a completely new network, as most competing technologies would require. CDPD also offers a transmission rate that is four times faster than most competing wide-area wireless services, many of which are limited to 4.8K bps or less.

In addition to supporting enhanced messaging services, including multicast, cellular paging, and national short-text messaging, CDPD extends client/server-based applications from the LAN environment into the wireless environment in support of mobile computer users. This extension can be used for such applications as database updates, schedule management, and field service support. However, the ultimate success of CDPD is closely tied to industry efforts to standardize its implementation. Using a universal standard for cellular packet data would allow users to roam and would simplify the introduction of wireless data services.

T1 AND T3

Traditional T1, which operates at 1.544M bps, is also undergoing innovation. For example, local exchanges are now being equipped to support switched T1 for on-demand (e.g., dial-up) service. Setup takes less than two seconds, providing a fast, efficient, and economical alternative to dedicated lines, which entail fixed monthly charges regardless of how little they are used. Some local-exchange carriers offer switched fractional T1, operating at 384K bps.

Some interexchange carriers offer fractional T3, in which a number of T1-equivalent pipes can be selected by customers to meet the bandwidth requirements of bandwidth-intensive applications without having to oversubscribe.

Nx64. A related innovation is Nx64 service, available from all major carriers. This allows users to build switched data pipes in bandwidth increments of 64K bps to support such applications as videoconferencing, CAD/CAM, or LAN interconnection. Channels of 64K bps can be added or dropped as necessary to support an application.

Inverse Multiplexer. A relatively new type of T1 device is the inverse multiplexer or bandwidth controller. Inverse multiplexing is an economical way to access the switched digital services of interexchange carriers because it provides bandwidth on demand, without having to subscribe to ISDN, which by comparison is more expensive and more complicated to configure.

Users dial up the appropriate increment of bandwidth needed to support a given application and pay for the number of 56K bps local-access channels needed. Channels can even be added or dropped during the transmission if bandwidth requirements change. Once transmission is completed, the channels are taken down. This eliminates the need for private leased lines to support temporary applications.

Fractional T3

T3 represents the equivalent of 28 T1 lines operating at the DS3 rate of 44.736M bps. With T3, users gain the additional bandwidth needed for a new generation of bandwidth-intensive applications, as well as traditional LAN-to-LAN and host-to-host interconnection. The absence of an optical standard for DS3 restricts the user's ability to mix and match equipment from different manufacturers. Customers must negotiate the types of optical interfaces to be placed in the interexchange carrier's serving office. In contrast to the more widely available T1 lines, T3 requires special construction for the local channel, from CPE to POP. Thus, T3 local-access lines are provided on an individual basis and usually entail high installation costs.

To broaden the appeal of T3, some carriers are offering fractional T3. With fractional T3, users can order bandwidth in T1 increments up to the full T3 rate of 44.736M bps. This service is designed for users who need more than the 1.544M-bps rate offered by T1, but less than the full bandwidth offered by T3 to support the interconnection of Token-Ring or Ethernet LANs. This enables corporate locations to share such high-bandwidth applications as document imaging, CAD/CAM, and bulk file transfers between LANs or hosts. In the case of LANs, a bridge or router is used for interconnection through the public network. The public network appears as an extension of the LAN.

X.25

X.25 was developed before digital switching and transmission technology became available. Because networks suffered at that time from interference from noise, X.25 relied on a store-and-forward method of data communication to ensure error-free transmission. When errors arrive at a network node, a request for retransmission is sent to the originating node, which retains a copy of the packets until they are acknowledged. This process is repeated at each network node until the data is delivered to its destination.

Although X.25 is highly reliable, today's digital networks have rendered unnecessary its stringent error-correction and other overhead functions. Network throughput can be greatly increased by leaving out these processing-intensive functions and relegating them to the customer premises equipment, as is done with frame relay. Despite the advances made with frame relay technology, the popularity of X.25 remains high.

Because frame relay is often compared to X.25, managers have become more informed about X.25 and its role in supporting value-added and dial-up applications, data entry, short file transfers, and financial and point-of-sale transactions. X.25's error correction is particularly useful for data communications to international locations where high-quality digital facilities still are largely unavailable. Although X.25 has been eclipsed by frame relay and switched multimegabit data services (SMDS), there have been advances in X.25.

Most X.25 networks operate at 56K bps, but some vendors have increased the transmission speed of their X.25 offerings to T1 rates and faster, making them more effective for LAN interconnection. Speeds as high as 6M bps performance are supported by some packet switches. Currently available are integrated switches that support both circuit and packet switching — the most appropriate switching method is selected in real time according to applications requirements. Also available are X.25 gateways to frame relay, SMDS, and other data services.

FRAME RELAY

Frame relay is a packet technology that offers performance advantages over X.25 while allowing users to more easily interconnect high-speed LANs over the WAN.

The concept behind frame relay is simple: protocol sensitivity, unnecessary overhead functions, and associated processing at each network node — all characteristic of X.25 — are eliminated to obtain higher transmission rates. The reliability of digital links enables frame relay service, because error correction and flow control already exist at the network and transport layers of most computer communication protocol stacks. Because these functions have been relegated to the edges of the network rather than placed at every node along a path, as in X.25, bad frames are simply discarded. Upon error detection, customer premises equipment at each end of the path requests and implements retransmissions.

Frame relay is optimized to transmit traffic in bursts, which is the way applications traverse the LAN. Therefore, when interconnecting geographically separate LANs, organizations should consider frame relay service. It is often cost-justified for sites only 750 miles apart, roughly the distance between New York City and Chicago. Frame relay also allows a variable frame size to make the most efficient use of available bandwidth. Frame relay's variable-length frames also mesh well with the variable-length packets used in TCP/IP, OSI, and DECnet.

Today's frame relay services are based on permanent virtual connections (PVCs) that correspond to the organization's network nodes. Node addresses are stored in each switching point on the network so that frames can be routed accordingly. For each PVC, the customer chooses a committed information rate (CIR) that supports the application, and the carrier bills for it accordingly. In frame relay, a 256K bps virtual connection can handle bursts of up to 1M bps. However, too many users exceeding their CIRs at the same time creates the possibility of the network becoming congested and of frames being discarded. Fortunately, carriers overprovision their frame relay networks to guard against this situation.

As companies continue to move from the host-centric data center to the distributed computing environment, the major carriers are starting to offer managed services that address the specific needs of System Network Architecture users. The advantages of frame relay over leased lines are clear-cut, especially for SNA users with many remote locations that must be tied into one or more hosts. Among them are the following:

- Frame relay PVCs replace expensive SDLC and BSC multidrop networks between the host and branch offices.
- Consolidating connections through frame relay eliminates costly serial line interface coupler (SLIC) ports on FEPs while increasing performance.
- WAN access extends the useful lives of SDLC/BSC controllers and 3270 terminals.

- The availability of systems network architecture (SNA) connections is increased by allowing controllers to take advantage of WAN connections with multiple host paths.

A managed frame relay service includes the frame relay access devices (FRADs) — leased or purchased — that transport SNA traffic over the PVCs. FRADs are more adept than routers at congestion control and ranking traffic according to priority. Some FRADs multiplex multiple SNA/SDLC devices onto a single PVC, instead of requiring a separate PVC for each attached device, resulting in even greater cost savings.

For a legacy SNA shop that does not have the expertise or resources, a carrier-managed frame relay service is a viable option, especially because frame relay networks are much more difficult to configure, administer, and troubleshoot than private lines. All of this activity can be outsourced to the carrier. The frame relay services themselves are priced attractively. On average, the frame relay service costs about 25 percent less than the equivalent private network. In some cases, discounts of up to 40 percent are possible.

INTEGRATED SERVICES DIGITAL NETWORK

Services built around the Integrated Services Digital Network (ISDN) primary rate interface (PRI) rely on switched T1 facilities. Of the 24 64K bps channels, 23 are bearer channels used for voice or data applications, and the twenty-fourth — the D channel — supports call-management functions.

ISDN has enabled early users to eliminate modem and infrequently used dedicated lines and to economically back up dedicated lines. The ISDN automatic number identification feature has also enabled some users to build new applications that integrate the traditionally separate domains of computer databases and voice communications. In this type of application, customer data is retrieved from a database and displayed at a terminal as the call is routed to a customer service representative. This arrangement improves customer response and employee productivity.

Another innovative use of ISDN comes in the form of improved call routing. Without actually connecting the call, ISDN's signaling channel first determines whether a PBX or automated call distributor (ACD) can handle it. If not, the call is forwarded to a PBX or ACD at another location that can take the call. This arrangement is useful for businesses spread across different time zones in that they can extend normal business hours. It also provides failure protection, so that if one location experiences an outage, another location can take the calls.

After a slow start, ISDN PRI is finally gaining user acceptance for such practical applications as network restoral, performance control, and peak traffic handling. The ISDN basic rate interface (BRI), which offers two bearer channels of 64K bps each and one 16K bps signaling channel, also is undergoing a resurgence, supporting such high-demand applications as computer-telephony integration (CTI), telecommuting, and Internet access. Many communications servers on the LAN now support ISDN, as do communications controllers in the host environment. Because ISDN service uses digital lines, users benefit from improved reliability, as well as from faster call setup time.

SWITCHED MULTIMEGABIT DATA SERVICES

Switched Multimegabit Data Services (SMDS) is a high-speed, connectionless, cell-based service offered by the regional telephone companies. It is used primarily for linking LANs within a metropolitan area. It offers customers the economic benefits of shared transmission facilities, combined with the equivalent privacy and control of dedicated networks. SMDS is much easier to provision and manage than frame relay and, over short distances, SMDS can be more economical than frame relay.

Despite its advantages, however, SMDS has not fared well against frame relay. One reason for frame relay's popularity is that it became available nationwide at a very early stage, whereas SMDS was promoted as a regional service. Only recently has SMDS become available from long-distance providers. This may alleviate user concerns about being able to link far-flung corporate sites using SMDS. Another sticking point for SMDS has been that access was not available at speeds lower than T1. Now SMDS is routinely offered by the regional telephone companies at access speeds between 56K bps and 34M bps. With these improvements, the demand for SMDS should grow at a much faster clip in the foreseeable future.

ASYNCHRONOUS TRANSFER MODE

Asynchronous Transfer Mode (ATM), also known as cell relay, is a general-purpose switching method for multimedia (e.g., voice, data, image, and video). Whereas frame relay and SMDS use variable-length frames, the cell size used by ATM is fixed at 53 bytes. This fixed size facilitates the switching of cells by hardware-based routing mechanisms, enabling operation at extremely high speeds. ATM speeds are scalable and can exceed 2.5G bps over optical fiber.

Despite the need to break larger variable-rate frames into fixed-size cells, the latency of ATM is orders-of-magnitude less than frame relay alone. For example, on a five-node network spanning 700 miles, ATM exhibits 0.3m-second latency vs. 60m-second latency for frame relay at T1 speeds. (At T3, the latency of ATM is only 0.15m seconds.) Thus, ATM makes for fast, reliable switching and eliminates the potential congestion problems of frame relay networks.

A nonblocking switching method, ATM virtually eliminates the buildup of congestion that can hamper the performance of campus LANs and inter-campus backbones. ATM hubs also allow networks to grow smoothly. Only switching capacity needs be added to handle increases in traffic; the user interfaces are not changed. ATM hubs are star-wired with direct links to every attached device. This configuration not only minimizes network management overhead but facilitates the collection of statistics for fault isolation, accounting, administration, and network planning.

ATM provides the features necessary for successful multimedia applications. Specifically, it has the ability to define different traffic types, with each traffic type delivering a different quality of service based on the unique properties associated with it. The traffic type that supports multi-media applications is called constant bit rate (CBR) service. CBR supplies a fixed-bandwidth virtual circuit, which addresses the special handling needs of delay-sensitive multimedia applications — those that contain real-time video and voice, for example. The quality of service is negotiated with the network. The applications themselves can do the negotiation through native ATM interface, or such interfaces as LAN emulation, an ATM Forum standard, and classic IP can perform the negotiation for the applications over ATM.

When the quality of service is negotiated with the network, there are performance guarantees that go along with it: maximum cell rate, available cell rate, cell transfer delay, and cell loss ratio. The network reserves the full bandwidth requested by the connection. There is no data rate limit for CBR connections, nor is there a limit on how long a connection can transmit at the maximum cell rate, otherwise known as the peak cell rate (PCR). The PCR is the maximum data rate that the connection can support without risking data loss. Any traffic above the specified rate risks being dropped by the network, whereas traffic below the specified rate will fail to satisfy the needs of the application.

These and the other advantages of ATM — including low latency, high throughput, and scalability — will one day make it the network of choice for supporting new, high-bandwidth multimedia applications, as well as legacy LAN and TCP/IP traffic. Meanwhile, ATM has been slow to take off because of the start-up costs of implementation. On the WAN side, carriers must invest in a new overlay infrastructure — something they have been slow in doing. Likewise, on the LAN side, companies must invest in new hubs, server interfaces, and workstation adapters. In some cases, new cabling may also be required.

SYNCHRONOUS OPTICAL NETWORK

Synchronous Optical Network (SONET) technology allows the full potential of the fiber-optic transmission medium to be realized. SONET standards specify transmission rates that start at 51.84M bps and reach to 2.488G bps and make provisions for transmission rates of 13G bps. Throughout this decade and beyond, SONET will gradually replace the proprietary T3 asynchronous networks of today.

With the same fiber cable that supports asynchronous networks, transmission capacity can be increased one-thousandfold by using end-to-end SONET equipment. SONET also supports a variety of current and emerging carrier services, including ATM, SMDS, and BISDN, increasing their reliability through embedded management functions.

Most of the activity in SONET deployment has been in building fiber rings that offer customers fail-safe data communications in major metropolitan areas. SONET equipment can reroute traffic instantly if a section of the network fails or becomes disabled. This level of reliability is increasingly becoming a critical requirement for businesses whose networks are becoming more data intensive with each passing year.

Today's self-healing SONET ring networks are capable of operating at 622M bps. Within 50m-seconds of a cable cut, customer traffic running over the primary path is automatically routed along the backup path, with no loss of data. This recovery process is implemented by the SONET Add-Drop Multiplexer (ADM), which duplicates and sends the data in opposite directions over the dual paths. When the signals reach a common point on the network, they are compared, then one set is discarded, while the other is delivered to the destination. If the primary path is disrupted, the data on the backup path is passed on to the destination.

Although the carriers have been installing SONET rings in major metropolitan areas at a pace that has been keeping up with customer demand, they are expected to step up their deployments of SONET. For many telcos, the cost-benefit threshold has been crossed; that is, the financial incentives of SONET deployment now exceed the costs of new installations.

FIBER DISTRIBUTED DATA INTERFACE

There is no question that traditional Ethernet and Token Ring LANs are beginning to get bogged down by the added bandwidth requirements of CAD/CAM, document imaging, collaborative computing, and multimedia applications. Fiber Distributed Data Interface (FDDI) backbones offer 100M bps of bandwidth that can alleviate potential bottlenecks. FDDI uses a token-passing scheme similar to Token Ring and a dual-ring fault protection scheme similar to SONET.

Normally considered a private networking solution for office environments, FDDI is now being offered as a wide-area network service by some carriers. Bell Atlantic, for example, provides a service to extend 100M-bps FDDI LANs across WANs. The service, called Full FDDI, is a response to requests from financial firms that wanted to use this kind of service together with a similar one offered by New York Telephone. The financial companies wanted to interconnect offices in New York City with data centers in New Jersey. The only difference between the two services is that Bell Atlantic places FDDI concentrators on customers' premises, while under New York Telephone's service, called Enterprise Service FDDI, concentrators are located at the carrier's central office.

Optical fiber equipment and adapters are still too expensive for FDDI deployment throughout the enterprise. An economical alternative to FDDI in the office environment is the twisted-pair distributed data interface (TPDDI). TPDDI offers the same speed as FDDI over ordinary twisted-pair wiring at distances of up to 100 meters (328 feet) from station to hub, which is enough to accommodate the wiring schemes of most office environments. TPDDI is designed to help users make an easy transition to 100M-bps transmission at the workstation level, in support of bandwidth-intensive data applications.

For companies with large investments in Ethernet, other 100M-bps technologies worth considering are 100Base-T, also known as Fast Ethernet, and 100VG-AnyLAN, a non-standard Ethernet extension technology. The major difference between the two is that 100Base-T preserves the contention access scheme of pure Ethernet, while 100VG-AnyLAN dispenses with it.

CONCLUSION

Data center managers are under increasing pressure to get all the value possible out of communications equipment and services, as well as to control the cost of networks. Despite these pressures, companies continue to make investments in applications and technologies out of a desire to gain competitive advantage. In implementing new applications and running them over various combinations of services, media and equipment, a balance of efficiency and economy can be achieved to obtain or sustain that advantage.

Telephone companies and interexchange carriers recognize that their financial futures hinge on their ability to provide data communications services that can support new and emerging applications. With data traffic already surpassing voice traffic on many corporate networks, the arrival of efficient and economical data communications services, such as frame relay and SMDS, is welcome and timely.

At the same time, digital communications over fiber-optic networks is becoming more available and cost justifiable. Such older forms of data communication as X.25, ISDN, and T-carrier have also undergone innovation in recent years. Data communications already play a major role in data center operations, and developments in this field will strengthen this role.

Chapter 57
The Emerging Advantage of xDSL Technology
Andres Llana, Jr.

SOME OF THE FLAVORS OF XDSL TECHNOLOGY have been around for awhile but sold under a different label. However, for the most part, end users just do not care what it is called, so long as it provides more bandwidth at less cost than before. Currently, Digital Subscriber Line (DSL) technology comes in several popular flavors: asymmetrical DSL (ADSL), high bit-rate DSL (HDSL), symmetric DSL (SDSL), or very high speed DSL (VDSL). There is also rate adaptive ADSL (RADSL). All of these are collectively referred to as xDSL, where x is the designator for the service.

In the proper setting, xDSL is capable of supporting any specific user bandwidth requirement given the local availability of copper. This is fine as long as one is the local exchange carrier (LEC), and one owns the copper. (See Exhibit 57-1.)

As a result of earlier initiatives by state and federal agencies to deregulate the "local loop," a new group of end users has emerged to benefit from this largesse. This emerging group of digital subscriber line (DSL) service users has now become accustomed to the "always connected" convenience of high-speed access to the Internet. These charter users, joined by an expanding group of Internet users, continue to want "more for less."

While these initiatives have not been well received by the incumbent local exchange carrier (ILEC) and the Regional Bell Operating Companies (RBOCs), these changes have altered forever the provisioning of copper local loops.

Because the RBOCs and their LECs have been slow to deploy DSL services, a new breed of aggressive service provider has come on the local scene. With little in the way of traditional organizational structures to get in the way, Competitive Local Exchange Carriers (CLECs) and Internet

Exhibit 57-1. xDSL.

xDSL technology is potentially a lower-cost replacement for dedicated 56Kbps local loops used to tie into a frame relay service. Enterprise network owners should investigate the availability of dry copper within their serving Central Office as one alternative to the more-expensive dedicated service. In addition, enterprise network architects might also negotiate with their competitive local exchange carriers (CLECs). Some enterprise network operators have been able to greatly improve their network access arrangements using lower-cost xDSL links to their frame relay service provider's POP. In addition, where there was a requirement for Internet access or a shadow network to back up the primary network, xDSL links provided full-time online access at less cost. Some network operators found that they could deploy a DSLAM behind their DMARC and use dry copper to link LANs or desktop terminals to the Internet for an "always on" connection.

Service Providers (ISPs) are charging ahead to get new local loop business at reduced prices.

Thus far, they have been able to provide local loop access on an unbundled basis, utilizing the local embedded copper. These CLECs and ISPs, deploying xDSL technology, have been able to provide their customers with a very cost-effective, high-speed data service.

WHAT HAS CHANGED

The original Digital Subscriber Line (DSL) service was introduced as ISDN in the 1980s. This technology compressed 160Kbps into an 80KHz bandwidth of the local loop. ISDN utilized a four-level PAM modulation (2 Binary, 1 Quaternary) "2b1Q" to reach the range of 18,000 feet.

High Bit-Rate Digital Subscriber Line (HDSL) came along in the early 1990s and used the same 2 Binary, 1 Quaternary (2b1Q) line coding to support T1 services. HDSL made it possible to provision loops of up to 12,000 feet long using 24 AWG. Some vendors are offering equipment that can extend this reach to 18,000 feet.

HDSL is more robust than the old T1 service, which required repeaters every few hundred yards. More advanced HDSL equipment, on the other hand, has eliminated many of the problems associated with provisioning T1 service, which resulted in much lower rates for local T1 access.

SOME OTHER FLAVORS OF DSL

Asymmetrical Digital Subscriber Line (ADSL) service came about in the 1992/1993 timeframe as a vehicle for offering video services to the home. Another DSL technology, Rate Adaptive Digital Subscriber Line (ADSL), came along as a means of allowing a transceiver to automatically adjust line speed to attain the highest level of speed over a given loop.

ADSL and RADSL promise to deliver rates of about 7Mb downstream with upstream links of about 1Mb; and while ADSL and RADSL are supposed to run up to 18,000 feet, to get the promised 7Mb downstream, the user would have to be very close to the serving central office (CO). While all of this technology sounds great, one needs to focus on the real-life application of technology for thousands of end users. Today, the majority of domestic use is focused on the World Wide Web; however, there is a growing number of Small Office Home Office (SOHO) users that require multi-network access as a means of directly or indirectly earning a living. Therefore, it is ADSL/RADSL service that ultimately offers a solution to the needs of the SOHO user.

Today, business applications have grown to stress higher speed access to public and private network infrastructures. The real-life issue is providing access to the corporate or public network without spending large amounts of money for local loop access.

Initially, HDSL technology reduced the cost for provisioning T1 services because it eliminated the need for extensive engineering, expensive repeaters, and the huge labor costs associated with deploying traditional copper wire T1 services. The adoption of HDSL technology allowed the LECs to make use of their copper infrastructure to offer more competitive T1 local loops without the burden of high provisioning costs.

Symmetrical Digital Subscriber Line (SDSL) is similar to HDSL in that vendor equipment supports the same line encoding scheme: 2 Binary, 1 Quaternary (2b1Q), which avoids any conflict when installed on the LECs' local copper. In addition, depending on vendor equipment and desired line speed, SDSL differs from HDSL in that the loop reach for an SDSL line has the potential of being somewhat greater than HDSL.

Like its predecessor, SDSL technology has become an enabler for high-speed services at a much more affordable price. This is due to that fact that the application of SDSL technology, like HDSL, causes no change in services and uses the same embedded copper infrastructure as HDSL. Potentially, SDSL technology, where applicable, provides lower install and monthly recurring costs for the installation of a circuit capable of supporting up to 1.5Mb of service.

Perhaps the largest demand for service has come from the Internet community of users and their access to the World Wide Web for the conduct of their business. Today, access to the Web has become the medium of choice for the dissemination of information to business associates and customers alike.

SDSL ENABLES ISP SERVICES

Historically, the gateway to any network — either private or public — was through a local copper loop that connected the end user to the network through the central office. The service providers or networks contracted with the serving utility to provide connectivity at the edge of their network. The end user or customer paid a high price for connectivity to the network, with the monthly price being determined by the available bandwidth of the line. The arrival of SDSL equipment, together with enabling legislation that supports competition at the local level, has changed the service arrangements at the local level. Because SDSL equipment requires a physical connection to the local loop, an ISP must locate a Digital Subscriber Line Access Multiplexer (DSLAM) within 12,000 to 18,000 feet of a subscriber. The ISP can do this by locating a DSLAM adjacent to the central office. Unconditioned "dry copper" is ordered from the LEC to connect the subscriber's location through the central office to the ISP's DSLAM adjacent to the central office.[1] T1, multiple T1, or T3 facilities connect the DSLAM to the ISP central hub. This arrangement gives the end user a direct link to the Internet at speeds of from 64Kbps through to 1.5Mb depending on the distance from the DSLAM. (See Exhibit 57-2.)

Another variation is the location of a DSLAM on the premises of an industrial park or campus. Located at a central location (usually the facility's demarcation point [DEMARC]), DSL lines are extended to users around the industrial park or campus area. (See Exhibit 57-3.) The DSLAM serves to concentrate all of the DSL lines and provide high-speed access to the Internet via T1/T3 access to a central ISP hub. In a multitenant industrial park, it is estimated that at least 200 or more users would be required to make this business model a success, although fewer tenants would work where higher-speed access is required. On the other hand, enterprise network operators have found that the application of dry copper can be used to support the connection of local offices or remote buildings that are served by the same central offices. They have also used dry copper and a local DSLAM as a more cost-effective method for concentrating a number of LANs or desktop terminals into the Internet.

Until the advent of more advanced xDSL technology, local loop lengths were limited to end users located within a 2.5-mile radius of the central office. However, the newer SDSL equipment utilizing proprietary technology can potentially lengthen the reach of a dry copper circuit's effectiveness to 30,000 feet at a lower bandwidth of 64Kbps. However, with incremental speed increases to 1Mb, the circuit length conversely would get shorter. For example, Bellcore, the former research arm of the Regional Bell Operating Companies, has conducted SDSL tests with single pair service, which was extended out to 24,700 feet at 192Kbps. These extensions are possible through continual advances in SDSL technology. For example, TUT Systems of Pleasant Hill, California, deploys a patented process called FastCopper™ technology that removes ambient electronic noise and other distortions in the environment where copper pairs are used. The focus of

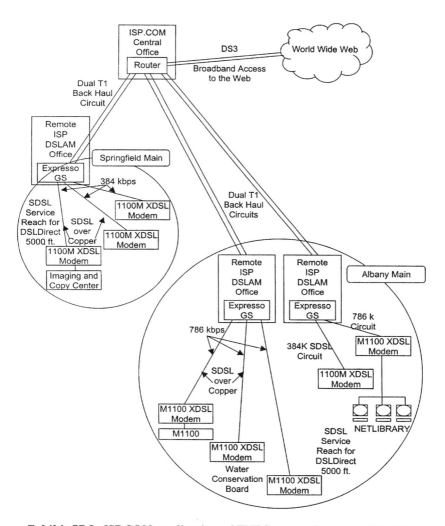

Exhibit 57-2. ISP.COM application of TUT Systems Expresso SDLAM.

this technology is aimed at noise reduction circuits, analog and digital signal processing circuits, and digital modulation. This technology makes possible the deployment of dry circuits to within a radius of five to six miles, rather than the more limiting factor of one to two miles. An extension in the central office service range provides support for increased bandwidth for private metropolitan networks as well as access to the Internet at high speeds for power users.

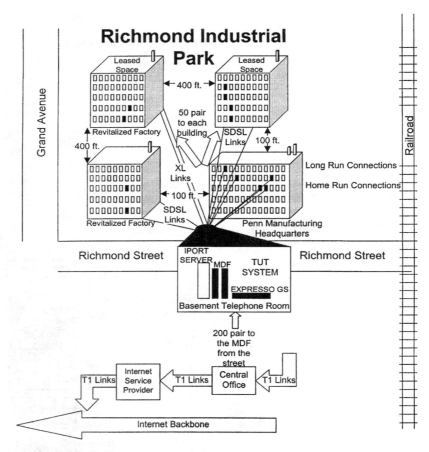

Exhibit 57-3. Richmond Industrial Park redeploying copper lines using DSL technology.

DSLDirect AND ISP.COM

ISP.COM is an Eastern Internet Service Provider, serving eastern businesses with high-speed Internet access. ISP.COM provides direct support to a number of downtown office buildings in several eastern cities. At present, these internal connections are brought to an Ethernet switch at the DEMARC and then in turn brought back to a TUT Systems Expresso DSLAM that is connected to the ISP.COM DS3 central hub via a fiber link. (See Exhibit 57-2.)

DSLDirect

ISP has recently introduced DSLDirect for direct high-speed Internet service for small and medium-sized Albany and Springfield businesses. The

DSLDirect service utilizes TUT Systems Expresso DSLAM units to provide direct access via dry copper, which is a more cost-effective solution than previous provisioning methods. Using these low-cost copper circuits, the ISP is able to provide 384Kbps and 768Kbps Internet connection speeds in direct competition with other larger service providers. The ISP service is not a bridged connection, as is the local RBOC service offering. All of the ISP DSLDirect end-user packets are shipped directly to the Internet, without being routed over several switches to the designated Internet switch.

With ISP DSLDirect service, the customer is linked directly to ISP Expresso DSLAM, which, in turn, is linked via multiple T1 links back to the ISP hub and their DS3 connection to the Internet. This in effect provides customers with their own dedicated circuit into the Internet.

The Expresso DSLAM, when first put on a dry copper pair, will adjust its speed depending on the line condition. When it finds its level, the speed remains constant. This has been a very helpful feature because customers can order a 384Kbps line but get a slightly better level of service. Because the level of service on the Expresso DSLAM is software adjustable from 64Kbps through to 1.2Mb in 64Kbps increments, ISP has a great deal of flexibility in serving the needs of its customers using SDSL technology. To use this service, the customer must purchase or lease a TUT Systems 1100M DSL modem/router for about $495, or $30 per month. There is also an ISP charge of about $175 (384Kbps), $275 (786Kbps), or $375 (1.2Mb per month) for the desired level of Internet service. These charges can vary from one region of the country to another.

Presently, DSLDirect is available to businesses located in the immediate vicinity of the Albany Main and Springfield Main (central office) locations. Additional central office sites will be added to the DSLDirect service offering in the future. (See Exhibit 57-2.)

ANOTHER SERVICE MARKET

Just about every service provider and equipment manufacturer is expanding into the enhanced multiple dwelling units (MDU) Internet service provisioning market. This market is comprised of over 40,000 office buildings, 3.5 million hotels, and as many up-market apartment complexes whose tenants have two or more PCs. Companies like Copper Mountain, Paradyne, and TUT Systems have organized special marketing efforts to support the multiple-dwelling market.

For example, TUT Systems has put together an integrated support service through a network of value-added resellers (VARs) that will provide the hotel or a multiple-dwelling property owner like a real estate trust (REIT), with a turnkey operation. This turnkey solution utilizes the TUT Systems HomeRun™ 2 technology together with an IPORT™ Internet

Access System premium Content Billing Platform System to provide an integrated solution called the Connected Community. This is a complete service package sold by local VARs that provides a full package of services.

The advantage of the Connected Community package to the property owner is the fact that there is nothing for the property owner to do. The VAR handles all the arrangements for Internet access with the local CLEC/ISP service provider. All arrangements for equipment configuration and installation are arranged by the VAR. In addition, the equipment can be configured and priced based on the property owner's immediate requirements. Therefore, costs for equipment can be based on present need. As the property owner's end-user requirements expand, additional equipment can be purchased as needed. Another cost-saving feature is the ability of the TUT Systems HomeRun™ technology to use existing standard telephone lines to deliver service without affecting the existing voice service. This solution eliminates much of the cost associated with rewiring a hotel or MDU for data transmission and Internet access.

MORE THAN JUST SPEED

The xDSL market focus until recently has been on speed and low-cost access. While DSL is a very compelling technology, it is worth mentioning that there are other competitors that offer other products and services. For example, a growing number of companies offer cable modems and Internet appliances that will support delivery of competing services over cable.

Recognizing the requirement for something more than bandwidth, service providers like GTE, U.S. West, Bell Atlantic, and others have announced an ADSL product. With over 700 million phone lines worldwide, service providers can take advantage of this technology to offer an extensive number of voice and data services.

ADSL offers great promise as an alternative to cable because it supports voice and data over the same twisted pair. Further, advanced xDSL line coding algorithms allow for the effective division of the frequency spectrum on copper telephone wire to support voice and data. (See Exhibit 57-4.) With the voice spectrum confined to the 4KHz baseband, the upstream and downstream channels can be dedicated to data. This allows the service provider to offer multimegabit data service while leaving voice service intact. Thus, ADSL connects two different entities — voice and data — all over the same physical wire pair. Recently, the International Telecom Union (ITU) has determined G-lite (G.992.2) to be the standard for ADSL-based service products. Many of the DSLAM manufacturers and service providers have settled on this standard so as to support interoperability. This will greatly simplify the acquisition of CPE (customer premise equipment) and the cross-integration of services across the country and internationally.

Exhibit 57-4. SDSL technology at risk.

Not all of the RBOCs have been happy with the rush by the CLECs and ISPs to take advantage of dry copper tariffs. For example, hearings were held before the utility commissions in some western states in an effort to drop the dry copper tariff, as it is known. While Nebraska allowed the discontinuance of the dry copper tariff, Colorado did not allow this measure to take place. Other states are considering the matter. Utility commissioners in other jurisdictions throughout the United States should be mindful of this because the Telecommunications Act of 1996 did specifically provide for competition at the local level. SDSL offers a number of opportunities for Competitive Local Exchange Carriers (CLEC), Independent Telephone Operating Companies (ITOCs), Internet Service Providers (ISPs), and enterprise network owners to deploy dry copper circuits to the advantage of the subscribing end user. For this reason, one should protect the embedded base of dry copper that forms much of the basic infrastructure of the U.S. communications system. This is a resource that has long been paid for by subscribers and should really be declared part of the public domain.

THE NEXT FRONTIER

As the ADSL G-lite services begin to take hold among the service providers, a new segment of the networking marketplace is poised for rapid deployment. Networks in the home represent the next window of opportunity for all service providers because ADSL splitterless services make it possible to support the delivery of service over a single pair of telephone cables.

To address this market, AT&T Wireless, AMD Networking, Hewlett-Packard, IBM, Lucent Technologies, Rockwell, and TUT Systems have come together to establish the Home Phoneline Networking Alliance (Home-PNA). This alliance was formed to develop the specifications for interoperability for all home network devices.

Subsequently, TUT Systems, who had announced their HomeRun™ technology early in 1998, licensed this technology to Lucent Technologies. As a result, the other members of the HomePNA group adopted HomeRun™ technology as the first specification for home networking. This move will serve to greatly facilitate the introduction of more than just bandwidth to the consumer market. HomeRun™ provides support for splitterless 1Mbps Ethernet transmission over existing telephone lines already in the home. When the proper customer premise equipment (CPE) is deployed, the consumer can establish a home-based local area network (LAN). In this operating environment, multiple applications can be run in the home with "always on" access to the Internet where there may be access to specific databases.

Notes

1. An ISP DSLAM can only be used to transport the subscriber to the Internet. It cannot be used to switch traffic at the CO.
2. The HomeRun™ technology has been adopted by the Home Phoneline Network Alliance as the standard home network LAN technology.

Chapter 58
Preparing for Cable Modems
Gilbert Held

DURING 1995, THE USE OF THE INTERNET EXPANDED CONSIDERABLY, with tens of thousands of corporations, universities, government agencies, and individuals creating home pages on servers, while tens of millions of users surfed the World Wide Web. As corporations began to recognize the value of the Internet for building software applications, promoting products and services, and locating as well as disseminating information, the addition of graphics to World Wide Web home pages literally slowed Web surfing operations to a crawl, adversely affecting user productivity. Whereas the replacement of 14.4K bps modem by state-of-the-art 28.8K bps devices has assisted many users in speeding up their Internet search operations, even at that operating rate the display of a typical Web page containing one or two graphic images can result in a delay of 10 to 15 seconds as the picture is "painted" on a monitor.

Recognizing the operating limitations associated with transmissions via the public switched-telephone network, as well as looking for an additional source of revenue, several cable television (CATV) companies initiated broadband access trials to the Internet during 1995. Each of these trials involved the use of cable modems, which enable a personal computer (PC) to access the Internet via a common CATV coaxial cable at operating rates up to tens of millions of bits per second. Although cable modems are in their infancy, both independent market research organizations and many cable operators predict that within a few years, the installed base of this new type of communications device will rapidly grow to over 10 million modems.

Due to the advantages associated with obtaining high-speed Internet access, as well as the potential economics associated with the use of cable modems to obtain such access, data center managers should consider preparing their facility for the infrastructure required to use cable modems.

This chapter discusses the nature of cable modems and describes their operation. The scope of the discussion also includes the cabling infrastructure being developed to provide a megabit transmission facility

0-8493-0859-3/00/$0.00+$.50

to residences and businesses. The chapter outlines the cabling requirements for installation within buildings, requirements that are necessary to access this new high-speed information highway via the use of cable modems. The data center manager should have a background of knowledge concerning a rapidly evolving new technology and be able to support its use when corporate policy begins to include Internet issues.

MODEM FUNDAMENTALS

The ability to appreciate why cable modems are able to provide a transmission capability that is an order of magnitude or more than conventional modems used for transmission on the switched telephone network, requires knowledge of certain transmission concepts, including the Nyquist theorem. This section concentrates on the operation of conventional analog modems that are used on the switched telephone network. This can provide the data center manager with an understanding of why analog modems' operating rate is limited and how they may be able to overcome that operating rate limitation.

A conventional analog modem commonly used to transmit information over the switched telephone network is limited to a maximum operating rate of between 28.8K bps and 33.6K bps, with the rate achievable dependent upon the quality of the connection and according to the modulation technique employed. In theory, the maximum operating rate of an analog modem that has been designed for use on the switched telephone network is limited by the 4K Hz bandwidth provided by the communications carrier for a switched telephone channel.

In 1924, Nyquist proved, in what is now referred to as the Nyquist theorem, that the maximum signaling rate of a device is limited to twice the available bandwidth; beyond that rate, inter-symbol interference occurs and adversely affects the transmission. As an example, for the 4K Hz telephone channel, this means the maximum signaling rate of a modem used to transmit on that medium is limited to 8000 baud. Baud is a term used to indicate signal changes per second.

The Quadrature Amplitude Modulation Technique

The most commonly used modem modulation technique, quadrature amplitude modulation (QAM), uses a combination of phase and amplitude to convey the settings of a group of bits in one signal change, enabling four bits to be represented by one baud change. This in turn enables an 8000 baud signaling rate to transport data at a rate of 32K bps when QAM is used for modulation.

Due to the 4K Hz telephone channel limitation, however, data transmission rates are limited to approximately 32K bps, with a slightly higher rate of 33.6K bps recently achieved by a few modem vendors using a modified QAM technique. Although the incorporation of data compression into modems provides a potential doubling to quadrupling of modem throughput, to between 67.2K bps and 134.4K bps, the ability of a modem to compress data depends upon the susceptibility of data to the compression algorithm being used. Because that susceptibility varies considerably as a modem user performs different operations, the end result is a variable compression rate; even though it is not noticeable during file transfer operations, that variable rate becomes extremely noticeable during interactive operations. In addition, even with the ability to compress data at a high rate, the resulting information transfer rate of 134.4K bps pales by comparison to the operating rate obtainable through the use of cable modems. It is clear, however, that advances in modem and cabling technology are limited with respect to increasing the performance of modems used to communicate via the switched telephone network.

CABLE MODEMS

The key difference between an analog modem designed for use on the public switched telephone network and a cable modem is in the bandwidth of the channels they are designed to use. Cable TV uses RG-11 cable for the main CATV trunk and RG-59 cable from trunk distribution points into and through residences and offices. Both types of coaxial cable have 75 ohms impedance and support broadband transmission, which means that two or more channels separated by frequency can be simultaneously transported on the cable.

From Unidirectional to Bidirectional Systems

A cable TV broadcasting infrastructure uses 6M Hz channels within the bandwidth of RG-11 and RG-59 cable to transmit a TV channel. Most CATV systems are currently unidirectional, which means that TV signals are broadcast from the CATV system operator without any provision for receiving a return signal. This transmission limitation is gradually being overcome as CATV operators begin to add bidirectional amplifiers to their networks that, when they are installed, will support transmission from subscribers in the reverse direction to conventional TV signal broadcasts. This will enable CATV systems to support the standardized transmit frequency range of 5M Hz to 42M Hz, and receive a frequency range of 54M Hz to 550M Hz, with 6M Hz cable TV channels.

By using one or more 6M Hz cable TV channels, a cable modem obtains the use of a bandwidth that is 1500 times greater (6M Hz/4K Hz) than that provided by a voice channel on the switched telephone network. This means that the modem can support a signaling rate of twice the bandwidth, or 12M baud, on one TV channel, based upon the Nyquist theorem, before the occurrence of inter-symbol interference.

The primary difference between cable modems currently being used in field trials is in their use of one or more 6M Hz TV channels within the band of channels carried by a coaxial cable, and their methods of attachment to the CATV network. One cable modem manufactured by Zenith Network Systems, a subsidiary of Zenith Electronics of Glenview, Illinois, operates on 6M Hz channels at 4M bps to the subscriber, using a special filtering technique to prevent data channels from interfering with adjacent information, which can be in the form of either data or video, that would coexist with the data transmission provided by the cable modem. The uplink or return data rate occurs at 500K bps. Modem modulation is biphase shift key (BPSK), which means that two bits (bi) are encoded in each phase change, and the modem's phase changes are shifted in phase from one to another. This modem is also frequency-agile, which means it can be set to operate on any standardized channel on a broadband CATV system.

The Zenith cable modem is actually one portion of a series of components required for a PC to use the modem. A complete transmission system requires the use of a Zenith cable modem, Ethernet 10Base-T adapter card with a 15-conductor pin connector, and a 15-conductor shielded cable to connect the cable modem to the adapter. Exhibit 58-1 illustrates the cabling required to connect a PC to a CATV network via the use of a Zenith Network Systems cable modem.

When the adapter card is installed in the PC it, in effect, turns the computer into a client workstation. Because the adapter is an Ethernet 10Base-T card, this means that the channel being used by the cable modem operates as one long CSMA/CD Local Area Network, with each PC user competing

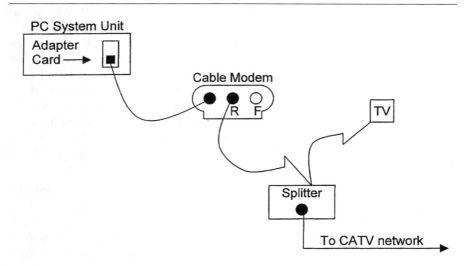

Exhibit 58-1. Cabling for a Zenith Network Cable Modem System.

with other PC users for access to the channel. Because of this, the CATV operator should segment its cable distribution system to limit the number of cable modems attached to any segment, similar to the manner in which conventional LANs are limited with respect to the maximum number of workstations that can be connected to the LAN.

The connector labeled "R" on the rear of the cable modem is a reverse cable connector designed for networks that use a single coaxial cable. The second connector, labeled "F," represents a forward cable connector that would be used if the modem were connected to a cable system that uses two cables. In such a system, one cable is dedicated to conventional CATV broadcasting through one-way amplifiers, which precludes reverse transmission on the same cable. This type of system also requires the use of a second cable to obtain a transmission capability in the reverse direction.

A High-Speed Cable Modem Architecture

In addition to the previously described cable modem based upon the exclusive use of RF technology and biphase shift key modulation, Zenith Electronics Corporation announced a high-speed cable modem architecture. This architecture is based on the use of 16-VSB (vestigial sideband), a technique developed by Zenith as part of the organization's high-definition research, as well as the 256 quadrature amplitude modulation technology. Through the use of more complex modulation techniques for which more data bits can be represented by one signal change, the Zenith modem architecture can support data rates up to 40M bps on a 6M Hz cable channel.

Recognizing the fact that many cable TV systems will be limited to one-way transmission in the foreseeable future because of the time and cost associated with upgrading the CATV infrastructure, Zenith plans to support a range of options and speeds for upstream data transmission. According to Zenith, both telephone (analog modulation) and RF return path transmission capabilities will be incorporated into different versions of this new family of cable modems. For many cable modem applications, such as Internet operations, the use of the switched network for a return path should provide an acceptable level of performance. The rationale for this is best noted by examining the communications interaction between a potential cable modem user and the cable network as a user searches out and accesses various points on the World Wide Web.

On the Web

When users access a Web page, they transmit a universal resource locator (URL) address that represents the document they wish to view. This address is transported using the HTTP within a packet. The HTTP consists of an address that totals fewer than 100 characters, which are used to frame the address to which the message is being transported, as well as the address of the originator of the request. The destination Web server uses the document address to locate the requested page on the server, retrieves it from disk, and forms a packet using the source address from the incoming packet as the destination address for the outgoing packets. If the requested document contains a full screen of text, the packet contain close to 2000 characters, because a full screen of text consists of 80 columns by 24 rows of data (i.e., 1920 characters). However, because a typical Web page contains one or more graphics, the total amount of data transmitted from the server to the user will be, in actuality, substantially more than 2000 characters. For example, it is assumed that the Web page in question includes a 3 in. x 3 in. photograph, drawing, or schematic diagram that has been scanned using a resolution of 300 dots per inch. Regardless of the color of the image, each square inch of the image requires 11,250 bytes of storage. If the image was scanned using a 256-color resolution, each pixel requires a byte to represent its color, resulting in 90,000 bytes of storage per square inch. Thus, a 3 in. x 3 in. color image requires 270,000 bytes of storage.

Because HTTP breaks large files into small packets for transmission, the image might be carried by a sequence of approximately 100 packets, each roughly 2700 bytes in length, to include packet overhead. Thus, the short, 100-character transmission from a user can result in a response of 280,000 bytes. Because a user connected to the Web typically clicks on hotlinks that represent document addresses to view other documents, most Web operations represent asymmetrical transmission, that is, more transmissions return to the user than the user actually originates. Thus, a high-speed cable channel with a low-speed reverse path occurring over the switched telephone network may actually be sufficient for most data transmission applications.

The previously described asymmetrical transmission operation of users was also recognized by Intel Corporation, which took it into consideration when designing its CablePort cable modem system. That cable modem is designed to provide an average downstream data rate of 27M bps and a 96K bps upstream rate. One interesting difference between Zenith and Intel concerning their cable modem systems is in the type of adapter card required to be used in the PC. Because Intel provides a higher downstream operating rate than what is usable by a 10Base-T adapter card, the user must install a Fast Ethernet(100M bps) adapter card in the PC to be able to use the Intel cable modem. Although no commercial costs were provided by Zenith or Intel for field trial operations, it is worth noting that a Fast Ethernet adapter has a retail cost of approximately $250, whereas a 10Base-T adapter can be obtained for less than $50.

A second difference between the Zenith and Intel modems concerns their upstream capability. Although Zenith's new architecture permits support of the switched telephone network for locations where CATV operators cannot provide reverse direction transmission, the Intel system did not offer this capability when this chapter was researched.

RECOMMENDED COURSE OF ACTION

Although the technology of cable modems is in its infancy, the data center manager can still plan for their use. Whereas the type of cable modem offered will depend upon the CATV operators' cable infrastructure (i.e., either unidirectional or bidirectional), as well as the cable modem vendor the data center manager selects, each cable modem requires the use of RG-11 coaxial cable. Thus, if the manager has previously installed such cabling as part of a legacy terminal to mainframe or legacy LAN wiring system and are considering its removal, he may wish to leave the cabling in place. If RG-11 cabling has not been installed, the data center manager may wish to consider contacting the local CATV operator to determine when cable modems will be supported and the type the operator intends to use. If it intends to use bidirectional transmission via RF modulation, the data center manager can develop a wiring plan that requires only the use of RG-11 cable. If the CATV operator says it intends to provide reverse transmission via the public switched telephone network, the wiring plan must be modified to ensure that each cable modem user will have an available telephone jack. By understanding how cable modems operate and planning the organization's wiring infrastructure to use this evolving technology, the data center manager will be prepared for its future use.

Chapter 59
Voice and Video on the LAN
Martin Taylor

VOICE AND DATA CONVERGENCE IN THE LAN has become a hot topic in the industry, thanks to advances in switching and processors, as well as the H.323 standard. This chapter first looks at the business reasons for considering the deployment of voice and video over the LAN and then discusses the technical issues and requirements. Topics include the value of voice and video on the LAN, infrastructure efficiencies, LAN technologies for integrated voice and video, and standards for LAN-based voice and video applications

Most desktops in enterprises today are equipped with two network connections: a LAN connection to the PC or workstation for data communications and a phone connection to the PBX for voice communications. The LAN and the PBX exist as two separate networks with little or no connectivity between them. Each has evolved to meet the very specific and differing needs of data and voice communications, respectively.

Despite much talk in the industry about the convergence of computers and communications, LANs and PBXs have not really moved any closer together during the last decade. In the mid-1980s, some PBX vendors sought to bring data services to the desktop via ISDN technology, but the advent of PCs requiring far more than 64K-bps communications bandwidth favored the emerging LAN standards of Ethernet and Token Ring. So far, most LAN vendors have not attempted to support voice communications on the LAN. But all this is about to change.

There are three key factors at work today that suggest why voice and data convergence in the LAN has become a hot topic in the industry:

1. the widespread acceptance of advanced LAN switching technologies, including ATM, which makes it possible for the first time to deliver reliable, high-quality, low-delay voice transmissions over the LAN

2. the emergence of the first standard for LAN-based videoconferencing and voice telephony, H.323, which removes objections about the use of proprietary protocols for voice and video over the LAN
3. the deployment of the latest generation of Intel processors, featuring MMX technology, which makes high-quality software-based, real-time voice and video processing feasible for the first time, and the new PC hardware architectures with Universal Serial Bus that permit voice and video peripherals to be attached without additional hardware inside the PC

This chapter first looks at the business reasons for considering the deployment of voice and video over the LAN and then discusses the technical issues and requirements.

THE VALUE OF VOICE AND VIDEO ON THE LAN

There are essentially two main kinds of motivation for considering voice and video on the LAN: the need to support new types of applications that involve real-time communications and the desire to improve the overall cost effectiveness of the local communications infrastructure.

New Types of Applications

Desktop videoconferencing, real-time multimedia collaboration, and video-based training are all examples of new kinds of applications that can benefit from the delivery of voice and video over the LAN.

The uptake of desktop videoconferencing has been held back by a combination of high costs and the difficulty of delivering appropriate network services to the desktop. Standards-based H.320 desktop videoconferencing systems require costly video compression and ISDN interface hardware, as well as the provision of new ISDN connections at the desktop alongside the LAN and the phone system. New systems based on the H.323 standard and designed to run over the LAN will leverage the processing power of the latest PCs and the existing switched LAN infrastructure, to lower cost and simplify deployment dramatically.

Desktop videoconferencing may be used either to support internal meetings and discussions between groups located at remote sites or to support direct interaction with customers and clients. For example, some enterprises in the mortgage lending business use videoconferencing to conduct mortgage approval interviews with potential borrowers, so as to greatly reduce the overall time to complete a mortgage sale.

Real-time collaboration applications, involving any mix of video and voice with data conferencing to support application sharing and interactive whiteboarding, provide a new way for individuals and small groups to collaborate and work together remotely in real time. This emerging class of applications, typified by Microsoft NetMeeting, is being evaluated by many enterprises, particularly for help desk applications.

By contrast, video-based training is already widely used in enterprise LANs. By delivering self-paced video learning materials to the desktop, training needs can be met in a more timely and less disruptive fashion than traditional classroom methods.

The growing popularity of these kinds of applications should be noted by network planners and designers. A preplanned strategy for local LAN upgrades to support voice and video will reduce the lead time for the deployment of these applications and enable the enterprise to move swiftly when the application need has been identified, to obtain the business benefits with the least possible delay.

Infrastructure Efficiencies

A single local communications infrastructure based on a LAN that handles data, voice, and video has the potential to cost less to own and operate than separate PBX and data-only LAN infrastructures.

The average capital cost of a fully featured PBX for large enterprises is between $700 and $750 per user, according to TEQConsult Group, a leading U.S. telecommunications consultancy. Furthermore, this is expected to rise slightly over the next few years as users demand more sophisticated features from their phone systems. It is not difficult to see how a switched LAN that has been enhanced to handle voice could provide a solution for telephony at a fraction of this cost.

Most large PBX installations are equipped with additional facilities such as voice mail and Interactive Voice Response systems for auto-attendant operation. These systems are typically connected directly to the PBX via proprietary interfaces, and they, too, represent major capital investments. With voice on the LAN, such voice-processing applications could be based on open server platforms and leverage the low-cost processing power and disk storage that is a feature of today's PC server market, thereby lowering the system's capital cost still further.

Separate PBX and LAN infrastructures each incur their own management and operational costs. For example, moves, adds, and changes require separate actions to patch physical LAN and voice connections and to update LAN log-on and voice directories. With telephony provided over a voice-enabled LAN supporting combined directory services, the management effort required to administer moves and changes would be substantially reduced.

These cost of ownership benefits come with a raft of usability improvements for telephony. The PC (with phone handset attached) becomes the communications terminal for making and receiving phone calls, and the processing power and graphical user interface of the PC can be leveraged to provide point-and-click call launch and manipulation. Features of PBXs such as call transfer, divert, and hold, which are hard to invoke from a phone keypad, become very easy to use from a Windows interface.

Incoming callers can be identified on the PC display by matching Calling Line Identifier with directory entries. And with voice mail and e-mail supported on a unified messaging platform such as Microsoft Exchange or Lotus Notes, all messages are accessible and manageable via a single user interface.

These usability benefits for voice telephony over the LAN also extend to videoconferencing — a single consistent user interface may be applied to both video and voice-only calls.

LAN TECHNOLOGIES FOR INTEGRATED VOICE AND VIDEO

The LAN technologies in widespread use today — Ethernet, Fast Ethernet, FDDI, and Token Ring — were not designed with the needs of real-time voice and video in mind. These LAN technologies provide "best effort" delivery of data packets, but offer no guarantees about how long delivery will take. Interactive real-time voice and video communications over the LAN require the delivery of a steady stream of packets with very low end-to-end delay, and this cannot generally be achieved with the current LAN technologies as they stand.

Asynchronous Transfer Mode (ATM)

At one time, there was a belief that ATM networking to the desktop would be embraced by LAN users to solve this problem. ATM is a networking technology that was designed specifically to handle a combination of the low-delay steady-stream characteristics of voice and video and the bursty, intermittent characteristics of data communications.

The ATM Forum, the industry body responsible for publishing ATM specifications, has developed a number of standards that enable desktops connected directly to ATM networks to support existing LAN data applications as well as voice telephony and videoconferencing. The ATM Forum standards for the support of voice and video over ATM to the desktop typically avoid the use of traditional LAN protocols such as IP, and instead place the voice or video streams directly over the ATM protocols.

While it is clear that ATM to the desktop provides an elegant and effective solution for combining voice, video, and data over the LAN, this approach does imply a "forklift" to the LAN infrastructure and the end station connection. The cost and disruptive impact of such an upgrade tend to limit its appeal, and as a result desktop ATM is not expected to be widely adopted.

However, the ability of ATM to provide "quality of service" — that is, to deliver real-time voice or video streams with a guaranteed upper bound on delay — makes it an excellent choice for the LAN backbone where voice and video over the LAN is needed.

Shared and Switched LANs

It is generally accepted that shared LANs are unsuitable for handling real-time voice and video because of the widely varying delays that are seen when multiple stations are contending for access to the transmission medium. The CSMA/CD access method used in shared Ethernet is particularly poor in this respect. Token Ring, on the other hand, is based on a token-passing access method with multiple levels of priority. Stations waiting to send data packets can be preempted by other stations on the ring with higher priority voice or video packets to send. As a result, Token Ring has excellent potential to handle real-time voice and video traffic, though this potential has yet to be realized in currently available networking products.

LAN switching does much to overcome the limitations of shared LANs, although today's products are still a long way from providing an answer for voice and video over the LAN. It is now cost-effective to provide users with dedicated 10M-bps Ethernet connections to the desktop and 100M-bps Fast Ethernet uplinks from the wiring closet to the backbone.

However, despite the vast increase in bandwidth provision per user that this represents over and above a shared LAN scenario, there is still contention in the network leading to unacceptable delay characteristics. For example, multiple users connected to the switch may demand file transfers from several servers connected via 100M-bps Fast Ethernet to the backbone. Each server may send a burst of packets that temporarily overwhelms the Fast Ethernet uplink to the wiring closet. A queue will form in the backbone switch that is driving this link, and any voice or video packets being sent to the same wiring closet will have to wait their turn behind the data packets in this queue. The resultant delays will compromise the perceived quality of the voice or video transmission.

The only way to overcome this problem is to find a way of treating real-time voice and video packets differently from data packets in the network and to give them preferential treatment when transient data overloads cause queues to form on busy network links. In practice, this means that LAN packets must be tagged with some kind of priority information that enables switches to identify which packets need to jump the queue.

CONSIDERING EVOLVING TECHNOLOGIES

The IEEE 802, which oversees standards for LAN technologies, has initiated a project identified as 802.1p, which is concerned with "Traffic Class Expediting" in LAN switches.

The principal problem faced by 802.1p is that there is no spare information field in the standard Ethernet packet format that could carry the required priority tag. As a result, it has been necessary to propose a new Ethernet packet format with an additional 4 bytes of information in the packet header that can contain a 3-bit priority tag field (offering eight levels of priority), together with some other information concerned with virtual LANs.

With the new Ethernet packet format containing a priority tag, end station applications can identify real-time voice or video packets by assigning them a high-priority value in the tag. LAN switches that have been enhanced to process the priority tags can separate high- and low-priority traffic in the switching fabric and place them in separate queues at outgoing switch ports. The LAN switches need to implement a queue scheduling algorithm that gives preference to the higher priority queues on outgoing ports, and by this means it is hoped that real-time voice and video can be carried over the LAN without incurring unacceptable delays during periods of heavy data traffic.

Hybrid ATM Networks

The discussion of ATM described how it offers guaranteed quality of service for real-time voice and video streams. Today, ATM is increasingly used as a LAN backbone for pure data applications, because it offers greater scalability and fault tolerance than other LAN technologies. Ethernet and Token Ring LANs are connected to ATM via "edge switches" equipped with ATM uplinks, typically supporting the ATM Forum standard for carrying LAN traffic over ATM, know as LAN emulation.

It is possible to enhance ATM edge switches to enable desktops connected via Ethernet or Token Ring to enjoy the benefits of ATM quality of service across the LAN backbone. Two techniques have been proposed to achieve this.

The first technique, known as "Cell-in-Frame," extends the native ATM signaling protocols over dedicated Ethernet connections from the edge switch to the end station. The voice or video application in the end station places the voice or video stream in ATM cells using the ATM Forum standards for native ATM transport, and then encapsulates the ATM cells in Ethernet packets for transport to the edge switch for onward transmission onto the ATM network. Effectively, this is ATM to the desktop, but using physical Ethernet with standard Ethernet adapter cards as a kind of physical transport layer for ATM traffic.

The second technique makes use of an emerging standard protocol for end stations to request quality of service for IP-based voice or video applications, known as the Resource Reservation Protocol, or RSVP. The enhanced edge switch intercepts RSVP requests originated by end stations and converts them into ATM signaling to request the setup of connections across the ATM backbone with the appropriate quality of service. The edge switch then distinguishes between IP packets containing data and those containing voice or video, using the information provided by RSVP, and steers voice and video packets onto ATM connections that have quality of service.

At the time of writing, the technique described here for RSVP-to-ATM mapping enjoys somewhat broader industry support than cell-in-frame, perhaps because of its relationship with Internet technology.

Until LAN switches supporting 802.1p priority tagging have proved themselves capable of meeting the very stringent end-to-end delay requirements for real-time voice and video communications, hybrid approaches based on ATM in the backbone and switched Ethernet or Token Ring to the desktop are likely to find acceptance as the solution of choice for voice and video over the LAN.

Standards for LAN-Based Voice and Video Applications

Standards for voice and video over the LAN fall into two categories: those designed for native ATM protocols and those intended for general-purpose LAN protocols, particularly IP.

Standards for native ATM protocols, such as the ATM Forum's Voice Telephony over ATM (VTOA), are appropriate only for ATM-connected desktops or desktops running Cell-in-Frame over Ethernet.

Standards for applications that run over IP are applicable both to ATM-connected desktops as well as desktops in general Ethernet or Token Ring environments. The most important standard in this space is H.323, which was developed by the International Telecommunications Union. While H.323 is designed to be independent of the underlying networking protocol, it will most often be deployed running over IP.

H.323 references other existing standards for the digital encoding and compression of voice and video signals and describes how audio and video streams are carried in the payload of IP packets with the aid of the Real Time Protocol (RTP), which provides timing and synchronization information. H.323 also covers the handling of data streams for application sharing, shared whiteboarding, and real-time file transfer (referencing the T.120 standard) and includes signaling based on ISDN messaging protocols for call setup and teardown.

The H.323 standard is flexible and accommodates any combination of real-time voice, video, and data as part of a single point-to-point or multi-point conference call. It may be used with a voice stream alone as the basis of a LAN telephony solution. H.323 enjoys the broadest support in the industry as a proposed standard for Internet telephony.

Additional Components: Gateways and Gatekeepers

Creating a LAN infrastructure that can consistently deliver voice and video streams with sufficiently low delay is an absolute prerequisite for integrating voice and video on the LAN, but it is by no means the complete answer to the problem. There are two other key components of a complete voice and video solution, which in H.323 parlance are known as the gateway and the gatekeeper.

An H.323 gateway provides interconnection between voice and video services on the LAN and external voice and video services typically provided over circuit-switched networks such as ISDN and the public telephone network. The gateway terminates the IP and RTP protocols carrying the voice and video streams and converts them to appropriate formats for external networks. For videoconferencing, the conversion is most likely to be to H.320, another ITU standard that specifies how voice and video are carried over ISDN connections. For voice-only connections, the conversion will be to the G.711 standard for digital telephony. This allows voice interworking with any phone on a public network or connected to a PBX.

An H.323 gatekeeper is a pure software function that provides central call control services. While it is possible to run H.323 voice and video communications over the LAN without a gatekeeper, in practice this function is extremely useful. At the most basic level, the gatekeeper provides directory services and policy-based controls applied to the use of voice and video communications. For example, the gatekeeper can bar stations from accessing certain types of external phone numbers at certain times of day. The gatekeeper can be thought of as the "server" in a client/server model of LAN-based telephony and videoconferencing.

At a more sophisticated level, the gatekeeper may be able to support supplementary services, including call transfer, hold and divert, hunt groups, pickup groups, attendant operation and so on — features that are typically found in high-end PBXs for controlling and managing voice calls. While the H.323 standard does not explicitly describe how supplementary call control features may be supported, the standard does provide a framework for the addition of these advanced capabilities.

CONCLUSION

This chapter has explained the value of voice and video integration on the LAN in terms of both application-driven needs and the desire for infrastructure efficiencies. It has looked at the technology issues surrounding the transport of real-time voice and video streams over LAN infrastructures and concluded that ATM backbones provide a solution in the near term, with the possibility of a later solution based entirely on switched Ethernet or Token Ring.

Finally, the chapter has described some additional functional elements, such as gateways and gatekeepers, that are an essential part of a complete solution for voice and video over the LAN. Over the last decade, the open standards-based environment typified by PCs and LANs has revolutionized the way data is handled and processed in enterprise environments. Now this open and standards-based approach is set to tackle the challenge of voice and video, formerly the exclusive domain of the PBX. The history of LAN evolution is set to repeat itself, and we can expect the traditional proprietary mainframe PBX to diminish in importance to the enterprise, giving way to client/server telephony and videoconferencing, just as the mainframe computer has been pushed into the background by client/server techniques for data processing.

Chapter 60
Internet Voice Applications
Frank J. Bourne

OF THE MORE INTRIGUING TECHNOLOGIES to be hurled into the networking universe from the Internet "big bang" phenomenon, Internet telephony and audio transport seem to be garnering the lion's share of consumer attention.

Home and business users are eagerly delving into a dreamworld filled with unlimited free long-distance telephone calls, teleconferencing, and real-time audio Web applications. While direct experience with these fledgling applications often pales when compared with the promise, adventurous users are nonetheless happily exploring creative ways to apply new technologies to everyday problems.

A BRIEF HISTORY OF VOICE COMMUNICATIONS

Communications via telegraph, radio, telephone, and cellular technology each struggled through an early period of disbelief, limited acceptance, and technical hurdles. Each communication medium also had the potential to provide substantive solutions to real needs. Commercial acceptance and widespread deployment came only with the creative and effective application of these technologies.

For the moment, available Internet telephony packages have captured the curiosity and excitement of consumers in the same manner citizens band (CB) radio entranced the American public in the 1970s. CB was a convenience technology that lured users by the millions with the promise of free and easy communication with friends, family, and business associates. Demand grew so dramatically that the Federal Communications Commission (FCC) was forced to open the citizens band spectrum from 23 to 40 channels.

While CB is still active as a commercial and emergency communications tool, the vast majority of radios built now lie dormant in closets, garages, radio repair shop parts bins, and landfills. What happened?

0-8493-0859-3/00/$0.00+$.50
© 2000 by CRC Press LLC

How Unpredictable Service Can Doom a Good Idea

Congestion happened, among other things. For many once-impassioned CB cowboys, cowgirls, and rangers, the thrill of the fad wore off quickly with the realities of use. The excitement of anonymous pranksterism was dulled when users became equally susceptible to the same.

Security was nonexistent. Solar noise often relegated useful medium- and long-range communications to late-night hours. Hackers with illegal 100-watt linear amplifiers would dominate the channels with the best propagation and flame anyone who dared to talk. The inconveniences of terrain, keeping antennae properly tuned, and coordinating important calls were also discouraging to many once enthusiastic CD users.

Worse, there simply was too much demand for limited bandwidth. The sheer number of simultaneous users on a given channel produced background noise levels that were difficult or impossible to communicate over, even using the best equipment at short range.

The unregulated load placed on the spectrum resulted, effectively, in lost or errored information that made the medium nearly unusable. Without quality of service guarantees, commercial implementation was limited to the very few whose needs were well-suited by this unpredictable service.

STATE OF INTERNET TELEPHONY TODAY

The Evolution

Internet telephony is evolving through a period of CB radio-like application. Wander into one of the Internet Relay Chat (IRC)-based voice call servers and you will find hundreds of users chatting about a wide variety of interests.

Some users coordinate offline to meet in private conversations in lieu of a standard telephone call. Many congregate in multiuser chat sessions on numerous topics of common interest — a natural evolution of the IRC relay chat channels. A few, cutting their teeth on limited demo versions of software, place calls randomly into any open channel in search of a modern "radio check."

Current Audio Products and Applications

But these applications represent old technology now. In fact, updated, improved versions of Internet audio and telephony software surface almost daily.

The energy in this industry manifests itself with an intense competitive urgency. New players and products are introduced and fade, accepted, rejected, or absorbed. The dominant vendors seek to outpace each other and grab market share. Alliances are struck, technologies acquired, and Web page press releases trumpet feature lists that would make a PBX salesperson envious. This industry is vibrant, alive, and here to stay — but in what form?

There are three basic audio product types approaching maturity on the Internet:

1. *Audio broadcast.* Products in this category provide real-time, one-way transmission of press conferences, announcements, or entertainment such as music and talk radio.
2. *Group conferencing.* These products enable multiuser voice conferencing.
3. *Telephony.* Such products enable person-to-person telephony via a personal computer or workstation, conference calling, and voice mail. Some products provide whiteboarding capabilities, permit multiple simultaneous calls, and support collaborative computing.

THE WORKINGS OF INTERNET VOICE TECHNOLOGIES

Internet audio and telephony applications employ efficient software-driven codecs on a personal computer or workstation to digitize and packetize voice information for transport via internetwork protocols such as SLIP, PPP, TOP, or UDP. These applications use the computer's multimedia hardware for input/output devices (e.g., microphones and speakers) and analog-digital conversion.

Delay. Delay-handling mechanisms are implemented in most commercially available packages, since voice communications are particularly intolerant of delay and delay variation. While not as disconcerting as propagation delay over satellite, significant but tolerable delay is noticeable in these applications at most connection speeds. Delay is only significant in two-way communications.

Delay is accounted for by buffering a certain amount of voice information in order to compensate for variations in network transit time between callers. While this actually adds slightly to the overall delay perceived by the user, it is a necessary acknowledgment of the random, unpredictable delay present in today's Internet.

One-Way Audio Broadcasts. Broadcast applications enable entities such as radio stations, news services, or corporations to transmit one-way audio to a potentially unlimited number of users. A centralized server digitizes the audio and either transmits it in real time to Internet-attached users, or stores the compressed audio on the server.

If users are unable to attend the broadcast, they may later access a compressed audio file on the server. Users are not required to download the file to their local workstation in order to listen; the file may be played out in real time by the server, avoiding a long, unproductive wait.

781

Several Internet-only "radio stations" have already sprung into existence, offering an eclectic variety of music, talk, and commentary programming. One intriguing advantage of Internet-based audio programming is the ability to archive shows for access when the user finds it convenient to listen. If a favorite show or episode is missed at broadcast time, it may be accessed remotely at a later time or even downloaded to the user's local disk drive for repeated listening.

Two-Way Conferences. Two-way conferencing applications are very popular among noncommercial users. A modified chat-server implementation is used to connect multiple users. Half-duplex communication is the norm, but some available applications allow limited whiteboard and collaborative computing capabilities.

Connection Speeds and Sampling Rates. Voice quality is directly affected by connection speed and the quality of the codec design. While some of the available codecs are capable of sampling rates above 35 KHz, only a minority of users currently have Internet access speeds that top 14,400 bps. All available software specifies a minimum connection rate of 14,400 bps, which provides usable but grainy voice quality.

With the better codec implementations, voice quality approaches then surpasses that of toll-quality conventional public telephony because higher connection speeds allow greater sampling rates. This is an exciting promise when contrasted with the fixed 300 Hz to 3,000 Hz bandpass and 8 KHz sampling rate used in conventional telephony.

Software Enhancements. Because Internet telephony applications are software-based, creative enhancements to the virtual telephone set are possible. These enhancements come in the form of integration of familiar tools, such as autodialing, address lists, directory services, caller ID, notepads, and voice mail. More sophisticated users may opt for concurrent support of whiteboarding and other image transfer and collaborative computing. The potential for integration with other software applications also warrants consideration.

USAGE ISSUES AND IMPEDIMENTS

Several success factors have been achieved as Internet voice applications have matured. Codec design, voice quality potential, and usability have been well-received if shelf sales and trial downloads are any indication of market interest.

The response of power users and techno-junkies does not, however, necessarily indicate a broad, long-term acceptance of these technologies. For Internet voice products to continue to thrive, several obstacles have yet to be overcome.

Support for Full-Duplex Operation. Only a small portion of existing sound cards support full-duplex operation, limiting even full-duplex-enabled telephony software to half-duplex capability. Given the rapid growth in home computer sales, and the dearth of installed multimedia hardware in existing business computers, this should not be a long-term concern.

Likewise, 28.8K bps modems are rapidly becoming the norm, and high-speed cable access technology trials promise greater availability of usable multimedia bandwidth. (What user wants to abandon a multiuser role-playing Net game or telecommuting session to take an Internet phone call?)

Interoperability Standards. Of greater concern is the general lack of standardization in codec and transport implementations. Few Internet voice implementations interoperate, requiring callers to use the same software to communicate.

Ease of use leaves much to be desired. Currently, both users must have an active Internet connection in order to place a call, which for many requires that a dial-up modem connection be made to the Internet before attempting to locate and connect a voice call to another user. One notable exception at this time is an Internet service provider (ISP) that proposes to allow a user to connect across the Internet through a server to a conventional telephone switch, from which users of traditional telephones may be dialed.

IP Addresses. Divining a user's Internet "telephone number" can also be challenging. All of the approaches currently available require significantly more coordination between users than conventional telephony.

Some products currently require users of a given application to use a private IRC-based server network. Some products allow "dialing" of a specific IP address, which gives more universal access to other users, should their client software be compatible with yours and they have a fixed address. Newer releases allow scanning a wide range of IP addresses for user IDs, which makes it possible to locate a specific called party, should they actually be online with their ISP at the time you wish to call.

An alternative approach to locating users with dynamically assigned public IP addresses employs an e-mail page to notify the called party that you wish to place a call to them.

Unpredictable Nature of the Internet. Perhaps the greatest limiting factor is the unpredictability of the Internet itself.

Traffic management is almost nonexistent, providing little or no quality of service guarantees to users. The vast majority of Internet voice applications are designed to manage delay and traffic loss only within strictly defined limits.

Internet provisioning practices do not account sufficiently for traffic loss, congestion, and delay. Current practices almost universally involve throwing more bandwidth and routers at the problem, which only provides temporary relief and does not ensure fairness among users. Retransmission of lost broadcast audio packets is somewhat acceptable within strict limits, but multisecond delays and large-scale discards render two-way voice communications unusable.

Multiplatform Support. Support for non-PC platforms is currently very limited, though it is only a matter of time before broader support of Macintosh and UNIX-based platforms is common.

Internet access capabilities are also being delivered in PBX platforms and PC-based telephony servers. While the PBX approaches are primarily aimed at 56K bps integrated services digital network (ISDN) Internet data access, it is only a small jump to providing Internet voice services on the same platform.

FUTURE DIRECTIONS

Technology Outlook

Rapid advances in hardware and software technology offer much hope for Internet telephony. Faster, more capable platforms will enable more sophisticated codec implementations, and improvements in peripherals such as sound cards, microphones, and modem speed will enhance voice quality. Multitasking and collaborative applications will benefit from increased platform capacity and connection speed as well.

Given sufficient processor power and connection bandwidth, sophisticated multimedia capabilities may be integrated with Internet telephony, bringing the capabilities of the corporate conferencing center to the desktop.

In addition to conversation, applications that employ images, video, whiteboarding, and console-sharing may be performed in real-time. Newer high-end home and business PCs approach these capacities today. Internet access speeds are increasing steadily and will achieve widespread availability in megabit increments within the next 10 years.

The growing acceptance of telecommuting will have a complementary impact upon the acceptance and deployment of Internet voice applications.

Success Factors

If Internet voice is to gain broad and permanent acceptance, it must offer value equivalent or superior to the existing public switched telephone network. Like the common telephone, interoperability must be universal and without question. Directory services, numbering, and billing must be effectively dealt with. Dialing must be effortless and intuitive, and feature sets must be standardized. While competitive pressures are understandably high, vendors and service providers must come to agreement on core standards and interoperability issues.

ALL-IMPORTANT INFRASTRUCTURE ISSUES

Quality of Service Is Everything

Commercial radio, the public-switched telephone network, and cellular telephony have survived because commercial providers have taken the steps necessary to ensure that a minimum quality of service (QOS) can be guaranteed of their respective offerings.

Quality of service encompasses many factors that vary by the service offered. For voice communications, the most important factors are:

- *Reliability.* The service must be functioning at least 99.8 percent of the time. Users must have an extremely high degree of confidence that the network will function and provide the desired service every time it is used.
- *Performance.* The service must provide a minimum guaranteed level of performance that the user finds desirable and of value.
- *Predictability.* The service must provide consistent, predictable performance at or above a specified minimum level of quality.
- *Fairness.* The service must provide fair, equal access to network resources for all users.
- *Accessibility.* The service must be readily and easily available to a number of users sufficient to make the service of value to subscribers.

Each of these quality of service factors is affected by a number of infrastructure design issues that require analysis, planning, and monitoring by the service provider in order to ensure the long-term viability of the service.

Becoming as Reliable as the Telephone. During the years of federal regulation of the public telephone network, the telephone came to be considered an essential item of daily life for more than conversation. To be more than another household or business accessory, Internet telephony must at least come close to meeting the reliability of the conventional telephone.

Telephone networks have been designed and built for decades to have sufficient redundancy to function in all but the most catastrophic circumstances. Floods, earthquakes, tornadoes, hurricanes, and other natural disasters are examples of conditions that challenge even minimal network operation yet place a terrible urgency upon the provision of at least a marginal level of service. Telephone switch central offices operate on self-sustaining, battery-backed power systems for this reason.

Redundancy in power systems, switching hardware, cable capacity, and cable paths are all considered to be essential and critical baseline design criteria for any public telephone system. While federal deregulation has somewhat eased the metrics by which public telephone networks are built, a deeply ingrained cultural design ethic exists within the telephony community that preserves such conservative design practices.

Likewise, the public customer base has for generations grown up with an unquestioning dependence upon the reliability of the network. If the power goes out, one generally expects to be able to pick up the telephone and notify the power company. Day after day, customers depend on the telephone and think nothing of it, unless it fails to function.

Responsibilities of Service Providers. Despite federal deregulation, the telephone service industry remains heavily regulated. Service providers are required to contribute significantly to infrastructure development, to maintain minimum service levels, and to guarantee universal access to all users, including accommodation of special needs such as TDD terminals for the hearing-impaired or low-cost basic service to the infirm.

As of this writing, the rapid rise in Internet telephony has caused many public telephone service providers to protest to regulatory bodies. The perception is that if Internet telephony is to be given a free ride without contribution to infrastructure pools such as the Universal Service Fund, conventional service providers will be at a competitive disadvantage.

Notably absent from the protest are telephone service providers who were adventurous enough to also have well-established Internet service offerings. These regulatory issues are sure to be addressed as the Internet matures.

It seems unlikely that Internet telephony will completely supplant the existing telephone network for quite some time. Internet voice quality and service levels require dramatic improvement. To achieve this level of quality and service, massive investments made over decades by the public telephone service providers would need to be matched. Internet access devices and circuits must be simplified to an appliance level and match the reliability and survivability of the existing network.

Moreover, the core infrastructure of the Internet itself requires switching equipment and design practices that make efficient use of wide-area bandwidth while providing redundancy in switching capacity, subsecond rerouting, and intelligent, dynamic bandwidth allocation. All of these core network factors depend on the inclination and ability of the service providers to develop the Internet infrastructure to such a level.

Performance Metrics — Quantifying "Perception." Service performance includes many elements, such as the time required to connect a call, peak instantaneous call capacity, voice quality, noise levels, and the ability to support enhanced services. The capacity of the overall network to support calls at a guaranteed minimum level of quality under normal and disaster conditions is also significant.

Traditional metrics used in the design and benchmarking of data network performance focus on objective factors such as error rate, throughput, and latency. Voice networking exposes an entirely different range of subjective, human perception factors that are difficult to quantify yet are critical to the practicality of a commercial voice offering.

Bell Labs long ago developed a standard, the Overall Reference Equivalent (ORE), to attempt to bring the human factor to bear in the design of the public telephone network. The ORE metric quantifies the user's tolerance for circumstances, such as time to connect to another user, blocked calls due to network overload, echo, volume, and noise. These metrics are a fundamental component of all current voice network design and testing processes.

A successful mass deployment of Internet telephony will hinge on the same factors. The Internet infrastructure and user devices will require low delay to inhibit echo and double-talk. Low delay variation and low data loss will be necessary to avoid distortion and noise.

High-performance switching and efficient utilization of switching, trunking, and access capacity in the Internet backbone will be essential to achieving these goals. Backbone switching hardware and software must be scalable to accommodate high-capacity, long-term growth of the network that will be necessary to effectively meet user demand.

Predictability — Key to a Universal Service. While performance and reliability are paramount, consistent performance of the network is also of extreme importance.

Users will expect a universal service to perform in essentially the same manner every time it is called upon. If a significant variance in performance exists from call to call, the lower range of performance will be perceived as unacceptable. This will be cause for contention between service providers and clients and can only be addressed through effective service network design and provisioning practices.

As Internet access and traffic grow, we are already witnessing dramatic variances in a given server's performance as a consequence of demand on the host processor and contention for transport bandwidth. Much like today's commercial telephone switches, sufficient resources must be provisioned at the host site to ensure that the desired level of service is provided to users.

In addition, wide-area transport and switching capacity in the Internet backbone require significant improvement in order to avoid the unpredictable network overloads and outages seen today. Delay, throughput, and error rate must remain relatively consistent not only throughout a call, but from call to call.

Fairness — Meeting Guaranteed QOS Levels. What is fairness? Users should be able to depend on a level of service proportional to their investment in the service, regardless of the state of the network at any given moment.

For example, a user with an expensive high-speed connection should expect more total throughput during network congestion or impairment than a user with a less expensive low-speed connection. Each user should receive a degree of service that is directly proportional at all times to their contracted quality of service.

In a similar fashion, active user connections should not have their throughput, delay, or error rate reduced below minimum guaranteed levels at any time as a result of new connection requests or variance in demand by other established connections.

Fairness also includes the assurance that once a call is placed and in progress, quality of service cannot be disrupted or usurped by new calls. Fairness of this sort equates to an "all circuits are busy" message from the public switched telephone network. The implicit message is that other users were there first, and courtesy (quality of service) dictates that an in-progress call may not be disconnected or impaired in preference for a new call.

The current frame-switched Internet backbone architecture generally allows unfair, unpredictable degradation of service to established connections due to its minimal support and enforcement of quality of service metrics.

Accessibility to a Broad User Base. Virtually universal access exists in today's public switched telephone networks. Practically anyone in the world desiring connection to telephone service may obtain it.

Likewise, while the worldwide telephone network is composed of multitudes of independent local, regional, national, and international service providers, interoperability is truly universal. Any caller on any telephone service may connect to anyone in the world with a telephone, including cellular and commercial mobile-radio telephones. Internet telephony requires the same degree of interoperability.

Of course, public telephone networks were of value long before such wide access was provisioned. Internet access is today sufficiently broad to support an Internet telephony user base. The promise of interoperability with the billions of installed conventional telephones is extremely encouraging. In fact, Internet-style telephony seems to have quite a strong chance of becoming the dominant voice communications medium in the next century. Instrument costs (e.g., PC sound cards and software) will certainly be driven continually downward, and stand-alone consumer Internet telephone instruments are absolutely feasible.

SUMMARY

An advanced, cell-based asynchronous transfer mode (ATM) backbone is an absolute requirement for a profitable, efficient, high-performance public multimedia network. Frame-switching technology cannot guarantee the distinct quality of service requirements of mixed voice, video, and data without costly overprovisioning of bandwidth and switching capacity.

Conversely, profitable operation of a frame-switched architecture in an intensely competitive deregulated environment will beg oversubscription by service providers, resulting in poor performance, unpredictability, and unfairness to users — as is increasingly seen in today's Internet.

A well-designed ATM infrastructure with low delay, large per-virtual circuit and by-traffic-class buffering, advanced adaptive queue service algorithms, scalable capacity, and effective, closed-loop traffic management will be mandatory for the continued growth of the Internet as a profitable, commercially feasible service.

The same switching infrastructure can provide not only extremely high-performance Internet services, but also guaranteed performance for conventional and packetized voice services, all manner of data delivery services, video broadcast and conference services, and true multimedia service across the wide area.

Chapter 61
Building an IP PBX Telephony Network

John Fiske

INTERNET TELEPHONY HAS BEEN INCREASINGLY EXPLORED and implemented as a viable communication tool in large corporations. A main component of enterprise IP voice is the IP PBX, which functions the way a traditional PBX does. It allows calls to be transferred throughout the organization, it allows easy intra-enterprise calls, and it operates automatically.

An IP PBX is different in almost every other respect. Not only is it easier and less costly to operate and maintain, it operates with different technology. The IP PBX has paid off for the corporations using it through reduced manpower and by eliminating an entire (telephone) network. This chapter provides other payoff ideas and an explanation of the technology behind the IP PBX.

THE PBX

Yesterday's PBX fulfilled a simple need: it allowed users to talk together, and also allowed users to talk out to the PSTN (public switched telephone network). PBX (premise branch exchange) manufacturers fulfilled this need by installing a mainframe computer into the enterprise and connecting a proprietary line card interface to either analog phones or proprietary digital phones. The connection out to the PSTN was established through a trunk interface card.

Today's PC-based PBX similarly fulfills a need. Phones on the enterprise side and the PSTN on the outside can be connected together. The approach with a PC-based PBX is fundamentally the same as the mainframe PBX architecture. The big difference is the use of relatively inexpensive PCs instead of hefty mainframe computers.

The third generation, tomorrow's PBX, is the IP (Internet Protocol)-based PBX. Again, it fulfills a by-now well-known need, but with a lot of other benefits. Instead of using a line interface card and circuit-switched card, it uses the TCP/IP network switching voice packets through an Ethernet, ATM, frame relay, ISDN, or whatever satisfactorily carries TCP/IP.

THE IP-PBX

Full PBX capabilities over IP LAN/WAN networks promise to substitute and replace traditional enterprise PBXs, and are an important step toward full voice and data convergence. In the IP PBX, voice traffic is digitized and compressed, placed into data packets, and transmitted across the packet network directly between the stations or WAN interfaces. End stations communicate with a call control server only when a call processing function, such as transferring a call, creating a conference call, or sending a call to voice mail, is required or requested.

Standards and the IP PBX

An IP PBX operates within the ITU (International Telecommunications Union) Standards (H.323 and T.120) that define how data equipment works in a data environment and define the signaling, call control, and audio compression for packet delivery of voice and video communications on IP networks. Without these standards in place and strictly followed, interoperability would not be possible.

Components

An IP PBX requires three components: the desktop telephone, call manager software, and a WAN/IP gateway. These three components are attached to existing LAN/WAN infrastructure.

The Desktop Telephone. Users have two desktop phone choices:

1. an IP Ethernet phone that plugs directly into an Ethernet jack
2. handsets or headsets that plug into their PC

The IP Ethernet telephone resembles a normal digital PBX set, but instead of connecting to a proprietary PBX port, it plugs into a standard Ethernet LAN jack. An IP telephone delivers audio quality comparable to that of a PBX telephone and is easy to use with single-button access to line appearances and features. The IP telephone can operate as a standard IP device with its own IP address. A fully H.323-compatible IP phone can talk to any other H.323 device. The following are key characteristics of the IP telephone.

- connects directly to any 10 Base-T Ethernet (RJ45) network
- programmable buttons for features, speed dialing, or line appearances
- IP address and signaling (TCP/IP) to call manager
- H.323 standards

- built-in compression: G.711; G.723 (ITU standards), on a call and feature basis
- IP address assignment and configuration with DHCP keypad or BootP
- administration and button configuration through a Web browser
- built-in encryption for privacy protection during voice conversation
- 3rd-pair or phantom powered to permit power backup in the event of building power failure
- one-button collaboration (T.120) with PC and NetMeeting for features such as application sharing, video, chat, and whiteboarding
- built-in repeater port for cascading Ethernet devices

The Call Manager. The call manager provides the network intelligence to enable simple-to-use and feature-rich IP communications. Call manager software is designed to work seamlessly with existing telephony systems (PBX or Centrex) or can provide full PBX functionality on its own. It can be deployed as a single IP PBX in a single office, or as a single IP PBX with multiple geographically dispersed users. With total switch and network independence, administrators can create a truly virtual campus environment utilizing a common Web browser.

By installing the call manager software on a Windows NT server in the IP network, features such as call, hold, call transfer, call forward, call park, caller identification, and multiple line appearances are provided to the IP phone. The SMDI interface on the call manager provides connectivity to various voice mail and IVR systems along with CDR reporting for call accounting and billing.

The call manager provides the call processing functionality for the IP PBX. It manages the resources of the IP PBX by signaling and coordinating call control activities. The call manager sets up a call by instructing the calling party to set up an RTP audio stream to the other device, either telephone or gateway. Once an audio stream is set up between two devices, the call manager is idle until a new request (such as transfer or disconnect) is made. In the event the call manager fails during a call, the two parties stay connected and can complete their call. Various signaling protocols, such as Q.931 for ISDN WAN control and H.225/H.245 for IP packet control, are managed and controlled by the call manager.

The call manager also manages calling zones to ensure efficient bandwidth performance at the maximum audio quality. When a call is routed over a low-bandwidth IP pipe, the call manager will instruct the IP phone to use a lower bit rate audio compression, such as G.723. For calls toward the PSTN, the call manager will have the phones use G.711, which is the compression required for PSTN calling.

The call manager offers a standard directory service that allows other applications on the network to access the call directory. It can be overseen via a Web browser and provides remote management for diagnostics and maintenance from anywhere in the world. The browser provides an intuitive interface for administrators and users. Upon administrator approval, users can access and configure their own phones. Call records are kept in a standard CDR database for billing and tracking activity.

The Gateway. IP-based telephony systems today need to connect to the PSTN and the existing PBX. Gateways are specifically designed to convert voice from the packet domain to the circuit-switched domain.

The gateway converts packetized voice to a format that can be accepted by the PSTN. Since the digitized format for voice on the packet network is often different than on the PSTN, the gateway will provide a type of conversion called transcoding. Gateways also pass signaling information.

Based on the various PSTN interfaces, there is a need for both a digital and analog trunk version. Gateways must all support supplementary services, such as call transfer and hold across subnets in the IP network and should be easily configured using the Web browser. Support for supplemental services is in the H.323 Standard and allows for the RTP audio stream to be redirected to different IP ports.

Configurations and Applications

The IP PBX is not defined by physical hardware limitations, as is a traditional PBX or even the newer "un-PBX" systems. Traditional PBXs or un-PBXs have constraints that limit scaling the system. For example, the circuit switch matrix that defines how many connections can be made at one time is based on the specific model of the PBX that has been installed. Once the limit has been reached, the entire PBX usually must be replaced.

Another limitation is the hardware line cards required for every telephone device or trunk interface. These cards fit into cabinets and, when the growth of the system requires more cards than cabinet space the entire system again must be replaced.

IP PBXs are very different in their architecture. Instead of a circuit switch matrix to make connections, the IP PBX uses LAN bandwidth to make voice connections. For telephone calls, the voice traffic does not pass through a central server or call manager. The call manager only performs signaling to set up and manage call states. Therefore, it can handle a large number of calls with fewer restrictions or limitations.

In addition, because of the scalability of LAN architectures, the IP PBX can scale linearly from one port to thousands of ports. When more ports are needed, additional hubs and switches can be added to grow the system without replacing the current investment.

IP Telephony off an Existing PBX. This configuration extends the existing PBX within the campus using the IP network as transport. The IP PBX connects to the PBX using either an analog or digital gateway, depending on the expectations of voice traffic and the number of users. The call manager software runs on an NT server in the data center.

This application allows a business, enterprise, university, or other large organization to extend normal telephony services using the existing IP LAN. The call manager provides feature functionality to the IP telephones, with features such as transfer, secretarial call coverage, and parallel dial plan used by the PBX. With the gateway interface to the PBX, users can call users with PBX telephones or call to the PSTN with the same privileges and restraints set by the enterprise administrator.

Remote Offices over an IP Network. This application is simply an extension of the previous configuration with the inclusion of IP WAN connectivity to remote sites. The same basic rules apply for the IP PBX, just as they would for a single-site deployment. The call manager can remain on the central site, or a secondary call manager can be deployed at the remote location.

This configuration is a common initial application for the IP PBX product line. Companies with multiple sites can now easily install full telephony systems while leveraging the IP data network already in place. This saves costs for long-distance calling, as well as eliminates the cost to install a second network at each remote location. This option also enhances flexibility for growing or shrinking locations based on business conditions and making changes.

Using the analog access gateway at the remote site, the remote workers have local calling. Long-distance calling can be muted over the IP WAN link and consolidated from the central site to maximize long-distance calling costs and administration. With the IP PBX capability to configure audio compression based on call routing, calls destined to the main location would use a lower bit rate compression to conserve bandwidth.

Network Deployment

The configuration of an IP PBX as a network-based service (such as an ISP) has characteristics similar to the previous configurations, except the call manager and the gateway are located in the WAN. On premise would be IP phones and possibly a smaller analog gateway for local calling and backup, in case the IP link to the network is unavailable.

In addition to local and long-distance calling, the network provider can also provide traditional services like voice mail and call center services with the applications residing either at the remote location or in the network.

The provider can also provide billing and management services for the customer: a range of telecommunications services in addition to long-distance routing and Internet access. The configuration options are based on the flexibility and power of IP networking.

PRACTICAL ADVANTAGES OF THE IP PBX

The IP PBX is expected to offer significant advantages in large-scale telephony. The earliest advantages pertain to cost. The benefits multiply, however, and include:

- *Cost.* Using the existing datacom network for voice transport, there is no need for the circuit-switched card or line interface card, and those expenses are avoided.
- *Total cost of ownership.* When one moves a phone on a circuit-switched PBX, one must call a PBX administrator, who makes an entry in a database that moves the phone from one physical port to another. It is logistical agony! IP phones are simpler and less costly in every way.
- *Maintenance.* One can plug in an IP phone directly out of the box. It automatically configures with a call management server, and it gets a directory number. Maintenance and configuration are simpler and easier.
- *Support.* There is no need for external support from field technicians from a proprietary PBX manufacturer. Additionally, there is a vast hiring pool of people who know Windows NT, TAPI, and TCP/IP — much greater than the number of people who know a particular vendor's circuit-switched PBX.
- *Extensible.* On a distributed campus with a unified dial plan and unified feature management, one can browse into the call processing server and manage the database from any point on the network.
- *Availability.* It is not necessary to pay for the extra availability the PBX vendors design into the system. One can pay a lot of money for very good PBX design work. But with an IP PBX, one does not pay for the extra capacity if it is not needed.
- *Capacity.* Using a dual Pentium Pro 300MHz server, one can run 500 to 600 phones. With the advent of inter server signaling, it will be theoretically possible to scale the system up to 100,000 lines, or larger.

Payoffs

There are several ways an IP PBX will save a company money.

- *Long-distance charge savings.* In many international markets, especially highly regulated ones, communications carriers have artificially high tariffs, as compared to carriers in deregulated markets. Additionally, these carriers have lower tariffs for data connections. There is short-term opportunity to exploit these differences — until carriers close the gap between voice and data costs. Longer-term cost savings will come from consolidation and management of all WAN connections, the Internet, local calling, and long distance through a single gateway/router device.

- *Data and voice convergence.* Data and voice conversion will facilitate new business practices, enabling people to work more effectively. This technology will release customers from barriers imposed by proprietary solutions, allowing organizations to develop.
- *Cutting acquisition and operating costs.* In 1997, the capital cost of building a LAN PBX system was slightly higher than the cost of building a traditional PBX. The changing marketplace has changed this model, however. The cost of swiftly evolving LAN equipment has fallen below the also-declining cost of traditional PBX equipment.
- *Administration costs.* This is the single largest opportunity to reduce costs. One will manage a single network instead of two parallel networks. Today's PBX requires a full-time staffer to manage the PBX database. In the traditional PBX, it costs $60 to $80 to move a phone. With the IP PBX, this cost is eliminated. It is also easier and cheaper to add a phone extension. General management of the IP PBX is identical to that of the IP network, which means that the same people with the same knowledge can be used in both arenas.

CONCLUSION

Corporate IP networks are becoming increasingly pervasive and essential. Consequently, the business LAN no longer occupies a niche department. Those departments are always looking for ways to improve the network's capabilities. Rapid improvement in technology and standards is driving these efforts. It was not long ago that companies started trials for IP telephony with gateways between their PBXs and the IP networks. Now they are moving to the next step by integrating telephony services and IP telephones controlled by call manager server software. The revolution has begun, and the momentum to converge voice and data networks reveals a new value paradigm. For many companies, the real value comes not from lower (or eliminated) long distance charges, but from the reduced cost of operating and managing a separate voice network.

The IP PBX is a pillar in this revolution. Connectivity spells efficiency and productivity. The traditional PBX provided the connectivity; but the IP PBX is cheaper to acquire and easier to operate and maintain. The IP PBX, evolving still, suggests a new way for businesses to communicate. As this latest communications revolution sweeps across the land, one may want to join it.

Chapter 62
Fax over IP
John Fiske

FAXING IS ONE OF THE MOST COMMON FORMS OF COMMUNICATION IN THE BUSINESS WORLD. Faxing does what no other form of communication can: it provides hardcopy information in realtime (almost) anywhere there is a telephone. Studies have shown that most people select a communications method based primarily on the urgency of the message, and faxing is still the preferred method for important documents. With 55 to 65 million fax machines worldwide generating a phone bill of about $30 billion per year, faxing represents a crucial part of the telecommunications industry.

Growth Industry

Recent studies show that faxing accounts for about 40 percent of a typical Fortune 500 company's yearly phone bill, with the average fax machine shared by 21 to 23 people. In the United States, the annual spending on fax long-distance has been estimated at about $12 to $15 billion (Murata Business Systems, 1996). One industry touchstone, the annual Gallup/Pitney Bowes fax study, estimates that U.S. long-distance fax minutes grew to 140 billion in 1999. With the advent of e-mail, express mail, overnight delivery services, courier services, voice mail, and even videoconferencing, one might expect the use of faxing to decline, but it has not. Fax usage is growing, not shrinking. In fact, according to a major polling organization of users who fax on a daily basis, 60 percent were faxing more than in the previous year.

Preferred Form

Studies show that faxing is preferred for immediate hardcopy transmission of urgent documents and documents under review, where handwritten comments must be passed along. Companies also widely prefer fax for sending documents internationally. Large companies use fax extensively within their own organizations, sending almost half of their fax traffic from one company location to another. Finally, faxes get more attention and quicker response than any other medium except the live phone call.

Many desktop fax software packages are available today, but using them requires a dedicated phone line and fax modem (to connect the desktop to the Public Switched Telephone Network). Studies show that only 20 percent of corporate PCs have a dedicated phone line (Gallup/Pitney Bowes, 1996).

Thus, it is apparent that bringing together the power of the desktop PC with the unique advantages of the departmental fax machine is highly desirable, but requires a somewhat different approach from the traditional modem-and-dedicated-phone line method.

Corporate Fax

According to Gallup/Pitney Bowes, about 37 to 40 percent of the typical Fortune 500 company's telecom bill results from fax. This is often a difficult expenditure to track, due to the difficulty of distinguishing voice from fax charges. In addition, corporations face many fax-related infrastructure expenses, including high-cost LAN fax servers, dedicated phone lines for fax machines (with an average of over 300 fax machines per F500 company), and fax modems and phone lines for PCs equipped to do traditional PSTN-based desktop faxing.

The average fax machine in the average medium-to-large business supports 23 people. It is often considered to be a less-than-efficient device, requiring that "trip down the hall" to use, sometimes a wait for access, often manual phone number entry, and then busy-signal retries. On the receiving end, there are several well-known drawbacks as well. It is no secret that faxes are not private; in fact, it is impossible for co-workers not to "peek at" faxes while sorting through jobs looking for their own (another time-consuming task). It is also not possible to retrieve faxes when traveling away from the office with the ease that one collects e-mail. From the standpoint of the corporate IS manager, every analog phone line that comes into the organization is a potential "open window" for intruders to hack their way into the corporate infrastructure.

Broadcast Fax

Certain groups in the organization send out faxes to groups of recipients. Investor relations, human resources, PR, sales, legal, and marketing departments must often contract outside fax service bureaus at significant expense to handle broadcast faxing. Technically, a broadcast fax is any fax sent to more than one recipient, although broadcasts typically reach dozens, hundreds, or even thousands of destinations.

Most broadcast faxers are business organizations that need to send the same message to a large constituency, or to a smaller but very important one. Broadcast faxing is commonly used for financial results, news releases, or important internal information for the organization. Normally, one would like to have complete control over such important and urgent communications, but the time-consuming, serial nature of traditional faxing makes that impractical.

Even preprogramming a fax machine to send out many jobs overnight one-at-a-time falls short of the bandwidth needed to complete a medium-sized broadcast in time. Fax bureaus harness many fax devices in parallel in order to speed up the process, and provide assurances of delivery within a certain timeframe.

However, outsourcing broadcasts to fax service bureaus takes away control of important (often mission-critical) projects from in-house departments. Control and feedback are necessarily reduced. And it is also expensive, with typical charges running to 30 cents per page or more.

Small Office Fax

Small businesses, branch offices, and consulting/vendor organizations rely on faxing in their own crucial way. Faxing may be more locally focused, but that is not always the case. Many small organizations do broadcast faxes and therefore make high expenditures on fax service bureaus. The desire to get the most out of every capital equipment dollar is very high, and installing dedicated phone lines and fax modems is an expensive proposition.

Small businesses often pay higher international and long-distance phone rates than large corporations, so they are even more motivated to gain control over fax charges, while lowering expenditures on equipment and service bureaus.

ADVANTAGES OF INTERNET FAX

Using the Internet to transmit fax documents from one computer or fax machine to another computer or fax machine should be as natural as sending e-mail, a form of communication that is already used by millions around the world. In fact, e-mail has become an easy way to share documents that originate in electronic form, such as word processing or electronic spreadsheets. Desktop scanners are available that allow users to scan in hardcopy documents containing written material such as signatures, comments, and corrections. Scanned documents in graphical format can be sent from desktop to desktop as e-mail attachments.

But what if hardcopy, in the form of fax output, is desired or required at the receiving end? Desktop fax applications that require a fax modem and dedicated phone line have drawbacks: the difficulty and expense of providing the phone line, the need to disconnect from other communications in order to use the fax phone line, etc.

Internet fax connects the PC (or a standard fax machine) to a fax server in the Internet. The fax server routes jobs through other servers in the Internet to a final server located physically near the destination. That server then makes a phone line connection to the destination fax machine and delivers the job at the lowest possible cost. Alternatively, the delivering fax server may send the job to a fax application in a desktop system, or as a graphic file e-mail attachment to a destination e-mail account.

There are three basic fax "on ramps" to the Internet:

1. LAN-connected computer to Internet
2. fax modem dial-up connection to Internet via PSTN
3. fax machine to Internet via PSTN

At the receiving end, there are also three types of "off ramps:"

1. Internet to LAN-connected computer
2. Internet via PSTN to computer with modem
3. Internet via PSTN to fax machine

The key to Internet faxing is the network of specialized fax servers inside the Internet. These servers accept fax jobs from PCs or specially equipped fax machines, then either deliver the jobs directly to the destination device, or route the jobs over the Internet (using least-cost routing) to a server near the destination for delivery.

Internet fax servers are connected both to the IP network and to the analog PSTN simultaneously. Each server can accept incoming fax jobs from the Internet or over analog phone lines. Likewise, they can send fax jobs over the Internet through the IP connection or deliver them via PSTN to destination fax devices.

When fax jobs are handled by computer, rather than telephony equipment only, many benefits become available. Users can view the status of all faxes, send faxes to large recipient lists, print faxes out on high-quality printers, forward faxes electronically, and distribute documents to a mix of fax devices and e-mail systems. By receiving faxes through an Internet server, users can ensure that they capture all their faxes, and can access them electronically at all times, even while away from the office.

Individual User Advantage

Individual users gain by faxing over the Internet. By adding fax send and receive capability to the PC, users come one step closer to a universal messaging center (adding voice to the PC will one day complete the solution). Low-cost desktop scanners that take up very little desktop "real estate" (some are built directly into a keyboard) can give the PC full "fax machine" capability. Because the average worker sends up to 25 fax pages per week, personal productivity goes up by eliminating trips to the stand-alone fax machine. Receiving faxes via an electronic inbox gives another boost to productivity and security, as the user previews faxes privately online and prints hardcopy from a high-quality laser printer.

Power User Advantage

Groups such as investor relations, PR, sales, and marketing send out faxes to large lists of recipients (broadcast faxing). Internet-based faxing lets users manage the entire process right from an in-house PC, including setting up recipient lists, sending the broadcast, and monitoring status of each broadcast fax job. And because the Internet "does the work" of transmitting the fax document to each recipient, the in-house PC is freed up immediately for other work, as soon as one copy of the document, and the recipient list, is sent to the Internet.PC

Organization Advantage

Organizations view Internet fax as an opportunity to outsource a significant piece of their communications infrastructure. Many IS and telecom managers welcome the chance to shift capital equipment and technology investments to the hands of specialized service providers. Faxing is a particularly good candidate for outsourcing. The combination of empowering individuals in the organization to do more while at the same time increasing control over usage and saving money on capital equipment and telco charges is a powerful incentive.

Many fax machines connected to dedicated analog lines actually bypass the corporate PBX, and may in fact cost the organization more than the official corporate rate. So, Internet faxing can produce dramatic savings while capitalizing on the investment made to put all those PCs on all those desks.

From a security standpoint, fewer analog phone lines into the organization means fewer "open windows" for intruders to hack their way into the corporate infrastructure. Getting visibility into the usage of 40 percent of the organization's phone bill is also a good thing. The key ingredients that corporate managers look for are reliability and quality. Here, the NSP is uniquely positioned to leverage its track record as an infrastructure service provider.

Smaller organizations can win big as well. They often pay higher international and long-distance phone rates than large corporations. Savings gained through lower rates, lower equipment costs, and elimination of service bureau charges hit the bottom line very quickly.

Top Ten Advantages

1. The PC is easier to use, and more convenient than a fax machine.
2. It is faster: no trip to the fax machine, redials, etc.

3. It is less disruptive to send faxes directly from within applications such as word processors, or from paper using a handy desktop scanner.
4. Inbox users never miss a fax, retrieving their faxes like e-mail or as e-mail attachments. Inbox faxes are private and secure, and easily previewed on the PC.
5. No dedicated phone line, fax modem, or LAN fax server is required.
6. Performing broadcast faxing easily from the desktop eliminates service bureau charges.
7. It automatically captures and reports online status of faxes.
8. Saves money on transmission costs, especially internationally.
9. Faxes can be sent to fax machines or converted to e-mail for delivery to PCs.
10. NSP-based service produces itemized billing for easier usage tracking.

BUILDING AN INTERNET FAX SERVICE

Take a step-by-step look at how an Internet fax service offering can be created. Why offer Internet fax? Every network service provider (NSP) is asking itself where to put its future emphasis. There are many competing demands for resources and priorities. But a few facts stand out:

1. The most valuable resource the NSP has is its customer base.
2. Creating new revenue streams from that existing customer base is not easy. Today, connectivity is a commodity. Where is a new, profitable offering going to come from?
3. Establishing an infrastructure for metered, "pay-as-you-go" services is essential to break out of the current "flat monthly fee" pricing environment.

Every major service industry, from telecommunications to overnight deliveries to airlines, relies on sophisticated rate structures and pricing packages to optimize charges against usage. Usage-based pricing funds improvements in the infrastructure and enables the creation of additional offerings. Network service providers need the ability to authorize and authenticate users, allocate resources, meter transactions, and charge for measured usage of their service offerings.

Internet fax is a great "first value-added-service" opportunity. Fax transmission lends itself to the current technology of the Internet. Internet faxing is an "easy reach" from current desktop capabilities, and, as pointed out, fits right in with the current suite of communications activities. Faxing is an extremely large business, international in scope, that offers great revenue potential. Internet-based faxing is the first of many billable value-added services that can be offered by an NSP. Future offerings could include streaming video, videoconferencing, voice applications, data access services, Internet-based metered gaming, information "push" services, and more.

KEY REQUIREMENTS

Here are the key requirements for a successful Internet fax service offering: Offer a compelling value proposition to the end user. Customers perceive value from improvements in their daily lives and business operations. Many of these benefits were listed in the previous section, including personal productivity, privacy, and security, easier and more manageable IS/telecom, better usage of computer resources, and greater control over important/urgent hardcopy communications.

Savings on capital equipment costs are important, reducing dependency on LAN fax servers, dedicated analog phone lines, fax modems, etc., and provide savings over telco fax transmission rates. By "letting the Internet do the work" of long-haul fax deliveries, most users can experience a price advantage from Internet fax versus a traditional telco service. Rather than positioning Internet fax as a premium service, it can be promoted as way to reduce the overall cost of fax transmissions.

Provide Both Outbound (Sending) and Inbound (Receiving) Services

To completely outclass the traditional fax environment, NSPs should deploy fax services that beat the fax machine "coming and going." Fax receiving services offer personal fax numbers, privacy, security, 24-hour-a-day coverage, and unmatched accessibility. The power of a complete send-and-receive solution is both dramatic and easily marketed.

DEFINING THE IP FAX SERVICE

Every service business begins with the customer. The implementation of Internet fax will depend on how one estimates two specific customer characteristics:

1. What will the adoption rate be over time for the service? The rate of acquisition of new customers will depend on many factors, including how many business vs. consumer users are in the customer base, how aggressively one plans to promote the service, and what kind of introductory offers one plans to implement, if any.
2. What is the overall faxing profile of the customer base? According to Gallup/Pitney Bowes, corporate faxing patterns are roughly: 10 to 12 percent international, 50 to 60 percent long distance, 25 to 40 percent local/regional.

The average fax user sends five fax pages per business day. These figures are a good starting point for estimating traffic loads. Over time, one will develop an accurate model of the particular customer base.

Look at three different adoption-curve scenarios based on a 20-day "business month." For now, exclude broadcast users and assume that everyone sends an average of five fax pages per business day. Note that the following rates of adoption are estimates. They are presented here for purposes of comparison only, and are not based on data gathered through experience.

Deploying Internet Fax Servers

At first, it makes sense to do a limited rollout of servers to high-traffic POPs, because servers deployed in high-traffic localities provide immediately profitable local fax delivery. Meanwhile, a centralized pool of servers delivers all other fax traffic via long-distance lines. However, as in the above service analysis, inbox accounts can increase revenue when configured into the network of deployed servers. So, a sensible strategy is to deploy local fax servers to provide inbox accounts and local fax deliveries, as well as a pool of "long-distance" servers. (The deployed servers provide local area code numbers for inbox customers.)

Over time, additional servers can be deployed to expand the local coverage of the system and to fine-tune it for greatest efficiency and profitability. This "division of labor" between distributed "local only" servers and pooled "long distance only" servers makes the provisioning of each server straightforward. In this approach, each server is set up with either local T1 and ISDN ports or with long-distance T1 ports.

A sophisticated least-cost-routing algorithm behind the scenes ensures that servers are delivering packetized fax jobs in the most reliable, time-efficient manner, adapting flexibly to changes in network traffic loads and other operating variables. The more fax servers an NSP deploys, the greater geographical coverage it can achieve. By deploying a fax server to every POP in the NSP network, the vast majority of local user faxes will be delivered locally, and more long-distance faxes will also be delivered for the cost of a local call. The ultimate goal of the service is to establish an essentially "distance-independent" alternative to the "distance-sensitive" model offered by traditional telco networks.

SUMMARY

Internet fax promises big savings. Documents would be sent directly from a user's desktop computer to the remote user's desktop. The time spent preparing and sending faxes would be reduced. There would be no need for dedicated phone lines, fax modems, or LAN fax servers. Broadcast faxing from the desktop would eliminate service bureau charges. Money would be saved on transmission costs, especially internationally. Internet fax is the next wave in cost-effective, efficient document transmission and telecommunication.

Chapter 63

Videoconferencing over IP Networks

Christine Perey
Matthew Feldman

ACCORDING TO LARRY IRVING, ASSISTANT SECRETARY FOR COMMUNICATIONS AND INFORMATION, in a May 8, 1996 letter to Reed Hundt, chairman of the Federal Communications Commission, "The Internet now connects more than 10 million computers, tens of millions of users, and is growing at a rate of 10 percent to 15 percent a month. This growth has created opportunities for entrepreneurs to develop new services and applications such as video-conferencing, multicasting, electronic payments, networked virtual reality, and intelligent agents. Perhaps more important, it creates a growing number of opportunities for users to identify new communication and information needs and to meet those needs."

Most engineers designing networks today recall that the world's largest system of interconnected networks had ambitious roots: to define how transmission would take place over networks connecting dissimilar computers. Chances are that few of those who developed internetworking protocols in the Department of Defense 25 years ago foresaw the variety and vast number of applications their protocols would be called on to support. Today, the protocols that together are the basis of the Internet continue to evolve to accommodate the demands of new media types.

This chapter reviews the underlying principles of Internet protocols in the context of one of the most demanding application sets to date: real-time videoconferencing and visual collaboration. It discusses the advantages and disadvantages of choosing Internet protocol (IP) networks for real-time multimedia communications and how real-time videoconferencing is achieved on IP networks — today and in the near future.

BASIC INTERNET PROTOCOL CONVENTIONS

Protocols that together manage packets on the Internet build on several widely accepted conventions/foundations. The principal components of the network are data connecting equipment (DCE), such as routers, and data terminating equipment (DTE), such as desktop computers (also called "hosts").

Without any special adjustments for the unique requirements of different media types, the network layers work in concert to transmit packets of user information. In its simplest implementation, the flow of the data from and to end points over an IP network is monitored or verified by a simple layer 3 communications protocol (e.g., Transmission Control Protocol, or TCP).

The advantage is that there is very little communications overhead associated with components in IP networks "talking" to one another. TCP running over IP in effect takes care of this. Each packet allocates the maximum number of bits to the user's information.

Together, protocols ratified by the Institute of Electrical and Electronics Engineers (IEEE) and the Internet Engineering Task Force (IETF) ensure that packets of data are reliably transmitted under any condition, as quickly as possible (e.g., bandwidth or network load on the segments of the networks tying together two or more points).

Several protocols have been developed to manage the unique requirements of real-time streaming data. To understand the importance of these developments, this chapter begins with a high-level discussion of video-conferencing and visual collaboration using networked multimedia desktop computers.

PRINCIPLES OF VIDEOCONFERENCING AND MULTIMEDIA COMMUNICATIONS

When a video camera and microphone pick up real-life events, the imagery and sound can be turned into digital formats for communications between Properly enabled end points over local or wide area networks. For the user to perceive the moving images and intelligible sounds, the digital information moves from transmitter to receiver (transmitters are simultaneously receiving in the case of two-way videoconferencing) in a highly consistent fashion. Compressed in real time, the data streams over a network in such a way that frames of video can be reconstructed and synchronized with audio with the least end-to-end delay.

Quantitative Quality of Service Parameters

End-to-end quality of service (QoS) in videoconferencing and visual collaboration is defined as the level of satisfaction a user has with a given session. It is a function of many independent and interdependent factors (e.g., window size, processor speed, network bandwidth), which together influence frame rate, bit depth, image clarity and resolution, audio clarity, lip synchronization, and latency.

In contrast to conventional data applications in which data transmission is bursty, digital video and audio applications require continuous data transmission. In IP environments, precise bit rates during the transmission vary. In the following list, the factors influencing bit rates (bandwidth) during videoconferencing and collaborative computing are presented as a function of the media (i.e., video, audio, and data):

Video factors include:

- Bit depth (number of colors)
- Resolution (size of the image being captured, compressed, transmitted, and decompressed) — Resolution is contrasted with window size, which is the size of the image that is displayed for viewing. If the window size is different from resolution, then interpolation is used to generate a new image that fits the window.
- Q factor (sharpness of edges in any given frame)
- Smoothing (this is a result of — and dependent on — motion estimation algorithms and content changes from one frame to the next)
- Frame rate (frames per second) — For example, NTSC video, the U.S. standard, is 30 fps; PAL, the European standard, is 25 fps.

Audio factors include:

- Sampling rate (the number of audio samples captured, compressed, and transmitted, expressed in KHz cycles per second) — For example, telephony is 6.3 KHz, FM radio is 36 KHz, music CDs 44.1 KHz (See Exhibit 63-1).
- Bit rate (the number of bits the system has in order to accurately represent different tones; for example, 8-bit or 16-bit)
- Mono and stereo sound

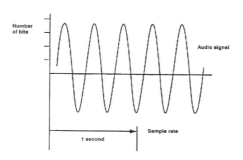

Note:
Frequency response is how high and low the audio signal can go. Clipping occurs if the actual audio signal becomes higher or lower than the signal the analog-to-digital or other chips can handle. Sample rate refers to how many audio samples are taken in a 1-second interval. Numbers of bits (usually 8 or 16) represents the accuracy of each audio sample.

Exhibit 63-1. Audio sampling.

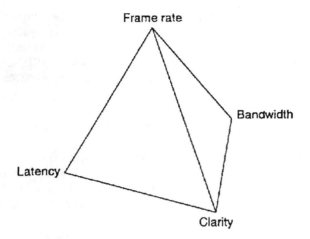

Note:
The four-sided pyramid represents quality of service (QOS) for videoconferencing. By choosing a single plane (triangle) of the pyramid, one corner remains constant. The remaining three corners are closely dependent; if any one corner changes, the others are affected. Usually systems can be optimized for any two of the three.

Exhibit 63-2. Interdependence of quality of service parameters in time-dependent streaming media.

Data factors include:

- Quantity of data
- Frequency of transmissions
- Latency of transmission (how long it takes to send at a given bit rate)

The central processor, any additional compression/decompression (codec) circuits, network infrastructure, and the user's network connection directly affect these quantitative factors.

Qualitative QoS Experience

Depending on the quantitative parameters, the user's experience with multimedia (which is a combination of audio, video, and data) may be qualitatively different. Exhibit 63-2 is intended to help readers understand the interdependence of various quality-of-service parameters in time-dependent streaming media.

The user's experience with bidirectional live video and visual collaboration over any network can be expressed quantitatively and qualitatively; in general, though, the objective is to reproduce a live meeting or conversation.

For the interaction to be as close to natural as possible, it is especially important that both (or all) users in a videoconference experience a uniformly low latency (minimum delay). Any variation in the frame rate between points is perceived as jitter. Poor synchronization between lips and audio is also distracting.

Thus, the most important factors in the user's qualitative experience of videoconferencing system are:

- synchronization of audio, video, and data
- end-to-end latency
- window size
- jitter
- richness and clarity of audio
- image clarity (bit depth, sharpness, smoothing, and resolution)

All these quality-of-service concepts are critical to the reader's overall understanding of the pros and cons of selecting IP networks for videoconferencing.

PROS AND CONS OF VIDEOCONFERENCING OVER IP NETWORKS

Founders of the Internet were academics driven by four guiding principles:

1. reliability (guaranteed delivery of packets), not efficiency
2. end systems' interoperability, and information or packet loss recovery
3. variable quality of service, not guaranteed bandwidth, so that any network bandwidth can be accommodated by a single protocol
4. no support for charging mechanisms, since commercial traffic was not envisioned

Internet protocols have withstood the test of multiple applications at the user interface, new operating systems in end points, and ever-changing transport media in the physical layers (e.g., SONET, ATM). For videoconferencing and visual collaboration, there are fundamental principles that determine bandwidth use in any session.

Bandwidth Allocation

Exhibit 63-3 illustrates the following types of bandwidth allocation:

- *Total bandwidth*. This is the maximum bandwidth available for user data and network management overhead.
- *User-available bandwidth*. This is the total bandwidth minus the network management overhead.
- *Application-specific bandwidth*. This is the bandwidth requested by the application.

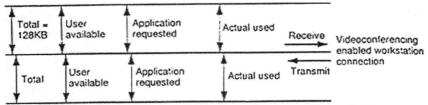

ISBN basic rate Interface (BRI) bandwidth allocation using H.320-compliant application – measured in each direction, therefore two times the bandwidth for each connection dedicated to a single user

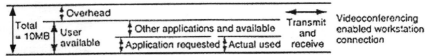

Ethernet-based bandwidth allocation using TCP/IP-compliant application – measured in both directions; connection shared between multiple users and applications

Exhibit 63-3. Examples of bandwidth allocation.

- *Actual used bandwidth.* This is the minimum bandwidth of either what the application requested or what is available over the end-to-end network during a particular session (whichever is lower).
- *Allocated bandwidth.* This is the portion of the total user-available bandwidth that can be reserved; it only applies when a reservation mechanism is in place, requested, and granted.

IP Network Advantages

Compared with other wide area network communications protocols, IP has four principal advantages for videoconferencing:

1. Low management architecture overhead and high carrying capacity make IP cost effective.
2. No guaranteed quality of service and low overhead make IP bandwidth scalable (64K bps to 100M bps and beyond).
3. IP architecture provides for many simultaneous virtual circuits, thereby enabling multiple services and multiple connections (through well-recognized sockets) at the same time.
4. Packet structure and network design make it possible for both broadcasting and multicasting to occur in the same network, without requiring packet redundancy.

Using extensions of IP to modify the payload format and reduce overhead associated with packet acknowledgment between end points, the communications between end points dedicated to user information is high.

In some cases as much as 95 percent of the bandwidth can be assigned to user traffic. The actual bandwidth a data stream uses is a function of the bit rate the end points have agreed to send upon call establishment.

When two endpoints have only very low bit rate capacity, owing to the local bus architecture or modem technologies over a POTS (plain old telephone service) line, the IP-based videoconference session operates within this constraint. On the other hand, when the same software (e.g., user application) is used over a high-bandwidth connection, a videoconference can take advantage of the increased capacity without any change in the application or communications protocol stack.

Networks without support for Internet Protocol Independent Multicasting (PIM) must recreate a data stream for each of the desktops to which the user wishes to communicate simultaneously. This puts extra pressure on the source (i.e., the host has to create, manage, and transmit the same packets more than once) and on the shared resources connecting all users, whether they are multimedia communications enabled or using traditional transactional functions between clients and servers. Multicasting on IP enables multiple participants (so-called multipoints) to experience the same real-time conference at the same time. The importance of this feature cannot be underestimated.

IP Network Disadvantages

Many practitioners believe that connectionless communications and best-effort delivery of packets is inappropriate for isochronous network traffic (e.g., where data needs to be sent sequentially and arrive at its destination at specific intervals). Such as that generated by digital video and audio. The principal disadvantages of IP network for videoconferencing are basically:

- Lack of guaranteed bandwidth, unless all the network components are controlled by a central manager that has chosen to implement network-wide bandwidth reservation schemes.
- Lack of international standard that would support interoperability of products from different vendors for intra- and intercompany communications.

The most common wide area network solution for videoconferencing has been integrated services digital network (ISDN). With a dedicated connection (i.e., a communications circuit) between two endpoints, bandwidth is guaranteed and, consequently, the quality of service remains consistent throughout a session.

The next most common wide area network for point-to-point desktop videoconferencing has been POTS, which despite its low bandwidth, ensures, like ISDN, a dedicated circuit for a conference between two end points.

Users find that they prefer running business applications over networks in which the bandwidth allocated, requested, and used are all the same (i.e., the circuit-switched environment). And there are many competitive, standards-compliant offerings for desktop videoconferencing over basic rate ISDN.

The natural consequence of a large — and especially a standards-compliant — installed base is that there are more people with which a system can interoperate without modification of any software or hardware. Until more vendors deliver standards-compliant, interoperable solutions for videoconferencing, the installed base will be confined to pockets of proprietary products that interoperate among themselves, but do not permit endpoint application independence.

Specifications for session setup, management, and compression were under development (e.g., IETF Audio/Visual Transport Working Group and the International Telecommunications Union's [IUT] H.323), and became commercial products during 1997. However, the standards have been revised three times since then, which makes it difficult for vendors to fully comply with the changing standard.

Compared to other protocols on the local area network for managing desktop videoconferencing (e.g., IsoEthernet or the specialized multimedia operating system, such as MOS, by First Virtual Corp., for 25M-bps ATM at the desktop), IP communications over 10Base-T Ethernets are prone to suffering from network contention and congestion. The relatively low bandwidth available for each user on a 10Base-T network has, to date, been unsuitable for business-quality videoconferencing using inexpensive software codecs.

GETTING STARTED WITH IP-BASED VIDEOCONFERENCING

Disadvantages and drawbacks aside, it is clear that many organizations will choose IP-based videoconferencing for its

- low cost of entry (e.g., integration into existing infrastructure)
- low cost of ownership (e.g., low maintenance and no telecommunications charges)
- ease of use (e.g., accessibility of the global IP network compared to ISDN provisioning)

For many years, real-time packetized audio and video over IP networks were tested and used on an isolated portion of the Internet: the multicast backbone (Mbone). The Mbone is operating, expanding, and improving. Some of the protocols used on the Mbone (developed by the Audio/Visual

Working Group of IETF) are being ratified by the IETF and have migrated from this relatively exclusive academic and industrial environment into commercial routers for Internet and intranet deployment. Subsequently, IETF protocols for managing video and audio packets would be widely incorporated in enterprises and on the Internet in general.

This section examines the components users need to add to their desktops for videoconferencing on IP. Local (LAN), metropolitan (MAN), virtual (VAN), wide area (WAN), and global network managers need to modify and prepare their networks to support the types of traffic generated by video-enabled desktops. The scope of these networking component changes and alternatives is discussed in more detail later in the chapter.

Desktop-enabling Technologies

To experience desktop videoconferencing on the Internet (or intranet) firsthand, the user needs only a camera for video input, a microphone for audio input, speakers (presuming the user wants to hear what others say), software to give the user access to connection initiation and answering, session management, compression algorithms, a video display board, an IP network interface, and a premium CPU.

CU-SeeMe and Other Software Supporting Multicasting. One of the more unique and proprietary of these desktop components is the user application and interface software. The first, and consequently one of the most widely deployed, application designed for videoconferencing on the Internet CU-SeeMe, originated at Cornell University. Distributed as freeware/shareware for the first several years, the application satisfied the needs of many Macintosh users in academic and nonprofit institutions for distance learning and research applications.

In 1995, Cornell University issued an exclusive license for commercial distribution of CU-SeeMe to White Pine Software. Since then, White Pine Software has ported the application to other platforms and greatly enhanced the functionality (e.g., adding color video, password security, and whiteboard capabilities).

Cu-SeeMe, like three or more competing user applications currently offered on the Internet — for example, VDOnet's VDOphone, CineCom's CineVideo/Direct, Apple Computer's QuickTime Conferencing, and Intelligence at Large's Being There — provides a directory management system, call initiation, answering and management software, and some utilities for controlling video and audio quality during a session.

The Desktop's Connected to the Mbone. Percept Software had developed multicast audio/video server and viewer products for Windows 3.1.1, Windows 95, and Windows NT to help enable the PC/Windows world to join the

Mbone community. The viewer, called FlashWare Client, can receive Mbone sessions transmitted with Livermore Berkeley Laboratory's vat 4.0 in real-time transport protocol (RTP) mode (selected via the –r option) using PCM, DVI, or GSM audio-encoding algorithms and vic 2.7 using its default H.261 video codec.

On the Precept Web site is a program guide that lists Mbone sessions using these protocols; users can launch the client automatically from there. The client is built as a media control interface (MCI) device driver so it can be invoked through Microsoft's Media Player, a Netscape plug-in, or other applications using the MCI A-PI. Playback of audio and video is synchronized using the time-stamping mechanisms in RTP and real-time transport control protocol (RTCP).

The IETF Audio/Visual Transport Working Group's RTP and RTCP protocols have been developed to facilitate the smooth transmission, arrival, and display of streaming data types. When end point applications support RTP, packets leave the sender's desktop with a time stamp and content identification label. Using this information, and through congestion-monitoring facilities at either end, the proper sequences of frames can be more reliably recreated at the receiving station, using a specified delay buffer (generally less than 100 milliseconds). Netscape's Cooltalk is another example of an architecture for streaming video and audio with RTP-ready endpoints.

Compressing Audio and Video Streams. In all but the most exceptional conditions (e.g., broadcast-quality production requirements), digital video and audio need to be compressed for superior management. Subsequently, the information must be decompressed (decoded) upon arrival so that it can be displayed on its destination screen.

A comprehensive discussion of compression technology and the ensuing debates over the virtues of different algorithms are not within the scope of this chapter; however, it must be noted that digital video compression has a marked impact on the quality of the experience users can expect when videoconferencing over an IP network.

All freeware applications for IP-based videoconferencing bundle a software codec for encoding and decoding the audio and video streams at the appropriate bandwidth for the station. Software codecs deliver lower quality audio and video than hardware in which there are optimized digital signal processors (DSPs) for these functions. Currently, there are no standard compression algorithms for use on the IP-based networks, so users receive the codec specified by the desktop application.

In the case of freeware developed by Livermore Berkeley Laboratory, as well as Apple's QuickTime Conferencing, the architecture can accommodate any number of compression algorithms, including H.261, which is the basis of all H.320 systems. The products comply with a new specification — H.323 — for videoconferencing over IP networks and use H.261 as a codec; however, a new and more efficient version (H.263) is less bandwidth consumptive and will quickly replace H.261 on IP networks.

Hardware Implementations for Business-Quality Videoconferencing. In general, videoconferencing on IP networks is like any other commodity: the customer gets what he or she pays for. The software packages mentioned so far are considered suitable for academic, nonprofit, and perhaps "personal" applications. For now, customers who seek "business-quality" video and audio will need to evaluate and select desktop videoconferencing systems that have been implemented in hardware.

Video and audio compression hardware for IP-based conferencing is available for Industry Standard Architecture (ISA) as well as Peripheral Component Interconnect (PCI), Sbus interfaces, and all major operating systems. Examples include those offered in Intellect Visual Communications Corp.'s TeamVision family of products (using very large scale integration [VLSI] chips and Mosaic's own design) and Netscape's Communique Line of products (using an Osprey Technology board and Lucent Technologies' AVP chips for DSP-assisted compression and decompression of audio and video).

Network Interface Hardware. All vidioconferencing systems require a network interface adapter for LAN or WAN access. Most institutions with intranets or T1 access to the Internet provide an Ethernet adapter at each desktop. The bandwidth and suitability for video depend on whether this interface adapter is 10Base-T, IsoEthernet, or 100Base-T and an assortment of network design issues. IP-based videoconferencing can also run locally over Token Ring networks with routers providing connectivity to and from the wide area networks.

For those who do not have a dedicated connection to an IP network, dial-up access to the Internet is accomplished with a point-to-point protocol (PPP) or serial line IP (SLIP) connection via a modem or an ISDN terminal adapter through an Internet services provider (ISP). In general, dial-up IP network interfaces accommodate consumer applications adequately, but are not suitable for business-quality video and audio supported with specialized hardware.

VIDEO-READY NETWORKS

In the previous connectivity scenarios, an Internet communications protocol stack in the host operating system negotiates and monitors connections. This section, however, focuses on the steps needed to address bandwidth, as well as the IP facilities and the internetworking software commonly used and currently being proposed for desktop videoconferencing in IP environments.

Network Upgrade and Management Issues

Preparing a network for any new application, including multimedia, requires careful analysis of existing components and user requirements. As far as network upgrades for videoconferencing are concerned, an intranet is quite different from the public Internet.

In the private network (e.g., intranets over LANs, MANs, VANs, and WANs), technologies can be more consistently deployed, more effectively maintained by a central IT group, and are often more economical to purchase when large site licenses are negotiated. This said, jurisdictional (i.e., workgroup) management of LANs is increasingly popular.

In contrast to the situation with LANs and private WANS, new protocols and architectures take much longer to deploy in the public/commercial IP environment. There is an inherent lack of control in this progress, especially if new management challenges are associated with upgrades. Video-enabling upgrades clearly fall in this category.

One way for LAN administrators and managers to approach the design of a video-ready network is by working from the endpoints toward the common infrastructure (e.g., the Internet).

Endpoint Performance. Initially, users and planners should evaluate the endpoint CPU performance. If the CPU is involved in any general data application management and compression or decompression tasks (which is almost always the case in the desktop videoconferencing applications distributed as freeware, and less the case when add-on compression hardware is necessary), then low performance at the desktop will translate to poor quality of service and less efficient bandwidth usage patterns. When endpoints are enhanced and capable of compressing video frames, bandwidth will be more efficiently utilized between desktops.

Network bandwidth requirements for desktop videoconferencing vary with applications as well. Some applications — especially precision medical or surgical applications or high-quality entertainment and advertisement production — require many megabits per second to transmit lossless (i.e., compressed without any loss of information) or nearly lossless video between points.

In most business scenarios, however, the combination of efficient compression algorithms, network management software, and user tolerance of less than TV quality video keeps the bandwidth requirement (per bidirectional session) between 28.8K and 768K bps.

Because, in general, users' lowest level of tolerance is the highest performance they have had the privilege of using, it is safe to assume that IP networks in place today need modification to deliver acceptable business-quality video in real time. On a shared network, such as an Ethernet, Token Ring, or fiber distributed data interface (FDDI) network, or the commercial Internet today, all stations have equal opportunity to send and receive data. This is known as "time division multiplexing."

Several options exist for changing network designs to accommodate the demands of streaming data types. One of these is to supplant or augment bewst-effort protocols in order to prioritize video and audio streams in such a way that end points receive consistently low latency. This approach is discussed in greater depth a little later in this chapter.

If, prior to changing the data management, an enterprise decides to deploy high-speed LAN technologies (e.g., 100Base-T, 100VG-AnyLAN, ATM), there also needs to be upgrades to WAN infrastructures. Options and issues in this arena are the focus of many books and current articles and outside the scope of this chapter.

Evolving Bandwidth Management Protocols. From an integration perspective, however, one of the most important advantages of planning the netwok using IP is that IP is well adapted to LAN as WAN environments.

DVMP. At the netwok achitecture level, piorritization schemes in the IP specifications issued by IETF working groups hold the greatest promise for improved management and distribution of video over IP networks. In the late 1980s, the IETF ratified the distance vector multicast routing protocol (DVMRP) to transport live video feeds in IP multicast mode over the Mbone. DVMRP works by essentially "flooding" all available routes with a broadcast message, something which could be tolerated more easily before the Intenet grew in popularity.

Ipv5 or Streaming II Protocol. About the same time DVMRP was introduced, the Steaming II (ST-II) protocol was proposed by Bolt Beranek and Newman (BBN). A connection-oriented routing protocol, ST11, is used in endpoint and router software and offers a call setup facility that lets the originator control bandwidth in a video and audio session by allocating bandwidth through the router upon request. Virtual links are established for the duration of the session and resources are allocated along the virtual links.

ST-II, also known as Ipv5 and sometimes called ST-II+, is evolving to address connection setup delays and options for allowing both receivers and senders to open sockets without a conference administrator's approval. Today's version of ST-II+ is not backward-compatible with ST-II.

Protocol Independent Multicasting (PIM). To address the inherently "unscalable nature of DVMRP," the PIM system was proposed. This protocol designates so-called rendezvous points for registration of both senders and receivers of multimedia multicasts.

Because the protocol (implemented in routers such as those shipping from Cisco Systems) is not restrictive, it also works with any unicast routing protocol (as in the case in a private videoconference over an IP WAN). Dense mode PIM, which applies where the volume of multicast traffic is high and senders and receivers are in close geographic proximity to one another, uses reverse path forwarding and operates much like DVMRP.

RSVP. The bandwidth management protocol with the most enthusiastic following to date is known as the reservation protocol (RSVP). Implemented in endpoint and router software on the Mbone and currently under review for IETF ratification, RSVP guarantees bandwidth allocation in connectionless networks according to a receiver-driven model.

RSVP is fixed-bit-rate allocation, with routines to handle available bit rate in the future. It is also technology independent and can run on ISDN and private network connections such as Ethernet-based intranets.

Prototype support for RSVP has been demonstrated by several different router vendors and became available in many products in 1997. With these products, RSVP was quickly deployed throughout intranets.

Billing and Related Issues. In addition to the inpediments cited so far — namely, complex management challenges associated with video — current Internet pricing models do not reflect guaranteed bandwidth allocation. As a result, most commercial Internet service providers will be reluctant to implement RSVP in their routers because, in using this protocol, a few users could potentially monopolize router resources without appropriately compensating the service provider. Research at BBN and in the IETF's Internet Services Working Group has addressed the problem with specific billing protocols built into endpoints and routers.

Researchers at the University of Illinois-Champaign are exploring a solution to circumvent the successive layers of management code over IP. The video datagram protocol (VDP) eliminates TCP and works at the IP level to move video, audio, and data simultaneously. The protocol itself addresses the delivery timing issues by dynamically using a best-effort adaptive flow control methodology.

HOW DESKTOP-TO-DESKTOP VIDEO AND AUDIO CONNECTIONS OPERATE IN IP NETWORKS

Given the large number of freeware and shareware solutions for videoconferencing on IP networks and proposed standards, and the rapidity of new developments on the IP landscape, it is difficult to make generalizations about the manner in which desktop-to-desktop connections are negotiated, maintained, and torn down in all user applications. This section explores some of the approaches different products use to enable videoconferencing and collaboration over IP networks.

Negotiating/Establishing Desktop Connections

Some applications have relied primarily on Internet (and later intranet) servers for negotiating desktop connections over LANs and WANs. White Pine Software's Reflector or software, for example, supports unicast, broadcast, and multicast sessions.

Unicasting and multicasting are achieved by specifying a reflector as the destination and sharing (publishing) the appropriate IP address of the reflector in question with other conference participants. To control unwanted participants, the reflector lets network managers issue passwords for different conferences. In addition, a roster of conference participants (one for a unicast, more for multicasts) is published dynamically to all participating desktops.

Several freeware and shareware programs are available to initiate and administer online conference over IP networks. Confman is one such tool for conference initiation and monitoring that employs certain Mbone tools: vat (for audio data), vic and nv (for video transmission), and wb (for whiteboarding) on the Internet.

Confman does not handle multimedia data, but helps the user to plan, setup, and control a conference by letting the network manager choose meeting participants (by IP address), the start time, and the tools (and codecs) the session members need to run on their endpoints. Conferences can be held in two different modes:

1. *Closed mode.* Using this mode with more than two participants requires a server process to route the multimedia data. This process might be regarded as a conference room. All connections are unicast connections; no multicast features are required.
2. *Multicast mode.* Multimedia data is sent via multicast. To restrict access, data has to be encrypted. A conference management tool distributes the encryption key to the selected participants in advance.

Microsoft's and Intel's Internet telephony products (and subsequent IP-based videoconferencing offerings) use the standard User Locator Service (ULS) to negotiate/establish calls between desktop videoconferencing users on IP networks. In June 1996, ULS was submitted to the IETF for consideration to become a standard and incorporated with LDAP (lightweight directory addressing protocol).

Ideally, all intranet and Internet service providers will have standards-compliant directories. For users not on a corporate network, the ISP's directory will automatically associate the e-mail address with a person. Every time users connect to the Internet, the network service can then pick up the IP address and initiate a local call to the end point nearest the recipient.

In a corporate environment, where there is a Novell network with ULS and computer telephony integration, simply having a desktop computer turned on and connected to the network should suffice to identify the end point for any incoming video and audio (or audio-only) sessions.

Maintaining/Modulating a Videoconference Session

As long as the sockets between endpoints, or between the endpoint and server, are open, the IP session is maintained. Another way of expressing this is that within a conference, the virtual circuits are always present.

Some applications use a single circuit for all audio, video, and data; other applications use a separate circuit for each media type. Having a separate socket for each permits higher error recovery and, therefore, fewer chances for problems to occur during a live conference.

Multicasting

The focus of this chapter is bidirectional real-time video and audio between two or a few desktop systems, otherwise known as desktop videoconferencing or, in Internet terms, strictly a unicast transaction.

For most who participate in unicast or simple point-to-point sessions, there comes a time when applications, especially meetings, require more than two participants. To execute on a network limited to unicast sessions, applications must generate a unique copy of each packet and send those packets to each participant's desktop (by specifying the endpoints' IP address). This is inherently inefficient if there is an alternative. With Internet multicast protocols, an application generates a single copy of each packet and sends it to a group address. Endpoints (e.g., clients on the client/server network) can selectively choose to listen to the multicast address. Multicasting minimizes network traffic and gives all users on a network grreater flexibility.

For an application to take advantage of multicasting, the IP stack in the network software on the host must support multicast and broadcast addressing. Multicast is implemented at both the data link layer (layer 2) and the network layer (layer 3). For multicast confined to a single LAN, the data link layer implementation is sufficient.

When a multicast application extends into different network media, such as frame relay, FDDI, or Ethernet, network layer implementations are recommended. Therefore, multipoint applications with both LAN and WAN participants must implement in both layers.

For all vendors of endpoint applications and network components to interoperate in multicast IP networks, several parameters must be defined. The IETF has standards specifying the addressing (i.e., network-layer address mapping onto data link layer multicast addresses), dynamic registration (i.e., a mechanism for clients to inform the network that they wish to be a member of a specific multicast group), and multicast routing (e.g., DVMRP and PIM).

Monitoring and Managing a Videoconference Session

In general, reflectors, as the servers are sometimes called, provide network bandwidth control, video "pruning," audio prioritization, and a range of conference control software. Using network management utilities, the reflector/server can adjust transmission rates of specific individual users on-the-fly, if packet loss is running too high because of heavy network traffic.

If contention is too heavy for a reliable conference, the transmission remains at the lowest setting and only moves up when the network is less congested. This is an important tool for network managers and ISPs who have to be concerned with balancing the needs of their other nonvideoconferencing network users during peak load.

Network monitoring utilities allow network managers to control the maximum bandwidth allocated per videoconference and the maximum number of simultaneous videoconferences. In this way, sufficient bandwidth is reserved for other users who have conventional network applications.

One of the freeware network monitoring tools for videoconferencing is Rtpmon.Rtpmon is a tool for viewing RTCP feedback packets from a session using the real-time transport protocol. It presents loss rate and jitter information from RTCP receiver report (RR) packets in a tabular format. The table can be sorted by various parameters and the recent history of reports from a particular receiver can be viewed in a stripchart.

SUMMARY

There are advantages and disadvantages in any network selection for any set of applications. The popularity of the IP for enabling a vast number of applications for users, as well as the advantages inherent in this network protocol, are fostering the development of new tools and technologies for real-time data types. Simultaneously, videoconferencing is coming to the desktop in force, largely because computers in business leverage LANs extensively and their users are interested in adding videoconferencing applications.

As a result, network managers must become more familiar with the underlying real-time technologies for their IP networks. This chapter has introduced the basic terminology and concepts of videoconferencing, as well as the components that enable the desktop for real-time video and audio. The network must be prepared for maximum quality of service in videoconferencing without compromising other application users, as is a requirement in any high-bandwidth application.

In the future, enterprise network managers can anticipate the very rapid deployment of new technologies as a result of:

- ratification of protocols by the IETF and ITU, and the subsequent implementation of standard protocols
- reduction in cost of all video network system components, including those for end points, LANs, gateway (internetworking), and WANs

Those who manage enterprise resources, from the CFO to the IS director, will experience a profound shift in the way "best-of-class" companies do business in the near future. The reduced cycle times and increased creativity and productivity made possible with real-time conferencing locally, nationally, and globally will justify — to different degrees — the investments necessary to deploy technologies such as are described throughout this chapter.

About the Editor

Gilbert Held is the Director of 4-Degree Consulting, a Macon, Georgia-based firm specializing in the areas of data communications, personal computing, and the application of technology. Gil is an award-winning author and lecturer, with over 40 books and 300 technical articles to his credit. Some of Gil's recent titles include *Frame Relay Networking, Enhancing LAN Performance, 3rd ed., Ethernet Networks, 3rd ed.,* and *Data Communications Networking Devices, 4th ed.,* all published by John Wiley & Sons of New York City and Chichester, England.

Mr. Held is a frequent contributor to several industry publications and was selected to represent the United States at technical conferences in Moscow and Jerusalem. He received his BSEE from Pennsylvania Military College, and MSEE from New York University, and the MSTM and MBA from American University. He is currently a member of the adjunct faculty of Georgia College and State University, teaching several graduate courses covering the various aspects of data communications.

Index